The Security Risk Assessment Handbook

The Security Risk Assessment Handbook

A Complete Guide for Performing Security Risk Assessments

Douglas J. Landoll

CRC Press
Taylor & Francis Group
Boca Raton London New York

CRC Press is an imprint of the
Taylor & Francis Group, an **informa** business

First edition published 2005
by CRC Press
6000 Broken Sound Parkway NW, Suite 300, Boca Raton, FL 33487-2742

and by CRC Press
2 Park Square, Milton Park, Abingdon, Oxon, OX14 4RN

Second edition published 2011
by CRC Press
6000 Broken Sound Parkway NW, Suite 300, Boca Raton, FL 33487-2742

and by CRC Press
2 Park Square, Milton Park, Abingdon, Oxon, OX14 4RN

Third edition published 2021
by CRC Press
6000 Broken Sound Parkway NW, Suite 300, Boca Raton, FL 33487-2742

and by CRC Press
2 Park Square, Milton Park, Abingdon, Oxon, OX14 4RN

CRC Press is an imprint of Taylor & Francis Group, LLC

The right of Douglas J. Landoll to be identified as author of this work has been asserted by him in accordance with sections 77 and 78 of the Copyright, Designs and Patents Act 1988.

ISBN: 978-1-003-09044-1 (ebk)
ISBN: 978-0-367-54747-9 (hbk)
ISBN: 978-1-032-04165-0 (pbk)

DOI: 10.1201/9781003090441

Typeset in Times
by SPi Technologies India Pvt Ltd (Straive)

To my parents, Jim and Dorothy, one of the greatest gifts you gave me is the love of learning. You continue to inspire me today.

Thank you

Contents

List of Tables

List of Figures

Author

Douglas J. Landoll has over three decades of information security experience. He has led security risk assessments and established security programs for top corporations and government agencies. He is an expert in security risk assessment, security risk management, security criteria, and building corporate security programs.

His background includes evaluating cybersecurity at the National Security Agency (NSA), North Atlantic Treaty Organization (NATO), Central Intelligence Agency (CIA), the Federal Bureau of Investigations (FBI), and other government agencies; co-founding the Arca Common Criteria Testing Laboratory, co-authoring the systems security engineering capability maturity model (SSE-CMM); teaching at NSA's National Cryptologic School; and speaking at national and international cybersecurity conferences.

Doug has founded or directed four information security firms including the southwest security services at Exodus Communications, Veridyn (sold to EnPointe Technologies), the Risk and Compliance Management division at Accuvant (now Optiv) and Lantego. Doug is currently the CEO of Lantego, specializing in risk assessment, policy development, and training. He is a CISSP. He holds a BS degree from James Madison University and an MBA from the University of Texas at Austin.

In his 30+ years in the industry he has performed over 100 cybersecurity risk assessment, written policies for scores of organizations, and instructed over 2500 CISSP and CISA candidates. Doug Landoll is dynamic speaker, perceptive author, and information security expert, who always brings a unique mix of business strategy, keen insight, and technical know-how to current cybersecurity topics.

1 Introduction

1.1 THE ROLE OF THE CHIEF INFORMATION SECURITY OFFICER

Most organizations have realized the need for a senior position within the organization to be accountable for information security. While the job description and even the placement within the organization will differ in each industry and each organization, a familiar set of responsibilities are typically associated with this role. These responsibilities include:

- **Establishing information security program strategy**: The CISO identifies the business cyber threats, industry and customer requirements, business drivers, information security requirements, framework upon which to build the information security program, and the people, process, and technology in which to assemble the program. Activities associated with this responsibility include:
  - Working with executive management to understand and document the organization's information security risk appetite.[1]
  - Designing information security architecture and selecting appropriate controls to meet the established information security risk appetite.
  - Keeping current on information security and privacy regulations.
  - Keeping current on changes to the threats impacting the organization.
  - Establishing and managing security policies.
  - Implementing effective security awareness and education; and
  - Planning effective information security incident and disaster response.
- **Assessment of the current information security program**. The CISO establishes means to measure the effectiveness of the current controls in implementing the information security program. Activities associated with this responsibility include:
  - Ensuring current access management strategies and implementations appropriately restrict access to authorized individuals.
  - Establishing information security metrics, collection processes, and monitoring program; and
  - Managing a security assessment program to include vulnerability assessments, penetration testing, and security risk assessments.
- **Ensure appropriate governance of the security controls**. The CISO creates oversight activities and processes to check on the compliance within (and external to) the organization to be sure that appropriate controls are implemented.
  - Establishing appropriate oversight controls such as separation of duty, job rotation, peer review, and sanctions for non-compliance with organizational policy; and
  - Reacting to security incidents and security assessment findings by ensuring appropriate remediation and prioritization of security initiatives.

There can be some debate as to the inclusion of these responsibilities with all information security officers or officers as organizational structures may place responsibility of fraud or business continuity in other departments, but one responsibility remains clear. The senior most security person must be able to determine, from the myriad of available security projects, the most advantageous projects to initiate.

Despite the structural differences between organizations, the threat or regulation environment, or even across economic conditions, there is always a limit to the available funding and staff required to perform security initiatives. It is not enough to know a set of desired security projects for the organization to improve its security posture. Information security officers need to be able to justify their next project and defend these decisions.

> Implementation of the information security strategy (through the selection and prioritization of security initiatives) is the fundamental CISO responsibility.

There are several approaches to identify and prioritize the organizational security initiatives to be funded. Each of these approaches is discussed briefly below.

1.1.1 AUDIT AS A DRIVER FOR SECURITY INITIATIVES

An information security audit is an external review of current information security controls against organizational security policies or an established standard. These information security audits result in a list of findings and recommendations. It is important that these findings and recommendations be reviewed and potentially remediated (depending on severity level). However, when the information security audit results are the primary driver for determining the next security initiative in an organization, the organization has no clear security strategy. Reliance on the audit results as the guide for improving the organization's security posture is necessary but not sufficient. Audits by their nature are reviews of current controls against policies and procedures (or regulations) that have already been established. A security strategy based only on what the auditors find will be in a constant state of catch-up and limited to a previous and narrow vision of minimum-security controls. Moreover, information security priorities stemming from these audits will be "audit-based" (or backward looking only), which is limited to the threats to our organization that we already know about and have written policies and procedures to address.

1.1.2 TECHNOLOGY AS A DRIVER FOR SECURITY INITIATIVES

Another approach to developing a security strategy that is often arrived at by default is a technology-based security strategy. A technology-based security strategy is an overreliance on information technology to provide the security controls to implement the organization's security strategy. It is clear that technologists and information security product vendors have been able to supply the industry with a steady stream of features, improvements, and new security products. Many times, these products are just what an organization needs to enact protection measures for their assets. However, a security strategy that relies too heavily on technologist and information security product vendors to dictate the security solutions will find the administrative and physical areas of their protection measures lacking. This leads to an unbalanced and ineffective implementation of the organization's information security strategy.

1.1.3 COMPLIANCE AS A DRIVER FOR SECURITY INITIATIVES

Information security regulations specify and even require a minimum set of information security requirements for organizations within specific industries. The information security regulations or standards such as Payment Card Industry Data Security Standard (PCI DSS) or Health Insurance Portability and Accountability Act (HIPAA) Security Rule seem a natural place to start when creating a security strategy for an organization in the related industries. However, these requirements likely represent a small portion of the organization's information security requirements to be addressed. Organizations need to address customer and business mission requirements as well. Relying only upon the information security requirements listed in industry regulations and standards will fail to take into account current threats, business drivers, and executive management risk appetite for the organization. Those organizations limit their information security strategy by adopting a compliance-driven strategy to security may find themselves battling the silo approach (e.g.,

HIPAA security effort, PCI DSS effort, and Privacy effort). Reliance on compliance regulations leads to the inevitable discovery that regulations do not provide adequate guidance for implementation. Furthermore, it is difficult to plan for the next iteration of changes to regulations.

1.1.4 Security Risk as a Driver for Security Initiatives

Even though each of these approaches offers some benefit, a more complete security strategy can be created based on the documentation of the organization's risk appetite, a complete understanding of the organization's information security requirements, and a thorough analysis of information security risk. It is the overall information security risk to the organization's assets (not those limited to audit findings, missing vendor features, or non-compliance) that needs to be appropriately addressed in the proper execution of the organization's information security strategy. The single best way to execute the information security risk strategy is to appropriately measure information security risk. As clear as this statement seems it is still surprising that security risk assessment is not always the driver for creating a security strategy.

In determining the effectiveness of an organization's ability to implement an information security strategy, it is useful to ask the following question of information security officers (or have them ask it of themselves):

> Given your limited resources, are you confident that your initiatives are addressing the largest security risks to your organization's assets?

At first blush this seems an innocent enough question and is often answered quickly in the affirmative. Following this question with a more probing question often gives the information security officer pause:

> How do you demonstrate that your initiatives are addressing the largest security risks to your organization's assets to management?

The reason the question above is a more difficult question is that is seems hard to demonstrate that the limited resources are being utilized to address security risk efficiently if security risk is not measured or not measured adequately. The above question essentially asks for proof or evidence that information security initiatives are appropriately prioritized. Overreliance on ineffective drivers (such as audit, vendors, and compliance) builds information security programs which are difficult to defend against such probing questions. Information security risk, therefore, stands out as the most effective driver for establishing information security initiatives and ensuring an effective information security program.

Building an information security program on the basis for information security risk requires a solid and effective security risk assessment. Afterall, the results of the security risk assessment are the input and direction to the establishment and management of the information security strategy. With so much riding on the results of security risk assessment it is important that they are done right.

1.2 ENSURING A QUALITY INFORMATION SECURITY RISK ASSESSMENT

If the information security officer has properly aligned his security strategy with the results of security risk assessment, then it is easy to demonstrate that the planned security initiatives are addressing the largest organizational security risks. The security risk assessment is, therefore, a critical tool in the monitoring and management of the information security program. When security risk assessment is used as the basis for security decisions, the quality of the security risk assessment becomes critical. A weak security risk assessment method can lead to inaccurate conclusions, bias results, a false sense of security (or fear), and eventually to significant planning errors, ineffective expenditures of limited resources, and increased information security risk.

There are many projects to be executed properly to ensure that information security programs effectively protect the organization's assets. For the reasons stated above, none is more important than the security risk assessment. When the security risk assessment is the driver for determining the prioritization of information security initiatives, it's proper execution cannot be taken lightly. Security risk assessments done without solid methods and accurate data collection (e.g., surveys, internal self-reviews, and checklists) can lead to costly mistakes and inaccurate strategic directions. The security risk assessment is the most highly leveraged activity performed within the information security organization (Figure 1.1). Security risk assessments are not commodities. There is a vast difference between a security risk assessment performed by an experienced team utilizing a strong security risk assessment method and an inexperienced team utilizing a weak method. The strength of the security risk assessment method is imperative if the resultant security risk assessment report is to be used as a management tool. Some of the benefits of a security risk assessment report based on a strong method include:

- Security Control Measurement—As the central element of a security risk assessment is to gather data and assess the strength of existing security controls, a security risk assessment based on a strong method provides an accurate measurement of existing security control effectiveness.
- Security Program Strength Measurement—The results of a security risk assessment based on a strong method provides insights into the strength of the existing security program.
- Basis for Improvement—When the results of a security risk assessment are based on a strong method the results and recommendations can be confidently used to determine actions and decisions for improvements in the organization's security controls.
- Understanding of Threats and Risks—A security risk assessment report based on a strong method provides all stakeholders a clear understanding of the security threats and risks to the organization.
- Senior Management Tool—A security risk assessment report based on strong methods is a powerful tool for senior management in planning, decisions, and oversight of the overall security program.

The realization that there was little guidance on the appropriate execution of security risk assessment and the collection of quality data it is the reason for the creation of this book. Security risk

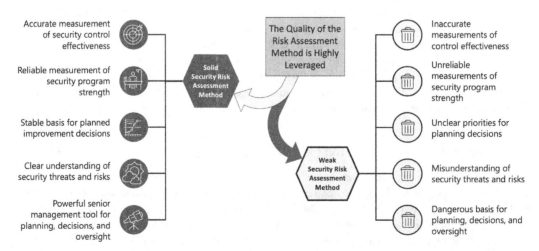

FIGURE 1.1   Importance of Security Risk Assessment Method. When a security risk assessment is used as the basis for making security decisions in the organization, the risk method is highly leveraged. Weaknesses in the risk assessment method can eventually lead to planning errors and increased security risk.

assessments should not be merely performed to check a box or to satisfy a regulatory requirement. Instead, security risk assessment should be performed in a professional manner that provides accurate results. It is my hope that this book will guide and inspire more professional information security assessments.

1.3 SECURITY RISK ASSESSMENT

An information security risk assessment determines the value of information assets, measures the strength of the overall information security program, and provides the analysis necessary to make planned improvements based on information security risks. The security risk assessment is the tool of senior management that gives them an effective measurement of their security controls and an indication of how well their assets are protected.

1.3.1 THE ROLE OF THE SECURITY RISK ASSESSMENT

A security risk assessment is an important element in the overall information security risk management process. Information security risk management involves the process of ensuring that the security risk posture of an organization is within acceptable bounds as defined by senior management. There are four stages of the information security risk management process: security risk assessment; controls test and review; information security risk mitigation; and operational information security (see Figure 1.2).

- Information Security Risk Assessment—This is an objective analysis of the effectiveness of the current security controls that protect an organization's assets and a determination of the

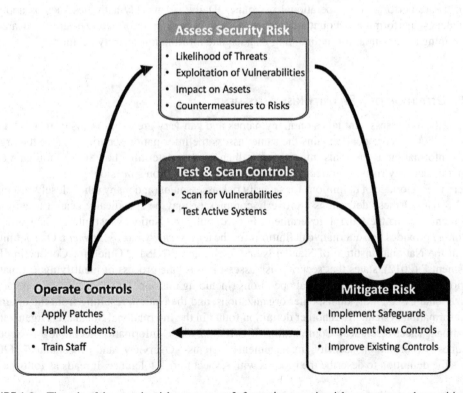

FIGURE 1.2 The role of the security risk assessment. Information security risk assessments play a critical role in the information security management process, providing information on the threats, assets, and information security risks to an organization.

probability of losses to those assets. A security risk assessment reviews the organization's threat environment, the asset values, the system's criticality, the information security controls' vulnerabilities, and the expected losses' impact, and also provides recommendations for additional controls to reduce information security risk to an acceptable level. Based on this analysis, the organization's senior management can determine if additional information security controls are required.

- Controls Test and Review—Information security testing is the examination of the information security controls against the information security requirements. The need for additional information security controls to obtain an acceptable level of information security risk is determined during the security risk assessment. Information security testing can be applied to any number of or subset of information security controls, such as physical controls testing (e.g., doors and access control), vulnerability scanning (e.g., external interfaces), or social engineering (e.g., user behavior). Typically, information security testing is performed more frequently than security risk assessments.

- Information Security Risk Mitigation—Either the reported information security risks are accepted or information security risks to an organization's assets are reduced through the implementation of new information security controls or the improvement of existing controls. Information security risk assessments provide information to allow the senior management to make information security risk-based decisions for the development of new controls or the expenditure of resources on information security improvements of existing controls. Information security test and review efforts provide information on how to keep existing controls up to date. Information security risk can be mitigated through corrections and additional controls, accepted or transferred.

- Operational Information Security—The implementation and operation of most security controls are performed by operational personnel. Daily and weekly activities such as applying patches, performing account maintenance, and providing information security awareness training are essential for maintaining an adequate information security posture.

1.3.2 DEFINITION OF A SECURITY RISK ASSESSMENT

The security risk assessment takes on many names and can vary greatly in terms of method, rigor, and scope, but the core goal remains the same: assess the information security risks to the organization's information assets. This information is then used to determine how best to mitigate those information security risks and effectively preserve the organization's mission.

There is no shortage of definitions for security risk assessment (and many other closely associated names). Many of these definitions are overly complex or may be specifically geared to an industry segment such as the federal government. For example, the National Institute of Standards and Technology provides two alternative definitions for the term *security risk assessment*. One definition, found in the National Institute of Standards and Technology (NIST) "Guide for Conducting Risk Assessments" (2012), states that security risk assessment is "the process of identifying, estimating, and prioritizing risks to organizational operations (including mission, functions, image, reputation), organizational assets, individuals, other organizations, and the Nation, resulting from the operation of an information system." Yet another definition found in the International Standards Organization/International Electrotechnical Commission (ISO/IEC) 27000 "Information technology—Security techniques—Information security management systems—Overview and vocabulary" (2018) expands the definition to describe the process with respect to risk tolerance. It reads as follows:

> Risk Assessment—the overall process of finding, recognizing and describing risk to comprehend the nature of risk and to determine the level of risk and of comparing the results of risk analysis with risk criteria to determine whether the risk and/or its magnitude is acceptable or tolerable.

Other uses of the term risk assessment are geared toward a specific use, such as complying with the PCI DSS. The PCI Security Standards Council defines risk assessment as a formal process used by organizations to identify threats and vulnerabilities that could negatively impact the security of cardholder data.

The ISO 27001/2 takes an integrated approach to security management and recognizes the value of security risk assessments in that process. The basic structure of security management involves selecting security requirements, assessing the risks, and selecting controls. The security risk assessment is central to this approach, as it assesses the risks that the security requirements may not be met and provides the basis for a risk-based decision for selecting security controls.

In all the regulations, guidelines, and standards, *security risk assessment* has been defined in numerous ways. Some definitions are more detailed than others in terms of how an assessment is performed. Some definitions focus on the result of the assessment, while others focus on the approach. For our purposes, a simpler *security risk assessment* definition is needed to cover any such approach or detail. Because this book will discuss the various methods of performing a security risk assessment, the definition used here is designed to fit all such methods. For the purposes of this book, *security risk assessment* is defined as follows:

> Security Risk Assessment—A probability determination of asset losses based on asset valuation, threat analysis, and an objective review of current security controls effectiveness.

1.3.3 THE NEED FOR A SECURITY RISK ASSESSMENT

A security risk assessment is a basic requirement for most information security regulations (e.g., PCI DSS, Gramm-Leach Bliley Act (GLBA), Sarbanes-Oxley (SOX), and NIST Cybersecurity Framework (NIST CSF)). Aside from being required, a security risk assessment is an essential element of any corporation seeking to protect its information assets. A security risk assessment has the following benefits to an organization.

1.3.3.1 Checks and Balances

A security risk assessment provides a review of the organization's current information asset protection implementation. The work of the information security officer and the security operations staff should be assessed by an objective party to determine the adequacy of the program and to note areas for improvement. Those who have architected the security program and those who are administering security controls are too close to the decisions that have been made and are not likely to be able to provide an objective analysis. (More on this in Section 12.1.3 Project Resources.)

1.3.3.2 Periodic Review

Even the most carefully constructed information security program requires a periodic review. A periodic review can provide a program effectiveness measure and information necessary to properly adjust the program for the changing threat environment and business mission.

Many elements of an information security program require periodic review to measure their effectiveness. For example, the security awareness training program should be reviewed to measure and improve its effectiveness based on changes to regulations, staff members, environmental threats, and recent security incidents within the organization. Such measurements should not be limited to student evaluations of security awareness training or courses delivered, but the actual security awareness that has been instilled into the culture of employees and others who have access to an organization's information assets. Additional measurements on the security awareness program's effectiveness could be obtained through physical inspections, security policy quizzes, and social-engineering experiments, to name a few.

Moreover, the landscape in which an information security program is developed is constantly changing and the controls in place should change along with these threats to keep up. Threats to the organization's information assets change as technology advances, information is promulgated, skills (or tools) are acquired by would-be intruders, and interfaces to the organization's assets increase. For example, prior to widespread knowledge, tools, and tutorials, a Structured Query Language (SQL) injection attack on a database required the skills of a determined intruder. Nowadays, less skilled and more abundant script-kiddies possess the ability to launch the same attack through tools circulated freely on the Internet.

Similarly, a decade ago many organizations could state, with reasonable confidence, that they were aware of and controlled all interfaces to their networks. However, if an organization lacks the proper controls, the introduction of mobile devices or cheap wireless routers that can be added to internal networks or connected laptops can render the network boundaries unknown.

Lastly, your organization's mission may have changed through mergers, acquisitions, divestitures, spin-offs, or simply retooling since information security controls were first devised. Changes in mission can change everything from the reclassification of sensitive data and the addition of partners and extended networks to the development of new systems, connections, and security risks. Without a periodic security risk assessment, an organization's information security program would remain stagnant while threats, attacker skills, and business missions change. The result would be a steady decline of the effectiveness of the information security program and an increased risk, as illustrated in Figure 1.3.

1.3.3.3 Risk-Based Spending

Resource allocation can be based on security risk to assets. Organizations have limited resources to address their information security issues. If a security risk assessment is not performed, the organization does not have an understanding of the security risks to its information assets. In the absence of security risk information, resources are allocated on a variety of other factors, including convenience, existing familiarity or skill, or simply interest.

When deciding how to spend the information security budget, the decision-makers may choose the latest gadgets offered by vendors who have an existing relationship to the organization. Similarly, the decision-makers may choose to expand the organization's capabilities within an area with which they are familiar. For example, the information security team members may be expert in configuring

FIGURE 1.3 The eroding security posture. Applying security improvements such as security awareness training and security patching can lower the security risk of an information system, but the changing threats and environment will erode the security posture over time.

perimeter devices to filter the content of outgoing messages. There may be exciting advances within this field. It would be natural for this team to be drawn toward pursuing the integration of such advances into the existing information asset control architecture. Lastly, the decision-makers may simply be swayed by new technology. While many of these controls will likely improve the organization's security posture, they may not deliver the best "bang for the buck."

Consider an organization that currently has an inadequate security awareness program and lacks the proper information security policies. Recognizing that security programs break at the weakest link, it is not a stretch to imagine that a security risk assessment would point out that the lack of an adequate security awareness program and security policies poses the greatest security risk to an organization's assets. However, without an adequate security risk assessment providing consideration of which security controls would ultimately reduce the overall security risk to an organization, other more familiar or interesting controls will likely receive funding over such administrative controls. When is the last time you remember a security professional being interested in developing a security awareness program?

1.3.3.4 Requirement

A security risk assessment is a required element of a security program according to multiple information security regulations. These regulations include PCI DSS, HIPAA, GLBA, NERC (North American Electric Reliability Corporation)/CIP (Critical Infrastructure Protection) Cyber Security Standards, ISO 27001/2, OMB A-130 (Office of Management and Budget), FISMA (Federal Information Security Management Act), and many others. If for no other reason, many organizations obtain a security risk assessment simply because it is required.

1.3.4 SECURITY RISK ASSESSMENT SECONDARY BENEFITS

Aside from the obvious benefits mentioned in Section 1.3.3, a security risk assessment may provide some secondary benefits to an organization as well. Among those benefits are the transfer of knowledge from the security assessment team to the organization's staff, increased communications regarding security among business units, and increased security awareness within the organization. In addition, the results of the security risk assessment may be used as a measure of the security posture and compared to previous and future results.

There is an expectation that the members of the security assessment team will be experts in the field of information security. As we shall discuss in this book, the ability to observe, estimate, assess, and recommend is largely based on having experience with security mechanisms, how they work, and how they fail. An experienced security risk assessment team will be able to apply that knowledge to specific implementations of security mechanisms within the organization's unique environment. Throughout the data gathering process and the draft and final security risk assessment report, the experience of the team will be shared with the organization. Many of the insights shared may prove valuable to the organization and would not otherwise have been gained.

The fact that a security risk assessment team is focused solely on the security risks to the organization requires that the interaction of security mechanisms between business units need to be addressed—perhaps for the first time. The security risk assessment may allow for or even force a security discussion among the business units. For example, when assessing the effectiveness of termination procedures, the legal, human resources, physical security, and information technology departments will all need to work together to ensure an effective approach and execution of these procedures.

A security risk assessment includes many activities that may test the security awareness of the employees within the organization. A security risk assessment will include physical security walkthroughs, checks on perimeter controls, and interviews with employees and key personnel, and it may include social engineering. All of these activities will result in an indication of how effective security awareness training is within the organization. Making specific results known to the organization's employees will increase the overall security awareness. For example, if the security risk assessment team was able to "piggyback" through physical access controls (e.g., trailing behind someone who has swiped a badge to open a door), consider letting the organization's employees know the results of those tasks. This will increase their awareness that such breaches can actually occur and that it is their responsibility to help enforce current policies.

The security risk assessment should conclude with a list of security risks to the organization's assets and an indication of the organization's overall security posture. These results can be compared to the previous and future results to assist in tracking the progress of the information security program. Organizations that consistently find that their security posture indicates that they are taking a larger security risk than they are comfortable with should consider increasing the resources allocated to information security. The organization should also ask the security risk assessment team for a comparison of the organization's information security program with those of similar organizations. As mentioned previously, the members of the security risk assessment team will have experience with other organizations and should be able to provide a rough comparison of how this organization measures up to its peers in the industry.

1.4 RELATED ACTIVITIES

There is much confusion surrounding the terms used to describe an assessment of the security mechanisms within an organization. Although there are clearly different approaches, objectives, and levels of rigor within various assessments, there does not seem to be a well-understood and accepted method for describing each of these assessments. For the purposes of this book and for clearly describing our topic, the following descriptions are offered.

All of the services listed in Figure 1.4 and Table 1.1 are related but should not be confused with a security risk assessment. A security risk assessment and the services described may be performed by professionals with similar credentials who use similar tools and checklists. However, a security risk assessment is differentiated from the other services in that only a security risk assessment takes

Security Program Elements Reviewed	Vulnerability Scan	Penetration Test	Security Risk Assessment
External Interfaces	✓	✓	✓
Internal Interfaces	✓	✓	✓
Web Applications	✗	✓	✓
Security Awareness	✗	✓	✓
Operational Procedures	✗	✗	✓
Security Policies	✗	✗	✓
Physical Controls	✗	✗	✓
Personnel Controls	✗	✗	✓
Vendor Management	✗	✗	✓
Asset Inventory	✗	✗	✓

FIGURE 1.4   A Comparison of Security Assessment Activities. Vulnerability scans and penetration testing provide a review of some of the elements of a security program. However, many key elements of the security program are left unchecked. The security risk assessment provides a complete review of an organization's security program.

TABLE 1.1

Security Assessment Definitions

Term	Definition	Purpose
Gap assessment	A review of security controls against a standard	To provide a list of controls required to become compliant
Compliance audit	Verification that all required security controls are in place	To attest to an organization's compliance with a standard
Security audit	A verification that specified security controls are in place	To attest to an organization's adherence to industry standards
Penetration testing	A methodical and planned attack on a system's security controls	To test the adequacy of security controls in place
Vulnerability scanning	An element of penetration testing that searches for obvious vulnerabilities	To test for the existence of obvious vulnerabilities in the system's security controls

Note: There are a great many different ways to review the security controls of an organization. Terms such as *assessment*, *audit*, and *test* are commonly used as synonyms, yet it is important to understand the distinctive use and limitations of these industry terms.

a risk-based approach at identifying vulnerabilities within the organization's security controls. Only a security risk assessment provides recommendations for improvement based on the actual and perceived security risks to the organization.

1.4.1 GAP ASSESSMENT

A gap assessment is the comparison between what exists within a corporation and what is required. Typically, gap assessments are associated with specific criteria, for example, HIPAA Security Rule Gap Assessment or ISO 27001/2 Gap Assessment. These assessments compare the existence of security policies, procedures, and mechanisms, along with activities (which may include a security risk assessment), against the required security policies, procedures, mechanisms, and activities dictated in the HIPAA regulation or in the ISO 27001/2 guidelines. There is no measure of security risk associated with this assessment; it is merely a review of what exists against an interpretation of what the regulation or guideline requires.

A gap assessment is performed at the beginning of the organization's compliance pursuit with a standard or regulation. Since the gap assessment will result in a list of "gaps" or things that need to be done prior to declaring compliance, these assessments do not require verification of findings. If an interview with key personnel and a review of the materials reveal that the security awareness program is adequate, then the assessment team need go no further with this line of review. The point is to efficiently reach the point where the organization knows what the compliance project entails. An efficient gap assessment helps them get a quicker start with known project objectives. The organization being assessed should realize that deceiving the gap assessment team will only result in an inaccurate compliance plan.

1.4.2 COMPLIANCE AUDIT

When the time comes to attest to the organization's compliance with a regulation or a standard, a more in-depth review is required. This review requires that all findings be verified. The same interview and review of the security awareness training program would be followed up with review of a sample of employee training records and interviews with some employees. A compliance audit still does not result in a measure of the security risk to the organization's assets. A compliance audit is an objective review of the organization's compliance with a security standard, such as HIPAA Privacy and Security Rule, GLBA 501(b), Federal Financial Institutions Examination Council (FIEC) Cybersecurity Assessment Tool (CAT), ISO 27001/2, or other regulations and standards that specify security controls that need to be in place.

1.4.3 SECURITY AUDIT

A security audit, also called a security controls review, is a verification that the security controls that have been specified are properly implemented. Proper implementation may be further defined in existing organizational security policy and procedures or within industry standards, such as COBIT 2019 Framework, ISO 27001/2, and others. Depending on the standards, these security audits can be quite rigorous and even involve statistically relevant sampling techniques and complete verification of all findings.

One thing that is common to all security audits is the overhead implicit in the assessment to ensure consistency with the standard. Many information security standards have associated assessment standards that specify the degree to which the assessor must analyze the data, sample the controls, and complete other such requirements. Some information security standards also require the assessors to obtain the proper credentials or require the assessor's company to be an auditing firm. While these requirements ensure consistency, they also add significantly to the cost of the audit. In most cases a "security audit" would cost far more than a security risk assessment.

The major differences here are level of rigor and formality of the statement. For example, a security audit performed under the Statement on Standards of Attestation Number 18 (SSAE No 18) is said to be an "attestation." This means that a certified public accountant (CPA) has expressed a conclusion about the reliability of a written statement that is the responsibility of someone else. There are two key elements of this definition. First, a CPA provides a conclusion as to the reliability of a written statement. Security audits incur significant overhead, since they must be overseen by a licensed CPA, the reports are issued by a licensed CPA firm, and the report is a formal input into the accounting process. Second, the written statement (referred to as a Statement on Compliance or SOC) is a statement regarding the presence of reasonable assurance that control objectives are met. Control objectives are statements of the intended result or purpose achieved by implementing security controls. These statements are tailored to the organization and the security it is intended to provide.

It is important to understand that, because of the way it is structured, the SSAE No 18 audit (and most standards-driven audits) does not perform a security risk assessment. These security audit methodologies review an organization against a standard and do not provide an analysis of the effectiveness of the current security controls. Instead, these security audits review the current security controls against a standard or a statement produced by the organization being assessed.

1.4.4 VULNERABILITY SCANNING

Vulnerability scanning is the testing of the external or internal interfaces of a system in order to identify obvious vulnerabilities. At a bare minimum, this service involves running a vulnerability scanning tool to test the known interfaces to the system and providing the tool-generated report. These tools are constantly updated with the knowledge of common system vulnerabilities. A more in-depth vulnerability scanning service would perform additional analyses and checks to remove false positives generated by the tool. False positive can be removed from a vulnerability scanning report upon the review and conclusion of a security engineer, using additional knowledge of the system, if the vulnerability identified by the tool does not really exist. These false positives are typically quite numerous in tool-generated reports.

1.4.5   PENETRATION TESTING

Also called ethical hacking, white-hat hacking, security testing, red team testing, and attack and penetration studies, this service is provided by an objective team who attempt to penetrate the defenses of an organization in order to demonstrate current controls effectiveness. A vulnerability scan is typically performed as the first stage of a penetration test. The vulnerability scan would provide one information source to the security testers for their use in attempting to penetrate the system. Penetration testing actually comprises several elements, including vulnerability scanning, ad hoc testing, war dialing, social engineering, and other techniques. These elements can also be performed as a stand-alone test or as part of the security risk assessment data gathering phase.

1.4.6   AD HOC TESTING

Whereas vulnerability scans test for obvious vulnerabilities, ad hoc testing is a search for less obvious vulnerabilities. This type of testing must be performed by experts who use various techniques and knowledge gained from years of experience. This is more of an art than a science, but methods and some tools are available or developed in-house to assist in the process.

1.4.7   SOCIAL ENGINEERING

This type of testing involves an assessment of the organization's security training, policies, and procedures by attempting to gain unauthorized access through the human element. Social engineering by its nature is ad hoc and varies each time. Examples of this testing include gaining unauthorized physical access through walking closely behind an authorized staff member through a physical entry gate to gain unauthorized entry (i.e., "piggybacking,") obtaining user identification and passwords through the help desk and gaining unauthorized information through temporary or new employees. Remote social engineering may include spoofed e-mail campaigns to lure the staff members into revealing sensitive information, called phishing; or using a phone call to perform similar deceptions, called vishing. Basically, social engineering involves gaining the confidence of authorized users in order to obtain sensitive information or gain access.

1.4.8   WAR DIALING

Another way of threatening an organization's assets is to gain access to its information systems or control systems through unprotected modems. This method is referred to as *war dialing*. A war-dialing effort consists of identifying all organizational phone numbers that have modems attached (foot printing), determining the vulnerabilities of these various modems (preparation), and finally gaining access to the organization's systems through vulnerable modems. Systems targeted include not only information systems but also environmental systems such as the High-Volume Air Conditioning (HVAC), security systems, and telephone systems (or private branch exchanges—PBXs). Although the use of modems has plummeted since the introduction of wireless access points (WAPs), these doors into your organization's critical systems still exist in many facilities.

1.5   THE NEED FOR THIS BOOK

The proliferation of information security and privacy laws, not to mention lawsuits, has mandated that businesses perform security risk assessments. Decades ago, an analysis of the effectiveness of security controls was rarely performed outside of government agencies and those organizations with the highest security concerns. Now most organizations are incorporating a security risk assessment into their information security programs as a way to continually improve their controls and remain compliant with information security regulations. At the same time, the demand for security risk assessments has exploded, but the supply of experienced information security engineers to perform them has not kept up with the demand.

In order to provide relief to this situation, there have been several promising advances in the area of security risk assessments. There are many sources of information that describe various security risk assessment processes. These resources include (a) general security program guidance, which includes discussions on security risk assessments; (b) descriptions of security risk assessment methodologies; and (c) information on security risk assessment tools. These resources are useful to most information security professionals involved with commissioning or performing a security risk assessment. Below are a few examples of resources for those looking to professionally perform a security risk assessment:

- General Security Program Guidance—Groups such as ASIS International and federal agencies such as the NIST have provided general guidance that covers some aspects of performing security risk assessments. Below are a few examples.
  - NIST Special Publication 800-30, Rev 1: Guide for Conducting Risk Assessments—This publication provides a detailed discussion of a four-step process for security risk assessments. The four-step process includes preparation, conducting the assessment, communicating the results, and maintaining the assessment. Step 2: "Conducting the Assessment" is expanded to describe the substeps of identifying threats, vulnerabilities, likelihood of occurrence, magnitude of impact, and finally determination of risk. For each of these steps, the NIST publication provides a discussion of the relevant points, offers some advice, and references several other useful sources of information. This publication offers a simplistic approach to calculating the security risk level for each system procedure/vulnerability pair. The publication offers a list of general categories of security risk prevention, detection, and recovery controls and advice on cost–benefit analysis.
  - ASIS International: The General Security Risk Assessment Guideline—This guideline was published to obtain a consensus regarding general practices for performing security risk assessments. It is a bit dated, 2002, but many of the concepts are still applicable to physical security assessments. The document outlines a seven-step process that comprises system and asset identification, specification of vulnerabilities, determining security risk probabilities and event impact, developing security risk mitigation options, studying the feasibility of options, and performing a cost–benefit analysis. The bulk of the ASIS security risk assessment guideline is the practice advisories contained in "Appendix I: Qualitative Approach." These practice advisories include several examples to help illustrate the seven-step process. The ASIS guideline also provides many useful references.
  - Security Risk Assessment Methods—Other groups and individuals, such as Carnegie Mellon University, and the Factor Analysis of Information Risk (FAIR) Institute have produced general security risk assessment models and methods that are designed to be used in the performance of a security risk assessment. For a more complete discussion of security risk assessment methods, see Chapter 13.
  - Security Risk Assessment Tools—There is even a good set of security risk assessment tools available to those looking at providing a security risk assessment service or with performing a security risk assessment within their own organizations. Security risk assessment tools include everything from simple checklists to complex software packages. For a more complete discussion of security risk assessment methods, see Chapter 14.

However, none of these resources are able to provide a complete and detailed explanation of the security risk assessment process sufficient to assist an information security professional in actually performing the work. Sufficient process details are missing and the information security professional is unable gain a comfort level that they would know what to do when assessing physical security controls, interviewing the Human Resources director, or writing an effective report.

Although many security risk assessment products, services, and approaches exist, little guidance is available to those who need to perform them. For all the conferences, seminars, tools, and literature that exists on the topic, there still is little available advice or guidance that tells the security practitioner how to get started, how to behave, how to present the results, or how to acquire any one of several dozen skills required to actually perform a security risk assessment. There is a frustration commonly experienced by information security professionals when attempting to perform a security risk assessment. Although existing material describes in detail the components of a security risk assessment, little information is available on how to execute those components. The "why" and the "what" are well explained, but there seems to be no information on the "how."

For example, most guidance currently available outlines the step in which the security risk assessment team must determine the impact of an event. The available guidance provides the structure for a security risk assessment team to work within by informing that losses may be direct and indirect, by emphasizing that the team must understand the business mission and consider the various security policies that could be threatened, and even by giving sample qualitative categories and descriptions such as "low," "medium," and "high" or even more complex quantitative formulas and spreadsheets. However, none of the guidance documents tells the team exactly how to come up with the impact classification for each of the security risk statements. No examples are given. No guidelines on ideal team size or decision techniques. No specific guidance on how to actually get this job done exists. Until now, that specific guidance has only been developed by experienced information security professionals and absorbed by less experienced team members during an actual engagement.

This book will attempt to document just that experience and advice. By providing real examples, step-by-step descriptions, checklists, decision techniques, and other tricks of the trade, this book will provide a detailed insight into precisely how to conduct security risk assessment from a practical point of view.

1.6   WHO IS THIS BOOK FOR?

This book is designed and intended for anyone who wants a more detailed understanding of how to perform security risk assessment. The audience for this book includes security professionals who want a more in-depth understanding of the process of performing a security risk assessment and for security consumers who want a better understanding of what goes into completing a security risk assessment project.

Security professionals will benefit from this book, as the information will help them to become more valuable members of—or perhaps even to lead—a security risk assessment team. The information in this book in based on nearly three decades of experience conducting security risk assessments for a variety of organizations and contains practical real-world advice that will help develop the experience of the security professional reader. This book has found its way onto the shelf of many security professionals who refer back to it as their experience level increases.

Security consumers will benefit from this book by having greater insight into the security risk assessment process. The process descriptions and examples in this book will give the security consumer a more in-depth understanding of the entire process. Enlightened security consumers are then better educated to negotiate the scope and rigor of a security assessment, interface with the security assessment team more effectively, provide insightful comments on the draft report, and have a greater understanding of the final report recommendations.

As a result of reading and using this book, it is envisioned that the reader will save both time and money. Students of this text can expect to save time since they will spend less time figuring out what activities to do next and precisely how to perform them. In addition, the charts, checklists, examples, and templates included in this text can speed up the process of data gathering, analysis, and document development for the security risk assessment effort.

It is also expected that students of this text can save money as well. In the world of information security consulting, time is money. This text is designed to increase the quality of a consultant's product and reduce the amount of effort it takes to create that product. Such advances can lead to consultants providing a better, less expensive service for their customers and perhaps even making a larger profit in the process.

The security service consumer will benefit from reading this book as well. In addition to being the recipient of better, cheaper, faster security risk assessments, security consumers who have a more in-depth understanding of the security risk assessment process will be able to more confidently scope their security risk assessments to meet their objectives in the most effective manner. Security assessment services can range from a low of about $35,000 to a high of well over $350,000, depending on various factors (see Section 2.2 for a discussion of these factors).

A more educated consumer will be better suited to solicit, and review proposals presented by various security service consultancies. Security service consumers who understand the process, components, skills, required experience, and other factors of a security risk assessment will be well positioned to commission a security risk assessment that meets their needs from a quality security service provider at a competitive price.

EXERCISES

1. Security testing can be applied to any number or subset of controls. What controls are being tested during each of the following tests? (Be as specific as possible.)
    a. Vulnerability scanning
    b. Penetration testing
    c. Social engineering
    d. Physical penetration testing
    e. War dialing
2. Review the definition of *security risk assessment* in Section 1.4.2 and compare/contrast with another definition you or others have used.
3. List the primary benefits of a security risk assessment.
4. Why would each of the following stakeholders request or commission a security risk assessment?
    a. a prospective customer
    b. an existing customer
    c. a newly appointed CISO
    d. executive management
    e. a regulatory body (e.g., PCI SSC and OCR/HIPAA)
5. Find an example of a security risk assessment Request for Proposal (RFP) online. Review the required services and
    a. Be prepared to discuss if this is truly a security risk assessment or a related activity.
    b. How would you modify or amend the RFP to align it with the goals of a security risk assessment?
    c. If the RFP is truly a security risk assessment, work as a group to estimate the hours it would require to perform the assessment and submit a bid. For any unknown variables required to provide an estimate, document assumptions or ask your instructor for clarification.
6. If security spending is not based on a security risk assessment, how are spending priorities typically determined?
7. What other security assessment activities that measure control effectiveness could be implemented, that are not already listed in Section 1.4?

NOTE

1 A security risk appetite is the level and type of security risks an organization is prepared to take or accept.

BIBLIOGRAPHY

American Institute of Certified Public Accountants. "Clarified Statements on Standards for Attestation Engagements (SSAE) No. 18: Concepts Common to All Attestation Engagements," AT-C Section 105, May 1, 2017.

ASIS International. *The General Security Risk Assessment Guideline.* November 13, 2002.

Department of Health and Human Services, Office of the Secretary. "Health Insurance Reform: Security Standards; Final Rule," 45 CFR Parts 160, 162, and 164, Federal Register, Vol. 68, No. 34, August 14, 2002.

Department of Health and Human Services, Office of the Secretary. "Standards for Privacy of Individually Identifiable Health Information; Final Rule," 45 CFR Parts 160 and 164, Federal Register, Vol. 67, No. 157, February 20, 2003.

Federal Deposit Insurance Corporation, "501(b) Examination Guidance: Examination Procedures to Evaluate Compliance with the guidelines to Safeguard Customer Information," November 13, 2018. https://www.fdic.gov/news/financial-institution-letters/2001/fil0168.html

Federal Financial Institutions Examination Council (FFIEC), "Cybersecurity Assessment Tool (CAT)," May 2017.

Federal Trade Commission. "Standards for Privacy of Individually Identifiable Health Information; Final Rule," 45 CFR Parts 160 and 164, Federal Register, Vol. 67, No. 157, August 14, 2002.

Federal Trade Commission. "Standards for Safeguarding Customer Information; Final Rule," 16 CFR Part 314, Federal Register, Vol. 67, No. 100, May 23, 2002. Payment Card Industry (PCI) Security Standards Council: Risk Assessment Special Interest Group, "Information Supplement: PCI DSS Risk Assessment Guidelines," November 2012.

International Standards Organization/International Electrotechnical Commission (ISO/IEC), 27000:2018 Information technology – Security techniques – Information security management systems – Overview and vocabulary," February 2018.

International Standards Organization/International Electrotechnical Commission (ISO/IEC), 27001:2013 Information technology – Security techniques – Information security management systems – Requirements," October 2013a.

International Standards Organization/International Electrotechnical Commission (ISO/IEC), 27002:2013 Information technology – Security techniques – Information security management systems – Code of practice for information security controls," October 2013b.

ISACA, "COBIT 2019 Framework," 2019.

National Institute of Standards and Technology (NIST): U.S. Department of Commerce, "Guide for Conducting Risk Assessments" NIST Special Publication 800-30, Revision 1, September 2012.

National Institute of Standards and Technology (NIST): U.S. Department of Commerce, "Framework for Improving Critical Infrastructure Cybersecurity," Version 1.1, April 16, 2008.

North American Electric Reliability Corporation (NERC), "Reliability Standards for the Bulk Electric Systems of North America," July 29, 2020.

Office of Management and Budget, Circular No. A-130, "Managing Information as a Strategic Resource," July 2016.

Payment Card Industry (PCI) Data Security Standard, "Requirements and Security Assessment Procedures," Version 3.2.1, May 2018.

U.S. General Accounting Office, Accounting and Information Management Division, "Information Security Risk Assessment: Practices of Leading Organizations," A Supplement to GAO's May 1998 Executive Guide on Information Security Management, GAO/IAM-00-33, November 1999.

U.S. Government Printing Office. "Federal Information Security Modernization Act of 2014," Public Law 113-283, 113th Congress, December 18, 2014.

U.S. Government Printing Office. "Sarbanes-Oxley Act of 2002: Corporate responsibility," Public Law 107-204, 107th Congress, July 30, 2002.

2 Information Security Risk Assessment Basics

It is the aim of this book to provide an extensive discussion of the elements and performance of an information security risk assessment. As such, you will find detailed information, discussion, and advice on all elements of the security risk assessment. Many of the sections of this book will provide a rather detailed discussion of a single element of security risk assessment. However, before we get into this level of discussion, it would be useful to provide a brief overview of the security risk assessment process.

For the purposes of this book, the security risk assessment process is defined as follows:

Security Risk Assessment—An objective analysis of the effectiveness of the current security controls that protect an organization's assets and a determination of the probability of losses to those assets.

There are many security risk assessment methods available and currently in use. Depending on the specific one employed, a security risk assessment may have any number of steps or phases, and each of these phases may have slightly different names. However, the overall security risk assessment process is largely similar in all these methods. The generic phases of a security risk assessment are shown in Figure 2.1.

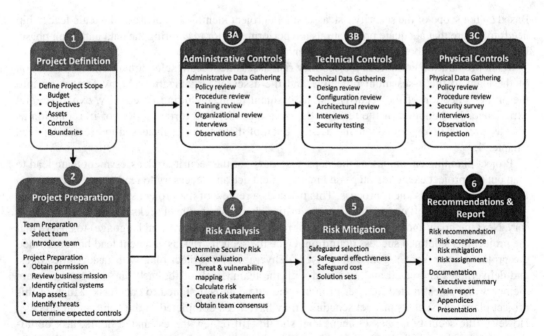

FIGURE 2.1 The Security Risk Assessment Process. The security risk assessment process comprises the following phases: project definition, project preparation, administrative data gathering, technical data gathering, physical data gathering, risk analysis, risk mitigation, and recommendations. These phases are described in more detail in the remaining chapters of this book.

2.1   PHASE 1: PROJECT DEFINITION

The first phase of a generic security risk assessment process is the project definition phase. As with many projects, the success of the security risk assessment project relies not only on the assigned security risk assessment team's skill and experience, but also on the project management effectiveness. A key component of project management is arriving at an agreement as to the scope and content of deliverables. Within the project definition phase, the project is properly scoped and documented.

The scoping of any project includes a clear understanding of the cost and time frame of the engagement. The security risk assessment team leader needs to ensure that the project budget and time constraints are well understood between the customer and the team lead, prior to conveying the project objectives to the team members. Documentation of this understanding is captured in the project plan and in the contract, if this involves an external customer. A project plan not only documents the budget, time constraints, and deliverables, but breaks down the overall project into manageable tasks and allocates resources to those tasks.

Beyond the project budget, time constraints, and deliverables, the scoping of a security risk assessment can be more complex than the scoping of some other projects. Unique variables to the security risk assessment process include the assessment objective, the assets and controls to be covered, and the assessment boundaries. Obtaining clarity on the security risk assessment objective is necessary to understand the customer needs. For example, a security risk assessment performed for contract compliance has a different objective than one performed for program review. The team must also seek clarity on the boundaries of the assessment through an identification of assets, systems, and other boundaries of the project. Each of these tasks is discussed in greater detail in Chapter 3.

2.2   PHASE 2: PROJECT PREPARATION

Based on the scope of the security risk assessment project identified in phase 1, the team leadership needs to ensure that adequate preparations are performed prior to entering the data gathering phase. Preparation includes both team preparation and project planning.

Team preparation comprises the security risk assessment team selection and the introduction of the team to the assessment objective and the assessed organization. Many factors go into the proper selection of the security risk assessment team, including objectivity, expertise, and experience. Introduction of the team to the customer includes formal letters of introduction as well as a request for permission and access. Each of these tasks is discussed in greater detail in Chapter 4.

Project planning encompasses the steps necessary for the security risk assessment team lead to map out the project execution steps and management actions necessary to lead, track, and manage the security risk assessment process. This includes a review of the project scope and deliverables to ensure they are well understood. The security risk assessment lead seeks clarification if necessary. Next the goals and objectives are set (or reaffirmed from contractual language) to ensure that the project has a defined success definition. Once the security risk assessment lead has confirmed the project basics (scope, goals, objectives, deliverables) a project plan with tasks, milestones, and deliverables is created and reviewed with the team. Each of the tasks are assigned to team members and an estimated number of hours and due date is assigned to each task. Much of this project planning (such as project schedule) may have been completed in the contractual process. However, the security risk assessment lead should still review the estimated hours, task definitions, and due dates with the team members to ensure understanding and agreement as to the tasks assigned to them.

2.3 PHASE 3: DATA GATHERING

The data gathering phase is the stage in the security risk assessment process in which the team acquires evidence regarding the security controls in place within the scope of the security risk assessment. This stage may be performed remotely (via conference calls, surveys, and even remote testing) or on-site (via system inspection, observations, physical site inspections, and on-site testing). Whether remote or on-site, the data gathering stage results in the information collection concerning the current administrative, physical, and technical security controls effectiveness.

Administrative controls are policies, procedures, and activities performed to enforce security controls (e.g., acceptable use procedures, sanction policy, and the investigation process). The security risk assessment team will review the administrative controls through the collection, review, and analysis of available policies and procedures as well as observation and interviews with staff regarding the implementation of those policies and procedures.

Physical security controls are barriers, physical monitoring, and the support of environmental (e.g., clean electric power, and air conditioning), and building and fire safety controls. The physical security controls will be assessed through techniques such as on-site inspections, observation, testing, and analysis of available data.

Technical security controls are automated identification, authentication, authorization, and audit controls implemented within the computer systems. The technical security controls will be reviewed through configuration review, technical analysis, testing, and review of logs.

The data gathering phase is the most comprehensive of all of the phases and is discussed in more detail in Chapter 5. Specific advice on how to perform data gathering for administrative, technical, and physical controls are found respectively in Chapters 6 (Administrative Data Gathering), 7 (Technical Data Gathering), and 8 (Physical Data Gathering).

2.4 PHASE 4: RISK ANALYSIS

The risk-analysis phase involves a review of the data gathered in the previous phase and an analysis of this data and the organization's threat landscape to determine the resulting organizational risk. During this phase, the security risk assessment team must determine the value of assets (data and systems), the existence and likelihood of threats to the organization's assets, and the existence and criticality of vulnerabilities based on the data gathered. Using this information, the team must calculate the organizational risk for each asset/threat/vulnerability combination. Although the calculation and presentation of these risks can vary greatly, depending on the security risk assessment method being used, three key components exist in nearly all industry accepted methods: assets, threats, and vulnerabilities Each of these key components to determine security risk are discussed in greater detail below:

2.4.1 ASSETS

The first element to be considered and discussed in a security risk assessment is the organizational assets. Assets are any items considered valuable by the organization, but in the context of a security risk assessment assets are those items (tangible or intangible) that are protected by the information system or the components of the information system itself. Later in this book, we shall discuss asset classes, asset valuation, and asset grouping, but for now it is important to understand that assets are the information, resources, system components, and other items that have value to the organization. Examples include buildings, equipment, personnel, organization reputation,[1] business documents, and many other tangible and intangible items.

Assets are an important element of a security risk assessment for several reasons. First, the enumeration of assets helps to scope the security risk assessment by concentrating on the controls that protect the assets in scope. Scoping of the security risk assessment will be discussed later as well, but for now, consider the following example. If an organization has commissioned a security risk assessment and has dictated that the buildings and equipment are not among the assets within the scope of the security risk assessment, then a review of the administrative and physical security controls protecting the buildings and equipment would not need to be performed. In this way, the enumeration of assets helps to scope the security risk assessment.

Second, the valuation of assets helps to determine the countermeasures employed. A countermeasure is simply a control (activity, technique, or technology) that reduces the possible loss to an organization's assets (see Table 2.1). While the appropriate selection of countermeasures can be somewhat involved, it is clear that we should not spend more on the countermeasure than the possible reduction in the organizational loss. Later in the book, we shall discuss both asset valuation and countermeasure selection.

2.4.2   Threat Agents and Threat Actions

The next elements to be considered and discussed in a security risk assessment are the threat agents and the threat actions. A threat action is an event with an undesired impact. A threat agent is the entity that may cause a threat to happen. Threat actions and threat agents are inextricably linked, in that it is the threat agent that causes a threat action to happen. A more in-depth discussion of threats, threat classes, threat environment, and threat analysis is provided in Chapter 4 (Section 4.5). The basics of threats actions and threat agents are presented here as a primer on the topic. Threat agents include Mother Nature and mankind. Threats actions can be anything caused by threat agents that may cause damage to the organization's assets. Examples of threats include humans-intentional, humans-accidental, and nature. Examples of threat actions include invoking malware, theft, and sabotage, being hacked, or error.

The main reason that threat actions and threat agents are important elements of the security risk assessment is that they help to determine the scope of the system vulnerabilities being assessed. To begin a security risk assessment, we must understand the threat actions from which we plan to protect the assets. It is rather naive to believe that something undesired will never happen, and it is equally naive to believe that you can possibly anticipate or even list every possible threat action. However, we can describe the types and capabilities of threat agents and threat actions that are most likely or foreseeable in the target system's threat environment. This approach helps the security risk

---

TABLE 2.1
Asset Summary

Key Concepts	Definition
Asset	Resource, data, system component, or other item of value to the organization.
Asset enumeration	A listing or grouping of assets under assessment. Asset enumeration helps to scope the information security assessment.
Asset valuation	The placement of a relative or dollar value on each asset. Asset valuation is useful in determining potential loss and countermeasure selection.
Asset grouping	The logical grouping of assets in order to simplify data analysis. For example, workstations assigned to staff members of a department could be considered a single asset grouping or class.

Note: Assets are those items the organization wishes to protect. The enumeration and valuing of the assets scopes and guides the security risk assessment.

---

assessment team to consider those threat agents and actions that are most likely to impact the security risk assessment target and to ignore those that are least likely to impact the security risk assessment target. Those threat actions that are considered relevant for a specific security risk assessment are called "valid threat actions."

For example, a security risk assessment being performed on an organization in Austin, Texas, would not need to consider the threat actions of earthquakes, snow blizzards, or perhaps even hurricanes. However, it would need to consider flooding, tornadoes, and severe thunderstorms. In this example, the threat agent is Mother Nature, and we consider some of her threat actions valid and others not valid for this portion of the country.

2.4.2.1 Threat Agents

Threat agents are the catalyst for the threat action. A threat agent is the entity that causes a threat action to happen. A list of threat agents is provided below:

- Human-Accidental—The most frequent threat agent is the trusted individual who performs (or neglects to perform) an action accidentally.
- Human-Intentional—Humans may also perform actions (or neglect to perform) an action intentionally. These humans can be insiders abusing trust or outsiders attempting to gain access or otherwise damage the organization's assets.
- Natural—Mother nature presents threats to an organization and the organization's assets. These threats include earthquakes, tornadoes, high winds, flooding, volcanoes, and landslides.

2.4.2.2 Threat Actions

A threat action is an undesired event that may result in the loss, disclosure, or damage to an organizational asset (see Table 2.2).

- Invoked Malware—A threat may introduce malicious software (e.g., malware) on their organizational computer.
- Theft & Sabotage—A threat actor may steal an organizational asset such as a laptop or a mobile device.
- Socially Engineered—A threat actor may use psychology (instead of technical approaches) to gain the trust of the employee and trick them into violating the organization's security policy.
- Hacked—A threat actor may use hacking methods to circumvent the security controls on an employee's computer or account.
- Abused Trust—A threat actor may abuse the trust given to them and utilize this misplaced trust to take actions against the organization.

TABLE 2.2
Threat and Threat Agent Summary

Key Concepts	Definition
Threat agent	The entity that may cause a threat action to happen
Threat action	An undesired event that may result in the loss, disclosure, or damage to an organizational asset
Valid threat	Threat agent/action pairs that are considered relevant for a specific security risk assessment
Threat environment	Determining the physical, geographical, and other aspects of the organization's system helps to determine the scope and extent of applicable threats

Note: Threats and threat agents are the actions and entities the organization would like to avoid. Threats and threat agents are determined by the physical geography and mission of the organization.

- Environmental Damage—Organizational assets may succumb to environmental damage from severe weather (e.g., floods, tornados, and earthquakes), infrastructure failures (e.g., power outages), or even infestations (e.g., rats). This threat action applies only to nature.
- Erred—Lastly, a threat actor may simply make a mistake that results in the loss of confidentiality of sensitive data, or in the misplacement of an organizational asset such as a laptop.

2.4.3 Vulnerabilities

A vulnerability is a flaw or oversight in an existing control that may possibly allow a threat agent to exploit it to gain unauthorized access to organizational assets. In Chapters 6, 7, and 8 we shall discuss in detail how to find and describe vulnerabilities in administrative, technical, and physical controls. In Chapter 9, we shall discuss how to assess and rate these vulnerabilities. For now, it is important to understand the relationship of vulnerabilities to other elements of the security risk assessment and the importance of the vulnerability in this effort.

Vulnerabilities are important elements of a security risk assessment because they are instrumental in determining existing and residual risk. Without vulnerabilities, there would be no risk. However, we know there is no such thing as a system without vulnerabilities, so it is the task of the security risk assessment team to assess the existing system controls to determine existing system vulnerabilities and those vulnerabilities that are likely to still exist if the safeguard recommendations are implemented. When assessing system vulnerabilities, it is useful to categorize the vulnerabilities according to administrative, physical, and technical areas, since the departments or personnel are likely to be distributed similarly.

Administrative vulnerabilities are those vulnerabilities that exist in policies, procedures, or security activities. Examples include missing acceptable use policies, gaps in termination procedures, or the lack of independence in security testing.[2] Physical vulnerabilities are those vulnerabilities that exist in the physical, geographical, personnel, or utility provisioning controls. Examples include holes in the fence line, a building located in a flight path, the lack of background checks for sensitive positions, and the lack of redundant power supplies. Technical vulnerabilities are those that exist in the logical controls in the organization's system. Examples include misconfigured routers, backdoors in programs, and weak passwords (see Table 2.3).

TABLE 2.3
Vulnerability Summary

Key Concepts	Definition
Vulnerability	A gap, ineffective element, flaw, or oversight in an existing control that may allow a threat agent to exploit it to gain unauthorized access to organizational assets
Administrative vulnerability	Gaps or ineffective elements in policies, procedures, or security activities, for example, missing acceptable use policies, gaps in termination procedures, or the lack of independence in security testing
Physical vulnerability	Gaps or ineffective elements in physical, geographical, personnel, or utility provisioning controls, for example, holes in the fence line, location in a flight path, lack of background checks for sensitive positions, and lack of redundant power supplies
Technical vulnerability	Gaps or ineffective elements in the logical controls in the organization's system, for example, misconfigured routers, back doors in programs, and weak passwords

Note: Vulnerabilities are weaknesses or absences of security control. These vulnerabilities can exist in administrative, physical, or technical controls.

2.4.4 SECURITY RISK

A security risk is the loss potential to an organization's asset(s) that will likely occur if a threat is able to exploit a vulnerability. In this book, we shall discuss various ways to assess (Chapter 9), reduce (Chapter 10), and report security risk (Chapter 11). Security risk (and residual security risk) is *the* key element of the security risk assessment because it is the culmination of all the other assessments, calculations, and analyses. Security risk is the key measurement that the organization's management really cares about; the rest of the security risk assessment elements are just a way to get to the key measurement of security risk.

There are many key factors to consider when discussing security risk, but the most important factor of security risk to consider right now is the manner in which the security risk is derived and presented. There are many ways to derive and present that security risk to stakeholders, but all of these approaches can be categorized as either quantitative or qualitative.

The quantitative approach to deriving and presenting security risk relies on specific formulas and calculations to determine the value of the security risk. A quantitative approach to determining and even presenting security risk has the advantages of being objective and expressed in terms of dollar figures. However, such quantitative calculations can be rather complex, and accurate values for the variables in quantitative formulas may be difficult or costly to obtain.

The qualitative approach to deriving and presenting security risk relies on subjective measures of asset valuation, threats, vulnerabilities, and ultimately the security risk. A qualitative approach to determining and presenting security risk has the advantage of being easy to understand and, in many cases, provides adequate indication of the organization's security risk. However, a security risk measurement derived from such qualitative measures is, indeed, subjective and may not be trusted by some in management positions (see Table 2.4). More detail on security risk analysis and methods involved in deriving quantitative and qualitative risk measurements is provided in Chapter 9.

TABLE 2.4
Security Risk Summary

Key Concepts	Definition	
Security risk	The loss potential to an organization's asset(s) that will likely occur if a threat is able to exploit a vulnerability	
Quantitative risk	A method of determining and presenting security risk that relies on specific formulas and calculations to determine the value of the security risk	
	Advantages	**Disadvantages**
	• Objective; • Security risk expressed in terms of dollars	• Security risk calculations are complex; • Accurate values are difficult to obtain
Qualitative risk	A method of determining and presenting security risk that relies on subjective measures of asset valuation, threats, vulnerabilities, and ultimately of the security risk	
	Advantages	**Disadvantages**
	• Easy to understand; • Provides adequate indication of the organization's security risk	• Subjective; • May not be trusted by some in management positions

Note: Security risks are a measurement of the likelihood that the organization's assets are susceptible. Security risk assessment methods can be either quantitative or qualitative.

2.5   PHASE 5: RISK MITIGATION

Based on the security risks defined in the risk analysis phase, the team must develop recommendations for safeguards to reduce the identified risks to an acceptable level. The safeguard selection process involves mapping safeguards to threat/vulnerability pairs, determining the risk reduction, determining the safeguard cost, and potentially grouping safeguards into solution sets.

The key concepts of the risk mitigation phase are the selection of safeguards and determination of residual risk.

2.5.1   SAFEGUARDS

Next, we consider the selection and recommendation of security controls, or safeguards, to be put in place to protect the organization's assets from the derived security risk. A safeguard (also called a countermeasure) is a technique, activity, or technology employed to reduce the risk to the organization's assets. A safeguard will reduce the security risk to an organization through the prevention, detection, or correction of a threat agent/threat action/vulnerability event. For this reason, safeguards are generally categorized as preventive, detective, or corrective measures.

Preventive measures are controls that are designed to deter undesirable events from happening. Examples include access controls, door locks, and security awareness training. Detective measures are controls that identify conditions that indicate that an undesirable event has happened. Examples of detective measures include audit logs, security testing, and intrusion detection systems. Corrective measures are controls designed to correct the damage caused by undesirable events. Examples of corrective measures include security guards, termination policies, and file recovery. Note that safeguards (also referred to as controls) may be classified as being in multiple categories, such as security guards, which can be considered a preventive, detective, and corrective measure.

Safeguards are an important element in security risk assessments for two reasons. First, all existing safeguards must be considered when determining the present vulnerability of the organization's system. If the security risk assessment team fails to consider all the safeguards in place to protect the organization's assets, then the security risk assessment results will be inaccurate and will likely err on the side of overestimating the risk. Such errors can be costly, as decisions for implementing additional security measures should be based on the results of security risk assessments.

Second, safeguards are an important element of security risk assessments because the final report should recommend safeguards to be implemented to bring the residual risk within tolerance levels of the organization's senior management. Safeguard recommendations are key to the results of a security risk assessment and must be carefully considered (see Table 2.5).

TABLE 2.5
Safeguard Summary

Key Concepts	Definition
Safeguard	A technique, activity, or technology employed to reduce the risk to the organization's assets. Safeguards protect the organization's assets from the risks of threats
Preventive	Controls designed to deter undesirable events from happening, for example, access controls, door locks, and security awareness training
Detective	Controls that identify conditions that indicate that an undesirable event has happened, for example, audit logs, security testing, and intrusion detection systems
Corrective	Controls designed to correct the damage caused by undesirable events, for example, security guards, termination policies, and file recovery

Note: Safeguards are security controls recommended by the security risk assessment team to address known vulnerabilities to reduce security risk.

TABLE 2.6
Residual Risk Summary

Key Concepts	Definition
Residual Risk	The security risk that remains after implementation of recommended safeguards. Residual risks are the leftover risks to the organization's assets after safeguards have been applied
Static risk	The security risk that will always exist
Dynamic risk	Security risk that may be reduced through the implementation of safeguards

Note: Residual risk is the amount of security risk present in the organization after safeguards have been implemented.

2.5.2 Residual Security Risk

Residual security risk is the security risk that remains after implementation of recommended safeguards. The objective of security risk management is to accurately measure the residual security risk and keep it to a level at or below the security risk tolerance level.

Residual security risk is an important element of security risk assessments for several reasons. First and foremost, residual risk is the security risk that the organization will inherit when safeguards are implemented. It is important that the organization's management fully understands the concept of residual security risk and is comfortable with staffing and budgeting decisions that determine the residual security risk level.

Second, the security professional and the organization's management must clearly understand that there is no such thing as 100% security (or 0%residual security risk). Even if the organization implements everyone of the information security professionals' recommendations, the organization still has some residual security risk to its assets. More detail about security risk mitigation is provided in Chapter 10. Table 2.6 provides a definition of residual security risk as well as some key concepts.

2.6 PHASE 6: RISK REPORTING AND RESOLUTION

The final phase of a security risk assessment is the risk reporting and resolution phase. During this phase, the security risk assessment team develops a report and a presentation to the project sponsor that clearly identifies the security risks found and the safeguards recommended. The final security risk assessment report should provide clear information for the executive, management, and technical personnel. The executives of the assessed organization must then determine the resolution of the identified risks. The security risk resolution element within this phase is considered a key concept within security risk assessments.

2.6.1 Risk Resolution

At the conclusion of a security risk assessment project, the senior management of the assessed organization must determine the resolution of each of the identified security risks. In other words, the senior manager must decide to reduce the security risk, accept the security risk, or delegate the security risk to someone else.[3]

A security risk can be reduced by implementing additional security controls or even by improving existing security controls. Suggestions for security risk-reducing safeguards for each identified risk should be documented in the final security risk assessment report. Along with these recommendations, cost and effectiveness estimations should be included to assist in the senior manager's decision.

TABLE 2.7
Risk Resolution Summary

Key Concepts	Definition
Risk resolution	The decision by senior management of how to resolve the risk presented to them
Risk reduction	The reduction of risk to the organization to an acceptable level through the adoption of additional security controls or improvement of existing controls
Risk acceptance	The deliberate decision by senior management to accept an identified risk based on the business objectives of the organization
Risk transference	The contractual transfer of risk to another organization through outsourcing or insurance

Note: Safeguards protect the organization's assets from the risks of threats.

A security risk can be accepted if the senior manager believes that it is in the best interest of the organization to accept the risk rather than to accept the cost burdens of implementing additional safeguards. The acceptance of this risk must be performed by a senior manager of the organization, because this decision impacts the organization as a whole and not just a single department or project.

Lastly, a security risk can be transferred to another organization such as an outsourcing company or an insurance agency. The transfer of security risk is a contractual agreement that clearly spells out the risk and the burden accepted along with the conditions and limitations of such an agreement (see Table 2.7). More detail on security risk assessment reporting is provided in Chapter 11.

EXERCISES

1. Tasks performed within a security risk assessment have some flexibility in terms of order performed (consider Figure 2.1). Indicate the order of the tasks below by listing prerequisite tasks (tasks that must be completed prior to starting) and successors (tasks that cannot begin prior to completion of current task) for each of the tasks listed below:
   Be Prepared to Justify Your Answers

Pre-requisite Tasks		Successor Tasks
	a. Project scope	
	b. Asset valuation	
	c. Threat identification	
	d. Policy review	
	e. Vulnerability scan	
	f. Schedule interviews	
	g. Perform interviews	
	h. Assess risk	
	i. Develop recommendations	
	j. Present report	

2. Research: Perform a market analysis on current providers of an information security risk assessment service. Review website resources, interview providers, and/or review your own

organization's resources or recent bids to determine methods or approaches used at several competitive organizations. Using parameters given by your instructor (or if not given create your own assumptions), obtain price quotes or estimates on the cost and time (estimate hours) for a security risk assessment with the given parameters?

    a. Determine the current market price for a security risk assessment.

    b. What factors are involved in the scoping of a security risk assessment?

    c. Are service organizations reluctant to give pricing information? Why or why not?

    d. Is there any confusion in terms of security risk assessments, vulnerability scans, security audits, security reviews, etc.?

3. Brainstorm: As a group or a class exercise, list the typical organizational assets. Attempt to group or categorize the assets.

    a. Consider the multiple grouping schemes and specificity of the assets. What are the pros and cons to the various schemes you created? For example, what are the pros and cons to treating all Web applications as a single asset?

    b. Are you able to find industry examples of asset classification guidance that can assist in this exercise?

4. Threat Trees: Threat trees are a way of organizing threats using tree structures.

    a. Using the threat agents and threat actions listed in Section 2.4.2 as a basis, create a threat tree. Start with tree "roots" (main nodes) of "natural" and "human-made" threats.

    b. What is the relationship between threat agents and threats (many–many, one–many, one–one, or many–one)?

5. In the News: Find an article on a recent computer security incident or breach.

    a. Identify as many of the following elements as possible:

        i. Threat agent/threat action

        ii. Vulnerability

        iii. Assets affected

        iv. Countermeasures applied

    b. What other safeguards could you recommend?

6. Choose a specific security control within your organization (e.g., badged physical access, two-factor authentication, and reporting of lost laptops). List the valid threat agents and actions this security control is designed to address.

NOTES

1 Although reputation is not a tangible asset, it does have measurable economic value to the organization. On the balance sheet, this value is generally called "goodwill."

2 Administrative security controls comprise policies, procedures, and security activities. Often, the term *administrative* has a bad connotation among security engineers. Those that come from a technical background may tend to think that *administrative* means paperwork, but this is not the case. Administrative security controls include controls that require technical skills such as risk assessments, security testing, and code review.

3 Another valid management action for an identified risk is to obtain additional data. This would be especially valid in cases where a security risk assessment was performed with little rigor (e.g., survey-based) and the potential mitigation strategies are expensive. Additional data supplied by a more rigorous review (e.g., interviews, observations, and testing) can give management a more appropriate amount of information for decisions involving large expenditures.

BIBLIOGRAPHY

Common Criteria for Information Technology Security Evaluation. Version 3.1, Revision 5 CCIMB-2017-04-001, April 2017.

3 Project Definition

A security risk assessment project can mean many things to many people. If there is not a common meaning between the security risk assessment team and the security risk assessment consumer (or other stakeholders) then it is rather difficult to ensure a successful project. Within the context of this book, a security risk assessment is defined as:

> An objective analysis of the effectiveness of the current security controls that protect an organization's assets and a determination of the probability of losses to those assets.

Various regulations, guidelines, and other information sources sometimes call the security risk assessment by another name. Terms used include *security audit*, *risk assessment*, *security testing*, and so on. Other times, *security risk assessment* is used to mean something different from what is described in this book.

Realizing the confusion surrounding these terms, it is important that the security risk assessment project be well-defined prior to project initiation. Definition of a security risk assessment project requires knowledge of the budget, objective, scope, and the level of rigor of analysis expected. Each of these areas is discussed in the following sections of this chapter. This chapter is dedicated to review how to ensure a successful security risk assessment project.

3.1 ENSURING PROJECT SUCCESS

Performing a security risk assessment is a project and, as such, anyone seeking to be an effective member of a security risk assessment team should understand how such a project is run successfully. Moreover, the leader of the security risk assessment team needs to be able to plan, track, and ensure the success of the security risk assessment project.

3.1.1 SUCCESS DEFINITION

Success cannot be achieved until we define the meaning of success, or the elements that make for a successful conclusion of the project. For a security risk assessment project (and, for that matter, most technical projects), success is defined as achieving customer satisfaction, quality technical work, and project completion within budget.

3.1.1.1 Customer Satisfaction

The customer of a security risk assessment includes the "sponsor" of the security risk assessment and additional stakeholders within the assessed organization. Each of these stakeholders has a unique point of view and a distinct definition of what they expect from a successful security risk assessment project. In order to ensure customer satisfaction, the security risk assessment team should be aware of the various customers of the security risk assessment project and seek to understand the success factors from the point of view of each of them.

3.1.1.2 Identifying the Customer

Regardless of whether the security risk assessment is performed by internal resources or is contracted out to a security consulting firm, the primary customer of a security risk assessment is the individual responsible for commissioning it. If the security risk assessment is performed by a contracted security consulting firm, the project sponsor should be explicitly stated in the contract. If not explicitly stated, consider the project sponsor the most senior official who will be at the final briefing. For internal security risk assessments, the project sponsor is the board of directors, internal audit department, the office of the Chief Information Security Officer, or other department manager or director who commissioned the project.

- Project Sponsor—The project sponsor is the person internally responsible for the success of the project. If this is a contracted effort, then the project sponsor is typically the signature authority for the project. Either way, the project sponsor will define the success of the project in terms of the quality of the technical work and project completion within time and budget constraints.

The quality of the technical work can be ensured through careful selection of project members and following the guidelines in this book. Project completion within budget can be ensured through following the guidelines in Chapter 13.

The secondary customer for the security risk assessment project includes any other stakeholder in the process. These stakeholders are numerous and play a vital role in the ultimate acceptance of the security risk assessment and, in turn, customer satisfaction. Each of these secondary customers is listed and discussed below.

- **Security Officer or Security Team**—The most senior security officer in the organization may be a chief information security officer, with a staff, visibility, and a security budget, or it may be a systems administrator who enjoys the security aspects of setting up the network. Regardless of the position within the organization, the most senior security officer will be very interested in the security risk assessment project. This person can be either the biggest critic or the most ardent supporter of the security risk assessment. Typically, the senior information security officer will be a supporter of the security risk assessment effort and may even be the project sponsor.

  The most senior security officer will be concerned that the security risk assessment is properly scoped, accurate, and performed by professionals with the appropriate experience and credentials. Many of these concerns can be addressed through proper negotiation and development of the statement of work (SOW). The accuracy of the security risk assessment can be ensured through careful data gathering, testing, analysis, and review. The professionalism and credentials of the security risk assessment team can be addressed through the presentation of their résumés, past performance descriptions, and certifications.

  Be aware that the most senior security officers will likely have their own set of security controls and priorities that they are trying to get adopted within the organization. The security risk assessment can point out the specific benefits of implementing these controls from a security risk-based approach. Therefore, the security risk assessment may be able to give the senior security officer the support needed for upcoming projects, or the security risk assessment may recommend other projects with a larger return on investment (ROI) than the ones currently planned. Be careful to ensure that you gain the necessary information from the security team, but remain objective and credible by forming your own opinions and recommendations.
- **Business Unit Managers**—Organizations divide responsibility for corporate governance among business units. These units may take on various names, such as groups, departments, or divisions. Here they are referred to simply as business units. The business unit will have a single individual in charge—sometimes referred to as the division chief, director, or even department head. Here we shall refer to them as the business unit managers. The business unit manager will be concerned with several factors, including proper understanding of the business unit, accurate security risk identification, clarity and usefulness of recommendations, and cost of implementing recommendations.
  - Understanding the Business Unit—The security risk assessment team will need to ensure that they offer the opportunity for an interview with each of the business unit managers.

This interview will give the managers a chance to explain the business unit functions and to voice concerns about existing security risks. Granting the business unit manager an opportunity to explain and voice these concerns will help to ensure acceptance of the results.

- Accurate Identification of Security Risks—The business unit managers are likely to be among the sharpest critics of security risk results that affect their business unit. This should not be surprising, as security risk results and their accompanying recommendations will affect the business unit manager's budget. The security risk assessment team should take the necessary steps to ensure that security risk findings are accurate. These steps include the interview with the business unit manager mentioned previously, interviews with other representatives for the business unit, and the ability for each business unit manager to review draft findings of the security risk assessment.
- Clarity and Usefulness of Security Risk Recommendations—A security risk assessment that simply states that the organization is at a certain level of security risk is of little value. The most valuable component of a security risk assessment is a prioritized list of actions that may be taken to reduce the security risk. Unclear, high-level, or ambiguous recommendations such as "increase security staff" offer little guidance to those who need to act on these recommendations. Security risk recommendations need to be clear, unambiguous, and ultimately useful to the customer.
- Cost of Implementing Security Risk Recommendations—Clearly, business unit managers would rather hear that the actions recommended are cheap and easy. But that might not always be the case. The project team cannot and should not artificially reduce recommendation cost estimates for reducing security risk. Although the true cost may lead some segments of the customer population initially to be disappointed in the results, ultimately an underestimate of recommendation costs would lead to a greater disappointment. The security risk assessment team should be straightforward and as accurate as possible when stating the cost of a security risk recommendation.
- **Compliance Officer Legal Department**—In many organizations, a security risk assessment is a legal requirement. Organizations with a legal requirement for obtaining a security risk assessment include health-care entities, financial institutions, government agencies, retailers, critical infrastructure organization, and organizations with specific customer requirements for a security risk assessment. In these cases, the individual within the corporation responsible for compliance with these laws or contractual obligations would certainly be interested in the method and results of the security risk assessment.
  - Security Risk Assessment Method—The organization compliance officer will be concerned that the security risk assessment will meet the legal or contractual specification and obligations. Some customers may have strict requirements as to the security risk assessment methodology. These requirements will typically state that the security risk assessment must follow certain guidelines or methods that are spelled out explicitly in the governing law or in the contract. The security risk assessment project manager should be familiar with the governing laws affecting the customer and should ask specifically for contracts that have specific requirements for a security risk assessment.
  - Security Risk Assessment Team—Although most governing law and contracts will not explicitly call for a specific security risk assessment methodology, there are some indirect requirements on the objectivity and credentials of the security risk assessment team. Several governing laws call for an *objective review* by *security professionals*. While not stating exact requirements for these terms, the following guidelines could be applied:
    - Objective Review—Objectivity requires the lack of real or perceived conflict of interest. Conflict of interest arises when the security risk assessment team has a stake in the outcome of the assessment. Namely, a conflict of interest occurs when the security risk assessment team includes members who have designed, operate, or are in charge

of portions of the security program. This includes any element of the security program that is to be assessed; for example, security policies, security awareness programs, security architecture, system hardening, audit log review, physical access control, logical perimeter controls (firewalls, routers), and managed security services. Anyone representing or involved in these functions will have a vested interest in how well they are perceived. This vested interest and the interest in uncovering all flaws that present a security risk to the organization are at odds and culminate in a conflict of interest.

To some, the exclusion of these members from the security risk assessment team may seem inappropriate or overkill. After all, these members know the systems better than anyone and can identify possible security risks with great efficiency. It is for this reason that, they argue, these members must clearly be involved in the security risk assessment process. While these are valid points, the need to ensure accurate and objective results outweigh any such benefit. These "insiders" should be interviewed, consulted, and possibly even included in many of the discussions that lead up to the findings of the security risk assessment. However, they should not be "voting" members or leaders of the security risk assessment team. In the end, those who make the final recommendations must be objective or the validity and credibility of the security risk assessment will be questionable.

- Security Professionals—The security risk assessment team needs to be composed of members who understand the concepts to be applied in a security risk assessment, needs to bring a measure of expertise to the project, and will act in a professional manner.

  An understanding of the concepts in a security risk assessment is required simply to be a productive team member. Without such an understanding, a team member may become lost in the process, misinterpret results, and be unable to be a productive member of the team.

  Some measure of expertise is required from each team member. The team will require members who can draw from experience to provide reasonable measurements of threat frequency, impact, and overall security risk. Furthermore, the team should include members with different areas of expertise so that all controls within the scope of the assessment may be adequately covered. Depending on the scope, the security risk assessment team requires experts in the areas of administrative, physical, and technical controls, such as locks, safes, and badges; database administration; security testing; secure code development; log review and monitoring; security policies and procedures; disaster recovery plans; and many other areas and controls.

  Each security risk assessment team member will need to behave in a professional manner. This includes showing the proper respect for the customer and those interviewed. Even more importantly, professional behavior requires the ethics necessary to ensure that information uncovered during the assessment will not be misused. Members of the security risk assessment team will uncover vulnerabilities in the customer's system. Unauthorized access or disclosure of these vulnerabilities could lead to external exposure to sensitive company information, account names, and passwords, and other realized threat actions that could pose a severe security risk to the customer's organization if this information is not properly handled and controlled.

- **Technicians, Operators, and Administrators**—These are the people in the organization who are relied upon to maintain and operate security controls. The network administrator is relied upon to apply up-to-date security patches to affected systems, the systems operator maintains user account information, and the network engineers set the firewall rules that implement the security policy. All of these people within the organization have a vested interest in the perceived quality of their work. A security risk assessment that results in findings that point out gaps within their area of responsibility may be seen as unjust or unkind. Security risk assessment team members must understand that care must be taken to ensure that all findings are accurate and worded appropriately. Properly worded findings clearly indicate the problem, its potential impact, and how to fix it. Do not point fingers or attempt to place blame. Failure to recognize this population, to ensure that their concerns are addressed, and to carefully word findings could result in an unsatisfied customer. Understand that these people are not typically the direct customer, but the direct customer is influenced by them. Moreover, a security risk assessment team should always strive to be fair and accurate.

3.1.1.3 Quality of Work

The success of the security risk assessment project will be based in large part on the quality of the technical report. After all, this is the project deliverable, and it will far outlast any other tangible evidence that such a project ever occurred.

Most consumers of a security risk assessment will judge the success of the project based on what they see as a result. The result seen by most security risk assessment consumers is the final security risk assessment report. The importance of the real quality of work and the perceived quality of work reflected by this document must be well understood by the entire security risk assessment team.

Information security engineers sometimes lose sight of the objective of their activities. They sometimes give the technical activities of their project precedence and leave little time to complete a quality report for delivery to the project sponsor.

SIDEBAR 3.1   WHAT DO WE SELL?

At a previous company I have been known to ask seemingly obvious questions at staff meetings in hopes of uncovering some greater truths. One such question provided our group a useful insight into the needs of our customers and their perceived value of our services. The following question was posed at one such meeting:

"What do we sell?" I asked.

The first answer was rather expected and went down the list of services we offer, such as policy development, security risk assessments, security training, and other services.

"No, what do our customers want to buy?" I asked, hoping the slight rephrase would spark some creative thought.

This rephrased question elicited more of the same descriptions, with only slight changes to the titles we gave them.

"Let's try this another way," I said. "Our customers don't want a security policy; they don't want a security risk assessment; they don't even want security training."

"But they buy our services? Why would they buy them if they don't want them?" answered the team.

"Because our services are a means to an end. What our customers really want is confidence," I explained. "Our customers buy our services because they want confidence that they are secure, or knowledgeable, or compliant," the enlightened audience interrupted.

BINGO!

It is important to understand that although we, as information security professionals, may be very excited about our techniques, methods, and tools, our customers' expectations do not center on these elements. Their expectations center on our providing confidence that they are doing the right thing.

The takeaway from this slightly offbeat discussion is that the quality of the security risk assessment project is not solely reliant on the quality of the technical work but also heavily reliant on any element that may influence the confidence of the project sponsor. It is for this reason that correct formatting and spelling in the final deliverable—the security risk assessment report—are just as important as adequate security testing.

Inattention to the details of the final deliverable is unfortunate and short-sighted, and in the end will not accomplish the goal of either party. In the pursuit of obtaining the best configuration for your scanners, getting the most up-to-date threat estimates, and determining the precise words for acceptable-use policy statements given the organizational culture, information security engineers are apt to forget that the consumer of the information security risk assessment really does not care about such details. This is not to say that consumers do not care about quality work; of course, they do. It is just that the consumer does not generally care about how the quality work gets done, just that it is quality.

For example, consider having a house built. This process involves a great many professional trades to design your house, install systems, and build to the specifications. The typical consumer of a newly constructed house judges the quality of the house on the result of inspections and a walk-through. Although it is important for the electrician to use the appropriate tools, supplies, and electrical code, the consumer only sees the exposed electrical components (e.g., switches, lights) and the inspection certificate that the system meets the electrical code. If the system did not meet the expectations of the consumer, it would not matter how great the electrician's tools or techniques were; the consumer would be dissatisfied.

Now consider the final security risk assessment report. If the final report contains the name of a previous company the consultant did work for (i.e., a "cut and paste" error), the consumer of the report is likely to lose confidence in the entire project. At this point, it does not matter how good the tools, techniques, and tests were. Many information security engineers would defend this work by saying, "That is just a typo—the results are still right." These engineers would be technically correct but would also fail to see the importance of a quality report delivery.

In general, all consumers care about is that the work they have commissioned is done by professionals, and they care about the quality of the work, but they do not generally care about the details of the tools, methods, and techniques that go into the work. As consumers, we expect that professionals keep up with the latest trends and obtain the appropriate tools for the job. We do not expect to have to be experts in the activities that we outsource.

3.1.1.3.1 Quality Aspects

The consumer of a security risk assessment report includes the "sponsor" of the security risk assessment and additional stakeholders within the organization being assessed. All of these stakeholders have unique points of view and a distinct definition of what they expect from a successful security risk assessment. These were discussed in the previous section. Regardless of the stakeholder role, several quality aspects are universally expected.

- **General Quality Expected in Any Report**—The following is a discussion of the quality aspects that are expected in any report, whether the report is technical or not. These general quality aspects include grammar, format, audience, and an understanding of the topic. Each of these is discussed briefly below.
  - Grammatically Correct—Any correspondence that ever goes to a customer is a representation of the author and the organization associated with the author. A formal project deliverable such as a report, or even a draft report, must be grammatically correct. What the author should consider is that even though a small grammatical error may not change the meaning of the sentence, it will make an impression on the reader. As unfair as it may seem, that impression may have as much weight in customer satisfaction as the underlying analysis. Furthermore, grammatical errors involving the customer's name, interviewees' names, system names, and the like are likely to make an even less favorable impression.
  - Visually Pleasing—Without even changing the words, a report can be vastly improved during document production and the formatting process. Improvements in the formatting of the report will make the report look professional. Reports that look like they have been

put together in a hurry do not convey professionalism. Moreover, it is likely that the acceptance of the conclusions of such a report will be subtly affected. When a report looks professional, it also looks more authoritative. The security risk assessment team should appoint one member of the team to produce the report. The report producer should be familiar with techniques to create a professional report. This book does not cover this topic in any detail, but you should expect the report producer to be familiar with the following elements of a professional report:

- Selection and consistency of a font
- Consistent treatment of tables, figures, bullets, etc.
- Appropriate styles for headings
- Spacing between paragraphs, graphics, and headers and footers
- Proper use of headers and footers
- Generation of a table of contents and table of figures.

- Addresses Its Intended Audience—As discussed earlier in this book, the security risk assessment report is intended for several different audiences. These audiences will have differing levels of familiarity with the project and differing levels of technical expertise. For this reason, the report must be written for several different audiences.
  - Executive Summary—The executive summary is written for the audience that wants to know the bottom line. An executive summary should be short and to the point. For a security risk assessment, it should answer the following question: "What are the security risks to my organization, and what should we do about them?" As a rule of thumb, since the executive summary summarizes the body of the report, it should be written after the body of the report has been completed. The executive summary should not contain any findings, graphs, or tables not included in the body of the report.
  - Technical Appendices—Technical details and supporting documentation to the security risk assessment report belong in an appendix or even an attached or accessible data file. The more technical readers of the report will want to review these technical details when implementing countermeasures. Examples of typical appendices to a security risk assessment report are as follows:
    - Vulnerability Scan Results—The results of a vulnerability scan run on the systems being assessed.
    - Evidence—A list of evidence used to draw conclusions. This would include interviews, test results, worksheet calculations, etc.
    - References—A list of sources of information and guidance used in the security risk assessment.
    - Documents reviewed—A list of customer-provided documents that were reviewed as part of the security risk assessment.
    - Solution Descriptions—Additional descriptions on proposed solutions. This could include product literature or a review of available solutions.
    - Calculations—Mathematical calculations supporting the findings.
- Understanding of the Organization—It is important that the reader of the report realizes that the security risk assessment team not only knows how to perform a security risk assessment but has a grasp of the relevant background necessary for performing the work. The introduction of the report can be used to reiterate relevant background information, including a description of the organization and the need for the security risk assessment.
- **General Quality Expected in Technical Reports**—Technical reports have their own unique requirements, and the audience reading a technical report has additional expectations. Technical reports, such as a security risk assessment, are expected to contain technical data and draw conclusions based on a technical data assessment. For this reason, it is important to ensure that the technical data presented in the report is accurate, the approach is presented and the conclusions are clear.

- Technically Accurate—Technical reports are based on technical data. Any inaccuracies in the data could lead to incorrect conclusions. It is important that the technical members of the security risk assessment team review all technical data to ensure its accuracy. This includes removal of false positives in vulnerability scanning and ensuring that account names, system names, and IP addresses are correct.
- Approach Described—The security risk assessment approach used by the team should be described in the final report. This has several benefits. First, it gives the report credibility. If the report references and follows a well-known or well-developed approach for performing security risk assessments, then the customer will be less likely to question the methods employed to determine the conclusions. Second, a description of the approach will allow the customer to follow the process and the logic of the analysis more closely, which will allow the customer to provide a better review of the draft report and a better understanding of the process.
- Clearly Presented Conclusions—The conclusions of a technical report are the most important element. These are likely the items that will be implemented. It is important that these conclusions be well articulated so that the implementer of the conclusions will know what is expected. For example, it is not very useful to simply recommend that the organization develop security policies. This advice provides little insight or direction and is an indication that the security risk assessment team may not clearly understand how to write security policies. A better recommendation would be a description of the security policies that are currently missing and perhaps an outline of the basic structure for each.
- **Quality Expected in Security Risk Assessment Reports**—A security risk assessment report is a specific type of technical report with its own unique quality requirements. A security risk assessment report is expected to provide a clear and accurate identification of the security risk to an organization's assets. Furthermore, the security risk assessment report is expected to contain adequate and relevant evidence to support its findings, clear and relevant recommendations, and clear compliance results for relevant information security regulations. For this reason, it is important to ensure that the security risk identified in the report is clear and accurate, evidence presented is accurate and relevant, recommendations are clear and relevant, and any compliance results are clearly stated.
  - Clear and Accurate Identification of Security Risk—The identification of security risk is the basic objective of the security risk assessment. Therefore, it is not surprising that customers would expect an identification of security risk as part of the security risk assessment report. However, it is important to convey the security risk in a meaningful way to the customer. The description of the residual security risk can be presented in a quantitative or qualitative manner, depending on the overall approach of the security risk assessment. In either case, the residual security risk should be presented in a context that is understandable by the customer. As such, a description should accompany the residual security risk statement, for example, a range for quantitative security risk measurements or managerial description for qualitative security risk approaches.
  - Adequate and Relevant Evidence—The results of a security risk assessment are recommendations for changes in an organization. Prior to those changes being implemented, the organization will likely scrutinize elements of the security risk assessment report to ensure that the recommendations are well founded. A quality security risk assessment report will contain adequate and relevant evidence for its conclusions and recommendations.
  - Clear and Relevant Recommendations—Hopefully many of the recommendations from the security risk assessment report will be implemented. Most organizations will have set aside resources to implement the recommendations of the security risk assessment, but these recommendations cannot be implemented if they are not clear, and they are not likely to be implemented if they are not relevant to improving the organization's security risk. The security risk assessment team must ensure that all recommendations are based on

relevant data and solid analysis. If it is unclear why the recommendations would improve the security posture of the organization, then the recommendations have not been clearly articulated. Also, the security risk assessment team should include cost and effort estimations for implementing each of the recommendations. Organizations typically require such estimations prior to moving forward with a project.

- Clear Compliance Results—For those organizations operating within regulated industries (e.g., health care, energy, and government), an analysis as to their compliance with the regulation is useful, if not a requirement of the security risk assessment project. If such an analysis is performed, the security risk assessment report should contain a table that clearly indicates those areas that meet the regulations and those that do not.

3.1.1.4   Completion within Budget

The biggest success factor of any project is whether it is completed on time and within budget. The project leader of the security risk assessment team must manage the project carefully to ensure that the project is completed within the time allotted and with the resources granted. Any project not completed within time or budget constraints is in danger of being canceled or completed too late to have an impact. Moreover, a project with significant overruns is typically an indication of the project team's inexperience.

The goal of completing within budget is not limited to outside consultants performing a security risk assessment. This goal applies equally to internal security risk assessment projects. In either case, the project has been granted a limited amount of resources (e.g., time and money) and must be completed within those constraints. Project leaders of security risk assessments must ensure that they meet this most important quality aspect of their project.

3.1.2   Setting the Budget

One of the biggest gating factors for scoping a security risk assessment is how much is in the budget for the security risk assessment. If no such line item exists in the budget, consider how much you plan on spending. Exact figures are not required here, but there is a huge difference in the scope and rigor of a $450,000 security risk assessment and a $45,000 one. The fact is, the more time that the team spends reviewing the security controls, the more rigorous the security risk assessment will be. So, if you plan on spending over $250,000 on a security risk assessment, then you would expect (and demand) more rigor than if you wanted to keep the cost down to less than $50,000.

In addition to the rigor of analysis, the amount of money you plan to spend on the security risk assessment will also be affected by the size of the organization, the geographical separation of organizational elements, the complexity of the security controls, and the threat environment in which your organization operates.

- Organization Size—A small organization, up to 500 employees, is likely to have many factors that simplify a security risk assessment. The organization structure is likely to be relatively simple and centrally located. This brings down the cost/effort in obtaining interviews with key personnel and gaining approval for testing and access to information. A small organization is also likely to be more centralized and to have fewer complex controls, which may reduce the effort required to assess their effectiveness. A larger organization is more likely to have a more complex organizational structure, and decentralized and complex controls.
- Geographic Separation—If your organization has just one location, then the effort to gather the information required to perform the security risk assessment is significantly reduced. An organization with multiple sites and geographically separated systems and key personnel will require additional funds for travel and information gathering.
- Complexity—The more complex the security controls, the more effort required to assess their effectiveness. For example, an organization with physical access controls that include

perimeter barriers, armed guards, biometrics, IP cameras and recording, zoned areas, smart card badge access, and multiple types of intrusion detection is going to require some effort to effectively review. An organization with a simpler physical security control that includes locked doors and visitor control will clearly require less effort.

- Threat Environment—Certain organizations operate within a higher security risk environment than others. For example, a high-profile and controversial national lobbying organization will clearly be exposed to a greater number of serious threats than the headquarters of a nationally franchised sandwich shop. A security risk assessment for an organization existing within a more serious threat environment will require more careful consideration of the threats. An organization existing within a less serious threat environment is likely to be affected by the standard array of threats that affect most organizations.

The other factor to consider for scoping a security risk assessment is the size of the overall information security budget. An organization should plan to spend only a portion of their overall security budget on an assessment. This sounds rather obvious, but it remains overlooked by many organizations. Consider an organization that spends nearly its entire information security budget in a given year on a widely scoped and rigorous security risk assessment and has little or no budget left to fix anything. A main benefit of a security risk assessment is to provide guidance for security risk-based spending, so that ultimately the security risk to the organization is lowered to a reasonable level. If the entire budget is spent on a security risk assessment, the organization may be unable to implement any of the recommendations. The result is that the organization is more aware of their security risks, but their assets are in the same danger as before.

A better approach is for the organization to determine a percentage or ratio of the budget that should be spent on the security risk assessment (see Figure 3.1). As with many elements of establishing and maintaining an information security program within an organization, there is no well-known or accepted ratio or percentage. Furthermore, it is not recommended that such a ratio or percentage be the only factor in determining how much to spend. However, an organization should carefully review their budget allocation if they are spending more than 25% of their security budget on a security risk assessment.

3.1.3 Determining the Objective

A security risk assessment can provide many possible benefits: a basis for risk-based spending, a periodic review of the security program, and a part of a system of checks and balances for sensitive tasks. Understanding and documenting the objective of a specific security risk assessment helps

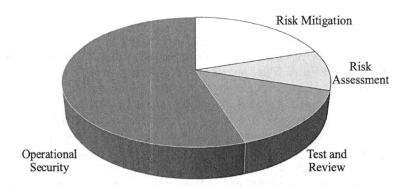

FIGURE 3.1 Security spending ratios. The exact spending ratios for elements within a security program will differ greatly among organizations. However, the relative spending ratios shown here are likely to be applicable to most organizations.

to focus the project on meeting the needs of the organization. The core aspect of a security risk assessment remains an analysis of the effectiveness of the current security controls that protect an organization's assets. This is the objective of the security risk assessment.

Security Risk Assessment Objective—accurate analysis of the effectiveness of current security controls that protect an organization's assets.

Most organizations simply want an objective review of their security controls. This may be provided by an independent team of security professionals who understand the security risk assessment methodology, possess the proper experience and credentials, and are provided the resources to adequately perform the assessment.

3.1.4   LIMITING THE SCOPE

The scope of the security risk assessment is the boundary of the security controls and assets included in the review. The definition of what is "in" and "out" of the scope of the assessment may be rather easy in some organizations but more difficult in others. In either case, the project sponsor and the security risk assessment team should carefully and clearly define the scope of the assessment in terms of the security controls to be reviewed, the assets to be protected, and the system boundaries of the security risk assessment target.

Every security risk assessment is limited: limited by budget, limited by time, and so forth. Project members of a security risk assessment will constantly find themselves reaching the limitations of the project. After all, could we not all do more in-depth analysis, more insightful recommendations, and more accurate risk measurements given unlimited time and money? But, no matter how much time or budget or skill is possessed by the security risk analysis team, if a discovered security risk exists outside the boundaries of the security risk assessment, it should not be documented in the security risk assessment. The single biggest limitation of a security risk assessment is the definition of the system being assessed.

The boundaries of a security risk assessment are determined by the sponsor of the security risk assessment. Identifying the security risk assessment boundaries is essential for the security risk assessment team to ensure that neither Under-scoping nor Over-scoping occurs.

3.1.4.1   Under-scoping

Under-scoping of a security risk assessment is a dangerous practice that can happen all too often. It occurs when the security risk assessment team does not address all security concerns of the sponsor. The term *Under-scoping* is from the perspective of the security risk assessment team and not the project sponsor. In other words, the security risk assessment team is not addressing the needs of the project sponsor because some of the organization's assets and relevant threats are not assessed within the security risk assessment.

Under-scoping typically results in high-risk items left unaddressed and, eventually, exposure of the organization's assets. Consider the following common scenario: An officer of a financial institution recognizes that his organization is legally required to comply with the Gramm-Leach-Bliley Act (GLB Act). The GLB Act clearly requires a security risk assessment among other information security requirements. The organization hires Fly-By-Nite Security to perform what they call a security risk assessment. Fly-By-Nite Security only knows how to run a vulnerability scan, but they have found that these services sell much better when they call them security risk assessments. The officer of the financial institution is unknowingly Under-scoping his security risk assessment by declaring (again unknowingly) administrative, physical, and most other elements of technical controls out of bounds for this assessment.

Although this example is a little extreme, similar problems can exist simply from dismissing other elements of a security risk assessment without ensuring that they are covered elsewhere. For example, it is relatively common in many organizations for physical security to be considered beyond the bounds of a security risk assessment. If the physical security controls are reviewed as a part of a separate security risk assessment, there is little to be worried about. However, if the physical security of an organization is ignored by all security risk assessments within the organization, then serious breaches in the security of multiple systems could occur. What good is writing the perfect firewall rules if a thief can walk away with the box?

3.1.4.2 Over-scoping

Over-scoping of a security risk assessment is dangerous as well. Over-scoping occurs when the security risk assessment team assesses threats, vulnerabilities, or security risks that are outside the bounds of the security risk assessment. The term *Over-scoping* is from the perspective of the security risk assessment team and not the project sponsor. In other words, the security risk assessment team is assessing organizational assets and threats that are beyond the needs of the security risk assessment sponsor. If a project sponsor fails to clearly indicate the bounds of the security risk assessment, the team may perform activities that end up wasting time and money. Another danger of Over-scoping is that the security risk assessment team may overstep its authority to test elements of a system that are not covered under the security risk assessment. Such out-of-bounds behavior could, by itself, be a serious breach of security. Consider the following out-of-bounds activities allowed by the practice of Over-scoping:

- *Example 1*: What's in a Name?—Fly-By-Nite Security is hired by the XYZ organization to test the security of its website. Fly-By-Nite Security obtains permission from XYZ to perform security testing, but the XYZ organization fails to properly scope the test and simply asks for a "zero-based" (an assessment approach that relies on the security tester to determine to IP addresses and URLs in scope for the assessment) review. When Fly-By-Nite Security performs its research, it finds www.xyz-org.com and www.xyz_co.com. When performing the security testing of these websites, Fly-By-Nite unknowingly performs security testing on both the XYZ organization (www.xyz.com) and the unrelated XYZ Manufacturing Company (www.xyz_co.com). Depending on the level of testing performed, Fly-By-Nite could end up on the wrong end of a lawsuit or criminal prosecution.
- *Example 2*: Take Out the Trash—Fly-By-Nite Security is again hired by the XYZ organization, but this time to perform a security risk assessment at their physical location. The project manager believed that the assessment would cover only the information security systems, but the industrious Fly-By-Nite employees diligently searched the trash cans for sensitive information, checked the security of the doors to sensitive areas, and reviewed the visitor and escort procedures. The security risk assessment sponsor was disappointed that the Fly-By-Nite team spent so much time "off task," since physical security is controlled by another department altogether that had just completed an assessment the previous month. Although this behavior did not trample on another organization's assets, it still wasted time and money, and it diverted analysis from within the intended boundary of the security risk assessment.

3.1.4.3 Security Controls

An organization may have implemented a wide variety of security controls to protect its assets. These security controls can range from policies and procedures to lighting and fences to firewalls and anti-virus solutions. Rather than list these controls one after the other, it is useful to group these controls into the categories of administrative, physical, and technical. These groupings provide a common approach to define or limit the scope of the security risk assessment.

3.1.4.3.1 *Administrative Security Controls*

Administrative security controls are defined as policies, procedures, and activities that protect the organization's assets. Policies include the information security policies such as acceptable use policy, system monitoring policies, and security operations policies. Procedures include emergency response procedures, computer incident response procedures, and procedures for hardening and testing the security of servers, for example. Activities include any activity performed to ensure the protection of the organization's assets, even if these activities do not have an associated policy or procedure. These could include activities requiring "technical" expertise, such as audit log review or penetration testing, or "nontechnical" activities, such as exit interviews for terminated employees. Administrative controls should be within the scope of any security risk assessment. An assessment that does not include these types of controls should be referred to as security testing or a limited assessment instead, as it would not give an accurate measurement of the security risk to the organization's assets.

3.1.4.3.2   Physical Security Controls

Physical security controls are those controls that are associated with the protection of the organization's employees and facilities. These protection measures include facility perimeter controls such as fencing, lighting, gates, and access controls; surveillance such as guards and cameras; facility protections such as seismic bracing and fireproofing; and personnel protection such as evacuation procedures and patrolled parking lots.

3.1.4.3.3   Technical Security Controls

Technical security controls are those mechanisms that logically protect the organization's assets, such as routers, firewalls, anti-virus solutions, logical access controls, and intrusion detection systems. A security risk assessment should consider the capabilities of the technical security controls, their current configuration, and their arrangement within the system to provide protection of assets (i.e., system architecture).

3.1.4.4   Assets

An organization has numerous assets of value that warrant protection. Assets are defined as the resources by which the organization derives value. These can include hardware, software, systems, services, documents, capital equipment, personal property, people, goodwill, trade secrets, and many other elements of the business process. Although it is clear that many factors create value for an organization, it is not always easy to define its assets. An attempt to simplify the enumeration process includes discussing both tangible and intangible assets.

3.1.4.4.1   Tangible Assets

Tangible assets are those assets that you can "touch." These assets include hardware (or equipment), systems, networks, interconnections, telecommunications, wiring, furniture, audit records, books, documents, cash, and software. However, the number one tangible asset is always people (employees, vendors, customers, guests, visitors, and others). These assets tend to be easier to list because they are visible and perhaps even accounted for in auditing records or asset tracking systems.

3.1.4.4.2   Intangible Assets

Intangible assets are those that you cannot "touch." These assets include employee health and safety, data, customer and employee privacy, image and reputation of the organization, goodwill, and employee morale. These assets tend to be rather difficult to list or enumerate, as they are not visible or accounted for. Nonetheless, an organization must seek to protect these intangible assets as well.

3.1.4.5   Reasonableness in Limiting the Scope

As discussed previously, not all security controls or assets may be within the scope of the security risk assessment. Although, as security professionals, we typically like to see the security risk assessment process not being hindered by a smaller scope than is warranted, there are a variety of adequate reasons for limiting the scope of a security risk assessment.

Many organizations rely on other entities to supply some of their infrastructure components. These supplied components could be physical security within a shared tenant building or an outsourced managed security service. If the security risk assessment team or the customer decides that an assessment performed by another team that covers the supplied component meets their needs, they may decide to adopt the report findings or to place the supplied components outside the scope of the security risk assessment.

In the following example, some of the network components and the procedures for clearing individuals are considered outside the scope of the security risk assessment. For this example, the customer determined that the clearance process for personnel with SECRET clearances was outside the scope of the evaluation for an information system on a single military base. Furthermore, the customer decided that the system boundary did not include the MILNET or the firewalls connecting the MILNET to the information system being assessed; these components were considered part of another evaluation.

Many other scope combinations and limitations are common in the industry. Common security risk assessment scopes include geographic, functional, and technology limitations.

3.1.5 IDENTIFYING SYSTEM BOUNDARIES

It should now be clear that the failure to properly scope a security risk assessment can have disastrous consequences. One important element of scoping a security risk assessment effort is to identify the system (or systems) being assessed. An information system is any process, or group of related processes, under a single command or management control that reside in the same general operating environment. The information system comprises the processes, communications, storage, and related resources necessary for the information system to operate.

Even though a security risk assessment may be limited to a single business unit, the information systems within that business unit may be one or many. Each information system to be assessed should be properly identified by explicitly stating its physical and logical boundaries.

3.1.5.1 Physical Boundary

Physical boundaries of the security risk assessment project are the physical demarcation between in-scope and out-of-scope physical locations and controls. Identifying the physical boundaries of an information system (or systems) to be assessed both clarifies and limits the scope of the security risk assessment. Such a limitation is appropriate, as security risk assessments should be limited to those resources under the control of the project sponsor. Besides, a system without boundaries cannot be assessed.

The physical boundaries of an information system properly identify those elements within the scope of the evaluation and those outside of the scope of evaluation. These diagrams not only provide the boundaries but also identify some of the key physical security elements that will be part of the assessment, see Table 3.1.

For exterior diagrams, or site plans, a physical boundary diagram defines the limits of the assessment in terms of the property elements such as parking garages, fences, outbuildings, and walls. Additional physical security elements may include parking garages, walkways, camera placement, and fire exits, see Figure 3.2.

For interior diagrams, or floor plans, a physical boundary diagram defines the limits of the assessment in terms of the interior property elements such as other tenant spaces, fire exits, camera coverage, telephone closets, and hazardous storage, see Figure 3.3.

Although physical boundaries are typically identified by the property demarcation (property line) these boundaries can be more complex. Consider an organization within a shared building. The in-scope and out-of-scope elements may not be as simple as a property line and instead the organization

TABLE 3.1
Physical Security Diagram Elements

Exterior Diagram Elements	Interior Diagram Elements
• Streets, Parking Lots	• Public and common areas
• Property boundary	• Non-public areas (office, conference rooms)
• Walls, Fences	• Secure rooms within buildings
• Garage, Parking	• Hazardous storage
• Gates	• Evacuation routes
• Bollards	• Fire exits
• Lighting	• Fire extinguishers
• Pathways	• Shelter zones
• Building entrances	• Offices
• Guard posts	• Hallways
• Camera placement	• Camera placement

Note: Physical boundary diagrams assist the team in understanding the boundaries of the assessment and provide some detail regarding physical controls in place.

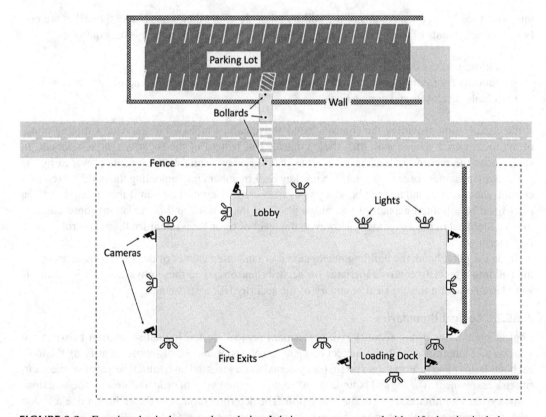

FIGURE 3.2 Exterior physical system boundaries. It is important to properly identify the physical elements that are inside and outside the security risk assessment boundary. This exterior diagram shows the physical elements inside the physical boundary.

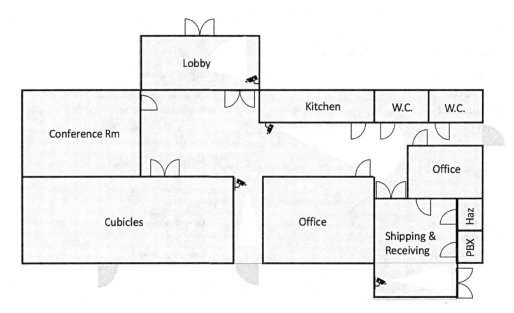

FIGURE 3.3 Interior physical system boundaries. It is important to properly identify the physical elements that are inside and outside the security risk assessment boundary. This interior diagram shows the physical elements inside the physical boundary.

must specifically list the elements of the building that are under their control and those that are not. For example, tenants of shared buildings many times share the following physical controls:

- Building access controls and procedures
- Building environmentals (e.g., air conditioning, power conditioning, and fire protections)
- Telephone closets and connections

If the organization providing the controls listed above can be included in the data gathering phase of the security risk assessment, then these controls can be part of the security risk assessment. In such a case the security risk assessment team would review available documents provided by the building management organization, interview key staff members implementing the building security controls, and inspect and test the building's physical security controls. Even if the organization can participate in a limited capacity (e.g., allow physical inspections and observation) these controls may be included in the assessment. However, the level of rigor assessment for those controls would be rather low.

If, on the other hand, the building management organization cannot or does not allow a review of the building's security controls (perhaps for security reasons) then these physical security controls would not be within the physical boundary of the security risk assessment.

3.1.5.2 Logical Boundaries

Logical boundaries of the security risk assessment project are the logical separation between the systems and functions within the subject being assessed and those out of scope. Identifying the logical boundaries of an information system (or systems) to be assessed also limits the scope of the security risk assessment. The logical boundaries of an information system properly identify the functions of the systems within the scope of the evaluation. The determination as to the inclusion or exclusion of system functions in the scope of the security risk assessment must be carefully considered.

By default, the logical boundaries of a security risk assessment should be inclusive of all functions within the information systems identified (see Figure 3.4).

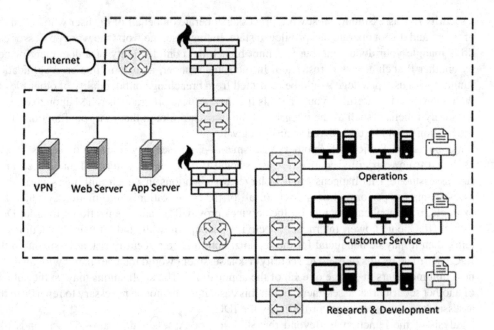

FIGURE 3.4 Logical system boundaries. It is important to properly identify the logical elements that are inside and outside the security risk assessment boundary. This diagram shows the logical elements inside the logical boundary by the longer dashed line surrounding the covered elements.

Logical boundaries can most effectively be enumerated and documented by the use of a system diagram containing the following elements:

- Workstations and laptops
- Servers (listed by function: database, file, e-mail, etc.)
- Network infrastructure (switches, routers, firewalls, load balancers)
- Internal network connections (including Local Area Networks (LANs) and Virtual LANs (VLANs))
- External network connections (including Virtual Private Networks (VPNs), dedicated circuits, Wireless Access Points (WAPs), and Internet connections)
- Removable media and mobile computing (laptops, smart phones, portable external drive)

Just as physical boundaries sometime contain limitations, the customer of the security risk assessment may also impose a logical boundary. A limitation in scope based on logical boundaries is also appropriate, as security risk assessments should be limited to those system functions under the control of the project sponsor. However, a reasoned approach for excluding certain logical systems, connections, or functions should be executed by both the security risk assessment sponsor and team. Specific reasons for the exclusion of system functions should be documented by the project sponsor or the security risk assessment team, and the identification of these functions should be included in the security risk assessment report. Specific reasons for the exclusion of system functions should accompany this discussion. The project sponsor and the security risk assessment team should refrain from excluding important system functions and should only exclude functions for good reason. Below are some possible reasons why a system function might be excluded from a security risk assessment:

- Function Is Not Security-Relevant—Some system functions (or applications) are not relevant to a specifically targeted security risk assessment. Such non-relevance should not be confused with non-importance. For example, a word-processing application or a custom application for creating and submitting time cards may not be security-relevant and can be safely ignored in a security risk assessment. Most word processors operate on behalf of the user who called the program and do not operate in a privileged state. In this case, the worst the word processor can do is mangle your document, but it cannot breach the confidentiality of a document owned by another if such access is restricted. In the same manner, a custom time card application running with user privilege would be restricted from breaching confidentiality of other files as well. However, be careful in your analysis if either of these programs is relied upon to enforce a security function, such as the integrity of the time card file; in that case, the function of the application would be considered security-relevant.

- Function Is the Subject of Another Assessment—Even security-relevant functions maybe excluded from a specific security risk assessment if they are the subject of another security risk assessment. This happens often in larger organizations in which multiple security risk assessments are performed on subsets of all of the organization's information systems. For example, if all applications rely on the services provided by an organization's Internet Data Center (IDC; e.g., power, Internet connectivity, backup, firewall, and intrusion detection system), then it may be beneficial for the organization to have a security risk assessment on the IDC itself. The results of the IDC security risk assessment would then be shared with the business unit managers in charge of each of the applications. The applications may be the subject of another security risk assessment, but in this case, it would not be necessary to reperform the assessment on those services provided by the IDC.
- Analysis of the Function Is Beyond the Skills of the Assessment Team—This sounds like something you would typically like to avoid, but it is not as bad as it seems. It is not uncommon for security risk assessments to be scoped according to the rigor requested by the organization. Scoping of the security risk assessment can include security-relevant functions that require specific skills not within the experience of the security assessment team. For example, many security risk assessments do not include the code review or penetration testing of Web applications. It is clear that many Web applications (if not all) are security-relevant. However, the skills required to review code for common errors is not possessed by all security risk assessment teams. It may be beneficial to "carve out" that portion of the assessment and bring in the experts.
- Physical or Environmental Control Makes the Function Non-Security-Relevant—Ensuring security functions that are enforced does not always have to be satisfied by logical means. Physical or environmental controls may adequately enforce security functions and therefore obviate the need for analysis of that function. For example, protection of the confidentiality and integrity of information while in transit on the internal LAN is certainly an important security function. However, if the internal LAN is physically protected (e.g., encased in pressurized conduit), then other logical controls to protect that information in transit are not required and therefore not relevant to the assessment.

3.1.6   SPECIFYING THE RIGOR

Any team of security engineers could spend as little as a week or as much as 6 months assessing the ability of the organization's security controls to protect its assets. A quick assessment that lasted only a single week would be forced to review the security controls with less rigor, while a security risk assessment scheduled for 6 months could afford to perform a more in-depth review of the existing security controls.

The organization contracting the security risk assessment project and the security risk assessment team will need to determine the appropriate rigor for the security risk assessment project. While available budget could certainly limit the extent of the security risk assessment, it is not necessary to simply spend the available money. In fact, from the point of view of the security risk assessment team hired to perform the security risk assessment, this may be considered unethical. The determination of rigor should instead be based on the complexity of the controls and the maturity of the security program.

One way to determine the required depth of analysis is to consider the perceived strength of the existing controls or the maturity of the organization's security program. Information security programs that have just recently been established are considered to have a low maturity level. When organizations with such information security programs have a security risk assessment performed, they are generally looking for the identification of gaps and oversights. Such an organization is typically not ready for a rigorous security risk assessment or the "white-glove test." A less rigorous security risk assessment on a less than mature security program will result in nearly the same recommendations because the findings are rather easy to uncover. Therefore, it is unwise and wasteful to spend money or perform a security risk assessment that simply increases the certainty of what was probably already known within the first several weeks of the security risk assessment. For example, if an internal vulnerability scan of a representative sample of workstations reveals that none of them is hardened, then it is unnecessary to continue to perform vulnerability scans on the remaining workstations. The conclusion that hardening policies are non-existent or ineffective is already formed, and additional vulnerability scanning adds nothing to the analysis.

There are many approaches to specifying the level of rigor to be performed within a security risk assessment. One of the easiest and most effective methods is to specify the activities to be performed in the data gathering portion of the security risk assessment. For example, a security risk assessment SOW could call out the following activities to be performed in order to specify the level of rigor in which the assessment is to be conducted, Table 3.2.

Documenting precisely the activities to be performed during the security risk assessment ensures that both the customer and the security risk assessment team share an understanding of the level of rigor of the data gathering portion of the security risk assessment project. A customer of the security

---

TABLE 3.2

Specifying Security Risk Assessment Level of Rigor

Data Gathering Activity	Scope of Activity	Description of Activity
Document Review	Approximately 50 documents including information security policies, procedures, and processes. Total page count less than 1,000 pages.	Documents shall be reviewed for clarity, content, correctness, consistency, and compliance with applicable regulations.
Key Staff Interviews	1–2-hour interviews with department heads, lead engineers, system administrators, and representatives from each department.	Interview topics shall cover the following: • Department mission • Job function • Key systems, applications, and sensitive data • Security controls entrusted to interviewee • Knowledge of recent security incidents • Review of job function processes involving security controls or protection of sensitive data and/or systems
Physical Inspections and Process Observations	Buildings at three locations (limited to buildings with physical controls designed to protect information and information systems)	Inspections shall include review of physical controls (barriers, access control, logging, monitoring, and response) for obvious vulnerabilities both during business hours and after hours. Observations shall include a review of observable processes (e.g., visitor control, sensitive data disposal, and clean desk policy).

(Continued)

TABLE 3.2 *(Continued)*

Data Gathering Activity	Scope of Activity	Description of Activity
Testing	Security testing shall be performed on the systems and applications within the scope of the assessment by an experienced and credentialed security tester.	Security tests shall include the following: • Security Functional Testing: Selected systems and functions (e.g., logging, access control, and encryption) shall be tested in ensure they operate as indicated. • Penetration Testing: Testers shall perform information gathering to identify attack targets from external sources; perform scanning and probing activities; perform host diagnostics assessments, perform firewall diagnostic assessments, use information gathered to attempt exploitations of the system and applications; and document all methodologies, test cases, and results.

Note: Assets are those items the organization wishes to protect. The enumeration and valuing of the assets scopes and guides the security risk assessment.

risk assessment project could alternatively provide a high-level description of the data gathering activities (e.g., "perform key staff interviews, onsite observations, and security testing of systems and applications in scope"). This approach allows prospective service providers to describe their own service techniques and allows the customer to choose from a larger variety of approaches (as opposed to dictating the approach and choosing from a larger variety of prices). Either way the customer must choose between dictating the price and allowing prospective service providers to specify the level of rigor or dictating the level of rigor and allowing the prospective service providers to specify their price. Choose one.

3.1.7 SAMPLE SCOPE STATEMENTS

As discussed previously, the creation of a proper scope statement is an important step in defining the security risk assessment project. The scope portion of the SOW specifies the elements of the organization that are the subject of the security risk assessment project. A proper scope statement will specify the target system(s) and applications, threats to be considered, assets, and controls that are to be the subject of the security risk assessment. Table 3.3 shows an abbreviated example scope statement that provides the information necessary to properly define a security risk assessment project. A proper scope for the security risk assessment project ensures an effective communication between the customer and the security risk assessment team regarding the boundaries of the security risk assessment.

TABLE 3.3
Sample Scope of Work Statement

Systems and Applications: The scope of the assessment includes all the physical premises at 1313 Mockingbird Lane, the automated information systems (AISs) located on premises, the employees and staff members of ACME, all users of the AISs located on the premises, and all policies and procedures governing AISs, AIS users, and ACME employees and staff members.

The security risk assessment includes consideration of risks related to the following:

Threats

- Natural disasters, including fire, flood, earthquake, windstorm, and snow/ice storm
- Authorized personnel, including insufficient or unqualified personnel, insufficient personnel training or supervision, and malicious insider activity
- Unauthorized personnel, including cybercriminals, script-kiddies, competitors, thieves, and vandals
- Malicious software, including viruses, worms, Trojan horses, and backdoors

Assets

- Personnel, including ACME staff and guests
- Computer systems, including databases, system software, hardware, network communications, and application software for existing and new implementations
- Internet applications, including cloud storage, meeting, and customer relationship management
- Data, including data in transit and storage; hard copy or soft
- Equipment, including capital equipment, laptops, and office equipment

Controls

- Existing countermeasures; safeguards already in place to address risks
- Security awareness and communication, including insufficient security awareness and communications, unclear assignment of security roles and responsibilities, and insufficient security plan documentation
- Data controls, including insufficient controls for data integrity, data retention and backup (short-term and long-term), system access, and system logging/auditing
- Maintenance controls, to include those for preventive maintenance, hardware failures, and remedial maintenance
- Physical and logical access controls
- Systems architecture, including previous analyses of architecture in regard to security
- History of security and disaster incidents at the facility and the surrounding area

The security risk assessment analysis shall include a review of the effectiveness of security controls, including the following tasks:

- Policy and procedure review
  - Organizational structure review
  - Social engineering
  - Vulnerability scanning
  - Application vulnerability scanning (but not application penetration testing or code review)
  - No penetration testing

Note: A proper scope for the security risk assessment project ensures an effective communication between the customer and the security risk assessment team regarding the boundaries of the security risk assessment.

3.2   PROJECT DESCRIPTION

Once the security risk assessment project is properly defined in terms of budget, objective, level of rigor, and scope, the project should be described in the security risk assessment project contract or SOW.

3.2.1   PROJECT VARIABLES

Not all security risk assessments are created equal. Security risk assessments can vary greatly from one to another based on the project variables. The specification of these variables is an important element of ensuring that both the customer and the security risk assessment team have the same vision for the appropriate engagement. The following project variables are discussed below:

- Project Scope
- Deliverables
- Security Risk Assessment Method
- Level of Rigor

The customer should decide on the appropriate "values" for these project variables for their needs. The customer does have a perceived need for the security risk assessment and understands what they want from the executed project. Therefore, the customer should certainly specify the project scope (logical and physical boundary) and the deliverables (e.g., executive summary, main report, and presentation). Regarding the security risk assessment method and the level of rigor, it is a bit more difficult to specify, or perhaps the customer should not specify at all and let prospective service providers describe that for them given a fixed budget.

To the customers in this situation, I have the following advice: Be careful of sole-source bids. Obtain several bids from several different companies. These bids should explain as best as they can the level of rigor for the assessment and the security risk assessment method to be applied. Note that the approach of sole sourcing may be a responsible approach if you are working with a trusted partner.

3.2.2   STATEMENT OF WORK (SOW)

The SOW is a portion of the contract that specifies the work to be performed. This may be as simple as a single paragraph or as complex as a multiple-page document covering the expectations and the bounds of a security risk assessment. Regardless of the length or complexity of the SOW, it should document the parameters of the security risk assessment to be performed. At a minimum, these parameters should include the service description (method and level of rigor), project scope, and description of the deliverables.

3.2.2.1   Specifying the Service Description

A security risk assessment should be clearly defined in the SOW. There should be no confusion as to whether this service is a vulnerability scan, penetration test, compliance audit, or security risk assessment. Using our definition above, the security risk assessment should be defined as:

> A probability determination of asset losses based on asset valuation, threat analysis, and an objective review of the effectiveness of current security controls.

A more complete service description would include the more detailed definition of the security risk assessment. This can best be accomplished by briefly describing the elements of a security risk assessment. By adding the following sentence, the definition of a security risk assessment becomes even clearer:

> The security risk analysis shall consist of an identification of tangible and intangible assets under protection, an identification of the threats to and vulnerabilities of the current system controls, an analysis of the threat/vulnerability likelihood, the impact of the threat to the identified assets, and recommendations for security controls to mitigate the security risks.

3.2.2.2 Scope of Security Controls

The SOW should further describe the scope of the security risk assessment by clearly stating if administrative, physical, and technical controls are included in this assessment. Physical boundaries are typically defined by building address. If various elements of the physical controls are handled by different organizations, it may be necessary to provide further refinement and identification of the physical controls to be reviewed. For example, if an organization is located within a shared facility, the building grounds, security force, and building entry control may not be under the control of the organization seeking the assessment. Furthermore, this organization may not be able to grant sufficient access for the security risk assessment team to effectively assess the adequacy of these controls. Either the organization should obtain permission and adequate access for the security risk assessment team, or they should request the organization that does control the building's physical security controls to obtain and share an objective security risk assessment covering those elements.

Administrative boundaries are typically defined by a description of the policies and procedures covered by the assessment. The complete set of policies that impact the administrative security controls within an organization can very often be owned by various departments within the organization. For example, a complete set of security policies will likely include policies from human resources, legal, help desk, network administration, business development, and operations. Moreover, many policies and procedures may be implicit, that is, practiced but not documented. It is important to specify all policies and procedures to be considered in the assessment.

Technical boundaries are defined by the systems, communication devices, and networks that are to be assessed. These boundaries are typically defined by system and network names. Often some systems or selected system components are determined to be outside the boundaries of a security risk assessment by the organization. Reasons for ignoring portions of the systems can range from recent reviews having been conducted, to control by another organization, to a planned rollout of new controls. Be sure to clearly identify all technical elements as either within scope or out of scope, for example, VLANs, VPN pool, and wireless networks. The technical boundaries of the system are best described in a well-labeled system diagram.

3.2.2.3 Specifying Deliverables

The deliverables for a security risk assessment always include the security risk assessment report. Other deliverables may be various drafts of the report, risk calculation worksheets, interview notes, etc. An SOW can go to great lengths to describe a security risk assessment report, but it simply contains four major elements. To be valuable to the customer, security risk assessment reports should clearly document the security risk assessment process, results, recommendations, and evidence.

- Process: The security risk assessment report should describe the process or methodology used in the security risk assessment. The description of the process should be no more than a few pages. The security risk assessment methodology description provides the reader with the confidence that an adequate methodology was used and gives a roadmap for understanding the results. Depending of the security risk assessment method employed, many security risk assessment results may seem coded. For example, the security risk assessment may conclude that there exist eight "level I risks" and 14 "level II risks." Without a description of how these security risk levels were determined and what they mean, the security risk assessment report is less useful.

- Results: The security risk assessment report should also have a section that clearly presents the results. This section should be understandable by the senior manager and the technical readers. The results section should include a title or short description of the security risk, an indication of its likelihood and impact, a resultant level of the security risk, and a recommendation for mitigating the security risk.
- Recommendations: The recommendations in the security risk assessment report should be described in enough detail that those who decide to implement them understand what is requested. This is not to say that the recommendations should provide step-by-step instructions for implementing the change, just enough that it is clear. For example, instead of saying "Improve logical perimeter security," state "Perimeter security should be improved through the addition of firewalls on all external interfaces and the development of a demilitarized zone (DMZ) architecture."
- Evidence: Many times, the results of a security risk assessment are questioned by members of the organization who commissioned the assessment. The security risk assessment team should keep careful notes and collect evidence to defend its findings. Evidence includes documents, interviews, and the results of inspections, observations, and testing. Evidence notations need not be elaborate. A simple notation such as "interview with Bob Smith, system administrator, on March 16, 2020" or "physical inspection of doors, windows, and gates (3/16/2020)" should be fine.

3.2.2.4   Contract Type

The direction of the negotiation and even the execution of the project depends directly on the type of contract that is used to govern the security risk assessment project. Contracts can be either a FPP or based on time and materials (T&M). The difference between these two types of contracts is a matter of who is taking the risk.

3.2.2.4.1   Time and Materials Contract

In a T&M contract, the risk belongs to the contracting organization. The contracting organization and the contractor come to an agreement as to an estimated number of hours required to complete the security risk assessment. If the security risk assessment comes in at the estimated amount of time, then all is fine. If the security risk assessment takes more time than expected, then the contracting organization can decide whether they would like the contractor to continue or not. If the security risk assessment takes less time than expected, then the contracting organization pays less than expected. The risk and reward (less likely) belong to the contracting organization.

Variations and other measures exist, such as a "not to exceed" limit, but the T&M contract still places the risk on the contracting agency, because the real deliverable here is hours. If the contractor delivers hours toward the development of the security risk assessment report, then, according to the contract, the contractor should be paid even if the report is not quite finished. T&M contracts are well suited for tasks where it is difficult to define the task upfront or if there may be considerable unknowns. For service provider organizations that are experienced in delivering security risk assessments the time required to complete a well specified security risk assessment should not be a mystery. It is a rare case when a security risk assessment project is best suited for a T&M contract.

SIDEBAR 3.2   NEGOTIATION

Coming to an agreement of terms and documenting the agreement for a security risk assessment effort requires negotiation skills. Negotiation skills can be learned in many different forums, including business school and professional education. Describing these skills is beyond the scope of this book, but the major elements required to adequately negotiate are described here:

- Understanding the Customer's Needs—Negotiation is a process of discovering the needs of others and modifying the arrangement in an attempt to meet everyone's needs. Negotiation cannot even start until the customer's needs are understood. The possible needs for a security risk assessment are numerous and should not be assumed. It is far too easy to assume that a customer simply wants a security risk assessment to identify the possible security risk to the organization's assets.
- Identifying Next-Best Alternatives—An important concept in negotiations is being aware of the other party's next-best alternative. The next-best alternative for the contracting organization is typically your competition or even an in-house effort. Understanding the market and the competitive advantages of the competition is essential to the consulting firm in contract negotiations. The next-best alternative for the contractor is typically other consulting work. Having a good understanding of the consulting firm's utilization rate, current backlog, and sales pipeline is useful to the contracting organization in contract negotiations.
- Finding Win–Win Solutions—If the negotiating parties are able to discuss the needs of each organization, many win–win situations can occur. Negotiating parties often assume that the other party's desires are in conflict with their own. If the negotiators are able to open up the discussion, many discoveries regarding mutual and complementary needs can be uncovered. For example, after some open discussion, many parties find that the concerns of each party are not solely focused on money. Important issues for both parties other than money include: project start and completion times, individuals assigned to the project, report details and complexity, and ability to follow up with assessor long after the report is complete. When these issues are important to the customer organization and easy for the consulting organization to arrange then negotiations are expanded from a mere discussion of price.
- Giving a Little More than Was Negotiated—Even after a negotiated contract, the consulting organization should strive to give more than is expected. Look for opportunities to impress the customer by taking on additional research, providing links for more information, comparing results to named competitors or industries, or other items that may be especially appreciated. The ability to provide this extra touch is relatively easy for organizations in the business of providing these services and goes a long way to customer satisfaction.

3.2.2.4.2   *Firm-Fixed-Price Contract*

In a firm-fixed-price (FFP) contract, the risk belongs to the contractor. The contractor and the contracting organization come to an agreement as to the description of the project and the price to be paid when the project is complete. If the security risk assessment is completed within the effort expected, then all is fine. If the security risk assessment takes more effort than expected, then the contractor must continue to expend effort until the project is complete to the satisfaction of the contracting organization within the definition of the contract. If the security risk assessment takes less effort than expected, then the contractor still gets paid the originally agreed price. The risk and reward belong to the contractor.

In a FFP contract, the description of the deliverables is very important. The completion of the project is completely defined by the description of the deliverables. Because the scope and level of rigor for a security risk assessment are so difficult to describe, most contracting organizations do not want to own the risk in the contract. Therefore, most security risk assessments are performed as a FFP effort. Both parties would be well-advised to carefully describe the deliverables in the contract. To clarify understanding here, it is recommended that both parties review a sample deliverable from a previous similar effort.

3.2.2.5   Contract Terms

First, let us assume that the security risk assessment is a FFP contract. Negotiation is the process of determining the needs of each party and coming to an agreement that comes as close as possible to meeting the needs of both parties. In order to negotiate, you must first understand the other party's needs and their next-best alternative.

3.2.2.5.1   Determining Needs

The contracting organization wants a quality security risk assessment performed by an objective and experienced team that results in an accurate security risk assessment report with clear and effective recommendations. The contractor wants to be fairly compensated for his work. From a contractor's point of view, he is just as happy to perform a 3-week-long security risk assessment as a 6-month-long one.[7] As you can see, the needs of the contractor are rather simple. Given an accurate description of the security risk assessment required by the contracting organization, the contractor simply wants to be compensated for the effort required to complete the task. The definitions of the scope, rigor, and overall level of effort of the security risk assessment are all in the contracting organization's court.

The contracting organization should clearly describe the scope of the security risk assessment. The remaining factors of level of rigor and overall level of effort can be difficult to describe. Most requests for proposals (RFPs) that go out fail to address the level of effort or rigor expected. As stated previously, a description of the security risk assessment that mentions only the scope of the project can be interpreted in many ways. A team could spend as much as 6 months on a rigorous assessment and as little as a few weeks on the same project at a much higher level. The level of rigor required by the contracting agency should depend on their needs and their budget, both discussed earlier in this section.

The most direct way to describe the level of rigor is to list the activities to be performed during the data gathering phase of the security risk assessment, see Table 3.1. The contracting organization could alternatively simply state how long the contractor think it would take a team to perform the assessment. For example, "The level of rigor on the assessment should be consistent with a team of three experienced professionals spending four weeks gathering data, interpreting the results, and producing the report." Of course, not all teams will take the exact same amount of time, but at least now both the contracting organization and the contractor are all in the same ballpark. This will provide a much better understanding of needs and make negotiation and the completion of an acceptable and appropriate contract much smoother.

3.2.2.5.2   Determining Next-Best Alternative

Many approaches to contract negotiation discuss the benefits of understanding the next-best alternative available to the other party, see Sidebar 3.2. Understanding the next-best alternative for both the contracting organization and the contractor can help to ensure a smooth negotiation process.

The next-best alternative to a contracting organization is the "next-best" contractor. The next-best contractor is likely very close in terms of quality and price to the preferred contractor. Contractors should be aware that there are many qualified companies waiting in line to take the job if negotiations break down. However, there are some exceptions that must be explored when determining the value of the next-best contractor:

- Familiarization—The preferred contractor may stand out above the crowd if he possesses a unique familiarization with the contracting organization's systems or the technology deployed. Familiarization is both an advantage and a disadvantage and, as such, may either increase the value of the familiar contractor or actually decrease the value. On the one hand, a familiar contractor is able to spend less time and effort in learning the organization's systems or specific technology. This ability will allow the contractor to perform a similar security risk assessment for a little less money than an otherwise equally qualified competitor. On the other hand, the familiar contractor may no longer be independent and possibly has lost the ability to be objective. A contractor who has developed the systems to be assessed or who sells the technology being used fails to be objective. If familiarity with the systems comes from actually developing them, or if familiarity with the installed technology comes from being a vendor for the technology, then the case for loss of objectivity seems rather clear. A contractor, no matter how well meaning, cannot objectively review his own work or technology upon which he relies for his financial reward. If, however, familiarity with the systems and technology comes from other experience with the client or the technology, then the contractor could successfully argue that he can remain objective. To the extent that the preferred contractor remains objective despite this familiarization, that contractor could be a much better choice than the next-best alternative.
- Expertise—Contractors possessing expertise within the organization's industry, with the specific security risk assessment requirements, or with the activities to be performed with the security risk assessment have a distinct advantage when it comes to delivering the best value to the organization.
  - Industry Expertise—Many industries, such as education, health care, energy, financial, gaming, retail, telecommunications, and e-commerce, have specific concerns, terminologies, and practices that are unique to that industry. A familiarization with these aspects of the industry will allow the contractor to more efficiently and effectively serve the contracting organization. The contractor with industry expertise will be able to comprehend system functions and connections more easily, since industry terms, expected systems and functions, industry regulations, and the threat environment of that industry are all well-known to the experienced contractor. The contractor will also find it easier to interview key personnel and anticipate their concerns, since the contractor has experience discussing the concerns with other industry leaders. Lastly, the contractor with industry experience is likely to be able to discuss and present the findings of the security risk assessment to those within an industry with whom the contractor has worked previously, because the contractor is able to correctly use the industry terminology and avoid terminology within the information security industry that may be used in a different context within the industry.
  - Regulation, Requirement, and Framework Experience—If the security risk assessment is being performed to meet specific requirements, regulations, or frameworks, a contractor who has had experience with those requirements, regulations, or frameworks may be able to provide security risk assessment services better than other similarly qualified individuals. Specific requirements, regulations, or frameworks such as HIPAA, the GLB Act, PCI DSS, Sarbanes-Oxley, FFIEC CAT, COBIT Framework 2019 , and others may have similar wording associated with the requirement for a security risk assessment, yet each of these regulations has its own unique set of expectations based on interpretations

of the requirements, case history, and the current expertise and expectations of the auditors. A contractor who has experience in the requirements, regulations, or frameworks will not need to spend copious amounts of time coming up to speed on the requirements, regulations, or frameworks and their interpretations that affect the nature of the security risk assessment. Furthermore, a contractor with experience in specific regulations, such as HIPAA, PCI DSS, FFIEC CAT, or the GLB Act, will already be familiar with how these requirements are being interpreted within the industry, the depth of analysis accepted by reviewers, and the scope of the requirements on the various system components and controls.

- Security Risk Assessment Activity Expertise—There are many different techniques, methods, and activities that may be performed within a security risk assessment in order to determine the overall security risks to the system. Depending upon the customer requirements, some of these aspects may be required within a specific security risk assessment. Key aspects include specific security risk assessment methods such as ISO 27001 or NIST SP 800-30 and techniques such as interviews, physical walk-throughs, and use of checklists; and activities such as social engineering, penetration testing, code review, architectural analysis, and organizational structure review. For those security engineers who have no experience with specific security risk assessment methods, techniques, or activities, the learning curve for these is likely to be steeper than for those security engineers with previous experience with these aspects.
- Security Risk Assessment Expertise—As unlikely as it may seem there are many security provider organizations that will include a security risk assessment as a catalog service without the appropriate experienced personnel to carry out an adequate security risk assessment. Any organization seeking to contract a security risk assessment should weed these providers out quickly. Techniques for eliminating unqualified vendors from the pool of service providers considered for the security risk assessment project include reference checks for similar projects, named project resources with resumes, and technical interviews with the proposed project leads.

The next-best alternative to the contractor is not to take the job. A contractor may choose to refuse to contract with the organization requiring a security risk assessment if there appears to be unreasonable expectations, requirements outside of their scope of expertise, or a perceived inadequate compensation for the effort expected. Since most security risk assessments are performed as a FFP contract, the contractor can end up spending a lot of hours attempting to obtain sign-off on a project with unreasonable expectations. Professional and experienced contracting organizations would sooner walk away from such a project than risk poor customer satisfaction or an unprofitable project that utilizes key resources.

3.2.2.5.3 *Negotiating Project Membership*

Occasionally, the contracting organization may find it necessary to specify the team that will be performing the assessment. This is typically a result of getting burned in a "bait and switch" routine. For example, consider the following scenario. A large consulting firm sends around its "big guns" to present proposals to clients. The clients become enamored by the skill, experience, and depth of knowledge possessed by the presenter. Then, when the time comes for the project to begin, the large consulting firm sends out recently indoctrinated entry level consultants to perform the project. The "big gun" presenter only plays a review role in the project. The result is a mismanaged, low-quality project that goes over budget and underdelivers on quality.

A good way to avoid this problem is to specify the qualities, experience, or credentials of the individuals on the project. Occasionally, the contracting organization may even require that named individuals be assigned to the project. Specifying named individuals can ensure a quality project, but it may unnecessarily tie the hands of the contractor. Remember that the contractor may have several bids out at once and experiences turnover from time to time. A preferred method of ensuring quality personnel is to allow substitution of named individuals with similar credentials and experience or upon the approval of the contracting organization.

EXERCISES

1. Consider the various audiences (stakeholders) for a security risk assessment.
   a. Who is the primary audience of a security risk assessment?
   b. Who are the secondary audiences of a security risk assessment?
   c. How does each audience member view the deliverables of the security risk assessment (process, results, recommendations, and evidence) differently?
   d. How does this differing audience view affect their attitude toward these deliverable elements?
2. How will the various audiences likely react to the following errors in a final security risk assessment report?
   a. Misspelling of interviewee's name
   b. False positive vulnerability in scanning data and conclusions
   c. Instance of another client's name in a footer of the report
   d. Missing document in list of documents reviewed
   e. Incorrect security risk category for a finding (based on method)
3. Describe an approach for defining the boundaries of a security risk assessment. What are the dangers of improperly scoping the security risk assessment?
4. Find a physical diagram of your school campus or organization's building(s). Choose a single business unit (or school) and define the physical boundaries. What assumptions did you make?
5. There are four reasons given in Section 3.1.5.2 for why it would be reasonable to exclude a system function from a security risk assessment. Can you think of any other reasons (legitimate or not)?
6. Consider the SOW in Table 3.3.
   a. What improvements can you define?
   b. What elements seem unnecessary?
   c. Would you like to see a required method for the security risk assessment? Why or why not?
7. Create an outline (or review one provided) for a security risk assessment report. Identify the primary audience of each section.
8. Why are most security risk assessments performed on a FFP basis? In what situations does a T&M contract make sense?

BIBLIOGRAPHY

American Institute of Certified Public Accountants, "Clarified Statements on Standards for Attestation Engagements (SSAE) No. 18: Concepts Common to All Attestation Engagements," AT-C Section 105, May 1, 2017.

Department of Health and Human Services, Office of the Secretary, "Health Insurance Reform: Security Standards; Final Rule," 45 CFR Parts 160, 162, and 164, Federal Register, Vol. 68, No. 34, August 14, 2002.

Department of Health and Human Services, Office of the Secretary, "Standards for Privacy of Individually Identifiable Health Information; Final Rule," 45 CFR Parts 160 and 164, Federal Register, Vol. 67, No. 157, February 20, 2003.

Federal Deposit Insurance Corporation, "501(b) Examination Guidance: Examination Procedures to Evaluate Compliance with the guidelines to Safeguard Customer Information," November 13, 2018. https://www.fdic.gov/news/financial-institution-letters/2001/fil0168.html

ISACA, "COBIT 2019 Framework," 2019.

National Institute of Standards and Technology (NIST): U.S. Department of Commerce, "Assessing Security and Privacy Controls in Federal Information Systems and Organizations: Building Effective Assessment Plans," NIST Special Publication 800-53A, Revision 4, December 2014.

National Institute of Standards and Technology (NIST): U.S. Department of Commerce, "Risk Management Framework for Information Systems and Organizations: A System Life Cycle Approach for Security and Privacy," NIST Special Publication 800-37, Revision 2, December 2018.

Payment Card Industry (PCI) Data Security Standard, "Requirements and Security Assessment Procedures," Version 3.2.1, May 2018.

4 Security Risk Assessment Preparation

Prior to the security risk assessment team's arriving on-site at the customer location, there are a number of activities to be performed to ensure an efficient project. These activities include introducing the assessment team to the organization, obtaining permission for testing and data gathering, and reviewing available information.

4.1 INTRODUCE THE TEAM

The introduction of the security risk assessment team to the customer organization is important in establishing a good start for the project. Providing an introduction to the security risk assessment team, along with contact information and credentials of individual team members provides the customer confidence in the professionalism of the effort to come. In some cases, the customer organization may have already been introduced to the team. For example, the security risk assessment team may have presented to the customer organization during the bidding and negotiation process. In many cases, however, the members of the security risk assessment team are unknown to the customer organization. Either way, a letter of introduction or a project kickoff call should be used to formalize the start of the security risk assessment project.

SIDEBAR 4.1 OPEN COMMUNICATIONS VERSUS COVER STORY

Occasionally, a security risk assessment team is asked to perform its work under the cover of an unrelated project. The unrelated project is purely a distraction from the main purpose of the assessment. This type of security risk assessment is meant to provide the security risk assessment team a better view of the actual security controls and current operations without the influence or suspicion of the current personnel. Although this type of assessment may be necessary during an investigation of a suspicious employee, it is of little use in a general security risk assessment. Security risk assessments described in this book depend on the involvement and support of current personnel, and their opinions and information relayed during interviews is an essential element of data gathering. The "undercover" security risk assessment would be unable to depend on the involvement and support of current personnel and would result in a completely different type of assessment.

4.1.1 INTRODUCTORY LETTER

The form and content of an introductory letter may vary a little, but there are several key elements that must be contained within this letter. Key elements of the introductory letter include primary points of contact for both the customer and the security risk assessment team, a reference to the statement of work, a start date and projected end date for the project, a date for the on-site portion of the assessment, the data to be requested at that time, and access required for the on-site visit.

- Points of Contact—The introductory letter should provide points of contact for all security risk assessment team members as well as contracting officers and management responsible for oversight of the project.

- Reference to the Statement of Work—The letter should also reference the specific contract and statement of work that contains the detailed requirements for the project.
- Start Date and End Date—The letter should inform the organization to be assessed of the desired or selected dates to begin the project, perform on-site data gathering, and complete the project.
- Data Requested from the Customer—The security risk assessment team should request any available information to reduce the amount of time required on-site. Information that would prove useful includes system diagram, policies, procedures, previous risk assessment reports, system configuration files, or other evidence that will provide the team with the necessary background of the organization, the organization's security program, and the security controls.
- Access and Other Requirements for On-site Assessment—Lastly, the introductory letter should list the on-site requirements for the team so that the sponsor may begin preparations. On-site team requirements typically include desks, phones, whiteboards, physical access, logical access (accounts required), and access to a point of contact while on-site.

The introductory letter should be addressed to the primary point of contact as specified in the statement of work.

4.1.2 Project Kickoff Call

Alternatively, the security risk assessment team can be introduced through a project kickoff call. The agenda for the kickoff call should follow the same topics as suggested for the introductory letter (team members, points of contact, SOW reference, important dates, document and data request, and access and other on-site requirements). A kickoff call can be more difficult to schedule as all parties involved in the assessment must find available time. However, the advantage of the kickoff call is that team members and the customer may experience a more interactive introduction which may make the project activities run more smoothly.

4.1.3 Pre-Assessment Briefing

It is always better to let people know what to expect rather than surprise them. A pre-assessment briefing can help to set the expectations of the organization to be assessed and also to listen to their concerns and adjust the security risk assessment approach accordingly. A pre-assessment briefing is performed on-site and at the beginning of the data gathering portion of the security risk assessment project. The pre-assessment briefing should cover the following topics:

- Introduction—The briefing should provide an introduction of the assessment team (or several representatives) to the organization, a review of the assessment objective, a schedule of the on-site assessments, and the final briefing.
- What to Expect—The presenter should let the members of the assessed organization know what to expect. The best way to improve the usefulness of the security risk assessment results is to make the following expectations known:
  - Not a Scorecard but a Planning Tool—The organization being assessed should understand that the security risk assessment is not a scorecard. The finding of a high-risk posture should not be an indication that people are not doing their jobs. Instead, it should be received as an indication of the need for an increased budget and staff for security. Such increases in staff or other changes such as improvements to existing controls require planning. A security risk assessment is the first step in the planning process.
  - First Step in Risk Management Process—The audience should be introduced to the risk management process and told where a risk assessment fits in that process. Risk assessments are the input into the determination of security controls, but periodic testing and operational controls play an important role as well.

- Many Findings—There will likely be many findings. The organization should not be surprised (or disappointed, shocked, or depressed) at the number of findings yielded by the security risk assessment. The process is such that many items will be listed; some will be major findings and some minor, but the number of findings is less important than the overall risk level.
- Not Always a Quick Fix—Some findings will be operational in nature and will require a quick fix. For example, a finding of obvious vulnerabilities in an externally available Web server will require immediate patching. Other findings will be tactical or strategic in nature and will require longer-term planning to fix.
- What the Team Needs to Know—The presenter should give the members of the assessed organization a forum to provide information to the assessment team that will likely impact the assessment. The presenter may want to ask open-ended questions to encourage the organization to share information. Information that would be useful includes special events during the on-site schedule, procedures for access, past experiences with assessments, possible architectural changes, and plans for additional security controls.

4.1.4 OBTAIN PROPER PERMISSION

Prior to gathering data, the security risk assessment team must obtain the proper authorization for certain data gathering activities. These activities include monitoring of user communications and access to information systems.

4.1.4.1 Policies Required

First, if the security risk assessment will include, or possibly include, the monitoring of user communications, then the security risk assessment team must ensure that their activities do not violate applicable laws and regulations, such as the Electronic Communications Privacy Act of 1986 (ECPA), international privacy protections such as the General Data Privacy Regulation (GDPR), and state privacy laws. The ECPA protects the electronic privacy of an individual and prohibits the monitoring of e-mail, voice mail, and cellphone conversations. These protections extend to users of the organization's information and telecommunication systems, and the security risk assessment team is precluded from accessing these communications without the proper authority and treatment. The GDPR establishes digital privacy rights for European Union citizens (even outside of the European Union) and limits data collection and monitoring. State privacy laws such as the California Consumer Privacy Act (CCPA) of 2018 may restrict the collection of some online information collection approaches.

For practical purposes, many of these regulations will not apply to the data collection stage of a security risk assessment project. Most security risk assessments need not monitor or even sample employee e-mail, voice mail, or cellphone conversations; or collect information online. The only reason to monitor or sample such conversations is to ascertain if there is a risk to the organization's information systems through the use of these communication methods. The risks are as follows:

- Authorized users could be sending unauthorized information (e.g., sending sensitive information to a competitor).
- Authorized users could be receiving unauthorized information or files (e.g., executables with malicious code).

In either case, a review of the current security controls in place would give the security risk assessment team adequate information to ascertain the risk. For example, if the organization does not have content filtering and anti-virus protection on the mail server, then the chances are pretty high that these things could happen. In the event that the security risk assessment team feels that it really needs to monitor these communications in order to sample data and obtain a more accurate assessment of the risk, then the following business processes must be confirmed. Failure to confirm these business processes could result in a violation of the ECPA or other applicable laws.

The organization must have an existing policy that states the organization's rights to monitor communications. The policy must be applied according to procedures that ensure that monitoring will be employed only to ensure availability and quality of the service and not to single out any individual without due cause. The security risk assessment project lead should be well-versed in the implications of collection methods and the applicability of data privacy laws. All members of the security risk assessment team shall ensure that data collection methods are approved by the security risk assessment team lead.

4.1.4.2 Permission Required

If the security risk assessment team plans to access or attempt access to the organization's information systems, then the security risk assessment team must ensure that they obtain the proper authorization. Proper authorization includes the following elements:

- Identification of System or Site Owner—Caution must be exercised here, since the determination of the owner is not always a straightforward task. First, ensure that the security risk assessment is being done with the permission of the system owner. The system owner should be independently verified through a trusted source. For example, my company was asked to perform penetration testing for a financial institution in a foreign country. The contract and the standard permission forms were signed, and we had even confirmed that the IP addresses given to us indeed belonged to the financial institution in question. However, we had yet to confirm that the parties we were dealing with actually represented the financial institution. In order to confirm that we had the authority of the financial institution and the IP address owner, we independently obtained the name of the entity that owned the IP addresses (our customers) and a point of contact for the financial institution. We contacted the financial institution and received a confirmation that our customers indeed represented the financial institution in this testing effort. Then we got it all in writing.
- Authority of System or Site Owner—Proper identification of the system owner is necessary, but it is not sufficient to properly gain permission and bound a security risk assessment project. Consider the case when there are multiple owners of the information systems or the intermediate systems connecting you to them. For example, your customer's website may be hosted at a web hosting facility. The website in question may even be running on a shared server. The security risk assessment team may have already obtained permission from the owner of the website but not the owner of the system that hosts the website. Furthermore, the security risk assessment team would be remiss if they proceeded to run a battery of vulnerability and penetration tests against the website, possibly disturbing or disrupting the other sites on the shared server.

  The security risk assessment team must ensure that they have the permission of the owner of all of the systems they will need to access in order to test the systems. There is a limit to the authority possessed by the system owner, and it is the security risk assessment team's responsibility to understand that limitation and to properly limit their security risk assessment activities.

  Because of this concern, outsourcing organizations often obtain their own security risk assessment on their environment and systems and share the results with their customers. This allows their customers to accept the results of a security risk assessment performed by another organization. Customers who accept these results will save themselves the hassle of performing security testing and analysis on the outsourcing organization, provided that they trust the objectivity and quality of the security risk assessment performed.

In the case of the shared server, or in fact most outsourced environments, the security risk assessment team should consider using the results from a previously conducted security risk assessment. Before simply accepting the results of the previous security risk assessment, the team should consider the objectivity of the security risk assessment team that performed the assessment, the quality of their work, and the extent to which the systems and their environment may have changed since the assessment. In the event that the security risk assessment team still feels the need to test these outsourced systems, the team should obtain explicit permission to test from the owner of the outsourced systems.

TABLE 4.1

Sample Penetration Test Permission Form

Introduction: As a part of a current assessment the [assessed organization] has granted permission to the [contracted organization] to perform certain security tests on our buildings, personnel, and systems. The purpose of this form is to formally authorize and limit the security tests to be performed.

Testing Subjects: The following is the list of buildings, systems, applications, and websites in which the security risk assessment team has been given permission to perform the security test methods:

Test Subject/Detail	Approved Methods/Tools	System Owner
Headquarters Building 7129 Bardstown Rd, Hodgenville, KY 42748	• Physical barrier inspection • After hours of escorted walk-through • Supervised demonstrations of physical weaknesses and control bypass limited to: • Physical access controls • Badge duplication/imitation • Guard procedures • Sensitive data handling procedures • Sensitive room barriers	
www.example.com 93.184.216.34	External security testing limited to: • Gathering publicly available information • Network scanning • System profiling • Service profiling • Vulnerability identification • Privilege escalation Specifically excluded: • Denial of service • Sensitive data modification • Intentional service interruption	

Name of Testers: The following individuals are the authorized testers for this engagement:

Date of Testing: The approved testing is to be performed within the following dates:

Acknowledgments:

The system owners acknowledge that they have the authority to grant permission for the security tests listed in this agreement and that they are aware of the potential for affecting system user experience, slow response times, possible downtime, and potential changes to data stored on the system. The system owners further acknowledge that the authorized security testers may be exposed to sensitive data stored, transmitted, or processed on your system.

Building owners acknowledge that they have the authority to grant permission for physical security inspections and tests and that they are aware of the potential for affecting building occupant experience, the exposure of physical security control weaknesses, and the potential to modify or damage physical security controls in the exercise of performing physical security inspections or tests.

Signatures and Dates:

- Explicit Authorization—Permission to perform tests on a building, staff members, systems or applications must be unambiguously expressed and documented. Once the security risk assessment team has established the owner and confirmed the owner's authority an explicit statement granting authorization to test and the details of the types of testing allowed shall be documented, signed, and dated.
- Clear Limitations of Permission—Also useful in a document granting permission to test is a clear listing of the limitations of the test. The system owner should list specific test limitations such as testing methods, restricted times, or other limitations to the permission granted.

A sample Penetration Testing Authorization Form is shown in Table 4.1. In this example the form addresses the purpose of the testing, the testing subjects, approved methods and limitations, and system owner identification, acknowledgment, and signatures. The penetration testing team needs to be familiar with the scope, permissions, and limitations of this agreement and ensure that they act within the bounds of the agreement, see Sidebar 4.2.

SIDEBAR 4.2   PENETRATION TESTING LIMITATIONS

The task of penetration testing comes a with great responsibility to act honorably, responsible, lawful, and ethical. Because the team is tasked with breaking and attempting to break existing security controls, they will run right up against potentially unethical and unlawful behavior. Organizations performing these services need to be mindful of the need for a mature and formalized practice. Below are a few considerations:

- Trustworthiness—Activities performed while executing penetration testing (and social engineering) are clearly trust-needy. The organization should implement measures to ensure that those assigned these tasks are trustworthy. Measures include background checks, reference checks, drug testing, training, code of ethics, internal employment agreements.
- Permission and Authority—The assessed organization is responsible for granting appropriate approval for systems, applications, and buildings under their control and ownership. However, the service provider organization is the expert in this engagement and also bears a responsibility to ensure the assessment organization ownership and authority are understood. For example, the assessed organization cannot give permission to perform penetration testing on their application, when their application is hosted by another organization.
- Methods—It must be noted that the penetration testing objective is to determine and demonstrate the vulnerabilities of existing controls. Within the realm of physical penetration testing this may be accomplished through many passive penetration testing activities such as piggy-backing, motion sensor sensitivity testing, finding unlocked doors, and finding sensitive data outside of controlled areas. Active methods of physical penetration testing include techniques such as lock-picking, creating and using fake or duplicate badges, and crawling over partitions. When rules of engagement are not clearly understood, penetration testers are unescorted, or when approval and authority are misunderstood by the stakeholders, this can potentially place the penetration tester in a difficult position.

On September 11, 2019, two penetration testers found themselves learning many of these lessons when they set off an alarm by manipulating the lock mechanism from the outside of a <u>county</u> courthouse in Dallas County Iowa. The <u>state</u> of Iowa had hired a security testing company to test its physical and technical controls within the state judicial system. The company obtained a permission form that laid out the rules of engagement and listed buildings in scope. Unfortunately, one of those buildings was a county (not state) judicial building. The assessed organization gave permission to test the physical controls, but they were not the building owner or supervisor and had no authority to authorize such a test. Surprisingly, the security testing company was unfamiliar with how state and county organizations and jurisdictions work and did not see the inappropriate authorization issue.

When the two penetration testers set off the alarm, they waited for the response and explained their role in testing the state judicial system. The county Sheriff was unimpressed as this was a county courthouse and not a state building and the two penetration testers were arrested for burglary, possessing burglary tools, and trespass. The charges were later dropped, but only after a rather dangerous and embarrassing situation.

4.1.4.3 Scope of Permission

Organizations should not be asked to give outright permission for access to everything at all times. Security testing permission should only be requested and granted for specific systems, at specific times, and for a specific purpose.

The permission form should specify the IP addresses, physical address, and application names to be included in the test. The tests should be restricted to a specified time window. If possible, the time window should not be selected such that the organization can be ready and waiting for the test. A window of at least 7 days is typical. There also may be a need for some extended hours (over several days) to accommodate longer security scanning and test processes, especially if the testing window is restricted to several off hours for each of those days. Lastly, the type of testing should be described (e.g., vulnerability testing, penetration testing, social engineering, and physical penetration testing), see Table 4.1 for a sample penetration testing permission form.

4.1.4.4 Accounts Required

The security risk assessment team must specify to the sponsor the number and types of accounts that will be required. The accounts required for any particular security risk assessment are dependent on the processes to be used by the security risk assessment team and the permissions that the customer will grant. An example of the accounts that should be requested is provided in Table 4.2.

TABLE 4.2
Example of Required Accounts

Account Required	Privileges	Need
Guest account	User privileges only	User security functions
Privileged account	Administrator privileges	Administrator security functions
Network component account	Read access	Read configuration files
Network access	Network media access	Vulnerability scanning, network sniffing

Note: The security risk assessment team will require multiple accounts with various privileges and access to properly gather information for the assessment.

4.2 REVIEW BUSINESS MISSION

Before attempting to assess and report on the risks to an organization and its assets, the security risk assessment team must first acquire a basic understanding of the organization, its mission, its objectives, and its critical systems. The security risk assessment team will never develop as complete an understanding of the organization as the organization's executives, but there must be a basic understanding of the corporate mission, structure, businesses, and culture. The security risk assessment team must understand the business mission of the organization to have a basic understanding of the business assets, the potential risks, and the impact of risks on those assets.

4.2.1 WHAT IS A BUSINESS MISSION?

Every organization has a reason for existing outside of making money. Making money is a potential side effect of performing the mission well. Sometimes it can be difficult to determine the business mission. Other times, it is clearly stated and available. In either case, the security risk assessment team is looking for the answer to three simple questions:

1. Who Is the Customer?—The basic starting block for understanding a business is to understand the customers they serve. For example, consider the magazine publishing industry. A surface-level understanding of the business tells you that the readers and subscribers are the customers. However, the revenue generated from subscriptions and newsstand purchases typically covers only the cost of printing and distribution.

   The real customers of the magazine publishing industry are the advertisers and the customers of "non-advertising marketing." Understanding that these are the real customers of the magazine publishing industry will give the team members a better understanding of the assets, critical systems, and acceptable levels of risk for each of those assets.

2. What Does the Organization Offer the Customer?—Find out what they sell, how they make money, and what the product is. The business mission is not always clear, but if you want to find out how that mission is defined, follow the money. Business missions are defined by the various services or products offered by the organization. Ask about business units, organization charts, and sources of revenue for the organization.

3. What Makes the Organization Different from Its Competitors?—Even within an industry familiar to members of the assessment team, the assessed organization may have several unique characteristics that set it apart. Simply ask senior management how they differentiate themselves from competitors. For example, an organization may be the low-cost provider of e-commerce for certain items. In this case, you would expect them to accept more risk than most of their competitors. Although this organization would need to meet minimum standards set by regulations and customers, it is unlikely that they would want to expend a lot of resources to implement additional controls unless these controls had other clear benefits.

The business mission statement typically identifies the customers and how the organization plans to serve them. Beyond those simple elements, look for how this company sees itself as different from its competitors. There are only two ways to differentiate yourself:

- Offer a better product or service
- Offer a cheaper price

A better product or service can take on many forms. Better could mean higher quality (e.g., reliable, respected, and fast) or more convenience (e.g., better integrated and easy ordering process). A cheaper price could mean less cost initially or less cost in the long run. In either case, the security

TABLE 4.3

Business Mission and Security Need

Security Level	Business Mission Elements	Security Need
Tier 1	• Cutting-edge organization • High-quality provider • Critical systems with critical data assets • Sensitive customers	Low risk acceptance • High availability • Defense in depth • Redundancy • High-security culture • Cutting-edge security mechanisms • First-rate security organization
Tier 2	Average Just do what is right	Average risk acceptance • Standard security practices
Tier 3	• Cost leader • Minimalist • Bare bones	High-risk acceptance • Minimal security practices

Note: A governing information security principle is that security needs are based on business objectives. This table provides
a simplified illustration of how the business mission can affect the level of security required within an organization.

risk assessment team is looking for the company to fall into one of three tiers of security need (see
Table 4.3). In most cases, it becomes rather obvious into which tier a client falls, based on a cursory
review of the business mission. Because of the need to differentiate one organization from its competitors, few companies are "on the fence" when it comes to these categories.

4.2.2   OBTAINING BUSINESS MISSION INFORMATION

To the extent possible, the security risk assessment team should attempt to obtain the business mission prior to visiting the organization. A review of public and provided information may produce the
knowledge necessary to understand the organization's business mission. Public information available to the security risk assessment team includes the organization's website, news articles about
the organization, annual reports, and press releases. Other information that may contain statements
relevant to the organization's mission includes introductory letters from the organization's chief
executive officer, internal memoranda, or corporate training material. Any of these sources should
yield a statement as to the customers served and the products or services offered.

   The security risk assessment team leader should perform the basic research necessary to identify
the organization's business mission. If this mission statement is formally documented by the security risk assessment team, it should be reviewed and approved by the customer organization and, if
necessary, appropriately modified.

4.3   IDENTIFY CRITICAL SYSTEMS

The customer organization is likely to have multiple information systems within the scope of the
security risk assessment. All of these critical systems must be considered independently, as they
will have unique critical assets, missions, data, procedures, controls, and data owners. Once these
systems have been identified, the security risk assessment team may find some overlap between the
systems such as common controls or shared system owners. For example, there may be a single system owner for two or three systems supporting a business function. However, it is still important to
identify these individual critical systems if there are any unique aspects.

TABLE 4.4

Sample Critical System Identification

System Name	Functions	Data Owner	Data	Authorized Users	Boundary of Resources
E-mail	Provide e-mail services	Dir. of IT	Personal, company confidential, company sensitive	Employees and contractors	E-mail server, e-mail client, e-mail archive
Claims	Claims processing	Privacy Officer	Protected Health Information (PHI)	Customer service agents	Custom applications, data store, remote access
Accounting	Accounts payable, accounts receivable, and creation of balance statement	CFO	Company financial information, customer bank account information	Accounting department	Accounting department workstations, accounting software, financial data, and firewall separating system from the rest of the organization
Shared file server	Provide intracompany access to company documents and project resources	CIO	Company confidential, Company sensitive	All staff members	File servers implementing internal shared drives and backup servers
GSS	General office automation support	Dir. of IT	Personal, Company confidential, Company sensitive	Employees and contractors	Individual workstations with operating system and applications

Note: Critical systems must be identified and treated uniquely, as they have unique functions, data, users, and data owners.

Information systems are defined by their boundary of resources and characterized by their function, data, authorized users, and system or data owners. For example, a customer organization may have the information systems listed in Table 4.4 defined as part of the security risk assessment.

4.3.1 DETERMINING CRITICALITY

The security risk assessment team should seek to obtain an understanding of the criticality of the various information systems to the organization's success. This is an essential part of understanding the organization's mission.

The criticality of information systems is determined by their support for business objectives. More specifically, critical systems are those that automate critical business functions. The assignment and prioritization of system criticality are difficult tasks, especially for a security risk assessment team that may not have adequate representation from all the organization's business units. However, there are activities that may be performed by the security risk assessment team to appropriately identify critical systems. There are three basic approaches for determining the criticality of systems for a security risk assessment:

- Assessment Information Reuse—Many organizations may have already performed business continuity planning (BCP). As part of a BCP effort, they would have already identified and prioritized critical systems within the organization. The security risk assessment team can reuse this information, provided that it is still considered up to date and relevant by the organization. Furthermore, the BCP documentation is likely to have additional information that can be used elsewhere, such as likely threats, asset valuation, and other aspects that can be used in other phases of the security risk assessment.

- High-level Review—If a BCP is available, by all means use it, but if the security risk assessment team must take on the process of identifying critical systems, sometimes only a high level of information is required. It is enough for most security risk assessment methods to simply identify those systems that are critical, important, and of moderate importance. There is no need to determine a prioritization of these systems and a measurement of how long they can be down before the organization is in danger of going out of business.
- Classify Critical Systems—The information technology (IT) infrastructure of many organizations can be rather complex, making the identification of critical systems a daunting task. It is important to divide the organization's IT infrastructure into manageable parts. For several reasons, security risk assessment should not be attempted on the whole system for complex IT infrastructures. First, a security risk assessment based on a large and complex environment tends to become difficult to manage, and the results are difficult to compare, as they apply across diverse business units. Secondly, it is typically useful to divide security risk assessments into systems that are associated with each business unit, as they are likely to have unique findings, priorities, and budgets.

Even given the assumption that a security risk assessment is to be performed on a manageably sized network and infrastructure, the task of identifying critical systems can be difficult. One approach to simplify this process is to classify the systems. The following classification system is well documented in several National Institute of Standards and Technology (NIST) publications and is intended for government agencies, but it should work well for most organizations. Minor modifications have been made to the NIST text, but the general concepts are largely the same.

4.3.1.1 Determine Protection Requirements

These example requirements are derived from the need for protection among the three elements of the security policy, namely, confidentiality, integrity, and availability. The following scale may be used for rating the protection requirements of the systems:

- High—A critical concern for the system or major financial loss (greater than $1 million), or requires legal action up to imprisonment for correction
- Medium—An important concern, but not necessarily paramount in the organization's priorities, or could cause significant financial loss ($100,000 to $1 million) or require legal action for correction
- Low—Some minimal level of security is required, but not to the same degree as the previous two categories, or would cause only minor financial loss (less than $100,000) or require only administrative action for correction

4.3.1.2 Determine Mission Criticality

The next step is to determine the mission or business criticality of each system. Criticality is defined as the extent to which the system is integral to carrying out the mission of the organization. The following NIST[2] definitions are useful for providing guidance for the criticality assignments of the identified systems:

- Mission Critical—These systems are those that would preclude the organization from accomplishing its core business functions if they were to fail. A system should be considered critical if it meets any of the following criteria:
  - Supports a core business function
  - Provides the single source of mission-critical data
  - May cause immediate business failure upon its loss

- Important—These systems are those whose failure would not preclude the organization from accomplishing its core business functions in the short term but would if the system is not repaired in the mid or long term (3 days to 1 month). A system should be considered important if it meets either of the following criteria:
  - Serves as a backup source for data that is critical
  - Would have an impact on business over an extended period of time
- Supportive—These systems are those whose failure would not preclude the organization from accomplishing its core business functions but would reduce the effectiveness or efficiency of day-to-day operations. A system should be considered supportive if it meets either of the following criteria:
  - Tracks or calculates data for organizational convenience
  - Would only cause loss of business efficiency and effectiveness for the owner

4.3.1.3 Define Critical Systems

The final phase in the process of identifying critical systems is to define each system as a general support system (GSS), major application (MA), or application.

- Applications—These systems are defined as "the use of information resources to satisfy a specific set of user requirements" (NIST SP 800-60).
- Major Applications—These systems are defined as "an application that requires special attention to security due to the risk and magnitude of the harm resulting from the loss, misuse, or unauthorized access to or modification of the information in the application" (NIST SP 800-60). Applications are considered MAs if they have been determined to be "critical" or "important" or if they have been determined to be supportive but have at least one of the protection requirements rated as medium or high.
- General Support Systems—These systems are defined as "an interconnected set of information resources under the same direct management control which shares common functionality" (NIST SP 800-60). GSSs provide support for the applications that reside on them. The criticality of a GSS is based on the highest criticality of any application or MA that resides on the GSS.

4.4 IDENTIFY ASSET CLASSES

A key step in preparing for a security risk assessment is to identify the classes of assets to be protected. The identification of assets is a necessary precursor to understanding the overall risk to those assets.

The depth and rigor of the asset-identification process should be commensurate with the depth and rigor of the overall security risk assessment. Asset identification can be a rather easy exercise of listing the items requiring protection based on available checklists and engineering judgment, or it can be an involved process requiring an inventory of capital equipment, a traceability matrix of system resources, a review of legal documents, and an attempt at listing all intangible assets, such as the organization's reputation. Each of these asset identification approaches (checklists and judgment, asset criticality classification, and asset valuation), along with several methods are discussed in detail below.

4.4.1 Checklists and Judgment

Listing assets based on checklists and judgment will yield an adequate identification of the critical assets of the organization. For many security risk assessments, this is good enough, as the organization would be unwise to spend its entire budget on a security risk assessment. A security risk assessment team can efficiently develop a relatively good list of assets by reviewing general lists of assets and using judgment to apply the list to the organization they are reviewing. Consider the general asset list in Table 4.5.

TABLE 4.5
General Asset List

Asset Category	Subcategory	Examples
Information	Sensitive	• Employee applications, Employment records • Facility plans • Intellectual property • Security vulnerabilities and parameters • Financial data, Pricing information • Contingency procedures
	Protected	• Medical records • Financial inquiries • Health insurance applications, Prescriptions • Bank statements, Credit reports
	Public	• Website, Marketing materials • SEC filings
Equipment	Computing	• Servers • Workstations, Laptops
	Telecomm	• Cabling, Switches • Closets, Panels
	Transportation	• Vehicles, Trucking
	Network	• Cabling, Hubs, Switches • Routers, Bridges, Subnets • Firewalls, IDS appliance • Modems, VPNs
	Special purpose	• Check printing • Product manufacturing
Maintenance	Tools	• Specialized tools, Spare parts
Inventories	Material	• Raw material • Partial assemblies
	Finished goods	• Products
Personnel	Staff	• Executives, Managers • Security personnel • Employees, Field personnel
Outsiders	Contractors	• Temporary workers, Vendors • Visitors
Contractors	Cleared contractors	• Escorted contractors
Temporary workers	Front office worker	• Sensitive position
Services	Movement	• Equipment • Personnel
Training	Staff	• Outsiders

(Continued)

TABLE 4.5   *(Continued)*

Asset Category	Subcategory	Examples
Infrastructure	Power	• Communication • Water • Cooling • Fire suppression
	Research and development	• New product research • Optimization
Facilities	Headquarters	• Field offices • Utility buildings
	Financial resources	• Checks • Accounts • Cash

Note: It may be impossible and certainly futile to exhaustively list every asset in an organization for a security risk assessment. However, the security risk assessment team should endeavor to account for the general assets and asset classes, as they affect the organization's security posture. This table provides a list of general assets to aid the security risk assessment team in identifying a reasonable set of assets to review.

4.4.2   Asset Sensitivity/Criticality Classification

Assets are, by definition, those items that require protection. It is useful to categorize or classify assets to organize asset protection requirements and to assess the vulnerability of assets. There are three approaches for classifying or categorizing assets:

4.4.2.1   Approach 1: Find Asset Classification Information Elsewhere

Some organizations may have already performed an activity in which assets were classified. Such activities include previous security risk assessments, asset inventories, security policies, or system documentation. The security risk assessment team can reuse this information, provided that it is still considered up to date and relevant by the organization.

4.4.2.2   Approach 2: Create Asset Classification Information

If there are no documents or previous activities that have already classified the organization's assets, the security risk assessment team must take on the process of classifying assets, but only a high level of information may be required.

For most security risk assessment methods, it may be enough to simply identify basic classes of information. For example, most organizations have many different reasons for protecting data (e.g., personal data on employees, proprietary data about product pricing, and security data regarding protective measures), but it may be enough for the security risk assessment to simply determine if information is sensitive or not. Sensitive data requires protection and public data does not.

This may be an oversimplification for some organizations, especially those that must comply with information-security regulations such as the Health Insurance Portability and Accountability Act (HIPAA) or the Gramm-Leach-Bliley (GLB) Act. Healthcare organizations seeking to comply with HIPAA also need to know whether information assets contain Protected Health Information (PHI). Similarly, financial institutions seeking to comply with the GLB Act also need to know whether information assets contain customer information (see Table 4.6).

4.4.2.3   Approach 3: Determine Asset Criticality

Another approach for categorizing assets is by severity (e.g., critical, important, and supportive). Definitions similar to those used by NIST for system criticality can be used here as well. Using those definitions and applying them to assets, we derive the following definitions:

TABLE 4.6

Sample Asset Classifications

Classification	Description	Examples
Sensitive assets	Assets that contain any form of sensitive information, including personal information on employees, configuration information of security controls, and company proprietary information	Employee applications, account passwords, pricing information
PHI or customer assets	Assets that contain PHI or customer information • Customer information—any record containing non-public personal information about a customer of a financial institution • Protected Health Information—individually identifiable health information	Medical records, financial inquiries, health insurance applications, bank statements, credit reports, prescriptions
Public assets	Assets that contain neither sensitive information nor PHI or customer information	Website, marketing materials, SEC filings

Note: For many organizations, assets may be easily classified into relatively few categories, thus making asset classification a simpler task.

- Critical Assets—Assets that would preclude the organization from accomplishing its core business functions if they are not protected. Critical assets are those that meet either of the following criteria:
  - Required by a critical system
  - Backup is not provided elsewhere
- Important Assets—Assets whose compromise would not preclude the organization from accomplishing its core business functions in the short term but would if the assets are not restored. An important asset is one that meets either of the following criteria:
  - Serves as a backup for other critical data
  - Would have an impact on business over an extended period of time
- Supportive Assets—Assets whose compromise would not preclude the organization from accomplishing its core business functions but would reduce the effectiveness or efficiency of day-to-day operations. A supportive asset is one that meets either of the following criteria:
  - Tracks or calculates data for organizational convenience
  - Would only cause loss of business efficiency and effectiveness for the owner

4.4.3 Asset Valuation

One of the key steps to performing a security risk assessment is to determine the value of the assets that require protection. Asset valuation is an important element of business accounting and planning within the organization and may be performed for many reasons. These reasons may include compliance, contingency planning, insurance, legal claims, records management, budgeting, information classification, or criticality assignment. Within a security risk assessment, asset valuation is performed for information classification and criticality assignment. Asset valuation is a required element in determining critical systems and the impact on the organization if the asset is lost or compromised.

There are many approaches to determine the value of an organization's assets. These approaches range from simple binary decisions, semi-quantitative valuation, qualitative valuation, or complex quantitative valuation. Due to the complexity of this issue, there are eight asset valuation approaches covered below (see Table 4.7) to give the reader an overview of the possible techniques that could be

TABLE 4.7
Asset Valuation Techniques

Approach	Technique	Description	Comments
Qualitative	Binary	Determination if data belongs to a protected class	• Easy to apply • Applicable in regulated industries
	Classification	Data is classified as high, medium, or low	• Easy to apply • Generally applicable to any organization
	Ranking	Each asset is ranked against all other assets	• Relatively easy to apply • Results in an ordered list of assets
	Consensus	Consensus estimate by a group of experts	• Works well with small groups • Not scientific, difficult to replicate results
Quantitative	Cost valuation	Based on economic principle of substitution	• Quantitative valuation • Replacement cost
	Market valuation	Based on economic principles of competition and equilibrium	• Quantitative valuation • Market value
	Income valuation	Based on economic principle of expectation	• Quantitative valuation • Expected income

Note: Many asset valuation techniques are available to the security risk assessment team. Choosing the appropriate one requires an understanding of the various techniques and the project requirements of the security risk assessment.

applied to any given security risk assessment. (Four approaches are qualitative, one is semi-quantitative, and the other three are quantitative.) Choosing the asset valuation technique that best fits any particular security risk assessment depends upon the budget, time, and regulatory requirements of the assessment effort. The asset valuation techniques are presented in order level of rigor, starting with the least rigorous and therefore the approach that is less costly to apply.

The four qualitative asset valuation approaches are as follows:

- Binary asset valuation
- Classification-based asset valuation
- Rank-based asset valuation
- Consensus asset valuation

4.4.3.1 Approach 1: Binary Asset Valuation

A binary asset valuation involves a simple decision for each asset: yes or no? This type of asset valuation is applicable to situations in which specific security controls are required for strictly defined data. For example, within the HIPAA regulation, electronic Protected Health Information (e-PHI) is a protected class of data and must comply with specific requirements within the HIPAA regulation. A HIPAA-based security risk assessment requires the identification of PHI and non-PHI data.

4.4.3.2 Approach 2: Classification-Based Asset Valuation

An extension of the binary approach for asset valuation is the classification-based approach. In this approach, assets are classified as one of several value classifications. For example, all critical assets can be considered of high value; important assets have a medium value; and supportive assets have a low value. This approach is the classic qualitative approach. It is a more general application of

TABLE 4.8

Classification-Based Asset Valuation

Criticality Level	Asset Impact/Criticality Rating Criteria
Critical	Indicates that compromise of the asset would have grave consequences, leading to loss of life or serious injury to people and disruption to operation of a critical business function
High	Indicates that a compromise of the asset would have serious consequences that could impair the operation of a critical business function
Medium	Indicates that compromise of the asset would have moderate consequences that would impair the operation of a critical business function for a short time
Low	Indicates little or no impact on human life or the continuation of the operation of critical business functions

Note: Assets may be classified in one of several asset classifications that indicate their qualitative value. For many organizations, the qualitative approach to asset valuation provides adequate asset valuation with less effort than quantitative asset valuation approaches.

the binary approach; in that it is more flexible and can distinguish between multiple classifications instead of just one. Another example of classification-based asset valuation is shown in Table 4.8.

4.4.3.3 Approach 3: Rank-Based Asset Valuation

The ranking approach to asset valuation requires that each asset is ranked in value against all other assets. For example, if the security risk assessment team has identified 50 assets within the organization, then each asset will be ranked between one and 50. This requires a little more analysis and discussion than the binary or classification-based asset valuation techniques, but it provides the security risk assessment team with more information as well.

4.4.3.4 Approach 4: Consensus Asset Valuation

Another approach to determining the value of an organization's assets is to gain a consensus estimate by a group of experts. The Delphi method, which involves the use of at least three experts and a facilitator, is a popular technique for gaining consensus. The Delphi method was developed by the RAND Corporation in 1969 and continues to be the standard for consensus-based estimation. This method works well for small groups of experts but tends to be labor-intensive as the number of experts increases. Other criticisms of the method are that it lacks scientific rigor and that it is difficult to replicate the results.

4.4.3.5 Approaches 5–7: Accounting Valuation Approaches

In many security risk assessment efforts, it may be enough to simply assign a relative or qualitative value based on the asset classification. Notice that assigning a value in a qualitative security risk assessment approach can be done at the same time (and with the same effort) as assigning a classification to the asset. Many qualitative methods therefore skip asset valuation, because a value is inherent in the classification of the data.

However, assigning a value to an asset may be a more complex process. For security risk assessments that implement quantitative methods in the calculation of risk, assets must be assigned a monetary value. There are three quantitative approaches for determining the valuation of an asset:

- Cost Valuation—Base the value of the asset on replacement or alternative costs
- Market Valuation—Base the value of the asset on the market value income
- Valuation—Base the value of the asset on the expected income from the asset

4.4.3.5.1   Approach 5: Cost Valuation

This approach to determining the value of an asset uses the economic principle of substitution. The principle of substitution states that businesses strive for efficiency by substituting current arrangements for another arrangement that will get the job done better for the same amount of money or produce the same results for less money.

Applying this principle to asset valuation, an asset is valued at the cost of a substitute that performs the same job. For example, consider placing a value on intellectual property such as a security risk assessment training class. Under the cost valuation approach, the class material would be valued the same as a similar class. If you can contract a firm to produce a similar training class for $50,000, then this specific security risk assessment class is worth $50,000.

4.4.3.5.2   Approach 6: Market Valuation

Another approach to determining the value of an asset is market valuation. This approach is based on the economic principles of competition and equilibrium, better known as the law of supply and demand. The law of supply and demand states that (1) the greater the supply of courseware for sale, the lower the price is set, and (2) the greater the demand for similar courseware, the higher the price is set. Lower prices bring more customers; higher prices drive some away. The equilibrium is set at a market-clearing price, meaning that a price is reached such that the number of buyers and sellers is equal.

Applying this principle to asset valuation, an asset is valued at the price someone is willing to pay for it. Using the same example, if nobody is willing to pay $50,000 for the class materials and ownership, but they are willing to pay $45,000, then the class material is worth $45,000.

4.4.3.5.3   Approach 7: Income Valuation

The last approach covered in this book for determining the value of an asset is income valuation. This approach is based on the economic principle of expectation. This principle states that the value of an asset is equal to the expected income from that asset.

Applying this principle to our example, the class materials for the security risk assessment should be valued at the expected income. For example, if you were to license the materials to a training company that could sell 24 classes per year with an average of ten students per course at a price of $2,000 and get a 5% royalty, then the class materials would be valued at over $100,000 (see Table 4.9).

TABLE 4.9

Sample Asset Valuation—Income Approach

	Assumptions	
Useful life of materials	Class is based on general principles and does not require updates	5 years
Expected income from classes per year	• 5% royalty • 24 classes a year, ten students a class • $2,000 per student	Revenue: 24×10×2000 = $480,000 Royalty income: 5% × revenue = $24,000
Present value of expected income	Rate of return = 6%	$101,096.73

Note: The value of educational materials for a security risk assessment class is used here to demonstrate the income approach to asset valuation. Based on the assumptions documented in this table, such a class would be valued at over $100,000.

SIDEBAR 4.3 FUTILITY OF LISTING ALL ASSETS

No matter how hard you try, you can never list all of the assets, tangible and intangible. There are too many factors that go into creating value for an organization. Unless you are an auditor, you really should not even try to list them all. First, it is extremely time consuming to attempt to put together a list of everything that brings value to the organization. The time spent compiling a list of office equipment or trade secrets or workstations leaves less time for the remainder of the security risk assessment. Moreover, such a list is simply not very useful to the security risk assessment effort. When assessing the risk to data and programs on workstations from malicious software, is it really important whether there are 43 workstations or 435 workstations? Does it really matter what general office software is installed?[1]

An effective security risk assessment recognizes the assets under consideration in relative terms only, because the purpose of asset scope is to scope the security risk assessment to the areas intended to be assessed. For instance, because physical security is typically separated from information security, many security risk assessments are performed without regard to the safety of people or building structures. So, rather than attempting to list all physical assets, simply note that building structures and facility utilities and protection mechanisms are outside of the scope of this security risk assessment.

4.5 IDENTIFYING THREATS

The next step for the security risk assessment team in preparing for a security risk assessment is to identify the threats to the system to be considered. The identification of the threats is important because it bounds the assessment to the actions that can be performed by those threats. For example, if a security risk assessment team is told by the assessed organization to consider only human and not nature threats, then the assessment is bounded to those threats that can be performed by humans. Furthermore, if the security risk assessment team is told to consider only external threats, then the assessment team would not look at insider threats.

These examples are simple cases of identifying the threats, since the threats were treated in broad terms. A more in-depth review of the threats applicable to an assessment will show that there are a great many possible threats to the organization's assets. To provide some structure to the multitude of possible threats, threats are discussed in terms of their components.

4.5.1 THREAT COMPONENTS

A threat is commonly described as an event with an undesired impact on the organization's assets. The components of a threat include the threat agent and the threat action.

4.5.1.1 Threat Agent

A threat agent is an entity that may cause a threat action to happen, such as an earthquake or a disgruntled employee. Threat agents can be organized by three categories:

- Human-Insider-Accidental—The most frequent threat agent is the trusted individual who performs (or neglects to perform) an action accidentally.
- Human-Insider/Outsider-Intentional—Humans may also perform actions (or neglect to perform) an action intentionally. These humans can be insiders abusing trust or outsiders attempting to gain access or otherwise damage the organization's assets.

TABLE 4.10

Threat Agents by Type and Category

Human	Nature	Technology
• Insider	• Fire, Heat, Smoke	• Infrastructure Power
• Executive	• Toxic fumes	• Internal Power
• Management	• Weather	• Water
• Sensitive position	• Rain, Flood	• HVAC
• Employee	• Lightning	• Gas
• Security force	• Hurricane	• Telecomm
• Outsider	• Monsoon	• Internet
• Terrorist	• Tsunami	• Network
• Cybercriminal	• High winds, Tornado	• Electronic interference
• Ex-employee	• Volcano	• External
• Competitor	• Extreme heat	• Power
• Building crew	• Extreme cold	• Water
• Associate	• Snow/ice	• Gas
• Business associates	• Solar flare	• Telecomm
• Customer	• Humidity	• Internet
• Vendor	• Vibration, Earthquakes	• DNS
• Visitor	• Landslides	• Electronic interference
	• Wildlife, Insects, Rodents, Birds	• System
	• Biological threat	• Hardware
	• Virus	• Software
		• Application

Note: There are many different approaches for identifying threats to an organization's assets. One approach is to first consider the threat agent and then consider the action the threat agent can take. This table lists the various threat agents from humans, nature, and technology.

- Natural—Mother nature presents threats to an organization and the organization's assets. These threats include earthquakes, tornadoes, high winds, flooding, volcanoes, and landslides.

The depth to which a security risk assessment team should identify threat agents depends on the expected rigor of the overall assessment. In some cases, the list of threats to be considered may have been bounded or defined during the project definition phase; for example, only external threats are to be considered. In other cases, the breadth of threats to be considered is wide open. In either case, the security risk assessment team must now consider the depth to which these threats will be identified. If additional depth of analysis is required during the threat identification stage, the security assessment team should further break down the threat agent into subcategories. For example, instead of treating all types of human-intentional as a single threat, the team could break down this category into insiders, executive, security force, cybercriminals, ex-employee, competitor, and visitor. An example breakdown of this category is found in Table 4.10.

4.5.1.2 Threat Action

A threat action is what is caused by a threat agent (human-accidental, human-intentional, or natural). While there are many ways in which to categorize threat actions, the following seven categories of threat actions will be used throughout this book. They are briefly explained below:

- Invoked Malware—An employee may take a number of actions that lead to the introduction of malicious software (e.g., malware) on their computer. This may involve opening an e-mail, visiting a website, inserting removable memory into the employee's computer, downloading the malware, or the malware may have been put in place by the software manufacturer.

When the threat is intentional this could be an employee or an outsider introducing the malware to the organization.

- Theft & Sabotage—An employee may be the victim of a robbery in which an organizational asset such as a laptop or a mobile device may now be in the hands of an unauthorized person. Employees may be susceptible to theft while traveling to and from work, traveling for work, or at home or a hotel. When the threat agent is intentional, this could be an employee or an outsider causing or perpetrating the theft or sabotage.
- Socially Engineered—An employee may fall prey to a cybercriminal who uses psychology (instead of technical approaches) to gain the trust of the employee and then tricks them into violating the organization's security policy. This is basically a modern version of a confidence scam (e.g., used to by conmen.) When the threat agent is intentional, this could be an employee or an outsider causing or perpetrating the con.
- Hacked—An employee may fall victim to an attacker using hacking methods to circumvent the security controls on their computer or account. Hacking methods are numerous and ever-growing as attackers continually find new methods to gain unauthorized access. In this case the threat agent is an outsider or human-intentional.
- Abused Trust—An employee may abuse the trust given to them and utilize this misplaced trust to take actions against the organization. As outsiders are not trusted, this threat action category applies only to insiders within the human-intentional category.
- Environmental Damage—Organizational assets may succumb to environmental damage from severe weather (e.g., floods, tornadoes, and earthquakes), infrastructure failures (e.g., power outages), or even infestations (e.g., rats). This threat action applies only to nature.
- Erred—Lastly, an employee may simply make a mistake that results in the loss of confidentiality of sensitive data, or in the misplacement of an organizational asset such as a laptop. This threat action applies only to human-accidental.

The association between the three threat sources and seven threat action categories is summarized in Figure 4.1. The depth to which a security risk assessment team should identify threat actions depends on the expected rigor of the overall assessment. If additional depth of analysis is required

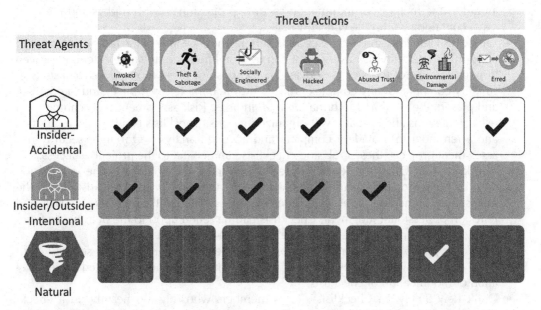

FIGURE 4.1 Threat Agent and Threat Action Association. The threat agents (human-accidental, human-intentional, and nature) are associated with the seven threat action categories.

during the threat identification stage, the security assessment team should further break down the threat actions subcategories. For example, instead of treating all environmental threats as environmental damage, this threat category can be broken down into the areas of structural damage, infrastructure damage, utility damage, water damage, and fire damage.

4.5.1.3 Threat Agent and Threat Action Pairing

Another more rigorous approach to identifying threats to an organization's assets is to create a list of threat agents and possible threat actions they may cause. This list could be quite extensive, as a single threat agent possesses the ability to cause any number of a multitude of threat actions. Therefore, it is important that the security risk assessment team adopts a disciplined approach to listing the threats. One such approach, threat agent and threat action pairing, is explained here.

Once threat agents and threat actions are identified, the security risk assessment team can identify the appropriate threat pairings to threat components. A pair is simply the logical association of a threat agent and a possible threat action that the threat agent may cause.

Given a list of threat agents, there are some threat actions that these threat agents may possibly cause and some that they could not. For example, a human being could cause threat actions in any category (i.e., health, physical exposure, logical exposure, and resource availability). On the other hand, severe weather can cause threat actions within the health, physical-exposure, and resource-availability categories, but cannot cause a logical exposure.

SIDEBAR 4.4   LIMITATION OF CHECKLIST-BASED APPROACHES

Checklists are an incredibly useful tool and are, in fact, highlighted throughout this book, with example checklists provided for many security risk assessment tasks. However, it is appropriate to provide severe warnings regarding the use of checklists as well. The following guidelines regarding checklists should be understood by any security professional considering their use:

- Checklists Are a Memory Aid—No security risk assessment team members should rely on checklists to tell them what to look for and how to look for it. Checklists instead are an aid to the memory of information security professionals who understand the concepts contained within the checklist.
- Checklists Help to Ensure Accuracy and Completeness—Many of the tasks involved with performing a security risk assessment can be simplified and, to some extent, improved through the use of tools or checklists. The purpose of these tools and checklists is to simplify computationally complex tasks, to ensure complete coverage, and to organize and present the wealth of information and findings. Risk assessment tools can perform risk calculations and prepare well-organized reports. Checklists can be used as a guide and a reminder to provide a complete and accurate analysis. On larger security risk assessment projects, these tools and checklists can be vital to the project's success.
- Checklists Can Drive the Results instead of Guiding the Engineer—The information security professional must use caution not to let the tools or the checklists "run" the assessment. In the end, a security risk assessment is filled with subjective analysis and relies on professional judgment. Checklists can be relied upon to the detriment of creativity and keeping your eye out for the unusual or new.
- Checklists Should Be Generated by Senior People—Senior information security engineers or experts within a key aspect of information security are best suited for the creation or modification of checklists.
- Don't Rely Solely on Checklists—Team members who rely too heavily on a checklist will find that their skills of observation, investigation, and perception can weaken.

An over-reliance on a checklist or a checklist-based approach for security risk assessments can lead to tunnel vision and a breakdown in the analytical process required for effective security risk assessment.

Checklists have received a bad reputation in some circles because of negative customer experiences. Checklists can be misused, as in the case of when a consultancy provides intensive training on the use of checklists to new recruits, followed by letting them loose on the customer with little or no supervision.

4.5.2 THREAT STATEMENTS

Threat components (threat agents and threat actions) can be combined with assets to create threat statements (see Figure 4.2). The creation of threat statements is a way to more clearly express the threats to be considered and countered during the security risk assessment process.

Threat statements can be further refined with the addition of intention of human threat agents. Human threat agents can cause threat actions on purpose or accidentally. Therefore, two threat statements can be generated for each threat statement that involves a human: one for the intentional cause of a threat action, and one for an accidental cause of a threat action (see Table 4.11).

4.5.3 VALIDATING THREAT STATEMENTS

The final action for the step of identifying threats is to validate the list of threat statements developed in the previous section. Among the threat statements that can be generated, only a portion of them is worthy of considering for any specific security risk assessment. Consideration for the appropriateness of a threat statement should be based on the threat environment of the organization being assessed. A security risk assessment should take the approach of validating only those threat statements that appear to be most likely, ignoring threats that appear to be a remote possibility.

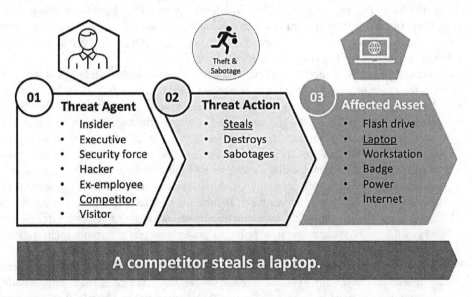

FIGURE 4.2 Threat Statements. Threat statements can be created by combining a threat agent, threat action, and an asset. Threat statements are a way to clearly express the threats to be considered during a security risk assessment.

TABLE 4.11
Multiple Threat Statements

Threat statement A	**An employee may cause the release of sensitive information**
Threat statement A1	An employee may accidentally cause the release of sensitive information
Threat statement A2	An employee may purposefully cause the release of sensitive information

Note: Multiple threat statements may be created from a single threat statement if the intention of the threat agent is considered.

The security risk assessment team is expected to use their experience, judgment, and common sense when assessing the validity of threat statements. Team members who are experienced in information security will have specific experiences with actual breaches at other organizations and can project the relevance of these past experiences to the current project. Judgment and common sense are built on the lessons learned from previous experience. Each of these attributes should be relied upon to determine reasonable threat statements. For example, a security risk assessment should probably include the following threat statement: "An employee may accidentally cause the release of sensitive information." However, a threat statement such as "A volcanic eruption may destroy critical equipment" may be considered beyond remote and thus dropped from consideration.

4.5.3.1 Factors Affecting Threat Statement Validity

That being said, the last threat statement above may be appropriate for some areas of the world. For example, organizations residing near Mount St. Helens in Washington state should consider the threat statement reasonable and thus include it. In fact, the security risk assessment team should consider a variety of factors when determining the validity of possible threat statements.

- History—It is hard to argue against the history of an organization. If considering whether or not it is likely that an executive laptop would ever be misplaced or stolen, simply ask the assessment sponsor if there is any history of this having occurred. If so, then a threat statement concerning the loss of an executive laptop is certainly valid. (Of course, it may be valid even if there is no history of it having happened.)
- Environmental Factors—Another important factor to consider in the validation of threat statements is the environment in which the organization resides. These factors include geography and climate, size and configuration of the facilities, and the social and political environment.
  - Geography and Climate—The geography and climate of the organization's facilities affect the validity of possible threat statements. Geography and climate can have an impact on the likelihood of natural threats occurring. For example, ice, snow, and extreme cold are not applicable in too many locations in the southern part of the United States. Also, natural disasters such as hurricanes, tornadoes, and earthquakes are more likely in some areas of the country and rather remote in others. In addition to affecting the likelihood of natural disasters, geography can affect infrastructure threats as well. Facilities located in certain areas of the country are more susceptible to power outages, electronic interference, and water shortages.
  - Facility Size and Configuration—The size and configuration of the organization's facilities can also affect the validity of possible threat statements. The size of the buildings and their configuration can have an impact on the likelihood of natural and human threats occurring.
  - Key aspects of facility size and configuration include construction material used in the buildings, the intended use of the facilities, square footage, working population during all shifts, number of visitors, number of cars parked on the premises, and to what extent the

structures may be below grade level. As many of these factors increase (e.g., number of visitors, number of employees, number of cars parked, and square footage), so does the organization's susceptibility to various threats. For example, a large facility with hundreds of visitors a day is more likely to have a valid threat of unescorted visitors breaching physical security than a smaller facility with few visitors. Social and Political Climate—The social and political climate of the organization's facilities affects the validity of possible threat statements.

- Social and political climate can have an impact on the likelihood of human threats occurring. Factors here include proximity to emergency and police services, local crime rates, and the stability of the local government. For example, facilities located in areas of a city with high crime rates should certainly consider any human threat statements regarding the safety of their employees from crime and theft of equipment.
- Business Factors—The last important factor to consider in the validation of threat statements is business factors. These factors include visibility of the organization, the type of services performed, the value of the equipment on the premises, and the value of the inventories.
  - Visibility—Some businesses may be more of a target than others. Organizations that provide services or produce products that may be considered controversial (e.g., research labs, world trade groups, clinics, political position organizations, and pharmaceutical companies) should seriously consider all human-based threats targeted at any protected asset such as employees, services, and financial resources.
  - Services Performed—Some services performed are more dangerous or susceptible to threats than others. Organizations that deal with hazardous chemicals, weapons manufacturing, or send their employees abroad need to consider all threats related to such activities.
  - Value of Equipment and Inventories—Organizations that house valuable equipment and inventories such as computer chips, financial instruments, and other assets need to consider threats related to theft of assets.

4.6   DETERMINE EXPECTED CONTROLS

By this stage in a security risk assessment, the team should have a good understanding of the business objectives, assets to be protected, and relevant threats to those assets. This information is adequate to determine high-level security requirements for an organization. Although traditional security risk assessment does not include a step for developing security requirements, this type of analysis has always been performed (perhaps unconsciously) by many information security professionals.

Consider the following scenario. During the data gathering phase of a security risk assessment, team members are surprised to find that a major pharmaceutical company has no security force on the premises. This is instantly written up as a vulnerability because it is clear to the team members that the value of information assets and the prevalence of industrial espionage within this industry warrants that physical security be strong.

Now consider the reason this vulnerability was identified. Was the identification of this vulnerability a weakness in existing controls? Or should it be considered the absence of an expected control? Some security risk assessment approaches are now formally recognizing this practice of expecting specific security controls within various risk situations. Specifically, a recently released guideline by the NIST recognized four risk situations and listed expected security controls for each ("The NIST Security Configuration Checklists Program," 2018). Table 4.12 shows expected security controls for various types of systems from the NIST guideline.

Members of the security risk assessment team may have additional expectations based on their experience. These expectations will ultimately impact the identification of vulnerabilities in the assessed system. Additional expectations may include any of the following security controls or security control areas, depending on the threat environment and organizational complexity of the organization to be assessed:

TABLE 4.12

Expected Security Controls

Environment	Description	Example Systems	Expected Controls
Small office/home office (SOHO)	Informal computer installation used for home or small businesses	Home office Small business	• Firewall appliance • Personal firewalls • Security updates • Anti-virus software • Malicious filtering on Web and e-mail • Disable unnecessary applications • Encrypt wireless traffic • System connection restrictions • User privilege restrictions • Resource-sharing restrictions • Backup and recovery procedures • Physical security procedures • Laptop encryption
Enterprise	Managed environments consisting of centrally managed workstations and servers protected from the Internet	Medium to large businesses	• Segmented internal networks • Centralized system management • Centralized security application management • Automated update management • Restricted access to printers • Centralized backup and recovery • Laptop encryption • Two-factor authentication • Strong encryption • Mobile device management • Automated inventory control
High security	An environment that is at a high risk of attack or data exposure. Security takes precedence over usability. Environment includes limited function computers and highly confidential information	Banking systems Health-care systems	• Single-function servers • Removal of unnecessary services and applications • Host-based firewall applications • Limited users • Two-factor authentication • Mobile device management • Automated inventory control • Restricted and encrypted remote access • Intrusion detection monitoring • Regular vulnerability scans • Skilled administrators

Note: The NIST guideline lists expected security controls for SOHO, enterprise, high security, and custom systems.

- Security Policy Expectations—Every organization is expected to have adequate information security policies. Depending on the size and industry of the organization, many security engineers would expect the following security policies to be documented, approved, distributed, and updated.
  - Senior management statement
  - Acceptable use policy
  - System development and deployment
  - Security maintenance

- Security operations
- Security logging and monitoring
- Incident response planning
- Business continuity planning
- Security Organization Expectations—Every organization should have some type of security organization. At a minimum, the role of the security officer should be described and assigned. In larger organizations, the effectiveness of the security organization can only be achieved if the organization has the proper authority, adequate resources, and a skilled staff.
- Security Procedure Expectations—In larger organizations, security procedures should be expected. The accuracy and consistency of security activities must be ensured through the development of and adherence to security procedures. These procedures should cover the initiation and continuous refining of the security organization as well as the programs and initiatives it institutes. Expected elements include account, system, and code maintenance; configuration management; security testing; interconnections with other organizations; security data management; and incident response. The lack of documented procedures for any of these security activities could be considered a vulnerability in most medium-to large-sized organizations.
- Physical Security Control Expectations—An organization is expected to have physical security controls commensurate with their physical security threats. Depending on the building location, business mission, asset valuation, and other factors a building may be expected to have a minimum set of physical security controls such as armed guards, fence lines, gates, badged access, guard procedures, and visitor control.
- Technical Security Control Expectations—Many technical security controls are an answer to technical threats and vulnerabilities. As attacks and techniques progress so do the expected technical security controls at an organization. An organization may be expected to have a minimum set of technical controls including two-factor authentication, strong encryption, mobile device management, and automated inventory control (to name a few).

If the security risk assessment team (or the security risk assessment methodology) decides to include the step of determining expected controls, then these controls should be documented as the expected security program for the organization. Organizations within some regulated industries, such as the federal government, health care, and banking, will have some of these expected controls documented in the form of requirements. Do not confuse the required security activities in these regulations with the expected elements of a security program. Many regulations provide only a baseline of minimum standards and protect a limited portion of all sensitive assets (e.g., cardholder data). Your security risk assessment team may determine that additions to the standard baseline are required.

EXERCISES

1. Discuss how the corporate use of cloud computing affects the "obtaining proper permission" process (see Section 4.1.3).
2. What are some examples of security controls that a low-cost e-commerce business would choose not to implement that a premium business likely would? Be specific.
3. Consider asset valuation techniques 5–7 (see Section 4.4.3.5). Which would be most appropriate and why for the following assets?
   a. Stolen wireless access point (WAP)
   b. Exposed intellectual property (IP)
   c. Phone service loss
   d. Web application breach involving privacy data

4. Create at least ten threat statements.
5. What natural threats are valid for your location? Name a few natural threats that are not valid for your location.
6. What are the most valuable assets at your organization?
    a. List the top three categories of assets at your organization in terms of value.
    b. Are there any current valuations on these assets? What documents would you review to find such valuations?
    c. Provide your own valuation on these top three categories.
7. How does your organization's business mission impact the expected security controls?

NOTE

1 These were intended to be rhetorical questions, but for those readers not yet convinced, the answer is "no" to each of these questions. Of course, it matters if the workstations are protected and if the general office software is up to date with security patches, but it is a waste of time to create a complete list of all such assets. This is a security risk assessment and not an asset audit.

BIBLIOGRAPHY

18 U.S. Code Chapter 119, Section 2510-2523: Wire and Electronic Communications Interception and Interception of Oral Communication.

American Institute of Certified Public Accountants, "Clarified Statements on Standards for Attestation Engagements (SSAE) No. 18: Concepts Common to All Attestation Engagements," AT-C Section 105, May 1, 2017.

ASIS International. *Protection of Assets: Physical Security*, 2019.

California Civil Code, Division 3. Obligations, Part 4. Obligations Arising From Particular Transactions. Title 1.81.5 California Consumer Privacy Act of 2018.

Dalkey, N. C. "The Delphi Method: An Experimental Study of Group Opinion," Rand Corporation, RM-5888-PR, 1969.

Department of Energy. "Energy Infrastructure Risk Management Checklists for Small and Medium Sized Energy Facilities." August 19, 2002. http://www.whitehouse.gov/omb/circulars_a130_a130trans4/

Federal Trade Commission. "Standards for Safeguarding Customer Information; Final Rule," 16 CFR Part 314, Federal Register, Vol. 67, No. 100, May 23, 2002.

Krebs, Brian, "*Iowa Prosecutors Drop Charges Against Men Hired to Test Their Security*," Krebs on Security, January 20, 2020. https://krebsonsecurity.com/

Marshall, Alfred. *Principles of Economics*, 1920.

Milton, Thomas J., James G. Rabe, and Charles Wilhoite. *Economic Analysis of Intangible Assets and Intellectual Properties*, 1999.

NIST. "Recommended Security Controls for Federal Information Systems." NIST Special Publications 800–53 Revision 3. August 2009.

National Institute of Standards and Technology (NIST): U.S. Department of Commerce, "Security and Privacy Controls for Federal Information Systems and Organizations," Revision 4, April 2013.

National Institute of Standards and Technology (NIST): U.S. Department of Commerce, "Volume II: Appendices to Guide for Mapping Types of Information Systems to Security Categories," NIST Special Publication 800-60, Volume II, Revision 1, August 2008.

National Institute of Standards and Technology (NIST): U.S. Department of Commerce. DRAFT National Checklist Program for IT Products—Guidelines for Checklist Users and Developers, NIST Special Publication 800-70, Revision 4 February 2018.

5 Data Gathering

One of the core phases of the security risk assessment project is the gathering of data on security controls within scope of the assessment. This phase involves the collection of evidence with respect to the security control existence and effectiveness within their existing environment and against the organizational security requirements. This phase of the security risk assessment is at the heart of the process and involves volumes of data, scores of activities, and many hours of effort. The data gathering phase is perhaps the most labor-intensive phase of the security risk assessment process and covers all of the organization's security controls within the boundaries of the project.

The preparation for the data gathering phase takes place in the project-preparation phase to ensure that the team's time off-site and on-site data collection will be effective and efficient. The scope of the data gathering phase is defined within the project-definition phase which defines the security risk assessment system boundaries, security controls, assets, and level of rigor. The activities performed within the data gathering phase are dictated by the representation of security controls and the depth of evidence collected on these controls.

- Security Control Representation—The security control representation is a decision as to the selection of instances that will represent the selected control. For example, for the security control of *termination procedures*, a security risk assessment team must determine how many and which instances of employee termination will be reviewed to determine the application of the control elements (e.g., every terminated employee in the history of the company, all terminated employees in the last 3 months, five random terminations within the last 12 months, or just the last termination).
- Evidence Depth—The depth of evidence collected is a decision as to the types of evidence that are collected. For example, using the same control, the team must determine what evidence types they will collect and review regarding termination procedures (e.g., review termination checklist, interview human resource department, interview hiring managers, and review accounts and permissions of departed employees).

Each of these elements of data gathering are discussed more in depth in the next sections.

SIDEBAR 5.1   DATA GATHERING: TOOLS VERSUS EXPERIENCE

Some security risk assessment tools and methods attempt to ensur5 the thoroughness of this effort through checklists and questionnaires. Although such tools and methods can help to guide this effort, there is no substitute for experience. An experienced security engineer possesses two critical skills required for an effective data-gathering effort:

- Application of Information Security Principles—The discovery and identification of vulnerabilities can be a complex process that involves the application of information security principles to situations not previously encountered. No matter how many times the team members have reviewed other organizations' security controls, there always seems to be something new. This may be new controls or simply a new application of an existing control. In these cases, the security risk assessment team cannot fall back on a questionnaire or a checklist but must assess the effectiveness of the security control based on well-understood security principles such as defense in depth, default deny all, and separation of duty. The application of these principles can often guide the assessment of new controls and result in a reliable conclusion. An overreliance on checklists, questionnaires, and tools can leave the security risk assessment team flat-footed and unsure of the next step when they encounter anything new.

- Observation Techniques Based on Experience—A good security engineer can probably spot 80% of the administrative and physical vulnerabilities in your organization by walking around the building and hanging out in the public areas. Such a cursory review of the administrative and physical security controls can later prove rather accurate, because the security engineer knew what to look and listen for. This skill becomes developed over the course of years of experience in reviewing other organizations, finding flaws, and expanding observational skills based on that experience. Although checklists, questionnaires, and tools can help to guide the observations, experience proves much more flexible, efficient, and accurate.

Those attempting to perform security risk assessments based solely on a security risk assessment process description, checklists, and a few weeks of training should reconsider their approach. A better approach would be to contract out the security risk assessment to an objective and experienced team. Alternatively, the security risk assessment team could be bolstered by the inclusion of one or more experienced security engineers.

Anyone who performs a security risk assessment using a checklist without an appreciation for how the checklist was developed and the principles reflected in it is working in the dark, without a clear understanding of the security risks in the system. Such an approach defies the whole reason for performing the security risk assessment in the first place.

Depending on the *breadth* of the scope of the security risk assessment, the data gathering phase can cover administrative, physical, or technical controls, or any combination. Depending on the *rigor* of the scope of the security risk assessment, the data gathering phase can provide in-depth analysis of security controls or a rudimentary review.

5.1 SECURITY CONTROL REPRESENTATION

For each security control within scope of the security risk assessment, the assessment team must determine how many instances and which instances are sufficient to represent the control being examined. The data gathered on each security control will either be all instances of the control (e.g., the population) or a subset of those instances (e.g., a sample).

If all instances of a security control are reviewed this is referred to as the population. The population of the security control instances may be used in cases where it is possible and reasonable to gather information on the entire population. For example, for the security control of exterior door locks, it is possible and reasonable to survey all exterior door locks at a single location office building as part of the data gathering process. Instances of exterior door locks would be fully represented by the survey as the survey includes every exterior door lock.

If a subset of those instance is reviewed, this is referred to as a sample. A sample of security control instances is used when it is not reasonable or efficient to review every security control instance and when that sample can reasonably represent the population. For example, for the security control of laptop system hardening, it may not be reasonable to check every instance of a laptop in a large organization. If that organization has a standard process for hardening laptops and all laptops follow the same procedure, then a sample of laptops may reasonably represent the larger population (e.g., all organizational laptops).

5.1.1 DATA GATHERING ON THE POPULATION

The simplest form of determining the instances in which to gather data is to include all instances of a security control. When it is possible and reasonable to gather data on all instances, the team may elect to simply perform data gathering on the population. When gathering data on all instances of a security control, there are no shortcuts. The team will need to acquire data on every instance of controls such as door locks, security incidents, or the exercise of termination procedures.

Population data gathering is typically limited to either small populations or automated data gathering. Examples of small populations include security control instances involving a small number of employees, security incidents, or third-party providers. In these cases, the security risk assessment team can effectively gather data by exhaustively reviewing each and every instance because the instances are typically limited to less than a dozen.

The security risk assessment team may also choose to collect data on the population of a security control when automated means of data gathering are available. Examples of automated data gathering include vulnerability scanners, IT asset inventory tracking software, security information and event management systems, and Identity Management (IdM) systems, to name a few. Almost all of these automated systems can provide information on the assets under their control in a variety of data ranges and formats. The security risk assessment team should determine the scope of the information required first (e.g., previous 12 months) and then either create those reports providing the required information or request reports from the automated systems under the assessed organization's control. If the automated system is not capable of presenting the information in the format required by the team, then the team should export a file (e.g., comma separated variables (CSVs)) into a data management system that they can manipulate correctly to give the required format.

5.1.2 DATA GATHERING ON A SAMPLE

Any testing, other than complete testing, is referred to as representative testing or sampling. If less than 100% of the population is tested, then this is sampling. If the selection of a random sample is performed correctly, the testing is practically just as accurate as complete testing. Sample testing is performed when there is time, budget, geographic, or other constraints that preclude complete testing.

Before sampling techniques are presented, some key statistical terms and concepts need to be introduced. These concepts are required within the area of sampling and sample selection, as many tasks within security risk assessments require a working knowledge of statistics and data analysis. Statistical sampling knowledge is generally useful to any security risk assessment team member. Some key terms and concepts that the security risk assessment team member should understand are as follows:

- Population—A population is the entire set of items being studied, for example, all the marbles in a bag, all the invoices in a given year, all the people voting in an election, or all the network components in a network.
- Sample—A sample is a subset of the population used to represent the population from which it is drawn. If it is impossible or simply too costly to gain information regarding every element of a population, then we try to gain an understanding of the population based on a representative sample of the population. For example, in a poll regarding early voting conducted prior to the 2004 elections, the Gallup organization sampled 1,866 registered voters. The poll showed that 21% planned to vote early and 77% planned to vote on Election Day. With a population of over 120 million voters, the Gallup organization was able to claim a 3% margin of error with a 95% certainty (www.gallup.com).

- Sample Size—A sample size is simply the number of instances in the sample. The trick is to select a sample size that is large enough to adequately represent the population yet small enough to provide significant time and effort savings over reviewing the entire population. Choosing the correct sample size can be a bit involved and is discussed in more detail in the next section.
- Confidence Interval—Since we are sampling the population and not reviewing every instance of a security control it is not possible to completely equate a finding on a sample to a finding on the population. Depending on our sample size (and a few other factors) we can be reasonably sure that the finding on the sample can be compared to a finding on the population. This is typically expressed as a "margin of error" (e.g., +/- 3%, 95% of the time). The "+/- 3%" refers to the range of a potential error in sampling and also as the confidence interval.
- Confidence Level—The confidence level is the amount of time we believe the sampling finding would fall within the margin of error (confidence interval) for the population. In our example above the confidence level is 95%.

5.1.2.1 Determining Sample Size

It is surprising to most people that the size of a sample selected from a population can be such a small percentage of the population yet still allow for accurate predictions regarding the entire population. For example, most political pollsters make predictions on the voting public based on 1,200 to 1,800 voters, out of a population of 210,000,000 voters. Within security risk assessments many data gathering activities can make use of a sample instead of the entire security control instance population to make the overall assessment more efficient.

Selecting sample sizes can be a complex calculation based on several factors including population size, desired margin of error, desired confidence level, and even considerations for what may be known about the distribution attributes of the population. There are also many approaches for sampling depending on the field of study or use of the result. For security risk assessments and audits, attribute sampling is typically used.

> Attribute Sampling: A sampling approach used to determine the presence or absence of an attribute in the samples.

For example, a given assessed organization has a requirement that all employees with access to sensitive data must receive security awareness training prior to being given access to the system. The assessment team needs to determine the effectiveness of the organization's controls. The population consists of all employees with access to the sensitive system (e.g., 500 employees); the attribute of the sample is the training completion date is sooner than the date in which they were granted access to the sensitive system.

The following general approaches are often used when determining the sample size for a data collection activity.

- Entire Population—The simplest approach is to simply use the entire population as the sample. The benefit of using the entire population is that it eliminates sampling errors or biases. However, there is no efficiency gain here as the security assessment team must collect data on all instances. This approach is best used for small populations or populations where using the entire population is automated (e.g., IT asset inventory tool and reporting software). For our example above, the sample size would be 500 records comparing the dates of training and system access.
- Use Published Tables—The security risk assessment team could alternatively use sample size tables published for the purpose of making the selection of a sample size easy. These tables typically provide reasonable population ranges and level of confidence variables to accommodate many needs. For security risk assessments and information technology audits the

American Institute of Certified Public Accountants (AICPA) has published tables that can be used to look up a sample size based on various factors such as error tolerance level and based on a confidence level of 90%, see Table 5.1.

The AICPA tables show an attribute sampling process which seeks to determine if the security control is operating effectively (or not). Based on the error tolerance (low or moderate) and the population size, a "round 1" sample size is suggested. If the assessor completes the review of the instances within the sample with no deviations (indications that the control was not implemented) then the control is considered operationally effective. If a deviation is found, the sample size is increased for round 2 and the assessor must be able to complete the review of the increased sample size without a second deviation for the control to be considered operationally effective. If a deviation is found during round 2, the sample size is increased one final time. If no deviations are found in the final round the control can be considered operationally effective, else the assessor concludes that the control is not effective.

- Use Formulas—There are a variety of formulas available to compute your own sample sizes. Selection of the most appropriate formula is beyond the scope of this text but such a selection will depend on size of the population (e.g., infinite, large, or small), the expected distribution of attribute values, and other elements. Some of the popular sample size formulas suggested by Cochran, Slovin, and Gay, see Table 5.2.

The objective of sampling is to make a statement regarding characteristics of the population based on testing a portion of it. A surprising degree of accuracy regarding the population can be gained using mathematical methods to select a random sample and then performing statistical tests on the sample. Some even argue that sampling provides a more accurate measurement of the population, because it can be shown to have a high degree of confidence, while measuring the entire population can lead to mistakes because of the tediousness of the process.

TABLE 5.1
AICPA Sample Size Guidance for Audits

		Population		
		<100	100-200	200+
Low Error Tolerance 5%-7%)	Round 1 (no errors)	30	35	40
	- Round 2, if needed	45	50	60
	- Round 3, if needed	65	75	90
Moderate Error Tolerance (8%-10%)	Round 1 (no errors)	20	22	25
	- Round 2, if needed	30	35	40
	- Round 3, if needed	45	50	60

Note: The smaller sample sizes in each cell are suggested for sampling when no deviations are expected (e.g., all instances of the security control will be found to be effective). The second number in each cell indicates the expanded sample size if a deviation is found in the first round of examinations. The third number in each cell indicates the expanded sample size if a second deviation is found. If a third deviation is found the security control should be considered ineffective, otherwise this security control is considered to be operating effectively (within a margin of error).

TABLE 5.2

Popular Sample Size Formulas

Suggested Sample Size Formulas Based on Population and Proportion		
Population Size	**<500**	**>500**
Proportion	**Known**	**Unknown**	
	Cochran	Slovin	Gay
Suggested Formula	$n = \dfrac{Z^2(p)(1-p)}{e^2}$	$n = \dfrac{N}{1 + (N)(e)^2}$	Descriptive Research $n = 0.2N$ Experimental Research $n = 15 - 30$

Note: The formulas above use the following notation: *n*=sample size, Z=Z score (1.96 for a confidence level of 95%), p=proportion, *e*=desired margin of error, and *N*=population.

- Accuracy—The accuracy of a sampling technique can be measured and reported. The mathematical terms used to indicate accuracy are as follows:
  - Standard Deviation—This is a dispersion measurement, that is, the distance of all values (x) from the arithmetic mean (average, x̄.) The formula for standard deviation (s) is (where n = number of values):

$$ s = \sqrt{\frac{\sum \left(x - \overline{x}\right)^2}{n}} $$

    This formula measures all samples and their distance from the mean. In order for larger distances from the mean to count more, the differences are squared.
  - Confidence Level—This is an accuracy measurement, i.e., the probability that the results of the testing sample are representative of the testing for the overall population. Specifically, the confidence level is the probability that any given element of the population will fall close to the average number (i.e., within a number of standard deviations). If a sample is a representative sample (i.e., a random sample) and the data exhibits a normal (i.e., bell-shaped) distribution, then we can assume the following:
    - ≈ 68% of the observations are within one standard deviation of the mean.
    - ≈95% of the observations are within two standard deviations of the mean.
    - ≈99.7% of the observations are within three standard deviations of the mean.
    The reporting on the results of many polls and surveys fail to express the confidence level itself, but it should be at least above a 90% confidence level. The results of the polls and surveys are typically expressed as "plus or minus" a specific measurement. For example, "58% of those polled will vote for candidate X, plus or minus 3%." The specific measure (3% in this case) is two standard deviations from the mean measurement (in this case 58%) if the confidence level is 95%.

5.1.2.2 Sampling Objectives

Sampling techniques can be used for several different objectives. Depending upon the objective of the test, different sampling techniques are more appropriate than others.

- Discovery (Exploratory) Sampling—Discovery sampling is used to uncover fraud or find a single instance of an infraction, error, or irregularity. Such a discovery would typically call for a more intensive investigation.
- Unit Sampling—Unit sampling is used when the tester wants to determine a characteristic or value of the population within a degree of confidence. This type of sampling is meant to answer the "How much?" or "How many?" questions regarding the population, for example, the value of inventories or error rates of controls.

5.1.2.3 Sampling Types

There are two basic types of samples: probability samples and judgment samples. Probability samples are selected at random through the use of a random technique such as a random number table. Judgment samples are selected by any other technique and are based on the selector's judgment. It is impossible to draw statistically relevant conclusions about characteristics of the population based on judgment samples, because these samples are not statistically representative and contain bias. For this reason, the sampling techniques discussed are all probability samples.

- Simple Sampling—This sampling technique involves the use of a random selection of sample units from a population. For example, if you wanted to select 20 random employees from a company of 2,000 employees (with employee numbers one to 2,000), you could use a random-number generator to generate 20 numbers between one and 2,000 and select 20 employees associated by their employee number.
- Systematic (Interval) Sampling—This sampling technique is based on a systematic approach to selecting sample units from the population. For example, to choose 20 employees from a company of 2,000 employees, a systematic approach could (a) divide the population into 100 sampling intervals, (b) select a random number between one and 100 (e.g., 37), and (c) choose the employee associated with the first random number and every 37th employee in each interval (i.e., 137, 237, 337, etc.). Systematic sampling is a simple approach that approximates random sampling and can be used if the order of the population has no relevance to the characteristics of the data being measured. For example, if you were measuring the salary or time at the company, it is clear that low-numbered employees will have been with the company longer, and it is more likely that very low employee numbers correspond with higher-level positions and therefore are more likely to earn more salary.
- Stratified Sampling—This sampling technique is based on the grouping of similar sample units into strata. This technique is useful when there is a potentially large variation between strata but a small variation within each stratum. Stratified sampling allows the observer to make different observations about each stratum.
- Cluster Sampling—This sampling technique selects clusters of sample units from the population to create a representative sample. Cluster sampling provides convenience for the surveyor in terms of proximity of sample units. For example, if it was determined that a vulnerability scan must scan 10% of the 500 IP addresses within a network, it would be easier to scan five groups of 10 IP addresses than 50 individual IP addresses. On the other hand, such a restriction in selection may skew the randomness of the sample if the proximity of IP addresses has relevance to the characteristic of the population being measured.
- Multistage Sampling—This sampling technique combines cluster sampling and simple sampling. Cluster sampling is used to determine the clusters of sample units, and simple sampling is used to determine sample units within the cluster. The Gallup organization uses multistage sampling in the typical Gallup poll.

5.1.3 Use of Sampling in Security Testing

Sampling can be an excellent technique for gathering representative security test data about a large number of network components. If the sample is selected correctly, then testing a small sample of the population can provide the security tester with the information regarding the network that is required for the security risk assessment. Proper selection of the sample, however, can be difficult and should only be undertaken by someone with an understanding of the basic principles of statistical sampling. Three approaches for selecting a security test sample are described in the following subsections.

5.1.3.1 Approach 1: Representative Testing

Within many information systems, there exist several components that are replicated many times. For example, in many information systems, a user workstation is created for each user in a department and is identical in terms of connectivity, operating system, configuration, and applications. Except for the data stored on the system, these systems are the same. If an information system consists of 20 file servers, five Web servers, three e-mail servers, and 800 workstations, a representative sampling approach would select to test a representation from each group (e.g., four file servers, two Web servers, two e-mail servers, and 50 workstations).

The advantage of representative sampling is cost savings and a reduction in repetitive data. Time and money are conserved through reducing the number of machines that would be tested. Repetitive data is reduced, since it is highly unlikely that a scan of the other 750 workstations would yield any different security risk findings.

The disadvantage of representative sampling is that in cases where the system components are different, the lack of testing may indeed miss a security risk finding. For example, if one of the file servers is dedicated to external users and it was not the file server chosen for scanning, some significant security risk findings could be overlooked.

5.1.3.2 Approach 2: Selected Sampling

Selected sampling is the technique of choosing areas of the infrastructure to test based on a belief that they may contain vulnerabilities. If it is not possible to test all areas of the infrastructure or all components within the information system, the assessor would choose the test sample based on the perceived likelihood that these specific components may contain vulnerabilities. For example, the assessor selectively samples the following 30 workstations:

- 10 workstations from the IT department
- 5 workstations from the R&D department
- 5 workstations from those who work on the night shift
- 5 workstations from the help desk
- 3 workstations for executive administrators and two workstations used as guest computers

The advantages of selective sampling include the same advantages of representative sampling, namely, cost savings and a reduction in repetitive data. An additional (possible) advantage of selective sampling is that the selected sample may be more likely to identify vulnerabilities that may have been overlooked through other sampling techniques. This last advantage is true only if the sample is selected wisely.

The disadvantage of selective sampling comes into play if the sample is not selected wisely. The assessor should be careful to choose areas that are likely to contain vulnerabilities but should also balance that with the recognition that vulnerabilities can turn up in unexpected places. If you only look for them in expected areas, you are not likely to uncover them.

5.1.3.3 Approach 3: Random Sampling

Random sampling is a technique of choosing areas to test based on a random selection of test subjects. In true random sampling, there is no bias toward or away from any area. The advantage of random sampling is that the test sample is unbiased, and results from the sample can be used to make statistical conclusions. The disadvantages of random sampling include the difficulty of choosing a truly random sample. To correctly choose a random sample, the selection process must be free of bias. This activity requires an understanding of statistics and survey principles, a skill that may not be present on the security risk assessment team.

5.2 EVIDENCE DEPTH

For each security control within scope of the security risk assessment, the assessment team must determine how much evidence is sufficient to appropriately assess each security control. The team can apply various techniques such as document review, interviews, observation, design review, and physical and technical testing to create evidence regarding the existence and effectiveness of the selected security control. The variety of activities that may be performed to gather data on security controls is quite extensive. The selection of these techniques can impact the quality of the results and ultimately the security risk assessment as a whole.

The more data collected and the higher the quality of the data, the more accurately the security control can be assessed. At the same time, the more data collection, the more of the limited time for the assessment to be completed is used up. The security risk assessment team must determine which data gathering activities are appropriate (and sufficient) given the scope of the assessment and the time/resources available to conduct the data gathering phase. However, the team determines to collect data the following key elements must be considered:

- Relevance—When attempting to gather evidence about a specific security control the security risk assessment team needs to ensure that the data gathering activities generate relevant evidence regarding the existence and effectiveness of the control. For example, when reviewing the security control of "assigned privacy officer" the activities of reviewing a job description for a current employee or interviewing a staff member, would generate relevant evidence. On the other hand, the activities of reviewing the privacy compliance procedures or a job description for a vacant position would not yield relevant evidence.
- Quality/Strength—Not all data gathering activities yield the same quality of evidence. The security risk assessment team should be careful to ensure that high quality and strong evidence is gathered on each security control within the scope of the assessment. Low-quality (or weak) evidence includes opinions, anecdotes, and conjectures. Strong evidence includes documented procedures and repeatable test results.
- Quantity—The more data points available for each security control, the better. A security risk assessment team can make up for low quality of some data on security controls by seeking more pieces of evidence. For example, a survey-based data gathering exercise will provide low-quality, opinion-based, and biased data on security controls from those responsible for implementing each of those controls. However, the security risk assessment team can increase the strength of the data they are available by implementing additional data gathering activities such as interviews, tests, and document reviews. Bringing all of the available evidence together will allow the team to provide a more accurate measurement of the strength of the security control.
- Accuracy—The ability for the security risk assessment team to acquire accurate data is an important element of planning the data gathering activities. Inaccurate data is any data that does not point to the correct conclusions on the strength of the security mechanisms being

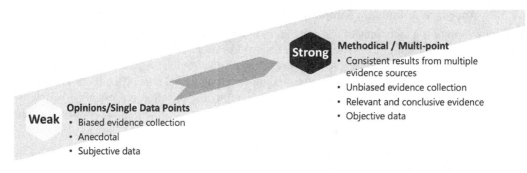

FIGURE 5.1   Strong vs. weak evidence. The strength and number of data gathering activities affect the quality of the evidence available for the team to determine the existence and effectiveness of the security controls.

assessed. For example, false positive indications of a vulnerability from a vulnerability scanner, incorrect guesses regarding encryption settings gathered from an interview, or inaccurate data from an out-of-date on-site audit; all provide no value to the security risk assessment team in drawing accurate conclusions.

Understanding these elements of strong data collection activities is important in the designing of the data gathering stage activities. The security risk assessment team lead should create a data gathering plan that results in strong evidence, see Figure 5.1.

5.3   THE RIIOT METHOD OF DATA GATHERING

For each security control within the scope of the security risk assessment, the team must determine the appropriate methods of data collection adequate to provide the intended evidence depth. This can be a complex task given the seeming vast number of choices there are for collecting data on a security control. Despite this complexity, few tools or methods have been developed that assist in the planning, performance, and coordination of these activities.

Introduced in the first edition of this book, the Review, Interview, Inspect, Observe, and Test (RIIOT) method of data gathering attacks the problem of organizing the data gathering activities. The RIIOT method simply breaks down the process of data gathering into one of five different approaches.

5.3.1   RIIOT Method Benefits

The value of breaking the task of data gathering into the RIIOT approaches is as follows:

- Organization—The RIIOT method helps to organize the data gathering effort into tasks that are easier to plan, assign, perform, and track.
- Project Management—The RIIOT method enables the definition and management of multiple tasks within the data gathering phase. Each approach can be assigned to different resources, and progress can be tracked individually.
- Coverage—The RIIOT method helps the planners of the security risk assessment data gathering effort to ensure that there is appropriate coverage of the threats and safeguards. A security risk assessment approach that uses only one of the RIIOT approaches without consideration for other approaches of gathering data is likely to fail to uncover key vulnerabilities and to reach erroneous conclusions.

5.3.2   RIIOT Method Approaches

The RIIOT method comprises five different approaches of data gathering and can be applied to the administrative, physical, or technical areas, see Figure 5.2. The RIIOT method approaches are as follows:

- Review Documents—The security risk assessment team reviews documents regarding the policies, procedures, rules, configurations, layouts, architectures, and other elements of the security controls. All available and relevant documents may be reviewed and can include policies, procedures, network maps, site layouts, backup schedules, and security awareness training slides.
- Interview Key Personnel—The security risk assessment team interviews key personnel to determine their ability to perform their duties (as stated in policies), their performance of duties not stated in policies, and observations or concerns they have with current security controls.
- Inspect Security Controls—The security risk assessment team members inspect specific implemented security controls such as visitor control, configuration files, smoke detectors, and incident response handling. These controls can be inspected against industry standards, with specific checklists of common vulnerabilities, or by using experience and judgment.
- Observe Personnel Behavior—The security risk assessment team members will observe the behavior of users, the security protective force, visitors, and others during the course of the assessment. These observations can provide keen insight into the effectiveness of the security controls in place.
- Test Security Controls—The security risk assessment team members will test specific security controls such as firewalls, servers, open-door alarms, and motion sensors. Almost all security risk assessment methods currently account for this approach. Testing involves the use of vulnerability scanners for logical security controls, but also specific methods for physical controls such as the shuffle test for motion sensors.

Each of the RIIOT approaches is described in more detail below. Additional guidance for performing each of these RIIOT approaches is contained within each section.

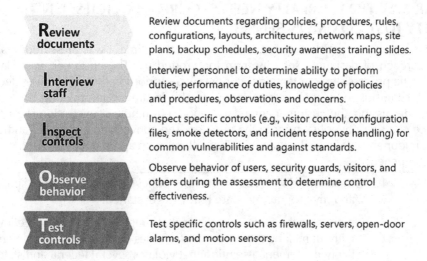

FIGURE 5.2   RIIOT data gathering method. The RIIOT data gathering method comprises five approaches to gather data for a security risk assessment. These methods are review documents, interview staff, inspect controls, observe behavior, and test controls.

5.3.2.1   Review Documents or Designs

The first approach in the RIIOT data gathering method is reviewing documents or designs. The process of reviewing documents to gather data for the security risk assessment involves knowing which documents to request and how to review the documents for adequacy. The process of reviewing designs to gather data for the security risk assessment involves an understanding of basic design principles and how to recognize their application, or lack of application.

But first, the member of the security risk assessment team assigned to review documents or designs must have an appreciation for the importance of security documentation. Reviewing information security documents and designs may be considered a "desk job," meaning that it can be performed without reviewing the IT infrastructure or the facilities. However, it is useful for this review to be performed on-site (or at least followed up on-site) so that the effectiveness of these policies can be ascertained. For now, the review of these documents and designs concerns only the existence of statements and not whether those statements are being followed.

5.3.2.1.1   The Importance of Security Documents

Many security engineers come to the profession through a steady succession of accomplishments from a technology-centric discipline, for example, systems administration or programming. Perhaps because of this experience, many information security engineers fail to understand the importance of documents—policies and procedures. Before discussing the review of documents provided by the organization to be assessed, it is useful to stress the importance of policies and procedures in the establishment and governance of a security program. The absence of solid, complete, and articulate security policies can be the root cause of many security vulnerabilities.

Security policies and procedures are the cornerstone of information security and the most important element of the security program for any organization. Without security policies, we may have strong security mechanisms implemented, but the policies they attempt to enforce will be a mixture of guesswork and confusion. Although the tenets of information security (confidentiality, integrity, availability) seem rather straightforward, the application of these tenets can be quite complex (see Sidebar 5.2). Effective information security policies can clarify the security objectives of the organization and ensure that security controls are enforcing a clear security policy.

SIDEBAR 5.2   DO WE REALLY NEED SECURITY POLICIES: ISN'T SECURITY JUST COMMON SENSE?

While advising an Internet start-up with more money than time, I was pressured to skip the normal approach of designing security from the ground up. The customer was adamantly opposed to the process step of creating security policies prior to advising on the selection of security mechanisms for a soon-to-be-released health insurance information Web service. After much discussion, the customer agreed to a short ten-minute conversation regarding the importance of a security policy prior to the first step. The conversation was brief and illustrative of the importance of these documents. What follows is an approximation of the conversation as it happened:

Customer:	OK, so why do we need a security policy? This stuff is rather simple, and my programmers are ready to get started.
Consultant:	I'm not sure the security policy is that simple at all. In fact, I believe that, without making the access control rules clear, your programmers will likely implement a solution that violates several federal and state laws.
Customer:	Oh, come on. It couldn't be simpler. If it is your information or your family's, then you can see it, and if it isn't, you can't. Write that down—that's your policy—are we done?

(Continued)

Consultant:	Hold on a minute. Let me ask a few clarifying questions to ensure I understand.

- What if you are legally separated from your spouse but still paying his medical bills, could you view his records then?
- What if you are given legal guardianship for a child, can you view the records prior to when you retained guardianship?
- What if you had an 18-year-old daughter enrolled in an out-of-state college but still under your health insurance; in what states are you allowed viewing of her health records for treatment at school? Does it matter where you live vs. where the service was performed?
- What if you pay cash for a treatment or test and don't claim insurance coverage; can the insurance company request to view those records or results?

Customer:	Uh, I don't know.
Consultant:	I don't know either, but we can start compiling this information, determining the attributes we need in the record to determine access, and deciding if we want to limit this service to certain states.

At this point the customer decided that he needed to rethink his entire business process and ultimately decided to change the direction of the company to supplying information to doctors on medical procedures. It is not that such a business should not be tackled, but that it should be well planned. It is important to identify the assumptions, obstacles, and requirements of the endeavor during the planning stage in order to properly plan and budget the project. Ignoring this type of planning does not make obstacles go away; it only postpones them until they surface painfully.

A security policy is not only a statement of the organization's security rules, but also a plan for behavior of the organization's systems and personnel. Organizations that create and install information systems or create departments and assign responsibilities without first planning the security with a set of security policies will soon learn of the painful surfacing of security issues.

5.3.2.1.2   Documents to Request

The security risk assessment team should request any document that may contain information relating to an administrative security control. It would be great if every organization had neatly titled documents that led the team directly to a description of a security control or policy; however, this is seldom the case. The team must be clear in its request for information by specifying the documents it requires through examples and a description of its contents. The assessed organization may find it necessary to provide multiple documents to cover the contents of what may typically be a single document. For example, many organizations have a single acceptable-use policy that is given to all employees upon hiring. However, some organizations have multiple documents covering what is typically contained in a single acceptable-use policy (e.g., e-mail use policy, software use policy, and network use policy). Prior to arriving on-site, the security risk assessment team should request all documents relevant to security controls at the organization, see Figure 5.3.

INFORMATION SECURITY DOCUMENT REQUEST FORM

We are preparing for our security risk assessment. As part of this preparation will we be reviewing available documentation (relevant policies, procedures, standards, guidelines, templates, processes, lists, and other documents that contain information security policy statements, guidance, processes, or procedures). Several of these documents are rather obvious but other documents containing information relevant to this engagement may be just a portion of a larger document. Please review the list of commonly titled information security relevant documents below and provide us with electronic copies of any of these documents you have. Once we have received all relevant documents, we will proceed with the document review process.

Area/Document

Company Information

- Mission statement
- IT strategic roadmap

Roles and Responsibilities

- Organizational structure (org. charts)
- Job descriptions and responsibilities of key staff
- Segregation of duties: policy, table, or analysis

Human Resources

- Screening/Background Investigation
- Terms and conditions of employment (NDAs, employment agreements)
- Disciplinary process/Termination procedures/Return of assets

Information Security Communication/Sr Level Involvement

- CEO/Board communication from senior security position (CISO)
- KPIs used to communicate to the board
- Copy of latest information security briefing to the board
- Contacts/Communications with authorities and security groups
- Information security project management (e.g., strategy, plans, and budget)

Network Information

- IT inventory (network and server assets with name, OS, and function)
- Network diagram (showing network architecture and external connections)
- Data flow diagram (showing sensitive information sources, storage, and transmission)
- Firewall and router settings (rule sets) and configuration standards
- List of data repositories for sensitive information

Technology and Application Information

- Inventory of technology assets
- Inventory of software assets
- List of shared business applications within the environment
- List of cloud services used
- List of IT technologies within the environment (e.g., DLP, e-mail filtering, and load balancing)

- List of third party service providers with service provided (agreements, documented, monitored, requirements responsibility matrix)
- Description of access authentication technologies (e.g., AD, two-factor auth, and OKTA) and where they are used
- Description of e-mail protection technologies (e.g., phishing, malware, and encryption)
- Description of incoming and outgoing network traffic protection (e.g., IDS/IPS and DLP)
- Description of file integrity monitoring solutions and where they are used

System Administration

- List (or description) of users with administrative access rights to workstations/laptops
- List of domain administrators

Policies and Procedures

- Data Classification, Handling, and Retention Policy and Procedures
- Disposal or transfer of assets/media
- Information Security Program Policy and Procedures
- Acceptable Use of Assets Policy
- Software Installation and Use Policy
- Mobile Device Policy
- Access Control Policy
- Cryptographic Control Policy
- Physical Security/Environmental Controls Policy
- Clean Desk Policy
- Malware Controls Policy
- Backup and Restoration Policy
- Vulnerability Management Policy
- Communications Security Policy
- Information Transfer Policy
- Vendor Security Management Policy
- Privacy Policy
- Operational procedures for managing firewalls
- Operational procedures for audit, logging, and monitoring
- Authentication and account management procedures (user registration, provisioning, reset, modification, privileged accounts)
- User access review procedures
- System component configuration standards and procedures
- Wireless component configuration standards and procedures
- Key management policy and procedures (if self-certifying)
- Secure transmission policies and procedures
- Policy and procedures for security patch management
- Software development process and procedures
- Change control procedures
- Business Continuity Plan
- Disaster Recovery Plan
- Incident response plan (roles, responsibilities, notification, backup, legal, response, procedures)
- Security awareness program and procedures (including anti-phishing training)
- Risk assessment process

Security Control Information

- List of encryption controls used to protect sensitive data
- List of assets monitored within current centralized log monitoring solution
- Description of any other security controls not otherwise listed (e.g., rogue wireless AP scanning, VPNs, virtual terminals, and IdM systems)

Frequent (Daily/weekly) Reviews

- Copy of latest report reviewing authorized changes
- Copy of latest report inspecting outgoing traffic
- Copy of latest report of potential security incidents

Audits and Assessments

- Copy of latest vulnerability scan
- Copy of latest penetration test
- Copy of latest web application scan/test
- Copy of latest firewall ruleset review
- Copy of latest user access rights review
- Copy of latest security audit or assessment
- Copy of latest System Security Plan
- Copy of latest Business Continuity/Disaster Recovery Test

FIGURE 5.3   Example document request list. It is useful to formally request documentation evidence that will be needed during the data gathering phase.

5.3.2.1.3   Policy Review within Regulated Industries

Many organizations within regulated industries may have policies developed for them or dictated to them from others, especially federal government agencies. In these cases, it may not be necessary to review security policies, as they have already been crafted by another entity and considered adequate for the threat environment of that organization. For example, within the federal government, the Federal Information Security Management Act (FISMA) provides minimum security standards for federal agency information systems. The FISMA is itself a policy that requires annual risk assessments, the appointment of a security official, and mandatory adherence to National Institute of Standards and Technology (NIST) guidelines, among many other requirements. The point here is that the policies for a federal agency have been developed outside that particular agency. In this case, the security risk assessment team should have a member familiar with federal agency information security requirements.

Other regulated industries may have portions of what is required for information security policies. For example, both the Health Insurance Portability and Accountability Act (HIPAA) and the Gramm–Leach–Bliley Act (GLB Act) require annual security awareness training. This is considered a security policy element. However, neither of these acts provides a security policy covering acceptable-use policy statements. The security risk assessment team should have a member familiar with the information security requirements for the specific industry, including what these regulations do and do not cover in terms of providing security policy.

SIDEBAR 5.3 POLICY PRESENCE VS. POLICY EFFECTIVENESS

The security risk assessment team members require the use of judgement when it comes to judging the effectiveness of security controls. When a security control is based on the existence of a policy, some inexperienced assessor may be tempted to simply confirm a policy with the right title exists for the assessed organization. However, assessing the effectiveness (and compliance of a policy requirement is a bit more involved. An assessment team member should strive to address the following issues when it comes to evaluating a policy:

- Policy Presence—At a bare minimum the assessor should ensure that the organization has a document with the appropriate title (e.g., acceptable use policy, business continuity plan).
- Empty Policy—Some organizational documents simply state that it is the policy of the organization to establish a policy. This is nonsense and does not implement any security controls worthy of assessment. The assessor should carefully examine organizational documents for the implementation of policy statements. The recognition that such a policy should be developed is simply a specification of requirements but does not count for implementation.
- Policy Adoption—The assessor should establish the extent to which the policy has been approved and adopted within the organization. Approval is required by the appropriate senior management role and the document should indicate the name, title, and data of the approval. Adoption of the policy requires that the organization enforces and/or utilizes the policy operationally. The assessor should look for customization of the policy that indicates its intended use for this organization (e.g., names, emails, specific organizational systems) and an absence of cut and paste errors or unfinished parameter place holders (e.g., [company_name], [organizationally-defined time period]).
- Level of Detail—A policy document that simply quotes requirements (e.g., "ACME develops, documents, and disseminates an incident response policy that addresses purpose, scope, roles, responsibilities, management commitment, coordination among organization entities, and compliance.") does not satisfy the requirement it quotes. The policy must actually address those requirement elements (e.g., document the scope of the incident response policy, identify the roles and responsibilities with respect to incident response, etc.)
- Implementation—A final sanity check on the effectiveness of a given policy is the level to which it is implemented. The assessment team will have a chance to discuss the topic of the specific policy with those organizational team members responsible for implementing its activities and functions. During these interviews it will become apparent if the policy is "shelf-ware" or is actually used as a guide during the execution of the activities in this area.

The security risk assessment team leader should ensure that experienced and trained team members adequately review the document effectiveness and do not stop at the title page.

5.3.2.1.4 RIIOT Document Review Technique

The following guideline provides the RIIOT technique for reviewing information security documents. The RIIOT technique can be used with any set of security document requirements, standards, or guidelines. The technique simply provides structure and process to an otherwise loosely structured process. Figure 5.4 depicts the RIIOT technique for reviewing documents.

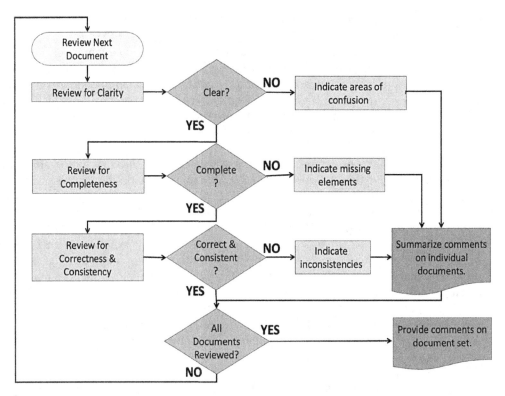

FIGURE 5.4 RIIOT document review technique. Each document is reviewed for clarity to the intended audience, completeness as measured against a standard, and consistency with other documents. Comments are provided on the complete documentation set and the individual documents.

The RIIOT document review technique is described in more detail as follows:

- Review Documents for Clarity—The security risk assessment team members should read through all policy documents to determine if they are clear and understandable. The team members must be sure to review the document from the perspective of the intended audience and not from his own perspective. For example, when reviewing security awareness training material, consider that the intended audience is not likely to have a technical understanding of the security controls they are asked to use. The assessors should use experience and judgment to determine if the governance and guidance is clear, free from unknown acronyms and technical jargon, and unambiguous.
- Review Documents for Content—The security risk assessment team members should analyze the document of each policy and procedure. Concentration on this task is on the completeness and correctness of the documents, and on the consistency between governance and guidance.
  - Completeness—The assessor should review the documents for set completeness and internal completeness. The set-completeness review ensures that the document set includes the entire set of policies, i.e., acceptable-use policy, business cataloging, security testing, etc. The internal completeness review ensures that all of the appropriate areas are addressed within each document. Appropriate areas are defined based on the threat environment, business objectives, and criticality of assets for the specific organization. The assessor can start with a checklist but should modify the checklist to meet the needs of the specific

TABLE 5.3
Expected Elements Completeness Review Example

Business Continuity

Policy Area	Expected Elements	Relevant Policy (example)	Document Review Comments (example)
Roles	• BCP Charter • Responsibility assigned	• Security group charter BCP initiative document	• Security group charter and BCP document have inconsistent roles assigned
Business continuity planning	• Business continuity strategy • Use of SaaS • Regulations addressed • Goals • Business impact analysis • Critical systems • MTD/Priorities • Dependencies • Preventative controls	• Latest risk assessment • Physical security handbook • Public Relations handbook	• No BCP strategy • BIA not documented (critical systems MTD and priorities are unclear) • Dependencies not listed for critical systems • Handbook covers physical threats only
Disaster recovery	• Recovery strategy • Backup, media handling • Equipment replacement • Alternative sites • Contingency Plan • Occupant emergency plan • Recovery procedures • Emergency response • Crisis management • Plan maintenance and testing	• Disaster Recovery Plan	• Backup and media handling well covered • No occupant emergency plan • Recovery procedures exist for only a few contingencies • Outdated contact information in emergency response procedures • Plan maintenance and testing addressed, but no lessons learned

Note: Each document that covers any of the business continuity expected elements is indicated in the chart. Once all documents have been reviewed, overlap and gaps can be more readily detected.

security risk assessment. Table 5.3 provides an example of using a template of expected elements in a completeness review.

- Correctness and Consistency—The assessor of the security policies should also review the documents with an eye on the correctness and consistency of the policies. The team member should ensure that policy statements are technically feasible, consistent with applicable regulations, and consistent with other policies and procedures.
- Indicate Coverage of Expected Elements—The assessor should review each document provided by checking off expected elements as they are located. Be sure to record where each element was found and in what document.
- Record Gaps—The team member should then compile a report showing the difference between the organization's current document set and the expected document set. This report should be organized according to the organization's existing document set and not the expected document set, see Figure 5.5.

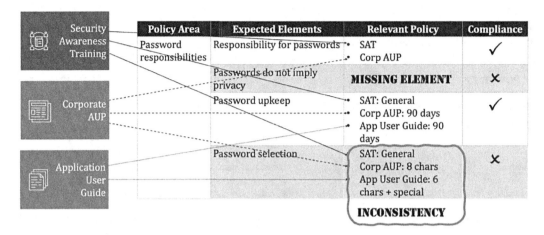

	Policy Area	Expected Elements	Relevant Policy	Compliance
Security Awareness Training	Password responsibilities	Responsibility for passwords	• SAT • Corp AUP	✓
		Passwords do not imply privacy	**MISSING ELEMENT**	✗
Corporate AUP		Password upkeep	• SAT: General • Corp AUP: 90 days • App User Guide: 90 days	✓
Application User Guide		Password selection	SAT: General Corp AUP: 8 chars App User Guide: 6 chars + special **INCONSISTENCY**	✗

FIGURE 5.5   RIIOT document review method. All policies should be reviewed for content and mapped to an expected elements table. Once all documents are mapped, the completed expected elements table can be used to note missing elements and inconsistent policies.

SIDEBAR 5.4   EVIDENCE TRACKING AND RECORDING

It is important to collect and retain the evidence for all data gathered during a security risk assessment. Evidence is used to support the claims made during the analysis portion of the security risk assessment process and provide a documentation trail for the findings and final report. Although this may sound like a lot of extra work, proper evidence collection and tracking does not need to place an undue burden on the project. Instead, collecting and tracking evidence properly can actually reduce the effort required to perform a security risk assessment. The security risk assessment team members should heed the following advice regarding the tracking and recording of evidence:

- Document Evidence as You Go—Writing down your review process and what you found while you are reviewing a security control is easy. Trying to recall these details is hard. Write down the evidence you collected as you go.
- Index Evidence against Security Controls—Evidence collected should also be associated properly with the controls to which they relate. In general, this is an easy step as you will be gathering data on a specific control as you review the available evidence. However, sometimes you will find evidence relating to other controls at the same time (e.g., during an interview or reviewing a large document). For each piece of evidence that relates to another control be sure to associate it appropriately.
- Be Specific—The data you gather on specific controls will be used later when the team analyzes the data to determine the effectiveness of each control. Be specific enough to provide useful data. Better data provides a better basis upon which to make judgments. It is easier to assess the value or certainty of data if you know how you got it, i.e., "I remember somebody said that control is not really in place" as opposed to "We found this north and west entrances susceptible to piggybacking on two out of three trials."
- Present Evidence—A presentation of findings backed with adequate evidence is a great way to avoid arguments with the customer. Specific evidence such as "the document contains out-of-date contact information for the consumer notification process" or "Server X has is missing the following critical patches" is typically good enough to move past any disagreements as to the effectiveness of the control and on to the more productive solution phase.

5.3.2.2 Interview Key Personnel

The second approach in the RIIOT data gathering method is interviewing key personnel. Interviews are conversations guided by a member of the security risk assessment team with key staff members in order to gain additional information on security controls and input on the security risk assessment process. The objectives of conducting interviews include the following:

- Confirmation of threat identification, asset valuation, and critical system identification
- Confirmation of security procedure execution
- Measurement of security awareness among staff members
- Measurement of role and responsibilities among staff members
- Identification of vulnerabilities in the area of the interviewee's expertise

Interviews can provide an incredible amount of information in a short amount of time. However, information gained during the interview should be considered as a single data point regarding vulnerabilities. Some data gathered from interviews may have a low value when compared to other data such as opinions and recollections. When the interview yields low-value data the security risk assessment team should seek to confirm that data through follow-up activities. Other data gained from the interview holds a much stronger value, such as a demonstrated lack of security awareness.

The process of conducting interviews to gather data for the security risk assessment involves selecting the interviewer(s), preparing for the interview, and the interview process itself. Each of these elements is described in more detail below.

SIDEBAR 5.5 INTERVIEWS: LIMITATIONS

It is essential that the security risk assessment team understand the limitations of the interview process. Information gathered during an interview should be considered as a way to identify areas for further study. Findings should not be based solely on the interview process.

This is a significant difference from other types of data gathering. Findings such as the absence of an acceptable-use policy, lack of separation of duty in the security organization reporting structure, and vulnerabilities found in the Web server can all stand on their own as a security risk assessment finding. No further corroboration is needed, since those findings are self-evident.

Findings resulting from an interview, however, should be followed up through additional data-gathering activities. Findings cannot stand on their own because both the interviewer and the interviewee are fallible.

The interviewer can make mistakes through misinterpretation of the questions or the answers provided, or through misreporting what was said. The interviewer may be unfamiliar with the industry or organizational terms used and may be confused by or mistake the meaning of the answer. Many security risk assessments are performed by teams with relatively little experience. In these situations, the likelihood is greatly increased that a question posed, or the answer provided is misinterpreted. Even experienced information security professionals can misinterpret what is said by the interviewee.

The interviewee can make mistakes as well. It is quite typical that the interviewee is unfamiliar with many of the terms used within the interview process, or the interviewee may have a different understanding of the question than the interviewer does. In these cases, the answer provided may not be accurate. Also, interviewees tend to be eager to please and will attempt to answer questions as much as they can. This process leads to guessing and "filling in the blanks." Again, this can result in inaccurate answers.

There are some security risk assessments that rely solely on questionnaires and interviews. The results of these risk assessments are completely contingent on the accuracy of the interview process and should be viewed with the appropriate degree of skepticism. In order to remove skepticism from your security risk assessment process, it is necessary to corroborate interview results with other data-gathering activities.

5.3.2.2.1   Selecting the Interviewer

Interviews should not necessarily be conducted by just anyone on the security risk assessment team. Performing one-on-one interviews is a difficult process and requires skills of perception, tact, and experience. This is true in almost all interview situations but is especially true during a security risk assessment. Interviews conducted within the security risk assessment process can be difficult for a number of reasons:

- Cynicism or suspicion on the part of the interviewee
- Use of unfamiliar terms and jargon (on the part of both parties)
- Difficulty in correctly recording information

The security risk assessment team should carefully consider the selection of team members who will conduct these interviews to ensure that the data gathering process goes well. A good interviewer must be able to put the interviewee at ease, use familiar terms, and seek clarification for unfamiliar terms, and be able to fluidly explore topics and possible findings. Although some of these skills can be taught, others are more prevalent among people with certain character traits and are unlikely to be trainable. Furthermore, the greatest teacher is experience. The security risk assessment team lead should avoid the temptation of filling the team with inexperienced surveyors to quickly gather data in large projects. The value of the data collected with such as approach is questionable.

Warning: Among all the other criteria for selecting interviewers, the security risk assessment team must also be careful to ensure that the interviewer can be objective and free from conflict-of-interest concerns. One such concern is the relationship between the interviewer and the interviewee. The interviewer must not interview coworkers, superiors, or subordinates.

5.3.2.2.2   Interview Requests

The security risk assessment team should request that the assessed organization schedule interviews with key personnel to cover the security control topics within the scope of the assessment. The assessment team may not know the appropriate titles, roles, or individuals responsible for each control, so it is best to let the security risk assessment sponsor arrange the interviews and assign the appropriate individuals to represent the requested areas and controls. The team can assist in this process by being clear in its request for interviews by specifying the key roles and topics it requires through an interview request form, see Figure 5.6.

INTERVIEW REQUEST FORM

We are preparing for our security risk assessment. As part of this preparation will we be interviewing key staff members that represent or control these various security safeguards. We have attempted to group interview topics into areas that are commonly controlled by a single person/role. It is likely that a single person could be responsible for several of these roles/topics (e.g., information security). In these cases, we would like to arrange a longer single meeting with those people if possible. In other cases, several individuals may be jointly responsible for a set of topics (e.g., BCP and incident response) and we would like to arrange a group interview. Please review the topics below and schedule interviews appropriately.

Typical Role(s)	Interview Area	Topics
C-Level Executives	Sr Management	• Enterprise Risk Management Strategy • Enterprise Treatment of Cyber Risk (appetite, escalation expectations, BoD involvement)
Dept. Leads	Other (all departments)	• Involvement in BCP/DRP • Involvement as data/system owner • Specific cybersecurity training requirements • Cybersecurity risks discussions • Segregation of duties requirements, if applicable
Chief Legal Counsel, Compliance Officer	Cybersecurity Regulations	• Privacy law applicability • Legal hold response • Data Classification, handling, and labeling • Cyber Security law applicability • Incident Response Strategy
CPO, Dir of Privacy	Privacy Controls	• Compliance with national and international privacy regulations • Privacy reviews of new applications • Compliant process
Department Heads IT Director	Business Continuity Planning	• Enterprise involvement in BCP • BCP Plan • Business Impact Assessment • BCP Plan • Alternative Processes • Communications Plan • DR Testing
IT Role, VP of Information Security, Incident Response Coordinator	Incident Response	• IR Plan • IR Team (roles and responsibilities.) • Backup Plan • Integration with DRP • Severity Levels • Containment strategies • Incident records • Mitigation strategies • Restoration strategies • Notification procedures • Lessons learned • Incident logging • Annual report of incidents • Escalation procedures • Communication procedures

(Continued)

Typical Role(s)	Interview Area	Topics
VP, Information Security CISO	Information Security Program	• Information Security Program Budget • Information Security Strategy • Information Security Program Roles and Responsibilities • IS Program Activities • IS Relationship with other departments • Data Classification, handling, and labeling
	Information Security Program Reporting and Assessment	• Annual reporting/review • Periodic reporting • Incident/Breach reporting • Annual risk assessment • Security program strategic plan
	Security Assessments and Testing	• Annual security risk assessment • Third-Party Risk Management • Independent reviews • External security testing • Internal security testing • Vulnerability scanning • Other security tests (SE, apps) • Risk Monitoring and Register • Security Program Metrics • Review of legacy system controls • Pen testing
	Information Security Policies	• Policy development and review • Third party risk management policies • incident response policies • Policy approvals and update • AUP • Standards of Conduct • Security Operations • Account Management • Third-party risk management • Logging and monitoring • Security Assessment and Testing Policy • Data Classification Policy (with corresponding controls) • Mobile Device Policy
	Investigations	• Forensic qualifications • Contact with authorities and special interest groups
	Threat Intelligence	• Threat Intelligence feeds • Latest Threat Intelligence report(s) • Agreements to share threat intelligence with peers/memberships in sharing communities • Collaboration and involvement with threat sharing communities and law enforcement • Membership in information sharing organizations • Threat Intelligence repository • Roles and responsibilities • Threat and vulnerability sharing protocols • Insider threat program • Threat intelligence summaries

(Continued)

Typical Role(s)	Interview Area	Topics
Internal Audit	Independent Audit Functions (with respect to security)	• Independent audit review of risk management • Independent audit review of information sharing • Independent audit review of cybersecurity controls • Independent audit review of third-party risk • Independent audit review of incident response
Dir of IT	Information Sharing and Connections	• Connections to third parties • Monitoring of connections • IDS for third-party connections
Dir IT Dir of Operations	Change Management	• Change Management Process • Approval process • Approval for system configuration changes • Access control of powerful utilities • Patch Management, maintenance • Third-party maintenance • Capacity management • Separation of environments (e.g., test, production, and development)
IT Role	IT Asset Management	• HW/SW inventory and updates • Asset management roles and responsibility • Asset life cycle process (acquisition to disposal) • End of life replacement process
IT Role	Configuration Management	• Baseline configuration standards • Baseline exceptions • Configuration monitoring • AV
IT Role	Account and Session management	• Session locking • Account management (creation, update, termination) • Separation of duty • Privileged accounts • Access rights reviews • Password complexity • Two-factor authentication • Use of privileged utility programs • Controlled access to source code
IT Role	Personal Laptops, Mobile Devices and Removable media	• Mobile device restrictions and protections • Removable media restrictions • Mobile device management • Remote wipe
IT Role	Logging and Monitoring	• Events monitored • Log review process and frequency
IT SOC	Security Operations Center /Security Operations	• Network Perimeter (FWs) • FW Architecture • Network segmentation • Port monitoring • Wireless networks • IDS • Endpoint protections • DDOS protections

(*Continued*)

Typical Role(s)	Interview Area	Topics
		• DNS protections • Remote access protections • Transmission encryption settings • Key management, if applicable • Data Loss Prevention • Remote conferencing device protections • E-mail protections • SPAM protections
Server Lead	Server Security	• Baseline configurations • Patching • Access approval • Vulnerability scanning
Workstation Lead	Workstation Security	• Baseline configurations • Patching • Access approval • Vulnerability scanning • Physical placement
Database Admin	Database Security	• Download restrictions • Separation of duty • Data at rest encryption
Application Lead(s)	Application Security	• Account management • Authentication • Access control • Logging • Patching • Vulnerability management
Dir of HR	Human Resources	• Employment screening • NDAs • Contractor screening • Cybersecurity recruitment • Sanctions with respect to cybersecurity rules • Performance plans includes accountability for cybersecurity • Disciplinary process, termination procedures
Dir of HR VP of Information Security	Security Training & Awareness	• Annual training • Situational awareness • Customer awareness • Cybersecurity staff training • Management cybersecurity training • Privileged account training • Business unit specific cybersecurity training • Training effectiveness measurements • Social engineering training • Training updates
VP of Security, Facilities Director, Data Center Manager	Physical Security Controls	• Protection of (IT) sensitive areas • Sensitive paper destruction • Access termination • Access log review • Recent incidents • Secure areas

(Continued)

Typical Role(s)	Interview Area	Topics
VP of Customer Service, CSR Lead	Customer Service Center	• Customer authentication • Specific cybersecurity training • Use of CSR applications (recording of sensitive data)
Development Lead, DevOps Lead	Code Development	• SDLC • Secure coding practices • App code review and testing • Code escrow

FIGURE 5.6 Example interview request list. It is useful to formally request interviews with key staff members of the assessed organization to make the best use of time for both the security risk assessment team and the assessed organization.

The assessed organization may choose to have interviews performed in groups of individuals with similar roles or choose to have interviews performed one-on-one. In either case, the security risk assessment team lead should ensure that the interviews are announced and scheduled to ensure the time allotted for interviews is efficient for everyone involved.

5.3.2.2.3 Preparing for the Interview

To conduct a successful and fruitful interview, the interviewer must prepare properly. Preparation involves the following items:

- Determine Interview Subjects—Based on the areas that require investigation, the security risk assessment team must select the subjects and business function areas that they would like to investigate. The team must carefully consider project time constraints as well as even and adequate coverage of all relevant areas when developing a list of interview subjects.
- Determine Interviewing Team—Following the advice of the previous section, the security risk assessment project leader must select appropriate team members to conduct interviews. Interviews should be conducted as one-on-one meetings, or at most as two-on-one meetings, to reduce suspicion and increase the candidness of the interview conversations. The security risk assessment team will need to determine the most effective number of interviewers for their specific environment. The benefit of having multiple team members is to have a witness to the information, thereby providing more robust observations. The benefit of having a smaller number of interviewers performing a single interview reduces effort required to conduct the interview and elicit more candid responses. Because recording of information can be a burden on the interviewer and distract from the flow of the conversation, the team should consider the inclusion of a transcriber or employ a recording device in the interview process. If a transcriber is used, they should strive to limit their interference in the interview process by sitting away from the conversation and quietly recording the responses of the interviewee. If a recording device is used be sure to ask the permission of the interviewee and ensure that the use of such a device does not violate any policies within the organization.
- Review Relevant Documents Prior—The objective of this activity is to obtain an understanding of the interviewee's position, responsibilities, concerns, and likely questions. Proper preparation for an interview includes the review of information relevant to the interviewee's function within the organization. Just as a potential employer reads a candidate's résumé prior to conducting an interview, the assessment team's interviewers must familiarize themselves with the security controls and functions relevant to the interviewees and their positions within the organization. Relevant documents include, but are not limited to, security policies and procedures, business function descriptions, job descriptions, and organization charts.

- Determine Objective of the Interview—Although all interviews are designed to gain additional information on security controls, the specific objective of individual interviews can vary
greatly. These objectives should be determined by the security risk assessment team for each
interview. The following points can be used as guidelines for interviewing different positions:
  - Staff Members—The objective of these interviews is to determine the security awareness
  of the general staff within the organization.
  - Key Personnel—The objective of these interviews is to confirm an understanding of roles
  and responsibilities, the execution of documented procedures, and draw out perceived
  vulnerabilities.
- Determine the Type of Interview to Be Conducted—There are several types of interviews that
are appropriate for use within the security risk assessment. Each of these types has its own
benefits and drawbacks. These interview types include the following:
  - Guided Interview—This type of interview is based on a standard set of questions. The
  advantage of this type of interview is that the answers can be more easily standardized and
  summarized. If the interview team plans to perform a lot of evaluations, this technique may
  be valuable.
  - Fixed Response—The interview technique consists of questions for which there are "yes,"
  or "no," or numbered answers. This technique may be used effectively in interview efforts
  that involve numerous responses and therefore require the compilation of many responses
  to draw conclusions. The interviewer should construct the interview questions to be consistent for each respondent and use common scales and definitions.
  - Conversational Interview—This type of interview has no set format and can be useful
  in obtaining a wide variety of information. The ability to put the interviewee at ease can
  elicit responses and information that may not have been forthcoming using other interview
  techniques.
  - Open-Ended Interview—This type of interview is based on a set of open-ended questions. These questions do not solicit "yes" or "no" answers but ask the interview subject
  to discuss an issue. These interviews are also effective at getting the interview subject to
  talk more about information security issues and reveal more information than the standard
  guided or fixed-response interviews.

A sample set of questions for the system development staff is provided in Table 5.4.

5.3.2.2.4 Conducting the Interview

The interview itself can result in an incredible amount of information if it is conducted properly.
There is a lot of advice concerning how to conduct a successful interview. Following is a compilation of that advice as it applies to the security risk assessment process.

- Establish a Productive Environment—The forum for the interview should allow for a dis-
traction-free conversation. The best approach is to acquire a small conference room reserved
for the interviews. When interviews are conducted within the interviewee's office, he may be
interrupted by phone calls and other distractions.
- Put the Interviewee at Ease during the Introduction—The quality and quantity of responses
from the interview subjects can be greatly increased by putting them at ease during the interview introduction.
  - The interviewers should introduce themselves to the interview subject and explain the
  purpose of the interview.
  - It should be made clear that the security risk assessment, and therefore the interview itself,
  are planning tools and not report cards.

TABLE 5.4

Sample Interview Questions for Key Personnel

System Development Staff Interview Questions

Objective	Key Topics	Example Questions
Determine existence and adequacy of security controls within system development	Separation of duty	• Who develops new code and who is responsible for reviewing it? • Who develops new code and who is responsible for putting it into production?
	Define security requirements	• How are security requirements defined and what groups are involved in the development? • How are they documented? • Who reviews the security requirements? • What regulations or customer requirements are addressed in the security requirements?
	System security plan	• How is assurance gained for systems with security requirements? For example, system documentation, threat assessment, vulnerability assessment, penetration testing.
	Operations plan	• How are the required security activities (e.g., audit procedures, backup, and monitoring) and security requirements for operating the system conveyed to those who will operate the system?
	Plan approval	• Who approves the system requirements, system security plan, and operations plan?
	Accreditation decision	• Who decides to "turn on the system?" • Who "owns" the risk? • Is this a formal and documented process?
	Software Development Life Cycle	• Please describe the software development life cycle. • Is this a formal, documented process? • How is security involved within the SDLC?
	Threat Modeling	• Do you have a threat modeling process? • Is it documented and updated? • How is the threat model used by developers? Reviewers?

- The interviewer should explain the degree of confidentiality that can be provided for information obtained during the interview and the intended use of the information. If no confidentiality can be promised—don't. The decision to provide confidentiality has the trade-off of the potential advantage of additional information gathered and the disadvantage of not being able to link findings to specific evidence.
- The interviewer should explain the format and time frame of the interview. Make it clear that the interview subject will have time at the end of the interview to ask any questions of the interviewer. If the interviewer is using a transcriber, the transcriber should be introduced. If the interviewer plans to use recording equipment during the interview, permission needs to be obtained. Lastly, the interviewer should leave contact information so that the interviewee can provide additional information at a later time if something comes to mind.
- Use Various Question Types to Elicit Required Response—The interviewer should be familiar with the different types of questions and use them appropriately to control the interview and guide the interview subject into providing relevant information.

- Knowledge Questions—This type of question seeks to gather specific knowledge from the interview subject. The objective is to better understand security controls for which adequate documentation may not exist.
  - Example: "Please explain your process for applying security patches to production systems."
- Behavioral Questions—These questions ask the interview subjects to indicate their behavior in certain situations. The objective of this type of question is to determine actual behavior and an understanding of how security controls are implemented and operated.
- Hypothetical questions—These questions allow the interviewer to explore an area in which processes are yet to be enacted or to discuss an area in which the interviewee has no experience. Example: "If someone were to steal a check and pay himself, how would this behavior be detected?"
- Opinion Questions—These questions ask the interview subjects their opinions on certain matters. The objective is to solicit their perspective or judgment regarding a specific security control.
  - Example: "Please explain the steps performed the last time a security patch was applied to a production system."
  - Example: "Do you believe that your security patch management process is effective?"
- Arrange Question Order—The interviewer should arrange the questions in an order that will result in the most effective interview session. Considerations for question arrangement include the following:
  - Ask Fact-Based Questions First—These questions are easy to answer and can break the ice. Getting the interview subject to start talking early on can lead to better and more in-depth answers for questions later in the interview.
  - Start with the Familiar—Questions regarding present behaviors should be asked first before moving on to questions regarding past or future behaviors. Bouncing around a timeline can become confusing and lead to inaccurate responses.
- Carefully Word Questions—The interviewer should spend some time ensuring that the wording of the questions is in line with the objective of the interview. Considerations for interview question wording include
  - Use Standard Terminology—The questions should be free of terminology that is not well understood by both parties. The interviewer should be on the lookout for perceived misunderstandings and have a standard set of definitions available.
  - Use Straightforward Questions—The questions and their delivery should be neutral, non-judgmental, and no leading.
- Elicit Candid Responses—Although it may not be obvious, the behavior of the interview team can greatly influence the candidness of responses from the interview subject. The following behaviors of the interview team should be considered:
  - Show Limited Emotion—Don't show emotion when asking questions or hearing answers. Security risk assessment team members may find it difficult not to show surprise, disappointment, empathy, or even amusement. Also be careful not to emphasize the note-taking process.
  - Show Appreciation—Non-verbal communication such as head nodding and an occasional "uh-huh" can keep the conversation going.
- Be Patient—Just prior to revealing insightful information, many respondents pause sometimes for what seems to be a long time. Wait—own the silence, be comfortable with the pause—the good stuff is coming.
- Provide Transitions—When moving from one topic to another, be clear that your questioning has changed direction. For example, "Moving on to… "

SIDEBAR 5.6   INTERVIEWING: TRICKS OF THE TRADE

Performing interviews effectively can be a complex process. The difference in results from an experienced and skilled interviewer and an inexperienced interviewer can be quite substantial. Although much of this skill will come in time as more interviews are performed, the following tricks of the trade are offered as a jumpstart to those who may structure and perform interviews as a part of a security risk assessment:

- Test questionnaires and checklists—If your interview process involves a pre-test questionnaire or a checklist for the interviewer, it is a good idea to perform a pilot test of the interview aide (e.g., list of questions). A pilot test with willing subjects (or a subset of those to be interviewed) will help determine the clarity and coverage of the questions and lead to the development of a better questionnaire and interview process.
- Dress like the interview subject—If you will be interviewing executives, you should wear a suit. If you are interviewing staff members, you should consider dressing in similar attire. Dressing reasonably alike puts the interviewee somewhat at ease. However, do not downgrade the formality of your clothes to below business casual. An assessor wearing a t-shirt and sandals gives a non-professional attitude and does not inspire confidence in the assessment.
- Beliefs vs. behaviors—Beliefs and behaviors often do not match. Someone may hold a certain belief but practice differently. For example, someone may state a belief in ethics and integrity but also illegally download songs, movies, and software. Let's say that a software developer states that "developers are pretty good at ensuring their code is secure" but there seems to be more to the story than that. Here are some approaches to get to the bottom of how people actually behave:
  - Ask a hypothetical question. Example: "If a vulnerability was discovered in public software library code tomorrow, how would that impact the code development process here?"
  - Ask about specific behaviors. Examples: Pick a specific activity such as code review and ask them to walk you through the process (including scheduling, checklists or tools used, and documenting results).
- Probing—If the interviewee defines or defends behavior based on an existing policy or on orders of another, ask if he always does what is in the policy. You will likely get a "no." Then follow up by asking for a specific instance where a policy was not followed.

5.3.2.2.5   Documenting the Interview

The results of the interview must be recorded for evidence and for sharing with the rest of the security risk assessment team. The interviewer or transcriber should be certain to record the name, position title, and contact information of the interviewee as well as the time, date, and location of the interview. Notes should be compiled and reviewed by the interview team as soon as possible. It is suggested that you schedule occasional breaks from interviews for this purpose. If this is not possible, notes should at least be reviewed and compiled by the end of the day.

5.3.2.2.6   Flexibility in the Process

Recall that the interview is a data gathering tool and is designed to confirm understandings of security controls, measure security awareness, or identify additional areas to review. The team's understanding of these controls becomes more astute as the security risk assessment progresses; therefore, the interview process must be flexible and fluid.

Flexibility is required because the team's understanding of the security controls is still incomplete. The topics covered and the questions asked in the interview should depend on the findings from these other activities. Following a questionnaire that was developed prior to digesting available information can be ineffective and make the interviewer and the team seem inexperienced. For this reason, the team and the interviewer need to be flexible when developing a set of questions for each of the key personnel to be interviewed.

Fluidity is required because an interview is an interactive process. The interviewer should react (not emotionally) to the answers to the questions and modify lines of questions accordingly to gain the most useful knowledge for the assessment.

5.3.2.2.7   Questionnaire Preparation

The development of a set of interview questions depends heavily on the security risk assessment method, scope, and budget being applied. Many security risk assessment methods (at least those that depend heavily on questionnaires and surveys) have a pre-developed set of questions to be asked. When performing a security risk assessment without a pre-developed set of questions, the security risk assessment team will need to develop their own set.

Specific questions should be developed based on the approach, style, and format of the interview process. The interviewer should also consider the security controls for which there is a lack of information. For example, if the security risk assessment team is unable to find an adequate termination procedure, the interview of the human resources director, the facilities manager, and the IT director should include questions regarding protection of assets upon termination of employment. Table 5.2 provides some sample topics that should likely be covered for different key personnel.

5.3.2.3   Inspect Security Controls

The third approach in the RIIOT data gathering method is inspecting security controls. Inspections are performed when security testing would be infeasible, ill-advised, or out of scope. For example, it is appropriate for the security risk assessment team to inspect a fire control system (i.e., examine the controls in place) but not to test it (i.e., light a fire in a trash can and see how long it takes for a halon discharge).

Many security controls, especially physical security controls, do not lend themselves well to the testing process. The testing of some security controls could possibly disrupt the organizational mission; if security testing were your only option, vulnerabilities within these security controls could go unnoticed. For this reason, it is important for the security risk assessment team to consider using the inspection approach of the RIIOT method. A security risk assessment that skips the inspection stage because it is inappropriate to test the security controls can leave out significant vulnerabilities in the security controls protecting the organization's assets and, therefore, result in an inaccurate measurement of risk.

The objective of the "inspect security controls" approach is to verify the information gathered during the document review and interview approaches. Specific inspection techniques will be discussed in the administrative, technical, and physical data gathering sections (Chapters 6, 7, and 8). The following steps provide general guidelines for the inspection approach:

- List Security Controls—Obtain or create a list of the security controls under review. Such a list can be requested, obtained during the interview process, or compiled through observation during a site tour. The list of security controls should give the security control, specific model number or configuration information, its objective, interfaces to other security controls, and the point of contact for further information.
- Verify Information Gathered—The information gathered in the security controls list, interviews, and other RIIOT approaches can be confirmed through inspection. Security risk assessment team members will find that many of the procedures, mechanisms, and other security

controls mentioned in documents and interviews may not operate as described or may even be completely missing.

- Determine Vulnerabilities—The goal of the inspection is to ensure that vulnerabilities of the security controls are discovered. The security risk assessment team should have at least one member who has experience and knowledge with the security controls to be inspected. Those with experience can likely determine vulnerabilities without the aid of checklists or other guidelines. However, a guideline or checklist is useful to both experienced and inexperienced members of the inspection team. A sample inspection checklist for the security control lighting system is provided in Table 5.5.

- Document and Review Findings—Preliminary findings of the inspection should be documented in as much detail as possible. Include dates and times of inspection and what characteristics or vulnerabilities were observed. The documented findings should be reviewed with the point of contact for each security control to provide that individual with a chance to clarify any possible misinterpretations.

TABLE 5.5

Sample Security Lighting Inspection Checklist

Objective	Key Topics	Example Questions
Determine existence and adequacy of security controls within lighting system	Sabotage	Tour areas critical to lighting systems to determine susceptibility to sabotage • Switchyards • Transformers • Circuit breakers • Power lines • Engine generators • UPSs
	Single point of failure	Inspect lighting system to determine if security lighting systems have any single points of failure • Single lighting circuit • Power supply on a single circuit breaker • Single power grid
	Access control	Inspect access controls on areas containing lighting system components
	Maintenance	• Inspect lighting in the evening to determine if any lights are out. • Follow up, if any lights are out, by asking for a copy of recent repair tickets and maintenance reports
	Settings	• Inspect lighting system setting (best in the evening): • Lighting levels (for building, walkways, and entrances) • Appropriate shielding • Coverage • Appropriate motion sensor settings

Note: When inspecting security lighting systems, the assessor should inspect their ability to control sabotage, single points of failure, access to critical components, maintenance, and appropriate settings.

5.3.2.4   Observe Personnel Behavior

The fourth approach in the RIIOT method for data gathering is to observe the behavior of the organization. The process of observation involves gathering information on the actual implementation of the security controls and determining if they are uniformly applied and effective. For example, the assessor may have already confirmed that a policy and procedure exist stating that unbadged visitors will be challenged. Furthermore, your interview subjects have confirmed that this policy is enforced. Now simply walk around in a new area without your badge and observe if anyone challenges you. This is essentially an analysis of the effectiveness of policies and procedures based on observation.

As with many data gathering activities during a security risk assessment, there are no complete and set guidelines on how to perform observation. Observation is a process in which the assessor observes behavior and situations and then develops a judgment regarding the observed behavior. Keen and useful observations to the security risk assessment process are more likely to come from more experienced team members, because they have more experience from which to draw observations and comparisons. However, other team members may have a naturally keen sense of observation. These members can prove just as useful in data gathering through the use of observation.

Advice: Team up less experienced members with more experienced members during the observation stage to develop the experience and observation capabilities of all members.

5.3.2.4.1   Observation Guidance

I once described the process of observation as "You walk around and look for stuff." Although that does not sound overly helpful, it is actually rather descriptive of the high-level process for gathering data through observation in a security risk assessment. A lower-level description of the process is difficult, because the observation process is flexible and based on specific circumstances and environments. However, a few examples of observations may illustrate the concept:

- Policy and Procedures—Observation of behavior to confirm or disprove that policy and procedures are followed. Examples include passwords posted on monitors, visitors walking around unchallenged, and changes not being documented.
- Physical Security—Observation of behavior of personnel and condition of controls to confirm or disprove that physical security requirements are met. Examples include gaps at the bottom of a fence, unlocked telephone closets, unenforced visitor registration process, and unlit parking lots.
- Security Awareness—Observation of behavior and knowledge of personnel to confirm or disprove security awareness assumptions and requirements. Examples include allowed piggybacking, unauthorized use of smart phones in sensitive areas, and unauthorized downloading.
- Media and Hard-Copy Disposal—Observation of behavior to confirm or disprove that disposal requirements for media and sensitive information are met. Examples include examining trash cans near fax machines.

The previous topics provide some guidance as to the areas of observation. Chapters 6 through 8 provide additional observation guidance based on administrative, technical, and physical controls.

5.3.2.5   Test Security Controls

Security testing of information systems within the scope of the security risk assessment is performed to identify the vulnerabilities of those systems. The inclusion of security testing in a security risk assessment is essential to identify the existence of these vulnerabilities and to provide this information to the organization so that they can address these vulnerabilities. It is important to understand both the abilities and limitations of security testing performed as part of a security risk assessment.

Depending on the type of security testing performed and the depth of testing, security testing can reveal many vulnerabilities that exist in systems protecting sensitive information. The results of a security test, however, only show the presence of known vulnerabilities at the time of testing. Security testing does not show the absence of any vulnerability. Furthermore, it must be recognized that the results of the security test are only accurate for the specific instance in which the test was performed. Almost immediately, the system and the threat environment begin to change. As these aspects of the system change, the results of security testing become less relevant.

It is with this background that the information security professional must recognize that security testing is a tool employed by the security risk assessment team to identify possible vulnerabilities in the system and organizational processes. For example, consider a system in which a security test reveals that the information system is susceptible to a well-known buffer-overflow attack, and an effective patch has been available from the vendor for over 3 months. This finding would reveal (1) that the system has a vulnerability that must be patched and (2) that the procedures for implementing patches are ineffective.

5.3.2.5.1   Security Testing Documentation

It is important to document all aspects of the security testing effort carefully and fully. The security risk assessment team will be testing a live system, so diligence in the security test documentation effort is required. All security tests should have documentation sufficient to support the repeatability of the test. Documentation should include, at a minimum, the following elements:

- Time and Date—Record the time each test was started and completed.
- Test Environment Setup—The test environment is the necessary preparations for executing the tests. Test environments may include establishing accounts, creating file folders, creating privileged roles, turning on specific logging and monitoring devices, establishing a local or network server connection, or white listing the testers' IP address with security devices.
- Tools Used—Identify the tools (or commands) used in each test. This should include any special instructions, parameters, add-ins, and version/build number.
- Tester—Document the name of the tester for each test.
- System—Document the systems and interfaces tested.
- Results—Indicate the results of the tests.
- Comments—If anything unusual or unexpected happened, include that in your notes as well.

Accurate and detailed security testing documentation is useful not only to demonstrate repeatability of the security tests but also to support the assessed organization's efforts to determine the system state or to perform troubleshooting.

- System Changes—Elements affecting the system security test can change during the security risk assessment engagement. Hopefully, the team is working with a stable system, and architectural changes are not being performed during the test process. However, other changes—such as users logged on, load to the system, emergency patches, and many other factors that may occur or change during the test effort—can change test results. Careful documentation can help to determine the relevance of the test results and recreate the test if necessary.
- Troubleshooting—When you are part of the security team performing tests on a live system, you must be aware that your team will be the first one blamed if anything goes wrong anywhere near the time or place you are testing. Be prepared to work with the assessed organization to help them determine the root of any problem. Detailed test documentation can save a lot of time and headaches when dealing with this situation. Also consider that, from time to time, your security tests may have actually been the catalyst for causing errors or system crashes. Even seemingly benign security tests such as a port scan can exercise some interfaces that have not been previously tested. In the case of custom-made applications, a simple security scan may cause delicate and untested applications to fail. Documentation comes in handy here in helping to resolve the problem.

5.3.2.5.2   Coverage of Testing

The complexity of an information system, the vastness of its interfaces, and the multitude of variables involved make comprehensive or exhaustive testing impossible. There is no way to completely test an information system. Therefore, any security testing effort is going to be less than complete. But that does not mean that testing should be considered inadequate. In fact, through thoughtful selection of the testing coverage, security testing can be performed effectively and efficiently.

There are several approaches to ensure proper coverage in performing security testing. The approaches covered include representative testing, selected sampling, and random sampling. Each has its own unique approach, advantages, and disadvantages. Each of these techniques may be used in isolation or in combination with each other. For more information on these sampling approaches, see Section 5.1.3, Use of Sampling in Security Testing.

- Complete Testing—A security testing effort may attempt to test all components of an information technology infrastructure. This approach is referred to as *complete testing*. The term *complete* here refers not to the rigor of the testing method, but instead to the number of network components included in the test. For example, if an information technology infrastructure is composed of 550 workstations, ten Web servers, five file servers, two e-mail servers, four database servers, three application servers, four firewalls, and ten routers, then all 588 network components would be tested.

The advantages of complete testing are rather obvious; complete testing provides security vulnerability information on all network components. This complete coverage allows the security risk assessment team to make reasonable conclusions regarding the network components, because all components were tested. When the network is relatively small (e.g., fewer than 200 servers) and the testing method is relatively simple (e.g., vulnerability scanning), it usually makes sense to perform a complete test.

Complete coverage for security testing has disadvantages as well. Clearly, complete security testing can be expensive and time consuming when the network is relatively large (e.g., over 500 servers) or when the testing method is more complex (e.g., ad hoc penetration testing).

5.3.2.5.3   Types of Security Testing

Security testing can be used to achieve many different objectives, such as testing that established procedure (system hardening or account maintenance) was followed by testing information accuracy to identify possible vulnerabilities (vulnerability testing) or to determine the system's resistance to attack (penetration testing). Each of these testing types is useful within the process of a security risk assessment.

It is important to understand the distinction between these security testing types and objectives, as not all security risk assessments will employ all three types. For example, a security risk assessment with a low level of rigor is unlikely to perform penetration testing. The security risk assessment team needs to understand where a vulnerability assessment leaves off and a penetration test begins. Each of these testing types is described in the following subsections.

5.3.2.5.3.1   Information Accuracy Testing

Information accuracy testing is performed to confirm the accuracy of data gathered within other stages of the assessment. Much of the data gathered within a security risk assessment relying on documents and interviews could be considered of low quality or uncorroborated information. This is not to say that we believe the information was purposefully misleading, just that interviews can result in inaccurate information, network diagrams can be out-of-date, and policies may not be strictly implemented. The objective of information accuracy testing is to corroborate information obtained during other data gathering activities. Several examples of how information can be corroborated or corrected are given as follows:

- Interviews—During an interview, subjects may, by nature, be eager to please, and rather than state that they do not know the answer, they guess at an answer. At other times, terminology gets in the way. The interviewer and the interviewee can be using the same terms but have different meanings associated with the terms. For example, an interviewee may state that passwords are never sent in the clear. The interviewee may truly believe this statement, because he has just finished a project on the upgrade of a legacy system that had passwords embedded in batch commands. Now that those commands are removed, the interviewee believes that passwords are never sent in the clear (unencrypted). However, it may be shown through the interception and analysis of packets that they are indeed still sent in the clear. The interviewee is not being dishonest; the individual just does not understand the implication of the implemented authentication protocols and protected communication paths.
- Network Diagrams—These are a representation of the logical arrangement (connectivity) of the network components. Network diagrams are useful during a security risk assessment to determine information flow, external and internal interfaces, and the architectural design of the network. As the network architecture can be in a constant state of change, the accuracy of a network diagram must be verified.
- Policies and Procedures—The organization may have a strict policy that every desktop must receive daily anti-virus updates. However, there may be some users within the organization who have figured out how to defeat the automatic updates ("because they slow down the machine too much").

5.3.2.5.3.2   *Vulnerability Testing*

The objective of vulnerability testing is to identify the vulnerabilities that exist in the currently deployed systems without causing a breach to the security of the system the security control is protecting. Within technical security controls, this is referred to as vulnerability scanning, because the use of tools allows for a quick scan of the system to identify any obvious vulnerabilities. Vulnerability testing can be applied to physical security controls as well. For example, a vulnerability test of a badge-access-activated entrance could entail the timing of the door mechanism to properly close. A long time to close would indicate a vulnerability that could allow an intruder without a badge to gain entry.

5.3.2.5.3.3   *Penetration Testing*

The objective of penetration testing is to exploit the vulnerabilities found during vulnerability testing. Within technical security controls, a penetration test would exploit a technical vulnerability such as weak encryption or insecure authentication mechanisms to gain unauthorized access to a system. Applying penetration testing to the physical security control in the previous example (the door that takes a long time to close), the assessor would attempt to actually gain access by utilizing this vulnerability.

5.3.3   USING THE RIIOT METHOD

As mentioned earlier in the chapter the planning, organizing, and execution of the data gathering phase can be challenging. The RIIOT method of data gathering assists the data gathering process by organizing the data gathering approaches (e.g., Review documents, Interview key staff, Inspect controls, Observe behavior, and Test controls), determining the appropriate approaches for each control, and then assigning and tracking the data gathering process among the team.

5.3.3.1 Determining Appropriate RIIOT Approaches

For every security control that may be employed in the enforcement of an organization's security policy, there are various RIIOT approaches available for data gathering. The security risk assessment team lead should select a number of approaches for each security control when developing the security risk assessment plan. However, since the level of rigor for the security risk assessment should already be established at this point some approaches may not be within scope for the assessment (e.g., security testing).

As an example, consider the abbreviated list of administrative controls in Table 5.6. For each administrative control listed, the table indicates the potential approaches to gather data. Data can be gathered on the security control of *asset tracking* through document review, interviews, and inspections; and data can be gathered on the security control of *vulnerability scanning* through document review, interviews, and testing.

The security risk assessment team lead needs to determine which of the available RIIOT approaches will be used for each security control. For example, the team lead may choose a subset of the RIIOT approaches as illustrated in Table 5.7.

5.3.3.2 Assigning RIIOT Activities

The team lead should then select the appropriate methods for this project and assign them to the team members. Assignments may not be as simple as illustrated in Figure 5.7, but the team lead can use the RIIOT terminology and organizational elements to provide clear assignments to each team member.

5.3.3.3 RIIOT Applied to Administrative, Physical, and Technical Controls

As security controls are typically divided into the administrative, physical, and technical areas, and different techniques and even skill sets are used to collect data in these areas, the team typically divides the data gathering process along the same lines. Chapters 6, 7, and 8 provide the reader with an overview of the threats and safeguards relevant to each of these areas. These chapters also provide a discussion of how the RIIOT approach can be applied to administrative, physical, and technical data gathering.

TABLE 5.6
Abbreviated RIIOT Method of Data Gathering for Administrative Controls

Controls	Review Documents	Interview Key Personnel	Inspect Controls	Observe Behavior	Test Controls
Acceptable-use policy	*	*		*	
Asset tracking	*	*	*		
Business impact analysis	*	*			
Data backup	*	*			*
Information labeling	*	*	*	*	*
Incident response plan and procedures	*	*		*	
Incident response training	*	*		*	
Server hardening	*	*			
Vulnerability scanning	*	*			*

TABLE 5.7

Selected RIIOT Approaches for Abbreviated Administrative Controls

Controls	Review Documents	Interview Key Personnel	Inspect Controls	Observe Behavior	Test Controls
Acceptable-use policy	*	*		*	
Asset tracking	*		*		
Business impact analysis	*				
Data backup	*	*			*
Information labeling	*		*	*	
Incident response plan and procedures	*	*			
Incident response training	*				
Server hardening	*	*			
Vulnerability scanning	*	*			*

Controls	Review Documents	Interview Key Personnel	Inspect Controls	Observe Behavior	Test Controls
Acceptable-use policy	★	★		★	
Asset tracking	★		★		
Business impact analysis	★				
Data backup	★	★			★
Information labeling	★		★	★	
Incident response plan and procedures	★	★			
Incident response training	★				
Server hardening	★	★			
Vulnerability scanning	★	★			★

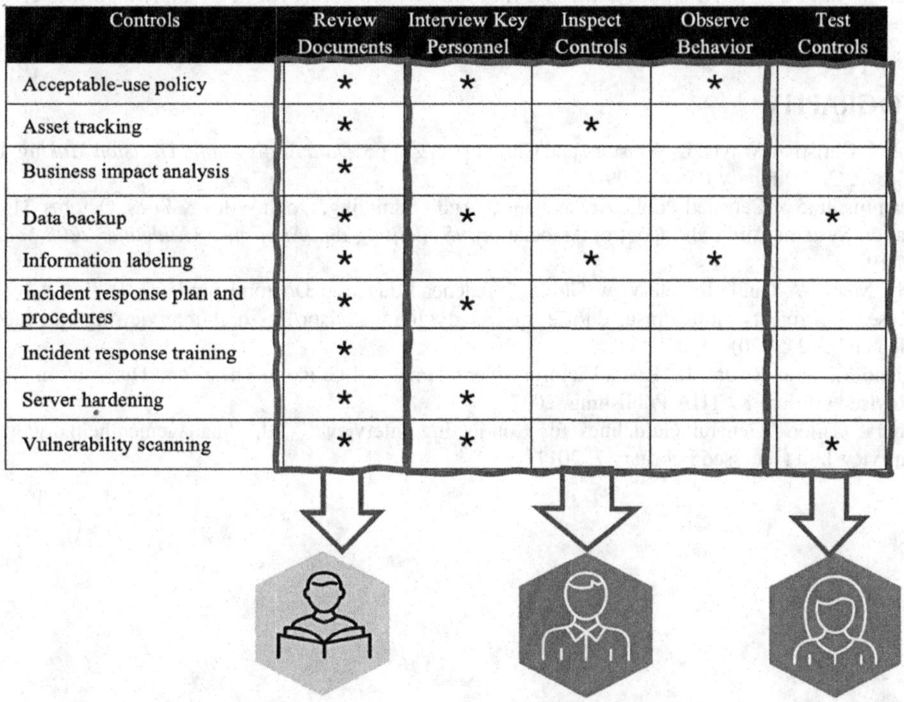

FIGURE 5.7 RIIOT activity assignments. The security risk assessment team lead can utilize the organizational elements of the RIIOT Data Gathering method to clearly assign tasks to team members.

EXERCISES

1. If the Gallup Poll decided to increase the size of its random sample of registered voters from 1,866 people to 4,000 people, what would be the effect on the following elements:
   a. Standard deviation
   b. Confidence level
2. True or False: Attribute sampling is quantitative in nature, and variable sampling is qualitative in nature.
3. What are the major limitations to utilizing interviews as a data gathering approach?
   a. Compare the interview limitations to the limitations of utilizing a questionnaire.
   b. How can combining the data gathered from an interview and a questionnaire address the limitations of gathering data from just a single activity?
   c. How would *reviewing documents* prior to the interview further reduce the data gathering limitations?
4. Compare/contrast the RIIOT method with the "examine, interview, test" assessment methods documented in NIST SP 800-53A.
5. Perform a review on the Acceptable Use Policy of your organization, school, or university.
   a. What documents make up the Acceptable Use Policy?
   b. Document your findings on the review of the AUP policy set.
      i.   What policy statements may be "missing?"
      ii. What policy statements are unclear?
      iii. What policy statements are inconsistent with other statements (or actions)?
   c. What other RIIOT data gathering methods would be useful in an analysis of the effectiveness of the AUP policy set?

BIBLIOGRAPHY

Albright, S. Christian, Wayne L. Winston, and Christopher Zappe. *Data Analysis and Decision Making*. Pacific Grove, CA: Duxbury Press, 1999.

American Institute of Certified Public Accountants, "Audit Sampling," John Wiley & Sons, October 31, 2016.

Information Systems Audit and Control Association. *IS Auditing and Assurance Guideline: 2208 Sampling*. 2019.

Kennedy, Mary. "A Guide to Interview Guides," Teacher Education Doctoral Students, Digital Advisor for Research Projects. https://msu.edu/user/mkennedy/digitaladvisor/Research/interviewing.htm (accessed September 2, 2020).

Maximiano Marquez Rivera, Jr., Roela Victoria Rivera, "Practical Guide to Thesis and Dissertation Writing," Revised Edition, KATHA Publishing, 2007.

McNamara, Carter. "General Guidelines for Conducting Interviews." http://managementhelp.org/evaluatn/intrview.htm (accessed February 7, 2011).

6 Administrative Data Gathering

Each of the next three chapters is dedicated to the topic (or security risk assessment phase) of data gathering. The topic of data gathering is a large one and encompasses many activities and security controls. In Chapter 5, the Review, Interview, Inspect, Observe, Test (RIIOT) data gathering method was introduced as a method of organizing, describing, and managing the data gathering effort. The RIIOT approach provides the organizational structure to discussions regarding the application of data gathering techniques for administrative, physical, and technical security controls. This large topic has been divided into three groups—administrative (Chapter 6), technical (Chapter 7), and physical (Chapter 8)—to facilitate the use of this book and to provide security risk assessment team members with target guidance on their area of review. The bulk of the next three chapters are dedicated to the description of how to gather data in these three respective areas: administrative, technical, and physical.

The ability to gather data efficiently is based on an effective data gathering approach and an experience and understanding of the security controls, their vulnerabilities, and threats. While this book cannot give the reader experience in these areas, it can provide a primer on the basics of the security controls and their respective threats and vulnerabilities for each of these areas. Therefore, each of the next three chapters will have a similar format of a discussion of threats and security controls designed to combat those threats, followed by the RIIOT method for data gathering. This chapter focuses on the administrative controls and the data gathering techniques for those specific controls.

6.1 ADMINISTRATIVE THREATS AND SAFEGUARDS

The definitions of threats, threat agents, and threat actions were covered earlier in Chapter 4. Administrative threats specifically are covered here as an approach to introducing administrative data gathering. This section, on threats and safeguards, is intended as a primer or introduction to security threats in the administrative area.

- Administrative Threats and Threat Actions—A member of a security risk assessment team requires a basic understanding of the threats and safeguards within the administrative security area to be an effective member of the team. There are numerous threat actions that can be addressed through the implementation of administrative controls. The list of specific threat actions is ever growing and difficult to completely enumerate. However, it is useful to have a basic understanding of the threat action categories. For administrative controls, those threat actions are categorized as invoked malware, theft & sabotage, socially engineered, hacked, abused trust, environmental damage, and erred, see Figure 6.1.
- Administrative Safeguards—There is a vast array of administrative safeguards that could be effective against the various threats to an organization. This chapter provides a brief introduction to many of these administrative safeguards to ensure that the security risk assessment team member is familiar with controls they may encounter during as assessment as well as available safeguards for recommendations to address high risk areas. The safeguards presented here are divided into the following categories:
- Human Resources—Safeguards in this category are typically implemented within the human resources department but may also be addressed or coordinated with other areas within the organization such as information technology and training. Safeguards are grouped into the classes of recruitment safeguards, employment safeguards, and termination safeguards.

FIGURE 6.1 Administrative safeguard threat actions. A variety of threat actions can be addressed through the implementation of administrative safeguards. These threat actions can be organized into the categories of invoking malware, theft & sabotage, being socially engineered, being hacked, abusing trust, suffering environmental damage, and committing an error.

- Information Control—Information control safeguards address controls that may be put in place to protect sensitive and critical information. These safeguards are grouped into the classes of sensitive information, user accounts, user error, asset control, and, audit.
- Business Continuity—Business continuity safeguards address the protection of sensitive data and critical systems during a disaster to ensure the continuity of business operations. These safeguards are grouped into the classes of contingency planning and incident response.
- System Security—System security safeguards address the protection of systems and applications. These safeguards are grouped into the classes of system controls, application security, change management, and third-party access.
- Organizational Structure—The organizational structure safeguards address governance and oversight functions that ensure the organization implements appropriate controls to safeguard sensitive information and protect critical systems. Safeguards in this area are grouped into the classes of senior management, security program, security operations, and audit.

The specific safeguards within each of these categories are discussed in the sections below and represented in Tables 6.1 through 6.5.

6.1.1 Human Resources

Organizations need to protect their assets from unqualified or untrustworthy personnel. Employees, through purposeful or accidental behavior, may expose sensitive assets to disclosure, compromise integrity of information, or block availability of critical systems.

6.1.1.1 Human Resource Threats

An organization's own employees (e.g., the insiders) pose a significant threat to the organization's critical systems and sensitive assets. In a recent study by Verizon, the insider threat was measured at 30% (all data breaches were traced back to "internal actors.") This is not to say that all cases of employee's actions leading to data breaches were deliberate. The insider actions exposing the organization to information security risk can be unintentional or intentional.

Unintentional actions of an employee can include the following threat actions:

- Invoked Malware—An employee may take a number of actions that lead to the introduction of malicious software (e.g., malware) on their computer. This may involve opening an e-mail, visiting a website, inserting removable memory into the employee's computer, downloading

TABLE 6.1

Administrative Threats and Safeguards: Human Resources

Class	Threat Action	Safeguard
Recruitment-unqualified/ untrustworthy personnel	• Socially Engineered • Abused Trust • Erred	• Application • Job requirements • Reference checks • Employment checks • Accuracy checks • Credit checks • Clearance procedures
Employment—unqualified/ unsuspecting personnel	• Invoked Malware • Theft & Sabotage • Socially Engineered • Hacked • Erred	• Employment policies • Training and education • Job description • Job requirements • Annual reviews
Employment—untrustworthy personnel	• Socially Engineered • Abused Trust	• Acceptable-use policy • Monitoring • Two-person control • Job rotation • Clearance refresh • Ethics training • Sanctions policy • Separation of duty • Job rotation
Termination—untrustworthy personnel	• Abused Trust	• Termination procedures • NDA, NCC • Out-briefing

Note: Threat actions applicable to human resources include invoking malware, theft & sabotage, being socially engineered or hacked, abusing trust, and committing errors. Administrative safeguards that can address these threat actions are policies, procedures, and activities described below.

the malware, or the malware may have been put in place by the software manufacturer. There are many types of malware. Below are a few examples:

- Ransomware—Is a type of malware that encrypts data files on the infected computer leaving the files or the computer itself in an unusable state for the victim until a ransom is paid.
- Command and Control Malware—Is a category of malware that can be controlled by the attacker through a command and control (e.g., C&C and C2) server operated by the attacker. C&C malware is especially damaging as the attacker can use the C&C methods to download additional malware components to the victim's computer or to exfiltrate sensitive information that has been collected.
- Trojan Horse—Is a type of malware that uses a seemingly useful program to deliver a hidden malicious function unknown to the victim. Trojan horse malware can many times evade malware detection mechanisms as they appear to be useful programs either needed for a job function or appears to provide an otherwise useful function.
- Password Dumper (AKA Credential Dumper)—Is the result of malware (and other hacking techniques) in which the user identification and authentication information (i.e., credentials) are published (dumped) online. These credentials are then wide open for other attackers to exploit user accounts.

TABLE 6.2

Administrative Threats and Safeguards: Organizational Structure

Class	Threat	Safeguard
Senior management	• Abused Trust • Erred	• Risk management • Assign duties • Understand responsibility • Governance and oversight
Security program	• Invoked Malware • Socially Engineered • Hacked • Abused Trust	• Assign duties • Authority, visibility • Budget • Risk analysis • Review of security activities
Security operations	• Invoked Malware • Socially Engineered • Hacked • Abused Trust • Erred	• Assign duties • Security operations policies • Maintenance procedures • Separation of duties • Dual control • Least privilege • Monitoring
Audit	• Abused Trust • Erred	• Separation of duties • Dual control • Least privilege • Monitoring • Internal audit • Third-party review • Security risk assessment

Note: Threat actions applicable to organizational structure include invoking malware, being socially engineered or hacked, abusing trust, and committing errors. Administrative safeguards that can address these threat actions are policies, procedures, and activities described below.

- Downloader—Is a type of malware that downloads and installs multiple instances of other.
- Backdoor—Is a type of malware in which attackers may gain unauthorized access to a system by going around typical security controls. Backdoors may be introduced through malware or may have been originally introduced into the system by the manufacturer as a way to gain access to the system after it has been deployed (presumably to assist customers).
- Theft & Sabotage—An employee may be the victim of a robbery in which an organizational asset such as a laptop or a mobile device may now be in the hands of an unauthorized person. Employees may be susceptible to theft while traveling to and from work, traveling for work, or at home or a hotel.
- Socially Engineered—An employee may fall prey to a cybercriminal who uses psychology (instead of technical approaches) to gain the trust of the employee and then tricks them into violating the organization's security policy. This is basically a modern version of a confidence scam (e.g., used to by conmen). There are many techniques used to implement social engineering. Below are a few examples:
  - Phishing—Is a technique used by criminals in an attempt to acquire sensitive data through a fraudulent solicitation in e-mail or on a website. The website/e-mail and the sender/website owner masquerade a legitimate business or reputable person. Phishing has been on the rise as the success of these attacks lead criminals to gain access to sensitive data and restricted accounts, and ultimately allows them to cash in on the ruse.

TABLE 6.3
Administrative Threats and Safeguards: Information Control

Class	Threat	Safeguard
Sensitive information	• Socially Engineered • Hacked • Abused Trust • Erred	• Criticality analysis • Information labeling • Media destruction • Access control review • Need-to-know • Separation of duty
User accounts	• Invoked Malware • Socially Engineered • Hacked • Abused Trust • Erred	• Account creation procedures • Account management • User account review • Account termination procedures • Need-to-know
User error	• Socially Engineered • Erred	• Security awareness • Job training • Job rotation • Policy and procedures • Monitoring • Double key data entry • Two-person control
Asset control	• Theft & Sabotage • Socially Engineered • Abused Trust	• Asset inventory • Asset tracking

Note: Threat actions applicable to information control include invoking malware, theft & sabotage, being socially engineered or hacked, abusing trust, and committing errors. Administrative safeguards that can address these threat actions are policies, procedures, and activities described below.

TABLE 6.4
Administrative Threats and Safeguards: Business Continuity

Class	Threat	Safeguard
Contingency planning	• Invoked Malware • Theft & Sabotage • Socially Engineered • Hacked • Abused Trust • Environmental Damage • Erred	• Business continuity strategy • Business impact analysis • Disaster recovery plan • Crisis management • Occupant emergency Plan • Data backup • Alternative services • DRP testing and maintenance
Incident response program	• Invoked Malware • Theft & Sabotage • Socially Engineered • Hacked • Abused Trust • Environmental Damage • Erred	• Incident response plan and procedures • Incident response training • Availability of experts

Note: Threat actions applicable to business continuity include invoking malware, theft & sabotage, being socially engineered or hacked, abusing trust, environmental damage, and committing errors. Administrative safeguards that can address these threat actions are policies, procedures, and activities described below.

TABLE 6.5

Administrative Threats and Safeguards: System Security

Class	Threat	Safeguard
System controls	• Invoked Malware • Socially Engineered • Hacked • Abused Trust • Erred	• Operating procedures • Server hardening • Vulnerability scanning • Penetration testing • Scheduled and emergency patches • Remote maintenance • Remote access • Security review/approval
Applications security	• Invoked Malware • Hacked • Abused Trust • Erred	• Architectural design • Authentication • Access control and data protection • Input validation • Cryptography standards • Error handling and logging • Configuration • Code review
Change management	• Abused Trust • Erred	• Configuration Item (CI) definition • CI protection • Change control • Status reporting
Third-party access	• Invoked Malware • Socially Engineered • Hacked • Abused Trust • Erred	• Vendor inventory • Vendor assessment • Vendor risk reduction • Security control assessment • Monitoring and performance measurements

Note: Threat actions applicable to system security include invoking malware, being socially engineered or hacked, abusing trust, and committing errors. Administrative safeguards that can address these threat actions are policies, procedures, and activities described below.

- Pre-texting—is a technique used by criminals to obtain their customer information under false pretenses. Pre-texting is a type of social engineer in which the criminal uses a story (e.g., a pre-text) to make the con more convincing. Pre-text attacks typically involve research by the criminal on the victim to make the back story more plausible and convincing.
- Hacked—An employee may fail victim to an attacker using hacking methods to circumvent the security controls on their computer or account. Hacking methods are numerous and ever-growing as attackers continually find new methods to gain unauthorized access. Below are a few examples of hacking methods that may impact the employee:
  - Brute Force—Is an attack method that continuously tries to guess a user's password through the use of attack tools that run through all possible combinations.
  - Exploitation of Vulnerabilities—Is a class of attacks that take advantage of known vulnerabilities in a system. The attacker may have determined the existence of these vulnerabilities through other attack tools or they may simply be guessing that the vulnerabilities may exist. Either way if the employee's computer has the exploitable vulnerabilities an attacker may take advantage of those vulnerabilities and gain unauthorized access.

- Use of Stolen Credentials—An attacker may simply use stolen account credentials of an employee. These account credentials could be the results of another attack (e.g., credential dumper).
- Abused Trust—An employee may abuse the trust given to them and utilize this misplaced trust to take actions against the organization. There are many such actions a trusted employee could take. Below are a few examples:
  - Privilege Abuse—The employee could use their account privileges to access sensitive data for which they do not have a need to know and are restricted from viewing.
  - Illicit Content—The employee could store or distribute illicit content on or using organizational systems.
  - Theft—The employee could steal organizational resources (e.g., money, equipment, and mobile devices).
  - Unapproved software—The employee could install unapproved software onto organizational resources potentially circumventing security controls.
- Erred—Lastly, an employee may simply make a mistake that results in the loss of confidentiality of sensitive data, or in the misplacement of an organizational asset such as a laptop. There are many types of errors that may result in a breach of the organization's security. Below are a few examples:
  - Loss—An employee may lose or misplace their physical access, badge, laptop, or mobile device. Without recovering the badge or device the organization must assume that it could be in the hands of an unauthorized person.
  - Misdelivery—A common mistake among employees is sending sensitive information to the wrong recipient. This may happen through e-mail, regular mail, fax, or even in person. Such a misdelivery may result in unauthorized access to sensitive data.
  - Misconfiguration—An employee may accidentally misconfigure their mobile device or system, leaving it susceptible to attack.
  - Publishing Error—An employee with the responsibility of publishing public information on the organization's website or responding to public inquiries for data may make an error and publish (or release) sensitive information.

6.1.1.2 Human Resource Safeguards

Given the wide array of potential threat actions that could be enacted on or by an unqualified, untrustworthy, or unsuspecting employee, organizations should implement an adequate set of security controls (e.g., safeguards) to address the insider threat. Table 6.1 lists an example set of safeguards that an organization may employ to counter the threat and threat actions of the employee. These safeguards are discussed within the employee time periods of recruitment, employment, and termination.

6.1.1.2.1 Recruitment

Prior to hiring an individual to become an employee within an organization, the human resources department has many opportunities to provide safeguards that may avoid or deter the employee being socially engineered, employee error, or abused trust. These safeguards include hiring procedures, job requirements, and a series of possible background checks that may be performed on the applicant. Each of these safeguards is briefly described below:

- Application—The application must collect the appropriate information and consent from each applicant to enable proper reference, background, and employment checking. Furthermore, the application will provide information on the applicant's experience and skill set that is intended to meet the requirements of the job description.
- Job Requirements—The hiring manager for each position must pay careful attention to the description of the job duties and employee requirements. The specific duties and requirements

recorded in the job description are what the human resources manager will use to screen candidates. An inaccurate description of the job requirements can lead to the hiring of an inadequate employee.

- Reference Checks—These checks include both professional and personal references who can attest to the skills, experience, and work ethic of the applicant. You should generally expect that such checks will come back quite positive because the applicant provided the names of whom to call. Nonetheless, such checks do provide some assurance that the applicant possesses the characteristics required for the position.
- Employment Checks—When called concerning a reference check, employers are only expected to provide information concerning the date of hire, date of termination, and job title. If the applicant has signed a "hold harmless" agreement with the previous employer, additional information may be provided. Although employers may provide this information without such an agreement, it is unlikely they will.
- Accuracy Checks—These checks provide an assurance that all the information provided on the application is accurate. Such checks cover employment dates, salary histories, education, professional affiliations, and other data that may be confirmed. Significant errors within the application could simply be a mistake but may also indicate either carelessness or deceit.
- Credit Checks—Credit checks provide a measure of the financial well-being of the prospective employee. This could provide insight into the candidate's dependability. In the case of sensitive government jobs, this could provide insight into the susceptibility the candidate may have to blackmail. A credit check may be conducted by ordering a credit check on the employee. However, such a check may be performed only if the employee is informed that a credit check will be issued and signs a consent form to be provided to the credit reporting agency.
- Background Checks and Clearance Procedures—Employers may access arrest and conviction records that are available as public information. The use of these records to make hiring decisions, however, varies from state to state. If the practice is legal within the governing jurisdiction, background checks can provide an immediate measure of the applicant's integrity. Within the federal government, additional checks will be performed to determine if the applicant is eligible for the required clearance.

6.1.1.2.2 Employment

Once an individual becomes an employee, the potential for the employee being socially engineered, invoking malware, being hacked, being robbed, or committing errors can impact the security of the organization's assets. There are many approaches for safeguarding the organization from the potential of such losses. Some of these are briefly described below:

- Employment Policies—The proper behavior of an employee begins with the organization's making the expected behavior clear. Policies such as acceptable use of equipment, non-compete agreements, and non-disclosure agreements define the security responsibilities and the sensitivity of organizational assets. These policies should be reviewed and signed as a part of the employment process.
- Training and Education—Many mistakes made by employees and susceptibility to cybercriminals, social engineers, and thieves are a matter of improper training and education. Programs such as security awareness training, process training, and regulation education help to ensure that employees understand their security responsibilities and how to carry them out.
- Job Description—The description of a job is not simply a human resources paperwork exercise. The job description itself is a security safeguard. An employee's expectations and limits of authority should be captured in the job description. Expectations set out the specific duties that must be performed and the duties for which the employee is responsible. Limits of authority document the NTK of the individual in the specific job position. For example, expectations

may include annual testing of the disaster recovery plan (DRP) plan; limitations may include account activation but not audit log review. Ensuring that these duties are performed and that privileges are not exceeded is a primary security concern.

- Job Requirements—Covered in Section 6.1.1.2.1
- Annual Reviews—The strength of the security measures set up during job description and job requirements is tested during an annual review. The annual review provides a measurement of the ability of the employee to meet the expectations of the position. Additionally, the supervisor should use the annual review as a method to review the job description and ensure that the job description properly identifies all of the duties performed in that position.
- Acceptable-Use Policy—The nature of work requires the use of the computer equipment, the corporate network, and possibly the Internet for electronic communication. "Acceptable Use" addresses employee use of the organization's resources for accessing the information, transmitting, or receiving electronic mail, general use of software, and system access. This policy communicates and documents the responsibilities and limits of privileges for employees.
- Monitoring—To further enforce the organization's security policies and procedures, the organization may employ monitoring procedures or automated monitoring equipment. Monitoring includes all activities that provide oversight of the employee's ability to follow stated security policies. These activities include supervision, review of the use of information resources such as e-mail, and automated monitoring of Web surfing behavior. As the laws in each state differ with regard to monitoring employee communications, the monitoring approach should be reviewed by the organization's legal department.
- Dual Control—This safeguard is applied to sensitive tasks and requires both individuals' approval before action is taken. This provides accountability and reduces fraud, waste, and abuse.
- Two-person Control—This safeguard employs the use of two employees to review and approve the work of each other. This provides accountability and reduces fraud, waste, and abuse.
- Separation of Duty—This is a concept that states that no single sensitive task should be able to be executed by a single individual from beginning to end. This concept may also be applied to any implementation task and requires that someone other than the implementer review the work.
- Job Rotation—This safeguard requires that employees perform a variety of job functions within a single department. Job rotation forces others' work to be reviewed and performed by their peers, thus reducing the chance for collusion and helping to prevent fraud. Job rotation has a side benefit of providing "bench strength" within a single department, because more than one person can perform critical duties.

The concepts of two-person control, dual control, separation of duty, and job rotation all help to reduce opportunities for fraud, waste, and abuse. Figure 6.2 illustrates the distinction between these concepts.

- Clearance Refresh—For those positions that require government clearance for access to sensitive information, the clearance process must be reperformed periodically. The clearance process involves background checks, credit checks, psychological screening, and other methods of determining the trustworthiness of an individual to keep secrets. Refreshing this process ensures that the individual continues to exhibit traits and evidence of trustworthiness.
- Ethics Training—Providing courses and training in ethics to the workforce is an effective way to ensure that employees understand the expectations of their ethical behavior. Ethics training should be customized to situations that apply to the employees and should be consistent with documented guidance and policies. Employers should include industry or organizationally relevant examples within the ethics training to increase the applicability of the training to the organization.

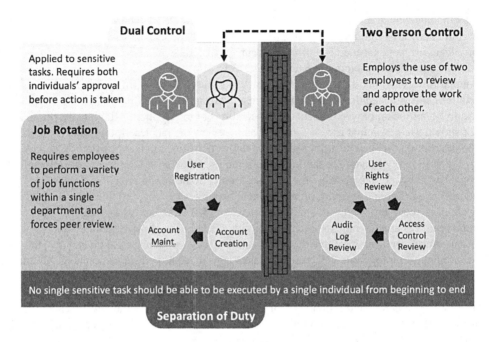

FIGURE 6.2 Administrative oversight safeguards. The concept of separation of duty states that one group should be responsible for reviewing another group's work. Job rotation requires that employees rotate positions within a department. Dual control requires two operators to perform a single function. Two-person control designates another individual to review the work of an operator.

- Sanctions Policy—All employee security policies should have specific and clear implications if violated. A sanctions policy provides the policy and procedures for the organization's actions upon violation of security policy. The sanctions policy should include, at a minimum, policies for documentation of incidents, definitions of prohibited actions, applicable policies and laws, and escalation procedures for incidents. The organization should ensure that the sanctions policies are applied equally to all employees and incidences.

6.1.1.2.3 Termination

When it becomes clear that an employee will no longer be employed at the organization, the termination procedures must be handled appropriately to avoid a breach in security. The potential for abuse of trust can be rather high, especially with disgruntled employees who have had access to sensitive information and critical systems. There are many approaches to safeguarding the organization from the potential of a security incident or breach in the event of an employee termination. Some of these are briefly described below:

- Termination Procedures—The organization should have a clear set of procedures to be followed upon an employee's termination. These procedures need to be tailored to the organization, because they will be dependent upon the industry, environment, and business structure. Some examples of items that should be included within termination procedures include the return of capital equipment and security access cards, termination of accounts, and the turnover of duties.
- Non-disclosure Agreements and Non-Compete Clauses—Upon termination the employee should be reminded of any non-disclosure agreements (NDAs) that have been signed with the former employer and any partners. A NDA identifies sensitive information (e.g., trade secrets

and customer lists) and the restrictions on its dissemination. A non-compete clause (NCC) specifies the restrictions placed on the future employment of the individual (i.e., restrictions on doing business with customers or even competing in the same industry).

- Out-Briefing—An out-briefing is a formal process during a non-hostile termination that can gather information from the terminated employee that could be used to improve the work environment or reduce vulnerabilities. Out-briefings are also performed to remind the employee of the contracts still in place (e.g., NDAs and NCCs) and their responsibility for continuing obligation.

6.1.2 ORGANIZATIONAL STRUCTURE

The structure of the organization includes creation of departments, reporting structures, allocation of budget and responsibilities, and the creation of governance and oversight activities. The organizational must establish a structure of security controls that address threats and threat actions such as error and abused trust within the organization.

6.1.2.1 Organizational Structure Threats

The structure of the organization plays a large role in the ability of the organization to effectively enforce security controls. The organization of departments, responsibilities, and reporting structures within the organization can affect the most basic of security controls. From security regulations compliance responsibilities to security activity coordination and execution, the effectiveness and efficiency of security controls can be thwarted by weak organizational structure controls. Threat actions addressed by organizational structure control include the following:

- Invoked Malware—As mentioned before an employee may take a number of actions that lead to the introduction of malicious software (e.g., malware) on their computer. Elements of the organizational structure can address these threat actions to the employees.
- Socially Engineered—Employees may be exposed to many attempts at social engineering. A strong organizational structure program can address many of these threat actions.
- Hacked—If an employee is hacked various activities within a strong organizational structure can address these threat actions.
- Abused Trust—An employee or more senior members of the organization may abuse the trust given to them and utilize this misplaced trust to take actions against the organization.
- Erred—An employee may simply make a mistake that results in the loss of confidentiality of sensitive data, or in the misplacement of an organizational asset such as a laptop.

6.1.2.2 Organizational Structure Safeguards

Given the wide array of potential threat actions that could be enacted organizations should implement an adequate set of security controls (e.g., safeguards) to address the threat actions applicable to the organizational structure. Table 6.2 lists an example set of safeguards that an organization may employ to counter the threat and threat actions applicable to the organizational structure. These safeguards are discussed within the safeguard classes of senior management, security program, security operations, and audit.

6.1.2.2.1 Senior Management

All security starts at the top. It is senior management that is ultimately accountable for the security of an organization. It is senior management that will be held accountable by the organization's stakeholders and for violation of laws and regulations. It is senior management that determines the organizational structure in which the security program and activities operate. If senior management does not establish an effective organizational structure for the security program, then the effectiveness of all other security controls is in question.

Specifically, the threat actions to the organization's assets that can be most attributed to senior management include error and abuse of trust. Senior management error includes negligence, poor management, ineffective security programs, and ignorance of applicable laws and regulations. Abuse of trust on the part of senior management includes embezzlement and abuse of privilege. The following safeguards can help to lessen the likelihood or impact of these threat actions:

- Risk Management—Risk management is the process of understanding, mitigating, and controlling risk through risk assessment, risk mitigation, operational security, and testing. As mentioned earlier, the objective of security risk management is to accurately measure the residual security risk and keep it to a level at or below the security risk tolerance level. Only senior management has the ability to define the organization's tolerance for security risk.
- Assign Duties—The senior management of the organization needs to determine the organizational structure most appropriate to enabling the risk management process. The structural decisions are implemented through an assignment and placement within the organization, establishment of roles and duties, and the granting of budget and staff.
- Understand Responsibility—It is imperative that senior management understand their security responsibilities and ensure that delegated duties are understood as well. Senior management needs to have an operating knowledge of the security regulations and controls within their industry and cannot simply delegate such responsibility. For example, the administrator of a hospital is not implementing this safeguard (understanding responsibility) if security duties have been completely delegated to the systems administrator. The hospital administrator needs to understand the components of the HIPAA (Health Insurance Portability and Accountability Act) regulations (and others) and understand that specific security activities and controls are required, many of which are likely outside the control of the systems administrators (e.g., business associate contracts).
- Governance and Oversight—Governance and oversight activities ensure that security control strategies and implementations are aligned business objectives. Governance and oversight controls are implemented through the proper placement of review functions, the granting of roles and responsibilities, and the approval of budget and resources that ensure implementation of the business objectives.

6.1.2.2.2 Security Program

The security program is functionally responsible for the management of the security controls within the organization. A well-structured, staffed, and funded security program can offer many security advantages to the organization. The threat actions to the organization's assets that can be most attributed to the security program include preventing the invocation of malware, protecting employees from being socially engineered or hacked, abuse of trust, and error. The security program prevention of social engineering, hacking, and introduction of malware is addressed by clear assignment of roles and responsibilities, appropriate risk analysis, and a review of the security activities. Abuse of trust on the part of the security program includes abuse of privilege and negligence. Specific elements of an effective security program are described below:

- Assign Duties—The security program must clearly assign duties to the members of the program. Duties include anything from running vulnerability scans, to creating security policies, to running the security awareness program. A clear and complete assignment of duties, coupled with annual reviews that measure individuals on how well they met their responsibilities, can provide effective safeguards against many threats to the organization's assets.
- Authority and Visibility—The security organization must have the ability to perform its activities effectively. Since security reaches across many departments, it can sometimes be difficult

for the security team to be noticed or for the security team to effect changes and enforce policy. The security team must be given the proper authority and visibility within the organization to effect changes and enforce policies.

- Budget—The security team will undoubtedly require an expenditure of money to implement some of its functions or acquire security technology. If the security budget is determined by another department (e.g., information technology), then the security team is, in effect, controlled by that other organization and loses its credibility and effectiveness to deliver the most cost-effective solutions.
- Risk Analysis—The security team should continually perform risk analysis on the security of the organization's assets. Based on available information (e.g., latest security risk assessment, scan, password cracking, and the latest incident), the security team must be able to articulate the security risk to the organization to senior management and other stakeholders. Furthermore, the security team should periodically report the security state of the organization to senior management and others.
- Review of Security Activities—If the security team is responsible for performing certain security activities, the principle of separation of duty dictates that someone else review the security team as to their effectiveness and adherence to policies and procedures. This can be performed by internal audit teams or as a part of a security risk assessment performed by an independent consultancy.

6.1.2.2.3 Security Operations

The security operations team is typically responsible for the implementation and maintenance of technical security controls such as account and access controls, firewalls, and anti-virus software. The security operations team may also be involved in reviewing new security products and contributing (or leading) the incident response team actions.

The threat actions to the organization's assets that can be most attributed to security operations include preventing the invocation of malware, protecting employees from being socially engineered or hacked, abuse of trust, and error. Security operations prevention of social engineering, hacking, and introduction of malware is addressed by clear roles and responsibilities, operational policies and procedures, and monitoring of the system security state. Security operations error includes data classification or data entry errors, maintenance or configuration errors, misdeliveries, and programming errors. Abuse of trust on the part of security operations includes abuse of privilege, data or e-mail misuse, or unapproved workarounds, hardware, or software. Some safeguards that may be applied to security operations are described below:

- Assign Duties—Members of the security operations team must have clearly assigned duties to ensure complete coverage and enforcement of separation-of-duties principles. Duties include account creation, account maintenance, file access controls, role definitions, and audit log reviews. A clear and complete assignment of duties, coupled with annual reviews that measure individuals on how well they met their responsibilities, can provide effective safeguards against many threats to the organization's assets.
- Security Operations Policies—Policies and procedures regarding the way in which the security operations team performs its functions help to ensure that individuals behave in a manner that benefits the organization. Policies are the foundation of security operations activities, because the policies define the expected behavior. Procedures further provide guidance as to how activities should be performed. The organization should have security operations policies that cover the activities of system or security administrators, such as account creation, server hardening, and file backups.
- Maintenance Procedures—These procedures provide additional guidance for those activities required to maintain security controls. Maintenance activities include account, software,

and access control maintenance. The modification of the parameters of these security controls must be carefully managed; maintenance procedures provide clear guidance and help to reduce errors and omission.

- Separation of Duty—Covered in Section 6.1.1.2.2.
- Dual Control—Covered in Section 6.1.1.2.2.
- Least Privilege—The concept of least privilege states that all employees should be given the least amount of privilege they need to perform their duties. Security operations must practice this concept when creating accounts and establishing access control rules. This concept can also be applied to the accounts of the security operations personnel themselves. For example, there is no reason for everyone in security operations to have all (or root) privileges.
- Monitoring—Covered in Section 6.1.1.2.2.

6.1.2.2.4   Audit

The audit function provides oversight for sensitive tasks and protection of organizational assets. Audit functions include the safeguards of internal audit, third-party review, and security risk assessments. The key to a successful audit function is to ensure that auditors are not involved in the development of what is to be audited, that auditors have access to all records, and that senior management must be formally required to respond to audit findings. The threat actions to the organization's assets that can be addressed to audit include abuse of trust, and error. Audit activities can find errors such as data classification or data entry errors, maintenance or configuration errors, misdeliveries, and programming errors; and instances of abuse of trust such as abuse of privilege, data or e-mail misuse, or unapproved workarounds, hardware or software. Some safeguards that may be applied though audit are described below:

- Internal Audit—The internal audit function is an in-house team of auditors who can review security controls and accounts. For those organizations large enough to have an internal audit team, security risk assessments are typically performed or commissioned out of these offices. This team should also have a direct report to a C-level executive, generally the Chief Executive Officer (CEO), board of directors, or Chief Financial Officer (CFO).
- Third-Party Review—If the organization has allowed outside organizations to connect to its network or share sensitive information, then the security boundary for the protection of the organization's assets has effectively increased to include that organization as well. A third-party audit is a security audit performed on a third party to ensure that they are properly safeguarding the organization's assets. These audits are typically bounded by specific requirements documented in a business associate contract. Third-party review can be conducted directly by the assessing organization, it can be conducted by hired external security experts, or the assessing organization can accept the audit reports of other qualified security experts.
- Security Risk Assessment—The security risk assessment is an objective analysis of the effectiveness of the current security controls that protect an organization's assets. Such assessments are carried out to determine the probability of losses to those assets.

6.1.3   INFORMATION CONTROL

Information is one of the most valuable assets of the organization. Many controls and safeguards exist, including controlling user accounts, restricting user error, controlling assets, and protecting sensitive information.

6.1.3.1   Information Control Threats

Adequate security controls should be placed on sensitive information to ensure that it is protected from various threat actions. Threat actions addressed by information controls include the following:

- Invoked Malware—As mentioned before an employee may take a number of actions that lead to the introduction of malicious software (e.g., malware) on their computer. Elements of the information control, such as information labeling, and media destruction can address these threat actions to sensitive data.
- Socially Engineered—Employees may be exposed to many attempts at social engineering and ultimately expose sensitive data. An information control program structure including user account reviews and NTK controls can address many of these threat actions.
- Hacked—If an employee is hacked various information control activities such as account management can address these threat actions.
- Abused Trust—An employee or more senior members of the organization may abuse the trust given to them and utilize this misplaced trust to take actions against the organization. Many information control activities, such as separation of duty, and job rotation can address these threat actions.
- Erred—An employee may simply make a mistake that results in the mislabeling of sensitive data, or unauthorized access to sensitive data. Many safeguards withing the information control area such as security awareness, and access control review can address these threat actions.

6.1.3.2   Information Control Safeguards

Given the wide array of potential threat actions that could be enacted organizations should implement an adequate set of security controls (e.g., safeguards) to address the threat actions applicable to the information control. Table 6.3 lists an example set of safeguards that an organization may employ to counter the threat and threat actions applicable to the information control. These safeguards are discussed within the safeguard classes of sensitive information, user accounts, user error, and asset control.

6.1.3.2.1   Sensitive Information

All data is valuable to the organization, but some data is more critical and sensitive than other data. The organization should identify this information and provide additional controls to protect it from disclosure.

- Criticality Analysis—Among the information and resources controlled by the organization, some are more critical than others. The organization can identify critical assets by analyzing the critical systems and the assets and resources required by those critical systems. The labeling of assets as critical allows the organization to more effectively track, control, and protect those assets, thus, ensuring their availability for critical systems.
- Information Labeling—All information is valuable to the organization, but some of the information is more sensitive. Sensitive data, however, is likely to be treated in a less strict manner than intended if the organization fails to properly classify and label sensitive information. The organization should create and implement a data classification scheme that takes into account the various levels of data sensitivity within the organization. For example, the organization may consider a scheme that dictates different controls for public, personal, partner-proprietary, and sensitive data.
- Media Destruction—Whenever a computer, hard disk, or magnetic media is to be disposed, transferred, or sold, it must be done in a way that ensures the confidentiality of the data. To ensure that media that leaves the control of the organization contains no sensitive information, extra efforts must be applied to remove any content. These efforts are referred to as *sanitization*:

- Sanitization of Data—All information must be erased or overwritten. Specifications for sanitization call for repetitious overwriting a specific number of rounds. Sanitization standards depend on the organization, its environment, and any regulations it may fall under. Typical sanitization standards include a provision for three to seven rounds of overwriting of the complete media, including the BIOS.
- Sanitization of Hard Drives—There are generally three acceptable methods for the sanitization of hard drives: overwriting, degaussing, and physical destruction. The method used for sanitization depends on the operability of the hard drives. Operable hard drives that will be reused are overwritten. If the hard drive is to be removed from service, it is preferable to physically destroy or degauss the hard drive.
- Sanitization of Other Media—The risk of disclosure of sensitive information also lies outside of computer hard drives. Specific attention should be paid to cell phones, CD-ROMs, tapes, DVDs, optical disks, and volatile and non-volatile memory components. These devices must be erased, degaussed if possible, or physically destroyed.
- Access Controls Review—The access controls for sensitive information should be reviewed more frequently than those controls for less sensitive information. For example, the access control lists (ACLs) for the payroll database should be reviewed more frequently than the ACLs for a users' home directory. Access controls applied to capabilities (e.g., account creation), applications, and files can also be misaligned. The system, application, or file owner should periodically review accesses and permission levels granted to the organizational assets for which they are responsible. The following schedule is suggested:
  - Review all system capability levels (e.g., administrative privileges) every 30 days.
  - Review all application permissions every 60 days.
  - Review all file permissions every 90 days.
- Need-to-Know—The principle of NTK states that each person shall have access to the minimal amount of information necessary to perform his duties. This principle is closely aligned with the concept of least privilege. The difference between these two safeguards is that NTK concerns access to information, while least privilege concerns capabilities. The implementation of NTK in handling access to information reduces the chances of disclosure.
- Separation of Duty—Covered in Section 6.1.1.2.2.

6.1.3.2.2 User Accounts

A user account contains a user's attributes such as name, sensitivity level, and account expiration. The user account provides the user access to organizational critical resources and files and should therefore be strictly controlled. The following safeguards can assist in ensuring that security is preserved through user accounts:

- Account Creation Procedures—The organization should have strict account creation procedures in place. These procedures should include approval from the information or system owner, a review of accesses required, and a notification to the information or system owner once the account is created.
- Account Management—User and administrative accounts on the organizations information systems require a documented and practiced management process to ensure appropriate access controls protections for the sensitive data accessible on those systems. Account management procedures should include the assignment of account managers, a documented process for account approval and access authorization, and a stricter approval and authorization process for privileged accounts such as database administrator.
- User Account Review—The privileges associated with user accounts are not always appropriate. A user account can be initially created with excessive privileges; the account can accumulate privileges as the user takes on additional assignments within the organization; or the termination procedures can be misapplied and fail to appropriately disable or remove

an account. A periodic review of user accounts and their associated privileges can help to ensure appropriate access rights are implemented for each account. The following schedule is suggested:

- Review all accounts every 180 days.
- Review all sensitive accounts every 90 days.
- Access Control Review—Covered in Section 6.1.3.2.1.
- Termination Procedures—Covered in Section 6.1.1.2.3.
- Need-to-Know—Covered in Section 6.1.3.2.1.
- Separation of Duty—Covered in Section 6.1.1.2.2.

6.1.3.2.3   User Error

Many controls and safeguards discussed so far have dealt with ways to stop fraud, waste, and abuse, but even well-meaning employees can breach the security of the organization's information through accidental means. The administrative controls discussed below are some of the ways to restrict user error as it would impact the security of the organization's information:

- Security Awareness—All employees and contractors should be made aware of their role in enforcing the security policy of the organization. Security awareness training educates all staff on acceptable use policy, common threats to the organization, and how to report security incidents.
- Job Training—The best way to ensure a lack of mistakes on the part of the users is to properly train them to perform their job. Assessors should be careful not to confuse education and experience with job training. Each organization has its own specific environment, policies, and ways of doing things. Job training ensures that users know what is expected and how to perform their duties.
- Job Rotation—Covered in Section 6.1.1.2.2.
- Policy and Procedures—For each position within the organization, there is a specific set of activities that are expected to be performed. If these activities are sensitive and can affect the security of the organization's assets, then the assessor should expect there to be some policies and procedures in place to ensure that the activities are performed in a manner that enforces the security policy of the organization.
- Monitoring—Covered in Section 6.1.1.2.2.
- Double-Key Data Entry—This is a data entry method in which each transaction is entered twice. The first data entry and the second data entry are checked for consistency with each other and the data is only considered valid if both entry values match. This control helps to reduce errors and fraud.
- Two-person Control—Covered in Section 6.1.1.2.2.

6.1.3.2.4   Asset Control

Asset control involves the explicit control and tracking of individual organizational assets. This includes both tangible assets and intangible assets. Organizations that employ asset control can easily keep tabs on critical assets, control theft of equipment, and handle assets according to their sensitivity.

- Asset Inventory—An asset inventory is a list of all of the assets of the corporation. This list typically has many fields, such as location, type of asset, asset owner, and serial number. For smaller organizations, such lists could be created manually, but large organizations will likely use an asset inventory software to automatically collect this information. The system may involve aspects such as bar codes, asset tag, or even Radio Frequency IDentification (RFID).

The asset inventory can be used as data to improve other security controls as well, such as termination procedures (ensure that all capital equipment is returned) and visitor control (ensure that visitors do not leave with an organization asset).

- Asset Tracking—Once an inventory has been created and the assets have identifiers (e.g., with serial numbers or asset tags), owners, and locations, the asset tracking system can be used to monitor the disposition of all organizational assets. These systems assist the organization in controlling and managing its inventory of assets through check in and checkout procedures, disposition tracking (e.g., documenting equipment transfers or destruction), and inventory checks and upkeep.

6.1.4 Business Continuity

Business continuity is the field of preparation planning undertaken by organizations to ensure that they remain a viable entity if and when a disaster impacts their critical systems. The possibility that a disaster will impact at least one critical system within an organization is rather large. In fact, a recent study found that 96% of companies surveyed had at least one outage in the past 3 years and 55% had five or more outages in the same time period. The cost of downtime includes lost revenue, brand damage, mitigation costs, and compliance failures. The cost of downtime has been estimated at $8,000 per hour for small businesses; $74,000 per hour for medium businesses, and $700,000 per hour for large enterprises. Regarding even more impactful disasters, an often-quoted statistic from the Federal Emergency Management Agency (FEMA) states that "roughly 40% to 60% of small businesses never reopen their doors following a disaster."

Business continuity planning is the process of identifying critical systems, identifying reasonable threats, and creating a long-term strategy for reducing the impact of interruptions to the business and stabilizing critical business functions. Adequate security controls should be in place to prepare for disasters and to ease the recovery process. Many controls and safeguards exist, including data backup, training, alternative services, and crisis management. Table 6.4 lists an example set of safeguards that an organization may employ to counter the threat and threat actions applicable during incidents and disasters. These safeguards are discussed within the safeguard classes of contingency planning and the incident response program.

6.1.4.1 Business Continuity Threats

The planning, strategy, preparation and other elements of business continuity planning and incident response preparedness enables an organization to avoid disasters and lessen the impact of disasters and incidents. Threat actions addressed by business continuity and incident response planning include the following:

- Invoked Malware—Malicious software invoked by an employee can have disastrous consequences for the organization and its assets. Incident response planning and business continuity controls can limit the impact.
- Theft & Sabotage—The threat action of theft &sabotage can cause security incidents and disasters severely impacting the organization. The organization may also be more suspectable to these threat actions during the time of a crisis. Planning and strategy in this control area can avoid and lessen the impact of the theft & sabotage threat actions.
- Socially Engineered—Successful social engineering attacks are themselves an incident and can lead to disasters. A strong incident response and business continuity program can address many of these threat actions.
- Hacked—If an employee is hacked various activities within a solid incident response and business continuity program can address these threat actions.
- Abused Trust—When employees and senior members of the organization abuse the trust given to them, their actions can lead to security incidents and disasters. The planning and preparation

activities within an incident response or business continuity program can address the impact of these threat actions.

- Environmental Damage—Impact from natural disasters (e.g., storms, floods, and fire) and external infrastructure disasters (e.g., power outage and disrupted water supply) can have severe consequences for the organization. The planning and response activities within incident response and business continuity can lessen the impact of these threat actions.
- Erred—Employee errors such as losing a laptop or accidently pressing the emergency power off (EPO) button in the data center can result in major losses to the organization and its assets. Activities within incident response and business continuity planning can address these threat actions.

6.1.4.2 Business Continuity Safeguards

Given the wide array of potential threat actions that could be enacted organizations should implement an adequate set of security controls (e.g., safeguards) to address the threat actions applicable to the business continuity and incident response planning. Table 6.4 lists an example set of administrative safeguards that an organization may implement to counter these threat and threat actions. These administrative safeguards are discussed within the safeguard classes of contingency planning and the incident response program.

6.1.4.2.1 Contingency Planning

The contingency planning process includes the business continuity planning (i.e., long-term strategy) and the DRP (i.e., near- and mid-term strategies) to handle specific situations:

- Business Continuity Strategy—A business continuity strategy is a plan to minimize the impact of realized risks on critical resources. The business continuity strategy is based on an analysis of the threats and critical systems (e.g., a business impact assessment (BIA)); a determination of alternative site requirements; and approval, implementation, and training of the plan.
- Business Impact Analysis—A BIA provides a measured impact assessment on business operations from a disastrous event. The steps involved in a BIA are, first, to establish priorities for which systems to bring up first in the event of a disaster and, second, to allocate the appropriate resources to those systems during an actual disaster.
- Disaster Recovery Plan—A DRP documents the business continuity process and provides a written plan in the event of an emergency. The DRP should contain emergency response guidelines for specific disaster scenarios, such as a computer virus outbreak, an internal cyber-criminal, a tornado, or an epidemic.
- Crisis Management—The procedures for crisis management should be part of the DRP; however, they are called out here because they are often left out of that document. Crisis management is a public relations program that proactively handles external agencies (e.g., emergency services and weather bureaus) and stakeholders (e.g., employees and key customers) in crisis situations.
- Occupant Emergency Plan—During a disaster it is important that everyone located at the facility in danger of environmental damage understands their role in ensuring the safety of all. Occupant emergency plans are provided to all those who may be located on the premises (including visitors) and cover a variety of foreseeable disaster which may take place at that location. The plan is a quick source of emergency information such as where to evacuate, whom to call, and how to secure the area, if applicable. The plan typically covers emergencies such as active shooter, hazardous materials spills, medical emergencies, natural gas leaks, fire and smoke, biological agent hazards, tornados, bomb threats, and earthquakes (and any other foreseeable local disasters or emergencies).
- Data Backup—Data required for critical systems on both the system level and the user level must be backed up periodically. Backup tapes of sensitive or critical information should be stored in a secure and separate location, but retrieval capability must be

consistent with required recovery times. The ability to restore data must be demonstrated periodically as well.

- Alternative Services—Many services are required of critical systems such as data centers, communications, transportation, housing, payroll, and manufacturing. The organization may engage in plans to have alternative services provides in the event of a disaster. This control is effective when it is accompanied by service contracts and involved in the testing of the DRP.
- DRP Testing and Maintenance—A DRP is not considered viable until it has been successfully tested. DRP testing verifies the adequacy of the team procedures and the compatibility with backup facilities and provides training for team members. Any inadequacies discovered in the testing phase or because of changes in the environment are handled within the scope of DRP maintenance.

6.1.4.2.2 Incident Response Program

An effective incident response program is essential to the organization to limit the potential for disclosure of confidential information, the subversion of critical systems, or the perpetration of fraud because of a security incident. Incident response programs include a response plan for each type of considered incident, incident response procedures to be followed by the organization's personnel in charge, incident response training, and the availability of experts when needed.

- Incident Response Plan and Procedures—The incident response plan and procedures provide the direction and authority to the incident response team for identification, containment, and recovery capabilities.
- Incident Response Training—All members of the incident response team should be well trained in the policy and procedures for incident response and reporting. Training should include how to recognize an incident, whom to notify in a given scenario, how to contain the damage, and how to recover the critical functions of the system.
- Availability of Experts—In the event of an actual disaster, the capabilities of the incident response team may not be adequate for certain situations. For example, the incident response team may have determined to pursue prosecution of an employee. If the incident response team does not have a staff expert in evidence collection, analysis, and court presentation of evidence, it may be wise to retain the services of experts in this field. Such arrangements should be made ahead of time during the planning, and not reacting process.

6.1.5 System Security

System security involves all of the activities an organization's information technology department performs to establish, configure, monitor, and maintain the security of deployed systems. The organization must implement adequate security control to protect its information systems from unscheduled changes, third-party access, system-level vulnerabilities, and application-level vulnerabilities. Table 6.5 lists an example set of safeguards that an organization may employ to counter the threat and threat actions applicable within system security. These safeguards are discussed within the safeguard classes of system controls, applications security, change management, and third-party access.

6.1.5.1 System Security Threats

The system controls, applications security, change management, and third-party access controls enable an organization to address the various threats and threat actions relevant to system security controls. Threat actions addressed by system security controls include the following:

- Invoked Malware—Malicious software invoked by an employee can have disastrous consequences for the organization's systems. System security controls such as system hardening can limit or eliminate the impact.

- Socially Engineered—Successful social engineering attacks can lead to system breaches but system security controls such as operating procedures may limit or avoid such incidents.
- Hacked—If an employee is hacked the system and its data may be severely impacted. System security controls such as vulnerability scanning, and coding standards may limit the frequency of successful hacks.
- Abused Trust—When employees and senior members of the organization abuse the trust given to them, their actions can lead to system and data breaches. The system security controls such as security and code review can address the impact of these threat actions.
- Erred—Employee errors such as misconfiguration and using insecure library routines in production code can result in major losses to the organization and its assets. System security activities such as scheduled patches and penetration testing can address these threat actions.

6.1.5.2 Organizational Structure Safeguards

Given the wide array of potential threat actions that could be enacted organizations should implement an adequate set of security controls (e.g., safeguards) to address the threat actions applicable to the system security. Table 6.5 lists an example set of safeguards that an organization may employ to counter these threat and threat actions. These safeguards are discussed within the safeguard classes of system controls, application security, change management, and third-party access.

6.1.5.2.1 System Controls

The organization's information systems can be further protected from rogue applications and unauthorized users through a set of system controls. These controls include policy, procedures, and security activities that discover, reduce, and avoid vulnerabilities within the organization's information systems:

- Operating Procedures—The system operating procedures establish the responsibilities of the system operations staff. These responsibilities include protecting of diagnostic ports, controlling changes to the system, maintaining operator logs, and creating emergency procedures.
- Server Hardening—System operators shall ensure that all systems have the latest approved patches, unused services are disabled, unused software is deleted, and any other known vulnerabilities of the system are addressed. This process is referred to as *server hardening*.
- Vulnerability Scanning—Since the systems operations personnel are responsible for hardening the systems, they should also perform a check of their work by running vulnerability scanners against the hardened machines.
- Penetration Testing—Performing security testing of applications can also be called *penetration testing*. This activity involves the rigorous analysis of the application and an ad hoc attempt to subvert the security controls of the application. Penetration testing should not be confused with vulnerability scanning, which is simply a search for obvious flaws. Penetration testing goes further by examining the design of the system, its interfaces, and its environment. Just like secure code review, organizations with experienced, skilled, and independent staff could perform a security code review in-house, but most penetration testing activities are performed by outside firms.
- Scheduled and Emergency Patches—The systems operations personnel are expected to test and apply all scheduled patches that have gone through the normal approval process. Additionally, the systems operations personnel shall apply all emergency patches; these patches may have been approved on an emergency basis by someone who normally has less authority than the identified approver in the normal process.
- Remote Maintenance—Systems operations personnel are not always trained or cleared to work on all systems and software that are a part of the organization's information systems. In the cases where systems or software is worked on by other personnel, this maintenance is sometimes performed remotely. The organization should ensure that this remote connection

does not significantly degrade the security of its systems. Several remote maintenance safe-guards and things to look for are listed below:

- Virtual Private Network (VPN) Protection—The VPN or other mechanism proving the gateway for remote access should have access controls such as two-factor authentication. Additionally, the VPN should have logging and monitoring of its functions.
- Access Controls—The passwords or other authentication used to gain access remotely should be issued to a single person within the maintenance company's staff. It is important to be able to trace audit events back to a single individual instead of a company. These authentication attributes should follow good security practices, for example, with strong passwords that are changed every 90 days.
- Remote Access—Many organizations find the need for their systems operations personnel or regular users to gain access remotely. Provided the organization implements appropriate safeguards, this practice should not lessen the security protections on the organization's assets. Here are a few additional safeguards that may be implemented for employee remote access:
  - Remote Access Policy—Employees must be informed of the responsibilities and security safeguards that accompany remote access. This can be added as a rider to an acceptable-use policy.
  - Strong Authentication—Users' authentication credentials should be based on at least two factors, for example, a password and a token device.
  - Use of Home Computers—Organizations must determine if employees shall be allowed to access the network using home computers. This is a dangerous practice, as VPN and other clients must reside on the system to gain access, and other family members share the same computer.
- Security Review and Approval—The systems operations personnel play an important role in implementing security controls for the information systems. However, the organization must implement policies and procedures that ensure that changes to the security-relevant aspects of the system are reviewed and approved by others. This increases oversight and reduces the chance of abuse of trust and error.

6.1.5.2.2 Application Security

Application security remains an important aspect of locking down the protections necessary to secure an organization's critical systems and sensitive data. Web applications in particular that are exposed to the Internet are a target of cybercriminals as their interfaces are available across the Web. Even though Web applications sit behind a firewall and perhaps even behind hardened operating systems, they are still vulnerable. This is because firewalls and hardened operating systems are not designed to restrict all access to Web applications (e.g., port 80 HTTP and port 443 HTTPS). Furthermore, exposed Web applications are likely to have errors. It has been estimated that close to 90% of Web applications contain major security holes. Below are a few security controls that may be employed to reduce the risk in applications:

- Architectural Design—The planning of how information security principles such as authentication and access control will be designed into a system is referred to as security architecture. This is not implementation (specific controls and coding) but a strategic approach to determining what the system will need to accomplish for the system to be secure. Examples of secure architectural design include a documented software development life cycle that integrates security activities, the use of threat modeling throughout development, documenting application interfaces and boundaries, and creating and abiding by a set of secure coding practices.
- Authentication—Ensuring the application has a strong method for the confirmation of authentic communication with people and devices is essential to implementing security policies

based on identification. This includes passwords and tokens, but also password strength, notifications of account usage, and secure and sound authenticator establishment and reset procedures.

- Access Controls and Data Protection—Once an identity is established and authenticated, a secure application shall ensure appropriate authorization rules are enforced to allow only that access that is explicitly permitted. Access and data protection controls include the implementation of least privilege and NTK, ensuring the reference monitor concept is appropriately enacted, and protecting data objects to ensure they are accessed only through appropriate transactions that enforce authorized access control.
- Input Validation—Web applications accept input from users and execute instructions based, in part on the value of that input. Hacking techniques such as injection and buffer overflow, and parameter manipulation take advantage of any web application program that does not effectively validate this input to ensure that the executed instruction behaves in the way it was intended. Techniques for validating input include sanitization, sandboxing, injection prevention, and deserialization prevention.
- Cryptographic Standards—Many elements of application security are reliant upon correct and sufficiently strong implementation of encryption routines. Application developers should follow established guidelines for the use of strong and secure algorithms, appropriate selection of key values, proper initialization, random value selection, and secure key management.
- Error Handling—Application developed within the organization shall include appropriate error handling and creation of logs. Logs created within the applications need to contain the necessary elements to allow for detailed investigations and need to be protected from unauthorized viewing.
- Configuration—The development of applications needs to include provisions for the secure configuration of the executable code and environment in which it executes. This includes the build environment, underlying system level hardening, and secure default configuration settings.
- Code Review—Application code review is one approach to ensure that applications are devoid of inherent vulnerabilities. Code review is typically an expensive alternative but is perhaps the best way to ensure a rigorous analysis of the security capabilities of the code. Code review can be assisted by the use of software tools, but it is still a semimanual activity. Organizations with experienced, skilled, and independent staff could perform a security code review in-house, but many security code reviews are performed by outside firms.

6.1.5.2.3 Configuration Management

An information system infrastructure is a complex and evolving system. Changes to the system affect its ability to effectively enforce the security policies and therefore protect the organization's assets. The process of managing the changes to the system and its components is referred to as *configuration management*. More specifically, configuration management is the process of identifying CIs, controlling their storage, controlling change to CIs, and reporting on their status.

- Configuration Items—CIs are unique work products that are individually controlled, tracked, and reported on.
- CI Protection—CIs must be protected from unauthorized changes. Without protection of the CIs, a configuration management system cannot function.
- Change Control—There must exist a process by which changes to CIs are reviewed, approved, and controlled.
- Status Reporting—Configuration management systems must be able to report the status of any CI and its history of changes. Moreover, the reporting feature must be capable of generating a version of the system based on the correct version of each of the CIs.

6.1.5.2.4   Third-Party Access

Despite any efforts the organization makes to secure its infrastructure, vulnerabilities can be introduced to the system through third-party access to the infrastructure or sensitive data. The organization must take precautions to ensure that the security posture of the system is equally protected by those given access outside of the organization itself. The organization should implement a strong vendor security risk management program. These third-party risk programs should be formalized with a definition of the program scope and roles and responsibilities of those entrusted to implement the program. Basic elements of a third-party risk program include:

- Vendor Inventory—The organization should identify a reasonable process to ensure that all vendors with access to sensitive data or critical systems are known. Sometimes referred to as a "choke point" a process such as procurement is typically a reasonable process element to tie in vendor inventory to ensure all vendors are known.
- Vendor Assessment—The vendors can be categorized according to risk levels based on their access, the goods or services provided, or the potential exposure they represent.
- Vendor Risk Reduction—The organization can reduce their risk exposure to vendors with pre-engagement activities such as reference checks, financial stability analysis, liability insurance requirements, and establishing contractual obligations. Prior to granting access or disclosing sensitive information to a vendor, the organization should legally bind the third party to provide adequate measures to safeguard the system and sensitive information. The vendor access contract should also contain a clause that allows the organization to review the security controls of the third party to ensure compliance with the contract and minimum-security requirements.
- Security Control Assessments—Once a vendor has been selected (but not yet contracted) the vendor program administrator can ensure that a security control assessment is performed on the vendor to measure their adherence to established minimum security control standards, based on the vendor risk categorization. Minimum control standards are the minimum set of security controls the vendor must implement to ensure the security of the system.
- Monitoring and Performance Measurements—The vendor risk program administrator also ensures that the vendors compliance with the vendor risk program is continuously monitored through service level agreement (SLA) reviews, periodic reassessments, adherence to notification requirements, and, if necessary, corrective actions to bring the vendor back into compliance.

6.2   THE RIIOT METHOD: ADMINISTRATIVE DATA GATHERING

As introduced in Chapter 5, the RIIOT method of data gathering can be applied to any security risk assessment technique and helps to ensure a more complete and well-managed data gathering process. The RIIOT method is applied to any area of security controls by reasoning about the most appropriate approach for gathering data on each security control under review. Applying the RIIOT method to the administrative area shows that a majority of the data gathering techniques to be applied to administrative security controls will be document review and key personnel interviews.

6.2.1   Determining Appropriate RIIOT Approaches for Administrative Controls

Recall from Chapter 5 that the RIIOT method of data gathering is used to assist the data gathering process by organizing the data gathering approaches (e.g., Review documents, Interview key staff, Inspect controls, Observe behavior, and Test controls) for the targeted security controls, selecting the approaches for each control, and then assigning the data gathering process among team members, and tracking their progress.

The number of methods and the selection of specific the methods to be used for data gathering will be based on the level of rigor specified in the security risk assessment project plan, the skills of the team members, and the approach determined by the security risk assessment team lead. These descriptions of data gathering activities against each of the listed security controls are intended to provide a general approach to be used by security risk assessment teams, and not specific answers to questions that may arise during a security risk assessment.

Table 6.6 provides a map to all of the possible RIIOT data gathering approaches that could be used to gather data on all of the administrative controls discussed in Section 6.1. The sections below

TABLE 6.6
RIIOT Method of Data Gathering for Administrative Controls

Controls	Review Documents	Interview Key Personnel	Inspect Controls	Observe Behavior	Test Controls
Application	*	*			
Job requirements	*	*			
Reference checks	*	*			
Employment checks	*	*			
Accuracy checks	*	*			
Credit checks	*	*			
Clearance procedures	*	*			
Employment policies	*	*			
Training and education	*	*		*	
Job description	*	*			
Job requirements	*	*			
Annual reviews	*	*			
Acceptable-use policy	*	*		*	
Monitoring	*	*		*	
Two-person control		*			
Job rotation	*	*			
Clearance refresh	*	*			
Ethics training	*	*		*	
Sanctions policy	*	*			
Separation of duty	*	*		*	
Termination procedures	*	*			
NDA, NCC	*	*			
Out-briefing	*	*			
Risk management	*	*			
Understand responsibilities	*	*		*	

(Continued)

TABLE 6.6 *(Continued)*

Controls	Review Documents	Interview Key Personnel	Inspect Controls	Observe Behavior	Test Controls
Business impact analysis	*	*			
Disaster recovery plan	*	*			
Crisis management	*	*			
Occupant Emergency Plan	*	*		*	
DRP testing and maintenance	*	*			
Data backup	*	*			*
Incident response plan and procedures	*	*		*	
Incident response training	*	*		*	
Availability of experts	*	*			
Operating procedures	*	*			
Server hardening	*	*			
Vulnerability scanning	*	*			
Scheduled and emergency patches	*	*			
Remote maintenance	*	*			
Remote access	*	*			
Security review/ approval	*	*			
Architectural Design	*	*			
Authentication	*	*			*
Access control and Data protection	*	*			*
Input validation	*	*			*
Cryptography standards	*	*			*
Error handling & Logging	*	*			*

(Continued)

TABLE 6.6 *(Continued)*

Controls	Review Documents	Interview Key Personnel	Inspect Controls	Observe Behavior	Test Controls
Governance and Oversight	*	*		*	
Assign duties	*	*			
Authority, Visibility	*	*		*	
Security team budget	*	*			
Risk analysis	*	*			
Review of security activities	*	*			
Security operations policies	*	*			
Maintenance policies	*	*		*	
Dual control	*	*			
Least privilege	*	*		*	
Monitoring	*	*			
Third-party review	*	*			
Security risk assessment	*	*			
Security awareness	*	*			
Job training	*	*		*	
Policy and procedures	*	*		*	
Double key data entry	*	*		*	
Two-person control	*	*		*	
Criticality analysis	*	*			
Information labeling	*	*	*	*	*
Review of access controls	*	*			*
Media destruction	*	*		*	*
Account creation procedures	*	*		*	*
Account termination procedures	*	*			*
Need-To-Know	*	*			*
Asset inventory	*	*	*		
Asset tracking	*	*	*		
Business continuity strategy	*	*			

(Continued)

TABLE 6.6   *(Continued)*

Controls	Review Documents	Interview Key Personnel	Inspect Controls	Observe Behavior	Test Controls
Configuration	*	*			*
Code review	*	*			
Penetration testing	*	*			
Configuration items	*				
CI protection	*				
Change control	*	*			
Status reporting	*				
Vendor inventory	*	*			
Vendor assessment	*	*		*	
Vendor risk reduction	*	*			
Vendor security control assessment	*	*			
Monitoring and performance measurements	*	*			*

Note: The application of the RIIOT method to administrative controls indicates that data gathering in this area will focus mainly on document review and personnel interviews.

describe each of these approaches and provide a description of how a security risk assessment team member may go about collecting that data.

6.2.2   REVIEW DOCUMENTS REGARDING ADMINISTRATIVE CONTROLS

As demonstrated in Table 6.6, gathering data on nearly every administrative security control involves the review of documents. The bulk of the document review will be a review of policies and procedures. The remaining document reviews will include a review of coding standards, information security policies, security awareness training, and various security work products.

6.2.2.1   Documents to Review

Using the RIIOT document review technique, the security risk assessment team should determine the set of documents to be reviewed. In many cases, the team will be able to review all documents obtained through information requests. In other cases, because of time or budget constraints, the team will need to narrow the evidence reviewed to determine the strength of administrative security controls (see Table 6.7).

6.2.2.2   Review Documents for Clarity, Consistency, and Completeness

All documents reviewed should be reviewed based on clarity, consistency, and completeness:

- Clarity—Determination of clarity depends on the intended audience. If the intended audience is considered technical, then the level of technical content within the document would be expected to be higher than in a document intended for a more general audience.

TABLE 6.7

Administrative Documents to Review

Document Type	Sample Titles	Expected Elements Table
General	• General Expected Elements • Senior Management Statement of Commitment	• Table 6.8 • Table 6.9
Policies	• Acceptable Use of Assets Policy • Access Control Policy • Authentication and Account Management Policy • Backup and Restoration Policy • Clean Desk Policy • Cryptographic Control Policy • Data Classification, Handling, and Retention Policy • Media Protection Policy • Mobile Device Policy • Physical Security/Environmental Controls Policy • Privacy Program Policy • Privacy—Web Privacy Notice • Systems and Communications Security Policy	• Table 6.10 • Table 6.11 • Table 6.12 • Table 6.13 • Table 6.14 • Table 6.15 • Table 6.16 • Table 6.17 • Table 6.18 • Table 6.19 • Table 6.20 • Table 6.21 • Table 6.22
Plans, Processes and Procedures	• Business Contingency Plan • Change Control Procedures • Disaster Recovery Plan • Incident Response Plan • Information Security Program Procedures • Other Operational Procedures • Security Awareness Program and Procedures • Software Development Life Cycle Process • Termination Procedures • Vendor Risk Security Management Program	• Table 6.24 • Table 6.25 • Table 6.26 • Table 6.27 • Table 6.28 • Table 6.29 • Table 6.31 • Table 6.31 • Table 6.33 • Table 6.34
Form & Process Documents	• Disposal of equipment form • Hardening procedures/guidelines • New account activation form • Operations manual • Security checklists	Review documents for consistency with policy or procedures that refer to them.
Contracts	• Service-level agreements • Business associate agreements	
Audits and Assessments	• Business Continuity/Disaster Recovery Test • Security audit or assessment • Penetration Test Results • Vulnerability Scan Results	Review these documents for indications of vulnerabilities.

Note: The security risk assessment should attempt to obtain and review as many relevant administrative documents as possible within the data gathering stage of the security risk assessment. This table provides a sample list of documents to request, but it is by no means exhaustive.

- Consistency—A measurement of the consistency of the documents will be determined once all documents have been reviewed. If more than one document covers a specific area or control and provides conflicting guidance or policy, then those policies can be said to be inconsistent.
- Completeness—Lastly, completeness will be determined based on the security risk assessment team's expectations for a given document. The expectations, or expected elements, could be dictated from a regulation or they could be based on the team's experience.

TABLE 6.8
General Security Policy Expected Elements

General Security Policy

The assessor should review all security policies provided as a set to determine the overall effectiveness of the security policy program.

Policy Area	Expected Elements	Discussion
Organized	• Organized in a logical manner to promote their use and distribution	Organization can take many forms such as online searchable policies, or well titled and indexed. In the end either the policy's organization promotes usability (e.g., employees know how to find and utilize policy elements) or not.
Documented	• Documented and revised as appropriate	Appropriate documentation can be assessed based on a perceived need of level of detail. The auditor's rule of thumb is "if it's not documented, it's not done," so if there are rules that should be enforced or procedures that should be followed, it should be documented.
Approved	• Appropriate authority has approved policies	Each policy document should have some indication of approval from the appropriate authority (e.g., a signature or name and date of approval).
Distributed	• Policies are made accessible to appropriate personnel	Accessibility of policies can be as simple as documented and placed in appropriate areas (e.g., offices, visitor control) or can be more sophisticated such as a document management system. It is important that appropriate staff members can gain access when needed and that they are aware or where to find these policies.

Note: All security policies are expected to be organized, documented, approved, and distributed to the audience intended.

6.2.2.3   Review Documents for Expected Elements

As discussed in the previous section, it is important to create a checklist or table of expected elements for each document or policy area. Expected elements are simply a listing of all the things a reasonable security engineer would expect to find in a complete document. For example, a complete account-creation approval form would be expected to have the following elements:

- name of requester,
- name of user,
- approval,
- username to be used,
- date of request,
- group access, and
- account privileges.

The expected elements should be used as a guideline for the assessor to ensure the document review process is complete. Missing elements are not necessarily something that would need to be remedied. The assessor should consider if each element is actually "expected" in the assessed organization's environment given their understanding of the threat environment for that organization. The expected elements for all of the documents listed in Table 6.7 are provided in Tables 6.8 to 6.34. An assessor may use these tables to guide their review of the documents. Note that all elements are not "required" but "expected." At this stage, data gathering, the assessor is collecting data on the access control policy to better enable the later stage of data analysis in determining the effectiveness of the control.

TABLE 6.9

Senior Management Statement Expected Elements

Senior Management Statement

A senior management statement (or statement of commitment) is an acknowledgment from senior management that security and privacy are business objectives within the organization. This may take the form of a memorandum, a separate policy, or an introductory paragraph that is present in all security and privacy policies.

Policy Area	Expected Elements	Discussion
Senior Management Statement	• Acknowledgment of importance	An acknowledgment of importance typically discusses the threat environment of the organization, the regulations and customer requirements that direct business objectives, and the importance of security controls within the organization.
	• Statement of support	A statement of support addresses the concern that security issues can be at odds with other business objectives. This statement commits to ensuring security controls are enabled to provide the necessary protections to organizational sensitive data and critical systems.
	• Commitment of authorization and funding	This statement will typically specify the security program office or chief information security officer and include a general commitment to provide appropriate resources to address the security needs of the organization.

Note: The senior management of the organization is expected to document their understanding and support for the security function within the organization.

In order to assist those performing security risk assessments, the set of expected element tables is listed in Table 6.7. These tables are an illustration of how to construct and use lists of expected items in security documents. However, the team must understand that not all documents are required for all environments, not all expected elements are necessary for all security controls, and not all documents provided will be as neatly titled as the documents discussed here.

6.2.2.3.1 Reviewing Information Security Policies

In general, the set of information security policies should be well organized, documented, approved by management, and distributed to the appropriate staff. The organization of the security policy set can take many forms. It is suggested that the policies be organized by audience first and subject matter second. For example, all of the policies regarding expected behavior of employees can go into a single manual because it is intended for the same audience. The single manual should be well organized to promote readability and usability (see Table 6.8).

Information security policies will generally contain statements regarding the required controls to be in place to protect the organization's systems, data, and protected areas. These documents should be clear in indicating what is required. For each of the information security policies reviewed the assessor may use Tables 6.9 through 6.22 for guidance as to the expected elements.

6.2.2.3.1.1 Senior Management Statement

All organizations should have a high-level statement of policy that acknowledges the importance of computing resources and organizational assets, provides support for the information security program within the organization, and commits management to authorize and ensure the implementation of an effective security program. This may seem like window dressing to some, but it provides the basis for all conversations regarding the implementation of information security controls. If an organization has a problem producing such a document, this may be indicative of much larger problems (see Table 6.9).

TABLE 6.10

Acceptable Use of Assets Policy Expected Elements

Acceptable Use of Assets Policy

An acceptable use policy is a statement of management intent as to how organizational assets are to be used, restrictions on their use, and minimum-security controls to protect these assets and systems.

Policy Area	Expected Elements	Discussion
Assigned Responsibility	• Responsibility for policy completion	Clear assignment of responsibility to a role or named person to ensure that all staff members and anyone with access to sensitive data, systems, or locations reviews and acknowledges their understanding and agreement to this policy prior to being granted access.
	• Responsibility to keep records.	Clear assignment of responsibility to a role or named person to keep records of acknowledgments and current and former versions of the policy.
Expected Behaviors	• Safe Computing Practices	List and description of expected security practices to be followed when using organizational assets such as • Use caution when opening attachments • Keep passwords secure • Keep desk and workstation secure • Challenge unauthorized personnel • Report security or privacy violations • Wear issued badges
	• Protection of Sensitive Data	Requirement to protect sensitive information in accordance with stated policies and procedures.
	• Marking of Sensitive Data	Requirement to mark sensitive information in accordance with stated policies and procedures.
	• Encryption of Sensitive Data	Requirement to encrypt sensitive information in accordance with stated policies and procedures.
	• Storage of Sensitive Data	Requirement to store sensitive information in accordance with stated policies and procedures.
	• Transmission of Sensitive Data	Requirement to transmit sensitive information in accordance with stated policies and procedures.

Prohibited Behaviors	List and description of prohibited practices to be avoided when using organizational assets such as
	• Computer tampering
	• Use of unauthorized equipment
	• Use of unauthorized software
	• Unauthorized use of software or services
	• Introduction of malware
	• System disruption
	• Circumvention of security controls
	• Using false identity
	• Mining cryptocurrency
• Unlawful Material	Description of inappropriate or unlawful material such as pornography or other offensive intimidating, hostile, or otherwise illegal material. The organization should utilize a legal or industry definitions where appropriate. In either case this section should have legal review.
• Unauthorized Use of Messaging	List and description of prohibited electronic messaging such as
	• Spam, Chain Letters
	• Unprofessional communications
	• Altered message content
	• False identity, Masked identity
	• Auto-forward to external accounts
	• Non-organizational e-mail account
	• Unencrypted sensitive data
	• Misrepresentation of organization
• Personal Use	Description of limitations of personal use of organizational resources.
• Violation of Intellectual Property Laws	Statement of prohibition of any violation of intellectual property laws.
• Unauthorized Access	Statement of prohibition of unauthorized access to sensitive information. Reference any applicable laws and regulations.
• Unauthorized Release	Statement of prohibition of unauthorized release of sensitive information. Reference any applicable laws and regulations.

(continued)

TABLE 6.10 (Continued)

Policy Area	Expected Elements	Discussion
Notifications	• User Responsibility	Statement of acknowledgment that the user understands their responsibility to abide by this policy.
	• Assets	Statement of ownership of assets such as "all system assets remain the sole property of the organization. Any data or intellectual property created by the user, including voicemail and electronic messages, shall remain the organization's property and shall not be removed, copied or shared except as part of the normal job responsibilities."
	• Monitoring	Statement acknowledging that the user's actions may be monitored and that the organization has the right to monitor activities that occur on its systems.
	• Content Blocking	Statement of any full or partial blocking of Internet content. The organization may block some content and fail to block all inappropriate content.
	• Record Retention	Statement of the records retention policies apply to the organization's systems and assets. There should be a reference to the full records retention policy/schedule.
	• No Expectation of Privacy	Statement that the user has no expectation of privacy on the system for any data created, stored, sent, or received. Comply with applicable laws and regulations.
Acknowledgment	• User Acknowledgment	An acknowledgment in the form of a signature or digital signature.

Not only is it essential to cover all policy elements, but the employee must sign and date the policy (see Table 6.10).

TABLE 6.11
Access Control Policy Expected Elements

Access Control Policy
An access control policy is a statement of management intent as to the correct use and management of logical access controls for the protection of organizational information systems and assets.

Policy Area	Expected Elements	Discussion
Access Enforcement	• Access Enforcement	Statement that the organizational information systems enforce logical access control based on a control policy (e.g., identity-based, role-based).
	• Assigned Responsibility	Clear assignment of responsibility to a role or named person for monitoring and controlling access to sensitive data.
	• Operational Procedures	Statement indicating that operational procedures are to be established, implemented, and maintained for the restriction of access to sensitive data.
Firewall Access Controls	• Information Flow Enforcement	Statement indicating only approved information flows shall be allowed between information system components and with external connections.
	• Perimeter Firewalls for Wireless Networks	Statement requiring perimeter firewall be installed and maintained between any wireless network and the organization's information system. These firewalls shall be configured to protect organizational information systems and to permit only authorized traffic between the wireless environment into the organizational information systems.
	• Personal Firewalls	Statement requiring personal firewall (hardware or software) on any portable computing devices that connect to the Internet when outside the controlled environment.
Privileged Account Restrictions	• Least Privilege	Statement requiring least privilege necessary for users and processes acting on behalf of users. (This is especially important with privileged accounts.)
	• Security Functions Access	Statement restricting access rights to specific security functions (e.g., account creation, audit log deletion).
	• Privilege Account Usage	Statement regarding the restriction of using a privileged account for non-privileged actions (e.g., checking e-mail, Internet access).
Access Monitoring and Auditing	• Audit of Privileged Functions	Statement requiring the monitoring and review of privileged actions.
	• Audit of Failed Access	Statement requiring the logging of failed access attempts.
	• Monitor Remote Access	Statement requiring the monitoring of remote access methods including failed remote access, false logins, and denial of service attacks.
System Use Notification	• Access Banner	Requirement and banner text that includes the following: • Notification of information system ownership • Users will be monitored; access is consent • Unauthorized use is prohibited Banner shall remain in place until the user takes an explicit action to acknowledge access conditions.
Session Controls	• Session Lock	Statement requiring session lock upon either user request or inactivity of a certain amount of time.

(Continued)

TABLE 6.11 *(Continued)*

Policy Area	Expected Elements	Discussion
Wireless Access / Mobile Device	• Wireless Authorization	Statement specifying requirements for authorizing wireless access connections to organizational information systems.
	• Wireless Encryption	Statement specifying minimum encryption requirements for wireless access (including encryption algorithms and strength requirements).
	• Mobile Device Requirements	Statement specifying minimum requirements for mobile devices (e.g., full disk encryption, report lost equipment).

TABLE 6.12
Authentication and Account Management Expected Elements

Authentication and Account Management Policy

An authentication and account management policy covers the baseline controls for the administration of information system accounts.

Policy Area	Expected Elements	Discussion
Account Types	• Group and Role-based Accounts	A complete list of group and role-based accounts (e.g., customer service representative, accounting, database administrator) within the organization's information systems and applications. This should include the conditions for group or role membership.
	• Account Specification	For each of the above account types, a description (or list) of access authorizations, privileges or other attributes associated with the account.
	• Privileged Accounts	Statement restricting assignment of privileged accounts to administrative roles.
	• Separation of Duties	If applicable, a list of sensitive transactions requiring separation of duty and an approach for. Implementing. For example, a separations of duty matrix.
Account Management	• Assign Account Managers	Clear assignment of responsibility to a role or named person for each organizational information system and application in which accounts are created.
	• Account Approval	Statement requiring documented approval for each account issued to a user.
	• Access Authorization	Statement restricting access authorization to users with a legitimate need for such access to the system. This restriction shall include the principle of deny-all in its implementation.
	• Database Access	Statement restricting direct database access to database administrators only.
Account Review	• User Rights Review	Statement requiring periodic review of accounts and associated privileges, Review shall be conducted by the information system or application owner.
Account Creation, Deletion, and Removal	• Account Creation	Statement requiring a process for the creation of user accounts.
	• Account Removal—Separated Users	Statement requiring a process for the deletion of user accounts for users separated from employment or transferred within a defined timeframe (24 hours maximum).
	• Account Removal—Temporary Accounts	Statement requiring a process for the removal of temporary or emergency user accounts.
	• Account Disable – Inactive Accounts	Statement requiring a process for the automatic disablement of inactive user accounts. Exceptions may apply but should be documented and approved.

TABLE 6.13
Backup and Restoration Policy Expected Elements

Backup and Restoration Policy

The backup and restoration policy covers the process of defining and ensuring the backup and restoration requirements for an organization.

Policy Area	Expected Elements	Discussion
Backup	• Responsibility for Backups & Restorations	Clear assignment of responsibility to a role or named person to ensure backups, restorations, and restoration testing are performed appropriately.
	• User-level Backup	Statement requiring the execution of user-level backups. This statement should include: • Frequency and method of backups • A list of critical systems and applications requiring backups.
	• System and Application-level Backup	Statement requiring the execution of system and application-level backups. • Frequency and method of backups should be included in this statement.
Restoration	• Restoration Capability	Statement requiring the recovery and reconstitution capabilities to a known state after file loss, disruption, or compromise.
	• Transaction Recovery	Statement requiring the ability to perform transaction recovery for any system that is transaction-based.
	• Restoration Testing	Statement requiring the testing of backup restoration capabilities. Frequency of testing should be included in this statement (maximum annually).

TABLE 6.14
Clean Desk Policy Expected Elements

Clean Desk Policy

A clean desk policy ensures that the work environment appropriately protects sensitive data and access to information systems from unauthorized access.

Policy Area	Expected Elements	Discussion
Clean Desk Policy	• Applicability	A section describing the work environments in which the clean desk policy applies.
	• Sensitive Data Restrictions	A section describing the requirements for protecting sensitive data. This section should include the following: • Period of time a desk may be left unattended (if any) • Protection measures for sensitive data (e.g., turn over and lock in cabinet)
	• Visitor Implications	A section describing additional controls in place when visitors (who are not authorized to view sensitive data) are present in the work environment. This may include escorts, indication lights, and additional protection measures (e.g., all sensitive data must be turned over).
	• Information System Restrictions	A section describing the requirements for protecting sensitive information systems. This section should include the following: • Period of time a system may be left unattended (if any) • Protection measures for sensitive information systems (e.g., screen lock, logout)

(Continued)

TABLE 6.14   *(Continued)*

Policy Area	Expected Elements	Discussion
	• Clean Desk Reviews	A section describing the process by which desks are reviewed for compliance with the clean desk policy. This process should cover the following elements: • Frequency • Steps involved in review • Actions involved when a non-compliant desk is found (including protection of data or systems) • Sanctions applied to non-compliant desk owners

TABLE 6.15

Cryptographic Control Policy Expected Elements

Cryptographic Control Policy

The cryptographic control policy (or cryptographic standard) covers the use of cryptography and establishes approved methodologies and use within the organization.

Policy Area	Expected Elements	Discussion
Cryptographic Standards	• Required Use	Statement indicating sensitive data storage, transmissions, and other uses where cryptographic controls are required.
	• Approved Algorithms	Description or list of approved algorithms. Description should include: • Approved algorithms • Prohibition of disallowed or deprecated algorithms • Minimum key length (per cryptographic algorithm type: symmetric, asymmetric, hash) • Exception process
	• Certificates and Keys	Requirements for cryptographic certificates and keys. These requirements should address the following: • Prohibited use of wildcard • Certificate signing process • Use of Public Key Infrastructure • Prohibition or restricted use of self-signed certificates • Approved trusted signing authorities • Minimum certificate signing algorithm strength • Certificate lifetime
	• Key Management	Requirements for key management. These requirements should address the following: • Approved hardware apparatus protection levels (according to the Federal Information Processing Standard (FIPS) 140-2) • Code signing • Database key access • Decryption services • Certificate authority private key protections • Minimum passphrase length • Key protection requirements

TABLE 6.16

Data Classification, Handling and Retention Policy Expected Elements

Data Classification, Handling and Retention Policy

The data classification policy provides a framework for the protection of data that is created, stored, processed, or transmitted within the organization's information systems.

Policy Area	Expected Elements	Discussion
Data Classification Controls	• Roles and Responsibilities	Clear assignment of responsibility to a role or named person for data ownership duties to ensure the appropriate marking and protection of sensitive data.
	• Classification Categories	Description or list categories of data classification levels. Each level should have the following: • a specified name (e.g., "Confidential"), • description, • examples, and • associated laws and regulations requiring the protection of this class of data
	• Protection Measures	Description of protection measures required for each classification category. Description should include: • Collection • Handling including requirements for hand carry, accounting, guardian, out-of-sight, conversations, and movement. • Transmission including requirements for encryption and encryption strength (see cryptographic control policy) • Processing – approved processing methods and devices • Media protection (see media protection policy)

TABLE 6.17

Media Protection Policy Expected Elements

Media Protection Policy

The media protection policy specifies the necessary controls to ensure the secure storage, transport, and destruction of sensitive information.

Policy Area	Expected Elements	Discussion
Media Protection Processes	• Roles and Responsibilities	• Description of roles and responsibilities within the media protection activities. • Clear assignment of responsibility to a named person for role, including accurate and up-to-date contact information.
	• Secure Delivery	Statement that requires specific controls when removable media with sensitive information is delivered. Controls may include a list of trusted delivery organizations, use of package tracking, and confirmation that package arrived in the hands of an authorized individual.
	• Media Inventories	Statement that requires an inventory of media containing sensitive data. Requirement should include frequency of inventories.
	• Media Sanitization	List of sanitization techniques for different forms of media. The document should cover all forms of media used within the organization (e.g., smart phones, Solid State Drives (SSD), Flash memory).

(Continued)

TABLE 6.17   *(Continued)*

Policy Area	Expected Elements	Discussion
	• Media Transport	Statement that requires specific controls for the protection of removable media with sensitive data when outside of controlled areas. Controls may include keeping removable media with you at all times, encryption, and marking.
Media Protections	• Media Access	Statement that requires access controls on removable media that contains sensitive information.
	• Media Marking	Statement that requires specific marking on removable media that contains sensitive information.
	• Media Storage	Statement that restricts physical storage of media storage to specified containers or controlled areas.
	• Media Use	Statement that specifies any restrictions on use of removable media such as prohibition of flash drives or prohibition of card holder data.

TABLE 6.18
Mobile Device Policy Expected Elements

Mobile Device Policy

The mobile device policy establishes a set of minimum controls necessary to secure the use of mobile device (e.g., laptops, smart phones).

Policy Area	Expected Elements	Discussion
Mobile Device Management	• Mobile Device Management	The organization should have a mobile device management program in place to manage the minimum controls for mobile devices with access to the organization's information systems and assets.
	• Inventory	The organization should have the ability to establish and maintain an inventory of mobile devices with access to the organization's information systems and assets.
	• Full Device Encryption	Mobile devices should implement full device encryption for the protection of sensitive information and applications.
	• Mobile device purge	The organization should have a process and permission to remotely wipe a mobile device if it is reported missing or stolen.
	• Authentication	Mobile devices should require authentication to access.
	• Report lost or stolen	Mobile device owners should be required to report lost or stolen devices immediately.

6.2.2.3.1.2   Acceptable-Use Policy

The acceptable-use policy covers the use of the Internet, network, e-mail, and software. This document provides the basis for the following security controls:

- Informing users of their security responsibility
- Informing users of the organization's right to monitor
- Informing users of prohibited activities and items
- Informing users of prohibited behavior and expected behavior

TABLE 6.19

Physical Security/Environmental Controls Policy Expected Elements

Physical Security/Environmental Controls Policy

The physical security protections policy ensures the physical protection of organizational assets through the enforcement of a minimum set of physical security controls.

Policy Area	Expected Elements	Discussion
Physical Security Plan	• Roles and Responsibilities	• Description of roles and responsibilities within the information security program. • Clear assignment of responsibility to a named person for role, including accurate and up-to-date contact information
	• Physical Security Plan	The organization should have a documented physical security plan that specifies the requirements and how they are set for the following areas: • Physical access control (entry and exits) • Physical control on network devices and system components • Quarterly key inventory • Intrusion alarms and response • Appropriate power systems and protections (e.g., Emergency power off) • Emergency lighting • Fire protection and suppression • Water damage protection • Temperature and humidity controls
Physical Control Operating Procedures	• Physical Access Authorization	The organization should enforce physical access into sensitive areas through the following documented activities: • Define sensitive areas • Document physical access request and approval process • Maintain a list of authorized individuals • Issue credentials based on access list • Review list quarterly to ensure inappropriate access have been removed • Remove access when individuals are separated or transferred
	• Monitoring Access	The organization should monitor access to organizational areas through the following activitiesmonitor physical access to detect and response to physical security incidents • Review video logs on a weekly basis and upon occurrence of a physical security incident • Store video logs for at least 90 days and have them available for review
	• Visitor Control Records	The organization should implement visitor control log controls through the following activities: • Maintain visitor access records, including name, firm represented, and onsite personnel visited • Review visitor access records monthly • Maintain visitor logs for 3 months.

6.2.2.3.1.3 Access Control Policy

The access control policy defines the correct use and management of logical access controls for the protection of organizational information systems and assets. The expected elements of an access control policy are listed in Table 6.11 to guide the assessors review of the document.

6.2.2.3.1.4 Authentication and Account Management Policy

The authentication and account management policy covers the baseline controls for the administration of information system accounts. The expected elements of an Access Control Policy are listed in Table 6.12 to guide the assessors review of the document.

TABLE 6.20

Privacy Program Policy Expected Elements

Privacy Program Policy

A privacy policy is a statement of the minimum controls in place to protection the privacy of sensitive data within the organization and organizational systems.

Policy Area	Expected Elements	Discussion
General Privacy Program Elements	• Authority to Collect	A statement regarding the organization's authority to collect personal data on individuals and store, process, and share that information.
	• Purpose Specification	A statement describing and listing the purpose and uses of the organization's personal data collecting activities.
	• Minimization of Personal Data	A statement that the organization will identify and collect only personal data that is necessary for legitimate business purposes.
Governance and Privacy Program	• Roles and Responsibilities	• Description of roles and responsibilities within the privacy program. • Clear assignment of responsibility to a named person for role, including accurate and up-to-date contact information
	• Monitor laws and regulations	A statement regarding the requirement that the organization monitor additions and changes in laws and regulations that may affect their personal data collection activities or their treatment of the data. The assessor should expect to see a listing of relevant laws and regulations in this section.
	• Operate privacy program	A statement that the organization formally recognizes and requires the establishment and maintenance of a privacy program.
Privacy Program Operational Procedures	• Privacy Impact Assessments	A documented process of privacy impact assessment performed within the organization. This process should be implemented for every new data collection activity that may involve private data or significant changes in the existing systems.
	• Privacy Monitoring and Auditing	A documented process of how privacy controls and internal privacy activities shall be monitored and reviewed annually for effectiveness.
	• Privacy Awareness Training	A documented process for the development, maintenance, and delivery of effective privacy awareness training. This process should include awareness of relevant laws and regulations, definitions of 'incident', 'breach' and other appropriate terms, restrictions on the collection and use of private data, and the organization's breach notification process.
	• Accounting of Disclosures	An accurate and up-to-date accounting of all disclosures of personal data within the organization. This accounting of disclosure can be limited to unauthorized disclosures in some cases. This documentation should be retained for six years.
	• Consent	A description of the organization's process for individuals to authorize the collection, use, maintenance, and sharing of their personal data.
	• Individual Access	A description of the organization's process for individuals to have access to their personal data maintained in the organization's systems.
	• Redress	A description of the organization's process for individuals have inaccuracies within their personal data within the organization's systems to be corrected.
	• Complaint Management	A description of the organization's process to document, track, and manage any complaints on the organization's collection or handling of personal data.
	• Personal Data Inventory	A description of the organization's process developing and maintaining an inventory of the personal data collection activities within the organization.
	• Privacy Incident Response	A description of the organization's process for managing incident response involving personal data.

TABLE 6.21
Web—Privacy Notice Expected Elements
Web Privacy Notice

A web privacy notice is a statement of privacy practices, rights and protections regarding the organizations collection, protection and use of private information online.

Policy Area	Expected Elements	Discussion
Information Collected	• Information Collected and Stored Automatically	A listing and description of information collected automatically by the user visiting the website. This information may include cookies, web server logs, browser information, and geographic location information.
	• Information Collected from Other Sources	A listing and description of information collected from social logins when access is granted based on registration on the website through login services provided by social media account; and information collected by other outside sources such as marketing lead generation databased or public databases.
	• Information Provided by the User	A listing and description of information provided by the user. This information may contain personal information disclosed by the user; account credentials; posted messages; and payment data.
Treatment of Online Submitted Data	• Non-Dissemination of Data	A statement that the data provided by the user will not be sold or otherwise disseminated.
Use of Personal Data	• Legitimate Business Needs	A listing and description of the legitimate business uses of the personal data collected. Legitimate uses include account creation, marketing, order fulfillment, targeted advertising, responding to requested feedback, enforcement of security, user-to-user communications, account maintenance, and legal response.
	• Information Protections	A description of how private data is protected. This section may point to a location where a detailed description of the security controls in place may be found.
	• Information Retention	A description of what elements of the private data may be retained and for how long. This section should state that when there is no longer a legitimate business need to retain the data that it will be purged (or anonymized).
	• Account Termination	A statement that private data will be deleted when the account is deactivated or deleted. If any data will be retained for a period of time after account termination, the data, and the reason (e.g., security purposes) should be stated here.
Sharing of Personal Data	• Reasons for Sharing	A listing and description of the reasons private data may be shared. Reasons for sharing private data may include consent, legitimate interests, performance of contract, legal obligations, and vital interests (e.g., security threats, fraud).
	• Types of Business with Whom Data May Be Shared	A listing and description of any business types in which the organization may share personal data. Business types may include vendors, consultants, third-party service providers, third party advertisers, affiliates, and other users (e.g., shared among users of the application).
	• Specific Businesses with Whom Data is Shared	A listing and description of all the businesses with which the organization shares personal data.
Privacy Rights	• Withdraw Consent	A statement regarding how a user may withdrawal consent to collect or share personal data. This statement should include contact information or a website address where the user may notify the organization of this withdrawal.

(Continued)

TABLE 6.21 *(Continued)*

Policy Area	Expected Elements	Discussion
	• Account Information Review	A statement regarding the process a user may take to review their account information. This statement should include contact information or a website address where this information may be reviewed.
	• Cookie Preferences	A statement instructing the user that they may change their preference for website cookies.
	• E-mail Preferences	A statement instructing the user that they may change their preferences to receive e-mails and instructions for how to do so.
Data Breach	• Data Breach Process	A statement regarding the data breach definition, data breach process, and data breach notification process. This statement includes information regarding how and when the user would be notified.
Additional Rights	• Specific Rights based on Regulations	This section(s) would include any additional privacy rights the user has based on specific states, nations, or unions (e.g., California, European Union).

TABLE 6.22

Systems and Communications Security Policy Expected Elements

Systems and Communications Security Policy

A Systems and Communications Security Policy establishes the minimum-security controls for the protection of organizational information systems and their communications.

Policy Area	Expected Elements	Discussion
Network and Architectural Controls	• Boundary Protections (firewall placement)	Requirements for the monitoring and controlled communication between the organization's information systems and external systems and at key internal boundaries. Minimum requirements likely include: • Firewalls required at all external interfaces • Firewalls required between internal networks and publically available network access • Implementation of subnetwork for publically accessible system components
	• Demilitarized Zone (DMZ)	Requirements for prohibiting direct public access between the Internet and any information system components. The DMZ implementation shall ensure: • Inbound traffic is limited to authorized public components of the information systems and IP addresses within the DMZ • Implementation of anti-spoofing measures to detect and block forged source IP addresses from entering the network • Outbound traffic is limited to unauthorized traffic • Systems containing sensitive data (e.g., database) are placed in an internal zone and not directly addressable from external networks
	• Firewall Configuration Standards	A section that provides configuration standards for the organization's firewalls. These standards should include: • A formal process for approving and testing all network connections and changes • Current network diagrams and sensitive data flows • A description of roles and responsibilities for network component management • A list of all services provided within the network components and a business justification for each service • A requirement to review firewall and router rule sets at least every 6 months.

(Continued)

TABLE 6.22 *(Continued)*

Policy Area	Expected Elements	Discussion
	• Firewall Configuration	Documentation that demonstrates that the network components are configured according to the documented configuration standards.
Server Controls	• Limited Functions	Requirement that network servers limit the services and functions provided to implement the concept of least privilege. At a minimum the following restrictions should be applied: • Single primary function for servers housing databases • Single primary function for servers housing sensitive data (e.g., card holder data)
	• Minimum and Secure Services	Requirement that servers only enable necessary and secure services as required for the function of the system. Description should include removal or disablement of: • unnecessary functions, • scripts, • drivers, • features, • subsystems, • file systems, and • unnecessary web servers.
	• Server Configuration	Documentation that demonstrates that the organization's servers are configured according to the documented configuration standards.
Secure Services	• Denial of Service Protections	Requirement that the organization's system protect against or limit the effects of denial of service attacks. Requirement should list the types of denial of service attacks for which it provides protections.
	• Cryptographic Services	Requirement that organizational systems and communication components implement strong and secure cryptographic services. (See Cryptographic Control Policy for details). Requirement should detail the following elements: • Approved algorithms and associated parameters such as key length and number of rounds where applicable • Requirements for key establishment and distribution • Requirements for key management and protection
	• Telecommunication Services	Requirements for the protection of external telecommunication services. Requirements should address: • Managed interface for external telecommunications service • Traffic flow policies for telecommunications traffic • Confidentiality and integrity controls • Documentation and annual review of exceptions
	• Transmission Confidentiality	Requirements for the protection of confidential transmissions. Requirements should address: • Physical protections (if any) • Cryptographic protections
	• Mobile Code Protections	Requirements for the protection of system components from mobile code. Requirements should address: • Acceptable and unacceptable mobile code (e.g., JavaScript, Flash, VBScript) • Usage restrictions and implementation guidance for acceptable mobile code • Authorization, monitoring, and controlled use of mobile code within organizational system components

(Continued)

TABLE 6.22   *(Continued)*

Policy Area	Expected Elements	Discussion
Workstation Controls	• Malicious Code Protections	A section describing the controls in place to protect workstations from malicious code. This section should include: • Centralized malicious code protections at all entry and exit points of the information system that can detect and eradicate malicious code • Automatic updates to malicious code protection software • Automatic and periodic scans for systems for malicious code • Generation of logs • System administrator alerts • Monitoring of status of all instances of malicious code software, its current state, and data of last update.
	• Workstation Configuration	Documentation that demonstrates that the organization's workstations are configured according to the documented configuration standards.

TABLE 6.23
Policy and Procedure Association Example

Statement Level	Description
Policy statement	*Employee termination*: All access and privileges to system and facility resources must be removed immediately upon termination of employment
Termination procedures	*Notification*: Human resources will ensure that all appropriate parties are notified and review non-disclosure and non-compete agreements with the terminated individual
	Logical access: Operations will terminate access to all accounts associated with the terminated individual
	Physical and communication access: Facilities will terminate all physical access (return of badge, revocation of access codes, lock, and combination changes) and communication access (cell phone, e-mail, voice mail)
	Duties: The supervisor will turn over duties to another individual and notify appropriate partners of the termination of employment

Note: The termination procedures implement the termination policy statements.

6.2.2.3.1.5   Backup and Restoration Policy

The backup and restoration policy addresses the process of defining and ensuring the backup and restoration requirements for an organization. The expected elements of a Backup and Restoration Policy are listed in Table 6.13 to guide the assessors review of the document.

6.2.2.3.1.6   Cryptographic Control Policy

The cryptographic control policy (or cryptographic standard) covers the use of cryptography and establishes approved methodologies and use within the organization. The expected elements of a Cryptographic Controls Policy are listed in Table 6.15 to guide the assessors review of the document.

TABLE 6.24
Business Contingency Plan Expected Elements

Business Contingency Plan

The Business Contingency Plan covers the controls required to minimize the risk of system and service unavailability due to a variety of disruptions by providing effective and efficient solutions to enhance system availability.

Policy Area	Expected Elements	Discussion
Business Continuity Plan	• Mission and Functions	A section that identifies the organization's mission and business functions.
	• Critical Systems and Data	A section that identifies the organization's critical systems, data, and resources required to implement the mission and execute the business functions. This should include: • Critical information system assets supporting missions and business functions. • Dependencies between information systems (e.g., e-mail required for customer support).
	• Recovery Objectives	A section that identifies the recovery objectives, restoration priorities, and metrics (e.g., Maximum Time Down, Recovery Point Objective).
	• Roles and Responsibilities	• Description of roles and responsibilities within the Business Continuity Planning activities. • Clear assignment of responsibility to a named person for role, including accurate and up-to-date contact information.
	• Maintaining Essential Functions	A section describing the organization's approach for ensuring essential mission functions are maintained despite a system disruption, compromise or failure. This section should include: • A list of foreseeable events that may lead to a disaster. • A description of the organization's general approach for ensuring continuation of business (e.g., cloud services, home offices, alternative locations).
	• Resumption of Services	A section describing the organization's approach for ensuring the eventual, full system restoration. [Note: This is not the same as "maintaining essential functions." This is returning to normal operations (e.g., return to restored facility).]
Business Continuity Plan Management	• Distribution and Protection	• A statement requiring the distribution of the Business Continuity Plan to appropriate personnel (e.g., distribution list). • An indication as to the sensitivity of the Business Continuity Plan (e.g., Confidentiality marking in the header or footer.)
	• Coordination	A statement or section of the Business Continuity Plan that indicates coordination between departments and security incident handling activities on the construction, review, and revision of the plan.
	• Review and Revision	An indication that the Business Continuity Plan is reviewed, and revised if necessary, annually.
	• Communications	An indication that changes to the Business Continuity Plan are communicated to appropriate personnel and organizational elements.
	• Testing	A statement regarding the required testing of the Business Continuity Plan. The testing section should include requirements for: • Annual testing • Documentation of test results • Review of test results • Documentation and tracking of correction actions arising from testing exercises.

(Continued)

TABLE 6.24   (Continued)

Policy Area	Expected Elements	Discussion
BCP Elements	• Alternative Storage	A section describing the organization's approach for alternative systems, processes, services, or products that ensure an adequate solution for providing storage needs during a disaster.
	• Alternative Processing	A section describing the organization's approach for alternative systems, processes, services, or products that ensure an adequate solution for providing processing needs during a disaster.
	• Alternative Communications	A section describing the organization's approach for alternative systems, processes, services, or products that ensure an adequate solution for providing communications needs during a disaster.

TABLE 6.25
Change Control Expected Elements

Change Control Procedures

Change Control (Management) Procedures establish the methods and standards for managing changes to organizational information systems.

Policy Area	Expected Elements	Discussion
General Change Control Elements	• Definitions	A section containing relevant definitions. Definitions should match the statements within the document but would likely include the following at a minimum: • Requester, Implementer, Reviewer, and Approver • Request Change, Approval • Change Control Board • Review • Impact
	• Roles and Responsibilities	Clear assignment of responsibility to a named person(s) for the roles of: • Change Control Board • Implementer • Reviewer • Approver
Change Request Process	• Request Criteria	A section documenting the required elements of a change request. Required elements should include: • Description of proposed change • Contact information for requester and implementer • Change Type [Normal, Important, Emergency] • Reason for Change Type and reason for change • Proposed timeline for start and completion • Expected impact (e.g., downtime, loss of data or service) • Pre-change testing and results, if applicable • Execution plan including post-test expected results • Back-out plan • Expected benefit of change
	• Test Plan	A section describing when a test plan is necessary and the required elements of the test plan. These elements should include: • A description of the test environment • Test conditions and required steps • Acceptance testing process and criteria, including test result review process

(Continued)

TABLE 6.24 *(Continued)*

Policy Area	Expected Elements	Discussion
	• Training Plan	A section describing when a training plan is necessary and the required elements of the training plan. These elements should include: • A description of the training necessary to enact or ensure appropriate staff members are trained on any changes • A plan for providing training • A description of determining the effectiveness of the training provided
Change Implementation Process	• Change Control Board	A section describing the change control board process for reviewing and approving changes. This should cover all change types (the process should be different for each).
	• Change Implementation Scheduling	A description or schedule of when changes may be implemented based on change type.
	• Change Protection	A description of how the system is protected from unauthorized changes.
	• Change Monitoring	A description of how the system monitors for unauthorized changes.
Documentation	• Affected Documentation Review	A description of how the change control process ensures that affected documents (e.g., incident response plan, security awareness training, backup procedures) are updated.

6.2.2.3.1.7   Data Classification, Handling and Retention Policy

The data classification policy provides a framework for the protection of data that is created, stored, processed, or transmitted within the organization's information systems. The classification of data is the foundation for the specification of policies, procedures, and controls necessary for the protection of sensitive information. The expected elements of a Data Classification, Handling and Retention Policy are listed in Table 6.16 to guide the assessors review of the document.

6.2.2.3.1.8   Media Protection Policy

The media protection policy specifies the necessary controls to ensure the secure storage, transport, and destruction of sensitive information. The expected elements of Media Protection Policy are listed in Table 6.17 to guide the assessors review of the document.

6.2.2.3.1.9   Mobile Device Policy

The mobile device policy establishes a set of minimum controls necessary to secure the use of mobile devices. The expected elements of a Mobile Device Policy are listed in Table 6.18 to guide the assessors review of the document.

6.2.2.3.1.10   Physical Security/Environmental Controls Policy

The physical security protections policy ensures the physical protection of organizational assets through the enforcement of a minimum set of physical security controls. The expected elements of a Physical Security/Environmental Controls Policy are listed in Table 6.19 to guide the assessors review of the document.

6.2.2.3.1.11   Privacy Program Policy

A privacy policy is a statement of the minimum controls in place to protection the privacy of sensitive data within the organization and organizational systems. The expected elements of a Privacy Program Policy are listed in Table 6.20 to guide the assessors review of the document.

TABLE 6.26

Disaster Recovery Plan Expected Elements

Disaster Recovery Plan

The disaster recovery plan is designed to reduce the risks to the organization when an event causes the disruption of a critical system or business function for a prolonged period of time and to provide for the timely recovery of critical data, applications, systems, and infrastructure.

Policy Area	Expected Elements	Discussion
Disaster Recovery Document	• Scope	A description of the scope of the disaster recovery plan.
	• Recovery Objectives	A section that identifies the recovery objectives, restoration priorities, and metrics (e.g., Maximum Time Down, Recovery Point Objective). This section is also in the Business Continuity Plan and should be identical (e.g., consistent).
	• Recovery Capability	Requirements for all information system and components to have the technical architecture, capability, capacity, and procedures in place to support recovery objectives.
	• Recovery Strategy	Detailed procedures for how the organization will meet the recovery objectives for a set of disaster scenarios. This will likely be an evolving document as the organization matures its process. At a minimum there should be a set of procedures for 3–5 foreseeable disaster and documentation to a level that someone meeting the minimum requirements for a position (but without experience in the position yet) can follow the instructions.
	• Testing	A section detailing the disaster recovery plan testing process. This process should include the following: • Testing requirements • Testing documentation (results, lessons learned, approval/certification) • Testing non-compliance process • Testing Approaches (e.g., table top exercise, full interruption)
Disaster Recovery Teams	• Disaster Recovery Teams	There are a number of teams responsible for different elements of disaster recovery. Each of these teams should be listed and covered in the disaster recovery plan. An example of these teams is listed below: • Damage assessment team • Site restoration team • Alternate site recovery team • Physical security team • Transportation and relocation team • Media relations team • Legal affairs team • Hardware recovery team • System software recovery team • Operating system administration team • Database recovery team
	• Disaster Recovery Team Process	There are a number of teams responsible for different elements of disaster recovery. For each of these teams there should be the following: • Team responsibilities • Team members currently assigned • Complete and up-to-date contact information for all team members • Procedures that the team follows to meet their objectives

TABLE 6.27
Incident Response Plan Expected Elements

Incident Response Plan

The incident response plan provides the organization the ability to rapidly detect incidents, minimize any loss due to destruction, mitigate the weaknesses that were exploited, and restore computing devices.

Policy Area	Expected Elements	Discussion
Incident Response Plan	• Roles and Responsibilities	• Description of roles and responsibilities within the incident response activities. • Clear assignment of responsibility to a named person for role, including accurate and up-to-date contact information.
	• Training	A section describing training necessary for those holding specified roles to correctly implement their responsibilities.
	• Testing	A section describing the testing of the incident response plan. Testing may include checklists, walk-throughs, tabletop exercises, simulations, or comprehensive exercises to determine the incident response effectiveness and document the results. The test elements should include the following: • Communication and contact strategies • Specific incident response procedures for common and foreseeable incidents • Data backup procedures • Legal requirements for breach notification analysis • Critical system component coverage and responses • References or inclusion of incident response procedures from external entities • Lessons learned
Incident Handling	• Incident Handling	A section describing the process for incident handling. This process should cover the following: • Steps involved within each phase of the incident handling process (preparation, detection and analysis, containment, eradication, and recovery). • Detailed process for common and foreseeable events
	• Privacy Incident Response Handling	A section describing the process for incident handling when personally identifiable information (PII) is involved. This process should cover the following: • Determination of involvement with PII • Involvement of privacy officer in incident handling process • Notification requirement analysis • Notification process
	• Incident Monitoring	A section describing the process for analyzing alerts, reported incidents and for tracking incidents. This process should include a description of roles and responsibilities including the security officer and privacy officer.
	• Incident Reporting	A section describing the process for reporting incidents. This process should cover the following: • Incident, reportable incidents, and breach definitions • Applicable laws and regulations • Timing requirements for notification • Other details regarding notification requirements such as media contacts and content of notifications.

6.2.2.3.1.12 Privacy—Web Privacy Notice

A web privacy statement is a notice of privacy practices, rights and protections regarding the organizations collection, protection and use of private information online. The elements required in such a statement depend on various jurisdictions, uses of the data, and the current state of privacy laws. The expected elements of a Web Privacy Notice are listed in Table 6.21 to guide the assessors review of the document.

TABLE 6.28

Information Security Program Procedures Expected Elements

Information Security Program Procedures

The information security program procedures establish the program and responsibilities for the overall information security program within the organization.

Policy Area	Expected Elements	Discussion
Information Security Program	• Roles and Responsibilities	• Description of roles and responsibilities within the information security program. • Clear assignment of responsibility to a named person for role, including accurate and up-to-date contact information.
	• Information Security Framework	A section describing the framework the information security program is based upon.
	• Applicable Law and Regulations	A listing of laws and regulations applicable to the content and effectiveness of the information security program.
Information Security Program Activities	• System Security Policies	A section describing the information security policies in place for the organization, responsibility for policy maintenance and distribution, and approval.
	• Security Risk Management	A section detailing the process of information security risk management within the organization. This process should cover the following: • information security's role in enterprise risk management • definitions for asset, threat, threat actor, threat action, vulnerability, impact, and risk • risk assessment • impact assessment • role of internal audit, third party review, and internal security team review. • security risk enumeration (e.g., security risk assessment, internal audit, security incidents) • third party security risk assessments • vulnerability scanning • penetration testing • Wireless access point testing • tracking security risks (e.g., risk register)
	• Security Metrics	A section describing the process of collecting, tracking, and presenting security metrics.
	• System ownership and Authorization Process	A section describing the ownership of data and systems within the organization. This should include the process system assessments and authorization process for approving the processing of sensitive information on organizational systems.

6.2.2.3.1.13 Systems and Communications Security Policy

A Systems and Communications Security Policy establishes the minimum-security controls for the protection of organizational information systems and their communications. The expected elements of a Systems and Communications Security Policy are listed in Table 6.22 to guide the assessors review of the document.

6.2.2.4 Reviewing Information Security Plans, Processes, and Procedures

Although security policies may be the most numerous documents the security risk assessment team reviews, they will not be the only ones. Another classification of documents for the security risk

TABLE 6.29

Other Operational Procedures Expected Elements

Other Operational Procedures

Additional operational procedures are instructions to work force members on the appropriate process for implementing operational controls within the organization that are not addressed in other expected elements tables.

Policy Area	Expected Elements	Discussion
Documented	• Documented and revised as appropriate	Operational procedures are also referred to as standard operating procedures. These are prescribed methods of performing operational activities in a standardized way. These procedures should be expected to be constantly undergoing changes and additions.
Approved	• Appropriate authority has approved policies	Each operating procedure document should have some indication of approval from the appropriate authority (e.g., a signature or name and date of approval).
Operational Procedures	• Account Management	Procedural-level instructions for performing the following activities: • Account request, approval, and activation • User access rights reviews • Account removal
	• Backup and Restoration	Procedural-level instructions for performing the following activities: • User-level backup and restoration • System-level backup and restoration • Application-level back up and restoration • Database backup and transactional restoration
	• Firewall Management	Procedural-level instructions for performing the following activities: • Firewall and router ruleset change requests and implementation • Periodic firewall and router ruleset review • Firewall configuration
	• Logging, Monitoring, and Auditing	Procedural-level instructions for performing the following activities: • Configuration of new installations to meet audit requirements • Log review process for each security event monitoring system within the organization
	• Patch Management	Procedural-level instructions for performing the following activities: • Operating system patch management process • Application patch management process • Scheduled patch process • Version updates process • Emergency patch management process • Remote maintenance process • Back-out procedure

assessment team to review are plans, processes, and procedures. The same approach as described for reviewing information security policies can be applied here:

- Review Documents for Clarity—The procedures should be useful to their intended audience without the need to research terms, definitions, and jargon.
- Review Documents for Content—The assessor should judge the content of procedures based on their completeness (coverage of the topic area) and the correctness and consistency with the policy it references. One approach to creating security procedures is to create one or more security procedure steps for each policy statement. The security procedures would then provide a mapping of procedures to security policy statements making a completeness and consistency argument.

TABLE 6.30

Security Awareness Program and Procedures Expected Elements

Security Awareness and Training Program and Procedures

The security awareness and training program documentation covers the organization's program to ensure that all employees and contractors are trained and educated on how to fulfill their information security responsibilities.

Policy Area	Expected Elements	Discussion
Security Awareness and Training Program	• Roles and Responsibilities	• Description of roles and responsibilities within the security awareness and training program. • Clear assignment of responsibility to a named person for role.
	• Identification of Sensitive Positions	A list of sensitive positions that require additional training to effectively perform their jobs (e.g., incident response, privacy officer).
	• Security Awareness Program Tracking	A description of the process by which the security awareness program(s) are tracked. This process should include training records, course contents, and course feedback and updates.
Security Awareness and Training	• Standard Security Awareness Training	Documentation used in the delivery of standard security awareness training (e.g., student manual). Review to ensure material covers adequate topics such as: • Acceptable use of assets • Restrictions on mobile devices and removable media • Online safety from malware, spoofing, phishing, and pre-texting • Clean desk policy • Use, selection, and upkeep of passwords/authentication • Employee responsibility for protection • Incident reporting procedures
	• Privacy Awareness Training	Documentation used in the delivery of privacy awareness training (e.g., student manual). Review to ensure material covers adequate topics such as: • Identification of personal data • Handling, collection, and sharing restrictions • Employee responsibility for protection • User's rights regarding personal information • Incident reporting procedures • Incident and breach investigations • Data breach notification process • Basic protection from malware, spoofing, phishing, and pre-texting.
	• Specialized Security Training	Documentation used in the delivery of specialized security training (e.g., student manual, course outline). Review to ensure material covers adequate topics.

The assessor can use this mapping technique to review the adequacy of the procedure content. There should be a one-to-many mapping from the security policy statement to the security procedure statements. For example, a security operations policy should have a security policy statement covering the termination of individuals. The associated security procedures should provide guidance (or requirements) on how to implement the policy statements. See the example in Table 6.23.

Not all security policies are expected to have associated security procedures. For example, the acceptable-use policy typically has no need for more detailed procedures implementing the policy.

TABLE 6.31

Software Development Life Cycle Process Expected Elements

Software Development Life Cycle Process

The software development life cycle is a documented process that governs the software development environment, process, and activities in place to ensure the reduction of risk in software developed within the organization.

Policy Area	Expected Elements	Discussion
General Software Development Program	• Roles and Responsibilities	• Description of roles and responsibilities within the software development life cycle program. • Clear assignment of responsibility to a named person for role.
	• Architectural Design	A description of the process the organization uses to ensure information security principles are designed into software and applications created within the organization. The architectural design should address: • The phases of the software development cycle and how security is integrated into each phase • Use of threat modeling throughout development • Documentation of application interfaces and boundaries • Secure coding practices (see Table 6.32 for examples)
	• Authentication	• A description of the process the organization uses to ensure the application has a strong method for the confirmation of authentic communication with people and devices is essential to implementing security policies based on identification. This includes processes to ensure the proper use of passwords and tokens, but also password strength, notifications of account usage, and secure and sound authenticator establishment and reset procedures.
	• Code Review	A description of the process the organization uses to ensure code review performed correctly within the organization. The process should include: • List and use of tools • Checklist of secure/insecure coding practices • Approval process
Secure Software Development Controls	• Access Controls and Data Protection	A description of the process the organization uses to ensure appropriate authorization rules are enforced to allow only that access that is explicitly permitted. Access and data protection controls include: • Implementation of least privilege • Implementation of need-to-know, • Ensuring the reference monitor concept is appropriately enacted Protecting data objects to ensure they are accessed only through appropriate transactions that enforce authorized access control.
	• Input Validation	A description of the process the organization uses to ensure that software that accepts input from users validate this input to ensure that the executed instruction behaves in the way it was intended. Techniques for validating input include: • Sanitization, • Sandboxing, • Injection prevention • Deserialization prevention
	• Cryptographic Standards	A description of the process the organization uses to ensure developers should follow established guidelines for the • Use of strong and secure algorithms • Appropriate selection of key values • Proper initialization • Random value selection • Secure key management

(Continued)

TABLE 6.31 *(Continued)*

Policy Area	Expected Elements	Discussion
	• Error Handling	A description of the process the organization uses to ensure software is developed with appropriate error handling and creation of logs. Logs created within the applications need to contain the necessary elements to allow for detailed investigations and need to be protected from unauthorized viewing.
	• Configuration	A description of the process the organization uses to ensure the secure configuration of the executable code and environment in which it executes. This includes: • Build environment, • Underlying system level hardening • Secure default configuration settings

TABLE 6.32

Secure Coding Practices Expected Elements

Policy Area	Expected Elements
Principles	Least privilege
	Fail-safe default
	Economy of mechanism
	Least common mechanism
	Open design
	Role separation
Good practice	Strip symbols from binary files
	Use program wrappers
	Self-limit resource consumption
	Sanity check input
	Use true random functions in encryption routines
	Plan maintenance and testing
	Use static links
	Use return codes
	Use privilege bracketing
Warnings	Do not hard-code passwords
	Do not echo passwords
	Do not store sensitive data unencrypted
	Do not transmit sensitive data unencrypted
	Do not invoke shells or command lines from within an application
	Do not use filenames (use file descriptors)
	Do not rely on IP address as authentication
	Do not create files in world-writable directories
	Do not make time-of-use/time-of-check errors
	Do not make race-condition errors

Note: The security coding standard should cover secure coding principles, good practices, and warnings.

TABLE 6.33
Termination Procedures Expected Elements
Termination Procedures

Termination procedures are a documented process that governs the departure of an employee to ensure the reduction of risk in ensuring there are no residual accesses allowed.

Policy Area	Expected Elements	Discussion
	• Roles and Responsibilities	• Description of roles and responsibilities within the privacy program. • Clear assignment of responsibility to a named person for role.
	• Notification	A description of the process the organization uses to ensure appropriate and timely notification of the employees departure to all appropriate parties including internal notification and partner notification.
	• Logical Access	A description of the process the organization uses to ensure appropriate and timely removal of logical access to organizational systems. This process is typically supported by a workflow, checklist, or ticketing process to ensure all accesses are removed including: • Central directory services • E-mail • File Server • Intranet • Cloud services associated with the organization • Logical accesses provided by partners • System password changes for any shared passwords
	• Physical Access	A description of the process the organization uses to ensure appropriate and timely removal of physical access to organizational locations. Physical access removal may include: • Return of badge, • Return of keys • Revocation of physical access codes, • Changes to locks and lock combinations • Removal from physical access lists at the organization • Removal from physical access lists at partner locations
	• Return of organizationally owned equipment and materials	A description of the process the organization uses to ensure appropriate and timely removal of service access to organizationally provided or sponsored services. Service access removal may include: • Return of laptop and other computer equipment • Return of cell phone • Return of other organizationally issued equipment • Return of company materials
	• Services Access	A description of the process the organization uses to ensure appropriate and timely removal of service access to organizationally provided or sponsored services. Service access removal may include: • Return of laptop and other computer equipment • Return of cell phone • Termination of cell phone contract • Termination of voicemail • Termination of VPN service

(Continued)

TABLE 6.33 *(Continued)*

Policy Area	Policy Area	Policy Area
	• Duties	A description of the process the organization uses to ensure appropriate turnover of duties. Turnover of duties may include: • Forwarding of phone calls, e-mails, and service tickets • Exit interview and update of job description • Retrieval of system, laptop or other passwords if required
	• Financial Settlement	A description of the process the organization uses to ensure proper financial settlement. This may include: • Last paycheck • Provisions for expenses

TABLE 6.34

Vendor Security Risk Management Policy Expected Elements

Vendor Security Risk Management Policy

The vendor security risk management program is the organizations standardized process for reducing or eliminating the risk of working with external entities (e.g., service providers, vendors, and other third parties).

Policy Area	Expected Elements	Discussion
Vendor Security Risk Management Program	• Roles and Responsibilities	• Description of roles and responsibilities within the privacy program. • Clear assignment of responsibility to a named person for role.
	• Vendor Inventory	A description of the process by which the organization ensures that it creates and maintains a complete list of all third parties with access to sensitive data, critical systems, or protected areas.
	• Vendor Assessment	A description of the process by which the organization assesses the security risk of granting the third-party access. This process should have the following elements: • Minimum set of security controls • Process to collect data regarding the vendor's adherence to those controls • Assessment method of scoring or otherwise determining the risk presented by the vendor • A decision process for accepting the vendor risk
	• Vendor Risk Monitoring	A description of the process by which the organization monitors the vendor's compliance with the vendor security risk management program. This process should include: • service level agreement (SLA) reviews • periodic reassessments • adherence to notification requirements • corrective actions
Vendor Security Risk Management Program Artifacts	• Vendor Questionnaires	Sample and/or selected vendor questionnaires. These artifacts should align with the described process.
	• Current Inventory	The current inventory of vendors granted access to organizational systems, data, and protected areas.

However, policy statements covering system hardening, account creation and termination, and incident tracking and reporting could certainly use more detailed description of how the policy statement will be enforced.

These documents will be highly individualized for the organization but will still need to adhere to a few simple elements to ensure their effectiveness.

- Assignment of Responsibility—Plans, procedures and processes are not performed by an organization or a department; they are performed by individuals. Many processes are ultimately ineffective because the activities within them are not assigned to an individual. Assessors should note when process activities are assigned to a department or worse to the organization as not one person or even role is responsible for its implementation.
- Up-to-Date Information—Plans, procedures and processes are detailed enough to require constant updating to ensure they are effective. The assessor should look for elements of the plan where out-of-date information would impact the effectiveness of the document. These areas include names, phone numbers, e-mails, system names, addresses, and other elements that should be under configuration management to ensure an effective document.
- Level of Detail—Plans, procedures, and processes are the documentation of a standardized process within an organization. They are used to enforce consistency and increase the maturity of the process. In order for these processes to work effectively they need to be documented, clear, and detailed enough to allow a qualified individual to be able to consistently perform the process in line with the organization's intentions. The assessor does not need to be an expert in these processes to be able to review them for the appropriate level of detail. Ask yourself, "could a new employee joining the organization follow this document without asking clarifying questions?"

For each of the information security plans, procedures, and processes reviewed the assessor may use Tables 6.24 through 6.34 for guidance as to the expected elements.

6.2.2.4.1.1   Business Contingency Plan

The Business Contingency Plan covers the controls required to minimize the risk of system and service unavailability due to a variety of disruptions by providing effective and efficient solutions to enhance system availability. The expected elements of a Business Contingency Plan are listed in Table 6.24 to guide the assessors review of the document.

6.2.2.4.1.2   Change Control Procedures

Change Control (Management) Procedures establish the methods and standards for managing changes to organizational information systems. The expected elements of Change Control Procedures are listed in Table 6.25 to guide the assessors review of the document.

6.2.2.4.1.3   Disaster Recovery Plan

The disaster recovery plan is designed to reduce the risks to the organization when an event causes the disruption of a critical system or business function for a prolonged period of time. The controls within the disaster recovery plan are designed to provide for the timely recovery of critical data, applications, systems, and infrastructure. The expected elements of a Disaster Recovery Plan are listed in Table 6.26 to guide the assessors review of the document.

6.2.2.4.1.4   Incident Response Plan

The incident response plan provides the organization the ability to rapidly detect incidents, minimize any loss due to destruction, mitigate the weaknesses that were exploited, and restore computing devices. The expected elements of an Incident Response Plan are listed in Table 6.27 to guide the assessors review of the document.

6.2.2.4.1.5   Information Security Program Procedures

The information security program procedures establish the program and responsibilities for the overall information security program within the organization. The expected elements of Information Security Program Procedures are listed in Table 6.28 to guide the assessors review of the document.

6.2.2.4.1.6   Other Operational Procedures

"Other" Operational procedures are instructions to work force members on the appropriate process for implementing operational controls within the organization that are not addressed in other expected elements tables. These procedures provide a consistent method of accomplishing routine tasks within the organization and help to increase the maturity of the process. There are other operational procedures mentioned within some of the policy documents above (e.g., incident response, data classification). The expected elements of Other Operational Procedures are listed in Table 6.29 to guide the assessors review of the document.

6.2.2.4.1.7   Security Awareness and Training Program

The security awareness and training program documentation covers the organization's program to ensure that all employees and contractors are trained and educated on how to fulfill their information security responsibilities. The expected elements of a Security Awareness and Training Program and Procedures are listed in Table 6.30 to guide the assessors review of the document.

6.2.2.4.1.8   Software Development Life Cycle Process

The software development life cycle is a documented process that governs the software development environment, process, and activities in place to ensure the reduction of risk in software developed within the organization. The expected elements of a Software Development Life Cycle Process are listed in Table 6.31 to guide the assessors review of the document.

An example of secure coding practices is provided in Table 6.32.

6.2.2.4.1.9   Termination Procedures

Termination procedures are a documented process that governs the departure of an employee to ensure the reduction of risk in ensuring there are no residual accesses allowed. The expected elements of a Termination Procedure are listed in Table 6.33 to guide the assessors review of the document.

6.2.2.4.1.10   Vendor Security Risk Management Program

The vendor security risk management program is the organizations standardized process for reducing or eliminating the risk of working with external entities (e.g., service providers, vendors, and other third parties). The expected elements of a Vendor Security Risk Management Program are listed in Table 6.34 to guide the assessors review of the document.

6.2.2.5   Security Work Product Review

Security work products are the output of a security-relevant activity. For example, signed acceptable-use policy forms are a work product of security awareness training. The review of security work products differs greatly, depending upon the security activity. Regardless, all work products should simply be reviewed as evidence that a security activity is performed regularly and completely.

The review of information security procedures should follow the review of policies. Procedures are the "next level down" from the security policies in that they provide guidance or instructions on how to implement security policy statements. The review of security work products should follow the review of procedures.

6.2.3 INTERVIEW PERSONNEL REGARDING ADMINISTRATIVE CONTROLS

Data gathering for administrative security controls also involves interviewing key personnel. The security risk assessment team can interview key personnel regarding nearly any aspect of administrative security controls. It is important that the security risk assessment team carefully plan the topics to cover, whom to interview, and what questions to ask.

6.2.3.1 Administrative Interview Planning

The interview process can be burdensome for the assessed organization. The security risk assessment team should be respectful of the staff's limited time they can give to this project and plan the interview process accordingly. The following elements should be considered in the interview process regarding administrative controls:

- Prepare for the Interview by Reading Administrative Control Documents—The security risk assessment team members conducting interviews should have read all associated documents regarding the administrative controls that are the subject of upcoming interviews. The assessment team members who have performed the document reviews will be well-versed in the administrative controls that are the subject of the interview and may be best suited as interviewers. It is also useful to have notes prepared for areas of the administrative control documents in which the assessor was concerned or unclear.
- Prepare for Interview by Reading Up on the Organization—The security assessment team should spend some time familiarizing itself with the organization. This should include reading the company website (especially recent news posts and executive profiles) reading available articles about the company in the news and ensuring that they are up-to-date on any industry trends, regulations, or recent threats.
- Plan Interview Dates and Times—The security risk assessment team should work with a project sponsor from the assessed organization to plan interview times and dates. The assessed organization can determine appropriate interviewees, check schedules, and arrange the calendar invites much more efficiently than the security risk assessment team can. The security risk assessment team should use the interview request form (see Chapter 5, Figure 5.6) to inform the assessed organization of the requested interview topics.
- Prepare and Share Questions Ahead of Time—To the extent possible, the security risk assessment team should be prepared to share the questions ahead of time. This is especially important when meeting with key executives as many of them do not like to go into meetings when they do not fully understand what will be asked of them. At a minimum prepare and share a list of topics (like the topics in the interview request form) for executives and key staff members as requested or required by the assessed organization, see Section 6.2.3.4.

6.2.3.2 Administrative Interview Topics

It is rare that the team has the luxury of interviewing personnel on every aspect of the security controls, so the team must prioritize topics and even specific questions to optimize the effectiveness of the interview process. A few key points to consider:

- Give Precedence to Questions Concerning Key Security Controls—The team may have discovered that the organization relies heavily on several key security controls. For example, the incident reporting and response process may be instrumental to the maintenance of the security posture. In this case, the interview of key personnel should include probing questions as to the effectiveness and maturity of this process.

- Get a Second Opinion—When asking about key security controls, obtain information from several parties involved in the process to compare views of the process effectiveness.
- Do They Walk the Walk?—Ask for specific steps involved in key processes. Specifically, ask what steps were followed recently so that you may compare those steps to the documented policy or process.

6.2.3.3 Administrative Interview Subjects

The security risk assessment team should interview those personnel best able to provide information regarding the topics they have selected to cover. Recalling that it is best to obtain several points of view on key processes, the team should also seek to interview those in various roles associated with key processes. Although the specific selection of whom to interview will depend largely on the organization's structure and the security risk assessment team's selected topic, the roles listed below should be considered:

- Users—The security risk assessment team should always interview a few representative users. If possible, these users should be picked at random, or at least the selection should be largely influenced by the security risk assessment team. Users can provide insight into the effectiveness of security awareness training, the efficiency of security controls, and the actual processes that are practiced.
- Human Resources Manager—Many administrative controls involve the human resources manager. Controls such as applications, job requirements, employment checks, accuracy checks, credit checks, clearance procedures, employment policies, training, job descriptions, job requirements, annual reviews, sanctions policies, and termination procedures are typically created by and administered by the human resources department.
- Senior Management—One of the principles of information security is that senior management is ultimately responsible for security. This principle is founded in the fact that senior management is in control of the budget, the organizational structure, and the ultimate decision to accept or reduce risk. A security risk assessment must include interviews with senior management to determine their risk tolerance and establish their role in risk management.
- Security Staff—Of course, the interview process must include interviews with those who perform the security activities such as system hardening, incident response, and account creation. The security risk assessment team should be looking for adherence to policies and procedures or evidence of good practices that do not happen to be documented. Be sure to include open-ended questions such as "What suggested safeguards are you hoping will come out of this security risk assessment?"

6.2.3.4 Administrative Interview Questions

Prior to any interview, the security risk assessment team (or interview team) should prepare a set of interview questions to ask each interview subject. To give the team an idea or example of such a set of questions, Tables 6.35, 6.36, and 6.37 provide a baseline set of questions that may be used, modified, or extended. These baseline interview questions cover the topics of incident response, security operations, and the security program, respectively.

6.2.3.4.1 Incident Response Interview Questions

The incident response questions in Table 6.35 can be asked of anyone involved in the incident response process. The questions cover the planning, detection, response, recovery, post-recovery, and reporting phases of incident response. If the organization has few incident response processes

TABLE 6.35
Incident Response Interview Guideline

Objective	Subtopic	Suggested Questions
Determine existence and adequacy of security controls within incident response area	Planning	• Under what circumstances would you pursue prosecution? • Who are the members of the incident response team? • How will the team communicate if the primary communication method is suspected of being compromised? • What credentials does anyone on the team have for computer forensic investigation? • For what common or foreseeable incidents do you have detailed procedures?
	Detection	• Do you have severity levels defined for incidents? • What severity level it be for a suspected account take-over? • What is an example of an event in which you would need to pull the CEO out of a board meeting? • Would someone on the night shift be able to make the same determination? • How are the terms "incident" and "breach" used in this context? • How are these terms defined?
	Response	• How do you go about deploying the team (specifically) in responding to an incident (a confirmed account take-over for example)? • Under what circumstances is a system owner's approval required for an investigation? • How is the request and approval documented? • To what extent is the privacy officer involved in incident response? How is that determined? • Describe the process for evidence collection. • How do you determine the cause of the breach?
	Recovery	• How are compromised systems restored? • How do you validate that the systems have been restored?
	Post-recovery	• How is evidence protected? • Is there a formal "lessons learned" process? What is an example of a recent lessons learned process and what changed as a result of it?
	Reporting	• What does an incident report look like? • How is the incident report classified/labeled/protected? • To whom would you report the following incidents: theft of trade secrets, imported child pornography, credit card numbers?

Note: The interviewer should structure the interview to determine the processes in place within each of the incident response phases and the extent to which these processes are followed.

TABLE 6.36

Security Operations Interview Guideline

Objective	Subtopic	Suggested Questions
Determine existence and adequacy of security controls within the system development environment	System operations	• What types of changes can be performed without approval or documentation? • How are hard drives disposed of? • Do you ever give systems away to employees or charities? How are they sanitized? • What is your backup plan? What about for laptops? • Where are the backups stored? • Do you test your backups?
	Server operations	• What guidance do you use or produce for system hardening? • What changes do you have to make to that guidance for some of your systems?
	File operations	• How do you control access to library code? • Are there shared drives within the organization? How is access to the drives and the files within them controlled? • How are the permissions on these files reviewed? How often and by whom?
	User operations	• How are changes in account privileges tracked? • What happens if a user forgets his password? Can they reset it on their own? • Is the temporary password used for password resets and/or new accounts the same or predictable? • Are user account permissions ever reviewed? How often? By whom?
	Emerging threats	• How do you learn about new vulnerabilities in your systems? • How do you test your possible solution?

Note: The interviewer should structure the interview to determine the processes in place within each of the security operations areas and the extent to which these processes are followed.

and does not clearly define these stages, the team should switch to a more open-ended interview that allows the interviewee to describe the current process by walking through a sample or the most recent incident.

6.2.3.4.2 Security Operations Interview Questions

The security operations questions in Table 6.36 can be asked of several representatives of the security or systems operations groups. The questions cover the system operations, server operations, file operations, user operations, and emerging threats. If the organization has few processes, the team should switch to a more open-ended interview that allows the interviewee to describe the current process by walking through patch management, account management, and system file management.

6.2.3.4.3 Security Program Interview Questions

The questions regarding the security program in Table 6.37 can be asked of several representatives of the security program group as well as the person to whom that group reports. The questions cover security awareness, policy development, risk assessment, security review, coordination and promotion, and program updates. If the organization has few processes, the team should switch to a more open-ended interview that allows the interviewee to describe the current processes by walking through training, the budgeting process, and how new security controls are selected and implemented.

TABLE 6.37

Security Program Interview Guideline

Objective	Subtopic	Suggested Questions
Determine existence and adequacy of security controls within information security program	Security awareness	• Do you have a list of all users who need training and have received it? • Where are the records kept? Do these records include a signature of the student and the instructor? • Is there a privacy awareness training offered as well? • Is there any specialized security training offered to sensitive positions?
	Policy development	• When were the policies last updated? How long did it take to get them approved? • How were users informed of their change? New signatures? • Upon which framework are the policies based?
	Risk management/ Risk assessments	• Describe your security risk management process. • Do you have a risk register (e.g., Plan of Actions and Milestones)? How is it tracked and managed? • How often are security risk assessments performed? • By whom? What is their relationship to the organization or any of its security controls? Did they recommend products? Did you buy them? • How are the security risks incorporated into the enterprise risk management process?
	Security review	• Do you think that other departments are following the policies you set for them (operations, monitoring, development)? Would it surprise you if I told you they were not? • Do you have any annual or periodic report on the security posture of your organization? • To what extent is the board of directors (or similar structure) informed on the security risk of the organization?
	Coordination and promotion	• Who is the security liaison within the development organization? (Follow up by reviewing that person's job description.) • What is your role in the BCP/DRP process? (Not leading it or sole member.) • Is the size of your security team adequate? If not, what areas are most lacking?
	Program updates	• To what extent do you research new security initiatives? What are you likely to recommend next? What did you recently decide not to implement or not recommend, and on what basis? • What is your role as a security liaison in another projects?

Note: The interviewer should structure the interview to determine the processes in place within each of the security program areas and the extent to which these processes are followed.

6.2.4   Inspect Administrative Security Controls

Data gathering for administrative security controls also involves inspecting administrative security controls. Recall that inspection differs from testing, in that inspection is performed when testing is inappropriate or infeasible. Inspection involves the review of the security control and such aspects as configuration or arrangements.

For the most part, the approach for performing a security control inspection includes the listing of the security controls under review, verifying information gathered, determining vulnerabilities, and documenting the results. Each of these phases is discussed within the context of administrative data gathering.

Special consideration must be paid, however, to the review of the security organization itself. This "inspection" is much more involved than the inspection of other security controls because it covers many activities, documents, roles, and even organizational structure. The inspection of the security organization is covered at the end of this section.

6.2.4.1   Inspection—Listing Administrative Security Controls

The relevant security controls to be inspected include only those that lend themselves to inspection. In the case of administrative controls, this includes the following:

- Asset and Inventory Tracking
- Information Labeling
- Change Control
- Two-Person Control
- Dual Control

Of course, only those controls actually implemented by the organization can be inspected. The list of administrative security controls to be reviewed for a specific organization comprises any of the controls that the organization has stated are in place. Statements regarding administrative controls in place could have come from interviews or been provided as part of the document review process. The team should obtain a point of contact for each of these controls.

6.2.4.2   Inspection—Verify Information Gathered

Information gathered regarding administrative security controls should be confirmed through the inspection process. Team members should use various methods to confirm the existence of each of these security controls.

- Asset and Inventory Tracking—If there is a policy in place that requires that all assets be tracked, then members of the team should check to see if all assets they come across are tagged. This does not need to be an exhaustive search. Instead, the inspection can be done throughout the time the team spends on site. The inventory tracking system can be spot-checked by tracing the disposition of a few assets. The inventory tracking system should be able to locate any item number in the inventory or produce a transfer or destruction document.
- Information Labeling—If the organization has instituted an information labeling program or has an information labeling policy, then the assessment team should inspect the administrative controls for their effectiveness in enforcing this policy. Inspection can be in the form of inspecting various documents or media containing sensitive information for the proper label. During the course of the on-site assessment, the team will come across many documents and media that contain sensitive information. The team merely needs to be cognizant of the

information labeling policy and determine if it is being followed. Specific documents that the team is likely to review include previous audit reports and internal documents.

- Change Control—If a change-control process is in place, the team should read available documentation to become familiar with the process. Then the team members should select several recent changes to the system, including at least one you know about through other data gathering processes. Ask to see the documents then walk through the process of change control for those selected changes.
- Two-person Control and Dual Control—If the organization has policies and procedures in place for two-person or dual control, the assessment team should inspect these controls to determine their effectiveness. Inspection of these controls can be accomplished through an understanding of the policies and job descriptions and then a review of any evidence of separation of duties. For example, if dual controls are in place for the creation of an account, the security assessment team members can review audit logs for the account-application and account-creation activities. If both activities are performed by unique individuals, then dual control could be deemed to be effective in this case.

6.2.4.3 Inspection—Determine Vulnerabilities

During inspection of the security controls, the security risk assessment team should look for vulnerabilities. Administrative security controls are policies, procedures, or activities, and not physical or logical controls. Therefore, the inspection process of these controls simply involves the determination of their effectiveness. If the controls are determined to be ineffective, then they have a vulnerability.

Work products of each of the administrative security controls (that lend themselves to inspection) can be inspected to determine if a vulnerability exists:

- Coding Standards—If instances are found where the code does not conform to coding standards or the code review does not take place, then the coding standards and coding procedures are ineffective.
- Asset and Inventory Tracking—If instances are found where assets or inventory cannot be tracked or accounted for, then the asset and inventory tracking policy and procedures are not effective.
- Information Labeling—If the team is able to find instances of information (media or documents) that do not have the proper labels, then the information labeling procedures are not effective.
- Two-person and Dual Control—If the team finds instances where the two-person or dual controls are not being enforced, then these procedures are not effective.

When the team finds any of these policies or procedures lacking, it is also important to determine the reason for the ineffectiveness of the policy. The team will need to use judgment to determine the root cause of the failures. Possible root causes are lack of sufficient training; lack of leadership; lack of sanctions, culture, or morale; lack of clarity in the document; insufficient time or resources to complete reviews; or lack of skills among the staff.

6.2.4.4 Inspection—Document and Review Findings

As with all findings, the security risk assessment team must be sure to carefully record their findings in the area of administrative controls through inspection. The team should include dates, evidence, team member names, and the vulnerabilities observed. These findings must be reviewed with the entire team and with the point of contact for the control, who should be given an opportunity to clarify any misunderstandings.

6.2.4.5 Inspection—The Security Organization

One of the most important administrative data gathering exercises the security risk assessment team can perform is assessing the effectiveness of the information security organization. The team must review the organization's security staff and the way in which the security staff is organized and reports within the organization. The security staff, after all, is the team responsible for the selection, application, and maintenance of the security controls within the organization. The composition and placement of this team within the assessed organization greatly affects the security posture of the organization.

The rise of threats to information assets and the development of information security regulations have led to a much greater appreciation for a strong information security capability within the organization. The way in which this capability is implemented in the organization can take many forms. Some organizations have created security teams, while others have appointed Chief Security Officers (CSOs) or Chief Information Security Officers (CISOs). Regardless of the form, the security risk assessment team requires an approach for measuring the effectiveness of the information security capability of the organization.

There are no hard-and-fast rules or numbers to follow when it comes to measuring the effectiveness of the information security capability of the organization, but the application of information security and business management principles can yield useful guidance.

6.2.4.5.1 Organizational Structure

The information security organization is functionally responsible for the security posture of the organization and the protection of the organization's assets. Execution of the security activities and other elements of an effective security program needs to be coordinated through a security organization and staffed by knowledgeable and experienced security professionals. Such an organization must have the proper organizational placement, adequate resources, and appropriate responsibilities consistent with its mission.

The regular and routine practice of risk reduction must be ensured through efficient operation of the security program. The principles by which any information security organization may be measured are listed in Table 6.38.

The importance of information security and the protection of the organization's assets are certainly understood within most organizations today. However, the proper placement and structure of the information security organization is not. It is useful to understand that information security can be divided into operations and oversight, as seen in Table 6.39.

- Security Operations—This function is responsible for the operations and maintenance of technical security mechanisms. This includes tasks such as server hardening, firewall ruleset maintenance, account maintenance, security patch application, and intrusion detection system maintenance.
- Security Oversight and Direction—Security oversight is responsible for the over-all information security program. This includes development of policies and procedures, security awareness training, and periodic review of security operations.

The placement, structure, and authority of the security organization can greatly influence its effectiveness. To be most effective, a security organization must have a direct reporting line to an officer of the company. Although almost any information security professional will agree that information security needs to report to (or be) a C-level position, few understand why. See Sidebar 6.1 for an explanation.

TABLE 6.38

Security Organization Inspection Guideline

Security Program Area	Expected Elements	Discussion
Organization	Visibility	The security risk assessment team should be able to determine the extent to which the security organization has visibility within the organization and the implications of that visibility on its ability to appropriately oversee the security program.
	Objectiveness	The security risk assessment team should determine the extent to which the security organization can be objective regarding the implementation of security controls and any limitations on that objectivity.
	Authority	The security risk assessment should determine the authority the security organization has to affect the security posture of the organization. Authority elements to look for include policy approval, role in change management, and access to the board of directors.
Budget and Resources	Adequate resources	The information security organization must have adequate budget and resources in order to ensure the development and maintenance of an appropriate security posture for the organization and the protection of the organization's assets
	IT security part of capital planning process	Does the security organization have its own budget?
Roles and Responsibilities	Responsibilities assigned	• Are the security organization's roles formally assigned? • Are there accurate and up-to-date job descriptions in place?
	Skills	Do the current security organization's staff members have the appropriate skills to perform their duties?

Note: The security risk assessment should inspect the effectiveness of the security organization through a review of the organizational structure, budget and resources, and roles and responsibilities.

6.2.4.5.2 Budget and Resources

The information security organization must have adequate budget and resources in order to ensure the development and maintenance of an appropriate security posture for the organization and the protection of the organization's assets. The key aspects of appropriate budget and resources are discussed as follows:

• Adequate Resources—The information security department must have adequate resources to get the job done. As there are no hard-and-fast rules as to what constitutes "adequate" resources, the security risk assessment team member must use interviews, observation, and judgment to determine the adequacy of the organization's information security resources. However, here are a few of the things to consider:
  • Does the security department have control of its own budget?
  • What percent of the overall IT budget is the security budget?
  • How many staff members are on the security team compared to IT?
  • How much does the company spend on legal costs as compared to information security costs?
  • How does the organization compare with its peers?

TABLE 6.39

Security Organization Structure

Security Organization	Functions	Reporting Requirement
Security Governance and Oversight	Overall internal security office. Overall security program including interface with other departments. Provide advice and guidance to other departments, create policy and awareness training, and periodically review security operations. Be in charge of resolving incidents. Report security posture to more senior management.	"C-level" executive—CIO, CFO, CEO, or even a CSO or the CISO itself—reporting to the CEO or board of directors. You could (should) have physical security reporting to the CSO.
Security Audit	Oversight for overall security program. Perform independent periodic risk assessment and security program review	This should be internal audit (if not reporting to CSO) or an outside firm.
Security Operations	Account maintenance, firewall and IDS configuration, operating system patching, anti-virus configuration and operations, etc.	It seems reasonable that this function reports to director of IT, although the security audit and governance should periodically review for compliance.

Note: The effectiveness of the security organization can be enabled or disabled by its placement within the security organization.

- Are resources distributed based on a risk model?
- Is information security part of the capital planning process?

6.2.4.5.3 Roles and Responsibilities

Lastly, the information security organization needs to formally recognize the roles and responsibilities of the team. These roles and responsibilities should be documented. The security risk assessment team member should review the current job descriptions of the information security staff to determine if the roles and responsibilities are appropriately assigned and documented. Again, there are no hard-and-fast rules as to what constitutes "appropriate" assigning of roles and responsibilities, so the security risk assessment team member must use interviews, observation, and judgment to determine the adequacy of the organization's information security resources. The assessor can use the following questions and observations as a guideline:

SIDEBAR 6.1   WHY SECURITY SHOULD NOT BE PART OF THE IT DEPARTMENT

One of the most important elements of a security program within an organization is the placement of the security personnel within the organization. There are a few key elements of information security that need to be considered for the organizational placement of the security department:

- Information security (IS) is a multifaceted concern. An information security department needs to consider the threats to the organization's assets no matter what the source. Therefore, the IS department will be working with many other departments such as legal, human resources, executives, department heads, and information technology (IT).

- The information security program develops information intended for C-level executives. Such information includes risks to the organization, trade-offs between usability and security, trade-offs between departments, and cost of adhering to contracts and regulations.
- The information security program is only effective if it is unbiased and protected. C-level executives need the information that the IS department can produce so that they can make informed decisions. If that information is tainted, swayed, or suppressed, then the organization is in danger of making decisions with the wrong information or without any information.

An information security department has three basic functions: governance and oversight, audit, and operations. The functions of the information security department can be divided across multiple organizations. In fact, such a separation increases the objectivity of the governance and audit functions. However, under no circumstances should the governance and oversight functions be inside the IT department. These functions must report directly to (or be) a C-level executive.

C-level executives, and not department heads, are trusted to make risk decisions for the organization. Furthermore, the IT department is the center of many security-relevant trade-offs and decisions. Placing the IS department inside the IT department effectively confirms that each trade-off will likely side with the budget and schedule constraints of the IT department and will not adequately consider the ramifications to the overall business.

The governance and oversight element of the security organization needs to be placed appropriately within the organization for it to be effective. The important aspects of the organizational placement of the governance function of the security organization are visibility, objectivity, and authority. Without these three aspects, the security organization is likely to fail in its mission.

- Visibility—In order to be effective, an information security organization must have visibility throughout all functions of the organization that can affect the overall security posture of the organization. If the security department is seen as "an IT thing," then it is likely that the security organization will be ineffective at controlling security risk in areas such as human resources, facilities, legal, and other business areas. The security risk assessment team should be able to determine the extent to which the security organization has visibility within the organization and the implications of that visibility on its ability to appropriately oversee the security program.
- Objectivity—An information security organization must be objective. This principle is a long-standing one in any function that provides oversight, audit, or compliance. The principle states, "You can't check your own work." Consider the security department that both hardens systems and provides the vulnerability scanning to ensure that the systems are hardened correctly or, worse, designs the network security model and provides the review of the network security architecture. The security risk assessment team should determine the extent to which the security organization can be objective regarding the implementation of security controls and any limitations on that objectivity.
- Authority—The information security department should also be given proper authority to provide oversight of the organization's security controls. Specific authority may include representation on the change-control board and reporting to a C-level executive. The security risk assessment should determine the authority the security organization has to affect the security posture of the organization. Authority elements to look for include policy approval, role in change management, and access to the board of directors.

- Does each staff member within the security organization have an accurate job description?
  - Are all of the responsibilities of the security organization assigned to individuals?
  - Does the description specify the qualifications required for each position?
  - Does the description specify the expectations and boundaries of the role?
- Are the staff members qualified and properly trained for their positions?
- Is there an adequate number of staff members to get the job done?

6.2.5   OBSERVE ADMINISTRATIVE BEHAVIOR

The process of gathering data through observation is a subtle one. With a few exceptions, this process is passive and depends on team members being aware of the organization's policies and procedures and keeping an eye out for opportunities to confirm or disprove the organization's adherence to policies and procedures. Some observations can be active in nature, such as placing a control badge in your pocket and seeing if anyone challenges you. However, more experienced team members will find observation to be second nature and a side effect of being on site.

With a little guidance and teamwork, these observations can be recorded by most team members, thereby adding additional data points to the data gathering process. Table 6.40 provides some guidance for observing the behavior of the organization's staff to determine the strength of some of the administrative controls. The security risk assessment team is encouraged to review Table 6.40 and add or modify table elements to suit its own needs and experiences.

6.2.6   TEST ADMINISTRATIVE SECURITY CONTROLS

The last phase of data gathering for administrative security controls in the RIIOT method is testing. Testing of administrative controls is the process of invoking conditions that should trigger the administrative controls and reviewing the response against the policies, procedures, and good practice. This type of data gathering provides excellent insight into the actual effectiveness of the controls, but it can only be applied in a limited fashion.

The administrative controls that lend themselves to testing include information labeling, media destruction, and account and access controls. An approach for testing each of these controls is presented below. The security risk assessment team is encouraged to adopt, modify, or add to these test methods.

6.2.6.1   Information Labeling Testing

Testing the procedures for information security labeling requires that the security risk assessment team perform activities that cause the information labeling procedures to come into effect (i.e., cause sensitive documents to be created). There are typically many activities that will cause a sensitive document to be created during a security risk assessment. In the event that the security risk assessment team has not performed any activities that would cause the creation of sensitive information, the team can simply ask for a document to be created that contains sensitive information.

Any one of the following events is likely to cause the assessed organization to create a sensitive document:

- Request Simple Mail Transfer Protocol (SMTP) strings for internal testing
- Request minutes of change-management control-board meetings
- Request latest incident handling report
- Create contractual documents for an independent security risk assessment

TABLE 6.40

Administrative Controls Observation Guideline

Administrative Control	Claim	Observation Test or Procedure Check
Ethics	All employees exhibit ethical behavior.	General observations from being on site: • Did any members of the team witness or overhear any unethical behavior?
Separation of duty	No sensitive transactions are performed by a single person. Security controls are independently reviewed.	Identify critical transactions requiring separation: • Development/production • Key generation/key delivery • Design and implementation/audit • PO creation/PO payment • Associate transactions with accounts or individuals • Check of conflicts of interest
Understanding responsibilities	All personnel understand their responsibilities.	General observations from being on site: • Did personnel generally understand for what they were responsible? • Were there any noticed gaps or overlaps in responsibilities?
Security team structure	Security program has the authority and visibility they need to accomplish their job.	General observations from being on site: • Did the security organization have the access and authority it needed to do their job? • Were any areas inappropriately excluded from the security risk assessment?
Least privilege	All personnel have the minimum privileges they need to perform their job.	Did personnel have more privilege than necessary? • Did anyone log in as root? • How many administrators have root access? • Who had access to audit logs?
Job training	All personnel have the proper training and skills to perform their duties.	Was there anyone who did not have adequate skills or training to do their job? • Were the available security tools being used to their full extent? • Did internal reviews, scans, and audits expose obvious vulnerabilities?
Policy and procedure	All policies and procedures are followed.	Were there any obvious breaches to security policies? • Were acceptable-use policies followed? • Were visitor control policies followed? • Was change management policy followed? • Did you see any passwords on monitors or other areas (e.g., under keyboards or phones)?
Double key data entry	Sensitive data is entered twice to ensure accuracy.	Ask to observe the data entry process: • Were the data entry procedures followed? • Did you witness any mistakes being caught?
Two-person control and dual control	Sensitive tasks are performed by more than a single person.	Ask to observe the sensitive process: • Does the process really require two people? • What would happen if a single person attempted to perform the whole process alone?
Information labeling	All sensitive information is labeled.	Find instances of unlabeled or improperly labeled information: • Check all documents reviewed for proper labels. • Witness documents being created (perhaps as part of the security risk assessment). Were the documents properly labeled?

(Continued)

TABLE 6.40 *(Continued)*

Administrative Control	Claim	Observation Test or Procedure Check
Media destruction	All sensitive information is removed from media released from control.	Ask to witness media destruction methods: • Were the media destruction procedures followed? • Query the inventory tracking system for disposed systems—check methods of disposal. • Check media destruction area or storerooms for unused media. Double-check stored media against the inventory tracking system for inaccuracies. • Check to see if processes are followed: • Check trash bins near fax machines or user work areas. Is there any sensitive information in them? • Check storage areas for older systems and system parts. Have all of these systems and parts been properly sanitized?
	Account maintenance is performed in accordance with policies.	Ask administrators if there are any group IDs or dormant accounts.
No weak passwords	Ask to see a list of accounts for selected network components.	Look for the following as good candidates: • Equipment requiring remote maintenance • Help desk functions • Any group accounts associated with the equipment? • Do these accounts conform to policies? Sufficiently strong passwords? Passwords changed and not shared?
Contractual obligations	All business partners with access to sensitive information properly protect information.	Ask for a list of contractors and list of signed contracts: • Were there any contracts that had significant modifications to the standard contractual obligations? • Do all contractors have a contract with the important elements of contractual security obligations? • Have any audits on the contractors been performed?
Security awareness and acceptable-use policy	All staff follow guidance.	Perform security walk-throughs. Be aware of: • Recorded passwords in workspace • Sensitive conversations in public areas • Sensitive information left on printers or in wastebaskets
	Staff understands how to recognize and guard against social engineering.	Perform social engineering (optional): • Attempt to gain sensitive information or access through social engineering methods
	All staff is security aware.	Ask some questions within the interviews to test security awareness: • Ask for information you should not receive • Ask who they would contact if they noticed a security breach
Incident response	Incident response policies and procedures are followed.	Ask for a walk-through of the last incident response: • Ask for documentation of the response. Check against the policy. • Also recall an incident from an interview or other source and ask to see where that incident was documented.

(Continued)

TABLE 6.40 *(Continued)*

Administrative Control	Claim	Observation Test or Procedure Check
Hiring and termination	• References are checked for all employees. • Background checks are performed for sensitive positions.	• Randomly select some employees and ask your HR contact to verify that references were checked for those persons. • Randomly select some employees with sensitive positions and ask your HR contact to verify that background checks were performed for those persons.
System monitoring	• Violations of the acceptable-use policy are monitored and reported. • Attempts to circumvent security are monitored and logged	• Attempt to violate the acceptable use policy by going to some forbidden Web sites. Ask to see the monitor logs later that day. • In conjunction with your external security testing, review system monitoring effectiveness.
Data backup	• Backups are performed for critical data.	• Ask to witness data backup procedures on a test system • Ask to witness any backup or restore procedure that is scheduled while you are on site.

Note: The security risk assessment team should be prepared to observe the behavior of the security staff, key personnel, and general employee population as a check against policies, procedures, and training.

The security risk assessment team can then simply check that the document was created according to the associated procedures. The team should specifically check for the proper label in the proper place and format.

6.2.6.2 Media Destruction Testing

Testing the media destruction controls requires that the security risk assessment team perform activities that cause the destruction of media that could possibly contain sensitive information. This can be a follow-on activity from the information-labeling testing, since that task involves the creation of sensitive information. The approaches for TRASHINT (short for Trash Intelligence) and sanitization testing methods below should be considered.

6.2.6.2.1 Approach 1: TRASHINT

This approach involves a simple test of the disposal and destruction procedures for sensitive information. The security risk assessment team should be familiar with the information-labeling and sensitive information and media disposal and destruction procedures. With those procedures in mind, the team should look for any deficiencies in the practice of the procedures. The TRASHINT approach tests these controls by looking for improper disposal of sensitive information or media.

- Where to Look—During a TRASHINT testing exercise, the security risk assessment team should search candidate areas for the possible presence of sensitive information. Sensitive information could be just about anywhere, but the following places are good candidates:
  - Trash Receptacles—Check trash bins for sensitive information, especially those bins near fax machines, sensitive areas, and shredding bins.

- Shredding Bins—Check for shredding bins that have not been properly secured.
- Out in the Open—Check for sensitive information left in unsecured areas. Places to look include desktops, executive floors, conference rooms, and outside security control areas.
- Outside Trash Receptacles—Check for unsecured outside trash receptacles. No need to scrounge through coffee grounds, but the team should look for boxes or stacks of paper or special forms.
- What to Look for—Sensitive information is typically quite easy to spot. Look for any papers with sensitive-information labels or with clearly sensitive information. Clearly sensitive information includes credit information, salary information, customer lists, personal data, and healthcare data.
- What to Do with It—Prior to participating in the TRASHINT exercise, the security risk assessment team must be briefed as to the protocol for handling sensitive information. The protocol should be developed specifically for the assessed organization's needs and approved by the organization. As a baseline protocol, the following are suggested:
  - Trash—If the sensitive information was found in the trash or discarded in an open area (e.g., hallway), then it should be collected, labeled, documented, and returned to the assessed organization.
  - Unsecured Shredding Bins—If the sensitive information is found in any container that is normally secured (or should be), then the information may be reviewed but should not be removed.
  - Workspace—If the sensitive information is discovered on someone's workspace when it should have been secured, then the information may be reviewed but should not be removed.

For those situations in which the material is not to be removed, the team should consider documenting the evidence by taking a digital picture. However, the process of taking pictures of sensitive information should be reviewed with the assessed organization and documented as a data collections activity that has the permission of the assessed organization.

6.2.6.2.2   Approach 2: Sanitization Test

The sanitization test requires that the security risk assessment team have tools to check the effectiveness of the assessed organization's sanitization methods. The security risk assessment team should be familiar with the media disposal and destruction procedures. With those procedures in mind, the team should collect samples of sanitized data, test the media for proper sanitization, and document the results.

- Collection of Samples—Samples of media that should be sanitized can be collected from storerooms, recycle bins, or work areas dedicated to this task. The team should seek only those devices that are believed to have completed the sanitization process.
- Test Media for Residual Data—The assessment team can test the data-sanitization measures to assess their effectiveness. The tests should start with simple read attempts, but could progress to low-level attempts to read data residuals with the use of tools. These tools can vary from the quality-assurance option in data-sanitization tools to disk recovery tools and data forensic tools.
- Document Results—The security risk assessment team needs to document the results of the attempts to read data from sanitized media. Any findings will be referenced as evidence in the final risk assessment report. It is important to record what data was captured as well as the effort and toil the team required in gaining access to the data.

6.2.6.3 Account and Access Control Procedures Testing

Whether or not a policy exists, the security risk assessment team should review the account-provisioning procedures and the account-maintenance procedures during the data gathering stage of the security risk assessment. Accounts on the systems within the organization represent the allowed accesses and privileges of users within the system. These security controls are central to the enforcement of any security policy. The following approaches are offered as examples of performing an account review.

6.2.6.3.1 Approach 1: Process Test

This approach involves a simple test of the account-provisioning process. Prior to the on-site portion of the security risk assessment, the team will have requested accounts for the team members. At this stage, the team can simply ask to see documented evidence on those requests and evidence of the account-provisioning process that was followed. For example, if the organization has a policy and specific forms and signatures that must be obtained prior to account provisioning, then the security risk assessment team would expect to find evidence that this policy and procedure were followed in their case as well. If no such policy or procedure exists, the team would document the process and note any deficiencies.

While all organizations are likely to have slightly different processes for account provisioning, the security risk assessment team should look for the following elements of the process as a minimum:

- Account-Provisioning Approval Form—This should include the name of the requester, the reason for the request, the accesses or privilege levels requested, the signature of the approver, and an indication that the candidate user has completed security awareness training.
- No Access Prior to Approval—The assessors (or any guest) should be denied access to information systems until approval is granted.

6.2.6.3.2 Approach 2: Process Audit—Sample

Another approach the security risk assessment team may use is a process audit in which the team samples elements of the account-provisioning and -maintenance program. Sampling is performed to gather some evidence quickly and efficiently on the account process. Sampling should be performed consistent with the team's sampling policy (see Section 5.1). Samples should be selected and reviewed in each of the account-provisioning phases:

- Phase 1: Account Creation—This phase covers the creation of accounts for new staff members and guests. As mentioned in the first approach, accounts created should follow the documented policy. Expected elements of the policy include an account-provisioning form that includes the requester's name, request type, privilege level, approval signature, and signature of account holder indicating that security awareness training has been completed.
- Phase 2: Account Maintenance—This phase covers changes in account status, for example, an increase in privileges for an existing account. To audit this activity, the assessor should ask for a list of personnel who recently changed positions within the company. The assessor should then ask for the documentation that was used to ensure that the process of changing accounts or increasing the privilege of the current account was performed appropriately.

  Another activity that could be performed during this phase is to review a list of all account status changes for the previous two months. This list should be reviewed with the information owners to determine if such changes were appropriate for each person listed in the report.

- Phase 3: Account Removal—Lastly, the termination of accounts must be handled appropriately. A discussion on expected policy elements was covered earlier in this book. The assessor should obtain a list from human resources on recent departures. Based on time available, the assessor should choose a number of terminations and walk through the termination procedures to determine if they were followed. Another approach to assessing account terminations is to review the account provisioning for the last guest or last set of auditors who should no longer have access. Then follow the same procedures as described previously.

6.2.6.3.3 Approach 3: Process Audit—Complete

The last approach for reviewing account maintenance is much like the second approach, process audit—sample, but it should be performed in a complete manner. This means that, during the account creation phase, all current accesses should be audited for the completion of an account-provisioning form. Also, all changes and terminations should be reviewed. Other than simply being more complete, this approach is basically the same as the second approach. However, there is one activity that should be performed during the complete process audit that has not yet been discussed:

- Zero-Based Review—When accounts are reviewed at random, or even when monthly changes are reviewed completely, some accounts can still slip through the cracks. Sometimes accounts are held open for the expected return of an employee. At other times, key personnel responsible for elements of the process are absent. A zero-based review is a review of all accounts on each critical system. The account review is simply a printout of all accounts on a system reviewed by the owner of the system. It may also be useful to cross-check the access list with human resources to ensure that all staff indicated on the access list are still employed and that all contractors have current access.

6.2.6.4 Outsourcing and Information Exchange

The security policies, procedures, and organizational structures we have discussed so far all have to do with the organization being assessed. But when the assessed organization outsources a critical function or shares sensitive information with another organization, then the security risk assessment must review the security controls being applied to those critical functions and sensitive data outside of the organization.

Almost all security risk assessments will be bounded such that the security risk assessment team would not be expected to travel to the other location and perform a security risk assessment there. However, there are several actions that should be performed by the security risk assessment team to gather data on the outsourcing and information exchange actions of the organization.

6.2.6.4.1 Outsourcing Review

If an organization has outsourced any of its critical functions, it may be difficult for the security risk assessment team to gather data regarding the adequacy of security controls within that outsourced function. The following approaches for obtaining appropriate data should be considered.

6.2.6.4.1.1 Approach 1: Review Contracts

The security risk assessment team member could simply review the contracts covering the outsourcing of the critical function. The assessor should look for the following elements in the contract:

- Is there a service-level agreement associated with the outsourced function?
  - Are reasonable and relevant security metrics defined?
  - Are these security metrics measured and reported?

- Is there a business associate agreement or other contractual agreement covering the sharing of sensitive information?
  - Does the organization have the ability to terminate the contract upon a material breach or violation of the outsourcing organization's obligations?
  - Does the contract specify appropriate safeguards for reasonably protecting the sensitive information and organizational assets from breaches of security?
  - Is the outsourcing organization required to report material security incidents that may impact the security of the organization's sensitive information and protected assets?
  - Does the organization have the right to audit or test the outsourcing organization's ability to provide adequate security?

6.2.6.4.1.2   Approach 2: Review Available Assessments

Many organizations that are in the business of performing critical business functions for other organizations (e.g., service organizations) or receiving sensitive information from other organizations (e.g., business partners) commission independent reviews of their security controls. The final report from these reviews is intended to be shared with organizations that must trust the security controls of the service organization or business partner.

If such a report is available, the security risk assessment team can simply review the results of the report. However, the assessor should also be careful to ensure that the report is recent, positive, and performed by someone knowledgeable and objective.

- Recent—An assessor cannot expect that the outside assessment be completed within the last 30 days, but a report more than a year old is probably no longer relevant. The assessor should use judgment to determine the extent to which there may have been significant changes in the business functions or threat environment and determine how recent a report should be to provide a measure of assurance that the service organization appropriately protects sensitive information and protected resources.
- Positive—The report should be rather clear as to the findings of the adequacy of the security controls. To be sure, the report will not make statements regarding "complete" or 100% security. The assessor should be looking for acceptable risk or adequate measures. Furthermore, the assessment report is likely to contain recommendations along with a timeline. The assessor should ask the sponsoring organization to follow up with the service organization to see if the recommendations have been implemented.
- Knowledgeable and Objective Author—If the assessment report is authored by the service organization itself, then this is not considered an assessment; instead, it is a statement. Such a report may still be useful in documenting the claimed security controls, but this does not provide a measurement of their adequacy, because the author would not be capable of providing an objective review. Moreover, the author of the document must demonstrate expertise and knowledge of security testing and security risk assessment methods. The assessor should expect to see the author's credentials, indication of experience, or an explanation and citation of the methodology that was used to perform the assessment.

6.2.6.4.1.3   Approach 3: Review Questionnaire Responses

A third approach would be to engage the service organization in communicating their claimed security controls through the use of a questionnaire or a phone interview. This questionnaire should solicit information using many of the same questions and report elements discussed in the other approaches. The following questionnaire may be appropriate for many service organizations.

- Does your organization have an information security policy?
- Does your organization maintain a firewall at the boundary of your network?
- Do you regularly apply security patches?

- Does your organization maintain anti-virus software?
- Do you protect stored and transmitted sensitive data through encryption?
- Are access controls used within your information systems?
- Is each person assigned a unique identification on the system?
- Are audit controls in place to associate security-relevant actions with a person or entity?
- Have default passwords and security parameters been overwritten?
- Are the security controls regularly tested?
- Is access to sensitive data and critical systems physically protected?

At the conclusion of the interview, the answers should be compiled, approved, and signed by the service organizations.

EXERCISES

1. What is the difference between two-person control and dual control? Give examples.
2. Create a threat statement complete with threat actors and threat actions and list the associated administrative controls that can address the risks caused by the threat actions.
3. Plan an interview with a systems administrator. (Limit the scope of the interview to administrative controls.)
   a. What controls would you cover in the interview?
   b. What questions would you ask?
   c. How would you prepare for the interview?
   d. What documents would you request from the systems administrator?
4. Review the security awareness training you have been given at your organization against the checklist provided in this chapter.
   a. Is the security awareness training complete?
   b. Are all of the directives governing your use of IT equipment and sensitive data clear?
   c. Are there any consistencies between the Acceptable Use Policy (AUP) and the security awareness training?
5. Is it appropriate to discuss security tips for home computer use during security awareness training?
6. Discuss the advantages and disadvantages of using phishing campaigns as a part of a security awareness and training program.
7. Plan a RIIOT-based data gathering to determine the effectiveness of the Acceptable Use Policy. Show the activities in all the appropriate RIIOT approaches.
   a. Include sufficient detail to guide a team to perform the analysis (e.g., how many hours would you allot to perform interviews, and who should be interviewed?)
   b. What questions would you ask of whom?
   c. Create an observation guideline.

BIBLIOGRAPHY

Balaouras, Stephanie, The State of Disaster Recovery Preparedness 2017, Disaster Recovery Journal, Spring 2017.

DoD, *National Industrial Security Program Operating Manual (NISPOM)*. DoD 5220.22-M, May 18, 2016.

Federal Deposit Insurance Corporation, *Outsourcing Technology Services: Service Level Agreements(SLAs)*, https://ithandbook.ffiec.gov/it-booklets/outsourcing-technology-services/risk-management/contract-issues/service-level-agreements-(slas).aspx, (accessed September 14, 2020.)

Federal Financial Institutions Examination Council, IT Examination Handbook: Audit AUD, April 2012. http://www.ftc.gov/documents/bus54-financial-institutions-and-customer-information-complying-safeguards-rule, (accessed September 14, 2020).

Federal Emergency Management Agency, "Make Your Business Resilient," Infographic, https://www.fema.gov/media-library-data/1441212988001-1aa7fa978c5f999ed088dcaa815cb8cd/3a_BusinessInfographic-1.pdf, (accessed September 20, 2020)

Gill, Mark, "10 Shocking Data Loss and Disaster Recovery Statistics," Comparitech, July 4, 2020.

LogicMonitor, "IT Outage Impact Study: A global analysis of IT downtime and its impact on businesses," 2019.

National Institute of Standards and Technology (NIST): U.S. Department of Commerce, "Assessing Security and Privacy Controls in Federal Information Systems and Organizations: Building Effective Assessment Plans," NIST Special Publication 800-53A, Revision 4, December 2014.

National Institute of Standards and Technology (NIST): U.S. Department of Commerce, "Guide for Security-Focused Configuration Management of Information Systems," NIST Special Publication 800-128, August 2011.

Microsoft Patterns & Practices Library. Walkthrough: Creating a Threat Model for a Web Application. October, 2005. http://msdn.microsoft.com/en-us/library/ms978538.aspx (accessed February 7, 2011).

Open Web Application Security Project (OWASP), "Application Security Verification Standard 4.0," Final, March 2019.

The Open Web Application Security Project (OWASP), *OWASP Secure Coding Practices Quick Reference Guide*, 2010. https://owasp.org/www-pdf-archive/OWASP_SCP_Quick_Reference_Guide_v2.pdf, (accessed September 14, 2020)

Verizon, *Data Breach Investigations Report*, 2020.

7 Technical Data Gathering

7.1 TECHNICAL THREATS AND SAFEGUARDS

The concepts of threats, threat agents, and threat actions were covered earlier in Chapter 4. Technical threats specifically are covered here as an approach to introducing technical data gathering. This section, on threats and safeguards, is intended as a primer or introduction to security threats in the technical area.[1]

- Technical Threats and Threat Actions—A member of a security risk assessment team cannot be effective without a basic understanding of the threats and safeguards within the technical security area. There are numerous technical security threats; some of the more frequent technical threats and safeguards are listed in Figure 7.1. The list of specific threat actions is ever growing and difficult to completely enumerate. However, it is useful to at a minimum understand the classes in which these threat actions may be organized and understood. Those threat actions that can be targeted at or mitigated by technical controls are categorized as invoked malware, theft & sabotage, socially engineered, hacked, abused trust, environmental damage, and erred, see Table 7.1.
- Technical Safeguards—There is a vast array of technical safeguards that could be effective against the various threats to an organization. This chapter provides a brief introduction to many of these technical safeguards to ensure that the security risk assessment team member is familiar with controls they may encounter during as assessment as well as available safeguards for recommendations to address high risk areas. The technical safeguards presented here are divided into the following categories:
  - Information Control—Information control safeguards address controls that may be put in place to protect sensitive and critical information. These safeguards are grouped into the classes of user error, sensitive information, and user accounts.
  - Business Continuity—Business continuity safeguards address the protection of sensitive data and critical systems during a disaster to ensure the continuity of business operations. These safeguards are grouped into the classes of contingency planning and incident response.

FIGURE 7.1 Technical safeguard threats. A variety of threat actions can be targeted at or addressed through the implementation of technical safeguards. These threat actions can be organized into the categories of invoking malware, theft & sabotage, being socially engineered, being hacked, abusing trust, suffering environmental damage, and committing an error.

TABLE 7.1

Technical Threats and Safeguards: Information Control

Class	Threat	Safeguard
User error	• Invoked Malware • Socially Engineered • Erred	• Anti-Malware • Monitoring technology • Audit logs
Sensitive/ Critical information	• Invoked Malware • Theft & Sabotage • Socially Engineered • Hacked • Abused Trust • Erred	• Anti-Malware • Logical access controls • Checksums • Encryption
User accounts	• Invoked Malware • Theft & Sabotage • Socially Engineered • Hacked • Abused Trust • Erred	• Anti-Malware • Single sign on systems • Two-factor authentication • Identity management systems • Automated password policies • Password crackers • Password generators

Note: Threat actions applicable to information control include invoking malware, theft & sabotage, being socially engineered or hacked, abusing trust, and committing errors. Technical safeguards that can address these threat actions are described below.

- System Security—System security safeguards address the protection of systems and applications. These safeguards are grouped into the classes of system controls, application security, and change management.
- Architecture—The architecture safeguards address the arrangement of network components and services. Safeguards in this area are grouped into the classes of topology, transmission, and perimeter network.
- Components—The component's safeguards address devices or subsystems within an organization's infrastructure that enforce a specific security policy. Examples include Identity Management systems (IdM), Intrusion Detection Systems (IDS), and Security Information and Event Management (SIEM) Systems. Safeguards in this area are grouped into the classes of access control and continuous monitoring.
- Configuration—The configuration safeguards address controls that implement or check the secure configuration of deployed systems. Safeguards in this area have a single class of system settings.
- Data—The data safeguards address controls that protect sensitive data. Safeguards in this area are grouped into the classes of storage and transit.

The specific safeguards within each of these categories are discussed in the sections below and represented in Tables 7.1 through 7.7.

7.1.1 Information Control

Information is one of the most valuable assets of the organization. Adequate technical security controls should be placed on sensitive information to ensure that it is protected. Various controls and safeguards are available, including restricting user error, securing sensitive information, and controlling user accounts.

7.1.1.1   Information Control Threats

One of the organization's most valuable assets is its own information. This asset can be a target of both internal and external threat agents. The insider actions exposing the organization's information can be unintentional or intentional. External actions are almost exclusively intentional. Intentional and unintentional actions of internal and external threat actors can include the following threat actions[2]:

- Invoked Malware—An employee may take a number of actions that lead to the introduction of malicious software (e.g., malware) on their computer. This may involve opening an e-mail, visiting a website, inserting removable memory into the employee's computer, downloading the malware, or the malware may have been put in place by the software manufacturer.
- Theft & Sabotage—An employee may be the victim of a robbery in which an organizational asset such as a laptop or a mobile device may now be in the hands of an unauthorized person. Employees may be susceptible to theft while traveling to and from work, traveling for work, or at home or a hotel.
- Socially Engineered—An employee may fall prey to a cybercriminal who uses psychology (instead of technical approaches) to gain the trust of the employee and then tricks them into violating the organization's security policy. This is basically a modern version of a confidence scam (e.g., used to by conmen).
- Hacked—An employee may fail victim to an attacker using hacking methods to circumvent the security controls on their computer or account. Hacking methods are numerous and ever-growing as attackers continually find new methods to gain unauthorized access.
- Abused Trust—An employee may abuse the trust given to them and utilize this misplaced trust to take actions against the organization. There are many such actions a trusted employee could take.
- Environmental Damage—Organizational assets may succumb to environmental damage from severe weather (e.g., floods, tornadoes, and earthquakes), infrastructure failures (e.g., power outages), or even infestations (e.g., rats).
- Erred—Lastly, an employee may simply make a mistake that results in the loss of confidentiality of sensitive data, or in the misplacement of an organizational asset such as a laptop.

7.1.1.2   Information Control Safeguards

Given the wide array of potential threat actions that could pose a threat to the organization's assets from an employee, an outsider, or even nature, organizations should implement an adequate set of technical security controls (e.g., safeguards) to address these threats. Table 7.1 lists an example set of technical safeguards that an organization may employ to counter the threat and threat actions impacting information control. These technical safeguards are discussed within the classes of user error, sensitive information, and user accounts.

7.1.1.2.1   User Error

Many controls and safeguards discussed so far have dealt with ways to stop fraud, waste, and abuse, but even well-meaning employees can breach the security of the organization's information through accidental means. The technical controls discussed below are some of the ways to restrict user error as it would impact the security of the organization's information.

- Anti-Malware Systems—Anti-Malware systems cover viruses, spam, and other malicious content. The extensibility of an organization's networks, e-mail systems, and user downloads, and the possibility of the introduction of malicious code make an anti-malware system an essential component of technical security controls. Anti-malware systems can be deployed at the network or workstation level. Both network- and host-based anti-malware systems depend on the diligent practice of signature updates (or anomaly detection) and active scanning.

- Monitoring Technology—Monitoring technology includes any technical device or program that can monitor a user's behavior on the organization's information system. Monitoring technology could focus on the user's Web-surfing habits, e-mail sent or received, or even down to the level of the user's input (e.g., keystroke). Universal Resource Locator (URL) monitoring (or blocking) can report on user Web-surfing habits or even block such behavior. E-mail monitoring systems can monitor the information received or sent by the user or even block certain e-mails. Keystroke monitoring can record and report on individual keystrokes at a specific user's machine.

- Audit Logs—Audit log files contain data recorded by the system at the time of a security-relevant event. The data contained in these logs should include, at a minimum, the following information: identification, time, event, success/failure. Additional information, such as performance metrics, warnings, and location, could be supplied in audit logs for certain events. The system events that produce audit logs are typically configurable and should strike a balance between performance impact and the availability of detailed audit data.

7.1.1.2.2   Sensitive and Critical Information

All data is valuable to the organization, but some data is more critical and sensitive than other data. The organization should implement technical security controls to protect it from disclosure or modification and to ensure its availability.

- Anti-Malware—Covered in Section 7.1.1.2.1.
- Logical Access Controls—Logical access controls are used to enforce the organization's intention of how critical and sensitive files may be accessed by users. These controls can be implemented through many different means, such as permission bits, access control lists (ACLs), capability lists, and passwords.[3] These types of logical access controls provide access control based on the identification of the user and the controls placed on the file. Some highly secure systems may employ the use of mandatory access control features, which control access to sensitive files based on the user's clearance and the file's sensitivity.
- Checksums—Checksums and cryptographic checksums provide a method for detecting unauthorized modifications to sensitive files. This service is provided by computing and separately storing a numeric value based on the contents of the file. The file's integrity is determined by recomputing the numeric value and comparing it against the stored value. If the values do not match, the integrity of the file has been compromised.
- Encryption—Specifically, encryption is the transformation of plaintext into another unrecognizable form. However, the term *encryption* is generally used to describe the application of one or more cryptographic techniques to ensure confidentiality, integrity, authentication, or non-repudiation. Encryption technology can be applied to sensitive and critical information to ensure its confidentiality and integrity.

7.1.1.2.3   User Accounts

A user account contains a user's attributes such as name, sensitivity level, and account expiration. The user account provides the user access to organizational critical resources and files and should therefore be strictly controlled. The following technical safeguards can assist in ensuring that security is preserved through user accounts:

- Single Sign-On Systems—A single sign-on (SSO) system is a networkwide system for user authentication based on client/server technology. Instead of having to remember an identification and password pair for every system on the network, a user of an SSO can simply remember a single identification and authentication pair (typically more than just a password). Such a system provides the benefits of consolidating authentication within the enterprise and encouraging better user habits because the user only has to remember one password.

- Two-Factor Authentication—Two-factor authentication, also called *strong authentication*, is the practice of requiring at least two forms of authentication information from a user prior to confirming the user's identity.[4]
- Identity Management Systems—Identity management systems identify individuals and provide systemwide access control. Identity management is a step beyond single sign-on, in that it provides a single identity for each individual (e.g., John M. Smith) and associates all of that user's system identities (e.g., jsmith, smithjm, and admin008) to that single individual.
- Automated Password Policy Enforcement—Many operating systems have password policy enforcement controls as a built-in function of the system. These controls allow the administrator to define password policies such as minimum length, expiration date, and complexity. The system will then enforce these policies for the user accounts under the control of the administrator.
- Password Crackers—User passwords are stored in a one-way encrypted form on the system. An administrator with access to the file containing these encrypted passwords (e.g., the password file) can use a program that tries to determine users' passwords by one-way encrypting candidate passwords and comparing the results to the data stored in the password file. Password crackers can use dictionaries of probable passwords or they can perform the cracking through a brute-force attack. Password crackers can be used as a method of testing the strength of user-selected passwords and informing those with weak passwords to choose a more secure password.
- Password Generators—Left to their own devices, many users are not good at selecting security passwords. Password generators can be implemented within the password reset routine to assist users in creating strong passwords for their use. There are many types of password generators. One such type provides pronounceable passwords made up of two-, three-, and four-letter combinations, such as "val-ton-mar" or "byt-me-jeff."

7.1.2 BUSINESS CONTINUITY

Business continuity is the field of preparation and planning undertaken by organizations to ensure that they remain a viable entity if and when a disaster impacts their critical systems. Business continuity planning is the process of identifying critical systems, identifying reasonable threats, and creating a long-term strategy for reducing the impact of interruptions to the business and stabilizing critical business functions.

7.1.2.1 Business Continuity Threats

The planning, strategy, preparation and other elements of business continuity planning and incident response preparedness enables an organization to avoid disasters and lessen the impact of disasters and incidents. Threat actions addressed by business continuity and incident response planning include the following:

- Invoked Malware—Malicious software invoked by an employee can have disastrous consequences for the organization and its assets. Incident response planning and business continuity controls can limit the impact.
- Theft & Sabotage—The threat action of theft and sabotage can cause security incidents and disasters severely impacting the organization. The organization may also be more suspectable to these threat actions during the time of a crisis. Planning and strategy in this control area can avoid and lessen the impact of the theft & sabotage threat actions.

- Socially Engineered—Successful social engineering attacks are themselves an incident and can lead to disasters. A strong incident response and business continuity program can address many of these threat actions.
- Hacked—If an employee is hacked various activities within a solid incident response and business continuity program can address these threat actions.
- Abused Trust—When employees and senior members of the organization abuse the trust given to them, their actions can lead to security incidents and disasters. The planning and preparation activities within an incident response or business continuity program can address the impact of these threat actions.
- Environmental Damage—Impact from natural disasters (e.g., storms, floods, and fire) and external infrastructure disasters (e.g., power outage and disrupted water supply) can have severe consequences for the organization. The planning and response activities within incident response and business continuity can lessen the impact of these threat actions.
- Erred—Employee errors such as losing a laptop or accidently pressing the emergency power off (EPO) button in the data center can result in major losses to the organization and its assets. Activities within incident response and business continuity planning can address these threat actions.

7.1.2.2 Business Continuity Safeguards

Given the wide array of potential threat actions that could be enacted organizations should implement an adequate set of security controls (e.g., safeguards) to address the threat actions applicable to the business continuity and incident response planning. Table 7.2 lists an example set of technical safeguards that an organization may implement to counter these threat and threat actions. These technical safeguards are discussed within the safeguard classes of contingency planning and the incident response program.

TABLE 7.2

Technical Threats and Safeguards: Business Continuity

Class	Threat	Safeguard
Contingency planning	• Theft & sabotage • Hacked • Abused trust • Environmental Damage • Erred	• Cloud storage • Cloud services • Data backup technologies • RAID
Incident response program	• Invoked malware • Theft & sabotage • Socially engineered • Hacked • Abused trust • Erred	• Anti-Malware • Forensic analysis tools

Note: Threat actions applicable to business continuity include invoking malware, theft & sabotage, being socially engineered or hacked, abusing trust, environmental damage, and committing errors. Technical safeguards that can address these threat actions are described below.

7.1.2.2.1   Contingency Planning

The contingency planning process includes the business continuity planning (i.e., long-term strategy) and the disaster recovery planning (i.e., short- and mid-term strategies) to handle specific situations.

- Cloud Storage—Cloud storage is a service provided over the Internet that allows users to store and access their files from anywhere with an Internet connection. In some ways these services can offer better protections on files stored in the cloud because of the business mission focus and resources. In other ways, users cannot completely control who has access to their files as they are stored under the control of another organization. The remote access benefits of cloud storage make this service a viable strategy for many organizations in ensuring viability of data during disasters.
- Cloud Services—In addition to simply storing files in the cloud, organizations can out-source applications and other services to cloud providers. These services may include business functions (e.g., customer relationship management), security services (e.g., cloud-based firewalls), and entire departments (e.g., out-sourced human resources). Understanding the ability for these services to offset some of the impact of disasters is important for the security risk assessment team members.
- Data Backup Technologies—Critical data should be backed up to ensure its availability immediately following a disaster. Depending on the recovery time objective (RTO) and recovery point objective (RPO) for the data or the system the data supports, there are many different backup technologies that may be appropriate. Simple solutions include traditional full and incremental tape backups stored on or off site. More complex solutions include journaling and remote backup.
- Redundant Array of Inexpensive Disks—A redundant array of inexpensive disks (RAID) is a technology used for redundancy and performance improvement. RAID technology combines several physical disks and integrates them into a logical array. There are many RAID levels that provide various levels of performance and redundancy improvements.

7.1.2.2.2   Incident Response Program

The technical controls within the incident response process includes anti-malware tools and logs, and forensic analysis tools.

- Anti-Malware—Covered in Section 7.1.1.2.1.
- Forensic Analysis Tools—In the event that the incident response requires investigation, the organization may need to employ forensic analysis tools to uncover additional evidence and perhaps even to support presentation of evidence in court. Forensic analysis tools have the capability to creating a forensic copy of a device (e.g., bit for bit copy), recover files marked for deletion, and uncover other key evidence necessary to piece together the events that led up to a security incident.

7.1.3   SYSTEM SECURITY

The organization must protect its information systems from unscheduled changes, system-level vulnerabilities, and application-level vulnerabilities, and application-level vulnerabilities. Any of these threats to the organization's information systems could lead to disclosure or corruption of sensitive information, subversion of network systems, or fraud.

7.1.3.1 System Security Threats

Adequate technical security controls should be implemented within information systems to ensure that they are protected from various threat actions. Threat actions addressed by information controls include the following:

- Invoked Malware—As mentioned before an employee may take a number of actions that lead to the introduction of malicious software (e.g., malware) on their computer. Elements of the system security controls such as anti-malware, logical access control, and vulnerability scanning tools can address these risks.
- Theft & Sabotage—The threat action of theft and sabotage can cause security incidents and disasters severely impacting the organization. The organization may also be more suspectable to these threat actions during the time of a crisis. Logical access controls in this control area can avoid and lessen the impact of the theft & sabotage threat actions.
- Socially Engineered—Employees may be exposed to many attempts at social engineering and ultimately expose sensitive data. System security controls patch management systems, and digital signatures can address many of these threat actions.
- Hacked—If an employee is hacked various system security control activities such as patch management and audit logs can address this threat action.
- Abused Trust—An employee or more senior members of the organization may abuse the trust given to them and utilize this misplaced trust to take actions against the organization. Many system security activities such as logical access controls and monitoring technology can address these threat actions.
- Erred—An employee may simply make a mistake that results in the mislabeling of sensitive data, or unauthorized access to sensitive data. Many safeguards within the system security area such as configuration management systems and monitoring technology can address these threat actions.

7.1.3.2 System Security Safeguards

Given the wide array of potential threat actions that could be enacted organizations should implement an adequate set of security controls (e.g., safeguards) to address the threat actions applicable to the system security. Table 7.3 lists an example set of safeguards that an organization may employ to counter the threat and threat actions applicable to the system security. These safeguards are discussed within the safeguard classes of system controls, application security, and change management.

7.1.3.2.1 System Controls

The organization's information systems can be further protected from rogue applications and unauthorized users through a set of technical system controls. These technical controls include logical controls and devices that discover, reduce, and avoid vulnerabilities within the organization's information systems.

- Anti-Malware—Covered in Section 7.1.1.2.1.
- Logical Access Controls—Covered in Section 7.1.1.2.2.
- Vulnerability Scanning Tools—Vulnerability scanning tools are used to gather information about possible vulnerabilities within the target system. These tools can provide both network mapping (listing available hosts and their open interfaces) and vulnerability scanning (providing an automated mapping of available hosts and ports to known vulnerabilities).
- Patch Management Systems—Keeping up with the latest vendor security patches can be a complex task, especially in a larger enterprise. Patch management systems provide an automated method for testing and tracking the application of vendor patches to workstations and servers within a security domain.

TABLE 7.3
Technical Threats and Safeguards: System Security

Class	Threat	Safeguard
System controls	• Invoked malware • Theft & sabotage • Socially engineered • Hacked • Abused trust • Erred	• Anti-Malware • Logical access controls • Vulnerability scanning tools • Patch management systems • Screen savers • Personal firewalls
Applications security	• Invoked malware • Theft & sabotage • Socially engineered • Hacked • Abused trust • Erred	• Anti-Malware • Penetration testing tools • Monitoring technology • Audit logs
Change management	• Invoked malware • Theft & sabotage • Socially engineered • Hacked • Abused trust • Erred	• Anti-Malware • Logical access controls • Checksums • Digital signatures • Configuration management systems

- Screen Savers—Password-protected screen savers provide default protection of a user's workstation if it is left unattended for a preset period of time.
- Personal Firewalls—A personal firewall is a software application designed to protect a single workstation from Internet-based attacks. Personal firewalls protect a single system's security by inspecting and controlling Internet connections to and from the workstation.

7.1.3.2.2 Application Security

Until recently, application security has been largely ignored by companies protecting their assets, but applications have not been ignored by cybercriminals. Even though Web applications sit behind a firewall and perhaps even behind hardened operating systems, they are still vulnerable. This is because firewalls and hardened operating systems are not designed to restrict all access to Web applications (e.g., port 80 HTTP and port 443 HTTPS). Furthermore, exposed Web applications are likely to have errors. Below are a few technical security controls that may be employed to reduce the risk in applications:

- Anti-Malware—Covered in Section 7.1.1.2.1.
- Penetration Testing Tools—Penetration testing is a methodical and planned attack on a system's security controls to test the adequacy of security controls in place. Some of the penetration testing is done "by hand," but there are many available tools, both commercial and shareware, that help to automate the process. The use of these tools can greatly increase the rigor of an application security review.
- Source Code Review—Source code review is a process of manually inspecting the code for custom-developed Web applications. The review searches for security weaknesses, such as insecure coding practices, and security breaches, such as the insertion of Trojan horses and backdoors. Source code review is the most rigorous and complete method for improving the security of custom-developed applications.

- Web Application Firewall—A Web application firewall is a firewall configured specifically to control the input and output of and the access to a Web application service. The Web application firewall intercepts and filters application-level requests from a Web client destined for a Web server. The Web application firewall seeks to protect the Web application from attack by reviewing Web service requests (and responses) for common attacks such as Structured Query Language (SQL) injection and cross-site scripting (XSS).

7.1.3.2.3 Change Management

An information system infrastructure is a complex and evolving system. Changes to the system affect its ability to effectively enforce the security policies and therefore protect the organization's assets. Following are a few technical security controls that may be employed to help enforce strict change management:

- Anti-Malware—Covered in Section 7.1.1.2.1.
- Logical Access Controls—Covered in Section 7.1.1.2.2.
- Checksums—Covered in Section 7.1.1.2.2.
- Digital Signatures—A digital signature is a cryptographic verification that a file or message was created or sent by a specific user or entity. Using asymmetric cryptography (e.g., RSA and ElGamal), the sender digitally signs the file or message with his private key. The recipient of the message can be sure of the authenticity and integrity of the message if he can verify the message using the sender's public key. Digital signatures are mentioned here as a technique of verifying the authenticity and integrity of a workflow message for change management. For example, imagine a change management process for changes to the firewall ruleset that is based on an e-mail from key personnel within the organization. Such e-mails could be easily spoofed, and the change management process could be bypassed. Incorporating digital signatures into critical workflow processes helps to ensure the security of the process.
- Configuration Management Systems—Configuration management systems implement change control on specific work products such as code, test suites, and user documentation. The implementation of a configuration management system formalizes and controls the process of change management to ensure that changes to the system are properly reviewed, documented, and implemented.

7.1.4 Secure Architecture

Much of the security in an information system is reliant upon the structure and services provided by the underlying architecture. Secure architectures are important because the lack of an adequate security architecture limits (or even negates) the security provided by other security mechanisms. The organization must ensure that the information system architecture is free from design flaws and protects itself from denial of service attacks, network attacks, disclosure of the internal network structure, and eavesdropping.

7.1.4.1 Secure Architecture Threats

Adequate security controls should be placed within the secure architecture to ensure that it is protected from various threat actions. Threat actions addressed by a secure architecture include the following:

- Invoked Malware—As mentioned before an employee may take a number of actions that lead to the introduction of malicious software (e.g., malware) on their computer. Elements of the secure architecture such as network segmentation, and defense in depth can address these threat actions to sensitive data.

- Theft & Sabotage—The threat action of theft and sabotage can cause security incidents and disasters severely impacting the organization. The organization may also be more suspectable to these threat actions during the time of a crisis. Use of secure protocols in this control area can avoid and lessen the impact of the theft & sabotage threat actions.
- Socially Engineered—Employees may be exposed to many attempts at social engineering and ultimately expose sensitive data. The implementation of security architecture controls including Data Loss Prevention can address many of these threat actions.
- Hacked—If an employee is hacked various secure architecture controls such as zero trust networks can address this threat action.
- Abused Trust—An employee or more senior members of the organization may abuse the trust given to them and utilize this misplaced trust to take actions against the organization. Many secure architecture controls such as defense in depth and zero trust networks can address these threat actions.
- Erred—An employee may simply make a mistake that results in the mislabeling of sensitive data, or unauthorized access to sensitive data. Many safeguards within the secure architecture control area such as network segmentation and security domains can address these threat actions.

7.1.4.2   Secure Architecture Safeguards

Given the wide array of potential threat actions that could be enacted organizations should implement an adequate set of security controls (e.g., safeguards) to address the threat actions applicable to the security architecture. Table 7.4 lists an example set of safeguards that an organization may employ to counter the threat and threat actions applicable to the secure architecture. These safeguards are discussed within the safeguard classes of topology, transmission, and perimeter network.

7.1.4.2.1   Topology

One of the key aspects of a secure system architecture is the topology of the network. A network topology is the physical and logical arrangement of the network components. Safeguards that can be applied within the network topology area are discussed below:

TABLE 7.4
Technical Threats and Safeguards: Architecture

Class	Threat	Safeguard
Topology	• Theft & sabotage • Hacked	• Defense in depth • Network segmentation • Security domains • Redundancy
Transmission	• Theft & sabotage • Hacked	• Evaluated products • Link encryption • Traffic flow security • Secure protocols
Perimeter network	• Invoked malware • Theft & sabotage • Socially engineered • Hacked • Abused trust • Erred	• DMZ segmentation • Data Loss Prevention • Zero Trust Networks

- Defense in Depth—Defense in depth is a security engineering principle which states that critical assets should not rely on single mechanisms for their protection. Applying this concept to security network topologies means that there should be multiple controls in the network to protect critical assets from compromise. For example, we would expect to see perimeter firewalls and internal firewalls on network segments, strong authentication, access controls, and audit log and review. These safeguards together provide a defense in depth for critical files stored within the network.
- Network Segmentation—A network segment is a subset of a larger network bounded by networking devices such as routers, switches, bridges, or gateways. By dividing a network into segments, or groups of computers, the organization can gain performance and security by limiting the traffic on the network segment to the traffic sent or intended for computers on the network segment.[5]
- Security Domains—A security domain is a logical grouping of computers on a network in which there exists a trust relationship among all those computers. For example, you may set up a security domain for the accounting group that includes all of the accounting group's computers and printers. By creating multiple domains and carefully implementing trust relationships between domains, the network architect can reduce the risk of unauthorized access and disclosure.
- Redundancy—When critical applications or systems rely on a resource for their security, the failure of such a component could be devastating. The absence of redundancy in such critical components is called a *single point of failure*. It is important to implement network architecture redundancies for critical components such as networkwide authentication servers, firewalls, and Internet connectivity.
- Evaluated Products—The U.S. government, specifically the National Security Agency (NSA) and the National Institute of Standards and Technology (NIST), long ago recognized that trusted computer systems or information-assurance products, which we rely on for the provision of security services, need to be analyzed beyond the simple interface tests that may be performed in a laboratory. Furthermore, to truly analyze the ability of these systems to enforce a security policy, in-depth analysis would need to be performed by skilled evaluators with access to vendor design documentation. The National Information Assurance Partnership (NIAP) oversees the Common Criteria Evaluation Scheme within the United States and licenses laboratories to perform these evaluations. Once a product has been evaluated, it is placed on the product compliant list (https://www.niap-ccevs.org/Product/).

7.1.4.2.2   Transmission

The transmission of data across the network may be secured through the use of link encryption, traffic flow security, and secure protocols.

- Link Encryption—Link encryption is implemented through intelligent switching nodes to set up encrypted links within a network. This provides confidentiality and traffic flow security on the link and is completely transparent to the user. Link encryption is implemented at layer 2 of the Open System Interconnection (OSI) model (e.g., L2F, PPTP, and L2TP) or layer 3 of the OSI model (e.g., IPSEC).
- Traffic Flow Security—If an eavesdropper is able to gain information about the messages sent to and from your network, this may give him or her relevant information about your operations. It is not always necessary for an eavesdropper to decrypt the messages in order to gain information. For example, consider the fact that all stations send messages to station A. This may indicate that station A is headquarters or at least a critical component of the network. Traffic flow security masks the ultimate source and destination addresses for packets and can

even mask the fact that any information was sent across a network segment at all (e.g., by filling dead spots with noise).

- Secure Protocols—A network protocol is a set of rules used by endpoints of a connection to communicate. Many protocols, such as HyperText Transfer Protocol (HTTP), File Transfer Protocol (FTP), and Password Authentication Protocol (PAP), are inherently insecure because they do not provide basic security services such as confidentiality. Use of secure protocols, such as HyperText Transfer Protocol + Secure Sockets Layer (HTTPS), Secure File Transfer Protocol (S-FTP), and Challenge Handshake Authentication Protocol (CHAP), will ensure confidentiality of the communication.
- Wireless Network Protocols—There are a variety of constantly evolving wireless network protocols. These protocols have different advantages to users, such as speed and bandwidth, but of note to us is the encryption technology and use that provides for confidentiality of communications. As vulnerabilities are found in the use of encryption within wireless networking protocols, a new standard is developed to provide better protection. Because the "old" protocol is then known to exhibit well-known vulnerabilities, it is then considered unsafe to use and is outdated. The term used in the industry is *deprecated*, meaning that the security features are outdated and superseded by the new protocol. Use of deprecated protocols such as Wired Equivalent Privacy (WEP) and Wi-Fi Protected Access II (WPA2) with its Temporal Key Integrity Protocol (TKIP) constitutes a vulnerability, as the security of the algorithms have been declared ineffective.

7.1.4.2.3 Perimeter Network

The perimeter of the organization's network is the part of the network that is directly exposed to untrusted users, such as the Internet or a modem bank. The protection of the network from these untrusted users is imperative and can be accomplished within the network architecture through demilitarized zone (DMZ) segmentation and Network Address Translation (NAT).

- DMZ Segmentation—The organization's critical assets can be better protected by separating Internet-accessible devices, such as the Web server, FTP server, and e-mail server, from the rest of the organization's network. This architectural component is called a DMZ, named after the military term for creating a buffer area between two enemies (see Figure 7.2).
- Network Address Translation—NAT allows a local area network (LAN) to use two sets of Internet Protocol (IP) addresses for each communication between the LAN and the Internet. An internal LAN computer is assigned a unique IP address used by the NAT box for communication between the NAT box and the LAN computer. The NAT box translates that address into an externally routable IP address for communication between the NAT box and the Internet. NAT technology provides the following benefits:
  - Internal Structure Masked—By using NAT technology, the internal structure of the network is masked from eavesdroppers.
  - Extends IP Address Space—The one-to-many mapping of external IP addresses to internal addresses means that a LAN with more than 256 hosts could use a C-class network.
- Port Address Translation—Port Address Translation (PAT) is a type of network address translation that provides a service similar to NAT through the use of port numbers.
- Data Loss Prevention (DLP)—DLP is a technology and service that reviews data leaving the organization and reviews it for potential violations of policy such as it contains sensitive information (e.g., health care data and credit card numbers) or that it sends information to the wrong destinations (e.g., blacklisted IP addresses). DLP technology is very good at reviewing exiting data for easy to profile sensitive data. This includes highly formatted data such as social security numbers or medical coding data. DLP can be applied to nearly any potential exit point in an organization's network including e-mail, file transfer, Internet browsers, and instant messaging.

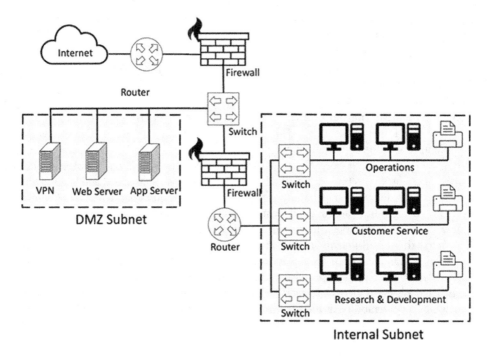

FIGURE 7.2   DMZ architecture. A DMZ is a secure network architecture configuration in which publicly accessible services are separated from the rest of the network by employing firewall technology.

- Zero Trust Networks—The Zero Trust concept incorporates the idea that any network component should treat all other network components as if they are untrusted and outsiders. In order to incorporate the concept of Zero Trust the organization must adopt a variety of enabling technologies that increase its ability to confirm user identity (e.g., multifactor authentication and identity management), secure transmissions (e.g., secure protocols and encryption) and implement strong access controls (e.g., file permissions).

7.1.5   Security Components

The components of an organization's network can provide security services to protect the critical resources. Components provide access controls and data security.

7.1.5.1   Security Component Threats

Adequate security controls should be placed within security components to ensure that the organization's assets are protected from various threat actions. Threat actions addressed by security component controls include the following:

- Invoked Malware—As mentioned before an employee may take a number of actions that lead to the introduction of malicious software (e.g., malware) on their computer. Security components such as Zero Trust networks and intrusion detection can address this threat action.
- Socially Engineered—Employees may be exposed to many attempts at social engineering and ultimately expose sensitive data. Security components including software asset management (SAM) and SIEM can address many of these threat actions.

- Hacked—If an employee is hacked various security components such as Zero Trust networks can address this threat action.
- Abused Trust—An employee or more senior members of the organization may abuse the trust given to them and utilize this misplaced trust to take actions against the organization. Many security components such as intrusion detection systems can address these threat actions.
- Erred—An employee may simply make a mistake that results in the mislabeling of sensitive data, or unauthorized access to sensitive data. Many safeguards within the security components area such as SIEM can address these threat actions.

7.1.5.2 Security Component Safeguards

Given the wide array of potential threat actions that could be enacted organizations should implement an adequate set of security components to address the listed threat actions. Table 7.5 provides an example set of safeguards that an organization may employ to counter the threat and threat actions applicable to security components. These safeguards are discussed within the safeguard classes of access control and continuous monitoring.

7.1.5.2.1 Access Control

Logical access control provides mechanisms that restrict access to critical resources to only those authorized to have access. Components that provide access control and information flow controls are called firewalls.

- Next Generation Firewall—These firewalls combine many of the information flow protections offered in other firewalls but combined in a single device. A next generation firewall reviews the packet contents (e.g., payload), header content, and transaction data (e.g., TCP handshake data).
- Application-Level Firewall—Application-level firewalls, also called *proxy firewalls*, are a type of firewall that processes data packets for specific applications. These packets are intercepted and analyzed and may be sent to the intended host. The advantage of an application-level firewall over other firewalls is that, because there is no direct communication between the external and internal host, there is no direct access granted to the internal network. Application-level firewalls can also proxy applications like strong authentication services.
- Session-Level Firewall—A session-level firewall, also called a *circuit level gateway* or a *stateful inspection firewall*, is a type of firewall that creates virtual circuits for permitted and

---

TABLE 7.5
Technical Threats and Safeguards: Components

Class	Threat	Safeguard
Access control	• Hacked • Abused trust • Erred	• Next Generation Firewall (FW) • Application-level FW • Session-level FW • Packet filter FW • Identity Management Systems
Continuous Monitoring	• Invoked malware • Socially engineered • Hacked • Abused trust • Erred	• Software Asset Management • Host-based Intrusion Detection Systems (HIDS) • Network-based Intrusion Detection Systems (NIDS) • Security Information and Event Management (SIEM)

established sessions between an external and internal host. The advantage of a session-level firewall over other firewall types is that, since it retains state information about established connections, it can be much faster than other firewalls. However, these firewalls provide only a moderate level of protection and should be used with other information flow controls.

- Packet-Filtering Firewall—A packet-filtering firewall is the simplest type of firewall. This firewall uses ACLs to determine permitted traffic flows based on the source and destination IP address and port. These firewalls can be inexpensive and relatively quick. However, they cannot provide protection against spoofing; they cannot proxy applications like strong authentication; and their audit logs are rather limited. Packet-Filtering firewalls do not provide a very good level of protection as they cannot check the contents (e.g., payload) of the packet.
- Identity Management Systems—Covered in Section 7.1.1.2.3.

7.1.5.2.2 Continuous Monitoring

Continuous monitoring components can provide protection against attacks to the information system based ensuring systems are up to date or by detecting attacks in progress. These systems provide an additional defense against attacks that may go unnoticed protected or unnoticed by other protection methods such as firewalls and audit log reviews.

- Software Asset Management (SAM)—SAM tools are centralized management tools that allow the organization to document and manage the software installed and used with the organization's computing resources. Within the objectives of information security these tools allow the organization to track licensing, software installations, and software updates.
- Host-Based IDS (HIDS)—A host-based intrusion detection system (Figure 7.3) is installed locally on host machines such as laptops, workstations, and servers. These IDSs inspect packets sent to the host for the potential of malicious attacks. HIDSs are deployed in areas in which specific host-level assets and attacks are the concern.

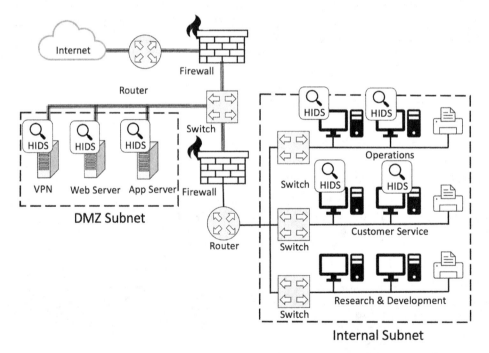

FIGURE 7.3 HIDS deployment. A host-based intrusion detection system (HIDS) inspects packets sent to the host. A HIDS is deployed as a software agent running on the host.

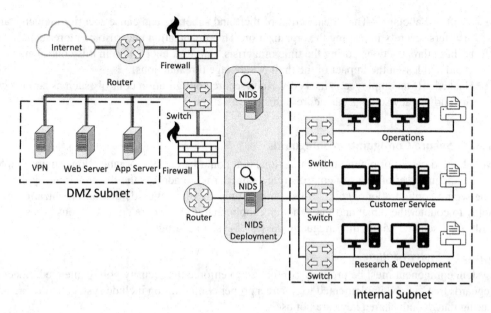

FIGURE 7.4 NIDS deployment. A network-based intrusion detection system (NIDS) analyzes network traffic. A NIDS is deployed as a network device running in promiscuous mode.

- Network-Based IDS (NIDS)—A network-based intrusion detection system (Figure 7.4) is installed on the network. The NIDS device has a network interface card (NIC) and is set up in promiscuous mode, meaning that it will analyze all traffic within its deployed network segment.
- Security Information and Event Management (SEIM)—SIEM software allows an organization to increase their ability to collect and aggregate log and event data from network components; identify and categorize security events based on the collected data; analyze the identified events; and provide reporting and alerting based on the results of the analysis.

7.1.6 Secure Configuration

Technical safeguards are designed to enforce a security policy over a defined set of critical assets, but the effectiveness of these safeguards can be limited or eliminated if the safeguards are not configured properly. Specific implementation and installation advice and guidance should be sought from the vendor of the device. A high-level discussion of safeguards aimed at ensuring that technical controls are properly configured is presented below.

7.1.6.1 Secure Configuration Threats

Adequate security controls should be implemented through secure configurations of organizational assets to ensure that they are protected from various threat actions. Threat actions addressed by secure configurations include the following:

- Invoked Malware—As mentioned before an employee may take a number of actions that lead to the introduction of malicious software (e.g., malware) on their computer. Elements of the secure configurations such as system hardening can address these threat actions to sensitive data.

- Theft & Sabotage—The threat action of theft and sabotage can cause security incidents and disasters severely impacting the organization. The organization may also be more suspectable to these threat actions during the time of a crisis. Full disk encryption in this control area can avoid and lessen the impact of the theft & sabotage threat actions.
- Hacked—If an employee is hacked various secure configuration controls such as strict security and privacy settings can address this threat action.

7.1.6.2 Secure Configuration Safeguards

Given the wide array of potential threat actions that could be enacted organizations should implement an adequate set of security controls (e.g., safeguards) to address the threat actions applicable to the secure configuration. Table 7.6 lists an example set of safeguards that an organization may employ to counter the threat and threat actions applicable to the secure configurations. These safeguards are discussed within the safeguard classes of system settings.

7.1.6.2.1 System Settings

A system component must be properly configured to enforce the security policy intended. Specific safeguards that may be implemented to ensure a proper configuration include system hardening and ensuring that default shared keys are not used.

- Full Disk Encryption—Laptops can be easily lost or stolen and with them 10s of thousands of sensitive data records or other sensitive information can be in the hands of unauthorized individuals. The implementation of full disk encryption (built-in to most operating systems) severely reduces the exposure of sensitive information stored on stolen or lost laptops, flash drives, or other removable media.
- System Hardening—System hardening is the process of securely configuring an operation system, application, or component. Elements of most system hardening processes include the removal of default passwords and accounts, the deletion of services and ports not used, and the setting of security parameters to meet the needs of the environment.
- Strict Security and Privacy Settings—There are many parameters that may be set with a computing resource such as browser settings, and application settings. The organization should ensure that individual systems (e.g., workstations and laptops) are properly secured through the correct understanding and setting of security and privacy settings.
- No Default Shared Keys—Many secure protocols (e.g., IPSec/IKE and WPA2) rely on a pre-configured shared key to initialize the secure communication between entities. Attackers armed with the knowledge of the default shared keys can compromise the secure communication. Organizations should ensure that no default shared keys are used.

TABLE 7.6

Technical Threats and Safeguards: Configuration

Class	Threat	Safeguard
System settings	• Invoked malware • Theft & sabotage • Hacked	• Full disk encryption • System hardening • No default shared keys • Strict security and privacy settings

7.1.7 Data Security

The security of the data itself can be further protected through safeguards that apply to both data in storage and data in transit.

7.1.7.1 Data Security Threats

Adequate security controls should be implemented through data security controls to ensure that the organizations data assets are protected from various threat actions. Threat actions addressed by data security controls include the following:

- Invoked Malware—As mentioned before an employee may take a number of actions that lead to the introduction of malicious software (e.g., malware) on their computer. Data security controls such as file encryption can address these threat actions to sensitive data.
- Theft & Sabotage—The threat action of theft and sabotage can cause security incidents and disasters severely impacting the organization. The organization may also be more suspectable to these threat actions during the time of a crisis. File encryption in this control area can avoid and lessen the impact of the theft & sabotage threat actions.
- Hacked—If an employee is hacked various data security controls such as checksums and e-mail encryption can address this threat action.

7.1.7.2 Data Security Safeguards

Given the wide array of potential threat actions that could be enacted organizations should implement an adequate set of security controls (e.g., safeguards) to address the threat actions applicable to data security. Table 7.7 lists an example set of safeguards that an organization may employ to counter the threat and threat actions applicable to data security. These safeguards are discussed within the safeguard classes of storage and transit.

7.1.7.2.1 Storage

When sensitive data are stored, they may be susceptible to attacks from others sharing the workstation or network, stealing a laptop, or finding a lost flash-memory device. Technical safeguards such as file encryption can help protect the confidentiality and integrity of the data.

TABLE 7.7
Technical Threats and Safeguards: Data

Class	Threat	Safeguard
Storage	• Invoked malware • Theft & sabotage • Socially engineered • Hacked • Abused trust • Erred	• File encryption • Checksums
Transit	• Hacked • Erred	• Network encryption • Virtual Private Networks • E-mail Encryption • Secure Protocols

- File Encryption—Individual files may be encrypted through the use of bulk encryption programs that can store an encrypted version of sensitive information and delete the plaintext file.
- Checksums—Covered in Section 7.1.1.2.2

7.1.7.2.2   Transit

When sensitive data are transmitted across the network, they may be susceptible to eavesdropping attacks. Technical safeguards such as network encryption, virtual private networks (VPNs), and e-mail encryption can help protect the confidentiality and integrity of the data.

- Network Encryption—Communication sessions can be encrypted to ensure the confidentiality and integrity of the network communication.[6]
- Virtual Private Network—A VPN provides remote users with a secure connection to one of the organization's servers sitting on the edge of the organization's LAN over an otherwise public network. To the user, this seems as if it is a point-to-point connection from the user's computer to the organization's LAN.
- E-Mail Encryption—E-mail encryption is a form of end-to-end encryption that is implemented at layers 6 and 7 of the International Standards Organization (ISO) model. End-to-end encryption allows users to select messages for encryption across the entire transmission. The advantage of end-to-end encryption is that the data is not susceptible to attacks at the intermediate nodes. However, a user must specify transmissions for encryption, as this is not performed automatically.
- Secure Protocols—Covered in Section 7.1.4.2.2

7.2   THE RIIOT METHOD: TECHNICAL DATA GATHERING

As introduced in Chapter 5, the Review, Interview, Inspect, Observe, Test (RIIOT) method of data gathering can be applied to any security risk assessment technique and helps to ensure a more complete and well-managed data gathering process. The RIIOT method is applied to any area of security controls by reasoning about the most appropriate approach for gathering data on each security control under review. Applying the RIIOT method to the technical area shows that a majority of the data gathering techniques to be applied to technical security controls will be document review and testing controls.

7.2.1   DETERMINING APPROPRIATE RIIOT APPROACHES FOR TECHNICAL CONTROLS

Recall from Chapter 5 that the RIIOT method of data gathering is used to assist the data gathering process by organizing the data gathering approaches (e.g., Review documents, Interview key staff, Inspect controls, Observe behavior, and Test controls) for the targeted security controls, selecting the approaches for each control, and then assigning the data gathering process amongst team members, and tracking their progress.

The number of methods and the selection of specific the methods to be used for data gathering will be based on the level of rigor specified in the security risk assessment project plan, the skills of the team members, and the approach determined by the security risk assessment team lead. These descriptions of data gathering activities against each of the listed security controls are intended to provide a general approach to be used by security risk assessment teams, and not specific answers to questions that may arise during a security risk assessment.

Table 7.8 provides a map to all of the potential RIIOT data gathering approaches that could be used to gather data on all of the administrative controls discussed in Section 7.1. The sections below describe each of these approaches and provide a description of how a security risk assessment team member may go about collecting that data.

7.2.2 REVIEW DOCUMENTS REGARDING TECHNICAL CONTROLS

As demonstrated in Table 7.8, gathering data on nearly every technical security control involves the review of documents. The bulk of the document review will be a review of manuals and diagrams. The remaining document reviews will include a review of hardening guidelines, network maps, technical policy statements, service level agreements, and various security work products.

TABLE 7.8
RIIOT Method of Data Gathering for Technical Controls

Controls	Review Documents	Interview Key Personnel	Inspect Controls	Observe Behavior	Test Controls
Anti-Malware	*			*	*
Monitoring technology	*				*
Audit logs	*	*		*	*
Logical access controls	*				*
Checksums	*				—
Encryption	*		*		*
Single sign on systems	*				*
Two-factor authentication	*				*
Identity management systems	*	*	*		—
Automated password policies	*				*
Password crackers	*				
Password generators	*				—
Cloud storage	*	*			—
Cloud services	*	*			—
Data backup technologies	*	*			*
RAID	*				—
Forensic analysis tools	*				—
Vulnerability scanning tools	*	*			—
Patch management systems	*	*	*		—
Screen savers	*			*	
Personal firewalls	*			*	*
Penetration testing tools	*	*			
Digital signatures	*			*	—
Configuration management systems	*	*		*	—
Defense in depth	*				
Network segmentation	*		*		*
Security domains	*				—
Redundancy	*		*		—
Evaluated products	*		*		

(Continued)

TABLE 7.8   *(Continued)*

Controls	Review Documents	Interview Key Personnel	Inspect Controls	Observe Behavior	Test Controls
Link encryption	*				—
Traffic flow security	*				—
Secure protocols	*				—
DMZ segmentation	*				—
NAT/PAT	*				—
Data Loss Prevention	*	*			*
Zero Trust Networks	*	*			*
Next Generation Firewall	*	*	*		*
Application-level Firewall	*	*	*		*
Session-level Firewall	*	*	*		*
Packet filter Firewall	*	*	*		*
Software Asset Management	*	*	*		—
Host Intrusion Detection System	*	*			*
Network Intrusion Detection System	*	*			*
Security Information and Event Management	*	*		*	*
Full disk encryption	*			*	—
System hardening	*	*			*
No default shared keys	*		*		
Strict security and privacy settings	*	*			—
File encryption	*		*		—
Network encryption	*				*
Virtual private network	*				*
E-mail encryption	*				*

Note: The application of the RIIOT Method to technical controls indicates that the data gathering in this area will focus mainly on document review and testing controls.

7.2.2.1   Technical Documents to Request

The security risk assessment team should determine the set of documents to be reviewed within the scope of the engagement. In some cases, the team will be able to review all documents obtained through information requests. However, in many cases, because of time or budget constraints, the team will need to narrow the evidence reviewed to determine the strength of technical security controls. The most useful technical documents for the security risk assessment team include general system information documents (e.g., network diagrams), previous assessment reports, and available service or application manuals (See Table 7.9.).

7.2.2.2   Review Technical Documents for Information

When reviewing technical documents, it is useful to create a checklist to guide the review of each document.[7] A checklist is simply a listing of all the things a reasonable security engineer would expect to find in a reviewed document. In order to assist those performing security risk assessments, baseline checklists for document review are provided in Tables 7.10 through 7.18. The team must understand that not all documents are required for all environments, not all checklist elements are necessary for all security controls, and not all technical documents provided will be as neatly titled as the documents discussed here.[8]

7.2.2.3   Review Documents for Clarity, Consistency, and Completeness

All technical documents reviewed should be reviewed based on clarity, consistency, and completeness:

* Clarity—Determination of clarity depends on the intended audience. If the intended audience is considered technical, then the level of technical content within the document would be expected to be higher than in a document intended for a more general audience.
* Consistency—A measurement of the consistency of the documents will be determined once all documents have been reviewed. If more than one document covers a specific area or control and provides conflicting settings, findings, architecture, or configuration, then those the documents can be said to be inconsistent and the quality level of evidence is diminished.

TABLE 7.9
Technical Documents to Request

Document Type	Sample Titles	Expected Elements Table
System information	• General system information review	• Table 7.10
	• Network diagram/Information flow diagram	• Table 7.11
Security assessment reports	• General security assessment review	• Table 7.12
	• Vulnerability scanning results	• Table 7.13
	• Penetration testing results	• Table 7.14
	• Security risk assessment	• Table 7.15
	• Security audit report/IT audit report	• Table 7.16
Technical manuals	• Administrative guide for security applications	• Table 7.17
Technical security design	• System specification	See Section 7.2.2.8
	• System design	
	• System architecture	

Note: The security risk assessment team should attempt to obtain and review as many relevant technical documents as possible within the data gathering stage of the security risk assessment. This table provides a sample list of documents to request, but it is by no means exhaustive.

TABLE 7.10

General System Information Document Elements

General System Information

The assessor should review all available system information to gain a better understanding of the effectiveness of the technical controls in place.

Policy Area	Expected Elements	Discussion
Documented	• Documented and revised as appropriate	Appropriate documentation can be assessed based on a perceived need of level of detail. The auditor's rule of thumb is "if it's not documented, it's not done," so if there is system information used to support a process (e.g., network maps are used to support architectural reviews) then it needs to be documented.
Accurate	• System information presented to the team needs to reflect the state of the system controls at the time.	The assessment team members should ascertain the accuracy of the documents presented to them based on other evidence already reviewed (or revisited these documents when presented with additional evidence). Potential inaccuracies include cut and paste errors indicative of documents created solely for the purpose of assessments; absence of new systems, interfaces, or applications; and reflections of the difference between planned strategy and implementation.
Up to Date	• System information should reflect current implementation and be up to date.	The assessment team should specifically ask if the information provided is up to date and also carefully review the elements of the system information provided to ensure it is current.

Note: All system information provided to the assessment team for review are expected to be documented, accurate, and up to date.

- Completeness—Lastly, completeness will be determined based on the security risk assessment team's expectations for a given document. The expectations, or expected elements, could be dictated from a regulation or they could be based on the team's experience.

7.2.2.4 Review Documents for Expected Elements

As discussed in the previous section, it is important to create a checklist or table of expected elements for each document or policy area.[9] Expected elements are simply a listing of all the things a reasonable security engineer would expect to find in a complete document. For example, a complete vulnerability scanning report would be expected to have the following elements:

- Scope—List of IP addresses, web applications, remote access, wireless and other systems included in the scanning activity.
- Scope Restrictions—List of any restrictions on the scope of the assessment and a statement of acceptable restrictions from the testing organization.
- Permission—Permission from system and/or data owners for all systems within scope
- Rules of Engagement—Statement regarding tests to be performed, how the tests will be conducted, and any restrictions on methods of testing.

- Testers and Tester's Organization—List of those who performed the test along with their credentials and organizational affiliation.
- Test Methods and Tools—List of test methods used (e.g., open port scans and OS fingerprinting) and tools used.
- Findings—List of all of the findings from the vulnerability scan with detailed enough information to support repeatability of the test.
- Severity Levels—For each finding the report should include a severity level or criticality of the finding.
- Recommendation—For each finding the report should include detailed instructions on how to address the finding.

The expected elements should be used as a guideline for the assessor to ensure the technical document review process is complete. Missing elements are not necessarily something that would need to be remedied just an indication as to the quality of the evidence provided by the document. The assessor should consider if each document element is actually "expected" in the assessed organization's environment given their understanding of the organization's threat environment. The expected elements for all of the documents listed in Table 7.9 are provided in Tables 7.10 through 7.17. An assessor may use these tables to guide their document review. Note that all elements are not "required" but "expected." At this stage, data gathering, the assessor is collecting data on the access control policy to better enable the later stage of data analysis in determining the effectiveness of the control.

In order to assist those performing security risk assessments, the set of expected element tables is listed in Table 7.9. These tables are an illustration of how to construct and use lists of expected items in security documents. However, the team must understand that not all documents are required for all environments, not all expected elements are necessary for all security controls, and not all documents provided will be as neatly titled as the documents discussed here.[10]

7.2.2.5 Reviewing System Information Documents

In general, system information should be documented, accurate, and up to date (see Table 7.10). System information can take several forms including hard copy documents, soft copy documents, online documents, and online reports or dashboards. The security risk assessment team members should be able to accommodate the review of technical documents in any format in which it is available. The only system information documents consistently provided as part of a security risk assessment is the network diagram and information flow diagram.

The security risk assessment team, or a member of the team, should review the available system information to determine the information system architecture. The objective of this review is to use information provided in the general system information documents such as network diagrams to double-check information already gathered and to gain insight into the information system's security architecture.

7.2.2.5.1 Network Diagram

A network diagram and information flow diagram provide a high-level architecture view of the overall information system. Network diagrams should include all network component classes (e.g., file servers, web servers, e-mail servers, and workstations), network connections, and system egress points (e.g., firewalls and wireless access points). An information flow diagram should show where sensitive data is stored, transmitted, and processed, and include encrypted links. See Table 7.11 for expected elements to guide the review of these documents.

7.2.2.6 Reviewing Previous Security Assessment Documents

The security assessment team is likely to receive reports from previous security assessments (e.g., vulnerability scans, penetration tests, and security risk assessments) as evidence of security controls. The form and style of these reports may vary greatly but the content of these reports provides the

TABLE 7.11

Network Diagram/Information Flow Expected Elements

Network Diagram/Information Flow Diagram Expected Elements

A network diagram and information flow diagram provide a high-level architecture view of the overall information system. An information flow diagram should show where sensitive data is stored, transmitted, and processed, and include encrypted links.

Document Area	Expected Elements	Review Tips
Document quality	• Accuracy	• Pick several connections shown in the drawings and inspect the actual equipment to verify the drawing (i.e., trace wires). • Use automated tools to develop a system diagram and compare against the drawings provided.
	• Up to date	• Inspect latest change management documents for changes that would affect the diagrams. Compare provided diagram against recent architectural changes. • Look at the date of the diagrams. The date should be relatively recent.
Document contents	• Identification of external interfaces	• Review the network diagrams for external connections such as Internet connections, VPN connections, connections to other systems, modem pools, and any network component that may be reached by a modem.
	• Identification of systems	• Check drawings against the system boundaries from the statement of work. Is there anything missing? Is there anything extra?
	• System architecture	• Defense in depth: Use network diagrams to determine the extent of security components protecting the network. Specifically, look for network wide authentication servers, placement of firewalls and IDSs, link encryptions, and NAT boxes. • DMZ: Review the network diagrams to identify the DMZ. Ensure that all components are identified and accounted for in the system identification from the statement of work. • Network segmentation: Review the network diagrams to identify any segmentation within the network. Note perimeter protection at each segment boundary and IDS sensors within each segment.
	• Data flow	• Sensitive Data Labels: Review the network diagram for an indication of sensitive data creation and/or storage. The assessment team should already have an idea as to what sensitive data is on the system (e.g., cardholder data) and even where that data is created (e.g., point of sale terminals) so the team should be able to spot check what they know against the information flow diagram provided.
	• Encrypted links	• Encrypted Link: Review the network diagram for links utilized by sensitive data (e.g., point of sale terminal to cash register applications). The diagrams should not only indicate an encrypted link but also state the algorithm and key strength of the link.

Note: The technical diagrams should be reviewed for accuracy, currency, and the implementation of system security architecture safeguards.

assessment team with valuable information regarding the effectiveness of the security assessment and other controls.

The security risk assessment team, or a member of the team, should review the available security reports to gain a perspective on the inputs to the current security risk assessment. The objective of this review is twofold. Firstly, the objective of the review of a previous security assessment is to

TABLE 7.12
General Security Assessment Report Expected Elements

General Security Assessment Report Expected Elements

The security risk assessment team may also be provided with reports from previously executed security assessments. These documents can be reviewed for several important pieces of evidence:

Document Area	Expected Elements	Review Tips
General security assessment report expectations	• Known vulnerabilities	• Use the list (and date) of vulnerabilities found to follow up with the assessed organization as to the current state of the vulnerabilities. • Where they addressed? • Did they get added to the risk register?
	• Consistency	• Review the security assessment reports provided by the assessed organization for details that may be used to check the accuracy of other documents provided such as the network map.
	• Completeness	• Review the report from the security assessment activity to determine the quality and frequency of the assessment as a security control. • How often is this activity performed? • When was it last performed? • Is this consistent with stated policy? • Does the security assessment report contain the expected level of detail? (see below)
Useful data for current assessment	• Mission statement	• Check mission statements recorded in other reports against the ones provided to you. If they are different, ask key personnel why this has changed.
	• System components and boundaries	• Review named system components and indicated system boundaries and compare them to the current statement of work. If they are different, ask key personnel for an explanation. • Look for any components, subsystems, areas, or interfaces that have not been included in the last or present assessment. For example, some organizations never include physical security as a part of the assessment. • Determine if the lack of review for organizational elements is a vulnerability.
	• Roles and responsibilities	• Look for definitions of roles and responsibilities from previous reviews. • Specifically, look for responsibilities such as running an internal vulnerability scan, account review, or other security activities.
	• Threats	• Review the threats considered during the previous assessment efforts. Review the threats identified for this effort and consider adding previously identified threats.
	• Assets and asset values	• Review the assets and the values assigned to those assets listed in previous assessment efforts. Consider listing additional assets previously identified. Reexamine asset values based on previous asset valuations.
	• Current safeguards	• Review the list, description, and vulnerabilities of existing safeguards from previous assessments. Determine if those safeguards are still in place. Consider the previous vulnerabilities within those safeguards and ensure that they are either addressed or listed in your current security risk assessment.
	• Recommended safeguards and timelines	• Review the recommended safeguards and suggested timelines for implementation from previous assessments. If such timelines have passed, look for evidence that these safeguards were implemented, addressed in another manner, or ignored.

Note: Security assessment reports should be reviewed for the uncovered vulnerabilities, consistency with other evidence, and completeness of the assessment effort. The assessment team should also review past security assessments for previously identified and relevant information that may impact the current security risk assessment.

judge the completeness or correctness of past reviews as the security assessments are a control and should be reviewed for their effectiveness. Secondly, the assessment team should use information gathered during past efforts to gain insights on threats, vulnerabilities, and past findings that may impact the current assessment. The assessor may use Table 7.12 for guidance as to the expected elements and useful information within these documents.

For each of the security assessment documents reviewed the assessor may use Tables 7.13 through 7.16 for guidance as to the expected elements.

7.2.2.6.1 Vulnerability Scan Report

The vulnerability scan reviews the network for open ports and available services and provides a report on known vulnerabilities in operating systems, applications, and services detected. The expected elements of a vulnerability scan report are listed in Table 7.13 to guide the assessors review of the report.

TABLE 7.13
Vulnerability Scan Report Expected Elements

Vulnerability Scan Report Expected Elements

The vulnerability scan reviews the network for open ports and available services and provides a report on known vulnerabilities in operating systems, applications, and services detected.

Document Area	Expected Elements	Review Tips
Scope	• Scope and scope restrictions	• Is there a list of IP addresses, web applications, remote access, wireless and other systems included in the scanning activity? • Are there any restrictions on the scope of the assessment? • Is there a statement of acceptable restrictions from the testing organization?
	• Permission	• Was permission from system and/or data owners for all systems within scope received and documented?
	• Rules of engagement	• Is there a statement regarding tests to be performed and how the tests will be conducted? • Were there any restrictions on methods of testing?

Methods	• Testers and tester's organization	• Is there a list of those who performed the test along with their credentials and organizational affiliation?
		  • Are they experienced and qualified to perform the testing?
		  • Are they independent of the assessed organization?

	• Test methods and tools	• Does the report list of test methods used (e.g., open port scans and OS fingerprinting) and tools used?
		  • Does these seem adequate?
		  • Are they up to date?

Findings	• Findings	• Does the report contain a list of all of the findings from the vulnerability scan with detailed enough information to support repeatability of the test? • Can the action taken on those vulnerabilities be traced to completion or acceptance?
	• Severity levels	• Does the report provide a severity level or criticality for each finding?
	• Recommendation	• Does the report provide detailed instructions on how to address each finding?

Note: Vulnerability scan report should be reviewed for appropriate scope, methods used, and vulnerabilities found.

7.2.2.6.2 Penetration Test Report

A penetration testing is a methodical and planned attack on a system's security controls to test the adequacy of security controls in place. A penetration test incorporates vulnerability scanning as just one of the techniques to gain information on the target system and goes beyond determination of vulnerability to exploit suspected vulnerabilities. The expected elements of a penetration testing report are listed in Table 7.14 to guide the assessors review of the report.

7.2.2.6.3 Security Risk Assessment Report

A security risk assessment is the subject of this entire text. The reader should have a good idea of what should be included in a security assessment report (See Chapter 11). The expected elements of a security risk assessment report are listed in Table 7.15 to guide the assessors review of the report.

TABLE 7.14

Penetration Testing Report Expected Elements

Penetration Testing Report Expected Elements

A penetration testing is a methodical and planned attack on a system's security controls to test the adequacy of security controls in place.

Document Area	Expected Elements	Review Tips
Scope	• Scope and scope restrictions	• Is there a list of IP addresses, web applications, remote access, wireless and other systems included in the penetration test? • Are there any restrictions on the scope of the assessment? • Is there a statement of acceptable restrictions from the testing organization?
	• Permission	• Was permission from system and/or data owners for all systems within scope received and documented?

	• Rules of engagement	• Is there a statement regarding tests to be performed and how the tests will be conducted?
		  • Were there any restrictions on methods of testing?
		  • Are Denial of Service (DOS) attacks allowed?
		  • Is social engineering allowed?

Method	• Testers and tester's organization	• Is there a list of those who performed the test along with their credentials and organizational affiliation?
		  • Are they experienced and qualified to perform the testing?
		  • Are they independent of the assessed organization?

	• Test methods and tools	• Does the report list of test methods used (e.g., injection, buffer overflow, and session hijacking) and tools used?
		  • Does these seem adequate?
		  • Are they up to date?

	• Completeness	• Does the testing continue until all methods are used or does the test come to a stop when the system is breached?
Findings	• Findings	• Does the report contain a list of all of the findings from the penetration test with detailed enough information to support repeatability of the test? • Can the action taken on those penetration test findings be traced to completion or acceptance?
	• Severity levels	• Does the report provide a severity level or criticality for each finding?
	• Recommendation	• Does the report provide detailed instructions on how to address each finding?

Note: Penetration testing report should be reviewed for appropriate scope, methods used, and vulnerabilities found.

TABLE 7.15

Security Risk Assessment Report Expected Elements

Security Risk Assessment Report Expected Elements

A security risk assessment is the overall process of finding, recognizing, and describing risk to comprehend the nature of risk and to determine the level of risk and of comparing the results of risk analysis with risk criteria to determine whether the risk and/or its magnitude is acceptable or tolerable.

Document Area	Expected Elements	Review Tips
Front matter	• Introduction	• Background: Does the report provide an introduction and background necessary to understand the context of the report. For example, is this an annual report, is it a response from an audit, etc.?
		• Scope: Does the report include enough detail to understand the scope of the assessment (e.g., IP addresses, systems, locations, and departments)
		• Does the assessment follow a specific method? If so, which method?
		• Requirements: Is this assessment intended to meet any organizational requirements? Are those requirements listed?
	• Qualifications	• Are the assessors listed on the report?
		• Are they independent of the organization?
		• Are they qualified to perform the assessment?
Main report	• Data gathering	• What were the data gathering activities (e.g., survey, interview, document review, and test)?
		• Were the data gathering activities sufficient?
		• Were sample sizes adequate?
	• Analysis	• Is the analysis demonstrated or shown in the report?
		• Was the analysis adequate?
	• Findings	• Are the findings in the report clear?
		• Can you trace the findings back to the analysis and data gathered?
		• Are the findings prioritized?
		• Is the prioritization process reasonable?
		• Can you find any prioritized findings that seem out of order?
	• Recommendation	• Are there recommendations for the highest priority findings?
		• Are the recommendations clear and detailed enough to support action?
Follow up	• Risk register	• Did the organization incorporate the highest priority findings into their risk register?
		• Did they assign and track mitigation of these findings?

Note: The security risk assessment report should be reviewed for appropriate front matter, main report elements, and the organization's follow-up.

7.2.2.6.4 Information Technology/Security Audit Report

A similar report to the security risk assessment report is the information technology (IT) or security audit report. This report will have a similar structure and therefore a similar set of expected elements, but it differs in the front matter and the risk register portions. The expected elements of a security risk assessment report are listed in Table 7.16 to guide the assessors review of the report.

7.2.2.7 Reviewing Technical Manuals

The security risk assessment team, or a member of the team, should review the available technical security manuals to gain a perspective on the inputs to the current security risk assessment. The objective of this review is to increase the security risk assessment team's understanding of the

TABLE 7.16

Information Technology/Security Audit Report Expected Elements

Information Technology/Security Audit Report Expected Elements

An IT/security audit report is similar to the security risk assessment report, but it differs in the front matter and the risk register portions.

Document Area	Expected Elements	Review Tips
Required contents	• Required contents	• Front Matter: An audit report will have a title (e.g., "Independent Auditor's Report"); an "Address" (the auditor's report to the board of directors so the report is addressed to them); and responsibility (a statement of a free and fair opinion).
		• Does the report have the expected front matter elements?
		• Scope: Does the report include enough detail to understand the scope of the audit (e.g., IP addresses, systems, locations, and departments)
		• Does the assessment follow a specific method or Statement on Auditing Standards (SAS)? If so, which ones are listed?
		• Requirements: Is this assessment intended to meet any governmental or industry requirements? Are those requirements listed?
		• Opinion: This is the main conclusion of the report.
		• Is the opinion other than unqualified (e.g., qualified, adverse, or disclaimer of opinion)?
		• What is the basis of the opinion?
		• Emphasis of Matter: If the auditors believe there is an area that warrants attention by the organization, the auditor generally documents those matters in this section.
		• What controls or other concerns are the subject of the emphasis of matter section?
		• Signature—this is the auditor that takes responsibility for the quality and accuracy of the report.
		• How are the auditor's independent?
		• Are they qualified to perform the assessment?
		• Is the firm they are associated with a CPA Firm?
Main report	• Data gathering	• What were the data gathering activities (e.g., survey, interview, document review, and test)?
		• Were the data gathering activities sufficient?
		• Were sample sizes adequate?
	• Analysis	• Is the analysis demonstrated or shown in the report?
		• Was the analysis adequate?
	• Findings	• Are the findings in the report clear?
		• Can you trace the findings back to the analysis and data gathered?
		• Are the findings prioritized?
		• Is the prioritization process reasonable?
		• Can you find any prioritized findings that seem out of order?
	• Recommendation	• Are there recommendations for the highest priority findings?
		• Are the recommendations clear and detailed enough to support action?
Follow up	• Risk register	• Did the organization incorporate the highest priority findings into their risk register?
		• Did they assign and track mitigation of these findings?

Note: The IT auditor's report should be reviewed for required contents, main report elements, and the organization's follow-up.

technology employed within the organization's information system. Table 7.17 provides a baseline checklist for reviewing technical security manuals.

7.2.2.8   Review Technical Security Designs

Security design review (also called architectural review) is an assessment of the system or architecture design to determine its ability to support the security requirements of the system. This is not a testing effort supported by the use of tools. Instead, this is an engineering review of the system and the design of its security controls.

TABLE 7.17
Technical Manuals Review Checklist

Technical Manuals Review Checklist

Technical manuals can increase the security risk assessment team's understanding of the technology employed within the organization's information system.

Document Area	Expected Elements	Review Tips
System functions	• Roles and accounts	• Systems and applications manuals should list the account types and roles associated with the system, application, or service. The assessment team should take note of privileged accounts. • Does the system have the ability to create administrative accounts with differing levels of privilege? • Can the ability to create new administrative accounts be restricted? • Is there an account with only the ability to review security activities within the system?
	• Configuration options	• Review technical manuals for configuration options of the equipment, for example, high-availability options for firewalls. • Review manuals for modes of operation for the equipment, for example, active mode for IDS.
	• Audit options	• What are the auditing options within the system? • What is the level of auditing selected in the deployed system?
	• Warnings and cautions	• Administrator warnings: Many manuals provide warnings to administrators for the security settings, or security functions, for example, ordering of firewall rules, or the existence of default accounts • User warnings: Many user manuals will provide warnings to users about the security features provided within the products; for example, digitally signed e-mail is not protected from disclosure. • Assumptions: Many manuals will state environmental assumptions that must be met to ensure security, for example, physical protection of the connection to the console
Other settings	• Encryption settings	• Symmetric keys: Symmetric keys less than 128 bits are generally considered weak. • Hash values: Hash values less than 160 bits are generally considered weak. • Asymmetric keys: Asymmetric keys less than 2,048 bits are generally considered weak. • There are many other cautions when it comes to encryption settings the assessment team should be up on the latest encryption algorithm vulnerabilities and ensure the organization has taken those into account as well.

Note: The technical manuals should be reviewed for configuration options, warnings, and cautions.

It is important to understand that this assessment is performed at the "design level," not the "implementation level." For example, a system design that places a critical database behind a packet-filtering firewall has a critical design error because the firewall cannot protect the critical database from direct communication with untrusted hosts outside the firewall. This is a design error, not an implementation error, because no packet-filtering firewall can protect the database in this design; this design requires a proxy-filtering firewall (at the least). Design-level errors cannot be corrected through a change in the implementation (e.g., harden the firewall and change the firewall ruleset); they require a change in the design (e.g., implement both a packet-filtering firewall and an application proxy firewall to protect the database).

As with many of the tasks within a security risk assessment, it is difficult to completely assess the security design of critical systems. Exhaustive assessments are typically considered unachievable. Furthermore, many security risk assessments are bound by scope and budget that limit the ability to delve too deeply into the security of the system design. However, given that the security design of the system can certainly contain critical vulnerabilities, the security risk assessment team should endeavor to review the security design of the critical system to the extent that time, budget, and expertise allow.

There are no known approaches to systematically review the security design of the system.[11] The ability to review a secure design is based on experience and analytical skill (but if I just left it at that, the readers would be disappointed). For the sake of extending the discussion of such approaches, the security risk assessment team should consider the following approach:

- Determine the security requirements of the critical systems.
- Assess the security design against basic security engineering principles.
- Assess the security design against a set of common mistakes or investigation areas

7.2.2.8.1 Determine Security Requirements

In government systems, this process can typically be accomplished without too much effort, because the security requirements should be documented in the certification and accreditation package. For those systems outside government agencies, determining the security requirements of the system may not be as easy, but the following approach can yield useful results quickly:

- Step 1: Recall System-Critical Assets—For each critical system, list the assets. This should have already been done during the preparation phase. It is best to identify categories of assets instead of specific ones. For example, it really does not matter that there are patient records, medical charts, admission forms, and medical test results on a system, but it does matter that there is protected health-care information on the system.
- Step 2: Identify Security Requirements for Each Asset—For each asset identified above, determine the security requirement for its storage, processing, and transmission. Again, no need to get too involved here, as we are assessing the system, not building it. Use categories of security requirements such as confidentiality, integrity, and availability. Some special-purpose systems may have additional or alternative security requirements. For example, trading systems have requirements for non-repudiation, and voting systems have requirements for anonymity.
- Step 3: Allocate Security Requirements to System Components—Systems can be deconstructed into subsystems to facilitate understanding. Subsystems could include network interface, storage, access control, administration, audit, and file management. Each of these systems will be responsible for a subset of the security requirements developed in step 2. For example, the confidentiality of protected health information should be allocated to the network interface, storage, access control, and file management.

- Step 4: Consider Additional Requirements for Components—Once you are able to view the security requirements allocated to system components, it may become obvious that some security requirements are absent. For example, each subsystem must be able to protect itself from tampering.

7.2.2.9   Basic Security Design Principles

One approach for reviewing a security design and determining if the security requirements are met is to assess the design against basic design principles. These principles are not always applicable to systems; instead, they should be viewed as a set of tools that may be employed when the situation warrants. However, it is useful to review each of these principles when considering the design.

- Defense in Depth—The principle of defense in depth states that the compromise of critical assets should require the compromise of more than a single security control. The use of multiple overlapping protection approaches means that the failure of any one mechanism will not result in the compromise of the protected asset. The jewelry in your home is likely protected by the following security controls: front-door locks, burglar alarm, barking dog, and a safe. Likewise, critical assets on a system are likely protected by multiple layers of security controls. Although this is not an exhaustive list, look for the following controls within a critical network:
  - Multiple levels and types of firewalls
  - Network anti-virus protection
  - Intrusion detection system and monitoring
  - Access controls
  - Network segmentation
- Encryption—For each critical asset within the system, the security risk assessment team should determine the adequacy of the security controls that must be breached to compromise the asset.
- Least Privilege—The principle of least privilege states that each person, role, or process is given no more privilege than required in order to perform the mission. The goal is to reduce the risk to the critical system by reducing the number of people and processes with access to critical system security controls. The application of this principle to the security design of the system means that user roles and privileged processes should only be given the privilege they need for the duties or functions they perform. For example, within an integrated system, a process that collects audit data from multiple network components needs the privilege of reading audit logs and creating a new one, but does not need other privileges such as reading password files and writing to sensitive databases.

  There is not much the security risk assessment team can do about reviewing the internal processes of commercial off-the-shelf (COTS) software, but many critical systems in operation also contain custom-developed code for the specific environment in order to make different pieces of off-the-shelf software work together. This type of code (sometimes referred to as "glue" code) seldom receives the same scrutiny and development controls as the commercial code. Programmers have been known to take the "shortcut" of giving a process all privileges and not just the ones it needs to perform its functions. This practice of loading processes with privileges leads to catastrophic security vulnerabilities when the process can be manipulated or compromised.

  The security risk assessment team should review the privileges of the processes within the system to determine if the principle of least privilege is enforced.
- Enforced Reference Validation Mechanism Aspects—A reference validation mechanism is a conceptual model of how access control should be performed within a computer system.

The model states that subjects may only obtain access to objects if they go through the reference monitor (see Figure 7.5). For the reference monitor to effectively enforce access control, it must possess the following attributes:

- Always Invoked—Every subject access to an object must go through the reference monitor. There must be no other communication path between a subject and an object.
- Tamper-Proof—The reference monitor must protect itself from tampering. No other process should be able to interfere with the reference monitor processes or security controls.
- Simple—The implementation of the reference monitor (called the security kernel) must be small enough to be verified. A complex security kernel evades analysis and likely contains vulnerabilities.

To the extent that the security kernel is analyzable, the assessor should review the security kernel's ability to enforce each of the reference monitor aspects.

- Enforce Domain of Execution—The principle of domain of execution states that a program in a privileged domain should be unaffected by programs in other domains. A domain of execution is enforced through the isolation of potentially shared resources, including memory, processes, the CPU, the bus, and other shared objects. Trusted processes require protection through isolation of resources from other untrusted processes. For example, Java applets run within a virtual machine called a sandbox. Processes within this sandbox are protected from processes running outside the sandbox because specific resources are dedicated to the Java applets running within the sandbox. However, if multiple Java applets are running in the same sandbox, it is possible that they could affect the operation of each other through shared and unprotected resources.

  The assessor should review the enforcement of domain of execution within critical systems to determine if trusted processes are isolated from untrusted processes.

- Assume Those Untrusted Will Seek to Do Harm—When assessing security controls to determine vulnerabilities, it is always a good idea to assume that the worst will happen. With that in mind, assume that non-administrative users will seek to gain unapproved access, and assume that those outside your control are untrusted. For example, during the security design review, the assessor should assume that external domains are insecure. Until an external domain has been deemed 'trusted,' system engineers, architects, and IT specialists should presume the security measures of an external system are different than those of a trusted internal system and design the system security features accordingly.

  With this assumption in mind, consider what vulnerabilities may exist. For example, when you assume that non-administrative users will seek to gain unapproved access, it becomes rather clear that a Trojan horse vulnerability that seeks to modify ACLs on critical files is a real possibility.

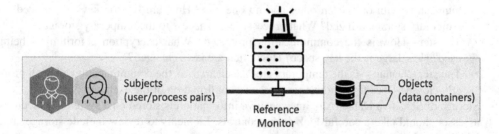

FIGURE 7.5 Reference monitor concept. The reference monitor is a conceptual model for access control that states that all subject accesses to objects must be approved by the reference monitor.

The security risk assessment team should review the connections to external networks and the interfaces of untrusted users with a critical eye. Ask yourself, "What is the worst they could do?"

- Keep It Simple—Complex designs for security mechanisms are more likely to contain design flaws. When reviewing the security design of a critical system, the assessor should pay careful attention to security mechanisms that seem overly complex. These areas are typically a good place to find design flaws.

  The security risk assessment team should critically review overly complex security mechanisms.

- Accountability—The principle of accountability states that the additions, modifications, and deletions of critical assets need to be audited and associated with the user or process that performed the action. For each critical asset within a critical system, an audit record should be cut when the file is viewed, deleted, modified, or created.

  The security risk assessment team should ensure that adequate audit records are generated for access to critical assets.

- Avoid Single Points of Failure—A single point of failure is defined as a resource whose loss will in turn result in the loss of a critical service. If a single system component or resource fails, then the critical system also fails. Systems with secure designs and availability requirements should be designed to avoid single points of failure for critical system services.

  The assessor should map critical systems to required resources and assess the extent of built-in redundancy for each of these required resources.

7.2.2.9.1   Common Areas for Investigation

Design analysis involves the review of the system design (not implementation) and its ability to enforce its security requirements. The best way to perform design analysis is to review the design of the system at a low level and create an argument for why it is able to enforce the security requirements. Unfortunately, such low-level design information is rarely available to anyone but the system developers. Moreover, such low-level analysis is not typically performed as a part of a security risk assessment. This discussion of security design analysis purposely takes a higher-level view.

The security design analysis approach described below concentrates on key areas in which system security design is typically flawed and areas in which the security risk assessment team is likely to be able to gain a view into the system design. These areas include transmission of sensitive data, storage of sensitive data, account setup and maintenance, perimeter controls, maintenance procedures, library routines, and backup procedures.[12]

- Transmission of Sensitive Data—Anytime sensitive information is transferred from one system to another, the security assessor should take a careful look at the controls. Elements to review include transfer setup, transfer, and transfer cleanup.
  - Transfer Setup—Determine how the transfer is initiated. How does each party know that they are communicating with the other? How does each party know that they are communicating with only each other and no one else? How are session keys exchanged? Is temporary storage utilized? What processes have access to the temporary storage?
  - Transfer—How is the communication protected? What encryption algorithm is being used? How large is the key space? How often are keys changed?
  - Transfer Cleanup—Is the temporary storage cleared? Is the communication channel properly closed? Does the sending party receive confirmation of the exchange?
- Storage of Sensitive Data—Anytime sensitive information is stored on a system, the security assessor should take a careful look at the controls. Elements to review include storage area, labeling, and retrieval.
  - Storage Area—Where is the data stored? How is the storage area protected from other processes? When is the data deleted? How is it ensured that no data is remaining?
  - Labeling—Is the data labeled? How is the label used in access control?

- Retrieval—How is sensitive data retrieved from long-term storage? What other processes have control over the data? When should data be deleted? How is deletion enforced?
- Use of Secure Protocols—There are many protocols for the transfer of information across a network that inherently do not provide confidentiality or integrity services. For example, the Password Authentication Protocol (PAP) uses a two-way handshake to establish communications and sends the password in the clear. The use of this protocol across a network that is assumed to be hostile is a design flaw. An authentication protocol that protects the confidentiality of the message should be used in this case, such as Challenge Handshake Authentication Protocol (CHAP) or Extensible Authentication Protocol (EAP).
  - Use of Secure Protocols—Ensure that secure protocols are used as appropriate. What security requirements have been allocated to the protocol? Is the protocol designed to address those requirements?
- Account Setup and Maintenance—When accounts are established, managed, or maintained, the security assessor should take a careful look at the controls. Elements to review include account privileges and rights, roles, resetting passwords, and administrative accounts.
  - Account Privileges and Rights—What privileges and rights are available for accounts? How are these assignments determined? How often are the rights and privileges reviewed? Is it possible to gain additional rights through other mechanisms (e.g., superzap)? To what extent is the granting of privileges audited?
  - Application-to-Application Access—How does one application gain access to another application? Is the application treated as "just another user"? If so, are passwords sent in the clear when accessing a password-protected application?
  - Single Sign-On—Is single sign-on (SSO) established within this design? What method of SSO is being used?
  - Roles—What are the privileged roles within the system? Are there separation-of-duty concerns among any of these roles? How are these concerns addressed? How are individuals assigned to roles? Are such assignments reflected in the audit records?
  - Password Recovery and Account Lockout—What does it take to lock up an account? Does it require administrator intervention to unlock the account? How are passwords recovered or reset? How does the administrator (or system) determine he is really talking to a user who forgot his password? How is the new password relayed to the legitimate user? Is he forced to change it?
  - Administrative Accounts—Do all administrative accounts have the same privilege? How are individuals associated with administrative accounts? Who audits the actions of the administrators?
- Perimeter Controls—The security controls that have been put in place to protect the perimeter of the system should be reviewed by the security assessor. Elements to review include perimeter coverage and protection strength.
  - Perimeter Coverage—Using a system diagram, identify all interfaces to the system. Now identify the protection used on each interface point (e.g., firewall, modem, and VPN). Ensure that all interfaces have some type of protection.
  - Protection Strength—Now assess the strength of each protection device. What type of firewall? Does remote access require two factor authentication? What encryption is used to support the VPN?
- Maintenance Procedures—Maintenance procedures associated with critical systems can sometimes represent an Achilles' heel to an otherwise secure system. Maintenance procedures are sometimes an afterthought and are performed when the system is outside its normal operating mode. It is for this reason that the maintenance process deserves some scrutiny.
  - Maintenance Access—Many systems allow remote maintenance access. The access can be provided through rather insecure means such as open modems, group passwords, or unencrypted communications.

- Maintenance Updates—Some systems receive maintenance updates through a physical means such as tapes in the mail. How does the administrator know from whom the tape really came?
- Proprietary Solutions—Be especially critical of proprietary solutions where open standards or well-known industry standards exist. A critical system that touts a proprietary encryption algorithm should be scrutinized.
  - Encryption Algorithms—Who developed the algorithm? To what extent has this algorithm been reviewed, tested, and analyzed? By whom?
- Group Identities—Although most users are likely to have unique identifiers for their accounts, many systems still have some group identities. The lack of unique identification for all accounts makes it impossible to enforce the following security principles: accountability, assignment of specific rights to individuals, non-repudiation services, access control decisions, and the prevention of masquerading.
  - Group Accounts—Which accounts have group identities (e.g., administration, maintenance, help desk, guest, and training)?
- Library Routines—Library routines are used by programmers to save the time it takes to rewrite subprograms that perform functions that are used by multiple programs. This practice is part of modular coding and is expected within well-designed systems. However, the system must carefully control access to the library routines. One easy way to compromise secure software is to replace a library routine with a Trojan horse. When this imposter routine is called, it will likely run with privilege.
  - Library Routines—Who has access to library routines? Are they protected through access controls? How would it be known if one was changed inappropriately? Checksums? Do programs that call library routines use the full path name?

7.2.3 INTERVIEW PERSONNEL REGARDING TECHNICAL CONTROLS

Data gathering for technical security controls also involves interviewing key personnel. For the most part, data gathering in the technical area involves testing the system. However, it is important to interview the key technical personnel to understand the network, troubleshoot the testing effort, and understand the technical controls employed.

7.2.3.1 Technical Interview Topics

As mentioned previously, the interviews with technical personnel are typically kept to a minimum. This is for several reasons. First, technical personnel are rarely available for formal interviews. You may find it easier to gain information by having several short and informal conversations. Second, the security risk assessment team is typically much more interested in how something really works than how someone says it works. Within the technical controls area, the security risk assessment team will find that interviews are useful as background information but should rely more on tests and inspections.

7.2.3.2 Technical Interview Subjects

The security risk assessment team should interview the technical personnel best able to provide the information required to understand the network and assist in setting up the test effort. The selection of interview subjects will depend on who has the responsibility for the safeguards in question. All questions will be directed to security operations staff.

7.2.3.3 Technical Interview Questions

Prior to any interview, the security risk assessment team should review the available documents and prepare questions based on the information provided or concerns that surfaced during the document review. If several members of the security risk assessment team were responsible for reviewing the documents, these members should get together to create a list of questions that they have compiled on the technical documents.

7.2.3.3.1 Security Testing and Review Interview Questions

Security testing and review activities are any practices conducted within the organization to ascertain the effectiveness of controls through testing. The security team within the organization likely has several activities such as password cracking, phishing exercises, and penetration testing that are performed on a regular basis. The security risk assessment team should interview those responsible for executing these security testing activities to determine the extent to which they are effective.

The security testing and review questions in Table 7.18 can be asked of anyone in the technical group who has the responsibility for the subjects discussed. The questions cover password cracking, vulnerability scanning, audit log review, and forensic analysis. If the organization has not implemented one or more of these controls, that section of the interview can be skipped, as it is not applicable.

7.2.3.3.2 Security Components Interview Questions

Security components are standalone devices (or services) within the organization's information system that implements one or more security services such as firewalls and intrusion detection systems. The security component questions in Table 7.19 can be asked of anyone in the technical group who has the responsibility for the subjects discussed. The questions cover firewalls, identity management systems, and intrusion detection systems. If the organization has not implemented one or more of these controls, that section of the interview can be skipped, as it is not applicable.

7.2.3.3.3 Security Operations and Procedures Interview Questions

Security operations are the everyday processes implemented by the security operations team to manage system security controls. The security operations and procedures questions in Table 7.20 can be asked of anyone in the technical group who has the responsibility for the subjects discussed.

TABLE 7.18

Security Testing and Review Interview Guidelines

Security Testing and Review Interview Guidelines

Security testing and review activities are any practices conducted within the organization to ascertain the effectiveness of controls through testing

Topic	Subtopic	Question
User testing	Phishing exercises	• What tools or services are used to conduct phishing exercises? • How often are phishing exercises executed? • How do you track the success of the exercises? • What changes have you seen in the hit rate of the phishing attempts sent over the last year? • Have you received any push back on the use of this technique? • What adjustments have you made?

	Password cracking	• What tools are used to test the strength of passwords?
		  • How often are these tools used?
		  • What account do you log into to use those tools?
		• Where are the results kept?
		  • How are they disseminated within the organization?
		• How is access to the tool and the password file protected?
		  • Is such access logged?

(Continued)

TABLE 7.18 *(Continued)*

Topic	Subtopic	Question
System vulnerability testing	Vulnerability scanning	• What tools are used to test the vulnerabilities of the system? • What account do you log into to use those tools? • Where are the results kept? • How are they disseminated within the organization? • How is access to the tool protected? • Is such access logged?
	Penetration testing	• What tools are used for penetration testing? • What techniques are used beyond the use of tools? • What account do you log into to use those tools? • Where are the results kept? • How are they disseminated within the organization? • How is access to the tool protected? • Is such access logged? • What credentials and/or training have you had in the use of the tools? • How are the scope, permission, and rules of engagement determined for the penetration testing exercises? • Is that documented? • What systems and technologies do you test within the scope a penetration test? • External interfaces? • Internal interfaces? • Web applications? • Database access? • Wireless access points? • Virtual Private Network?
System logging and monitoring testing	Audit log review	• How many different audit logs are created? • How often is each log reviewed? • Do you have any tools or processes that assist in the review of these logs? • What account do you log into to review these logs? • How is access to these logs protected? • Who else has access to these logs? • How much information (in hours or days est.) can these logs store? • What happens when the log file gets full? • Do you receive a warning when the file is nearly full? • What information is available for each audit event? (i.e., log-on/ log-off, policy changes, process tracking) • How are events on the same system correlated? How are events that happen on different parts of the network correlated? • How are audit files protected from deletion? How much audit log information do you retain and for how long? How are archived audit logs protected?
Incident response review	Forensic analysis	• What tools are used for forensic analysis? • What training have you had on these tools? • Do you hold any industry certifications in forensic analysis? • What account do you log into to use those tools? • How is access to the tool protected? • Is such access logged?

Note: The interviewer should compile a list of questions to ask the responsible party to ensure that the security risk assessment team has a clear understanding of the technical safeguards.

TABLE 7.19

Security Component Interview Guidelines

Security Component Interview Guidelines

Security components are standalone devices (or services) within the organization's information system that implement one or more security services.

Topic	Subtopic	Question

Information flow components	Firewalls	• What is the firewall architecture in place within the organization?
		• What types of firewalls are deployed?
		• How are the firewalls updated to protect against the latest attacks?
		• Who has authority/access to make these changes?
		• Are there unique IDs for each person authorized to make the change?
		• What is the process for making changes to the firewall ruleset?
		• How often is the firewall ruleset reviewed?
		• What is the naming convention used for firewall rule objects?
		• How are unused or temporary rules tracked and removed?
		• What inbound services are allowed through the firewalls?
		• Do each of the rules include a comment explaining the purpose and/or business justification of the rule?
		• What events are tagged for alerts?
		  • Who gets these alerts?
		  • How are the alerts delivered?
		• What events are tagged for audit?
		• Who reviews the audit logs?
		  • How often?

Identity components	Identity management systems	• Please explain the architecture of the identity management system. • How is the identity management system used for provisioning of user accounts? • How are these accounts updated? • How are these accounts disabled and terminated? • Is there a defined and documented set of roles and groups to which users are assigned? • How many privileged accounts and how many user accounts are managed within the identity management system? • How often are user access reviews performed? • Is multi-factor authentication implemented within the identity management system? • Are there any exceptions? • Are there any separation of duties that are implemented through the identity management system? • How is the identity management system used to ensure unnecessary user accounts? • Are there any systems, applications, or services that are not incorporated into the identity management system?
Software management	Software asset management	• To what extent is the software asset management (SAM) system deployed and operational? • Please explain how the SAM system authorizes and verifies that software installation media comes from a trusted source. • Please explain how software execution whitelisting is utilized within the organization through the SAM system. • How often is an inventory of installed software created and reviewed within the organization? • How often is a patch level aging report created and reviewed within the organization? • How many systems are not patched within 30 days of a security patch being made available?

(Continued)

TABLE 7.19 *(Continued)*

Topic	Subtopic	Question

Monitoring components	Intrusion detection systems	• Is the IDS in active or passive mode?
		• What has been your experience with false positives?
		• Did you make adjustments to the system?
		• How are IDS signatures updated? Do these signatures work well within your environment?
		• Did you make adjustments to the rules to accommodate your environment?
		• What attacks are tagged for audit?
		  • Who gets these alerts?
		  • How are the alerts delivered?
		• What attacks are tagged for alerts?
		  • Who reviews the audit logs?
		  • How often?

	Web and e-mail filtering	• Does web filtering create logs of accesses and attempted accesses?
		  • How often are these reviewed?
		  • Is the review of these logs logged?
		  • What has been your experience with false positives and false negatives?
		• Can users make their own adjustments to the system?
		• How are spam filters updated?
		• Is the blocked e-mail stored?
		  • Where?
		  • How long?
		  • Who has access?

Note: The interviewer should compile a list of questions to ask the responsible party to ensure that the security risk assessment team has a clear understanding of the technical safeguards.

The questions cover patch management, configuration management, hardening guidelines, and data backup. If the organization has not implemented one or more of these controls, that section of the interview can be skipped, as it is not applicable.

7.2.4 INSPECT TECHNICAL SECURITY CONTROLS

Data gathering for technical security controls also involves inspecting technical security controls. Recall that inspection differs from testing, in that inspection is performed when testing is inappropriate or not feasible. Inspection involves the review of security control and security control aspects such as configuration or arrangements. For the most part, the approach for performing a security control inspection includes listing the security controls under review, verifying information gathered, determining vulnerabilities, and documenting the results. Each of these phases is discussed within the context of technical data gathering.

7.2.4.1 List Technical Security Controls

The relevant security controls to be inspected include only those that lend themselves to inspection. In the case of technical controls, this includes the following:

- Audit logs
- Identity management system
- Data backup technologies
- Vulnerability scanning tools
- Penetration testing tools
- Patch management system
- Anti-spam tools

TABLE 7.20

Security Operations and Procedures Interview Guidelines

Security Operations and Procedures Interview Guidelines

Security operations are the everyday processes implemented by the security operations team to manage system security controls.

Topic	Subtopic	Question
System configuration	Hardening guidelines	• Do you have a hardening guideline or checklist? • Is there a specific checklist for each of your platforms and major COTS applications? • What is the source of information for the hardening guidance? • To what extent is the hardening process automated? • How do you check the configuration of deployed systems against hardening guidelines? • What components within the organization do not have hardening guidelines established? • How often is your guideline updated? • How do you keep track of changes to the guidance and application of the guidance to your systems? • How do you test the effectiveness of your hardening guidance?
	Patch management	• What is the scope of the patch management system? • What systems are not covered by the patch management system? • How do you verify the integrity of the patch? • How is the patch tested for correctness and effectiveness? • Is the system backed up prior to applying a new patch? • How do you ensure the patch worked? • How are patches prioritized and scheduled for application? • How do you inform other administrators that the patch was applied? • Do you require external partners to apply critical patches? • How often is a patch level aging report created and reviewed within the organization? • How many systems are not patched within 30 days of a security patch being made available?
System configuration management	Configuration management	• Is there a configuration management plan in place? • What tools are used to implement configuration management? • Which of the following elements are under configuration control? • network maps, • firewall rulesets, • IDS signatures, • user accounts, • operating system patches, • application versions? • Who reviews and approves these configuration changes? • Does "security" have a review or approval "voice" in the configuration process?
Backup	Data backup	• How often do you test your data backups? • What is your backup schedule? What is your tape rotation schedule? • How often do you update your backup software? • Where are your backup media stored? • Where do you store your backup software? • Is there encryption or other logical controls on the backup data? • Are your backups automated? • Do you ensure that all critical files are closed prior to performing a backup?

Note: The interviewer should compile a list of questions to ask the responsible party to ensure that the security risk assessment team has a clear understanding of the technical safeguards.

- Configuration management
- Firewalls
- Intrusion detection systems
- System hardening guidance
- Operating systems and applications

Of course, only those controls actually implemented by the organization can be inspected. The list of technical security controls to be reviewed for a specific organization comprises any of the controls that the organization stated are in place. Statements regarding technical controls in place could have come from interviews or been provided as part of the document review process. The team should obtain a point of contact for each of these controls.

7.2.4.2 Verify Information Gathered
Information gathered regarding technical security controls should be confirmed through the inspection process. Team members should use various methods to confirm the existence of each of these security controls.

7.2.4.2.1 Audit Logs
The security risk assessment team should review a sample of available audit logs. Specifically, the team can ask to see the audit reports of specific events they suspect or know have happened:

- Log files for security risk assessment team log-ins
- Log files associated with security risk assessment team testing
- Log files for last access to an excessive privileged application such as a password cracker
- Log files associated with the last documented incident

7.2.4.2.2 Identity Management System
The security risk assessment team should identify a member of the technical team who "wears several hats," for example, a system operator who also reviews the audit log files. Then the team members should ask the operator to list all of the accounts he has at the organization and ask for a report on his identity. The team members can then compare the report against stated accounts for that user. This same process can be repeated for several different positions.

7.2.4.2.3 Data Backup Technologies
A member of the security risk assessment team should ask to see where the backup tapes are stored. The team member can then compare the condition of the actual tape backup site against what was discussed during the interview. For example, the team member can ask, "Where are the tapes really stored?" The team member should also inspect the tape label to ensure that it contains the date of backup, the type of backup, the operating system version, and the retention period.

7.2.4.2.4 Vulnerability Scanning Tools
The security risk assessment team should compile a list of the vulnerability scanning testing tools that are used internally. Each of these tools should be checked for the latest updates. The team should ask the person responsible for running these tools a few questions to ascertain his experience and knowledge using these tools.

To ensure a complete coverage of vulnerability scanning testing tools within the organization, a member of the team should map each of the tools used against the following categories of internal checks that may be run:

- Operating system vulnerability scanning
- Web application vulnerability scanning
- Database vulnerability scanning
- Wireless LAN vulnerability scanning

7.2.4.2.5   Penetration Testing Tools

The security risk assessment team should compile a list of the penetration testing tools that are used internally. Each of these tools should be checked for the latest updates. The team should ask the person responsible for running these tools a few questions to ascertain his experience and knowledge using these tools.

To ensure a complete coverage of penetration testing tools within the organization, a member of the team should map each of the tools used against the following categories of internal checks that may be run:

- Operating system penetration testing
- Web application penetration testing
- Database penetration testing
- Wireless LAN penetration testing

7.2.4.2.6   Patch Management System

A member of the security risk assessment team should ask for a demonstration of the patch management system. During the demonstration, the team member should determine the features of the patch management system (e.g., enterprise-wide monitoring, report generation, delegation of duties, and automatic deployment of patches).

7.2.4.2.7   Web and E-mail Filtering Tools

A member of the security risk assessment team should check for false positives by asking to see the repository for filtered e-mail (i.e., e-mail identified as spam) and determining if filtered e-mail contains legitimate e-mail. Alternatively, the team member could send an e-mail to several points of contact containing text that might be inappropriately flagged as spam. For example, send an e-mail with the word "Middlesex" in the subject line.

7.2.4.2.8   Configuration Management

A member of the security risk assessment team should ask for a demonstration of the configuration management system. The team member can then determine the features of the configuration management system (e.g., change identification, change tracking, and integrated approval process). Also, the team member should ask to see the change management documentation for several recent changes.

The team should read available documentation to become familiar with the process. Then the team members should select several recent changes such as patch application, account creation, or firewall change, including at least one known about through other data gathering processes. Ask to see the documents that walk through the process of change control for those selected changes.

7.2.4.2.9   Firewalls

Firewall rulesets are the list of information flows allowed and blocked. The inspection of firewalls comes down to the inspection of the firewall ruleset. Use Table 7.21 to guide your review of the firewall rulesets. Of course, firewalls are not one-size-fits-all, so treat this table as a guideline, not a rule.

TABLE 7.21

Firewall Ruleset Inspection Guideline

Firewall Ruleset Inspection Guidelines

Firewall rulesets are the list of information flows allowed and blocked. The inspection of firewalls comes down to the inspection of the firewall ruleset.

Firewall Type	Subtopic	Question
All firewalls	Consistent with architecture	• Ensure rules are consistent with the documented network architecture (e.g., are there any rules that allow external access directly to the internal subnet, bypassing the DMZ?) • Are the VLANs in the provided network documentation properly implemented? • are there any rules that allow external access directly to the internal subnet, bypassing the DMZ?) • Is the Guest WiFi profile appropriately restricted?
	Firewall administration rule	• The rule(s) established for firewall management (destination = the firewall's IP address) should limit the source address to the firewall administrators address (or a small set of addresses).
	"Clean Up" rules	• Ensure there are no "any, any, any" permissive rules. • Ensure there is an "any, any, any" denial rule (i.e., "default deny all" rule)

	Rule management	• Do each of the rules include a comment explaining the purpose and/or business justification of the rule?
		• Review the naming conventions used throughout the firewall rules.
		  • Are they of a consistent format?
		  • Are there any redundant or duplicate rules?
		• How are unused or temporary rules tracked and removed?

	Blocked addresses	• Does the firewall block the following?
		• private addresses
		  • Unrouteable addresses
		  • Reserved addresses
		  • Illegal addresses
		  • Internal addresses over external ports

	Egress filtering	• Does the firewall apply egress filtering (i.e., outgoing traffic may only come from internal IP addresses)?
	User permitted behavior	• Are rules for user permitted behavior (e.g., https to Web server) appropriate?
	System management permitted behavior	• Are the rules for management-permitted behaviors (e.g., SNMP traps to the management server) appropriate?
	Malicious and vulnerable	• Is access to any vulnerable ports and services allowed? • Are malicious packets (e.g., UDP and TCP echo requests to the broadcast network address) identified and dropped?

Next generation and application firewalls	Rules	• Is URL filtering implemented?
		• Do the ruleset include rules for blocking the following commands:
		  • EXPN, VRFY, DEBUG, WIZARD
		  • PUT command for FTP servers

Note: The firewall ruleset is the collection of access control rules that govern the logical access control decision made by the firewall. Depending on the type of firewall, these rulesets can make access control decisions on IP address, protocol, and even recognized attacks.

7.2.4.2.10   Intrusion Detection Systems

The security risk assessment team should review the intrusion detection systems to ensure their effectiveness. Specifically, the team should examine the following elements of the IDSs for vulnerabilities:

- Definition Files—A member of the security risk assessment team should review the intrusion detection definition files. The team member can compare these definitions with vendor and Common Vulnerabilities and Exposures (CVE) latest known attacks.
- Adequate Coverage—The effectiveness of an intrusion detection system is based on the availability of the information it receives about network- or host-based activities. The assessor should ensure that IDS sensors are properly placed throughout the information system network to ensure proper coverage. The best approach to assessing adequate coverage is to indicate the presence of IDS sensors on a network diagram. The assessor should be cognizant of subnets, critical servers, and critical applications
- Capacity—An important element in ensuring that an IDS is effective is to ensure that it has the appropriate capacity for the network traffic (NIDS).

7.2.4.2.11   System Hardening Guidance

A member of the security risk assessment team should review the application of system hardening guidance to a sample of systems. Hardening guidance application can be reviewed by walking through the hardening guidance elements and checking the system being reviewed against each element. Also, the team member can check for documentation of who performed the hardening and when it was performed.

7.2.4.2.12   Operating Systems and Applications

Many operating systems and even some applications arrive from the manufacturer with a multitude of features and services that can result in security vulnerabilities (e.g., development tools and default settings). System hardening refers to the removal of those features, services, and default settings to establish a secure implementation of operating systems and applications. In addition, by ensuring that default settings are corrected, a configuration review also ensures that the services and features are properly used.

By far the most widely used approach for a configuration review is the use of a checklist. A checklist (also called lockdown procedures, hardening guidelines, or security technical implementation guide) is a document that contains instructions and procedures for the secure configuration of IT products. A security configuration checklist can assist the security risk assessment team in efficiently reviewing the parameters of the secure implementation of a security system component. Using the checklists as a guide in the examination is a quick way to ensure that a reasonable review of the possible vulnerabilities has been performed.

7.2.4.2.12.1   Sources of Checklists

Security configuration checklists are developed by government, consortia, vendors, academia, and private industry. Below is a list of some of the sources for security configuration checklists:

- Government Checklists—Agencies and departments within the United States Federal Government provide useful checklists for the secure configuration of many commercial systems and applications:
  - Defense Information Systems Agency (DISA) Security Technical Implementation Guides (https://public.cyber.mil/stigs).

- National Institute of Standards and Technology (NIST)—The National Checklist Program Repository contains checklists for just about any type of system component (e.g., VOIP, routers, firewalls, cell phones, biometrics, databases, applications, and domain name servers). The NIST security configuration checklists will be stored at the following link as they become available: https://nvd.nist.gov/ncp/repository.
- Vendor Checklists—Many security product vendors provide useful checklists for the security configuration of their systems and applications:
  - Microsoft Security Compliance Toolkit—Microsoft provides a set of tools to test installed servers for compliance with their recommended security baselines. The tools cover operating systems, servers, Microsoft Office, Microsoft Edge, and other products.
  - Oracle Advanced Customer Services—Oracle provide white papers on the topic of hardening Oracle installations.
  - Red Hat Linux—Red Hat provides a security guide for Red Hat Linux.
- Consortia Checklists—There are other information security groups and consortia that also provide useful checklists for common commercial systems and applications:
  - The SysAdmin, Audit, Network, Security (SANS) Institute SANS Security Consensus Operational Readiness Evaluation (SCORE) Effort (https://www.sans.org/score/checklists)—This site provides a set of security checklists, including ASP, firewalls, handheld computers, operating systems, databases, and wireless access points.
  - The Center for Internet Security (CIS) (http://www.cisecurity.org)—This site contains "benchmarks" for desktops operating systems, browsers, mobile devices, network devices, servers, virtualization platforms, and applications.

7.2.4.2.12.2   Use of Checklists

Checklists should not be considered as the only mechanism for performing a configuration review. A security configuration checklist can be used to assist or guide the security risk assessment team in reviewing the system components for possible vulnerabilities, but the assessors should use one or more of the following approaches:

- Approach 1: Review Components against a Checklist—If the organization being assessed has no documented procedure for hardening system components, then this is the only approach you can take. This approach involves the following steps:
  1. Select an appropriate checklist for the security components being reviewed. See the lists in the previous section for sources of such lists.
  2. Customize the checklist to account for unique environmental and organizational concerns. Just as all customers do not use off-the-shelf software in the same manner, a security checklist will not apply equally to all environments. For example, almost all checklists include a section for disabling used services. The services used for each environment may differ. Therefore, you must know the services offered by the system components to customize a security checklist for appropriate use.
  3. Walk through the customized security checklist indicating areas in which the actual implementation differs from the recommended implementation in the checklist.
  4. Determine the possible vulnerabilities within the system component based on deviations from the recommended checklist. Note that some deviations may not result in an actual or material vulnerability. Most of the checklists will provide information as to the vulnerability that each step within the checklist prevents. If no such information is available, you must determine the vulnerability through research, analysis, or testing.
- Approach 2: Review Components against Organization's Checklist—If the organization does have a documented procedure for hardening system components, then you can select a

component to review and follow the documented guideline. This approach maps to Approach 1 except the checklist is one produced by the assessed organization and not an outside source.

- Approach 3: Review the Organization's Checklist against a Checklist—Another approach to take if the organization has a documented procedure for hardening system components is to review their document against yours. This could be considered more of a procedure review, in that it is a "desk check" exercise, in which you will note deficiencies in the organization's procedure wherein they fail to close a known vulnerability considered in the selected checklist. This approach is rather straightforward. Place the documents (their checklist and yours) side by side and indicate any vulnerability that is addressed in your document but not in theirs.
- Approach 4: Use a Checklist-based Tool—Many commercial system and application secure configuration checklists have grown to a rather substantial size. Walking through an entire checklist can be time consuming and error prone. Many of these checklists can also be the basis of a tool-based check against an active system.

Next, determine the possible vulnerabilities within the system component based on the noted deviations. Again, some deviations may not result in an actual or material vulnerability. If your checklist provides information as to the vulnerability that each step within the checklist prevents, then record each vulnerability. If no such information is available, you must determine the vulnerability through research, analysis, or testing.

7.2.4.3 Determine Vulnerabilities

During inspection of the technical security controls, the security risk assessment team should look for vulnerabilities. The inspection process of these controls involves the recognition of ineffective mechanisms, configurations, or processes. The questions and tips within the previous section guide the security risk assessment team toward these vulnerabilities. For example, when inspecting the audit log features for adequate indication of potential security breaches, a vulnerability exists if the team determines that the audit logs are missing critical information (e.g., network time or access to critical files).

7.2.4.4 Document and Review Findings

As with all findings, the security risk assessment team must be sure to carefully record their findings in the area of technical controls through inspection. The team should include dates, evidence, team member names, and the vulnerabilities observed. These findings must be reviewed with the entire team and with the point of contact for the control to give that person a chance to clarify any misunderstandings.

7.2.5 OBSERVE TECHNICAL PERSONNEL BEHAVIOR

The process of gathering data through observation is a subtle one. With a few exceptions, this process is passive and depends on team members being aware of the organization's policies, procedures, and safeguards, while keeping an eye out for opportunities to confirm or disprove the organization's effective use of technology. However, some observations can be active in nature, such as performing activities that should be audited and checking the audit logs. More experienced team members will find observation to be second nature and a side effect of being on site.

With a little guidance and teamwork, these observations can be recorded from most team members and add additional data points to the data gathering process. Table 7.22 provides some guidance to the security risk assessment team for observing the behavior of the organization's staff in order to determine the strength of some of the technical controls. The security risk assessment team is encouraged to review Table 7.22 and add or modify table elements to suit their own needs and experiences.

TABLE 7.22
Technical Controls Observation Guideline

Technical Controls Observation Guideline

The effective execution of technical controls can be observed while onsite, engaging with technical staff members and while performing other data gathering activities.

Technical Control	Claim	Observation Test or Procedure Check
Audit logs	All security-relevant events are audited and reviewed	• Review audit logs for security-relevant events that transpired during the on-site inspection. • Wait a few days after an auditable event and check to see when the event was first reviewed.
Anti-virus systems	• System prevents virus infection • Updates are performed regularly • Users cannot block scans or updates	• Be aware of viruses that may be circulating during the time of the assessment. Determine from observation if the virus is having an effect on the information system. • When given the chance to interview users or inspect a workstation, check to see if the latest updates have been applied. Also check to see if scans or updates can be blocked.
Screen savers	All workstations have active screen savers with passwords	• General observations of user behavior and workstations viewed while on site.
Personal firewalls	• Users cannot override settings • Users understand how to use personal firewalls • Updates performed regularly	• Be aware of attacks that may be circulating during the time of the assessment. Determine from observation if the attacks have an effect on the information system. • When given the chance to interview users or inspect a workstation, check to see if the latest updates have been applied. Also check to see if scans or updates can be blocked.
Anti-spam filters	Spam is reduced or eliminated	• When given the chance to interview users, ask if they still receive any spam.
	False negatives are non-existent or do not impact business	• Ask if the spam filters have blocked any legitimate e-mail that they know of. Be careful of just taking the user's word for this. There can be many reasons for not receiving an important e-mail, including the possibility that it was never sent. Ask if the user opened a trouble ticket or asked someone in IT about it. Follow up on the complaint to confirm that legitimate e-mail was actually blocked.
Spyware removal	• Spyware is removed • Updates are performed regularly • Users cannot override settings	• Determine from observation if spyware has infiltrated workstations and affects the mission. • When given the chance to interview users or inspect a workstation, check to see if the latest updates have been applied. Also check to see if scans or updates can be blocked.
Digital signatures	Digital signatures are used for workflow processes	• Be aware of any security-relevant workflow process (e.g., account activation) that relies on e-mails. Confirm and document these processes, then ensure that each e-mail is accepted only if it has been digitally signed. Any instance where this is not the case should be documented as a finding, because e-mail may be spoofed, and the workflow process may be compromised.
Configuration management systems	Security-relevant changes are documented, reviewed, and appropriately approved	• Be aware of security-relevant changes that happen while the team is on site. Follow up during the configuration management inspection if those changes have appropriately gone through the process.

Note: The security risk assessment team should be prepared to observe the behavior of the security staff, key personnel, and general employee population to check the effectiveness of technical controls.

7.2.6 TEST TECHNICAL SECURITY CONTROLS

The last phase of data gathering for technical security controls in the RIIOT method is testing. Testing of technical security controls is the process of invoking conditions that test technical controls against their intended security functions. This type of data gathering provides excellent insight into the effectiveness of the controls.

The technical controls that lend themselves to testing include monitoring technology, audit logs, anti-virus systems, automated password policies, VPN, firewalls, IDSs, and system hardening. An approach for testing each of these controls is presented below. The security risk assessment team is encouraged to adopt, modify, or add to these test methods.

7.2.6.1 Monitoring Technology

The appropriate technologies to test include Uniform Record Locator (URL) blocking. Testing procedures for URL blocking require that the security risk assessment team perform activities that attempt to bypass the blocking controls in place. The following URL blocking tests should be attempted in order to gain a minimum level of confidence that the monitoring technology is effective:

- Attempt basic testing of various categories to be blocked:
  - Prohibited Content Sites—adult sites, hate groups
  - Prohibited Use Sites—gambling sites, Web-based e-mail
  - Waste of Resources—streaming media, shopping, real estate, dating, job search, games, financial, chats
  - Security Violations—hacking, downloads, personal websites
- Attempt to use remote proxies or Web anonymizers to bypass the URL blocking
- Attempt to defeat mechanism if it is a client-side device

7.2.6.2 Audit Logs

Testing procedures for audit logs require that the security risk assessment team perform activities that exercise security-relevant activities that should be audited. Additionally, the audit logs should be tested for protection from unauthorized modification. The following tests should be attempted in order to gain a minimum level of confidence that the audit log protections are effective:

- Audited Activities—The assessment team member should perform a sampling of security-relevant activities that should create audit records, for example, multiple authorization attempts, and attempted reading of protected files.
- Audit Log Information—The team member should review the created audit log files for the essential audit log event elements, for example, user identification, attempted access, success or failure, and network time stamp.
- Audit Log Protection—The team member should attempt to access audit log files from an unauthorized account.

7.2.6.3 Anti-Virus Systems

Testing procedures for anti-virus systems require that the security risk assessment team perform activities that attempt to bypass the anti-virus controls set for the system or workstations. The following tests should be attempted to gain a minimum level of confidence that the anti-virus technology is effective:

- Check Anti-Virus Settings—There are several settings essential to an anti-virus system that are important to its proper functioning. The assessment team member should review several deployed instances of the anti-virus software to check the following settings:

- Automatic Updates—The anti-virus software should be configured to receive automatic updates at least daily.
- Automatic Deletion—The anti-virus software should be set to automatically delete those viruses that it can.
- Automatic Scans—The anti-virus software should be configured to run automatic scans on all incoming e-mail and new files. The software should also be set to run a complete system scan at least once a week.
- Locked Settings—The anti-virus software should be configured to block user attempts to bypass scanning, updates, or complete scans.
- File Extension Settings—The anti-virus software should be configured to scan for the following file extensions: .exe, .com, .dll, .doc.
- Check Anti-Virus Currency—The assessment team member should check several deployed instances of the anti-virus software for the latest version and release.
- Check Anti-Virus Capabilities—The anti-virus software should be capable of scanning compressed (unencrypted) files.
- Run the Anti-Virus Test File (Optional)—To more completely test the anti-virus software, the security risk assessment team may elect to set up a test machine and run an anti-virus test file against it. The following website contains an updated anti-virus test file for just that purpose: www.eicar.org/anti_virus_test_file.htm.

7.2.6.4 Automated Password Policies

Testing procedures for automated password policies require that the security risk assessment team perform activities that attempt to bypass the policies set and enforced. The following functional tests should be attempted to gain a minimum level of confidence that the automated password policy enforcement technology is effective:

- Password Length—The assessment team member should attempt to change the password on an issued account to a length less than the specified minimum. The team member should also attempt to change the password to an extraordinarily long length.
- Password Complexity—The team member should attempt to reset the password to a character string that does not meet the complexity requirements. Also, the team member should attempt to set the password to a character string that includes illegal characters.
- Minimum Limit—The team member should attempt to change the password again within a short span of time (e.g., several minutes) to test any minimum password periods that may have been set.

7.2.6.5 Virtual Private Network

Testing procedures for VPNs require that the security risk assessment team perform activities that attempt to bypass the authentication and authorization controls on VPNs. The following tests should be attempted to gain a minimum level of confidence that the VPN authentication technology is effective:

- Username Enumeration—An assessment team member should test the VPN system for its susceptibility to user enumeration attacks. Some VPN systems respond differently to authentication attempts if the username is valid or invalid. Systems that exhibit such a behavior are more susceptible to dictionary and brute-force attacks on the authentication.
- IKE (Internet Key Exchange) Aggressive Mode Attack—This test is a little advanced, but tools exist that can largely automate the attack. The assessment team may consider testing the VPN through attempts to gain knowledge of the pre-shared key (PSK). If a VPN is set up to

accept IKE Aggressive Mode connections, then the PSK transmitted prior to authentication is unencrypted. This unencrypted hashed key can be captured. A brute-force attack against the hash can be performed within minutes. If the assessment team does not need to demonstrate this vulnerability, it may suffice to ensure that the VPN is set to IKE Main Mode.

- VPN Leaks—When a user of a VPN uses a Domain Name Server (DNS) that is outside of the VPN, then it is possible for the DNS to determine the user's IP address from the request. Therefore, the DNS can link a user with the websites they are visiting, and this may be a privacy concern. There are several websites that can be used to test for VPN leaks such as https://www.vpnmentor.com/tools/ip-leak-test-vpns-tor/ or https://www.dnsleaktest.com/ . To test for a VPN leak simply connect to the site of the tool without your VPN. The tool will display your current IP address. Next enable your VPN and repeat the test. If the site has the same IP address for you then your VPN leaks your IP.

7.2.6.6   Firewalls, IDS, and System Hardening

The testing of firewalls, intrusion detection systems, and system hardening can be combined here because security professionals all use the same tools and techniques for testing these devices. In short, these tools include vulnerability scanners and automated penetration testing tools, and these techniques include ad hoc penetration testing (see Section 7.2.6.8). This section provides an overview of these tools and techniques to assist security risk assessment teams in ensuring completeness in their technical data gathering effort.

Every security risk assessment team should have members who are expert in these tools and techniques. As any of these experts would tell you, these tools and techniques change all the time, and they can get quite complex. This book does not attempt to provide the level of detail required to actually perform these tests, for several reasons. First, there are many other books in print and websites online that can provide that information. Second, the tools and techniques change too often to possibly print relevant and up-to-date information on these techniques. Instead, this section provides a description of the tools and techniques and a high-level review of how they should be employed in the technical data gathering phase.

7.2.6.7   Vulnerability Scanning

Vulnerability scanning involves the testing of information system interfaces to identify obvious vulnerabilities.[13] A vulnerability scan is an important element of any security risk assessment because it provides a cost-effective way to identify vulnerabilities that exist within the system. All other data gathering approaches result in indications of possible vulnerabilities and can be costly, but a vulnerability scan is both inexpensive (relatively) and effective.

The objective of the vulnerability scan is to identify the obvious configuration vulnerabilities that exist in the currently deployed systems. A configuration vulnerability means that the vulnerability can be safeguarded through improvements in the configuration of the servers or workstations (e.g., system hardening). This section provides a description of the vulnerability scanning process.

7.2.6.7.1   Stages of Vulnerability Scanning

A vulnerability scan is not simply the process of running the tool and printing out a report. A vulnerability scan actually incorporates a multistep process that includes setup, mapping, scanning, and report generation. Most of these steps are described below.

- Setup—Setting up properly for a vulnerability scan is essential to the success of the scan itself. Several elements of the setup step need to be considered:
  - Administrator Presence—It is a good idea to have the administrator present during the setup process. This will give the assessor instant feedback if problems occur, and the administrator can assist in problem resolution.

- System Descriptions—The assessor should ask the organization to provide a list with each IP address to be scanned and the associated functions. Many vulnerability scanners can be set to scan only for relevant vulnerabilities given the function of the system or applications on the system. This can significantly reduce false positives from the vulnerability scan.
- Subnets—The assessor must be aware of the network architecture and the subnets in order to properly place the vulnerability scanning device or software.
- Network Mapping—This step is described in the following section.
- Vulnerability Scanning—This step is described in the following section.
- Report Generation—When generating the vulnerability scanning report, several elements need to be considered:
  - More than Raw Data—A vulnerability scan report should not simply be a dump of raw data generated by the vulnerability scanning tool. It should be a professional report that includes a description of the testing effort, the methodology, and the recommendations and timelines for correction.
  - Don't Point Fingers—The report should attempt to simply state facts and not overstep its bounds to guess at the cause. Keep it simple: State the vulnerability and the recommendation.
- Various Views—The report should provide various views of the data. For example, include an executive summary that states the number of vulnerabilities and the overall risk level. Also include mid-level views of the data that categorize vulnerabilities by class. Lastly, make the raw data available.

7.2.6.7.2 Vulnerability Scanning Tools

The availability and power of vulnerability scanning tools has increased tremendously over the past few years. These tools have automated tasks previously performed manually and have increased the level of rigor and the depth of analysis commonly performed in security testing. In the past, security testing activities would include manual procedures or proprietary scripts to look for commonly known (called "obvious") vulnerabilities in many protocols, operating systems, and applications. Many vulnerability scanning tools have advanced and continue to advance by incorporating these procedures and scripts into available tools, some with intuitive graphical interfaces. This process has significantly reduced the effort and skill required to perform the task of vulnerability scanning.[14] Moreover, with the availability of such tools, the depth of testing commonly performed on information security risk assessments has increased to a level that previously would have been prohibitively expensive to obtain.

As discussed previously, vulnerability scanning is a technique used to gather information about possible vulnerabilities within the target system. Vulnerability scanning tools support this task in one or more of the following areas:

- Network Mapping—Lists the available hosts and their open interfaces to be tested
- Vulnerability Scanning—Provides an automated mapping of available hosts and ports to known vulnerabilities

7.2.6.7.2.1 Network Mapping

The first phase of any vulnerability scanning activity involves the enumeration of the interfaces to be tested. This is generally referred to as network mapping. When the interfaces to be tested are unknown or when they need to be confirmed, network mapping is a useful technique.

- Definition—Network mapping tools run a port scan on the system to identify all reachable active hosts, network services operating on those hosts, and the name of the applications running those services.

- Result—The result is a list of IP addresses of the available hosts on the system and the associated ports, services, and applications run on those hosts.
- How They Work—Network mapping tools perform three tasks that together provide a listing of the hosts reachable on the system, their ports, and their services offered:
  - Finding Hosts—Network mapping tools generally determine available hosts through the use of ICMP_ECHO and ICMP_REPLY packets. The TCP/IP protocol states that when a host receives an ICMP_ECHO packet, it responds with an ICMP_REPLY packet to the host that was the source of the packet. Network mapping tools generate ICMP_ECHO requests for every possible IP address within a specified range. Once the network mapping tool has completed sending and receiving these packets, it will know which hosts are available.
  - Determining Open Ports—Network mapping tools find open ports through TCP and UDP scanning:
    - TCP Scanning—TCP scanning is straightforward because TCP is a connection-oriented protocol and guarantees delivery of packets. By attempting to establish a connection with every port on an available host, a network mapping tool can determine the ports that are open because those that are "listening" will respond with a successful connection.
    - UDP Scanning—UDP scanning is more difficult and unpredictable because of the nature of UDP. UDP is a connectionless protocol that does not provide reliable delivery of data packets. This means that no connection is established between the sender and the receiver, and that there is no guarantee that packets will be delivered either way.[15] Network mapping tools that implement UDP port scanning generally send UDP packets, with no data, to a port. If the port does not provide an open service, then an "ICMP Port Unreachable" response is generated. If the port does provide an open service, then either the port will respond with an error or it will drop the packet altogether. So, we can be sure of results that indicate ports are closed, but a result that indicates a port is open is only a guess, because either the UDP packet or the ICMP response could have been dropped. Network mapping tools that implement UDP scanning generally will retransmit packets that appear to have been lost. Even with this improvement, there are likely to be many false positives.
  - Determine Services and Applications Associated with Open Ports—There are over 65,000 possible ports for each IP address. Ports are used to establish a specific communication between the source host and the destination host. Different types of communication are performed on different ports. Many specific communication types are performed on specific ports. For example, HTTP, the protocol used to communicate with Web servers, is performed on port 80, whereas the secure version of HTTP (HTTPS) is performed on port 443. Simply by reviewing the port numbers open and used, network mapping tools can determine the available services on the targeted machines.
- Limitations—Network mapping tools are considered rather low-level data gathering devices. They can gather very useful information, but they can also be easily fooled or blocked. There are several important limitations of network mapping tools of which security testers should be aware:
  - No System Map—In general, network mapping tools do not provide a "map" of the system. All reachable hosts are simply listed without an indication of their arrangement within the internal system architecture.
  - Can Be Blocked and Fooled—Network mapping tools attempt to gain information through simple ICMP probing techniques. Many information systems that have been reasonably secured may have intrusion detection systems, honeypots, or even simple gateways that can block such inquiries or even send back erroneous data to confuse the suspected cybercriminals.

- Services May Be Different from Expected—The assignment of services to port numbers is administered by the Internet Assigned Numbers Authority (IANA), which coordinates the use of the available port numbers to lessen confusion. The adherence to these assignments is not universal. Still, low-numbered ports (0–1024) are generally regarded as having specific services associated with them, and many well-known ports (1025–49151) follow the general registration of ports and services. Regardless, the mapping of an open port to an expected service is an educated guess and not a certainty.
- Overcoming Limitations—To overcome some of these limitations, many network mapping tools have developed additional functions and techniques to obtain the network, port, and application information on the target network:
  - Fingerprinting—This technique is used to identify the operating system at the other end of a connection. Information may have been blocked by configuring the system to not announce the operating system. However, the operating system can still be guessed with reasonable certainty, based on several fingerprinting techniques, including response to invalid commands, port pairs, and banner grabbing.
    - Response to Invalid Commands—Almost all operating systems would respond in a generic way to expected commands, but error messages sent for unexpected commands tend to be unique to operating systems. Using this information, some network mapping tools are able to "fingerprint" the operating system and report this information back to the tester.
    - Port Pairs—Some operating systems can be spotted merely by the ports that remain open. For example, if a system has port 135 (DCE endpoint) and port 139 (NetBIOS), then the operating system is likely Microsoft Windows 2000 or NT.
    - Banner Grabbing—During the open connection, the server sends configuration information to the requesting host. This information is not typically seen by the user, but a network mapping tool could intercept this "banner" and use the information in it to determine the application name and version.
  - Stealth Scanning—As you may expect, the process of scanning a system would be quite noticeable to anyone looking for such activity. If the target network has a firewall or an intrusion detection system with the ability to spot scanning or probing, the network mapping effort is likely to be cut short. Stealth scanning is a way to slow down the scan to such a level that it is not likely to be detected as a "port scan." For example, suppose you try to scan 65,535 ports with a scanner that can scan 300 ports per second. Then you will be able to scan one IP address every 3.64 minutes. That is pretty fast, but a stealth scan will slow the scan down to one port per second (for example) and would take over 18 hours to scan a single host.
  - Strobing—This term refers to the scanning technique in which the system tester looks for only a specific set of open ports on the system. That set of open ports would include common ports where dangerous services are being offered but not secured, or where it is indicative of a Trojan horse having already been installed. This technique is useful when the testing effort is limited, fast scanning would likely be detected, and stealth scanning would take too long.
  - Fragmented Packet Port Scans—Some networks will be protected by a packet-filtering firewall with rules designed to limit or block port scanning. By fragmenting a packet, a port scan can still occur, even though the firewall is designed to block port scanning. This works by splitting (or fragmenting) the IP header into several different packets. The fragmented IP header may not be identified as part of a port scan because many packet-filtering firewalls do not reassemble the IP packet header before determining if the packets meet the ruleset for the firewall. Even packet-filtering firewalls with the ability to reassemble the header packet prior to determining the flow of the packet are typically configured to ignore this capability for performance reasons.

- SYN and FIN Scans—Another way around some firewalls' discovering a port scan is to ensure that the TCP connect operation never completes, and therefore the server process is not informed by the TCP layer that a connection was attempted. There are two approaches to port scanning while ensuring that a TCP connect never occurs:
  - SYN Scan—A SYN scan sends a SYN request to a port on the server. The SYN message is the first stage of the three-way handshake that occurs in opening a connection. If the server responds with a SYN-ACK message, then the port scanner assumes the port is listening. If the server responds with a RST, then the port scanner assumes there is no open service on that port. In either case, a connection is never made, and therefore the server process is not told of the messages by the TCP layer.
  - FIN Scan—A FIN scan sends a FIN request to a port on the server. If there is no open service on the port, then the server responds with a RST message. If there is an open service on the port, then the server ignores the message because it did not currently have a connection with the message sender. It is difficult to produce reliable results quickly with these scans because an open port is indicated by no response. There could be other reasons for no response, including accidentally dropped packets or packets blocked by the firewall.
- Network Mapping Tools—There are many network mapping tools available to information security professionals that can automate or significantly reduce the effort required to perform a listing of the network hosts and services. Below, one popular network mapping tool is discussed. There are other tools such as SuperScan and Siphon, but the discussion below provides a general overview of such tools:
  - Nmap—Nmap is a port-scanning tool that can identify active hosts and open ports on those hosts (i.e., services). Nmap supports the following port scans:
    - TCP connect( )—Uses connect( ) system call to attempt to open a connection on user-selected ports on a remote host.
  - TCP SYN—Uses root privileges of the host machine to initiate a connection (using a SYN packet). If a negative response is received (RST), then it is assumed that the port is closed. If a positive response is received (SYN/ACK), then it is assumed that the port is open, and a cancel connection response is sent (RST).

SIDEBAR 7.1   PORT NUMBERS AND RANGES

There is a total of 65,536 (0–65535) possible port numbers. The port numbers are divided into ranges: well-known ports, registered ports, and (dynamic) private ports.

Well-Known Ports (0–1024)

These ports, also called low-numbered ports, are assigned by the IANA. They are unique because most operating systems restrict the association (called binding) of any service with these ports to trusted processes, such as root. Table 7.23 shows a partial listing of the more common "well-known" port and service pairings.

Registered Ports (1025–49151)

These ports are not assigned by the IANA, but for convenience to the community, the IANA lists the registered uses of these ports. This means that, although you may suspect a certain service to be performed on a given port, this may not be the case.

These port numbers are not considered "trusted" because, in most operating systems, ordinary users may establish an association with any of these port numbers. So, if a user beats another process to the establishment of a service on port number 1050, a client system opening a connection to that port may be looking for the Common Object Request Broker Architecture (CORBA) Management Agent but will be connected to the user process instead. Table 7.24 contains a partial listing of the more common port and service pairings in the registered port number range.

Dynamic and Private Ports (49152–65535)

These ports are not assigned or registered. These ports are not assigned, registered, or controlled. Dynamic ports are used for temporary or private ports.

TABLE 7.23
Selected Well-Known Port Numbers

Port Number	Service
7	ECHO
20	File Transfer Protocol—Data
21	File Transfer Protocol—Control
22	SSH Remote Login Protocol
23	Telnet
25	Simple Mail Transfer Protocol
42	Host Name Server
43	Who Is
53	Domain Name Server
69	Trivial File Transfer Protocol
110	Post Office Protocol v3
118	SQL Services
137	NetBIOS Name Service
138	NetBIOS Datagram Service
139	NetBIOS Session Service
143	Interim Mail Access Protocol
156	SQL server
161	SNMP
179	Border Gateway Protocol
194	Internet Relay Chat
389	Lightweight Directory Access Protocol
443	HTTPS
458	Apple Quick Time
546	DHCP client
547	DHCP server
666	DOOM, Cain and Abel Trojan

Note: Port numbers below 1024 are important because they are associated with well-known services. Binding to well-known ports should be restricted to trusted processes.

TABLE 7.24
Selected Registered Ports

Port Number	Service
1050	CORBA Management Agent
1243	SubSeven—Trojan horse
1352	Lotus Notes
1433	Microsoft SQL Server
1494	Citrix ICA Protocol
1521	Oracle SQL
1604	Citrix ICA/Microsoft Terminal Server
2049	Network File System
3306	MySQL
4000	ICQ
5010	Yahoo! Messenger
5190	AOL Instant Messenger
5632	PCAnywhere
5800	Virtual Network Computing
5900	Virtual Network Computing
6000	X Windowing System
6699	Napster
6776	SubSeven—Trojan horse
7070	RealServer/QuickTime
8080	HTTP
26000	Quake
27010	Half-Life
27960	Quake III
31337	Back Orifice—Trojan horse

Note: Port numbers 1025–49151 are not considered trusted,
since associations with these port numbers are not
typically restricted.

7.2.6.7.2.2   *Vulnerability Scanners*

The second phase of the vulnerability scanning activity involves the identification of vulnerabilities of the hosts, operating systems, services, and applications identified during the network mapping phase. This is generally referred to as *vulnerability scanning*. When you need to confirm the existence of obvious vulnerabilities based on knowledge of available interfaces, a vulnerability scanner is a useful tool.[16]

- Definition—Vulnerability scanners attempt to identify vulnerabilities in identified hosts by looking for "obvious vulnerabilities." Vulnerability scanners are built by security engineers on the knowledge of how to identify vulnerabilities in specific systems. By coding this knowledge in an automated tool, these scanners can significantly reduce the work of the information security professional during this stage of security testing.

- Result—The result of running a vulnerability scan is a mapping between the results of the network mapping effort and known exploits for the systems it believes are present.
- How They Work—The vulnerability scanners are actually quite simple, in that they look up known vulnerabilities for each port, service, operating system, or application that is known to be running on the system. Many vulnerability scanners also provide a risk index indicating the severity of the vulnerability as well as safeguard recommendations.
- Limitations—The limitation of the vulnerability scanners lies in the limited knowledge developed during the network mapping exercise. The network mapping efforts can produce incorrect data, such as misinterpreting information and reporting back that an operating system is running on the system when in fact it is not. Such incorrect information can lead to baseless assumptions about the target system and result in what are known as *false positives*. False positives are reported vulnerabilities that do not exist on the system.
- Overcoming Limitations—The tester may reduce false positive readings by using multiple network mapping programs and comparing the results. Another technique is to create a document of the systems being scanned and the known services on these systems. If these documents can be trusted, then the network mapping information can be corrected, and therefore the vulnerability scanner will produce fewer false positives.

7.2.6.7.2.3   Virus and Pest Scanning

An optional phase of the vulnerability scanning activity within the security testing approach involves a search for executable code on the system that can lead to a breach in the protection requirements for the protected assets. This is generally referred to as *virus* or *pest* scanning. If the security risk assessment team needs to test for the presence of such software, virus and pest scanning tools are available.

- Definition—Anti-virus software, spyware, and pest scanners can be used to search for installed malware such as viruses, worms, spybots, keyloggers, adware, and other uninvited code.
- Result—The running of these tools results in the identification and possibly the removal of malware.
- How They Work—These tools typically work on the basis of signature definitions. These definitions or fingerprints allow the tools to detect the signature of the virus or other malware. As mentioned previously, some of these tools also have the capability of removing the malware. Removal is possible if the tool is programmed with the knowledge of where all the pieces of the malware are stored.
- Limitations—These scanners are limited in their ability to detect malware based on limitations of the signature definitions. If the definitions stored with the tool are out of date or do not otherwise contain a matching signature, then the malware will go undetected. The scanners are limited in their ability to remove malware if they do not know where all the pieces are stored or if the malware is integrated with another program that the user may not want deleted. Most of these programs are software that business users would not need, such as freeware games.
- Overcoming Limitations—The security assessment team member performing the malware scans should ensure that the signature definition files are up to date. Additionally, the team member may want to consider using at least two different malware scanners to increase coverage.

7.2.6.7.2.4 Application Scanners

Another optional phase of the vulnerability scanning activity within the security testing approach involves a search for vulnerabilities within deployed and custom applications. This is generally referred to as *application vulnerability scanning*. The security risk assessment team may elect to test for the presence of vulnerabilities within COTS and custom applications.

- Definition—Application scanners, also known as Web application scanners, are tools that automate the testing of applications based on a set of known vulnerabilities. Many Web application scanners comply with the OWASP Top Ten. The Open Web Application Security Project (OWASP) Top Ten Most Critical Web Application Vulnerabilities are now considered an industry standard as the minimum set of vulnerabilities for which an application should be scanned.
- Result—The running of these tools results in the identification of known vulnerabilities in the applications.
- How They Work—These tools typically work on the basis of signature definitions. These definitions or fingerprints allow the tools to detect the signature of the vulnerability.
- Limitations—These tools are limited in their ability to identify all application vulnerabilities based on limitations of the signature definitions and the inherent limitations in scanning. A more complete review of Web application security would include Web application code review.
- Overcoming Limitations—The security assessment team member performing the application scans should ensure that the signature definition files are up to date.

7.2.6.8 Penetration Testing

Penetration testing involves the exploitation of system vulnerabilities to gain system access or otherwise violate the organization's security policy. Penetration testing can take two forms.

The first form of penetration testing is simply an extension of vulnerability scanning. When vulnerability scanning is complete, the assessment team has a list of known vulnerabilities to the system. In this first form of penetration testing, the team simply exploits the discovered vulnerabilities. Typically, this is not recommended because the vulnerability is already known, and there is little or no benefit to the security risk assessment process in risking damage to the system or the organization's mission.

The second form of penetration testing is an ad hoc testing method to look for less obvious vulnerabilities. This type of penetration testing requires a skilled team member. Based on the nature of this type of testing, which is ad hoc, it also eludes description, but the basic approach is as follows:

- Information Probing—The penetration tester will attempt to gain additional information on the systems to be tested. This information could simply be given to the tester, or it could be gained through such efforts as reviewing newspapers and trade magazines, searching domain name registries, searching for information posted on Internet chat groups, and using network probing tools such as network sniffers.
- Vulnerability Scanning—This step was described previously and would probably already have been performed at this stage in the testing effort. However, if the vulnerability scans were not performed, the penetration tester would perform them now.
- Penetration Techniques—There are various techniques that may be used to penetrate the system based on known systems and vulnerabilities. Some of the techniques that may be employed include password cracking, privilege escalation, Web application hacking, social engineering, e-mail spoofing, and ad hoc testing.

SIDEBAR 7.2 ZERO-KNOWLEDGE TESTING: WHO IS REALLY BEING TESTED?

Many organizations assume that the external threats or cybercriminals to their systems must truly be outsiders. As such, they expect that when cybercriminals first begin to break into their systems, these cybercriminals start with no knowledge of the organization's systems, connections, partners, and employees.

The objective of an external penetration test is to test the adequacy of security controls in place and their resistance to attack from an external threat. Therefore, it is reasoned, such a test should emulate the external threat as realistically as possible. Using this reasoning, many organizations contract an independent security consultant to perform zero-knowledge testing. Zero-knowledge testing requires that the independent security consultants be given only the name of the company to be tested, a point of contact, a budget, and a few ground rules.

This zero-knowledge restriction on the external testing service is unnecessary, misleading, and costly, and will result in less useful results. The prevailing thought among organizations requesting this restriction on the service seems to be that the independent security consultants should "prove" themselves. The premise that a firm that is working for you should demonstrate its ability to find information necessary to perform a thorough test is misguided. The qualifications of the firm you intend to hire should be carefully reviewed and assessed prior to the signing of the contract—not during the performance of the contract.

Another driver for placing the zero-knowledge restriction on external testing seems to be a misplaced belief that external threats come from those who will target the organization specifically. Although such targeted attacks are possible, the majority of the threat to organizations is manifested in the masses of script-kiddies and other deviants, who exist in huge numbers. These pests are so ubiquitous that if your system exhibits a vulnerability for a small amount of time, chances are good that one of them will stumble upon it. For example, it is widely believed that an unprotected system exposed to the Internet will be compromised within three minutes. Therefore, a vulnerability in your system is more likely to be discovered by someone who stumbles upon it than it is by someone who targets your system. Restricting knowledge of your system to the security testers is not the best emulation of the real threats.

The work that must be performed to obtain knowledge of the organization's systems, connections, partners, and employees can be tedious, but it is not difficult. There is little doubt that any qualified security consultant could actually figure out the information typically given prior to testing anyway; it may take a bit of time though. Qualified security consultants know how to review public information (e.g., domain registries, press, bulletin boards, and annual reports) and perform social engineering to obtain the necessary information. Because it takes time to obtain this information, the security consultants will need to charge more for the service.

Lastly, the less information you give the security testers, the less complete the external testing can be. For example, your organization may have several areas that should be tested that may not be discovered in the initial search for information. These areas could include modem numbers on key equipment, systems registered under a different company name, and new interfaces. You can bet that these interfaces will be well exercised sooner or later by the masses of cyber-pests. If the security testers are not told about these interfaces and they go untested, the ultimate results of the test are questionable because of their incompleteness.

7.2.6.9   Testing Specific Technology

The following sections provide a description for how to perform testing on specific technology such as modems, wireless networks, and PBXs.

7.2.6.9.1   Modem Access Testing

Modem access testing, also known as *war dialing*, is a security-testing technique for identifying modems within the organization that may be attached to the information system and assessing the access controls of identified modems. The following tasks are performed during a war-dialing effort:

- Footprint—The assessment team member scans a range of phone numbers belonging to the organization to identify phone numbers that give back a modem/carrier signal. Initially, this sweep of phone numbers within the range provided will be performed during the off hours so as not to cause suspicion. Additional sweeps of numbers can be performed during business hours as well. The advantages of such a sweep include the ability to find modems only available during working hours. The disadvantages of this additional sweep include disruption of phone lines and workers during business hours and increased risk of detection.
- Preparation—The assessment team member should now sort through the numbers identified in the footprint effort to prioritize candidate phone numbers for penetration. Candidate phone numbers should be sorted according to the following categories:
  - Default Passwords—Many systems may have default passwords still enabled. Based on response signatures or screens, war-dialing tools may be able to identify the dial-up system.
  - Single Authentication/Unlimited Attempts—Systems at the other end of these phone numbers allow unlimited attempts at guessing log-in credentials. The modems will not disconnect after a threshold of failed attempts. Moreover, these systems either only ask for a password (log-in ID is supplied or assumed) or, worse, only ask for log-in ID (which is typically easier to guess than a password).
  - Dual Authentication/Unlimited Attempts—Systems at the other end of these phone numbers allow unlimited attempts at guessing log-in credentials. The modems will not disconnect after a threshold of failed attempts. These systems ask for both a log-in ID and a password.
  - Limited Attempts—Systems at the other end of these phone numbers will disconnect after a threshold of failed attempts.
- Penetration—The assessment team member should attempt to gain access to the organization's systems through modem numbers identified and sorted during the previous steps. The assessor should use a dictionary of default and easy-to-guess passwords to attempt to log in to these systems.
- Reporting—The assessment team member should log all war-dialing efforts and report the results. This report should include the range of numbers scanned, identification of modem/carrier signals detected, and identification of systems penetrated.

7.2.6.9.2   Wireless Network Testing

Testing procedures for wireless networking systems require that the security risk assessment team perform activities that attempt to discover wireless networks within the network and determine the access controls placed on those networks. This testing can be performed rather simply using what is known as a war-driving technique:

- War driving—A member of the security risk assessment team should configure a laptop or cell phone with a wireless scanning application such as AirMagnet, NetStumbler, or Wireshark. The assessor should then walk or drive around the organization's complex in search of discovered wireless networks. These applications will discover all networks within range and report on the network name (if broadcast), signal strength, and mode of protection. The mode of protection will be either open, WEP, WPA, or WPA2. Obviously, open networks are insecure, but WEP- and WPA-protected networks are also considered weak and insecure.
- Wireless Penetration Testing—Once wireless access points have been identified within the organization's network the security assessment team should determine the extent to which they will be performing wireless penetration testing. As with other more technical testing methods, this text will not be going deep into the process (as that would be a subject of another entire text). However, the basic areas of wireless penetration are as follows:
  - Access Control Attacks—When wireless access points (APs) control access based on the Media Access Control (MAC) address, the wireless penetration tester may elect to perform a wireless access point access control penetration test. This test sets up a sniffer to capture legitimate MAC addresses being used to connect to the wireless AP and then spoofs the MAC address from an unauthorized source to circumvent the MAC address access controls.
  - Rogue Access Points—The wireless penetration tester could install a wireless access point at any location within the organization's network for the purposes of creating an unauthorized access point. This unauthorized access point could then be used for the staging of other penetration testing methods or simply provide unauthorized access to the organization's network. The main test here is whether or not the wireless penetration tester can surreptitiously deploy the unauthorized device and whether or not the organization will detect (automatically or manually) and remove or block the device.
  - Evil Twins-Organizational users of wireless access points can either automatically or manually connect to available wireless access points based on the Service Set Identification (SSID). For example, an organizational user will connect to ACME_WiFi1 or ACME_WiFi2 assuming that each of these wireless APs provide access to the ACME network. However, a wireless penetration tester can simply create a wireless AP from the penetration tester's laptop with an expected or frequently used SSID (e.g., ACME_WiFi3). Even more effective is the penetration tester's use of the organizational user's Preferred Network List of frequently used and memorized SSIDs. Many organizational users would have SSIDs such as linksys, Home, WLAN, or FreeWiFi. If the wireless penetration tester creates a wireless AP with one of these SSIDs the organizational user's laptop may automatically connect to the wireless penetration tester's wireless AP and therefore subject themselves to various attacks such as Man-In-The-Middle (MITM).

7.2.6.9.3 PBX Testing

Testing procedures for private branch exchange (PBX) systems require that the security risk assessment team perform activities that attempt to bypass the access controls for the PBX system. Note that for many organizations the PBX technologies are considered old and may not be in use. However, this section remains here for the purposes of any organization that do still implement this technology. The following tests should be attempted to gain a minimum level of confidence that the PBX protections are effective:

- Attendant Terminals—The assessment team member should determine if attendant terminals are physically and logically protected. Attendant terminals provide access to the administration functions of a PBX and should be reserved for use by authorized individuals. Physical protection could mean locating the devices in a locked room. Logical protection could be accomplished through password or PIN codes.

- Remote Maintenance—The assessment team member should determine if remote maintenance is enabled on the PBX. If remote maintenance is enabled, the external access should be controlled; for example, turn off the modem when not in use, use a callback modem, or change default passwords. Unassigned Numbers—The team member should attempt to find an unassigned number by guessing extension numbers that may not have been assigned. Then, by calling into the extension number, he may be asked for a password to set up the mailbox. The assessor should try default passwords such as 1111, 1234, and the extension number itself.
- More Attacks—There are many more complex attacks that may be attempted as well. These attacks are well documented in the NIST Special Publication 800-24, "PBX Vulnerability Analysis" (2001).

7.2.6.9.4 VOIP Testing

Testing procedures for Voice Over Internet Protocol (VOIP) systems require that the security risk assessment team perform activities that attempt to bypass the access controls for the VOIP system. The following tests should be attempted to gain a minimum level of confidence that the VOIP protections are effective:

- Enumeration and Information Gathering—Identification of the Session Initiation Protocol (SIP) servers with which the VoIP phones communicate.
- Eavesdropping—Capturing packets between SIP servers.
- Authentication Attacks—Taking advantage of weak encryption to decrypt communication packets.
- Denial of Service Attacks—Flooding SIP servers with INVITE requests to overwhelm the service available to legitimate users.
- Voicemail Spoofing—Using unauthenticated INVITE requests to impersonate internal departments or individuals as part of a social engineering attack.
- VLAN Hopping—Use of hacking tools to jump from the VLAN designated for VoIP phones to other VLANs within the organization's network.
- Provisioning Servers—Using a sniffer tools to capture configuration files designated for the setup of new phones. These files may contain sensitive information such as initial passwords for the new phones.

EXERCISES

1. Discuss the implementation of Basic Security Design Principles (Section 7.2.2.9) with respect to the following topics:
   a. Cloud computing
   b. Virtual machines
   c. Outsourcing code development
   d. Outsourcing Web hosting
2. Based on current capabilities, what are the reasonable minimums for encryption key strength for each of the following encryption techniques (include sources of information)?
   a. Hashing
   b. Symmetric encryption
   c. Asymmetric encryption
3. How would the principle of "Assume those untrusted will seek to do harm" apply in a system connection between business partner organizations? What controls would you expect to see in place?

4. Which of the following can be considered a secure protocol?
   a. Telnet
   b. HTTPS
   c. TFPT
   d. BIOS
   e. WPA2
   f. CHAP
   g. SSH
5. Explain the difference between a vulnerability scan based on TCP and a vulnerability scan based on UDP.
6. How could the RIIOT data gathering method be used to specify the scope and rigor of a technical security risk assessment?
7. Write a data gathering plan for a selected technical control.
   a. Active Directory
   b. Mobile Device Management
   c. Centralized Patch Management

NOTES

1 For those who are experts in this field or have checklists they are already comfortable with you may skip this section without losing any context for the rest of the chapter.
2 These threat actions are described in greater detail (additional examples) in Chapter 5.
3 Protecting access to a file via a password mechanism is considered inherently weak within information systems, because of the lack of accountability and the inability to revoke access.
   Password protection for files sent over an insecure network medium are more common but still considered insecure, because an unauthorized user may intercept the file and perform unlimited attempts at guessing the password.
4 Two-factor authentication has an additional requirement that the two authentication methods must be of different types (i.e., something you know, something you have, and something you are). For example, a password and a personal identification number (PIN) are not considered two factor authentication because it simply reduces to a longer password.
5 This works well for threats such as eavesdropping, where network segmentation will limit potential eavesdropping to only those computers on the network segment. However, network segmentation must be accounted for when deploying safeguards such as intrusion detection systems. The system designer must be careful to include IDS sensors on all segments of the network to ensure complete coverage. A network segment is not bounded by hubs, since hubs are a layer1 device that does not even recognize MAC (Media Access Control) addresses.
6 A more detailed understanding of encryption is important to any information security professional. However, such a discussion is beyond the scope of this book.
7 Many experienced security consultants will be tempted to simply review documents and provide comments on discovered security deficiencies, but fail to spot missing key elements. It is for this reason that a checklist is used to guide the review and ensure a more complete analysis.
8 For a more complete discussion of how to use the "review documents" approach, refer to Section 5.2.2.1.
9 Many experienced security consultants will be tempted to simply review documents and provide comments on discovered security deficiencies but fail to spot missing key elements. It is for this reason that the discipline of completeness review, using a table of expected elements, is recommended to improve the review process.
10 For a more complete discussion of how to use the "review documents" approach, refer to Section 5.2.2.1.
11 Some would argue that the Common Criteria Evaluation Methodology (CCEM) provides a systematic approach to design review. However, the Common Criteria requirements and evaluation methods only specify the form and content requirements for design documents and the approach for evaluating the sufficiency of the documents. Design analysis occurs, but there is no formal process for such an analysis in the CCEM.

12 Each of these security design areas is treated at a rather high level. This is intended, because a security risk assessment is not the same as a system evaluation. System evaluations can afford the time and effort it takes to review these controls in much more detail. Remember that security risk assessments are a periodic check based on changes in the threat environment; a security evaluation is performed prior to acceptance of the system in the first place.

13 The Common Vulnerabilities and Exposures (CVE) dictionary is a list of standardized names for known vulnerabilities and security exposures. The CVE dictionary is a project run by the MITRE Corporation and sponsored by the US-CERT at the U.S. Department of Homeland Security (www.cve.mitre.org).

14 Vulnerability scanning can be applied to any network device with an IP address. This includes firewalls, VPN servers, IDS, etc. This section deals with vulnerability scanning as it applies to any network-connected device. More specific testing of technology is covered in a later section.

15 Vulnerability scanners have reduced the effort and skill required to perform the task of vulnerability scanning, but not eliminated them. A good amount of skill is still required to set up the tests and review the results. Also, in larger systems, the vulnerability scanning effort can easily be one of the largest tasks.

16 At first glance, this sounds like a useless protocol because it cannot guarantee anything. But this is not the case. The UDP provides fast delivery of packets with low overhead in processing. This type of service is extremely useful in services such as voice and video streaming that do not care.

BIBLIOGRAPHY

Common Criteria Evaluation Methodology. Version 1.0, CEM-99/045, August 1999.

Mitre Corporation. Common Vulnerabilities and Exposures. http://cve.mitre.org (accessed September 17, 2020).

National Institute of Standards and Technology, National Checklist Program for IT Products: Guidelines for Checklist Users and Developers, NIST Special Publication 800-70 Revision 4, February 2018. https://csrc.nist.gov/publications/detail/sp/800-70/rev-4/final (accessed September 17, 2020).

National Institute of Standards and Technology, National Cybersecurity Center of Excellence, "Software Asset Management: Continuous Monitoring," https://www.nccoe.nist.gov/sites/default/files/library/fact-sheets/sam-fact-sheet.pdf, (accessed September 14, 2020).

National Institute of Standards and Technology, Security Considerations for Voice Over IP Systems; Recommendations for the National Institute of Standards and Technology, NIST Special Publication 800-58, January 2005. https://nvlpubs.nist.gov/nistpubs/Legacy/SP/nistspecialpublication800-58.pdf (accessed September 17, 2020).

National Institute of Standards and Technology, Systems Security Engineering: Considerations for a Multidisciplinary Approach in the Engineering of Trustworthy Secure Systems, NIST Special Publication 800-160, November 2016. https://csrc.nist.gov/publications/detail/sp/800-160/vol-1/final (accessed September 17, 2020).

PBX Vulnerability Analysis: Finding Holes in Your PBX before Someone Else Does. August 2000. NIST Special Publication 800-24. http://csrc.nist.gov/publications/nistpubs/800-24/sp800-24pbx.pdf.

Practical VoIP Penetration Testing, Vartai Security, March 10, 2020, https://medium.com/vartai-security/practical-voip-penetration-testing-a1791602e1b4

Restore Privacy, VPN Tests and Checks, June 25, 2020. https://restoreprivacy.com/vpn/test-check-vpn-working/ (accessed September 17, 2020).

Reynolds, J., and J. Postel. Request for Comments: 1700, Assigned Numbers, IETF October 1994. http://tools.ietf.org/pdf/rfc1700.pdf

SANS, SCORE: Checklists & Step-by-Step Guides. https://www.sans.org/score/checklists (accessed September 17, 2020).

Wireless Security – WiFi Pen Testing, https://www.tutorialspoint.com/wireless_security/wireless_security_wifi_pen_testing.htm (accessed September 17, 2020).

8 Physical Data Gathering

Extending the security risk assessment to include the review of physical security mechanisms provides a more complete view of the overall security posture of the organization. Failure to consider physical vulnerabilities can lead to a false sense of security and increase the risk of a breach to capital or information assets. Attempts to breach the security of the organization can come from logical attacks or physical attacks. Ignoring the physical side of the security risk equation is an invitation to disaster.

There are some organizations in which the physical security and the logical security are handled by distinctly separate groups (e.g., military bases). Even if the organization does have a distinct separation between the physical and logical security, the project sponsor should consider a joint (physical and logical) security risk assessment as an improvement to the assessment process.

SIDEBAR 8.1   PHYSICAL SECURITY ASSESSMENTS

As with any project, it is important to note the objective of the security risk assessment, especially when it comes to reviewing physical security controls. The objective of the assessment is to provide an accurate analysis of the current security controls and not to inspect the security controls for adherence to building codes, fire codes, or other legal regulations. In fact, certain licenses and credentials are required for the inspection of fire systems and installation of physical security controls.

Therefore, the material in this security risk assessment book is at an appropriate level to provide a security risk assessment team the information and approach needed to spot threats and vulnerabilities in the current security posture and to make recommendations for improvement. However, the design, installation, and inspection of physical security controls are beyond the scope of this book. For more information on physical security controls and certifications, visit the following Web sites:

- ASIS International: www.asisonline.org
- Underwriters Laboratories Fire Alarm System Certification—Listing Process: www. ul.com/alarm systems/fire.html
- DOE Physical Security Inspectors Guide: www.oa.doe.gov/guidedocs/0009pssig/0009 pssigpdf.html

8.1   PHYSICAL THREATS AND SAFEGUARDS

The concept of threats, threat agents, and threat actions were covered earlier in Chapter 4. Physical threats specifically are covered here as an approach to introducing physical data gathering. This section, on threats and safeguards, is intended as a primer or introduction to security threats in the physical area.[1]

- Physical Threats and Threat Actions—A member of a security risk assessment team requires a basic understanding of the threats and safeguards within the physical security area to be an effective member of the team. There are numerous physical security threats; some of the more frequent physical threats are discussed in Figure 8.1. The list of specific physical actions is ever growing and difficult to completely enumerate. However, it is useful to at a minimum understand the classes in which these threat actions may be organized and understood. Those

FIGURE 8.1 Physical safeguard threats. A variety of threat actions can be targeted at or addressed through the implementation of technical safeguards. These threat actions can be organized into the categories of theft & sabotage, being socially engineered, abusing trust, suffering environmental damage, and committing an error.

threat actions that can be targeted at or mitigated by physical controls are categorized as theft & sabotage, socially engineered, abused trust, environmental damage, and erred, see Table 8.1.

- Physical Safeguards—There is a vast array of physical safeguards that could be effective against the various threats to an organization. This chapter provides a brief introduction to many of these physical safeguards to ensure that the security risk assessment team member is familiar with controls they may encounter during as assessment as well as available safeguards for recommendations to address high risk areas. The physical safeguards presented here are divided into the following categories:

TABLE 8.1
Physical Threats and Safeguards: Utility and Interior Climate Control

Class	Subclass	Threat	Safeguard
Power	• Power loss	• Theft & sabotage	• On-site power generation
		• Abused trust	• Uninterruptable power source
	• Degraded power	• Environmental damage	• Line conditioner
		• Erred	• Voltage regulator
	• Excessive power		• Surge suppressor
Cooling	• Unavailable cooling	• Theft & sabotage	• HVAC
	• Insufficient cooling	• Abused trust	• Temperature alarm
		• Environmental damage	• Temperature log
		• Erred	
Humidity	• Low humidity levels	• Theft & sabotage	• Humidifier
		• Abused trust	• Humidity level alarm
		• Environmental damage	• Humidity level log
	• High humidity levels	• Erred	• Dehumidifier
			• Humidity level alarm
			• Humidity level log

Note: Threat actions applicable to utility and interior climate controls include theft & sabotage, abusing trust, environmental damage, and committing errors. Physical safeguards that can address these threat actions are described below.

- Utilities and Interior Climate—Utilities and interior climate safeguards address controls that may be put in place to protect and ensure a steady and secure supply of utilities and climate control. These safeguards are grouped into the classes of power, heat, and humidity.
- Fire—Fire prevention, detection, and suppression safeguards address the protection of building occupants, sensitive data, and critical systems from fire and fire related impacts. These safeguards are grouped into the classes of fire exposure, fire detection, fire alarm, and fire suppression.
- Flood and Water Damage—Flood prevention and control safeguards address the protection of building occupants, sensitive data, and critical systems from water and water related impacts. These safeguards are grouped into the classes of water exposure and water damage.
- Other Natural Disasters—Other natural disaster prevention and control safeguards address the protection of building occupants, sensitive data, and critical systems from natural disasters other than fire and flood. Safeguards in this area are grouped into the classes of general natural disasters, landslides, earthquakes, volcanoes, and hurricanes.
- Workforce—Workforce protection safeguards address the protection of building occupants, sensitive data, and critical systems from untrustworthy staff members or former staff members. Safeguards in this area are grouped into the classes of personnel screening and personnel termination.
- Perimeter Protections—Perimeter protection safeguards address the protection of building occupants, sensitive data, and critical systems from outsiders. Safeguards in this area include barriers, lighting, intrusion detection, and physical asset control.

The specific physical safeguards within each of these categories are discussed in the sections below and represented in Tables 8.1, 8.3, and 8.8 through 8.11.

8.1.1 Utilities and Interior Climate

Protected assets, especially computer systems and components, need to be safeguarded from adverse climate conditions to ensure continuous operation. Of primary concern in areas that house computer equipment (e.g., data centers) is monitoring and controlling of heat and humidity conditions.

8.1.1.1 Utility and Interior Climate Threats

The services of utilities and interior climate can be the intentional target of internal and external threats or the unintentional result of natural forces or disasters. Intentional and unintentional actions of internal and external threat actors can include the following threat actions:

- Theft & Sabotage—An employee may be the victim of a robbery in which an organizational asset such as a laptop or a mobile device may now be in the hands of an unauthorized person. Employees may be susceptible to theft while traveling to and from work, traveling for work, or at home or a hotel.
- Socially Engineered—An employee may fall prey to a hacker who uses psychology (instead of technical approaches) to gain the trust of the employee and then tricks them into violating the organization's security policy. This is basically a modern version of a confidence scam (e.g., used to by conmen.
- Abused Trust—An employee may abuse the trust given to them and utilize this misplaced trust to take actions against the organization. There are many such actions a trusted employee could take.
- Environmental Damage—Organizational assets may succumb to environmental damage from severe weather (e.g., floods, tornadoes, and earthquakes), infrastructure failures (e.g., power outages), or even infestations (e.g., rats).

- Erred—Lastly, an employee may simply make a mistake that results in the loss of confidentiality of sensitive data, or in the misplacement of an organizational asset such as a laptop.

8.1.1.2 Utility and Interior Climate Safeguards

Given the wide array of potential threat actions that could pose a threat to the organization's assets from an employee, an outsider, or even nature, organizations should implement an adequate set of physical security controls (e.g., safeguards) to address these threats. Table 8.1 lists an example set of physical safeguards that an organization may employ to counter the threat and threat actions impacting utility and interior climate control safeguards. These physical safeguards are discussed within the classes of power, heat, and humidity. Each of these classes within the utility and interior climate control classes of power, heat, and humidity also have subclass that further describe the control area.

8.1.1.2.1 Power Utility

All other critical systems depend on adequate, consistent, and "clean" power. Power delivery systems within the building and within the computer rooms must take adequate precautions against risks. The following elements of power should be considered:

- Power Loss—Many factors, including weather, sabotage, and equipment failure, can cause a loss of power to the building. A loss of power will obviously impact all critical systems.
- Degraded Power—Many factors, including weather, power load, and equipment failure, can cause a momentary or continuing voltage drop. Many pieces of equipment are unable to perform correctly when experiencing a voltage drop.
- Excessive Power—Another problem sometimes experienced in the power delivered to the building is excessive power. This can be caused by many factors, including lightning strikes and equipment failure.

8.1.1.2.1.1 Power Safeguards

The following safeguards should be exercised within the power distribution plant inside the building or on the ground of the organization's campus:

- On-Site Power Generation (OPG)—Gasoline- or diesel-powered generators can be located on-site to protect against power outages that last beyond the capacity of the UPS system. These systems must have a supply of fuel on site to ensure that they can continue operation in the event of an emergency.
- Uninterruptible Power Supplies (UPS)—These devices sit between the AC power source (called "The Mains") and the electronic equipment (Called "the load"). UPS devices provide power conditioning, distribute the power load, and provide backup power in case of a loss for longer durations. There are three basic types of UPSs you may find in a data center or computer room:
  - Standby or Offline—During normal operation standby UPSs feed the mains directly to the load. When a power loss is detected a solid-state switch transfers the battery power to the load. If there are voltage fluctuations standby UPSs will pass low voltage (sags) or high voltage (surges) directly to the load. During the transfer to battery power there can be an interruption of service (break) of up to 25 ms. These are low cost and efficient options for providing UPS but there is no filtering of power in this type of UPS.
  - Line Interactive—During normal operation line interactive UPSs feed the mains directly to the load, but a line interactive UPS has the ability to detect sags and surges and switch to battery power. When voltages outside of pre-set tolerances occur the line interactive UPS feeds voltage from the battery. These UPSs provide a reasonable cost solution with better

protection measures, but they cannot completely protect against voltage fluctuations such as spikes and they exhibit a break in service when transferring to battery power.

- Online Double Conversion—During all operations of an online double conversion UPS the mains is converted to DC power to charge the batteries and the batteries charge the load. Since the AC mains is converted to DC to charge the battery and the battery converts to AC to power the load, all fluctuations are normalized. These more expensive UPS units provide continuous and total power conditioning with no break in power to the load.
- Regulate Voltage—Power regulation devices ensure consistent steady power. Devices include the following:
  - Line Conditioners—These devices regulate, filter, and suppress noise in AC power sources.
  - Voltage Regulators—These devices provide a constant DC output independent of input voltage, output load, or temperature.
  - Surge Suppressors—These devices protect against temporary excessive voltages.

8.1.1.2.2   Cooling Interior Climate

Computer rooms are filled with equipment that produce heat (e.g., monitors and Central Processing Units (CPUs)). As CPUs operate, they continue to generate heat and when those temperature get too high within the computers the CPUs can overheat and malfunction. Most manufacturers recommend that temperature levels for a CPU stay between 122°F and 158°F (50°C–70°C) but CPUs can generally run just fine at temperatures 10° higher or up to 163°F (73°C) and even up to 212°F (100°C) for some CPUs. While many computer systems may still function above these temperatures the danger to the computing components increases substantially the more and longer the computer room temperatures operate outside of this range. The CPU within the computer systems have temperature sensors that will instruct the CPU to slow down or even halt at certain temperature thresholds.

One of the major functions of a data center (or computer room) is to ensure that the CPUs remain within appropriate temperature levels. Traditional data center cooling technologies rely on air cooling and recommendations from the American Society for Heating, Refrigeration and Air-Conditioning Engineers (ASHRAE) for all classes of data centers is between 18°C and 27°C or (64°F–81°F). Within these data center classes ASHRAE also provided guidance for the temperature ranges at the front of the equipment rack (e.g., rack intake) and the rear of the equipment rack (e.g., rack outtake). Table 8.2 provides the recommended data center and CPU temperature recommendations.

The need to save on the cost of energy in providing cooling has led the industry to seek alternative, less costly, methods of cooling and allow for higher operating temperatures. ASHRAE added data center classes (A3 and A4) to accommodate the use of alternative cooling methods and an increased range of allowable temperatures. For A3 data centers using these cooling technologies the allowable ambient room temperature is between 41°F and 104°F (5°C–40°C) and for A4 data centers using these cooling technologies the allowable ambient room temperature is between 41°F and 113°F (5°C–45°C).

Heating and air conditioning systems serving these rooms must be specially designed to handle the cooling needs of this equipment but as mentioned above they may also be designed to be

---

TABLE 8.2

Traditional Data Center and CPU Temperature Recommendations

Ambient Room	Rack Intake	Rack Outtake	Average CPU	Maximum CPU
18°C–27°C	18°C–27°C	40°C–46°C	50°C–70°C	73°C–100°C
64°F–81°F	64°F–80°F	105°F–115°F	122°F–158°F	163°F–212°F

Note: Traditional data center cooling and maximum temperature ranges for CPUs provide guidance for data center managers to ensure for the correct operations of computing equipment.

efficient and reduce the overall cost of operating the data center or computer room. The following technologies may be employed in a data center or computer room to provide adequate and efficient cooling to the equipment:

- Computer Room Air Conditioner (CRAC)— CRACs are the least expensive but relatively inefficient method of cooling a computer room. These systems are similar to conventional air conditioning systems in that they draw air across a refrigerated cooling unit to deliver cold air to the computer room. The refrigerated cooling unit coils are cooled by circulating a refrigerant or through water cooling.
- Computer Room Air Handler (CRAH)— CRAHs use chilled water to refrigerate the coils. These systems can be very reliable and cost efficient for large data centers, but they also introduce a water source into the computer room.

Data center and computer room cooling solutions must take adequate precautions against risks. The following elements of cooling threats should be considered:

- Unavailable Cooling—The heating and air conditioning system could shut down completely leaving the computer room or data center with an inability to maintain a safe level of cooling and forcing the systems to shut down (or ultimately fail).
- Insufficient Cooling—The heating and air conditioning system lose its ability to maintain safe cooling levels in the computer room leading to system malfunctions or shutdowns.

8.1.1.2.2.1 Cooling Safeguards

An appropriate method of providing sufficient cooling to organization should be in place. The overall load of each rack and the entire data center should be tracked, and the cooling technology should be rated to handle the anticipated load within the computer room. Redundant systems and redundant sources of air help to mitigate some of the risks of failure. The following safeguards should be considered:

- Appropriate Cooling—The computer room or data center should have an appropriately designed and maintained cooling method for the needs of the equipment. This may be a CRAC, CRAH, or even a more modern solution such as liquid cooled directly to the CPU.
- Temperature Sensor—A temperature sensor can be installed in the equipment rack. It is recommended that each rack have temperature sensors for the air intake and air outtake, recommendations for the number of temperature sensors per rack range from three to six.
- Temperature Alarm—When room, rack intake, and rack outtake temperatures reach levels that exceed thresholds devices can alert those responsible. If such a device exists in the organization being assessed, the security risk assessment team should ask about frequency of alarms and the various responses.
- Temperature Log—Room, rack intake, and rack outtake temperatures can be recorded and stored over time. These logs can be used to track and identify cooling needs for planning purposes. If such a device exists in the organization being assessed, the security risk assessment team should review the logs for the previous 90 days.

8.1.1.2.3 Humidity

The equipment in computer rooms is sensitive to both high- and low-humidity environments. High-humidity environments can increase the risk of corrosion to sensitive equipment. Low humidity levels increase the chance of static buildup and discharge. Static discharge can reset or damage sensitive computer equipment. Most manufacturers recommend that humidity levels stay between 40% and 60% relative humidity (RH).

8.1.1.2.3.1   Humidity Safeguards

Safeguards for ensuring that the computer room stays within established thresholds include the following:

- Humidifiers/Dehumidifiers—A component can be added to the air-handling system to add or remove humidity from the air. If these are used in areas that have hard water (i.e., high mineral content), then the water should be softened prior to being introduced into this expensive equipment.
- Humidity Alarms—A humidity monitor can be set to alarm individuals responsible for the computer room climate when humidity thresholds are transcended. Recommended alarm thresholds for alarms are at 40% and 60% RH and critical alarms at 30% and 70% RH.
- Humidity Log—Special devices or computer peripherals can be installed to record the room humidity levels over time. These devices can alert those responsible when thresholds are transcended, but they can also be used to track and identify air conditioning needs for planning purposes. If such a device exists in the organization being assessed, the security risk assessment team should review the logs for the previous 90 days.

8.1.2   FIRE

The danger of a fire is ever present in the organization's buildings. Fire represents a major threat to building occupants, critical systems, and sensitive data. Fire is both a foreseeable and devastating event with major impacts to the organization.

8.1.2.1   Fire Threats

The assets of building occupants, critical systems, and sensitive data can be the intentional target of internal and external threats or the unintentional result of natural forces or disasters. In fact, a non-residential fire can have a myriad of different causes. The most prevalent causes of non-residential fires are cooking and playing with fire, see Figure 8.2. Intentional and unintentional actions of internal and external threat actors can include the following threat actions:

- Theft & Sabotage—A fire may be the result of intentional sabotage to the organization or the organization's buildings.
- Environmental Damage—Any number of natural events or disasters (e.g., lightning, wildfires, and storms) may cause a fire in the organization's buildings.
- Erred—Lastly, an employee may simply make a mistake (e.g., careless with smoking and malfunctioning space heater) that results a fire in the organization's buildings.

8.1.2.2   Fire Safeguards

A fire can be devastating and lethal to the organization and the organization's employees. It is important that the organization consider the controls available to combat this threat. Table 8.3 lists an example set of physical safeguards that an organization may employ to counter the threat and threat actions from fire. Organizations may protect their assets from the damaging effects of fire through limiting their exposure to fire, installing fire alarm systems, monitoring fire alarms, installing fire suppression equipment, and having fire evacuation plans. These physical safeguards are discussed within the classes of prevention, detection, alarm, and suppression.

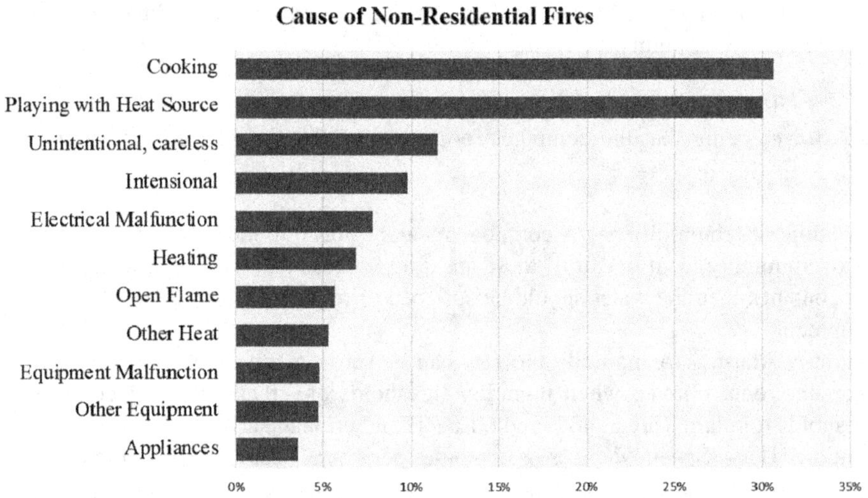

Cause of Non-Residential Fires

FIGURE 8.2   Causes of non-residential fires. The most common cause of non-residential fires, by far, are cooking and playing with fire.

TABLE 8.3
Physical Threats and Safeguards: Fire

Class	Threat	Safeguard
Prevention	• Theft & sabotage • Environmental damage • Erred	• Building construction • Fire exits • Storage of combustibles
Detection	• Theft & sabotage • Environmental damage • Erred	• Smoke detectors • Heat detectors • Flame detectors • Fire detector location
Alarm	• Theft & sabotage • Environmental damage • Erred	• Control panels • Local alarm • Municipal alarm • Auxiliary alarm • Proprietary system • Central station • Remote station
Suppression	• Theft & sabotage • Environmental damage • Erred	• Mobile • Water • Foam • Clean agent

Note: Threat actions applicable to fire controls include theft & sabotage, environmental damage, and committing errors. Physical safeguards that can address these threat actions are described below.

8.1.2.2.1   Fire Prevention

The best way to reduce the impacts of a fire on an organization is to avoid the fire in the first place. Organizations may reduce their exposure to fire through building construction choices, safety training, and careful storage of combustible materials.

8.1.2.2.1.1   Fire Prevention Safeguards

A fire can be avoided (or damage reduced) by reducing the building's exposure to fire components. Following are key factors for consideration in fire exposure reduction through building design:

- Building Construction—The materials used for construction of the building can greatly affect the combustibility of the building itself. Building construction types are classified according to the amount of time it takes a small fire to grow, consume the building, and lead to collapse. Fire safety standards and building codes for critical buildings call for a minimum fire resistance rating of 2 hours. An indication of the fire classification of various construction types is detailed in Table 8.3.
- Fire Exits—All buildings must comply with local and national fire codes, which require fire exits that comply with local and national building codes. The Occupational Safety and Health Standards (OSHA) for exit routes require the following:
  - Fire Resistance—The fire exit must be separated from the rest of the building using materials that will resist fire for 1 hour in buildings three stories or less and for 2 hours in buildings higher than three stories.
  - Two Exits—There must be at least two fire exits located as far apart as practical.
  - Exit Discharge—The fire exit must lead to an area that can safely accommodate all building occupants.
  - Unlocked Exit—The fire exit must be unlocked or able to be opened from the inside with no special knowledge or tools (e.g., keys) required.
  - Side Hinged Exit—The fire door must swing in the direction of exit.
- Storage of Combustibles—Organizations are restricted in the storage of materials that may create fire hazards. These materials are combustibles and flammables. A flashpoint is defined as the temperature in which the liquid vapor could be ignited. Flammable liquids have a flashpoint below 100°F (37.8°C) and combustible liquids have a flashpoint between 100°F and 200°F. These liquids can be found within most organizations' buildings and include cleaning liquids, paints, waxes, and polishes. OSHA has strict requirements for the storage of flammable and combustible liquids including no storage in exits or stairways and approved storage cabinets for large quantities (Table 8.4).

8.1.2.2.2   Fire Detection

If a fire event takes place the organization may reduce the effects of the fire by quickly detecting the event. Organizations may reduce the impact of fire or the risk of exposure to fire through the detection of smoke, heat, and flame.

8.1.2.2.2.1   Fire Detection Safeguards

Early fire detection can be accomplished through detecting elements of a fire (e.g., smoke, heat, and flame). Fire detection controls may be deployed with organizations to increase their ability of fire detection. There are three basic types of fire detectors: smoke, heat, and flame.[2]

- Smoke Detectors—Smoke detectors deployed in non-residential buildings should not be confused with those used in residential homes and apartment buildings. The devices used in homes are technically smoke alarms because they both detect smoke and signal with an audible alarm. Smoke detectors used in non-residential buildings only detect smoke and signal

TABLE 8.4

Fire Classification for Various Types of Construction

Type	Name	Description	Fire Classification
I	Fire resistive[a]	All structural material is non-combustible and fire-resistant (e.g., concrete and steel beams sprayed with insulation).	3–4 hours
II	Non-combustible	All structural material is non-combustible (but not fire-resistant).	2–3 hours
III	Ordinary	Exterior load bearing wall made of masonry; all other structural material is combustible.	1+ hours
IV	Heavy timber	Large wood beams and columns.	1 hour
V	Wood frame	All major structural components are made of combustible material (e.g., rich framing).	minutes

Note: Different types of construction provide vastly different protection from fire. A wood-frame construction provides little protection, while heavy timber and fire-resistive construction can provide 1–3 hours of protection.

[a] The only difference between fire-resistive construction and noncombustible construction is the presence of insulation on the beams. This may seem like a minor improvement in fire construction, but it is the insulation that protects the beams from the intense heat of the fire and slows the beam failure and the building collapse.

the information back to a control panel, where data from the smoke detector can be assessed. If an alarm is to be sounded, it can include the entire building. Smoke detectors can increase survivability chances in the event of a fire emergency by as much as 47%. All smoke detectors should be dual powered, interconnected, and have an indicator light.

- Dual Powered—Smoke detectors should be wired to a 120-V AC circuit and also have a battery backup.
- Interconnected—Smoke detectors should be connected to one another so that smoke detection in one causes an alarm in all (within a specific zone).
- Indicator Light—Smoke detectors should have an indicator light to signal that they have sounded an alarm. This is especially useful when the alarm annunciator is centrally controlled, and it may not be clear which detector has tripped.

There are three basic types of smoke detectors:

- Photoelectric Smoke Detectors—These detectors use a photoelectric eye that can detect visible by-products of combustion (e.g., smoke).
- Ionization Smoke Detectors—These detectors contain a small amount of radioactive material in a dual detection chamber. The radioactive material ionizes the air, making it conductive and permitting a flow of current between the two chambers. Invisible by-products of combustion (e.g., smoke particles) attach themselves to the air particles and reduce the conductance of the air. This interferes with the electrical conductivity between the chambers. Thus, ionization smoke detectors can detect smoke that is not visible to the human eye. An ionization smoke detector can cover 200 to 300 square feet.
- Very Early Smoke Detection Alarm or Apparatus (VESDA)—A VESDA is a fire detection system based on the ability to sample air and to detect degrading materials during the pre-combustion stages of a fire (smoke). Depending on the levels of smoke in the air, a VESDA can provide the appropriate signal to the on-site response team or to a control panel. Signals can range from an early-stage alert to a late-stage declaration of fire.

- VESDA systems have an advantage over other smoke detectors in that they can detect smaller levels of invisible smoke (called obscuration) than ionization smoke detectors. The ability to draw the air in for sampling and the use of processors to interpret the data allow VESDA to detect levels of obscuration as low as 0.003% per foot, whereas ionization detectors can only detect levels of obscuration as low as 3% per foot.
- A VESDA device can cover 5,000 to 20,000 square feet.
- A VESDA system should not be considered in an area that allows smoking.
- A VESDA system should not be considered in an area that is unattended (lights out) and is accessible within half an hour.

- Heat Detectors—Properly functioning smoke detectors will almost always give an earlier warning than heat detectors because detectable levels of smoke almost always develop before detectable levels of heat. Heat detectors, however, have the lowest false alarm rate. Heat detectors can be installed in areas that may experience non-threatening smoke, such as kitchens, or in other high-risk areas where there may be steam or fumes, such as boiler rooms, drying rooms, or other mechanical rooms. Each heat detector will have an effective radius (typically between 25 and 50 feet.). The effective radius is the maximum distance between detectors in a coverage grid. There are two basic types of heat detectors:
  - Heat Alarm—Heat alarms detect heat at a pre-defined level. Most heat detectors can be configured to trigger at common temperature ranges: Heat detectors may also be integrated into sprinkler heads in fire suppression systems and are typically color coded (see Table 8.5).
    - Low Temperature (100°F–134°/38°C–57°C)–designed for application that demand the best reaction time and provide the largest margin of safety.
    - Ordinary Temperature (135°F–174°/57°C–79°C)–designed for the most common application.
    - Intermediate Temperature (175°F + /80°C +)–designed for applications with high ambient temperatures are expected during normal conditions (e.g., attics and boiler rooms).
  - Rate of Rise—Rate-of-rise heat detectors are able to detect a rapid rise (e.g., 12°F–15°F [6°C–8°C] per minute) or extreme temperatures (e.g., 135°F [57°C]). Rate-of-rise detectors can cover up to 2,500 square feet. These detectors are typically deployed in areas where high heat may normally occur, such as kitchens or attics, since rate-of-rise detectors do not normally respond to slowly developing fires.

TABLE 8.5

Heat Detector Trigger Points

Temperature Trigger Point		Temperature Classification	Fuse Color	Glass Vial Color
F	**C**			
135°F	57°C	Ordinary	Black	Orange
175°F	79°C	Intermediate	White	Yellow
250°F	121°C	High	Blue	Blue
325°F	163°C	Extra high	Red	Purple
400°F	204°C	Very extra high	Green	Black
500°F	260°C	Ultra-high	Orange	

Note: Heat detector triggers can be set for the conditions of the protected area.

- Flame Detectors—Flame detectors, or optical detectors, detect radiant energy (wavelength between 1,800 to 7,700 angstroms). Flame detectors have a cone of vision outside of which they are unable to detect the presence of a flame. There are two basic types of flame detectors, UV, and IR:
  - Ultraviolet (UV) Flame Detectors—UV flame detectors are sensitive to both sunlight and artificial light. A UV flame, such as hydrogen, ammonia, or sulfur flame, radiates within the UV spectrum and is detected by the device. These devices can be used indoors or outdoors, but they must have a line of sight to the flame.
  - Infrared (IR) Flame Detectors—An IR flame detector senses a flame by detecting energy on a cell that is sensitive to IR radiation. These devices can detect a flame based on its light component or flicker frequency. IR flame detectors are sensitive to most hydrocarbon fires, but not burning metal or hot gases such as ammonia or sulfur. These devices may be used indoors or outdoors when shielded from the sun.

8.1.2.2.3　Fire Alarm

Many of the fire detection events are automated (e.g., smoke detector) and the detection alone does not allow for a response to the situation. An organization requires a method of informing responders (manual or automatic) of the event.

8.1.2.2.3.1　Fire Alarm Safeguards

Fire alarm systems are composed of fire detectors, pull stations, a control panel, fire suppression equipment, speakers, and bells, and possibly a link to the fire department (see Figure 8.3). Damage resulting from a fire can be limited or avoided if the building controls are capable of performing an early detection of a fire. Several types of fire detectors are described below, as well as considerations for their location and connection to a control panel.

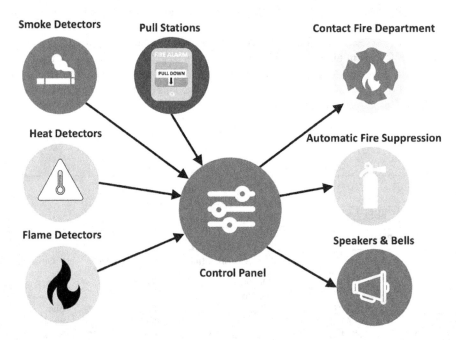

FIGURE 8.3　Fire alarm systems. A fire alarm system is an interconnected protection system consisting of fire detectors, pull stations, fire suppression equipment, speakers, a control panel, and optionally a link to the fire department.

- Control Panels—Fire alarm control panels are systems that receive inputs from a variety of fire detection equipment, process the data, and trigger a response (e.g., warnings or alarms). Control panels should be located near the building entrance, and the panel should be well labeled to identify which detector (or group of detectors) was alarmed.
  Control panels also have an annunciator, a device that signals a change in the protection zones under the control of the monitoring system. Annunciators may log alarms or display a status of the alarm that identifies the zone of the origin of the alarm signal with an indicator light. There are two types of control panels:
  - Simple—Simple control panels report on detectors that have tripped. Devices are typically grouped into zones through wiring circuits. The panel's report on specific alarms in specific zones, such as a smoke alarm in a storage room.
  - Addressable—These control panels are able to group individual devices into groups regardless of the wiring by use of a signaling technique. These signals allow the addressable (or intelligent) control unit to identify specific initiating devices or groups of devices. Some advanced control panels can report on the sensitivity setting of each sensor and even compensate for age, the accumulation of dust, or other factors.

8.1.2.2.3.1.1 Fire Alarm Installation Types

A fire alarm is the system that reacts to the detection of a fire. Fire alarms have a warning system and a response system. The warning system includes bells, speakers, and a visual alarm for the hearing impaired or in areas where there are high noise levels. The warning system signals the building occupants to evacuate. The response system for non-residential fire alarm systems can be installed to alarm and signal response teams in six different ways. Each approach has its own advantages and disadvantages.

- **Local Alarm Station**—A local alarm station is an alarm that signals at the location of the alarm. These systems are unmanned and typically turn off automatically after a short duration. Local alarm systems are the oldest type of systems and are typically found in schools and some hospitals. The basic system consists of manual fire pulls and bells. Local alarms may be linked to central or remote monitoring stations. Local stations must have a backup battery capable of 24 hours of standby power and able to sound an alarm for 5 minutes.
- **Municipal System**—A municipal system is an alarm system run by a municipality and distinguished by "pull boxes" directly connected to the fire emergency response units. These systems, also called public alarm reporting systems, were popular decades ago because it would otherwise have been difficult to contact the fire department through lack of available phones and interconnected networks. Although such a system provides a direct connection to the emergency responders, these systems were susceptible to malicious false alarms. With the advent of ubiquitous networks and the availability of phones, very few municipalities maintain public alarm reporting systems.
- **Auxiliary System**—An auxiliary system has an electrical circuit between the fire alarm control panel in the building and a municipal fire alarm box. When an alarm condition is detected, the municipal fire alarm box transmits an alarm signal to the dispatch center (just the same as if someone had manually pulled the municipal fire alarm box). This fire alarm system is the oldest remote alarm system.
- **Proprietary Systems**—Proprietary systems are monitored on-site by trained professionals. The on-site location must be isolated from other buildings and comply with national and local codes. It is rather costly to maintain a private proprietary system. Such systems are typically found in large industrial complexes, college campuses, and military installations.
- **Central Station**—A central station is a business approved to monitor subscribers' alarm systems from a central location rather than on-site. The central station notifies the police, fire,

or emergency services upon receiving an alarm signal. Only approved central stations may maintain a direct connection with fire and police stations. Fire alarm systems monitored by central stations are required to have a 24-hour backup battery capable of sounding an alarm for 5 minutes.

- **Remote Station**—A remote station is a secondary alarm station located on-site but at a distance from the primary alarm site. Remote stations were designed to serve those areas that were not close enough to be monitored by central stations because of limitations in signaling. Digital communications advances removed the limitations of central stations, and remote stations are rarely used anymore. Most remote stations have been turned into central stations. Remote stations must have a backup battery capable of 60 hours of standby power and be capable of sounding an alarm for 5 minutes.

8.1.2.2.4 Fire Suppression

Fire suppression is the act of taming and extinguishing the fire, including any lingering effect such as smoldering. An organization may efficiently ensure fire suppression through the use of extinguishers, both manual and automatic.

A fire is defined as the energy released in the form of light and heat when oxygen combines with a combustible material (fuel) at a suitably high temperature (heat). These three elements (oxygen, fuel, and heat) form what is known as the fire triangle (see Figure 8.4). The fire needs all three elements of the fire triangle to survive. Firefighting is based on the removal of one or more of these elements. For example, heat is typically removed by spraying water on a fire; oxygen is removed by coating fuel with a chemical "blanket" such as foam, thus blocking the fuel from oxygen; and fuel is removed from the triangle by removing fuel sources in the proximity of the fire (e.g., by digging a fire line).

There are four stages of a fire: the incipient stage, the established stage, the flashover stage, and the decay stage, as shown in Figure 8.5 and Table 8.6. The incipient stage begins with the fire source, but no flames evolve and there is only an initial low heat. With the ignition of one or more of the materials the established stage begins. This is a well ventilated and developing fire where the heat increases rapidly. Flashover refers to the point when all materials are at their ignition temperatures. This stage produces the hottest temperatures. The decay stage of the fire occurs when the fuel is burning out or the oxygen is becoming unavailable. At this stage the fire temperature slowly drops.

To avoid fires or limit their damage to the organization, the organization attempts to detect and suppress the fire at its earliest possible stage but once a fire has begun the organization or the firefighting professionals will need to practice fire suppression methods.

FIGURE 8.4 The fire triangle. A fire needs three things to survive: heat, oxygen, and fuel. A fire may be effectively suppressed by removing any of these elements but is more effectively suppressed by removing several or all of these elements.

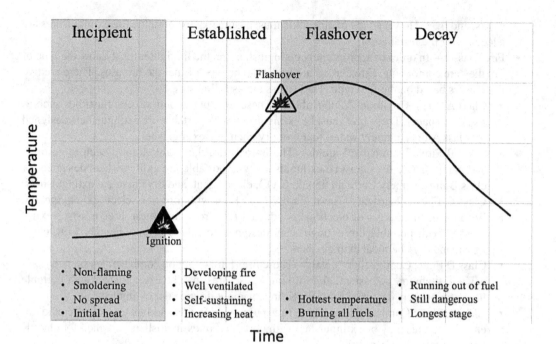

FIGURE 8.5   Fire stages. All fires go through four stages: Incipient stage, Growth stage, Development stage, and Decay stage.

TABLE 8.6
Fire Stages

Event	Indication	
Initial	Incipient	Non-flaming, smoldering, no spread, initial heat
Ignition	Growth	Developing fire, well-ventilated flaming, fire is self-sustaining, increasing heat
Flashover	Developed	Fire is at its hottest point, burning all its available fuels
Decay	Decay	Fire is running out of fuel. Fire is still dangerous. Longest stage

Note: Fires go through the stages of incipient, growth, developed, and decay based on available fuel source and heat level. The sooner fires are detected, the more efficient fire suppression methods can be.

8.1.2.3   Fire Suppression Safeguards

A fire suppression system consists of the hardware (e.g., pipes and nozzles) and the suppression agent. The fire suppression hardware must be properly designed for the specific installation and use of the building. Fire suppression hardware can be classified as a mobile suppression system or a stationary suppression system.

- Portable Fire Extinguishers—These devices, also called handheld fire extinguishers, are an important element of an overall fire suppression system. Handheld fire extinguishers are essential to responders and their ability to extinguish small fires in early stages. This is the key to successful fire risk management; any fire that can be extinguished prior to a dump of suppression agent from the stationary systems can potentially save time, money, information assets, and lives. However, the organization must ensure that the portable fire extinguishers are adequate for the installation.

- Fire Classes—In order to appropriately extinguish a fire, the firefighter must know the type of fire they are combatting. Fire classes are based on the type of fuel the fire uses. There are five fire classes based on the fuel type. These class are as follows:
  - Class A Fires: Common Combustibles—These fires burn common combustibles such as wood and paper. These fires must be extinguished with portable fire extinguishers designed for class A fires, namely water, foam, or dry chemical extinguishers.
  - Class B Fires: Flammable Liquids—These fires burn flammable liquids such as gasoline and paints. These fires must be extinguished with portable fire extinguishers designed for class B fires, namely Carbon Dioxide (CO_2), clean agent, and dry chemical extinguishers.
  - Class C Fires: Electrical—These are fires that burn within or near electrical equipment. Because of the danger of electrical conducted (electrocution) these fires must be extinguished with portable fire extinguishers designed for class C fires, namely CO_2, clean agent, and dry chemical extinguishers.
  - Class D Fires: Combustible Metals—These fires burn common combustibles such as magnesium, titanium, potassium, and lithium. These fires may be extinguished with portable fire extinguishers designed for class K fires, namely dry powder extinguishers.
  - Class K Fires: Combustibles—These fires burn cooking oils and fats in commercial kitchens. These fires may be extinguished with portable fire extinguishers designed for class K fires, namely wet chemical.
- Portable Fire Extinguisher Ratings—Mobile suppression devices (e.g., hand-held fire extinguishers) are labeled for the fire class(es) they are rated to extinguish. Some of these devices are rated for a single class of fire. For example, units that deliver water and foam are rated as a class A fire suppression device while units that deliver dry chemical are rated as an A, B, and C suppression device, see Figure 8.6.
- Device Placement—Portable fire extinguishers should be placed appropriately to allow building occupants to be properly prepared to extinguish fires in their early stages. This means that there should be a sufficient number of devices placed at appropriate distances from the hazard sources, see Table 8.7.

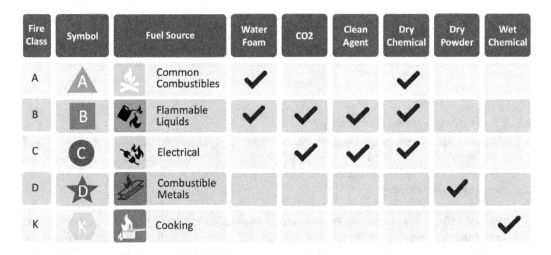

FIGURE 8.6 Fire classes and appropriate mobile fire suppression: It is important to ensure that the organization has the appropriate mobile fire suppression devices based on available fuel sources.

TABLE 8.7

Portable Fire Extinguisher Placement

Fire Class	Travel Distance Max	Installation
Class A	No more than 75 feet from hazard (at least two extinguishers for every 3,000 feet)	Extinguishers must be installed:
Class B	• Low Volume: No more than 30 feet from hazard • High Volume: No more than 50 feet from hazard	• No higher than 3.5–5 feet above the floor • A minimum of 4 inches above the floor
Class C	Based on class A or B hazard	
Class D	No more than 75 feet from hazard	
Class K	No more than 30 feet from hazard	

Note: Portable fire extinguishers must be placed appropriately to allow for building occupants to be properly prepared to extinguish fires in their early stages.

- Device Inspection and Maintenance—Portable fire extinguishers should be inspected monthly. Inspections include the following for portable fire extinguishers:
- Device Visible—Portable fire extinguishers should be in their designated place, clearly visible to building occupants and not blocked.
- Label Visible—The device label or nameplate with the fire class rating symbol should be facing outward. Instructions should be clearly legible.
- Fully charged—Portable fire extinguishers should be fully charged with extinguishing agent. This may be checked by ensuring that the pressure gauge needle is in the green zone.
- Untampered—The pull pin and tamper seal should be intact demonstrating that the device has not been tampered with or previously used.
- Good condition—Portable fire extinguishers should be free of obvious defects such as dents, corrosion, or leaks.
- Rock Powder—For dry powder devices (class D), portable fire extinguishers should be rocked top to bottom to ensure powder is not packing.

8.1.2.3.1 Stationary Suppression Systems

Stationary suppression systems are in place throughout a building and connected to the fire alarm system. The pipe size, nozzle type, and pressure within the system are dependent upon the suppression agent within the pipes. Various suppression agents include water, foam water, and clean agents.

- Water Suppression—Water suppression systems, also called sprinkler systems, suppress fires through the application of water mist or spray, thus cooling the fire. These systems are recommended by insurance companies, whenever the maximum possible fire loss (MPFL) exceeds $1 million, or when there are other circumstances, such as adjacent buildings, highly sensitive areas, or central control centers within the building. The use of these systems is a good idea whenever an environment could be exposed to a fire composed of common combustibles such as wood, paper, cloth, and rubber (i.e., a class A fire). Water suppression systems are not recommended below raised floors. Some studies have found that the presence of water suppression systems increases the chance of survival in a fire by 97%.

  There are four basic types of water suppression systems, wet pipe, dry pipe, pre-action, and deluge, see Figure 8.7.

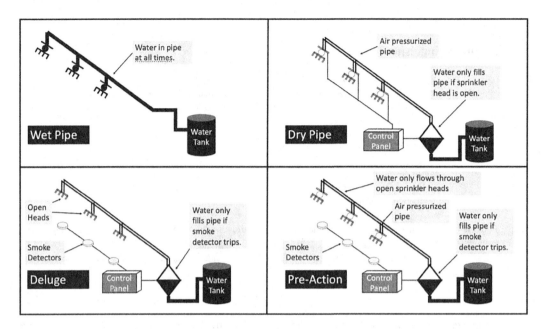

FIGURE 8.7   Four basic water suppression types: The four types are wet pipe, dry pipe, deluge, and pre-action.

- Wet Pipe—The term *wet pipe* refers to the configuration of the water suppression system that leaves pressurized water in the pipes at all times. These systems are simple and less costly than the dry pipe alternative but leave equipment or other assets beneath the pipes at risk in the event of a pipe leak or rupture.
- Dry Pipe—These systems store the water in tanks connected to the water suppression pipes, but the pipes are only filled with water when the fire detectors that are part of the system indicate a need. These systems are more expensive. Dry pipe systems have an increased fire response time and increased corrosion potential but are necessary for areas that may be cold enough to freeze such as parking garages and outside canopies.
- Pre-Action—These systems store the water in tanks connected to the water suppression pipes, but the pipes are only filled with water when the smoke detectors that are part of the system indicate a potential fire. At this point the pipe is filled with water but water will not flow until a sprinkler head opens. These systems are more expensive as well. This system addresses the response time by pre-filling the sprinkler pipes upon indication of a potential fire (e.g., smoke).
- Deluge—These systems are similar to dry pipe systems in that water is not present in the pipe until an alarm is triggered, however, the sprinklers attached to the pipe are always open. The deluge value, which holds back the pressurized water supply is a non-resetting value that stays open once it is triggered. Deluge systems are used in special areas where rapidly spreading fire is a concern, such as storage areas and building entrances and hallways.
- Foam Water Suppression—Foam is a made by mixing an additive to water that assists its firefighting capabilities by soaking in and breaking down the water tension on solid, combustible materials. This helps the water to penetrate the burning material and suppress the fire. These systems require a method for mixing the foaming agent with water. Proportioning equipment ensures the proper concentration of foam and water, while balancing valves (at the nozzle) regulate the foam concentrate pressure to match the water pressure. Foam suppression can be very effective because it fights the fire in four ways:

1. A foam blanket covers the fuel surface and smothers the fire.
2. The foam blanked gives the firefighters visible confirmation of covered areas making fire-fighting more effective.
3. The fire is cooled by the foam/water mix, which remains in contact with the hot surfaces for a longer period of time and absorbs more heat.
4. The foam blanket restricts the release of flammable vapors that could further fuel the fire.

   Foam water suppression can be used to fight class A or class B fires however specific formulations are used to create a class B foaming agent and only class B foams should be used to fight class B fires. These foaming agents are specifically designed to contain the explosive vapors produced by flammable liquids.

- Clean Agent—Clean agent suppression systems are specifically designed to be used in areas where special equipment resides. Clean agents do not leave behind water, foam, or dry chemicals that can damage sensitive equipment. These suppression agents not only have fire suppression capabilities, but are non-conductive, non-corrosive, dry, and clean. The other advantage of clean agents over water mist systems is that these agents are deployed as a gas and will penetrate shielded enclosures. There are many alternative clean agents that can be used, and some of the most popular ones are described below:

  - Carbon Dioxide (CO_2)—This suppression agent is an asphyxiant and therefore is extremely dangerous to human and is designed for non-occupied areas and special industrial applications. CO_2 extinguishes fires by producing a heavy blanket of gas that reduces the oxygen level to the point where combustion cannot occur. CO_2 works on class A, B, and C fires, leaves no residual, and has a negligible effect on the environment. It has an ozone-depleting potential (ODP) near zero and a global-warming potential (GWP) of one. CO_2 is inexpensive, but it does require ten times more agent than halon-based systems.

  - Halon—This suppression agent is a combination of hydrocarbons and halogen produced by the combination of the non-metallic elements carbon, fluorine, chlorine, and bromine. For example, Halon 1301 is a combination of 1-part carbon, 3-parts fluorine, and 1-part bromine. Halon is effective on class B (liquid) and C (electrical) fires. Halon suppresses the fire by cooling the fire, smothering the fire through the removal of oxygen, and disrupting the chemical reaction of combustion. Despite its fire-fighting capabilities, however, halon is not environmentally friendly. It has an ODP of 3–10 and a high GWP. Global treaties have mandated that halon is not used in new installations, and production of halon ceased in 1993. Halon agents are being replaced by halon alternatives.

  - Halon Alternatives—Three suppression agents that are commonly used as halon alternatives include Inergen, FE-13, and FM-200:

    – Inergen—Inergen[3] can be used for occupied and unoccupied areas; it has an ODP near zero and a GWP near zero. Inergen requires ten times the amount of agent as halon and has a longer discharge time: 60 seconds vs. 10 seconds.

    – FE-13—FE-13[4] can be used for occupied and unoccupied areas; it has an ODP near zero but a high GWP. FE-13 may be subject to future environmental restrictions. This agent is good for areas with ceilings as high as 25 feet. FE-13 requires 2.5 times the amount of agent as halon.

    – FM-200—FM-200[5] can be used for occupied and unoccupied areas; it has an ODP near zero and a low to medium GWP. FM-200 requires twice as much agent as halon. This agent cannot be used for areas in which the ceiling is higher than 12 feet unless two rows of nozzles are installed.

    – Novec 1230—Novec 1230[6] can be used for occupied and unoccupied areas; it has a zero ODP and a GWP of less than one. Novec 1230 has a large safety margin (margin between effective and fatal mixtures) and requires less volume than most inert gases. Novec 1230 has a quick discharge time of 10 seconds.

8.1.3 Flood and Water Damage

Next to fires, flooding is the most common and widespread natural disaster. A flood is defined by the National Flood Insurance Program as a general and temporary condition of partial or complete inundation of two or more acres of normally dry land or of two or more properties from overflow of inland waters, unusual and rapid accumulation of runoff surface waters from any source, or a mudflow. (FEMA, http://fema.gov/plan/prevent/floodplain/nfipkeywords/floor_or_flooding.shtm)
Accidental water leakage is also covered here, since many of the safeguards to protect against natural flooding and accidental water leakage are similar.

8.1.3.1 Flood and Water Threats

The threat of damage from water (e.g., spills, intentional flooding) can be the intentional or accidental target of internal and external threat actors. The threat of natural floods comes solely from natural causes[7]:

- Theft & Sabotage—An organization may be the victim of sabotage to their building of information systems through the threat of water and the threat action of intentionally flooding a computer room for example.
- Environmental Damage—Organizational assets may succumb to environmental damage from severe weather (e.g., floods, tornadoes, and earthquakes), infrastructure failures (e.g., power outages), or even infestations (e.g., rats).
- Erred—Lastly, an employee may simply make a mistake that results in the damage to organizational assets such as accidentally spilling water on sensitive equipment.

8.1.3.2 Flood and Water Safeguards

Given the wide array of potential threat actions that could pose a threat to the organization's assets from an employee, an outsider, or even nature, organizations should implement an adequate set of physical security controls (e.g., safeguards) to address these flood and water threats. Table 8.8 lists

TABLE 8.8
Flood and Water Threats and Safeguards

Class	Threat	Safeguard
Exposure	• Theft & sabotage • Environmental damage • Erred	• Building location • Land and building safeguards • Water restrictions • Dry pipe • Raised floor
Monitoring	• Theft & sabotage • Environmental damage • Erred	• Inspections and maintenance • Leak alarms • Water flow alarms
Response	• Theft & sabotage • Environmental damage • Erred	• Response procedures • Tarps onsite

Note: Threat actions applicable to flood and water threats include theft & sabotage, environmental damage, and committing errors. Physical safeguards that can address these threat actions are described below.

an example set of physical safeguards that an organization may employ to counter the threat and threat actions impacting flood and water safeguards. These physical safeguards are discussed within the classes of water exposure, monitoring, and response.

8.1.3.2.1   Flood and Water Exposure

The best way to reduce the impacts of a flood and damaging waters to an organization's assets is to avoid exposure to floods and damaging waters. Organization's may reduce their exposure to floods and damaging waters through building location, water restrictions, dry pipe installations, and raised floors.

8.1.3.2.1.1   Flood and Water Exposure Safeguards

Floods and damaging waters can be avoided (or damage reduced) by reducing the building's exposure. Following are key factors for consideration in exposure:

- Building Location—The best way to protect an organization's assets exposure to floods and damaging waters is to avoid the water altogether. Floods can be somewhat avoided by choosing the proper geographic site for the organization's buildings.
- Land and Building Safeguards—Both the land the building occupies and the building itself can have flood and damaging water protections such as levees, sump pumps, and drains.
- Water Restrictions—Accidental water spills can damage sensitive data. Restrictions of bringing beverages into data centers can reduce the frequency of accidental spills and the accompanying damage to sensitive equipment.
- Dry Pipe—Covered in Section 8.1.2.5.2
- Raised Floor—Many data centers have installed raised flooring to provide a space between the true floor and the data center floor. In addition to providing a space for air flow, the data center below floor plenum provides protections from flooding and other damaging waters.

8.1.3.2.2   Flood and Water Monitoring

The damage sustained by an organization from water increases as sensitive data continues to be exposed to the water. Monitoring of situations in which water is in danger of or is currently damaging sensitive equipment is important in reducing the impact of this threat.

8.1.3.2.2.1   Flood and Water Exposure Safeguards

The impact of water on sensitive equipment can be reduced by increasing the monitoring abilities of the organization to include monitoring of potential water damage. The following water monitoring safeguards should be considered:

- Inspections and Maintenance—Routine inspections of the organization's building should note signs of water damage and leaks. This includes discolored (or even wet) ceiling tiles and walls. When these are noticed they should be immediately investigated as the source of the leak should be detected and addressed.
- Leak and Water Flow Alarms—Damaging waters to organizational assets can come from the water supplied to the building. Water damage can come from supply line or fitting leaks, pipe bursts, or even a faucet being left on. Both leak detectors and water flow alarms can reduce this threat.
    - Leak detectors respond with either an audible alarm or a signal to a control panel when they detect the presence of water. Control panels can alert appropriate responders or even be configured to automatically shut off water control valves to limit the damage.
    - Water flow alarms may be installed in water suppression systems to detect when water is flowing through sprinkler supply lines. This can indicate a sprinkler head opening (e.g., tripped by heat) or a pipe leak or burst.

8.1.3.2.3   Flood and Water Response

The sooner an organization can respond to situations of water damage, the less damage will occur to the organization's sensitive equipment. An organization's ability to respond is an important element to safeguard their sensitive equipment.

8.1.3.2.3.1   Flood and Water Response Safeguards

The impact of water on sensitive equipment can be reduced by increasing the response abilities of the organization. Organization can prepare for quick and rapid response through the implementation of water response safeguard:

- Response Procedures—An element of the organization's incident response plans, guard procedure, and/or facility plans should cover response to damaging waters. Response plans should include proper procedures for water valve location and shut off, equipment protection measures, such as covering systems with a tarp when appropriate, and preparing for potential floods.
- Supplies Available— Along with response procedures, the organization should have the associated supplies (e.g., tarps, sandbags, and duct tapes) on hand and easily obtained.

8.1.4   OTHER NATURAL DISASTERS

There are a variety of other, natural threats that may damage an organization's assets. These include lightning strikes, earthquakes, volcanoes, landslides, hurricanes, and tornadoes.

- Lightning Strikes—Lightning is a giant spark of electric power discharged from the atmosphere. Lightning from severe thunderstorms can cause electrical damage, interruption of electrical service, fires, and injury or death to people.
- Earthquakes—An earthquake is the violent shaking of the ground resulting from a sudden release of energy in the Earth's crust. Earthquakes can cause massive damage to buildings and infrastructure.
- Volcanoes—A volcano is break in the Earth's crust that allows lava, volcanic ash, and gases to escape from below the surface. The hazard of volcanic activity includes local volcanic activity, lava flows, ash fall, and volcanic mud flows (called *lahars*) and can destroy buildings and infrastructure in the immediate area and cause damage to any other buildings affected by ash fallout.
- Landslides—A landslide is a movement of ground such as a rock fall, slope failure, mudflow, or debris flow. Landslides are typically caused by unstable land and gravity but can be triggered by rainfall, earthquakes, or excavation. The hazard of landslide incidents is greater in mountainous areas of the United States.
- Hurricanes—A hurricane is a storm that forms over tropical or subtropical waters. To be classified as a hurricane these storms must reach windspeeds of 74 miles per hour. The incidence of hurricanes within the contiguous United States is concentrated on the southeast coast.
- Tornadoes—A tornado is a violent rotating column of wind that touches the ground. Tornadoes can cause death and destruct buildings in its path within seconds. The incidence of tornadoes is concentrated along "tornado alley," but they also occur frequently in other areas in the eastern United States.

8.1.4.1   Other Natural Disaster Threats

Natural disasters occur because of nature and therefore the threat actions of these threat sources are limited to environmental damage.

- Theft & Sabotage—An organization may be the victim of theft from looting while the organization is exposed based on damage from natural disasters.
- Environmental Damage—Organizational assets may be damaged or destroyed from the impact of any of the natural disasters listed above.

8.1.4.2 Other Natural Disaster Safeguards

Organizations should be aware of their exposure to natural disasters and increase their ability to withstand their impacts. Depending on the natural disaster most relevant in their location, organizations can implement an array of safeguards. Table 8.9 lists an example set of safeguards that an organization may employ to counter the threat and threat actions of natural disasters. These physical safeguards are discussed within the classes of general natural disaster protections, lightning protections, earthquake protections, volcano protections, hurricane protections, and tornado protections.

8.1.4.2.1 General Natural Disasters

Many natural disasters may be weathered better by the organization if they have appropriately prepared. The following safeguards are generally applicable to most natural disasters.

8.1.4.2.1.1 Natural Disasters—General Protection Safeguards

The impact from most natural disasters can be lessened through the following preparation safeguards:

- Building Enhancements—The damage from many natural disasters may be mitigated through appropriate building construction. Buildings may be enhanced through seismic bracing, hurricane straps, uplift limiting design, and the installation of impact resistant windows and doors.
- Evacuation Procedures—The organization's evacuation plans should cover foreseeable natural disasters in their evacuation procedures.

TABLE 8.9

Other Natural Disasters Safeguards

Class	Threat	Safeguard
General Natural Disaster	• Theft & sabotage • Environmental damage	• Building enhancements • Evacuation procedures • Stockpile plywood • Communication plans • Shelter in place plans • Listen to emergency information and alerts
Lightning	• Environmental damage	• Lightning arrestors • Surge suppression
Earthquake	• Theft & sabotage • Environmental damage	• Earthquake zones • Avoid tall structures
Volcano	• Theft & sabotage • Environmental damage	• Supply of N95 masks
Hurricane	• Theft & sabotage • Environmental damage	• Clear gutters and drains • Move to highest floor

Note: Threat actions applicable to other natural disaster threats include theft & sabotage and environmental damage. Physical safeguards that can address these threat actions are described below.

- Stockpile Plywood—For many natural disasters, the organizational buildings can be hardened by covering windows with plywood to withstand potential damage from storms and high winds.
- Communications Plans—The organization should ensure that they have a communications plan in place that will work effectively during a disaster. This communications plan is typically part of a disaster recovery plan and procedures.
- Shelter-in-Place—Organizations should create an appropriately secured and protected shelter-in-place area sufficient to withstand local disasters and large enough to house potential occupants.
- Emergency Information and Alerts—During an imminent threat of a natural disaster, the organization should have the ability to listen to emergency information and alerts to have the most up-to-date information relevant to the weather situation. The emergency Alert System is a national public warning system that sends information through broadcasters, satellite digital audio services, direct broadcast satellite providers, cable television systems, and wireless cable systems. Additional information regarding weather information can be obtained from the National Oceanic and Atmospheric Administration (NOAA) Weather Radio All Hazards (NWR). NWR is a nationwide network of radio stations that continuously broadcast National Weather Service information.

8.1.4.2.2   Lightning

Lightning strikes may be weathered better by the organization if they are appropriately prepared. The following safeguards apply to lightning.

8.1.4.2.2.1   Lightning Safeguards

The impact from lightning strikes can be lessened through the following of the general preparation guidelines above and the specific lightning preparation safeguards below:

- Lightning Arrestors—Lightning arrestors are devices that can divert the high voltage delivered by a lightning strike to electric power or telecommunication systems. When the system experiences a current surge from a lightning strike the current is diverted through the arrestor to ground.
- Surge Suppression—A surge suppressor is really just a smaller version of a lightning arrestor and performs the same function.

8.1.4.2.3   Earthquake

Earthquakes may be weathered better by the organization if they are appropriately prepared. The following safeguards apply to earthquakes.

8.1.4.2.3.1   Earthquake Safeguards

The impact from earthquakes can be lessened through the following of the general preparation guidelines above and the specific earthquake preparation safeguards below:

- Avoid Earthquake Zones—Also called seismic or seismic hazard zones, these are areas where earthquakes tend to occur and have the largest hazard level due to earthquakes.
- Avoid Tall Structures—Organizations with buildings in earthquake zones should consider the avoidance of tall structures and buildings near other tall structures.

8.1.4.2.4   Volcano

Volcanoes may be weathered better by the organization if they are appropriately prepared. The following safeguards apply to volcanoes.

8.1.4.2.4.1   Volcano Safeguards

The impact from volcanoes can be lessened through the following of the general preparation guidelines above and the specific volcano preparation safeguards below:

- Mask Supply—Because of the potential difficulty and hazard of breathing unhealthy air due to ash fallout, organizations in areas affected by volcanoes should have a ready supply of N95 masks.

8.1.4.2.5   Hurricane

Hurricanes may be weathered better by the organization if they are appropriately prepared. The following safeguards apply to hurricanes.

8.1.4.2.5.1   Hurricane Safeguards

The impact from hurricanes can be lessened through the following of the general preparation guidelines above and the specific hurricane preparation safeguards below:

- Gutters and Drains—Prior to hurricanes, or better yet, prior to hurricane season, an organization should ensure that the runoff drains and gutters are clear of debris.
- High Floors—During a flood event, building occupants should move to the highest floors of the building, but not into an attic space with no exit.

8.1.5   WORKFORCE

The determination of physical security risks to an organization's building includes an analysis of natural and human hazards. The natural hazards were covered in previous sections. This section covers those hazards or risks that are initiated by the workforce. Physical security controls should be in place to deter, detect, and remove intruders. These controls cover employees, visitors, and outsiders.

8.1.5.1   Workforce Threats

Humans can represent a serious threat to organization's buildings and information assets. Threat actions of humans that can be addressed by physical controls can include the following:

- Theft & Sabotage—An organization may be the victim of sabotage to their building of information systems through the threat of water and the threat action of intentionally flooding a computer room for example.
- Abused Trust—An employee may abuse the trust given to them and utilize this misplaced trust to take actions against the organization. There are many such actions a trusted employee could take.

8.1.5.2   Workforce Safeguards

Given the wide array of potential threat actions that could pose a threat to the organization's assets from an employee, organizations should implement an adequate set of physical security controls (e.g., safeguards) to address the threat actions associated with the workforce. Table 8.10 lists an example set of physical safeguards that an organization may employ to counter the threat and threat actions of the workforce. These physical safeguards are discussed within the classes of personnel screening and personnel termination.

TABLE 8.10

Employment Threats and Safeguards

Class	Threat	Safeguard
Personnel screening	• Theft & sabotage • Abused trust	• Proof of identity • Background check • Proof of citizenship • Military clearance
Personnel termination		• Escort/removal

Note: Threat actions applicable to employment threats include theft & sabotage and abused trust. Physical safeguards that can address these threat actions include personnel screening and personnel termination safeguards.

8.1.5.2.1   Personnel Screening

Organizations with security concerns (this should be all organizations) should perform some measure of screening on personnel prior to employment and possibly perform periodic updates. Personnel screening controls include proof of identity, background checks, citizenship checks, reference checks, and criminal checks and military clearances.

- Proof of Identity—Prior to hiring an individual, employers are required to have a method by which they ensure the identity of the potential employee. Methods typically include checking a government-issued photographic identification card (e.g., driver's license and passport).
- Background Check—To confirm that information given on the employment application is accurate, employers should consider the performance of a background check. Such a review will require the permission of the applicant and will determine the accuracy of educational and professional qualifications, employment history, and personal references. The potential applicant should also be asked to sign a statement regarding criminal convictions.
- Verification of Citizenship and Right to Work—To be compliant with labor law, employers must determine the right of the potential employees to work and their citizenship. The employer should ask to see credentials that prove citizenship and right to work (e.g., birth certificate, passport, social security card, work permit, and visa).
- Criminal and Credit Checks—In some positions, it may be appropriate to request a criminal background investigation or a personal credit check.
- Military Clearances—For sensitive positions that expose the candidate to government-controlled sensitive information, much more rigorous personnel clearance processes are required. The procedures for such clearances are beyond the scope of this book.

8.1.5.2.2   Personnel Termination

Organizations with security concerns should be prepared to protect their assets from potentially disgruntled employees during a termination. Termination controls within the physical security controls area include escort and removal procedures.

- Escort and Removal—While termination is a difficult time for both the employer and certainly for the employee, the employer should take precautions when terminating employment of a worker that may cause damage to the building, information systems, or injury to employees. The organization should have a standard process of terminating potentially disgruntled employees to ensure the maximum protections. The following elements should be considered in the creation of a termination procedure for disgruntled employees:

- Time and place—the organization should schedule the termination meeting at the end of the workday to reduce potential disruption on the workforce. This can even allow any potential targets of the disgruntled worker to leave beforehand. The termination meeting should take place near an exit or even off-site to further reduce disruptions.
- Escort—The organization should have an escort capable of intimidating the potentially disgruntled employee. This is typically a security guard, but it could also be another individual within the organization, preferably someone who is not involved in any recent arguments with this terminated employee.
- Gather Personal Belongings—It is best to have another employee gather personal belongings and have them ready at the end of the termination meeting or mail them later. It is not advisable to allow the terminated employee to clear out their desk if there is a potential for arguments or damage to the system or building.

8.1.6   Perimeter Protections

The determination of physical security risks to an organization's building includes an analysis of the definition, control, and defense of the building's perimeter. This section covers those threat actions that attempt to breach the building perimeter or threat actions which may endanger the building's perimeter controls.

8.1.6.1   Perimeter Protection Threats

Humans can represent a serious threat to organization's buildings and information assets. Threat actions of humans that can be addressed by perimeter protections can include the following:

- Theft & Sabotage—An external unauthorized person pose a threat to the organization. These unauthorized individuals may seek to gain unauthorized access or steal organizational assets.
- Abused Trust—An employee may abuse the trust given to them and utilize this misplaced trust to take actions against the organization. There are many such actions a trusted employee could take including theft of organizational equipment.

8.1.6.2   Perimeter Protection Safeguards

Given the value of organizational assets and the potential exposure to unauthorized outsiders, organizations should implement an adequate set of perimeter protection controls (e.g., safeguards) to address these threats. Table 8.11 lists an example set of perimeter protection safeguards that an organization may employ to counter the threat and threat actions of the unauthorized outsiders and rogue and insiders. These perimeter protection safeguards are discussed within the classes of barriers, lighting, intrusion detection, and physical asset control.

8.1.6.2.1   Barriers

Barriers are used to control, limit, or exclude access to the physical premises. Control of access includes directing the flow of authorized pedestrian and vehicular traffic, providing entry points where identification can be checked, delaying forced entry, blocking visual inspection, and protecting individual assets. Physical access control is made easier by reducing the number of entry and exit paths for potential intruders and making more effective use of the protective force personnel.

- Fencing—Fences are used to indicate property boundaries and to enclose secure areas. To be effective, fences must be of the proper height, and the fence line needs to be in good condition.
- Buildings—The building itself provides barriers such as walls, ceilings, floors, windows, and doors. Some of these barriers are rather weak, for example, dropped ceilings and raised floors behind which walls do not extend to the hard deck. These are referred to as partitions.

TABLE 8.11
Perimeter Threats and Safeguards

Class	Threat	Safeguard
Barriers	• Theft & sabotage • Abused trust • Environmental damage	• Fencing • Buildings • Doors • Windows • Locks • Vehicle barriers
Lighting	• Theft & sabotage	• Continuous lighting • Standby lighting • Movable lighting • Emergency lighting
Intrusion detection	• Theft & sabotage • Abused trust	• Exterior sensors • Interior sensors • Video Surveillance
Physical access control	• Theft & sabotage • Abused trust	• Badges • Card readers • Biometrics • Visitor control • Property removal prevention

Note: Threat actions applicable to the building perimeter threats include theft & sabotage, abused trust, and environmental damage. Physical safeguards that can address these threat actions include barriers, lighting, intrusion detection, and physical access control safeguards.

- Doors—In addition to being a portion of the building barrier, some doors and windows are an extension of other systems such as the fire alarm system and the intrusion detection system. These doors have several control requirements and options to ensure that they work as an effective element of the overall system:
  - Door Hinges and Frames—A door cannot securely block unauthorized entrance if the hinges of door frame can be circumvented. Security hinges should be used on all exterior or doors.
    - Removable Pin – Butt Hinge—These are your standard hinges for interior doors or exterior doors with the hinge pin on the inside.
    - Non-Removable Pin—Butt Hinge—These hinges have non-removable pins and are recommended for any exterior or interior locking door with the hinge pin on the outside of the protected area.
    - Continuous Hinges—These hinges run the full length of the door.
    - Security Studs—Butt hinges can have security studs that interleave with a hole on the opposite side of the hinge. When closed this prevents the two sides of the hinges from separating even if the pin is removed, see Figure 8.8.
  - Door Locking Mechanisms—The locking mechanism is the element of the door that allows or prevents entry. There are several modes in which a locking mechanism can operate:

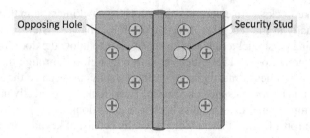

FIGURE 8.8 Security Stud Hinge. A security stud is a feature on some butt hinges that interleaves the two sides of the hinge together when closed. The security stud fits into the opposing hole blocking two sides from separating laterally.

- Fail Safe Lock—The lock on the door or window automatically opens during a power failure. This type of lock is essential to fire alarm systems to ensure the safe and speedy evacuation of personnel and is required for all fire exits.
- Fail Secure Lock—The lock on the door or window automatically closes during a power failure. This type of lock is essential for the protection of sensitive areas such as cash vaults. Areas with fail secure locks are considered uninhabited spaces. No person should ever be in one of these enclosures with the door closed.
- Fail Soft Lock—The lock on the door or window can operate with a reduced capacity during a power failure. This type of lock may be used as part of a fire alarm system such as an automatically opening sliding door that will open, but not automatically, and must be pushed open.
- Mantraps—Mantraps, also called air locks or sally ports, are a configuration of doors to create a small room or vestibule with two interlocking doors. The mantrap is configured such that it allows entrance into the vestibule but will not allow passage through the second door until the occupant is authorized. Authorization can take place through visual review or badged access control. Mantraps must be configured in a Fail-Safe mode if they are part of the designated fire exits.
- Door Locks—Locks are used to secure building entrances or security containers. The type and strength of the lock required depends on the information or area that it is safeguarding. Common vulnerabilities include weak locks and lose control over keys and combination changes.
  - Padlocks—Padlocks are self-contained locking mechanisms and are not permanently fixed to a door or cabinet. Padlocks can be operated with keys or combinations. These locks are best used for gates, with chains, or to secure cabinets.
  - Deadbolt Locks—Deadbolts are used to supplement existing locked doors to make a door more secure than the existing lock or a latch bolt lock. These locks are most commonly used on doors with glass or near windows.
  - Cylindrical Lever Locks—These locks are the most commonly used because their handles are ADA compliant and are best used for interior doors.
  - Cam Locks—These locks are cylinder locks with a post (or cam) at the rear of the cylinder that turns when the key opens the lock. These locks are best used for filing cabinets, mailboxes, and low security areas.
  - Mortise Lock—These locks require a mortise (cut out pocket in the edge of the door) in which to fit the lock case. They are best used on commercial-grade entry doors because of their strength and durability.
  - Interchangeable Core (IC) Cylinders—These locks allow key cylinder replacement without taking the lock apart. A control key is used to remove and install the interchangeable cores (ICs). These locks are best used in environments with a high turnover in occupancy.

- Strike Locks—An electronic strike lock is a locking system that uses a remote button (usually at the reception desk), a key fob, a badge system, and a motion sensor for exiting personnel to release the strike plate to allow the door to open.
- Magnetic Lock—These locks hold the door closed through the use of a strong magnet. The release mechanisms on these locks are usually the same as a strike lock (remote button plus motion sensor). These locks are typically installed on doors without functioning door handles such as a glass door.
- Electronic Locks—These locks typically consist of keypads in place of (or in addition to) a cylinder lock. They are useful in areas in which the issuance of keys is laborious.
- Panic Bars—Panic bars, also called exit bars, use a horizontal bar that can simply be pushed to unlatch the lock and allow for easy exit. These locks are designed to ensure easy and safe exit for fire exit doors.
- Keys—Many locks described above require the issuance and use of keys. There are various controls available for the keys.
  - Standard keys—The shape of the key (groves, thickness, depth) is called the keyway. These blank keyways (common called blank keys) are generally available through hardware stores and the keys can be readily copied.
  - Restricted Key Systems—Keys issued under a restricted key system are more difficult to duplicate because locksmiths are restricted from making copies of the keys that are issued to most staff members. Locksmith restrictions include authorized keyway distribution (the manufacturer will only supply keyways to authorized locksmiths) Another restriction on the key duplication is that the keyway is patented and locksmiths (or others) who make an unauthorized copy of the key are in violation of intellectual property rights.
  - Master Key System—A master key system is a hierarchical key system in which the master key can open all locks keyed within the system, while each lock can also have its own unique key issued to the occupant.
- Windows—Windows can provide for an increased ability for surveillance outside of the building. At the same time, windows can be the weakest point in a building's barrier and susceptible to breakage (shatter), impact, and penetration. In addition, there is a safety concern regarding plate glass in that when it breaks it produces large glass shards that may cause lacerations and severe injuries. To increase the protection properties of windows, organization may consider the use of alternative (or enhanced) glazing.
  - Security Window Film—Security window film may be applied to an existing window to increase its ability to withstand forced entry, severe windstorms, bomb blasts, and earthquakes. In addition to increasing the difficultly of breaching the window, window film reduces the flight path of glass in the event of breakage. However, security window film is not effective in stopping bullet penetration.
  - Security Glass—Reinforced glazing can also increase a window's ability to withstand forced entry, severe windstorms, bomb blasts, earthquakes, and, in some cases, bullets. Security glass (or glazing) comes in a variety of strengths designed for various applications, which include tempered glass, wired glass, laminated glass, acrylic, and polycarbonate sheeting, see Table 8.12.
- Vehicle Barriers—These are used to stop vehicles from entering the building. Barriers include bollards, pop-up barriers, cables, and natural terrain obstacles. Vehicle barriers, when employed, must be properly placed and monitored.
  - Permanent Bollards—A bollard is a short, sturdy, and reinforced vertical post designed to restrict vehicular traffic. These are used in areas in which road access needs to be controlled or buildings need to be protected from vehicle ramming attacks.

TABLE 8.12

Safety Glass Benefits

Glazing	Shatter Resistant	Impact Resistant	Penetration Resistant	Description
Plate Glass	✓	✗	✗	• Safety concerns • Glass shards may cause lacerations
Tempered Glass	✓	✗	✗	• Heat treated glass
Wired Glass	✓	✓	✗	• Embedded wire in glass • Also fire resistant
Security Window Film	✓	✓	✓	• Can be applied to existing windows
Laminated Glass	✓	✓	✓	• Highly shatter resistant
Laminated Security Glass	✓	✓	✓	• Highly penetration resistant
Acrylic	✓	✓	✓	• 2X strength of laminated glass • 17X impact resistance • Excellent light transmission
Polycarbonate sheeting	✓	✓	✓	• 30X strength of laminated glass • 300X impact resistance

Note: Glazing (referring to glass and other clear penetration resistant products) can provide a variety of safety benefits from shatter resistance to impact and penetration resistance.

- Removable Bollards—Removable bollards are used in areas where the barrier needs to be removed from time to time. Bollards are placed in an embedded sleeve and secured with a padlock.
- Pop-Up Bollards—Pop-up bollards are used in areas in which the barrier needs to be open at times to allow for authorized vehicular traffic. These bollards may be retracted to allow vehicle access and rise quickly to block traffic when needed.
- Barrier Arms—These are vehicle gates that can be raised and lowered to control access to a road, building, or other areas in which traffic is restricted. The standard parking garages are typically outfitted with breakaway arms but high security areas can install traffic control barriers that can stop hostile vehicular threats.

SIDEBAR 8.2   NATURAL AND ARCHITECTURAL BARRIERS

Providing physical security to the perimeter of a protected building does not have to involve jersey walls, high fencing, and other "ugly" methods. An approach to providing external barriers to the building through environmental design can be used to provide esthetically pleasing and physically strong barriers. This approach is called Crime Prevention Through Environmental Design (CPTED—pronounced "sep-ted").

There are four basic elements to the CPTED approach: territorial reinforcement, natural access control, maintenance, and natural surveillance, see Figure 8.9.

- Territorial reinforcement conveys the idea that the area is protected by ensuring that the grounds, seating areas, fence lines, and landscaping give the impression of a well-maintained and guarded area. This approach works two ways: (1) would-be intruders get the impression that exterior surveillance and barriers are well maintained and unlikely to have vulnerabilities, and (2) authorized personnel are more likely to challenge unauthorized visitors in a more defined and controlled area.

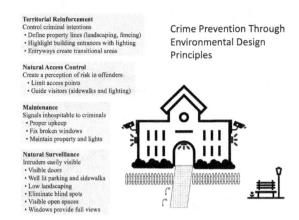

FIGURE 8.9   Crime Prevention Through Environmental Design (CPTED).

- Natural access uses architectural and landscape elements to guide access to and within the building. Design elements that implement natural access include location of parking lots, sidewalks, doors, signage, and lighting. These elements conspire to control and direct traffic to those areas where would-be visitors are better scrutinized. Possible attack and escape routes are also significantly reduced through natural access designs.
- Maintenance signals a clean image and that the property is well kept. This signals to would be intruders that the property is inhospitable to them and they are likely being watched. This CPTED element includes well-groomed grounds, and no broken windows or out of order lights or cameras.
- Natural surveillance incorporates building and landscape elements to ensure that all external areas are under constant surveillance. This CPTED element includes placement of windows, landscaping, and lighting to enable external and internal surveillance.

For more information, see the following Web sites:
- International CPTED Association (ICA): www.cpted.net
- National Crime Prevention Council: www.ncpc.org

8.1.6.2.2   Lighting

Lighting is an essential physical security control that helps to prevent intrusions and endangerment to employees. In addition, lighting can increase the surveillance capabilities of the security force by correctly lighting property lines, entrances, and other critical areas. There are several types of lighting, including continuous lighting, standby lighting, movable lighting, and emergency lighting.

- Continuous Lighting—This is the most common type of lighting. Continuous lighting is a series of fixed lights that flood an area with continuous light. It is important to have a minimum safe light level and to avoid dark patches by implementing overlapping cones of light. There are two types of continuous lighting: glare lighting and controlled lighting. Glare lighting is used to direct light across a field of view to illuminate potential intruders and to hide internal guards. Controlled lighting is used to illuminate a patch of land, such as a field or parking lot, or a strip of land, such as a pathway or fence line. Minimum and maximum lighting levels are determined by the governing laws and local ordinances. There is a lot of variation in these standards; however, the following figures can be used to provide a baseline understanding.

TABLE 8.13

Recommended Lighting Levels for Various Applications

Application	Recommended Lighting Level
Guard route	0.5 candle foot
Building, fence line, parking lot	1 candle foot
Walkway, loading dock	3 candle feet
Parking structure	5 candle feet

Note: Not all light applications require the same level of brightness (measured in candle feet). Guard routes require a low level to ensure night vision, while parking structures require a high light level to illuminate dark corners.

- Standby Lighting—Similar to continuous lighting in terms of arrangement of lights; however, standby lighting is configured to illuminate automatically when an intruder is detected or manually when guards become suspicious. This lighting can be motion-activated by integrating the lighting system with intrusion detection systems (Table 8.13).
- Movable Lighting—This type of lighting refers to portable, manually operated lighting devices such as spotlights and searchlights or areas that require temporary lighting.
- Emergency Lighting—This type of lighting is used during a power failure and other emergencies to facilitate continued protection and safe evacuation. It depends on an alternative power source such as batteries or generators.

8.1.6.2.3 Physical Intrusion Detection

Physical intrusion detection systems, also called *electronic security systems* (ESS), are designed to detect, delay, and respond to intruder activity. Unauthorized intrusion on the premises is a breach in physical security and is a risk to the organization's assets. Such intrusions should be detected by means of intrusion detection (alarm) sensors or visual surveillance. Regardless of the type of intrusion detection sensor, there should be a guard force capable of responding within a reasonable amount of time (e.g., 5–10 minutes).

The design and deployment of intrusion detection sensors depends on the site-specific characteristics of the building, such as terrain, geography, climate, and type of protection required. Many sites require both interior and exterior sensors to completely protect the organization's assets.

8.1.6.2.3.1 Exterior Sensors

Exterior sensors include fence sensors, line-of-sight (LOS) sensors, and video motion sensors. These sensors are placed on the exterior of the building. As such, they must be resistant to weather conditions (e.g., rain, snow, fog, and extreme cold) and possible nuisance alarms from external disturbances (e.g., windblown objects and animals). Each of these exterior sensors is described briefly below:

- Fence Sensors—Fences are practical barriers that cover a large amount of terrain and cannot always be continuously monitored through direct surveillance. A series of fence sensor technologies is available to extend the surveillance capabilities of the security protective force and detect breaches or attempted breaches to the fence line:
  - Strain-Sensitive Cable—These fence sensors are cables that run the length of the fence and can detect fence movement (e.g., from an intruder climbing the fence) or fence penetration attempts (e.g., fence cutting).
  - Taut Wire—A taut wire sensor is woven through a fence and protects the fence line by indicating when force is applied to the wire. Taut wires, when force is applied, signal

intrusions through the closing of mechanical switches or a change in the monitored electrical output of strain gauges.

- Fiber-Optic Cable—These sensors are established by stringing a fiber-optic cable of the length of a fence line and sending a modulated light signal through the cable. When force is exerted on the fiber-optic cable, the modulated signal is modified and detected. This causes an alarm to be sent. Fiber-optic cables are non-metallic and are not susceptible to electrical interference and nuisance alarms such as lightning.
- Electric Field—Electric field sensors utilize alternating current to establish a constant electrostatic field (typically within a few feet of the fence line). Intruders entering the field will interrupt the constant field pattern and signal an alarm.
- Capacitance Proximity—These sensors consist of a capacitance sensor and several capacitance wires. Interference between the sensor and the wires is detected and set to signal an alarm condition. These sensors can be effectively installed on fence lines and roofs of buildings by placing horizontal strands of capacitance wires along the tops of fences or roofs of buildings.
- Buried Line—These sensors consist of a buried cable or a set of underground detection sensors. Because they are hidden, they can be difficult to detect, but they are susceptible to environmental conditions such as a hard freeze or running water.
- Line-of-Sight (LOS) Sensors—LOS sensors detect intrusions when the field they protect is interrupted. LOS sensors work best on flat terrain with no obstructions.
  - Monostatic Microwave—This type of sensor incorporates a microwave transmitter and receiver at one end of the detection zone. Monostatic microwave sensors have a range of approximately 400 feet. Intruders are detected by a signal reflecting off their moving body. Monostatic microwave sensors provide volumetric protection for localized areas such as corners and around the base of a protected structure.
  - Bistatic Microwave—This type of sensor utilizes a separate microwave transmitter and receiver and has a range of up to 1,500 feet. This type of exterior sensor must incorporate overlapping zones because the area directly under and near the pole-mounted transmitter and receiver is not covered by the pair.
  - Passive Infrared (PIR)—Sensors can detect IR energy[8] and movement based on IR energy in its field of view. These are among the most widely used motion sensors.
  - Active Infrared (IR)—IR sensors provide alarms when IR beams are interrupted (active IR sensors).
- Video Motion Sensors—These intrusion detection systems work when an intruder enters a video camera's field of view. The sensor is able to process the video image and trip an alarm in the event that the images match pre-defined criteria. Video motion sensors are most sensitive when intruders walk along side (parallel to the sensor) as opposed to toward the sensors. This is because there is a greater change in the image from the point of view of the sensor when the intruder walks across the protected area instead of toward the sensor, see Figure 8.10.

8.1.6.2.3.2 Interior Sensors

Interior sensors include boundary penetration sensors, volumetric motion sensors, point sensors, and duress alarms. These sensors are placed on the interior of the building. Interior sensors are categorized by the structure for which they are intended to provide protection, namely, barriers and interior spaces. Each of these interior sensors is described briefly below:

- Boundary Penetration Sensors—These sensors are designed to detect penetration of barriers such as walls, ceilings, duct openings, and windows.
  - Structural Vibration—These sensors are designed to detect low-frequency vibrations that match the vibrations of attempted penetrations of a physical barrier (e.g., walls and

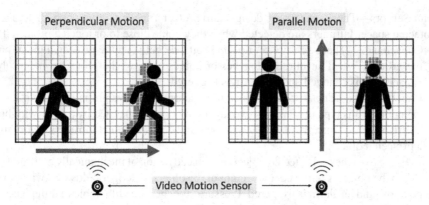

FIGURE 8.10 Proper placement of video motion sensors. Proper placement of video motion sensors ensures that the intruder walks across the protected area to increase the detection capabilities of the device.

ceilings). Structural vibration sensors detect attempts such as hammering, drilling, cutting, forcible entry, and explosive detonation.

- Glass-Break—These sensors listen for the sound of breaking glass. The sound is picked up by microphone transducers that respond to specific frequencies that match the sound of breaking glass. These sensors typically cover a maximum of 100 square feet of glass surface.
- Passive Ultrasonic—These sensors listen for sounds that could indicate the penetration of a barrier. Sounds detected by passive ultrasonic sensors include breaking glass, the snipping sound of bolt cutters, the hissing of an acetylene torch, the whining sound of a drill, and the shattering of brick or cinderblock. The effective range of passive ultrasonic sensors is between 3 feet (the sound of drilling) and 55 feet (the sound of bolt cutters).
- Balance Magnetic Switches—These sensors have two parts: a switch mechanism mounted to a stationary object such as a door frame and an actuating magnet mounted to a moving object such as a door. The switch is held open by a balanced magnetic force set up between the actuating magnet and a bias magnet mounted near the switch. This configuration is useful when an intruder may attempt to defeat the alarm with an external magnet. Either the door opening, or the presence of an external magnet will cause the switch to become unbalanced and trigger the alarm.
- Grid Wire—These sensors are composed of a single electrical wire arranged in a grid pattern with an electric charge placed on it. The grid is either attached to the surface that it is designed to protect (e.g., a window or wall) or placed over an opening (e.g., a duct). When the grid wire is broken, an alarm is sounded.
- Volumetric Motion Sensors—These sensors are designed to detect the presence of an intruder in an interior space. All three of these technologies were previously described in the exterior sensor sections. They are included here for convenience.
  - Monostatic Microwave—This type of sensor incorporates a microwave transmitter and receiver at one end of the detection zone. Monostatic microwave sensors have a range of approximately 400 feet. Intruders are detected by a signal reflecting off their moving body. Monostatic microwave sensors provide volumetric protection for localized areas such as corners and around the base of a protected structure.
  - Infrared (IR)—IR sensors provide alarms when IR beams are interrupted (active IR sensors) or when thermal IR radiation is detected within the field of view (passive IR sensors).
  - Video Motion—These intrusion detection systems work when an intruder enters a CCTV camera's field of view. The sensor is able to process the video image and trip an alarm in the event that the image matches pre-defined criteria.

- Point Sensors—These sensors are designed to protect a specific point or small area within the protected space. Intruders are detected when they come close to or touch a protected object.
  - Capacitance—These sensors set up a capacitance between the protected metal object and the ground. When an intruder touches or comes close to the protected metal object, the capacitance is changed and an alarm is triggered.
  - Pressure Mats—These sensors generate an alarm when weight is applied to the mat. An example of this type of sensor is two layers of copper separated by rubber with holes in it. These mats are typically placed at windows and doors to detect intruders before they get to a protected object.
  - Pressure Switches—Protected objects are placed on top of mechanically activated switches. When the object is removed, the weight of the object no longer holds the switch in the open position, and an alarm is triggered. Pressure switches are vulnerable to thin pieces of material slid underneath the protected object.
  - Duress Alarms—These are fixed or portable alarms that signal the security protective force or an external alarm location to indicate an intrusion or other emergency. Duress alarms must not annunciate at the point of alarm because an audible alarm may endanger the person tripping the alarm.

8.1.6.2.3.3 *Video Surveillance Systems*
The surveillance and alarm response capabilities of the security protective force can be extended through the implementation of a video surveillance system. A video surveillance system can have two distinct functions: alarm assessment and surveillance.

- Alarm Assessment—A video camera alarm assessment system is designed to enable the security protective force to respond rapidly to triggered alarms. The video surveillance system can be used to perform preliminary investigations of the area and dispatch the security protective force to the appropriate areas.
- Surveillance—A video surveillance system can effectively extend the surveillance capabilities of the security protective force. With a properly installed and maintained system, the standing security protective force can monitor more areas of the protected site and provide a greater frequency of physical and video monitoring.

8.1.6.2.3.3.1 Video Surveillance System Capabilities
The video surveillance system capabilities should be matched to the organization's surveillance needs. Video surveillance systems have a variety of capabilities:

- Resolution—The digital cameras that are part of the video surveillance systems provide a picture quality measured in pixels (short for "picture element"), which are the smallest elements of a digital image. The quality of a digital picture is measured in pixel counts. The more pixels used to represent an image, the higher the quality of the image. Currently video surveillance cameras are delivering between 2 mega-pixels (MP) and 5 MP. Images below 2 MP are generally adequate to detect motion or an intruder but inadequate to read license plates or confirm identifying faces. Organizations that use older analog video cameras are likely limited to less than 0.5 MP image, although there are some higher quality analog security cameras capable of 2 MP.
- Frame Rate—Frame rate is the number of frames per second (fps) the video surveillance systems are capable and set to record. The more fps, the easier it is to recognize details in an image. The trade-off here is network bandwidth.
- Lighting Level—Many cameras now have the capability to record in low light conditions using IR technology. Cameras using IR light emitting diodes (LEDs) capture IR waves from

the camera lens reflected off of objects in the cameras' field of view. The more IR LEDs the camera has, the better its low light capabilities.

- Audio—Many video surveillance systems include the ability to record audio. This provides better surveillance capabilities as the guards monitoring the area can hear discussions or sounds (such as breaking glass) through the surveillance system. Some systems include two-way audio that allows the guards to communicate (or warn) the intruder.
- PTZ—The Pan-Tilt-Zoom (PTZ) capabilities of a video surveillance system allows the guard to move the field of view and even zoom in on a subject. PTZ cameras are typically covered with a tinted doom to mask the current field of view as the intruder could potentially avoid detection by staying ahead of the camera pan.

8.1.6.2.4 Physical Access Control

Physical access control systems complement perimeter barriers, protective lighting, and other physical security safeguards by preventing unauthorized entry, the introduction of harmful devices, and the movement of information and materials from the protected location.

The protection of organizational assets relies on preventing unauthorized entry onto the premises and into sensitive areas. A variety of methods may be employed to prevent unauthorized entry. Identification methods are those mechanisms that use one or more methods of identification, together with authorization and access control, such as badge systems, card readers, or biometric controls. Visitor control procedures restrict the freedom by which visitors can access the premises and place controls on their movement.

For those people who are allowed to access the premises, identification methods provide a means to identify each individual, associate access authority with the identified person, and control access through integration with physical access devices. Examples of identification methods include badge systems, card readers, and biometric controls.

8.1.6.2.4.1 Badges

More-sensitive facilities require additional protection to ensure that only authorized personnel enter, occupy, or leave a designated area. Security badging systems are used to implement and enforce controls to keep unauthorized visitors out. These controls include accountability procedures, badge storage, badge recovery, photo updating, handling of lost badges, and ensure adherence to procedures.

- Accountability Procedures—The facility protective force must ensure that all badges are accounted for. Documentation specifying the disposition of badges should include date of issue, serial number, name of badge holder, organization, and date of destruction.
- Badge Storage—Facilities are especially susceptible if badges are stored in an insecure location. Badges should be stored in a locked drawer and protected at all times.
- Badge Recovery and Termination—When employees are terminated, facilities personnel must ensure that they retrieve and destroy the badge or otherwise terminate badge access immediately.
- Photo Update—Photo identification badges must be kept reasonably up to date such that the photo resembles the person to whom the badge was issued.
- Handling of Lost Badges—There must be complete and clear procedures for handling lost badges. These procedures should include rapid notification and termination of access on the lost badge. This can be accomplished automatically through a manual procedure of keeping up-to-date lost badge lists at all entrance points.
- Procedure Adherence—The safeguards listed above depend upon the establishment of and adherence to badge safeguarding procedures. The organization must ensure that the facility protective force and all employees and visitors understand and follow the established procedures.

SIDEBAR 8.3   BADGES

The use of badges in many organizations provides little to no security. Unless the badging system has a logical control element, most implementations of these systems have significant vulnerabilities that severely reduce their effectiveness. Examples of logical control elements integrated into a badging system include badge readers and entry systems. For example, all entry points to the organization's campus and individual buildings could have badge readers and turnstiles or mantraps activated by authorized badges.

Badging systems that only employ and procedural controls typically offer little added security. Consider the following vulnerabilities and possible observations:

- **Weak badge design and construction**. Replacement picture could be easily inserted without detectable damage to the badge.
- **Non-Picture badges**. Badges, even for permanent employees, have no identification picture. Lost badges Card readers are an improvement over picture-only badges. These authentication systems combine a badge (with or without a picture) with a mechanized system that further authenticates the badge holder or the badge itself. Simple card or badge readers encode information on the card through methods such as magnetic strips, smart cards, or proximity cards. The coded information on the card is compared with the information stored on the system, and access determination is based on the results.
- **Sticker visitor badges**. These badges can be easily forged. Furthermore, these badges are rarely collected upon leaving the building, and reusable badges can be found in the trash cans outside of visitor control.
- **Lack of inspection**. Badges are seldom reviewed close up by security personnel. Badges are viewed at a distance (i.e., badges are "flashed" as you drive by). In many cases, fake badges consisting of a white background and a colored blob in the middle would suffice.

Team members of the security risk assessment team should determine the effectiveness of the badging system through observation.

8.1.6.2.4.2   Card Readers

An additional control of a personal identification number (PIN) can be added to the automated card-reading system. The addition of this control makes the authentication mechanism stronger and is referred to as *two factor control*. Care should be taken to ensure that PINs can be entered without others observing the secret PIN.

Card readers may be vulnerable to the extent that badges become lost and not reported or the ease with which the data stored in the card can be manipulated. Cards in which the data is stored in plaintext on a magnetic strip are the most vulnerable because devices to read and write to these cards are cheap and readily available.

8.1.6.2.4.3   Biometrics

Physical access control to an organization's buildings and protected areas can be improved through the implementation and deployment of biometric controls. Biometrics encompasses any technology that automates the authentication process through the use of physiological or behavioral characteristics. Physiological characteristics are measured by devices that implement retina, iris, finger, facial, or hand scanning technology. Behavioral characteristics are measured by devices that implement voice, signature, and keystroke scanning technologies.[9]

- Biometric Authentication Vulnerabilities—The use of biometric systems to authenticate authorized individuals should be examined by the security risk assessment team to determine the level of risk incurred based on the biometric and implementation architecture of the authentication system. The following classes of biometric vulnerabilities should be considered:
  - Authentication Device Protection—The authentication device itself must be protected from adverse weather conditions and possible destruction by potential adversaries. Both weather conditions and vandalism can degrade or destroy the capability of the authentication device for performing access control. In most cases, such a threat would have a denial of service impact on the authentication service. The team should observe the general location and accessibility of the device to unauthorized personnel and its exposure to the elements. Furthermore, the team should determine the effectiveness of the procedures in place to deal with the loss of function of one or more devices.
  - Storage of Templates—A template is a distillation of the biometric characteristics measured and is unique to each catalogued individual. The storage of these templates must receive the same protection as the storage of system password files. The security risk assessment team should perform investigation and testing to ensure that the template files cannot be modified, replaced, or read through an unapproved process.
  - Transmission of Templates—Centralized biometric authentication systems that store template files on a central server typically send the template file generated at the point of capture to the central server for comparison. The central server then sends back an approval code to the point of capture. The transmission of the template files and approval codes must be secured through physical protection of the transmission media, or encryption, or both.
- Crossover Error Rates—Each biometric device or technique has inherent errors within the system. Error rates, which can be false negatives or false positives, are generally compared using the crossover error rate (CER), which is the error rate when false rejection and false acceptance rates are equal. Biometrics with a high CER should be considered somewhat vulnerable to the denial of access to authorized users and the allowed access of unauthorized users.[10] Furthermore, even higher CER values than may be reported by the manufacturer or industry sites may be present in a system deployed at the assessed site. Errors of implementation and configuration can introduce significant vulnerabilities for which tests should be conducted.

8.1.6.2.4.4 Visitor Control

The purpose of visitor control is to properly identify and control visitor access to the premises. The following elements of a visitor control program should be reviewed:

- Approval—All visitors should have prior approval to be on the premises from an authorized employee.
- Identification—The identification of a visitor should be established through the presentations and inspection of a government-issued identification card, such as a driver's license.
- Visitor Badges—All approved visitors should wear a conspicuous badge at all times. Visitor badges should be recovered when the visitor leaves.
- Escort—All visitors should be escorted in areas with high sensitivity.
- Restrictions—For most installations, visitor access should be restricted to daytime work hours and non-sensitive buildings.

8.1.6.2.4.5 Property Removal Prevention

The security protective force should also provide controls for the prevention of unauthorized removal of equipment. Possible controls include the following:

- Property Pass—Authorized removal of equipment requires that a property pass be issued by an authorized individual. Property passes should protect against forgeries and reuse.
- Package Inspection—In order to ensure that all equipment removed from the premises is authorized, the security protective force should have the ability to inspect all packages (e.g., boxes, briefcases, and purses).

8.2   THE RIIOT METHOD: PHYSICAL DATA GATHERING

As introduced in Chapter 5, the Review, Interview, Inspect, Observe, Test (RIIOT) method of data gathering can be applied to any security risk assessment technique and helps to ensure a more complete and well-managed data gathering process. The RIIOT method consists of five processes for gathering data regarding the effectiveness of a security control: Review documents, interview keep staff, inspect controls, observe behavior, and test controls (RIIOT). This method is applied to any area of security controls by reasoning about the most appropriate approach for gathering data on each security control under review. Applying the RIIOT method to the technical area shows that a majority of the data gathering techniques to be applied to physical security controls will be document review, personnel interviews, and inspection of controls. Table 8.6 provides suggested reasonable approaches to gathering data for each of the security controls described in this chapter.

8.2.1   Determining Appropriate RIIOT Approaches for Physical Controls

Recall from Chapter 5 that the RIIOT method of data gathering is used to assist the data gathering process by organizing the data gathering approaches (e.g., Review documents, Interview key staff, Inspect controls, Observe behavior, and Test controls) for the targeted security controls, selecting the approaches for each control, and then assigning the data gathering process among team members, and tracking their progress.

The number of methods and the selection of specific methods to be used for data gathering will be based on the level of rigor specified in the security risk assessment project plan, the skills of the team members, and the approach determined by the security risk assessment team lead. These descriptions of data gathering activities against each of the listed security controls are intended to provide a general approach to be used by security risk assessment teams, and not specific answers to questions that may arise during a security risk assessment.

Table 8.14 provides a map to all the potential RIIOT data gathering approaches that could be used to gather data on all of the administrative controls discussed in Section 8.1. The sections below describe each of these approaches and provide a description of how a security risk assessment team member may go about collecting that data.

8.2.2   Review Documents Regarding Physical Controls

As demonstrated in Table 8.14, gathering data on physical security control involves the review of documents. The bulk of the document review will be a review of logs, processes, and procedures. The remaining document reviews will include a review of architectural drawings and schematics.

8.2.2.1   Physical Documents to Request

Using the RIIOT document review technique, the security risk assessment team should determine the set of documents to be reviewed (see Table 8.15). In some cases, the team will be able to review all documents obtained through information requests. In most cases, because of time or budget constraints, the team will need to narrow the evidence reviewed to determine the strength of physical security controls.

TABLE 8.14
RIIOT Method of Data Gathering for Physical Controls

Controls	Review Documents	Interview Key Personnel	Inspect Controls	Observe Behavior	Test Controls
On-site power generation	*	*	*		
Uninterruptable power supply	*	*	*		
Line conditioner	*	*	*		
Voltage regulator	*	*	*		
Surge suppressor	*	*	*		
Computer room air conditioner	*	*			
Computer room air handler	*	*			
Temperature sensor/alarm	*	*	*		
Temperature log	*	*	*		
Humidifier		*			
Humidity sensor/alarm		*	*		
Humidity log	*	*	*		
Building construction	*	*	*		
Fire exits	*	*	*		*
Storage of combustibles	*	*	*		
Smoke detectors	*		*		
Heat detectors	*		*		
Flame detectors	*		*		
Fire alarm control panels	*	*	*		
Fire alarm installation type		*	*		
Portable fire extinguishers	*		*		
Stationary suppression-water	*		*		
Stationary suppression-foam	*		*		
Stationary suppression-clean agent	*		*		
Building location	*	*			
Levees and drains		*	*		
Water restrictions	*	*			
Raised floor		*	*		
Inspection and maintenance	*	*	*		
Leak and flow alarms		*	*		
Natural disaster response procedures	*	*			

(*Continued*)

TABLE 8.14   *(Continued)*

Controls	Review Documents	Interview Key Personnel	Inspect Controls	Observe Behavior	Test Controls
Disaster supplies			*		
Building enhancements	*	*	*		
Evacuation procedures	*	*		*	
Communications plans	*	*			
Shelter in place preparation	*	*			
Emergency information monitoring		*			
Lightning arrestors			*		
Escort and removal procedures	*	*		*	*
Proof of identity	*	*	*		
Background check	*	*	*		
Proof of citizenship	*	*	*		
Criminal check	*	*			
Military clearance	*	*	*		
Fencing		*	*		
Buildings			*		
Doors			*		*
Windows			*		
Locks		*	*		*
Vehicle barriers	*	*	*		
Continuous lighting	*	*	*		
Standby lighting		*	*		
Movable lighting		*	*		
Emergency lighting		*	*		*
Fence sensors	*	*	*		*
Line of sight sensors	*	*	*		*
Video motion sensors	*	*	*		*
Boundary penetration sensors	*	*	*		*
Volumetric motion sensors	*	*	*		*
Point sensors	*	*	*		*
Duress alarms	*	*	*		*
Video surveillance system	*	*	*		*
Badges	*	*	*	*	*

(Continued)

TABLE 8.14 *(Continued)*

Controls	Review Documents	Interview Key Personnel	Inspect Controls	Observe Behavior	Test Controls
Card readers	*	*	*	*	*
Biometrics	*	*	*	*	*
Guard procedures	*	*		*	
Visitor control	*	*		*	*
Property pass	*	*		*	*
Package inspection	*	*		*	*

Note: The application of the RIIOT method to physical controls indicates that the data gathering in this area will focus mainly on document review and inspection of physical controls.

TABLE 8.15
Physical Documents to Request

Document Type	Sample Titles	Expected Elements Table
Safeguard information	• Product manuals • System schematics • Inspection reports • Configuration settings	Table 8.16
Previous physical assessments	• Inspection • Physical audit • Industrial security audit	Table 8.17
Building and site architecture	• Physical site diagram • Building drawings • Blueprints	Table 8.18
Procedures and work products	• Procedures • Guard logs • Visitor logs • Incident reports	Table 8.19

Note: The security risk assessment team should attempt to obtain and review as many relevant physical documents as possible within the data gathering stage of the security risk assessment. This table provides a sample list of documents to request, but it is by no means exhaustive.

8.2.2.2 Review Physical Documents for Information

It is important to create a checklist to guide the review of each document.[11] A checklist is simply a listing of all the things a reasonable security engineer would expect to find in the reviewed document. In order to assist those performing security risk assessments, the checklists for document review are provided in Tables 8.16 through 8.19. The team should be aware that not all documents are appropriate or available for all environments.

TABLE 8.16
Physical Safeguard Document Elements

General Safeguard Information

The assessor should review all available safeguard information to gain a better understanding of the effectiveness of the security implications of the physical controls in place.

Control Area	Expected Elements	Discussion
Product manuals	• Capabilities	Determine the capability, type, and number of exterior and interior sensors. • Identify make, model, and version of equipment. • Review equipment capabilities online or in available manuals.
System schematics	• Architecture and integration	For any available system schematics that show the integration of multiple physical controls, review the following: • Consistency of physical site characteristics with schematics (e.g., accuracy and currency) • Consistency with number and placement of physical security controls (vs. physical/visually inspection) • Coverage of ingress, egress, and sensitive areas.
Inspection reports	• Findings and follow up	For any available inspection reports covering physical security controls, review the following: • Findings from the last 2 years • Documentation regarding mitigation of findings (e.g., maintenance reports and risk register entries) Make a note of any findings visible during physical site tours or inspections. Review physical with documented mitigation.
Configuration settings	• General	For all physical controls accessible remotely determine: • Secure configuration (e.g., authentication and secure transmission) • Level of integration with other surveillance systems • Latest update applied (if applicable) • Log location and capacity • Any features disabled
	• Power settings	Appropriate settings for these devices are dependent upon the business mission, environmental conditions, and threat of power loss. However, reasonable settings are typically as follows: • UPS capacity: 20–45 minutes OPG: 8–72 hours (be sure to inquire about on-site fuel capacity)
	• Fire detection	Appropriate setting for fire detection and suppression devices is conditional upon the placement and purpose of each device. Specifically, team members should look at the settings of the following devices: • Heat alarms. Typically set for 117°F (47°C), 135°F (57°C), 165°F (74°C), or 200°F (93°C) • Rate-of-rise detectors. Typically set for 12°F–15°F (6°C–8°C) per minute
	• Fire alarms	All alarms (e.g., fire, smoke, and heat) should be reviewed for the following capabilities: • Battery backup. 24–60 hours backup • Separate circuit • Line supervision. For alarms that dial out (e.g., remote systems) • Coverage. Review coverage capabilities of various alarms (e.g., smoke, heat, and intrusion). Compare coverage capabilities to the need of the environment

(Continued)

TABLE 8.14 *(Continued)*

Control Area	Expected Elements	Discussion
	• Fire suppression	Ensure that clean-agent suppression chemicals are appropriate for the application. For example, FM-200 cannot be used for areas where ceilings are higher than 12 feet.
	• Cameras	Determine the camera's ability to focus, zoom, pan, capture video, and distinguish characteristics in different lighting conditions.
	• Video surveillance system	Determine the system's capabilities for the following: • Camera control • two-way communication • Motion sensing, image masking • Video storage and replay capabilities

Note: The physical safeguard information should be reviewed for configuration options, current settings, warnings, and cautions.

8.2.2.3 Review Documents for Currency and Capability

All available documents regarding physical controls should be reviewed for currency and capability.

- Currency—Many physical security controls may have been in place for a long period of time. It is important to ensure that documents regarding those controls are updated and accurate. For example, fire evacuation plans need to accurately reflect the current building layout.
- Capabilities—Many physical security controls have specific capabilities that may only be observable through inspection of documents. For example, the capabilities of an Uninterruptable Power Supply (UPS) are most effectively reviewed through wiring diagrams and equipment manuals.

8.2.2.4 Review Documents for Expected Elements

As discussed in the previous section, it is important to create a checklist or table of expected elements for each document or policy area.[12] Expected elements are simply a listing of all the things a reasonable security engineer would expect to find in a complete document.

The expected elements should be used as a guideline for the assessor to ensure the physical document review process is complete. Missing elements are not necessarily something that would need to be remedied just an indication as to the quality of the evidence provided by the document. The assessor should consider if each document element is actually "expected" in the assessed organization's environment given their understanding of the organization's threat environment. The expected elements for all of the documents listed in Table 8.15 are provided in Tables 8.16 through 8.19. An assessor may use these tables to guide their document review. Note that all elements are not "required" but "expected." At this stage of data gathering, the assessor is collecting data on the access control policy to better enable the later stage of data analysis in determining the effectiveness of the control.

8.2.2.5 Reviewing Physical Safeguard Information Documents

In general, the model numbers, versions, and capabilities of physical safeguards should be documented, accurate, and up to date. Physical safeguard information can take several forms including equipment manuals, labels, or schematics, either online or hard copy. The security risk assessment team members should be able to accommodate the review of technical documents regarding the physical controls in any format in which it is available.

The security risk assessment team, or a member of the team, should review the available documents regarding the capability and currency of physical controls to determine the security implications of the equipment deployed. The objective of this review is to increase the security risk assessment team's understanding of the physical safeguards employed at the organization's site. Table 8.16 provides a baseline checklist for reviewing physical safeguard information manuals.

8.2.2.6   Reviewing Previous Physical Assessment Documents

The security risk assessment team, or a member of the team, should review the available physical security assessment reports to gain a perspective on the inputs to the current security risk assessment. The objective of this review is not to judge the completeness or correctness of past reviews, but to use information gathered during past efforts to double-check and improve the current effort. Table 8.17 provides a baseline checklist for reviewing previous physical security assessment reports.

8.2.2.7   Reviewing Building and Site Architecture Documents

The security risk assessment team, or a member of the team, should review the available building and site architecture to gain a layout of the physical site. There are two basic physical site diagrams: the exterior diagram (e.g., site plan) and the interior diagram (e.g., floor plan), see Figures 8.11 and 8.12 for example site plans and floor plans. The objective of this review is to provide an understanding of the current physical security boundary and controls. The assessment team should also be looking for potential vulnerabilities highlighted by these documents, but any potential vulnerability should be followed up with a physical inspection to ascertain the current physical security control implementation instead of what is on paper. Table 8.18 provides a baseline checklist for reviewing previous physical security assessment reports.

TABLE 8.17
Previous Physical Assessment Document Elements

Previous Physical Assessments

The assessor should review all available previous physical assessment reports to gain a better understanding of the physical controls in place, their previous vulnerabilities, and planned mitigations.

Control Area	Expected Elements	Discussion
Inspections	• Compliance	Inspections may be as simple as a check mark and initials or a longer report. Review available inspections for • Currency of inspection • Inspection findings • Planned mitigations
Audits	• Compliance	Audits will include material findings and recommendations. Review available physical security audits for • Audit findings • Planned mitigations
Physical assessment reports	• Controls • Capabilities • Findings	Physical assessment reports (or site surveys) will have a description of the physical environment, the surveyed controls, and include findings and recommendations. Review available inspections for • Description of physical security controls • Assessment findings and recommendations • Planned mitigations

Note: The physical safeguard information should be reviewed for configuration options, current settings, warnings, and cautions.

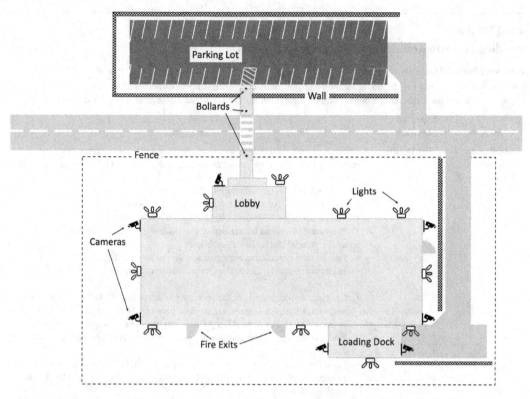

FIGURE 8.11 Site plan. The review of the exterior security controls of the assessed property can be aided by the use of a site plan. Site plans will typically show the property lines, the building outline, fences, gates, and building entrances and exits and may also include cameras, lights, and bollards.

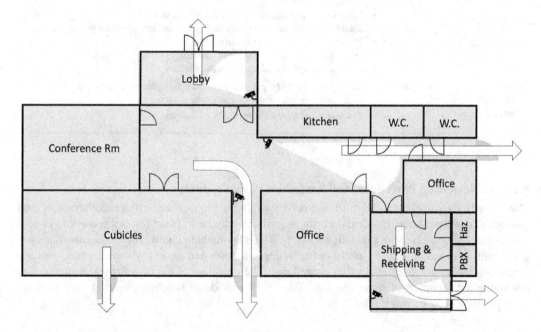

FIGURE 8.12 Floor plan. The review of the interior security controls of the assessed property can be aided by the use of a floor plan. Floor plans will typically show the building outline, building entrances and exits, evacuation routes, shelter in place areas, and may show hazardous storage, sensitive areas, and placement of cameras and motion sensors.

TABLE 8.18

Building and Site Architecture Document Elements

Previous Physical Assessments

The assessor should review all available building and site architecture documents to gain a better understanding of the physical site, the physical controls deployed, their location, and the identification of ingress, egress, and sensitive areas.

Control Area	Expected Elements	Discussion

Physical site diagram (exterior)	• Site Details	A physical site diagram should document the assessed property, gates, driveways, entrances, exits, and physical access and monitoring controls. Review physical site diagrams for:
		• Consistency in physical boundaries of the assessment
		• Identification and location of physical elements and controls
		  • Placement of gates, bollards, lights, motion sensors, and cameras
		  • Placement of critical infrastructure components (electric, water, gas, telephone)
		• Identify potential threats or vulnerabilities
		  • Low or high ground that may give an intruder an advantage
		  • Inadequate lighting, camera coverage, intrusion detection coverage, or guard coverage.
		  • Consider response times of the security protective force, when sensor activates, and what additional controls are in place between the breached sensor and the protected asset. For example, a good design would be a motion sensor in the yard leading up to a window, a window glass-break sensor, and a locked file cabinet.
		  • Look for opportunities for sabotage, such as critical components in public areas or unprotected critical components (e.g., lack of bollards, low light levels, and weak locks).

Floor plans (interior)	• Building Interior Details	Floor plans diagram the building interior walls, doors, sensitive areas (e.g., data center and telephone closet), and optionally the locations of physical security controls (e.g. cameras, motion sensors, fire extinguishers, and badge readers) Review floor plans for: • Identification and location of interior physical security controls • Identification and location public (e.g., lobby and cafeteria) and private areas • Identification and location sensitive areas • Data centers, equipment closets, hazardous storage • Evacuation routes and shelter in place locations
Emergency evaluation routes	• Emergency Procedures	Evacuation routes may be part of the available floor plans or may be a separate document. Review available evacuation routes for: • Evacuation routes and shelter in place locations

8.2.2.8 Reviewing Procedures and Procedure Work Products

The security risk assessment team should review available physical security procedures and their associated work products. Physical security procedures may be in place for any procedure or process in place to protect the organization's assets. This may include guard procedures, maintenance, and repair of physical security controls (including windows and doors), visitor control, package inspection, and emergency evaluation procedures. The objective of the review of procedures is to determine the adequacy of these controls. Table 8.19 provides a baseline checklist for reviewing these physical security procedures.

TABLE 8.19
Procedures and Procedure Work Products

Procedures and Procedure Work Products

The assessor should review all available physical security procedures and the work products of those procedures to gain a better understanding of the procedures in place to provide physical security protections and to review these procedures for expected elements.

Control Area	Expected Elements	Discussion
Physical security procedures	• Emergency procedures	*Fire evacuation procedures.* At a minimum, these procedures should have the following elements: • Fire and emergency drill training • Fire department notification • Evacuation procedures • Door-closing instructions • Fire extinguisher use instructions • Tarp use and storage instructions • Designated meeting areas • Free egress in emergency for all physical restrictions (e.g., metal detectors, mantraps, and doors). Depending on the location and organization type there should be emergency procedures for any other foreseeable emergency event such as: • Bomb threat • Active shooter • Weather emergency
	• Responsibilities	A physical security officer should have a very clear set of responsibilities. This may be a job description or be included in a standard operations manual. Job responsibilities should cover: • Change of shift duties (updating, reporting, logging) • Post-assignment • Emergency and law enforcement notification and assistance • Responsibilities (access control, material access, crowd control, patrol, key control, and surveillance)
	• Access control	These procedures cover company employees, and visitors and include the following: • Badge access procedures for employees • Visitor procedures including visitor log, identification checks, visitor badging, and required visitor agreements to be signed • Escort procedures for visitors
	• Material access	These procedures cover the removal of equipment from the site and include the following: • Package inspection • Property passes • Material removal procedures (permission, serial number recording, signature, log entry)
	• Crowd control	These procedures cover the rules of engagement for controlling any escalation of crowds that may occur on the property.

(Continued)

TABLE 8.19   *(Continued)*

Control Area	Expected Elements	Discussion
	• Patrol	These procedures cover the routine patrols and include the following: • Daytime vs. Nighttime patrols • Location of all shut off valves, electrical and alarm panels light switches, and emergency lighting. • Location and operation of emergency equipment (e.g., backup generators, first aid kits, fire alarms, hydrants, and extinguishers). • Patrol route, including check points and alternative routes, timing, and schedule • Patrol checklist (windows and doors, blind spots, equipment check, condition of alarms, damage to building, or security controls)
	• Key control	These procedures cover issuance and inventory of keys: • Key access control (lock box) • Key issuance, lost key procedures, and key replacement • End of shift key inventory • duties (monitors, recording review, reporting)
	• Surveillance	These procedures cover surveillance duties and include: • Surveillance monitoring • Equipment checks and reporting of damage or malfunction • Review of previous surveillance • Surveillance-based reporting requirements
Guard logs	• Contents	• Guard logs may be reviewed to provide evidence that guard procedures are followed. A sample of logs may be reviewed for expected elements based on specific procedures for the organization. • If any events (e.g., suspicious vehicle and alarm) or damaged controls (e.g., broken lock and burnt out light) were noticed by the assessment team, the logs may be reviewed to ensure that the events or maintenance requests were noted in the guard logs.
Visitor logs	• Contents	• Visitor logs may be reviewed to provide evidence that visitor control procedures are followed. Look for missing elements in the visitor log such as signatures, time out, or badge number issued.
Incident reports	• Recent incidents	• Guard incident reports may be reviewed to provide the assessment team with an understanding of the existing threats to the organization. Look for threat types (e.g., attempted break-ins and equipment theft) and frequency of occurrence. • The review of incident reports can also provide the assessment team with evidence of the guard procedures being followed. Review the incident reports for completeness and adherence to the guard procedures. • Review incident reports looking for frequency of incidents and possible weaknesses in security controls. • Review logs of alarm reporting devices and alarm plots. Look for large nuisance rates.
Control testing	• Testing frequency and results	• Review the control testing schedules and look for inadequate testing depth, rigor, or frequency. • Review test results and look for remaining vulnerabilities.
Badge disposition records	• Contents	• Look for inaccurate records and evidence of lax procedures, for example, missing badges, visitors who did not check out. • Look for active badges against a list of terminated employees. • Look for evidence of abundance of lost badges

Note: The physical security work products such as visitor logs and incident reports should be reviewed to give the team an indication of the relative threat levels and compliance with established procedures.

8.2.3 INTERVIEW PHYSICAL PERSONNEL

Members of the security risk assessment team should discuss the effectiveness of physical security mechanisms with key members of the physical security staff. Key members may include the head of facilities, members of the security force, and others involved in the selection, operation, or maintenance of physical security controls.

8.2.3.1 Physical Security Interview Topics

Within the physical security controls area, the security risk assessment team will find that interviews should provide a detailed understanding of the physical security safeguards employed at the site.

8.2.3.2 Physical Security Interview Subjects

The security risk assessment team should interview the facilities personnel best able to provide information required to understand the physical safeguards. The selection of interview subjects will depend on who has the responsibility for the safeguards in question. All questions will be directed to physical security staff.

8.2.3.3 Physical Security Interview Questions

Prior to any interview, the security risk assessment team should review the available documents and prepare questions based on the information provided or concerns that surfaced during the document review. If several members of the security risk assessment team were responsible for reviewing the documents, these members should get together to create a list of questions they have on the physical security documents.

8.2.3.3.1 Utilities Interview Questions

The utilities questions in Table 8.20 should be asked of facilities personnel in charge of various physical security controls. The questions cover utilities and alarms. If the organization has not implemented one or more of these controls, that section of the interview can be skipped, as it is not applicable.

8.2.3.3.2 Physical Security Procedures Interview Questions

The physical security procedures questions in Table 8.21 should be asked to facilities personnel in charge of various physical security controls. The questions cover utilities and alarms. If the organization has not implemented one or more of these controls, that section of the interview can be skipped, as it is not applicable.

8.2.4 INSPECT PHYSICAL SECURITY CONTROLS

Data gathering for physical security controls also involves inspecting physical security controls. Recall that inspection differs from testing, in that inspection is performed when testing is inappropriate or infeasible. For almost all physical safeguards, testing is inappropriate. Inspection involves the review of the security control and such security control aspects as configuration or arrangements.

For the most part, the approach for performing a physical security control inspection includes the listing of the security controls under review, verifying information gathered, determining vulnerabilities, and documenting the results. Each of these phases is discussed within the context of physical data gathering.

8.2.4.1 Listing Physical Security Controls

The relevant physical security controls to be inspected include only those that lend themselves to inspection. Many physical security controls are actively protecting critical assets, and it would be difficult to test them without interrupting operations. However, the security risk assessment team can still gain valuable information based on a carefully planned inspection of critical elements.

TABLE 8.20
Physical Security Controls Review Interview Guideline

Objective	Subtopic	Question
Increase knowledge of physical safeguards deployed within the organization	Utilities	• *Testing.* How often are these tested? How well have they performed in the tests? • *Capacity.* Has capacity significantly increased since the equipment was procured? • *Fuel.* How much fuel do you have on-site? How long can the generators run on that fuel? What is your process for obtaining more fuel?
	Alarms	• *Components.* Is there an alarm system? How many zones of protection? Where are the annunciating units? • *Coverage.* Are there any areas not covered by the alarm? • *Testing.* How often is the alarm system inspected and tested? • *Response.* Who responds to the alarm? What procedures do they follow? • *Protection.* Does the alarm have tamper-proof protection? Does the system have weather-proof protection? Does the system have its own circuit? Backup power? Line supervision? • *Maintenance.* Who maintains the equipment? • *Records.* Are records kept on all alarms (time, date, location, resolution)? Is there a specific part of the alarm system that has a high nuisance rate?

Note: The interviewer should compile a list of questions to ask the responsible party to ensure that the security risk assessment team has a clear understanding of the physical safeguards.

In addition to the review of physical security documents and the interview of key personnel, the security risk assessment team can survey the organization's premises to further determine the existing controls present. Basic steps in a physical security survey are as follows:

- Fence Line—Survey the site perimeter, noting fence lines. Include details such as type of fence, condition, number of openings, and manned and unmanned posts.
- Parking Area—Survey the outside parking area. Include details such as area enclosures, parking lot controls, and manned and unmanned posts.
- Building Perimeter—Survey the building perimeter. Include details such as pedestrian and vehicular entrances and access controls. Check all doors and note how they are secured. Check the ground floor and basement windows or ventilation grills, manholes, and fire escapes. How is each of these controlled?
- Building Interior—Start at either the top floor or the bottom floor. Note fire alarm systems and devices. Include details such as number and type. Check the telephone and electrical closets. Are they locked? Note any alarms. Include details such as the type, number, and location. Determine the location of manned posts and times manned. Determine guards' shifts and rotation procedures.

Physical controls within the building are numerous and can be complex. Inspection procedures for these interior controls are discussed in more detail in Table 8.22.

TABLE 8.21

Physical Security Procedures Interview Guideline

Objective	Subtopic	Question
Increase knowledge of physical safeguards deployed within the organization	Asset tracking and control	• *Asset tracking.* Are hardware assets (e.g., servers, telephones, laptops, and projectors) tracked in an asset database? Are they signed out when needed offsite? • *Portable assets.* Are portable assets (e.g., laptops and projectors) physically secure to protect from removal? • *Property control.* Is there a mechanism for property control (bringing and removing laptops from the site)?
	Visitor control	• *Visitor control procedures.* What are the procedures for visitor control? Are logs kept? • *Escort procedures.* What are the procedures for escorting?
	Security protective force	• *Duties.* What are the duties of the security force? Is there a job description? Is there a manual? Is there a daily/nightly checklist?

Note: The interviewer should compile a list of questions to ask the responsible party to ensure that the security risk assessment team has a clear understanding of the physical safeguards.

SIDEBAR 8.4   PHYSICAL SECURITY WALK-THROUGH

A physical walk-through was once described as "walk around and look for stuff." Even though this description is rather informal and could be viewed as treating the technique lightly, this is not how it was intended. If you ever witness someone who is very good at the physical security walk-through, it will seem as if he simply "walks around and looks for stuff," but he seems to notice everything. This is because he is going through a complex thought process in his head when analyzing the presence, condition, or absence of security mechanisms and the behavior of the organization through observation. This thought process is partly checklist and partly intuition based on experience.

In advising the reader on how to perform effective physical walk-throughs, checklists can be devised, but intuition must be learned on your own. The approach used in this book—to empower the reader to be a more effective security risk assessment engineer—is to expose the reader to both a proposed checklist and examples of results derived from pure intuition. The checklist presented here provides a logical dissection of physical security measures and essential elements and required aspects of those measures. Also included in this section are several examples of "things that were noticed" by experienced security engineers through their ability of perception. It is believed the exposure of these "things" will assist readers in developing their own intuition, but nothing compares to experience.

A physical security walk-through is an inspection through observation of the physical security access controls. In most cases, a physical security walk-through can be accomplished by one or two individuals in less than a single day. The walk-through itself is simply the gathering of information. This information must still be documented, assessed, and presented. However, a physical security walk-through adds a small amount of effort and cost to a security risk assessment and should be heavily considered for all security risk assessments.

TABLE 8.22

Physical Safeguards Inspection Guideline (Power, Fire, and Lighting)

Physical Control	Safeguard Inspection
Power	• *Monitor power fluctuations.* A strip chart recorder should be in place to log internal transients.
	• *Isolate power to critical systems.* Ensure that the computer room distribution panels are directly connected to primary feeder panels and do not share step-down transformers with other loads, especially high-horsepower motors.
	• *Clearly mark controls.* Both the distribution panel and the master control switch should be clearly marked. The master control switch (turns off all power) should be located near the room entrance but should be protected against accidental engagement.
	• *Protect power distribution rooms.* Rooms that house power distribution equipment should be physically protected from unauthorized personnel.
	• *Protect outdoor utilities.* Any elements of the power system that are housed outside the building should be protected. Transformer pods should be within locked rooms. Transformer pods and utility poles should be protected by barriers to prevent accidental or deliberate destruction.
	• *Protect master control switch.* The switch that shuts off all power should be clearly visible but protected (e.g., hinged cover).
Handheld fire extinguisher	• *Monthly inspection.* Check that fire extinguishers have recent inspections and are full. Extinguishers should be inspected monthly and tested annually.
	• *Placement.* Fire extinguishers should be placed within 50 feet of each piece of equipment and located near the entrance to the room.
	• *Marked location.* The location of the fire extinguishers should be clearly marked (e.g., red paint on the wall or top of column).
	• *Size.* Fire extinguishers should be 2.5-gallon water extinguishers or 15-lb CO_2 extinguishers. Smaller handheld extinguishers should be available if there is a concern about the ability of some occupants to lift larger extinguishers.
	• *Fire blanket.* A fire blanket for small kitchen fires or humans should be available in appropriate areas.
Fire resistant building construction	• *Penetrations.* When the building walls are penetrated by pipes, ducts, or conduit, the penetration must be sealed with a material that provides equal or better fire resistance.
	• *Walls and partitions.* Interior firewalls and partitions should be erected to slow the spread of smoke and fire in the building.
	• *Stairwells.* Stairwells should be fire rated and designed to reduce the spread of fire and smoke.
	• *Ducts.* Air-handling ducts should be fitted with shutters or dampers that are activated by the smoke and fire detection equipment to reduce the spread of smoke throughout the building (e.g., switch to outside air only).
	• *Material.* Building material such as paint and carpet should be low flame spreading.

(Continued)

TABLE 8.22 *(Continued)*

Physical Control	Safeguard Inspection
Storage of combustibles	• Separate storage, in addition to the inspection elements discussed in the previous item, "Fire resistant building construction."
Fire detectors	• *Smoke detectors.* All smoke detectors should be in good working order, i.e., firmly attached to ceiling or wall near ceiling, and with good batteries.
	• *Detector range.* All detectors (smoke, heat, flame, etc.) should be deployed in a manner that conforms to their specifications. For example, VESDA devices typically operate within an effective range of 5,000–20,000 square feet, with a rate of rise of 5,000 square feet; smoke detectors typically operate within a range of only 200 square feet.
	• *Detector location.* Smoke and heat detectors' ability to detect fire is based on the flow of air to the detector. Improperly placed detectors (e.g., not within 8 inches of the ceiling or near exit doors) are less effective than fire detectors placed on the ceiling or in central locations.
	• *Detector types.* Different fires behave differently; some smolder, others ignite quickly. All types of fire detectors should be centrally located or near potential sources of fire.
	• *Closed spaces.* Certain closed spaces such as telephone closets, raised floors, and hung ceilings could harbor a fire unnoticed in the early stages. These areas require dedicated fire detectors because electrical shorts are a major source of fire.
Water pipes	• *No water over computer room.* Water used for plumbing and drains should not be routed over the computer room or other sensitive areas.
	• *Shutoff valves.* All water pipes, including fire suppression pipes, should have shutoff valves properly placed and marked. These valves are used to limit the damage of an accidental leak or pipe burst.
	• *Avoid "wet columns."* All buildings must route plumbing pipes up and down floors somehow. Some buildings route these pipes near support columns and enclose the whole column. These columns are also called risers or wet columns. If possible, the computer room or other rooms with sensitive equipment should not contain these risers. Risers can be identified because they are generally thicker than other columns to allow room for the pipes.
	• *Supply of plastic sheeting.* Keep a supply of plastic sheeting handy. It can be used to cover equipment in the case of a fire or accidental leakage or pipe burst. Many insurance policies require that a supply of plastic sheeting be kept nearby.
Raised floors	• *Raised electric boxes.* Electrical boxes below raised flooring should be raised to a minimum of 8 inches off the floor.
	• *Unbroken conduit.* Conduit used beneath raised flooring should be a single piece or unbroken.
	• *Water detector.* Organizations should consider the use of water detectors underneath raised flooring to detect water in these closed areas.
	• *Drains.* The hard slab flooring beneath raised flooring should have drains about every 18 feet. These drains need to be plumbed correctly to ensure that drainage always flow away, i.e., positive drains.

(Continued)

TABLE 8.22 *(Continued)*

Physical Control	Safeguard Inspection
Natural hazard protection	• *Drains.* Low-lying areas that receive runoff, also called sumps, need to have adequate drainage to move excess water away fast enough so that the sump does not overflow. These drains should be fitted with check valves that ensure the water flows in only one way: out.
	• *Sump pumps.* In times of excess runoff, the drains within a sump may be inadequate to remove the excess water. A sump pump (or several sump pumps) is a good safeguard to keep the area clear of water and to prevent the excess water from overflowing the sump and damaging other parts of the building. The sump pump should have gasoline-driven motors, and a supply of gasoline should be available nearby.
	• *Levees, curbs, walls.* These building structures can divert or even hold back floodwaters to a limited degree. Organizations with buildings located within a floodplain should consider the construction of permanent flood protection systems.
	• *Sandbags.* In the event of an impending flood, sandbags can be used to create an emergency levee, raise an existing levee, or fill the gaps in permanent flood protection systems. Organizations should keep a supply of sandbags, sand, and filling devices (shovels) nearby in case of such an emergency.[13]
	• *Duct tape.* The handyman's best friend, duct tape, can come in handy in many situations. During a potential flood emergency, duct tape can be used to seal door frames. This is an extremely inexpensive and easy-to-implement safeguard.
Lighting	• *Building.* Buildings should be illuminated at a minimum of 1-foot candle. Lighting should be to a height of 8 feet above grade level or top of window or door, whichever is greater. The lighting should not extend to above the illuminated structure.
	• *Fence line.* The fence line should be illuminated at a minimum of 1-foot candle. Lighting should be controlled by motion sensors located 5 feet inside the fence line. Such a system should supply illumination only upon the detection of an intruder.
	• *Parking lot.* The parking lot should be illuminated at a minimum of 1-foot candle. Lights should be placed to avoid dark patches through overlapping cones of light.
	• *Pedestrian walkway.* The walkway should be illuminated at a minimum of 3-foot candles.
	• *Parking structure.* The parking structure should be illuminated at a minimum of 5-foot candles.
	• *Loading docks.* Loading docks should be illuminated at a minimum of 3-foot candles and a maximum of 5-foot candles. Lighting should be 25 feet out from the building.
	• *Guard route.* The route should be illuminated at a maximum of 0.5-foot candles. It is important to avoid over illumination, which can decrease the guard's ability to see clearly at night.

Note: The security risk assessment team should be prepared to inspect physical security devices to determine the effectiveness of physical safeguards. Physical security safeguard inspection is unique, in that many inspection elements are focused on determining the presence of a safeguard and not always on inspecting a specific safeguard for the correct configuration and working order. Of course, all safeguards should be visibly inspected and determined to be in good working order.

8.2.4.2   Verify Information Gathered

Information gathered regarding physical security controls should be confirmed through the inspection process. Team members should use various methods to confirm the existence of each of these security controls.

8.2.4.2.1   Logs, Records, and Audit Files

The security risk assessment team should review a sample of documents and other evidence that indicates the effectiveness and operation of physical security controls. Specifically, the team can ask to see the logs, log tapes, records, reports, and audit files covering the area and time of specific events they suspect or know have happened. For example, ask to see records of the team's badges being issued.

The team should also review temperature and humidity logs (e.g., tapes). The assessors should look for periods outside the ideal range. The ideal ranges are typically as follows:

- Temperature (computer room): 70°F–74°F (21°C–23°C)
- Humidity (computer room): 40–60% RH.

8.2.4.2.2   Perimeter Security

The goal of perimeter security is access control and employee safety. Access control is implemented through a series of security mechanisms to permit only authorized users to gain physical access to the building. Table 8.23 provides some guidance to the security risk assessment team for inspecting perimeter access control to determine the strength of the physical access controls. The security risk assessment team is encouraged to review the table and add or modify table elements to suit its own needs and experiences.

Of course, only those controls actually implemented by the organization can be inspected. The list of physical security controls to be reviewed for a specific organization comprises any of the controls that the organization stated are in place or that are observed by the security risk assessment team. Statements regarding physical controls in place could have come from interviews or been provided as part of the document review process. The team should obtain a point of contact for each of these controls and should be escorted for many of the inspections, because these controls safeguard critical business functions.

8.2.4.3   Determine Physical Vulnerabilities

During inspection of the physical security controls, the security risk assessment team should look for vulnerabilities. The inspection process of these controls involves the recognition of ineffective mechanisms, configurations, or processes. The questions and tips within the previous section guide the security risk assessment team toward these vulnerabilities. For example, when inspecting the badge-issuing process log features for adequate and accurate information being captured, stored, and retrieved when needed, a vulnerability exists if the team determines that the log process creates confusion or does not record critical information (e.g., driver's license number, point of contact, badge number, and type of access granted).

8.2.4.4   Document and Review Physical Findings

As with all findings, the security risk assessment team must be sure to carefully record their findings in the area of physical controls through inspection. The team should include dates, evidence, team member names, and the vulnerabilities observed. These findings must be reviewed with the entire team and with the point of contact for the control to give that person an opportunity to clarify any misunderstandings.

TABLE 8.23

Physical Safeguards Inspection Guideline (Barriers)

Physical Control	Claim	Inspection Elements
Property line	• Property line has the appropriate number and type of controls • Controls are in good repair	• *Fences.* Look for jump points (anything that can be used to circumvent property fence lines), for example, depressions in the earth, tunnels, pipelines, erosion, missing fence panels, trees or trash receptacle near the fence line, insecure attachment to poles, vegetation providing cover, or bent tops of fence wire. • *Fence heights.* Fences should be an appropriate height for the intended purpose. Use the following as a guide: • *Property demarcation:* 3–4 feet • *Barrier:* 6–7 feet • *Serious barrier:* 8 feet with three strands of barbed wire • *Gates.* Ensure that gates work and leave no gaps large enough for a person to fit through. • *Cameras.* Look for adequate coverage, especially for parking lots and all entrances. Adequate coverage includes camera existence, placement and quality and capture of image (lighting, focus, granularity, and frames per second [fps]).
Building perimeter	• Building perimeter has the appropriate number and type of controls • Controls are in good repair	• *Windows.* Look for broken or unlocked windows. • *Skylights.* Look for unsecured skylights. • *Doors.* Look for unlocked doors, specifically, loading docks and doors near smoking lounges. Look for telltale signs that controlled-access doors are held open. • *Lighting.* Look for consistent and adequate lighting in parking lots, walkways, perimeter walls, fence lines, and perimeter doors.
Vehicle barriers	• Vehicle barriers are appropriately placed • Barriers are in good repair	• *Bollard placement.* Vehicle barriers (bollards) should be placed in areas requiring protection of unauthorized vehicles, for example, power transmission boxes, utility sheds, pedestrian entrances. • *Bollard condition.* Visually inspect bollards to ensure that they are in good repair.

Note: The security risk assessment team should be prepared to inspect physical security devices to determine the effectiveness of physical safeguards. Physical security safeguard inspection is unique, in that many inspection elements are focused on determining the presence of a safeguard and not always on inspecting a specific safeguard for the correct configuration and working order. Of course, all safeguards should be visibly inspected and determined to be in good working order.

8.2.5 Observe Physical Personnel Behavior

The process of gathering data through observation is a subtle one. With a few exceptions, this process is passive and depends on team members being aware of the organization's policies, procedures, and safeguards, while keeping an eye out for opportunities to confirm or disprove the organization's effective use of physical safeguards. However, some observations can be active in nature, for example, placing an access badge in your pocket instead of wearing it. More experienced team members will find observation to be second nature and a side effect of being on-site.

The observation of physical security controls will include a review of internal security:

- Controlled Access—Controlling access to the building through well-defined, monitored, and defended entrances allows for effective protection of the organization's assets. The building entrances should have the appropriate number and type of controls.
- Shared Access—When a building is shared by multiple tenants, it is not always possible to provide access controls at the building entrance. Special consideration must be given to environments that share building access or that have public access to the building.
- Internal Access Controls—The goal of internal access controls is to provide additional access control among authorized personnel. Not all personnel authorized to be on the premises are authorized to be everywhere on the premises. For example, visitors to the building must be escorted and cannot enter designated sensitive areas. Access control is implemented through designation of controlled areas, internal access controls, internal monitoring controls, and work area controls.
  - Controlled Areas—Controlled areas are any areas that are not open to the general employees. These areas are restricted to a limited set of personnel who perform a specific function. Examples of controlled areas include telephone closets, computer rooms, shipping and receiving, secure compartmented information facilities (SCIF), and equipment rooms. When reviewing the controls in a controlled area, the security risk assessment team member should use judgment as to the effectiveness of the controls. For example, a padlock on an SCIF is a weak control because it could be easily defeated with a single blow of a hammer.[14]
  - Internal Access Controls—Internal areas are areas that are not open to the general public. These areas are restricted to employees and guests. Examples of internal areas include offices, workspace, and internal meeting rooms. When reviewing the access controls in an internal area, the security risk assessment team member should determine the effectiveness of the existing controls through test and observation.
  - Internal Monitoring Controls—Most governmental or corporate buildings have a variety of internal controls—for example, heat, humidity, intrusion—that are monitored. The effective monitoring of these alarms can be an important element of an organization's security posture.
- Work Areas—The protection of sensitive information is susceptible to bad user habits. An observation of work areas can reveal the effectiveness of awareness training and the security culture within the organization.

With a little guidance and teamwork, these observations can be recorded from most team members and add additional data points to the data gathering process. Table 8.24 provides some guidance to the security risk assessment team for observing the behavior of the organization's staff to determine the strength of some of the physical safeguards. The security risk assessment team is encouraged to review Table 8.24 and add or modify table elements to suit its own needs and experiences.

8.2.6 Test Physical Security Safeguards

The last phase of data gathering for physical security safeguards in the RIIOT method is testing. Testing of physical security safeguards is the process of invoking conditions that test physical safeguards against their intended security functions. This type of data gathering provides excellent insight into the effectiveness of the controls.

The physical safeguards that lend themselves to testing are limited to doors and locks and physical intrusion detection. An approach for testing each of these controls is presented below. The security risk assessment team is encouraged to adopt, modify, or add to these test methods.

TABLE 8.24
Physical Safeguards Observation Guideline

Physical Control	Claim	Observation Test or Procedure Check
Controlled access	Building entrances and exits have the appropriate number and type of controls	• *Entrances.* Are all entrances to the controlled area protected? • *Exits.* Are exits locked and are locks in good repair/ Check each exit door, especially those near outside employee break areas or areas that show signs of smoking, worn paths, or may be closer exists to employee parking.
	Controls are in good repair	• *Walls.* Are there other ways into the controlled area, for example, false ceilings, large vents, or false floors?
		• *Doors.* Look for unlocked doors. Are the doors properly and consistently locked? Specifically, in closets and areas where it is difficult to control the temperature. Look for telltale signs that controlled-access doors are held open. Is there an alarm for doors held open? Is there an access log?
		• *Door hardware.* Are the hinges for the doors on the inside of the controlled area? Are the door bolts shielded?
		• *Telephone closets.* Are modem numbers recorded? Are the modems always on?
Shared access	There are no gaps in the security opened up by sharing access to the building	• Are there any other people who can gain access to the controlled area, for example, shared access with other tenants? • Do others with access follow the same procedures?
Internal access controls	There is an appropriate number of building internal controls	• *Visitor controls.* Did you sign a visitor's form advising you of the procedures for visitors? Do employees enforce escort procedures? Are visitors challenged?
	Controls are in good repair	• *Badge control.* Is there unlocked or unprotected badge storage? • *Manned posts.* Determine location of manned posts and times manned. • *Public areas.* Are there any places to tap into the network or use the phone unnoticed? Are there any office computers or workstations in the area? Are they locked?
Internal monitoring controls	Physical location has the appropriate number and type of internal controls.	• Start at the top or bottom floor. Note fire alarm systems and devices. Record the number and type of each device.
	Physical location is adequately monitored	• Note any other alarm type, location, and number of devices (e.g., heat, humidity, and intrusion). • Determine location of monitoring facility. What alarms are being monitored and at what times?

(Continued)

TABLE 8.24   *(Continued)*

Physical Control	Claim	Observation Test or Procedure Check
Work areas	Sensitive data are always secured	• *Recorded passwords.* Casually look for passwords on "sticky notes" under phones and keyboards, in index files, and on various papers posted in plain view in individual work areas. Many users will clearly post their passwords on sticky notes stuck to their monitor, while others will attempt to hide or encode them by placing them on the last page of their calendar or writing them backward under their keyboard. Regardless of how they are hidden, they are typically within plain view or an arm's reach. • *Trash receptacles.* Look in several trash cans to see if sensitive information may have been improperly disposed. Focus on high-probability areas such as trash cans near fax machines, near meeting rooms, and in executive assistant areas. • *Desktops.* Look for papers or recordable media that may contain sensitive information that may be unsecured.

Note: The security risk assessment team should be prepared to observe the behavior of the security staff, key personnel, and general employee population to check the effectiveness of physical safeguards.

8.2.6.1   Doors and Locks

Testing procedures for doors and locks require that the security risk assessment team perform activities that attempt to bypass the blocking controls in place. The areas protected by these doors and locks are likely to be sensitive areas. It is for this reason that the security risk assessment team leader must be sure to gain permission from the organization to test such controls. The tests listed in Table 8.25 should be attempted to gain a minimum level of confidence that the doors and locks are effective.

8.2.6.2   Intrusion Detection

Testing procedures for physical intrusion detection controls require that the security risk assessment team perform activities that attempt to bypass or defeat intrusion detection controls. For physical intrusion detection systems, the security risk assessment team may consider testing the installed system through the imitation of a nuisance alarm (e.g., animals and windblown objects) or through the testing of known vulnerabilities of physical intrusion detection systems. Below is an introduction to the terms and techniques utilized in testing physical intrusion detection systems.

- Improper installation—Many intrusion detection sensors can be rendered useless if installed improperly. Improper installation includes mounting sensor on walls opposite hallway (instead of alongside), mounting too far away from protected object, or mounting in area affected by nuisance alarm sources such as vibrating machinery.
- Ambient Noises—If the area around the sensor is subject to noises that may set off the sensor such as industrial background noises, hissing pipes, ringing phones, or impact noises, the sensor may be triggered outside of actual intrusion events.
- General Bypass Terms—If the materials or earth near the protected object may be breached the sensor protections may be bypassed, see Figure 8.13. Bypass terms include:
  - Tunneling—Digging under the obstructions to bypass the sensor.
  - Planking (or Bridging)—Using a solid plank to bridge over the sensor.
  - Jumping—Leaping over the sensor or protected obstruction.
- Slow Movement—Many motion sensors are equipped with LEDs that light up when the motion sensor detects movement. If motion sensors are so equipped, the assessors can use this

TABLE 8.25
Doors and Locks Testing Guideline

Technical Control	Claim	Observation Test or Procedure Check
Door and locks	Doors and locks are in good working order	• *Timed closure test.* Open the door to a 90° angle and time how long it takes to close. A rule of thumb is that 6 to 8 seconds is reasonable. Doors that close more slowly are susceptible to tailgating.
	Doors and locks are adequately protected	• *Closing latch test.* Open door just 1 inch. Let go and witness if the door closes shut or stays open owing to the friction or pressure of the latch.
		• *Protected latch test.* Inspect door to determine if the door latch is exposed to the outside. This basically means there is a lack of shielding between the door frame and the door near the door handle. If latch is exposed, attempt to defeat the mechanism through the use of a credit card, butter knife, or other tool.
		• *Motion sensor activated doors.* Attempt to circumvent door lock through unprotected gaps in the door. Methods include sliding a coat hanger with a piece of foil on the end through the door gap. The motion and heat of the foil could trip the motion sensor to open the door as if someone from the inside was approaching.
Badge access	Doors controlled by badge access provide adequate protection	• *Failed access.* Test for audit or alarm upon successive failed accesses.
		• *Tailgating.* Test for prevention of tailgating through supervision or mantraps. Will attempts be prevented or detected?
		• *Tampering.* Test (if appropriate) for detection of tampering through line supervision or monitoring.
		• *Power loss.* Test (if appropriate) documented settings for controlled access to determine disposition (i.e., fail secure, fail safe, fail soft) upon power loss.
		• *Shoulder surfing.* Test to determine if the PIN can be observed without being noticed.

Note: The security risk assessment team should be prepared to test the functioning and strength of doors and locks to check the effectiveness of these physical safeguards.

signal as a method of testing for areas without coverage and the success of defeat tests. The typical motion sensor test is called the "four-step method." The tester takes four consecutive steps in single direction within 1 second per step. This is called a "trial," and the sensor should trip in three out of four trials. Trials are to be taken with 3–5 second rests in between each and started in a new direction.

• Camouflage—Intruder wears colors very similar to background to lessen the detectable differences from one frame to the next in video motion detection, see Figure 8.14.
• Defeat magnet—A reed switch is a door alarm held in an open state by an internal door magnet. When the door opens the spring-loaded reed (no longer held down by the internal door magnet rises to contact the alarm wire thus sounding an alarm. These simple intrusion detection sensors can be defeated by placing a strong magnet below the door frame to act as the internal door magnet, even when the door is opened thus defeating the reed switch, see Figure 8.15.

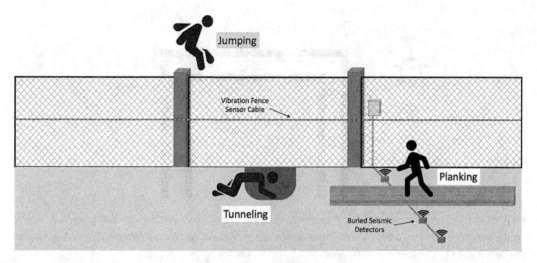

FIGURE 8.13 Bypass methods. Physical intrusion detection sensors may be bypassed in a variety of ways. Jumping, planking, and tunneling are rather effective bypasses.

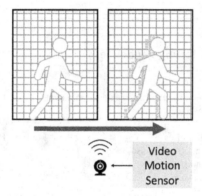

FIGURE 8.14 Camouflaged motion. Intruders can wear colors similar to the background of the protected area to lessen their chance of detection. The video motion sensor has a threshold for the number of detected changes allowed to occur without sounding an alarm.

- Shimming—Placing a thin object (a shim) between the protected object and the pressure switch.

In an effort to provide a more complete knowledge base, Table 8.26 provides many possible tests for these controls. The security risk assessment team is expected to review these tests and select the appropriate test for the required coverage and rigor of their specific security risk assessment.

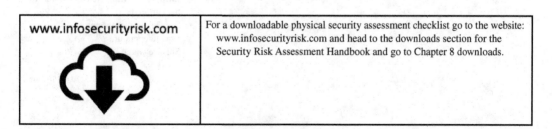

www.infosecurityrisk.com

For a downloadable physical security assessment checklist go to the website: www.infosecurityrisk.com and head to the downloads section for the Security Risk Assessment Handbook and go to Chapter 8 downloads.

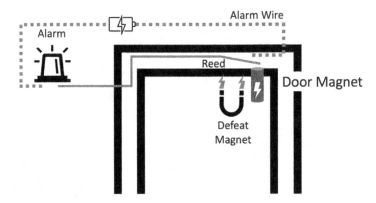

FIGURE 8.15   Defeat magnet. A defeat magnet may be used to bypass a reed switch door protection. A reed switch has a spring-loaded reed held away from an alarm wire with an internal door magnet. The defeat magnet can hold the reed away from the alarm wire even if the door is open.

TABLE 8.26
Physical Intrusion Detection Testing Guideline

Exterior Sensors	Nuisance Alarms	Vulnerable to
Structural vibration	• Mounting on walls exposed to external vibration • Vibrating machinery	• Bypass coverage area • Persistent random false alarms
Glass-break	• Sharp impact noises • Industrial background noise	• Bypass by cutting glass • Sound muffling
Passive ultrasonic	• HVAC air movement • Ringing telephone • Hissing pipes	• Sounds outside of range (e.g., drilling)
Balanced magnetic switches (BMS)	• Vibration • Improper installation • Poorly fitted doors and windows • Extreme hot and cold (expansion and contraction)	• Bypass protected opening • Line tampering • Cut door or window and hold actuating magnet
Grid wire	None	• Bypass protected wall • Line tampering
Monostatic microwave	• Movement beyond detection area (microwaves penetrate standard walls and glass) • Fluorescent lights	• Bypass coverage area • Slow movement • Metal obstacles
Passive infrared (PIR)	• Sunlight-heated objects • Target masking • Overheated room	• Bypass coverage area • Obstacles
Video motion	• Internal lights	• Very slow motion • Intruders wearing clothes similar to background
Capacitance	• Rodents	• Control unit tampering • Low temperature • Surface water

(Continued)

TABLE 8.26   *(Continued)*

Exterior Sensors	Nuisance Alarms	Vulnerable to
Pressure mat	• Nearby vibrating machinery	• Bypass (step over)
		• Planking over
Pressure switch	• Accidental object movement	• Shimming
Duress alarm	• Accidental alarms	• Surprise and defeat
Strain-sensitive cable (e.g., taut wire)	• Lightning • Vegetation • Animals • Vibrations (railroad, highway)	• Tunneling • Bridging
Fiber-optic cable	• Vegetation • Animals • Vibrations (railroad, highway)	• Tunneling • Bridging
Electric field	• Vegetation • Animals	• Tunneling • Bridging
Capacitance proximity	• Birds • Vegetation	• Tunneling • Bridging
Buried line	• Lightning • Low levels of seismic activity	• Sidewalks and roads • Frozen ground • Bridging
Monostatic microwave	• Movement beyond detection area (microwaves penetrate standard walls and glass)	• Tunneling • Bridging • Slow movement • Uneven terrain • Metal obstacles
Bistatic microwave	• Movement beyond detection area (microwaves penetrate standard walls and glass) • Fluorescent lights	• Tunneling • Bridging • Slow movement • Uneven terrain • Metal obstacles
Infrared	• Windblown objects • Sunlight-heated objects • Target masking	• Tunneling • Bridging • Uneven terrain • Obstacles • Heavy snow, fog, rain • Warm weather
Video motion	• Headlights, sunlight, sunset • Birds and animals • Windblown objects • Large bushes and trees • Cloud movement and shadows • Severe weather	• Very slow motion • Camouflage

Note: Susceptible physical intrusion detection systems are those that may be bypassed easily through various means such as magnet substitution or removal for balance magnetic switches, wearing dark clothing to fool CCTVs, and walking slowly to fool motion sensors.

EXERCISES

1. Activity. Perform a physical walk-through of a sensitive area such as a data center in your organization or school. See how many vulnerabilities you can find just through observation. Compare what you find with another team in the class. (Be sure to obtain permission from the data center manager or appropriate business unit manager.)
2. Consider the most likely natural hazards in your geographic region.
   a. What are the most likely natural threats?
   b. Has your school prepared you to deal with them?
   c. Can you locate emergency evacuation maps?
   d. Can you identify the closest safe room?
3. Your data center has recently been able to save significant floor space due to the implementation of blade servers and virtualization. A significant portion of the data center has been reallocated to a training center by adding a wall (true floor to true ceiling) and creating additional office space.
   a. What controls would be affected by this reconfiguration?
   b. How would you ensure that security has been preserved?
   c. What RIIOT data gathering methods would you perform on each of these controls?
4. Where would you locate a disaster recovery site if the main site was in the following locations:
   a. San Jose, California
   b. New York City
   c. Chicago, Illinois
   d. Singapore
   e. Your present location
5. Why would a data center have both VESDA devices and traditional smoke detectors?
6. How would you determine if a facility had adequate exterior lighting? Describe your process.

NOTES

1 For those who are experts in this field or have checklists they are comfortable with, you may skip this section without losing any context for the rest of the chapter.
2 Although it is still an area of research, development has begun on some devices that can detect the noise of a fire. As fires of different fuel types put out different sounds, these devices can detect those sounds and signal the presence and type of fire. These devices are limited to solid-fuel fires only.
3 Inergen is a registered trademark of the Tyco Fire Products LP.
4 FE-13 is a trademark of Chemours.
5 FM-200 is a registered trademark of the Chemours.
6 Novec 1230 is a trademark of 3M Company.
7 These threat actions are described in greater detail (additional examples) in Chapter 5.
8 All objects with a temperature above absolute zero generate thermal energy. Humans generate between 7 and 14 microns. Passive infrared (PIR) motion sensors typically operate within the 4- to 20-micron IR wavelength.
9 These are only the most popular biometrics in use today. Other biometric technologies currently being researched include gait (or walk), vein patterns, DNA, and even odor.
10 CER values can range from near zero to 50%. These values are difficult to obtain because there seems to be no freely available test data on a variety of biometric devices. One group, the International Biometric Group, does provide industrywide testing, but the results are contained within a report that must be purchased.
11 Many experienced security consultants will be tempted to simply review documents and provide comments on discovered security deficiencies, but by doing so they may fail to spot missing key elements. It is for this reason that a checklist is used to guide the review and ensure a more complete analysis.

12 Many experienced security consultants will be tempted to simply review documents and provide comments on discovered security deficiencies but fail to spot missing key elements. It is for this reason that the discipline of completeness review, using a table of expected elements, is recommended to improve the review process.

13 For more information on preparing for and using sandbags and other flood-fighting equipment, see the Flood Fight Handbook, U.S. Army Corps of Engineers, St. Paul District, 2009. (www.mvp.usace.army. mil/disaster-response/cemvp-Flood-Fight_Handbook_2009.pdf.)

14 The security controls required for the proper protection of SCIFs are beyond the scope of this book. The proper place to find this information is in the National Industrial Security Program Operating Manual (NISPOM).

BIBLIOGRAPHY

AFCOM Data Center Institute Standards Endorsed Whitepaper DCISE-001 September 2014

ASHRAE TC9.9, Data Center Power Equipment Thermal Guidelines and Best Practices, 2016. https://tc0909. ashraetcs.org/documents/ASHRAE_TC0909_Power_White_Paper_22_June_2016_REVISED.pdf (accessed September 21, 2020)

Defense Advanced Research Projects Agency (DARPA), 1997. *Perimeter Security Sensor Technologies Handbook.*

Director of Central Intelligence Directive (DCID). Physical Security Standards for Sensitive Compartmented Information Facilities. 6/9-Manual, November 18, 2002.

DoD, *National Industrial Security Program Operating Manual* (NISPOM) 5220.22-M, May 18, 2016, https:// www.esd.whs.mil/portals/54/documents/dd/issuances/dodm/522022m.pdf

Federal Emergency Management Administration, U.S. Fire Administration, Fire Estimate Summary: Nonresidential Building Fire Trends (2009–2018), March 2020. https://www.usfa.fema.gov/downloads/ pdf/statistics/nonres_bldg_fire_estimates.pdf (accessed September 18, 2020).

National Fire Protection Association, 2019. *National Fire Alarm Code.* NFPA 72(02). https://www.nfpa.org/ codes-and-standards/all-codes-and-standards/list-of-codes-and-standards/detail?code=72

Occupational Safety and Health Standards (OSHA), Design and construction requirements for exit routes, 1910 Subpart E, Exit Routes and Emergency Planning, 1910.36, https://www.osha.gov/laws-regs/regulations/ standardnumber/1910/1910.36 (accessed September 21, 2020).

U.S. Department of Energy, December 2016. *Physical Security Inspectors Guide.* https://www.energy.gov/ sites/prod/files/2017/02/f34/PhysicalSecuritySystemsAssessmentGuide_Dec2016.pdf

Viasala 2018 Annual Lightning Report, Vaisala, 2019. https://www.vaisala.com/sites/default/files/documents/2018%20Annual%20Lightning%20Report_1.pdf (accessed September 22, 2020).

9 Security Risk Analysis

The fourth phase of a security risk assessment is security risk analysis. The objective of this phase is to utilize the data gathered to determine both the security risks of individual scenarios and the overall security risk to the assessed organization. The depth to which the team performs this security risk analysis depends upon the agreed upon method between the assessment team and the assessed organization. The security risk analysis task can be rather straightforward or rather involved using more complex methods.

The objective of the security risk assessment analysis phase is to determine and convey the security risk to the organization's assets. The basic equation for security risk calculation is

$$Security\ Risk = Threat\ Frequency \times Expected\ Impact$$

In other words, how often will a bad thing happen (threat frequency) and how bad will it be (expected impact). Both the threat frequency and the expected impact are influenced by security control vulnerabilities. In fact, when determining the threat frequency or the expected impact the security risk assessment team needs to incorporate the evaluation of security vulnerabilities into these measurements, see Figure 9.1.

Therefore, many security professionals and security risk assessment methods consider the security risk equation to include vulnerabilities more directly as such:

$$Security\ Risk = Threat\ Frequency \times Controls\ Vulnerability \times Expected\ Impact$$

The security control vulnerabilities that tend to influence the threat frequency variable are typically different from those that influence the expected impact variable. In fact, preventative control vulnerabilities operate on the threat frequency, and detective and corrective control vulnerabilities operate on the expected impact variable, see Figure 9.2.

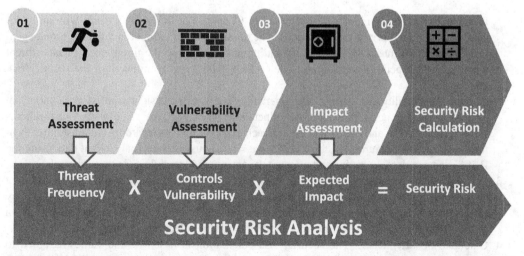

FIGURE 9.1 Security risk analysis components. The basic security risk equation computes the relationship between threats, vulnerabilities, and assets. The assessor's ability to understand and measure each of these components is essential for calculating security risk.

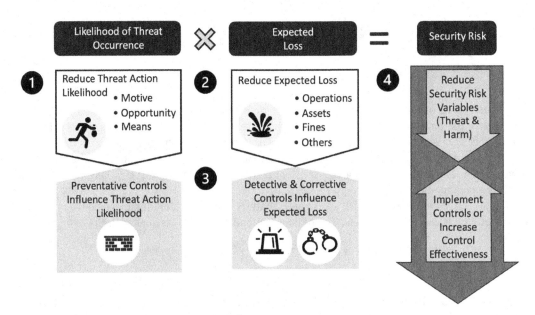

FIGURE 9.2 Security Control Influence on Threat Frequency and Expected Impact. The reduction of security control vulnerabilities among preventative controls reduces the threat frequency. The reduction of security control vulnerabilities among detective and corrective controls reduces the expected impact.

The security risk analysis depends on all the previous data gathering stages to supply the information required to analyze the security risk to the organization. The security risk analysis phase consists of techniques and approaches for determining individual and overall security risk levels. This process can take many different forms, depending upon the security risk assessment method performed. The security risk determination therefore is dependent upon the values applied to these security risk equation variables derived from an assessment of the threats, vulnerabilities, and assets; and the security risk calculation itself. Our discussion of the security risk analysis phase of the information security risk assessment will address all three of these elements of the risk equation and the security risk calculation. Specifically,

1. Perform Threat Assessment—As discussed in Chapter 4, a threat is an event with an undesired impact on the organization's assets. The components of a threat include the threat agent and the resultant threat action. Understanding and measuring the threat components (threat agent and threat action) is essential to determining the threat component of the security risk equation.
2. Perform Vulnerability Assessment—A vulnerability is a flaw or oversight in an existing control that may allow a threat agent to exploit the vulnerability to damage the value of the organization's assets. Chapters 6, 7, and 8 provided an approach to gathering data regarding administrative, technical, and physical controls. In this chapter we will discuss how to analyze that data using the RIIOT framework to determine and measure the extent of vulnerabilities in those controls.
3. Perform Impact Assessment—The basis of any security risk calculation is the value of the asset being protected. As mentioned in Chapter 2, assets in scope for security risk assessments are any items considered valuable by the organization protected by information systems. The valuation of these assets guides the security risk calculation and the selection of countermeasures.
4. Calculate Security Risk—The security risk calculation is based on the values assigned to assets, threats, and vulnerabilities. Different security risk assessment methodologies have different ways in which to calculate security risk, but they are all based on the assessor's understanding and measurement of assets, threats, and vulnerabilities.

Depending upon the security risk assessment method adopted by the security risk assessment team the approach for determining and specifying the values for the security risk equation will differ but no matter how in-depth the assessment team's security risk analysis approach, they will go through the same security risk analysis steps in determining the value of the variables associated with asset value (AV), threat, vulnerabilities, and the calculation of those values to determine risk.

9.1 OBTAINING MEASUREMENT DATA FOR SECURITY RISK ANALYSIS

The security risk analysis phase requires the security risk assessment team to provide measurements for the security risk variables associated with the security risks to be analyzed. In the case of simple security risk equations these measurements will be for the security risk variables of *loss probability* and *expected loss*. In the case of most complex security risk equations (e.g., expected loss with multiple elements) the security risk assessment team may be asked for measurement data on a wide array of data elements.

There are many methods the security risk assessment team may employ to obtain this data. A brief outline of these methods includes the RIIOT approach (see Chapters 5–8), asset valuation, estimation (see Section 9.3.2), checklists, online resources/research, and experience.

- RIIOT Approach—The Review, Interview, Inspect, Observe, and Test (RIIOT) approach presented in Chapter 5 and detailed in Chapters 6–8 provides a detailed approach to gathering data regarding any security control within the scope of the assessment. At this point in the security risk assessment, the assessment team should have compiled and organized a large set of data useful in the analysis of security risks. If the assessed organization has experienced recent security incidents, they would likely have a good idea as to the loss associated with those incidents. The security risk assessment team should be sure to include interview questions or surveys that gather this information from the appropriate personnel within the assessed organization or follow up on initial interviews when this data is required.
- Asset Valuation—The security risk assessment will have already performed an asset valuation exercise as part of the preparation for the security risk assessment, see Section 4.4.3. Using the data gathered during the asset valuation phase, the security risk assessment team can assign expected loss estimates to threat actions based on the likely effect on assets and the asset valuation.
- Estimation—Team members will be well acquainted with the security organization and controls being assessed and many of the security trends. This knowledge along with some acquired estimation skills and calibration allow the team members to provide useful estimated measurements for security risk assessment variables. This topic is described more fully in Section 9.3.2.
- Checklists—There are many available lists, checklists, and taxonomies that can be useful to the security risk assessment team when performing the security risk analysis. These checklists are organized and presented below by their topics of threats, impacts, and control sets:
  - Loss Probability (Threat Actions)—Threat lists or threat event catalogs that list threat agents and threats events along with pre-populated threat agent and/threat event aspects, such as motivation, and capability can be useful to the security risk assessment team in the performance of a security risk assessment. Creating this list for each security risk assessment would be a daunting task. There is literally no end to the number of ways an organization's system may be attacked by mankind or Mother Nature. When performing a security risk assessment, however, we must limit the threat agents and threats that we shall consider to those that are relevant.

    A checklist or catalog of possible threat agents and associated threats may be used to ensure that the security risk assessment team considers all relevant threat agents and threats. Much of the work here would be involved in compiling such a list, but that work

can be reused for each security risk assessment performed. While the security risk assessment team will need to reconsider the threat agents and threats that are relevant for the specific security risk assessment, there is no need to reinvent the list. Threat lists and catalogs provide a useful jump start to that process element. Examples of threat lists include:
  - NIST SP 800-30 Appendix D, Table D-1: Threat Source Identification
  - NIST SP 800-30 Appendix D, Table D-2: Taxonomy of Threat Sources
  - NIST SP 800-30 Appendix E, Table E-2: Representative Examples—Adversarial Threat Events
  - NIST SP 800-30 Appendix E, Table E-3 Representative Examples—Non-Adversarial Threat Events
  - IRAM2 Common Threat List: https://www.securityforum.org/
  - BSI Threat Catalogue—Elementary Threats: https://www.bsi.bund.de/SharedDocs/Downloads/EN/BSI/Grundschutz/download/threats_catalogue.pdf?__blob=publicationFile&v=2
  - Department of Homeland Security, IT Sector Baseline Risk Assessment: Appendix 3: IT Sector Risk Assessment Methodology—Manmade Deliberate, Manmade Unintentional, and Natural Consequence Threat Framework. https://www.dhs.gov/xlibrary/assets/nipp_it_baseline_risk_assessment.pdf
  - ISO 27005 Appendix C: Examples of Typical Threats
  - OCTAVE Allegro Table 7: Graphical Representation of Threat Trees
• Expected Loss (Impact, Harm)—Lists of assets and asset impacts along with consequence frameworks, harm factors, and other lists can be useful to the security risk assessment team in the performance of a security risk assessment. Creating this list for each security risk being assessed would be time consuming. A checklist or catalog of expected loss elements or other taxonomies may be used by the security risk assessment team to simplify the process. Expected loss lists and catalogs provide a useful jump start to that process element. Examples of expected loss lists include
  - NIST SP 800-30 Appendix H, Table H-2: Examples of Adverse Impacts
  - Department of Homeland Security, IT Sector Baseline Risk Assessment: Appendix 3: IT Sector Risk Assessment Methodology—Manmade Deliberate, Manmade Unintentional, and Natural Consequence Framework. https://www.dhs.gov/xlibrary/assets/nipp_it_baseline_risk_assessment.pdf
  - ISO 27005 Appendix B: Identification and valuation of assets and impact assessment
• Control Sets (Vulnerabilities)—Controls are all of the administrative, physical, and technical security controls established by the assessed organization in order to protect their assets. The listing of these controls for planning the review and assessment of them can be a large task and difficult to ensure that a complete list is created. Security controls sets can provide the security risk assessment team with a complete list of security controls upon which to base the security control (or vulnerability) assessment portion of the security risk assessment. Control strength or vulnerability frameworks provide an organization approach to aligning control strength (or lack thereof) to threats.
  - NIST SP 800-53: Security and Privacy Controls for Information Systems and Organizations. https://csrc.nist.gov/publications/detail/sp/800-53/rev-5/final
  - Department of Homeland Security, IT Sector Baseline Risk Assessment: Appendix 3: IT Sector Risk Assessment Methodology—Manmade Deliberate, Manmade Unintentional, and Natural Consequence Vulnerability Framework. https://www.dhs.gov/xlibrary/assets/nipp_it_baseline_risk_assessment.pdf
  - OCTAVE Catalog of Practices Version 2.0: https://resources.sei.cmu.edu/asset_files/technicalreport/2001_005_001_13883.pdf
  - ISO 27002 Annex A: Reference control objectives and controls
  - ISO 27005 Appendix D: Vulnerabilities and methods for vulnerability assessment

- Online Resources and Other Research—The research and compilation of the data necessary to estimate the threat action likelihood and its components is a significant effort in this phase of the security risk assessment. The team should utilize available online resources of relevant and up-to-date information to gather appropriate data. The team should consider the following sources of information to aid their research:
  - Natural Threat Agents—When considering Mother Nature as the threat agent, the assessment team should be able to find ample targeted data regarding threat action likelihood. Data is compiled and available for natural disasters and threats such as earthquakes, severe winds, and floods, see Figures 9.3, 9.4, and 9.5. Several government agencies provide up-to-date information on natural hazards that can be used by the security risk assessment team. Useful websites include the following:
    - United States Geological Service: www.usgs.gov
    - National Oceanic and Atmospheric Agency: www.noaa.gov
    - Federal Emergency Management Agency: www.fema.gov
    - National Fire Protection Association: www.nfpa.org
  - Infrastructure Threat Agents—When considering infrastructure services such as electrical power, Internet, and water service as the threat agent, the assessment team should be able to find data regarding threat action likelihood. Data is compiled and available for each of these threat actions. Several government agencies and industry groups provide up-to-date information on infrastructure outages that can be used by the security risk assessment team. Useful websites include the following:
    - United States Energy Information Administration: www.eia.gov
  - Human Threat Agents—When considering human-intentional threat agents such as employees (internal) and criminal cybercriminals (outsiders), the assessment team should be able to find recent surveys and annual reports that provide some insight and direction regarding the threat action likelihood. Data is compiled and available for many of the most

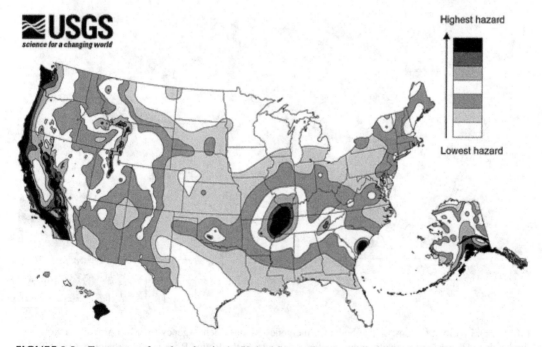

FIGURE 9.3 Frequency of earthquakes in the United States. Data compiled over the last 50 years allows for the United States Geological Survey to provide seismic hazard maps with hazard ratings, frequency, and scale of earthquake activity. www.usgs.gov.

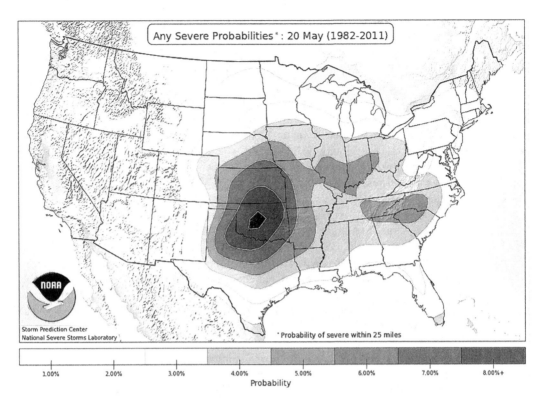

FIGURE 9.4   Severe winds probabilities. The Storm Prediction Center (SPC) at the National Oceanic and Atmospheric Administration (NOAA) provides prediction data for severe winds and tornadoes.

FIGURE 9.5   Flood risk maps. The Federal Emergency Management Agency (FEMA) provides a variety of flood risk and hazard products including this flood risk map of the Round Rock and Georgetown area of Texas.

prevalent threat actions. Several government agencies and industry groups provide up-to-date information on infrastructure outages that can be used by the security risk assessment team. Useful websites include the following:

- – Security Vendor Annual Reports
  - – CheckPoint Research Cyber Security Report: https://www.research.checkpoint.com
  - – Crowdstrike Global threat Report: https://www.crowdstrike.com/resources/reports
  - – Fujitsu Group Information Security Report: https://www.fujitsu.com/global/about/resources/reports/securityreport/
  - – IBM, Cost of A Data Breach Report: https://www.ibm.com/security/data-breach
  - – Sonicwall Threat Report: https://www.sonicwall.com/2020-cyber-threat-report/
  - – Sophos Labs Threat Report: https://www.sophos.com
  - – TrendMicro Midyear Cybersecurity Report: www.trendmicro.com
- – Security Consulting Firm Annual Reports
  - – Accenture Annual State of Cybersecurity Report: https://www.accenture.com
  - – EY Consulting Global Information Security Survey: https://www.ey.com/en_us/giss
  - – Herjavec Group Annual Cybercrime Report: https://www.herjavecgroup.com/the-2019-official-annual-cybercrime-report/
  - – Mandiant Security Effectiveness Report: https://www.fireeye.com
  - – Trustwave Global Security Report: https://www.trustwave.com
  - – PWC Global State of Information Security: https://www.pwc.com/
  - – Verizon Data Breach Investigations Report: https://enterprise.verizon.com/resources/reports/dbir/
- – Industry Organization Annual Reports
  - – ISACA State of Cyber Security: https://www.isaca.org
- – Government Annual Reports
  - – Australian Government: Australian Signals Directorate: Annual Cyber Threat Report: https://www.cyber.gov.au
- – Other Sources of Cybersecurity Statistics
  - – InfoSecurity Magazine State of Cybersecurity Report: https://www.infosecurity-magazine.com/
  - – Hiscox Cyber Readiness Report: https://www.hiscox.co.uk/cyberreadiness
  - – Ponemon Institute: https://www.ponemon.org/research/ponemon-library/
- • Experience—The security risk assessment team members should have experience in estimating elements of the security risk equation including loss probability and expected loss. The security risk assessment team can apply its experience here as part of the estimations for any security risk variable or component.

9.2 QUALITATIVE SECURITY RISK ANALYSIS TECHNIQUES

When the security risk assessment team performs a security risk assessment method that relies on qualitative data, the assessment team will need to estimate those values using qualitative techniques such as ranking, scoring, and lookup tables.

- • Ranking—Ranking is the ordering of a list of elements. For example, the assessment team may be asked to rank foreseeable threats from a threat agent/action list or to rank impact elements for the expected loss element of the security risk equation. The assessment method may require the ranking of the impact areas of reputation, financial impact, productivity losses, safety and health impact, and fines and legal costs in order using a rank score of one to five, five being the most important and most heavily weighted rank. In this example the ranking of impact areas may best be informed by the assessed organization as this is a business driver. The assessment team may provide a basic introduction and definition of these areas and the ability of threat agents to cause harm in these areas. The ranking could be a summation of the ranking from key staff members of the assessed organization or a ranking by the security risk assessment sponsor. In either case it is useful to include notes explaining or defending the ranking, see Table 9.1.

- Scoring—Scoring is a method of qualitative estimation that provides a qualitative scale along with a description for each of the scale levels. The security risk assessment team is expected to utilize their knowledge of the assessed organization, threat agents and actions, expected loss, and/or vulnerability severity to assign a scale level to the security risk equation elements. For example, the assessment team may be asked to assign a scale level to the likelihood of a threat action occurrence for non-adversarial threat agents. The assessment method may require an assignment for each of the threat actions based on a scale of very high, high, moderate, low, and very low. In this example the assignment of threat agents may best be informed by the assessed organization's experience with similar incidents in the past and the security risk assessment team's experience and research regarding the frequency of each of these threat action occurrences, see Table 9.2.

- Lookup Tables—Lookup tables implement a method of combining subelements of the security risk equation into a higher-level value. Lookup tables are implemented by a matrix or table with one subelement represented by the rows of the table and the other subelement represented by the columns of the table. The security risk assessment team uses the values of the subelements as an index to the appropriate row and column in the table. The intersection of the row and column determine the security risk equation element that is the subject of the lookup table. For example, the assessment team may already have scored both the likelihood and the impact for a security risk scenario and needs to determine the security risk. The security risk assessment team uses a lookup table and the threat likelihood value of low, the expected impact value of moderate, as an index to the Figure 9.6.

TABLE 9.1

Example Impact Area Ranking

Impact Area	Ranking	Notes
Reputation	4	As an advisory firm avoidance of reputational damage is important to us.
Financial	5	Most important as risk management is driven by cost benefit analysis.
Productivity	3	Many of our processes are quite resilient to interruption.
Safety and health	1	Least important when it comes to risk management. We comply with health and safety guidelines.
Fines and legal	2	We can manage fines and legal fees through our lawyers and adherence to due diligence.

Note: Ranking relies on the ordering of a finite list of elements. In this example, the security risk assessment team is asked to rank the threat impact areas of reputation, financial, productivity, safety and health, and fines and legal from 1–5, five being the most important impact area to the assessed organization.

Source: Adapted from NIST SP 800-30, Table G-3.

TABLE 9.2

Example Likelihood Assessment Scale for Non-Adversarial Threat Occurrences

Qualitative Value	Description
Very high	Error, accident, or act of nature is **almost certain** to occur, or occurs **more than 100 times a year**.
High	Error, accident, or act of nature is **highly likely** to occur, or occurs **between 10–100 times a year**.
Moderate	Error, accident, or act of nature is **somewhat likely** to occur, or occurs **between 1–10 times a year**.
Low	Error, accident, or act of nature is **unlikely** to occur, or occurs **between 0.1 and 1 time a year**.
Very low	Error, accident, or act of nature is **highly unlikely** to occur, or occurs **less than once every 10 years**.

Note: Scoring relies on the assignment of a scale level associated with a description of the level to each instance of a security risk equation variable. In this example, the security risk assessment team is asked to score the threat likelihood of a non-adversarial threat occurring using a scale from very low to very high.

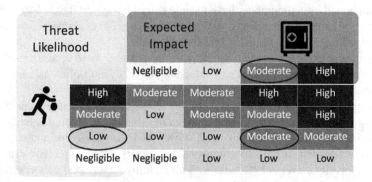

FIGURE 9.6 Example risk lookup table. Using a threat likelihood value of *low* and an expected impact value of *moderate*, the resulting risk is *moderate*.

9.2.1 Qualitative Security Risk Analysis Advantages

Qualitative methods, based on the subjective judgment of security risk assessment team members, have many benefits:

- Simple—Qualitative methods can be a welcome relief from the complexity of quantitative methods. The simplicity of these methods is their major feature and is the root of nearly all of their advantages.
- Simple Measurement Values—Using quantitative methods, it can be extremely difficult to derive exact numbers for each of the variables for assets, threats, impacts, and safeguards. Using qualitative methods, this task is still significant, but it can be performed with a lot less effort. Consider how difficult it would be to determine the impact of an e-mail server going down under the quantitative method. Now consider how easy it would be to get the team to agree that the impact of the e-mail server going down for a day would be a "major loss" as opposed to a "critical loss" or a "minor loss."
- Easy to Understand and Convey—The analysis and results of qualitative security risk assessment methods are easy to convey to others. Descriptive terms and relatively easy computations make it easy for others not involved in the analysis to review the results and comprehend the analysis contained in the security risk assessment report.

- Provide Adequate Identification of Problem Areas—In most situations, a qualitative security risk assessment will provide enough information at an adequate level to influence the improvement of the organization's security posture. Although there is not a dollar value attached to recommended safeguards, qualitative security risk assessment methods still provide enough information to let the organization know what improvements are required to reduce the security risk to their critical assets.

Whereas quantitative analysis relies on complex formulas and monetary or frequency values for the variables, qualitative analysis relies on the subjective judgment of the security risk assessment members to determine the overall security risk to the information systems. The same basic elements are required to determine security risk, such as AV, threat frequency, impact, and safeguard effectiveness, but these elements are now measured in subjective terms such as "high" or "not likely."

Qualitative security risk equation variables are sometimes expressed as numbers; however, these should not be treated in the same manner as numbers within quantitative analysis. When a qualitative analysis method utilizes numbers as values of security risk variables, these numbers are considered ordinal numbers. Ordinal numbers have meaningful order (e.g., High > Medium > Low), but there is no metric to determine the distance between categories. For example, it does not make sense to say that a "High" risk is twice as bad as a "Medium" risk.

Because these qualitative numbers or labels are only ordinal, these security risk values cannot (should not) be computed using mathematical techniques (e.g., multiplied and added) to produce security risk assessment results. These qualitative security risk equation variables are not treated as values in the way that quantitative analysis variables are treated. Qualitative security risk equation variables are not expressed in terms of monetary values, but as an ordered category of monetary loss such as "Critical," "High," "Medium," and "Low." The "formulas" for qualitatively determining security risk assessment results are simply tables, charts, or lookups. For example, in Table 9.1, an "Impact Severity Level" of "2" and a "Vulnerability Likelihood of Occurrence" of "C—Conceivable" results in a "Risk Level II", see Table 9.3.

Therefore, unlike quantitative security risk analysis, the results of qualitative security risk analysis cannot be used to directly justify costs through a cost–benefit analysis. Different qualitative security risk assessment methods have varying names, descriptions, and levels of qualitative values. An example of qualitative values is shown in Table 9.4.

TABLE 9.3

Example Qualitative Risk Determination

Impact Severity Level	Vulnerability Likelihood of Occurrence				
	A-Frequent	B-Probable	C-Conceivable	D-Improbable	E-Remote
1	Risk I	Risk I	Risk I	Risk II	Risk III
2	Risk I	Risk I	Risk II	Risk II	Risk III
3	Risk I	Risk II	Risk II	Risk III	Risk III
4	Risk III	Risk III	Risk IV	Risk IV	Risk IV

Note: Qualitative security risk analysis relies on lookup tables to determine results.

TABLE 9.4
Qualitative Values

Level	Attempt	Exploit	Impact
1	Likely	Easy	Exposure or loss of proprietary information
			Loss of integrity of critical information
			System disruption
			Major structural damage
			Loss of physical access control
			Exposure or loss of sensitive information
			Grave danger to building occupants
2	Conceivable	Moderate	Major system damage
			Significant structural damage
			Risks to access controls
			Potential exposure to sensitive information
			Serious danger to building occupants
3	Improbable	Difficult	Minor system damage or exposure
			Some structural damage
			Reduced access control effectiveness
			Moderate exposure to sensitive information
			Moderate danger to building occupants
4	Remote	Extremely difficult	Less than minor system damage or exposure
			Extremely limited structural damage
			Potential effect on access controls
			Control of sensitive information
			Safety of building occupants

Note: Qualitative analysis methods use levels, labels, and descriptions for qualitative values. The example shown here has qualitative values and descriptions for vulnerability measurements of attempt, exploitability, and potential impact.Source: Adapted from the IRAM2 residual risk rating matrix.

9.2.2 QUALITATIVE SECURITY RISK ANALYSIS DISADVANTAGES

Although qualitative methods have many benefits, the simplicity of this approach results in some substantial disadvantages as well:

- Subjective Results—There is no getting around the fact that the value of the security risk assessment variables is subjective and based more on experience and judgment than cold, hard facts. Therefore, the results are subjective as well, and one could always argue that they may be inaccurate.
- Subjective Asset Value—The same argument used above can be used for the valuation of assets. It is difficult to defend subjective values placed on assets other than to state that the judgment was based on experience. Although such estimates are typically accurate, the value can still be questioned, and this can lead to difficulties in getting the results accepted.

- Subjective Recommendations—If the analysis is based on subjective AVs and results, then it follows that the resulting recommendations are subjective as well. Many will argue that this makes the results no less accurate, but the results may be more difficult to defend.
- Difficult to Track Improvements—For security programs that want to track their improvement from assessment to assessment, this becomes difficult when the assessment results in a "high-medium" or "medium-low" security risk. Just how good an improvement would that be?

9.3 QUANTITATIVE SECURITY RISK ANALYSIS TECHNIQUES

Quantitative security risk analysis is a security risk analysis approach that relies on numeric values and mathematical calculations and methods to determine the value of the security risk decision variables. When performing security risk assessments using quantitative methods, the security risk assessment team should be aware of quantitative measurement techniques to provide quantitative estimates for the security risk equation variables and subelements.

9.3.1 CLASSIC QUANTITATIVE SECURITY RISK ASSESSMENT FORMULAS

There are several classic formulas that are commonly associated with quantitative security risk analysis. These formulas cover the expected loss for specific security risks and the value of safeguards to reduce the security risk. There are three classic quantitative security risk analysis formulas: annual loss expectancy (ALE), single loss expectancy (SLE), and safeguard value:

1. Annual Loss Expectancy (ALE) = Single Loss Expectancy (SLE) × Annual Rate of Occurrence
2. Single Loss Expectancy (SLE) = Asset Value × Exposure Factor
3. Safeguard Value = ALE Before × ALE After × Annual Safeguard Cost

Each of these formulas is explained in more detail below.

- Expected Loss—The expected loss is a useful concept because, when dealing with security risk, you are not dealing with certainty but instead with probabilities. Consider a situation in which a gambling friend proposes that he flip a coin to determine how much money you win. If the coin lands on heads you win $1.00; if the coin lands on tails, you win $2.50. Clearly this game provides you the opportunity to make money, but your friend intends to charge you for each coin flip. How much would you be willing to pay to play such a game?

    The value of this game (or your friend's expected loss) can be determined through the application of the concept of expected loss. First, note that the probability of your friend losing $1.00 or $2.50 is equally likely. Using statistics, we can compute your friend's expected loss for a single event of $1.75. This means that if you play this game you may end up winning as much as $2.50 or as little as $1.00, but on average you will win $1.75:
    - Expected Loss = [probability (heads) × $1.00] + [probability (tails) × 2.50]
    - Expected Loss = (0.5 × $1.00) + (0.5 × $2.50)
    - Expected Loss = $0.50 + $1.25
    - Expected Loss = $1.75
- Single Loss Expectancy—In business, we deal not with gambling friends, but with cyber-criminals, disgruntled employees, viruses, and other events that are not certain but have an element of chance or prediction. Because these threats may have an impact on our organization's assets, it is useful to predict and measure the expected loss. SLE is the expected loss as the result of a single incident. In the case of the gambling friend, the SLE for the event is $1.75. Many security risk assessment techniques use a specific formula for SLE that incorporates

an EF and the AV. An EF is the average amount of loss to the asset for a single incident. For example, a warehouse that catches on fire would, on an average, burn only halfway or lose only half of its value. This would equate to an EF of 0.50. SLE is defined as AV multiplied by the EF:

- Single Loss Expectancy = Asset Value × Exposure Factor
- Annualized Loss Expectancy—It is rare that a security risk event happens exactly once a year. Some security risk events, for example, computer viruses, happen several times a year, while others such as a fire in a warehouse happen only once every 20 years. Because budgets for avoiding or otherwise dealing with these incidents are on a yearly cycle, it is useful to compute the expected losses from these security risks within a single year. This number is referred to as the annualized loss expectancy (ALE). The ALE is computed by multiplying the SLE by the annual rate of occurrence (ARO). An ARO is simply a prediction of how often a specific security risk event is likely to happen each year. For example, the ARO for a virus may be six times in 1 year (or simply six), while the ARO for a fire in the warehouse could be 0.05 (or one time in 20 years).
  - Annualized Loss Expectancy = Single Loss Expectancy × Annual Rate of Occurrence
- Safeguard Value—Lastly, it is useful to determine how much you would be willing to spend on a countermeasure to reduce a specific security risk. A countermeasure is any administrative, physical, or technical security mechanism that reduces the security risk to the organization's assets. No countermeasure can completely eliminate the security risk to an organization's assets. Instead, a countermeasure may reduce the security risk to an organization's asset by reducing the SLE, the ALE, or both. A countermeasure can reduce the SLE by reducing the EF, or it may reduce the ALE by reducing the ARO. A countermeasure also costs money to implement. Sometimes a countermeasure may be worthwhile to implement because the expected losses to the organization's assets are severely reduced with a low-cost countermeasure. At other times, a countermeasure may not be worth the cost because the organization only experiences a slight drop in the security risk to their assets and a high cost of implementing the countermeasure.

  This brings us to the last basic equation for security risk assessment: countermeasure or safeguard value. Safeguard value is defined as the reduction experienced in the ALE minus the annual cost of implementing the countermeasure:

- Safeguard Value = (ALE Before—ALE After)— Annual Cost of Countermeasure

Some values may be easy to acquire as they are based on an inventory hardware or a statutory fine but other values are a bit more elusive and the assessment team may require the use of advanced quantitative analysis techniques. For these elusive values the assessment team will need to rely on several techniques for measuring security risk variables and computing security risk quantitatively:

- Estimation
- Probability Distribution
- Monte Carlo Simulation

9.3.2 Estimation

When using quantitative information security risk assessment methods, the security risk assessment team will first need to determine quantitative values (e.g., $50,000 loss) instead of qualitative values (e.g., low, moderate, and high). One of the biggest obstacles assessors experience when first introduced to quantitative analysis is a frustration with estimating these quantitative values. Afterall, how do you know exactly how much a ransomware incident is going to cost the assessed organization if it ever happens; and how do you know the probability that it will happen?

The approach used in many qualitative security risk assessment methods is not to provide an "exact" number but instead to estimate. For example, you probably do not know the exact impact or how often a ransomware incident will happen in the assessed organization. For quantitative values that are difficult to know, such as future events, the assessment team will need to estimate. Estimation is not a guess, but a judgment based on knowledge. Based on the data gathering performed by the assessment team, the assessment team is knowledgeable about the factors affecting quantitative security risk variables in the assessed organization and able to provide estimates on these variables.

- Single Point Estimates—An estimate may be a single point estimate such as "2 laptops will go missing next year" or "there is a 5% chance of a major security breach." The usefulness of single point estimates in security risk calculations are limited as they may not represent the full knowledge of the assessors on the variable nor the variation in the variable. However, they are used quite extensively in some current quantitative security risk assessment methods.
- Estimate Ranges—Estimate ranges (e.g., between zero and five laptops will go missing next year) are a good way to more accurately represent the security risk variable. Estimate ranges are expressed using a low and a high value representing the range of values for the risk variable. The low value should represent an event that has a low probability of occurring where most other events that occur have a higher value. The high value should also represent an event that has a low probability of occurring but where most other events that occur have a lower value. The example above of between zero and five laptops going missing in the next 12 months is a good example for using low and high values to describe an estimate range.
- Estimation Skills—Estimation can be a tricky area for some assessors to grasp. When confronted with creating estimate ranges it can be difficult for some to create reasonable ranges that support analysis. For example, an assessor may state, "there will be between 0 and 75 laptops that go missing next year." While this statement is most likely (ML) true, it is not useful as a measurement as the range is quite extensive and fails to provide data that accurately predicts the risk event to the level of the assessor's knowledge. The assessor has exaggerated the high number in order to always be "correct" but likely has more knowledge about the probability of lost laptops in the future. In order for the assessor to be useful in this stage of the security risk analysis they require estimation skills. A few approached to improving an individual assessor's skills are listed below:
  - Aggressive But Possible—One approach, born out of software estimation techniques, is the "aggressive but possible" estimate.[1] Here the assessor is asked to estimate the low and high numbers of the range as "…but possible" (e.g., five laptops missing next year is high but possible).
  - Confidence Levels—A better approach is to estimate a range with a 90% confidence level or in other words, "I am 90% confident that the number of laptops that will go missing next year will be between 0 and 5."
  - Calibration—The security risk assessment team members are now playing the role of estimators. In addition, the assessed organization's key staff members are interviewed and asked to provide estimation data and are estimators as well. Estimation is a tool and tools need calibration. The previously recommended book by Doug Hubbard does a very good job providing exercises and techniques to calibrate the team members through the use of calibration tests.[2] Your team and the assessed organization's key staff members are strongly encouraged to calibrate its estimators prior to providing estimation ranges.

9.3.3 Probability Distributions

A probability distribution is a mathematical function that produces range of values together with their associated probabilities for occurrence. Depending on the security risk equation variable (or subelement) that needs to be estimated there are several different probability distributions that may be used to model that variable most accurately.

- Discrete Variables—In many risk scenarios, the quantitative values sought are discrete numbers. For example, the number of laptops that may go missing in the next year could be zero, one, two, three, four, or five, but there is no chance that 1.8 laptops will go missing. There are two discrete distributions typically used in quantitative security risk assessments: binary distributions and frequency distributions.
  - Uniform Distribution—The uniform distribution is a flat probability distribution, where all of the values within the distribution have the same probability of being selected. This is an appropriate probability distribution for events in which all values in the range have an equal probability. For example, when rolling a six-sided die there is an equal chance of it landing on any value between one and six. If we apply a discrete uniform distribution to the number of lost laptops with values from zero to five we have an equal chance at losing zero, one, two, three, four, or five laptops, see Figure 9.7
  - Binary Distribution—The binary distribution generates only two possible outcomes. This distribution represents the probability that an event will happen or not. For example, there either will be a hurricane damage or destroy the organization's data center next year or there will not. The distribution is governed by a single parameter: probability of the event. This distribution is commonly used for events with large impacts that happen infrequently such as a natural disaster. For example, a major hurricane (e.g., Category 3 or higher) has a "return period" of 6 years for North Carolina, South Florida, and Southeast Louisiana coastal regions.[3] If your data center is located in one of these areas the probability of the event is equal to 17% and can be represented by a binary distribution, see Figure 9.8.
  - Frequency Distribution—The discrete frequency distribution generates any number of discrete outcomes. This distribution represents the probability of occurrence for each of the discrete numbers covered by the distribution range. For example, the probabilities for zero, one, two, three, four, or five laptops going missing next year can be represented by a discrete frequency distribution. This frequency distribution function is governed by a probability parameter for each of the discrete values in the range. This distribution is commonly used when there are expected to be more than one occurrence and the probabilities for each occurrence can be estimated, such as the number of lost laptops annually given and historical records that document such events, see Figure 9.9.
  - Binomial Distribution—The binomial distribution generates a discrete probability distribution that models the number of times an event will occur within a certain number of trials. In Excel, the normal distribution function is:

    ```
    BINOM.DIST(x,trials,probability_s,cumulative)
    ```

    - x: Value for which you want the distribution
    - trials: the number of independent events taking place within the time frame
    - probability_s: Probability that the event is "successful"
    - Cumulative: Enter TRUE or FALSE depending if you want a cumulative distribution function (probability that a value of x or lower will occur) or a probability mass function (probability that a value of x will occur).

      For example, the number of laptops out of 100 issued to be lost or stolen next year can be represented by a binomial distribution. This discrete distribution function is governed by the number of trials and the estimated probability of "success". In this example, we will use a 3% probability of success as many industry studies point to roughly 3% of all laptops going missing each year, see Figure 9.10.
  - Poisson Distribution—The Poisson distribution generates a discrete probability distribution that models the number of times an event will occur within a certain timeframe. In Excel, the normal distribution function is:

    ```
    POISSON.DIST(x,mean,cumulative)
    ```

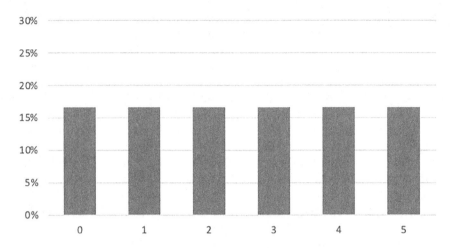

FIGURE 9.7 Uniform distribution of lost laptops. Uniform distributions can be used to represent events in which the likelihood of each outcome is equal. Here the uniform distribution is used to represent laptops lost annually.

Binary Distribution of Category 3 Hurricane Strike In Coastal NC, South FL, and SE LA.

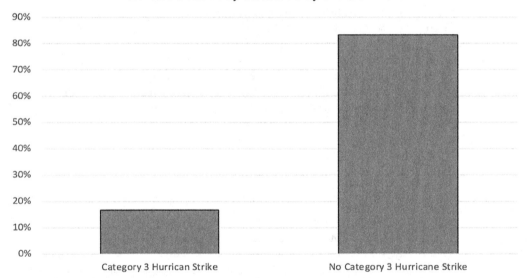

FIGURE 9.8 Binary distribution of major Hurricane strike. Binary distributions can be used to represent the probability of a major hurricane strike on a datacenter located in the coastal regions of North Caroline, Southern Florida, or Southeast Louisiana annually given the return period of major hurricanes for those regions.

- − x: Value for which you want the distribution
- − mean: Average number of occurrences
- − Cumulative: Enter TRUE or FALSE depending if you want a cumulative distribution function (probability that a value of x or lower will occur) or a probability mass function (probability that a value of x will occur).

For example, the assessor estimates the average number of laptops lost or stolen each year to be four. Using the Poisson distribution, we can create a probability distribution for the likelihood of lost laptops, see Figure 9.11.[4]

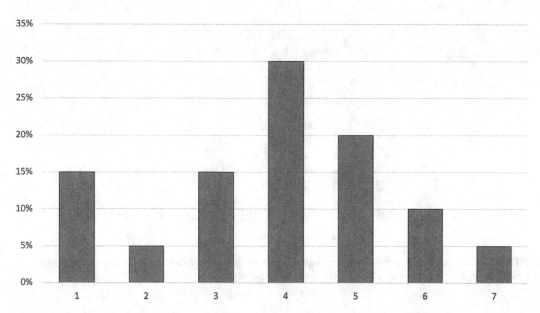

FIGURE 9.9 Frequency distribution of lost laptops. Frequency distributions can be used to represent the expected number of laptops missing annually given the organization has sufficient data to create probabilities for each of the discrete numbers within the given estimated range.

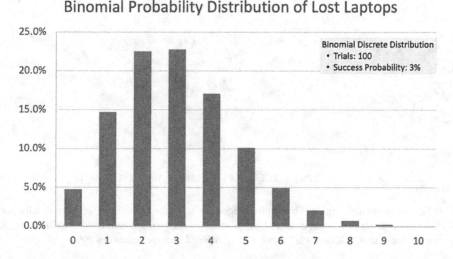

FIGURE 9.10 Binomial distribution of lost laptops. Binomial distributions can be used to represent the expected number of laptops missing annually given the number of trials (e.g., number of laptops) and probability of a laptop going missing in a year.

- Continuous Variables—In other risk scenarios, the quantitative values sought are continuous numbers or real numbers (not limited to integers), and the probability function that represents these numbers is a continuous probability function. For example, the impact ransomware attack could be estimated at between $312,000 and $1,248,000. In this example the variables are continuous and are best represented by a probability density function (pdf). A pdf represents the probability that a variable (e.g., ransomware impact) would be equal to a given value within the range of values. There are an infinite number of values between any two real numbers and instead of assessor attempting to specify the probability of each value between the lower and upper bound, a probability distribution function can be described by a limited set of parameters

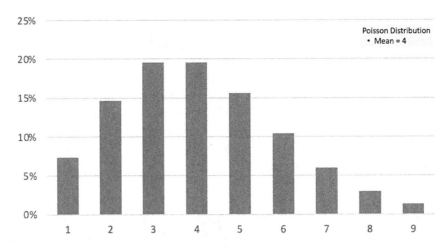

FIGURE 9.11 Poisson distribution of lost laptops. Poisson distributions can be used to represent the expected number of laptops missing annually given the estimated average.

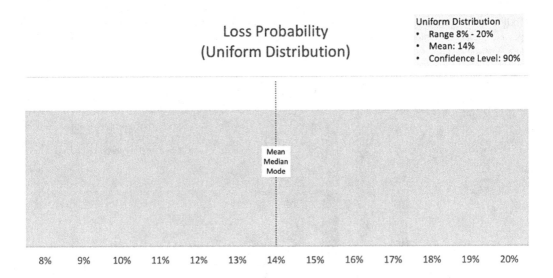

FIGURE 9.12 Uniform distribution. Probability ranges can be described using a uniform distribution if all values within the range have an equal chance. Loss probability is described here using a uniform distribution with a 90% confidence level with a lower bound (LB) of 8% and an upper bound of 20%.

that govern the individual values. There are many probability distribution functions used in quantitative security risk assessments. A few of the most popular are presented below.

- Uniform Distribution—A flat probability distribution, where all of the values within the distribution have the same probability of being selected, is called a uniform distribution. This is an appropriate probability distribution for events in which all values in the range have an equal probability. For example, when rolling a six-sided die there is an equal chance of it landing on any value between one and six. If we apply a uniform distribution to the loss probability (8% to 20%) we have an equal chance at every probability between 8% and 20%, see Figure 9.12.

  If the assessor feels that a uniform distribution does not accurately describe the estimate range, they may describe the estimate range probability distribution using other functions that may more accurately describe the estimate range.

- Normal Distribution—The most commonly used probability distribution is the normal distribution, also called the bell curve based on its symmetric shape. In Excel, the normal distribution function is:

$$\text{NORM.DIST}(x, \text{mean}, \text{standard\_dev}, \text{cumulative})$$

- – x: Value for which you want the distribution
- – Mean: Mean of the distribution (estimate)
- – Standard_dev: Standard deviation of the distribution if known, else calculate as (upper_bound – lower_bound) / 3.29
- – Cumulative: Enter TRUE or FALSE depending if you want a cumulative distribution function (probability that a value of x or lower will occur) or a probability mass function (probability that a value of x will occur).

In a normal distribution the highest part of the curve represents the most frequent value, also called the mode. The average of all of the values (called the mean) is equal to the mode, and the "middle" value of the data set is also equal to both the mean and the mode. The width of the bell curve is described by the standard deviation, 68% of the data set values are within one standard deviation; 95% are within two standard deviations; and 99.7% of the values are within three standard deviations. The normal distribution curve approximates many natural and economic data sets such as adult heights, intelligence quotient (IQ), and stock market returns. Normal distributions can be described by simply knowing the data set mean and standard deviation.

For security risk assessments, the assessment team is estimating the data set that describes the security risk assessment values (e.g., loss probability and expected loss). In these cases, the assessment team does not have a data set upon which to calculate the standard deviation. Instead, we use a mathematical trick to derive the standard deviation from the confidence level. If the assessor creates an estimate range and is 90% confident that a real-world value would fall within that range; the range is said to have a 90% confidence level. The standard deviation can be derived from the upper and LBs and the confidence levels of 90% or 95% using the following formulas:

- – Standard Deviation (90% confidence level) = (upper bound– lower bound)/3.29
- – Standard Deviation (100% confidence level) = (upper bound – lower bound)/3.92

In the example case of the loss frequency for ransomware the standard deviation would be computed as follows: (8%–20%)/3.29 = 3.65%, and the normal distribution would show a symmetric probability distribution centered on the mean (14%), see Figure 9.13.

Continuing with the example we can use a normal distribution to describe the expected loss for the laptop as well. Here we estimate the expected loss range from $200K to $1.2M with a confidence level of 90%. Standard deviation is computed to be $303K and the normal distribution of the expected loss values are depicted in Figure 9.14.

- Lognormal Distribution—Not all phenomena fits neatly into a normal bell curve distribution. Normal distributions assume a balanced "bell curve" (e.g., mean = median = mode) and allow for negative values. The modeling of many loss frequencies and impacts are not accurately modeled with a normal distribution. Many can be more accurately modeled using the log normal probability distribution. In Excel, the log normal distribution function is:

$$\text{LOGNORM.DIST}(x, \text{mean}, \text{standard\_dev})$$

- – x: Value for which you want the distribution
- – Mean: Mean of the distribution if known, else calculate as (LN(upper bound)_LN(lower_bound))/2
- – Standard_dev: Standard deviation of the distribution if known, else calculate as (LN(upper_bound)–LN(lower bound))/3.29

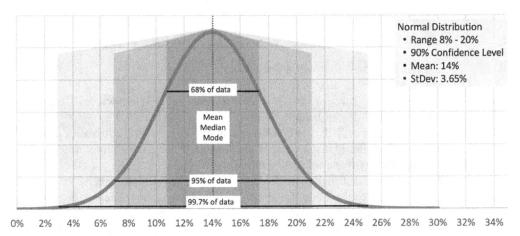

FIGURE 9.13 Normal distribution ("Bell Curve") of loss probability. Probability ranges can be described using normal distributions where mean, median, and mode are equal, and the probabilities are distributed symmetrically. In a normal distribution 68% of the data values are within one standard deviation; 95% within two standard deviations; and 99.7% within three standard deviations. Loss probability is described here using a normal distribution with a 90% confidence level with a LB of 8% and an upper bound of 20%.

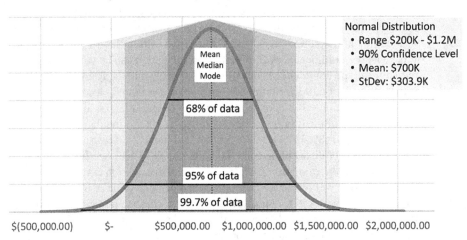

FIGURE 9.14 Normal distribution ("Bell Curve") of expected loss. Expected loss is described here using a normal distribution with a 90% confidence level with a LB of $200K and an upper bound of $1.2M. Notice that negative values are possible in this distribution, but negative values are not acceptable for expected loss.

The log normal distribution describes the log of variables from a normal distribution curve. Log normal distributions correct for some of the issues found in applying normal distributions to security risk variables. Log normal distributions created a "skewed" (not centered) distribution that exhibits the following features:

— Low mean values—For many expected loss scenarios a greater than average number of occurrences will result in a low loss value. For example, most lost laptops do not result in an ultimate data breach so the overall loss for this event tends to only include

Loss Probability (Log Normal Distribution)

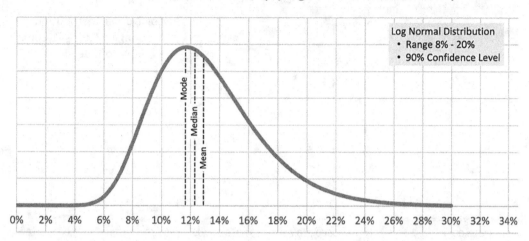

FIGURE 9.15 Log normal probability distribution of loss probability. Loss probability is described here using a log normal distribution with a 90% confidence level with a LB of 8% and an upper bound of 20%. Notice that this distribution is slightly skewed to the right allowing higher probabilities but favoring a lower probability of loss.

operational disruption and hardware asset loss. A distribution representing this loss event may be better modeled with a probability distribution that exhibits low average values.

– Large variances—For many expected loss scenarios there exist some elements of the data set that represent very large losses (e.g., the lost laptop that does result in a data breach of 100K records). The log normal probability distribution can be skewed right, meaning that is has a long right-sided "tail" representing the rare large losses.

– All positive values—When referring to either loss probability or expected loss security risk variables, neither of them would have a negative value. Log normal probability distributions have the feature that all values are positive and therefore these distributions are often a good choice for modeling the security risk variable.

The log normal distribution curve approximates many natural, scientific, and industrial data sets such as adult weight and blood pressure, bacteria survival time, mean time to failure (MTTF), and failure rates. Like normal distributions, log normal distributions can be described by simply knowing the data set upper and LBs and deriving the standard deviation. Using the same range, confidence level and a similar mathematic trick to derive the standard deviation we can create a log normal distribution for the ransomware loss frequency, see Figure 9.15.[5]

Continuing with the example we can use a log normal distribution to describe the expected loss for the laptop as well. Here we estimate the expected loss range from $200K to $1.2M with a confidence level of 90%. The log normal distribution of the expected loss values is depicted in Figure 9.16.

• Triangular Distribution—The triangular probability distribution is a useful alternative to the uniform, normal, and log normal distributions in some situations. When the assessor can represent the values with an upper and LB limit (the value will never fall below or rise above) and the mode (ML value) is not in the middle, a triangular probability distribution is quite useful. There is no function within Excel for the triangular distribution, but it can be created with the following formula:

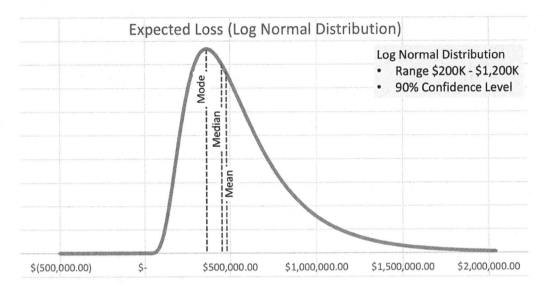

FIGURE 9.16 Log normal probability distribution of expected loss. Expected loss is described here using a log normal distribution with a 90% confidence level with a LB of $200K and an upper bound of $1.2MK. Notice that this distribution does not contain negative values and extreme losses are possible.

```
IF(x<lower_bound,0,
IF(x<mode,2*(x-lower_bound)/
((upper_bound)*mode-lower_bound)),
IF(x<upper_bound,2*(upper_bound-x)/
((upper_bound-lower_bound)*(upper_bound-mode)),0)))
```

- x: Value for which you want the distribution
- Mode: ML value (estimate)
- Lower_bound: Lower limit of value (estimate)
- Upper_bound: Upper limit of value (estimate)

  For example, if the assessor believes that the chance of a ransomware incident will never be below 8% and never above 20% and wants to set the most likely chance at 12% then the triangular probability distribution can be used to describe the loss probability value, see Figure 9.17.

  Similarly, if the assessor believes that the chance of a ransomware incident will never have an expected loss below $200,000 and never above $1.2M and wants to set the ML loss at $400K then the triangular probability distribution can be used to describe the loss probability value, see Figure 9.18.

- Beta Distribution—The beta probability distribution models a probability and therefore generates numbers between zero and one. The location and shape of the curve are dictated by the selection of the alpha (α) and beta (β) parameters of this function. The beta probability distribution can produce a wide variety of probability distributions and is best used when the assessor graphs the distribution through successive changes to the parameters until the resultant probability distribution equates to a 90% confidence. In Excel, the Beta distribution function is:

```
BETA.DIST(x,alpha,beta,cumulative)
```

- x: Value for which you want the distribution
- alpha (α): Required parameter that affects the "shift" of the distribution curve

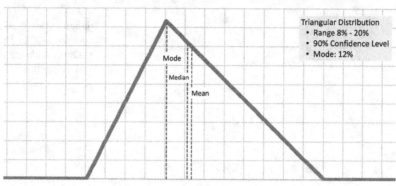

Loss Probability (Triangular Distribution)

FIGURE 9.17 Triangular probability distribution of loss probability. Loss probability is described here using a triangular distribution with a 90% confidence level with a LB of 8%, an upper bound of 20%, and a mode of 12%. Notice that this distribution is slightly skewed to the right allowing higher probabilities but favoring a lower probability of loss and strictly limited to probabilities between 8% and 20%.

- beta (β): Required parameter that affects the "spread" of the distribution curve
- Cumulative: Enter TRUE or FALSE depending if you want a cumulative distribution function (probability that a value of x or lower will occur) or a probability mass function (probability that a value of x will occur).

   In general, increasing the α parameter shifts the probability to the right, increasing the β parameter shifts the probability to the left; and the distribution narrows as both α and β increase. Using our ransomware example, lets say that the assessor wants to model a probability distribution for the loss probability of ransomware based on a target of around 8% to 20% probability with a more customized curve than can be created with the normal, log normal, or triangular probability distributions. Using the beta probability distribution, the assessor can make successive iterative changes to the α and β parameters until the probability distribution models the assessor's 90% confidence level, see Figure 9.19.

   The beta probability distribution can be applied directly to the security risk variable of *loss probability* as the values map easily to percentages (0–1). When using the beta probability distribution for the security risk variable of *expected loss* the result (between zero and one) will need to be used in an equation to achieve the probability distribution desired around the upper and LBs.

- PERT-Beta Distribution—The PERT-Beta probability distribution model is a Beta probability distribution based on the Program Evaluation and Review Technique (PERT) model for estimation. The PERT model improves estimation by weighing the ML (mode) estimate four times what the minimum and maximum estimates are weighed. For example, if you were to estimate the number of laptops that may go missing next year with a minimum of zero, a ML number of one, and a maximum number of five then a standard average would be two ((0+1+5)/3), but a PERT average would be 1.5 (((0+4*1+5))/6). This weighing of the ML is expected to produce a more accurate estimate.

   The PERT-Beta probability distribution uses the easy-to-estimate values of minimum, ML, and maximum to derive the alpha (α) and beta (β) parameters in a Beta distribution. This model is an improvement to the triangular probability distribution in that it smooths out the angles and more closely models natural phenomenon. Recall that the triangular

Expected Loss (Triangular Distribution)

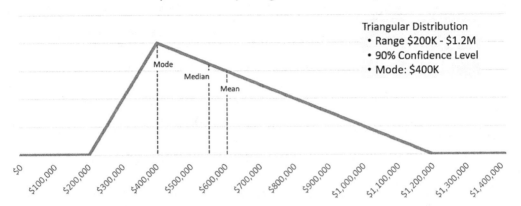

FIGURE 9.18   Triangular probability distribution of expected loss. Expected loss is described here using a triangular distribution with a 90% confidence level with a LB of $200K, an upper bound of $1.2M, and a mode of $400K. Notice that this distribution is slightly skewed to the right allowing losses but favoring a lower expected loss and strictly limited to losses between $200K and 1.2M.

distribution was based on equal weighting of the minimum, ML, and maximum values. In the PERT-Beta distribution the *ML* value is weighted four times what the other values weigh.

When the *ML* value is the average of the *most pessimistic* and *most optimistic* values there is little difference in this method over the simpler *low* and *high* range method. However, in cases where one of the values is farther away from the ML than the other, the PERT estimate moves toward the further value. In many risk scenarios many cases of the *most pessimistic* value tend to be farther out than the *most optimistic* values and their range of numbers tend to move toward the most pessimistic number.

The PERT-Beta probability distribution can produce varying probability distributions and is best used when the assessor can estimate the minimum, ML, and maximum with a 90% confidence level. There is not a specific PERT-Beta function in Excel, but the Beta distribution function can be used with the PERT variables. In Excel, the PERT-Beta distribution is implemented in the following way:

$$\texttt{BETA.DIST(x,alpha,beta,FALSE,min,max)}$$

- x: Value for which you want the distribution
- alpha (α): Required parameter calculated as follows:

$$\left(4*\left(mode-minimum\right)\right)/\left(\left(maximum-minimum\right)+1\right.$$

- beta (β): Required parameter calculated as follows:

$$\frac{4*\left(maximum-mode\right)}{maximum-minimum}+1$$

- Cumulative: Enter TRUE or FALSE depending if you want a cumulative distribution function (probability that a value of x or lower will occur) or a probability mass function (probability that a value of x will occur).

The standard PERT weight of four applied to the mode can be modified to flatten the curve. When this is desired a lambda value of two to 3.5 is typically applied. For

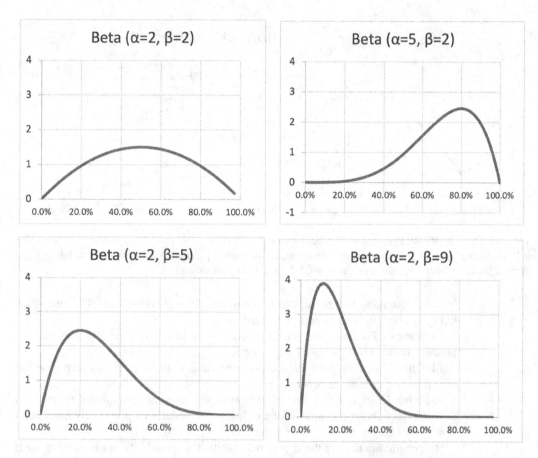

FIGURE 9.19 Beta probability distribution of loss probability. Loss probability is described here using a beta distribution. Notice the successive iterative changes to the α and β parameters (and the resultant probability distribution) until the assessor achieves a distribution at a 90% confidence level that represents the loss probability.

our example, however, we will stick with the standard weight of four and create a PERT-Beta probability distribution with minimum, mode, and maximum values of 8%, 12%, and 20% to represent the loss probability of ransomware, see Figure 9.20.

- Weibull Distribution—The Weibull probability distribution models reliability analysis such as the MTTF for devices. The location and shape of the curve are dictated by the selection of the function's alpha (α) and beta (β) parameters. The Weibull probability distribution can produce varying probability distributions and is best used when the assessor either knows the Weibull parameters (α and β) for a given hardware device or graphs the distribution through successive changes to the parameters until the resultant probability distribution equates to a 90% confidence. In Excel, the Weibull distribution function is:

```
WEIBULL.DIST(x,alpha,beta,cumulative)
```

- x: Value for which you want the distribution
- alpha (α): Required parameter that indicates time to failure with respect to the beta parameter. Generally, this is set to the median of the time to be studied. For example, 5,000 hours for studying the 1–4-year failure rates for a hardware device.
- beta (β): Required parameter that indicates the way in which time affects failure rates:

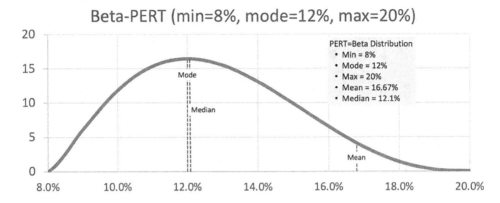

FIGURE 9.20 PERT-Beta probability distribution of loss probability. Loss probability is described here using a PERT-Beta distribution. In this distribution the Beta distribution parameters of alpha (α) and beta (β) are derived based on estimated values of minimum, ML, and maximum values.

- $\beta < 1$: Descending failure rates (referred to as "infant mortality") as defective items fail early and failure rates decrease over time
- $\beta = 1$: Steady failure rates that remain constant over time. This generally indicates that failure rates are most due to external forces
- $\beta > 1$: Climbing failure rates that increase over time. This indicates that parts wear out over time (e.g., the aging process)
- Cumulative: Enter TRUE or FALSE depending if you want a cumulative distribution function (probability that a value of x or lower will occur) or a probability mass function (probability that a value of x will occur).

  In general, increasing the α parameter shifts the probability up, increasing the β parameter affects the curve of the distribution. As an example, a hard drive that is known to follow a Weibull distribution with $\alpha = 5,000$ hours and $\beta = 2.6$ (climbing failure rates) is shown in Figure 9.21.

- Exponential Distribution—The exponential probability distribution models many natural (and other) phenomena that have an exponential decay rate such as number of years until the next earthquake or the damage incurred from natural disasters. The rate of decay is dictated by the selection of the function's lambda (λ) parameter. The lambda parameter is calculated as the inverse (e.g., 1/x) of the mean value. For example, if the return period for major hurricanes is 16 years then the λ parameter is 1/16. In Excel, the exponential distribution function is:

```
EXPON.DIST(x,lambda,cumulative)
```

- x: Value for which you want the distribution
- lambda (λ): Required parameter that indicates the rate of decay of the curve. This is set to the inverse of the mean (e.g., 1/16).
- Cumulative: Enter TRUE or FALSE depending if you want a cumulative distribution function (probability that a value of x or lower will occur) or a probability mass function (probability that a value of x will occur).

  An example of the loss probability distribution of a major hurricane with a return period of 16 years is shown in Figure 9.22.

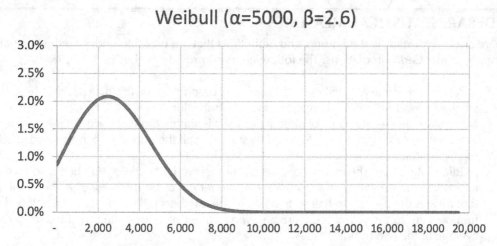

FIGURE 9.21 Weibull probability distribution of hardware device failure rates. Loss probability (caused by a hardware device failure) is described here using a Weibull distribution. This distribution has the parameters values of α = 5,000 hours and β = 2.6 (climbing failure rates).

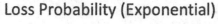

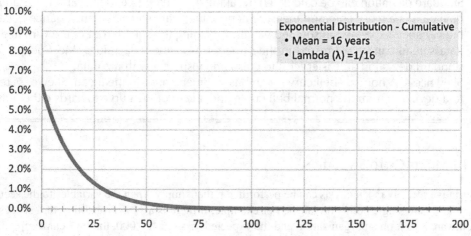

FIGURE 9.22 Exponential Probability Distribution of Hurricane Return Periods. Loss probability (the return of a major hurricane) is described here using an exponential distribution. This distribution has the parameters values of λ = 1/16 years.

SIDEBAR: STATISTICAL MEASURES

There are several statistical measures and definitions that are useful to understand when performing Monte Carlo simulations. The following terms provide the basics:

- Range (Confidence Interval) —The range is a description of the data set that lists the smallest (lower bound) and largest (upper bound) values.
- Mean (Average) —The mean of a set of numbers is simply the average of all the numbers in the set. The mean can be calculated by summing all the numbers in the set and dividing by the total numbers in the set.
- Median (Middle) —The median of a set of numbers is the "middle" number. If you were to arrange all the values in the data set in numerical order the median is the number that divides the data set in half so that half of the numbers fall to the right and half of the numbers fall to the left. If there are an even number of values, then the median is the average of the two middle values.
- Mode (Most Frequent) —The mode of a set of numbers is the value that appears the most. the average of all the numbers in the set. If the data set has more than one value with the most frequently occurring value, then the data set has more than one mode.
- Variance—A statistical measure of the spread between values in a set of data. Variance is calculated by squaring the difference between each value in the data set and the mean and then taking the average of those squares. Variance is a measure of the variability of the values in the data set.
- Standard Deviation—A statistical measure of the data dispersion relative to the mean. Standard deviation can be calculated by taking the square root of the variance. Standard deviation is a more common measurement of the "data spread" than variance because the variance expressed in squared values. By taking the square root of the variance the data spread can be expressed in the same terms as the data values. Most people find standard deviation an easier term to grasp and visualize with the data.
- Skewness—A normal "bell curve" exhibits symmetry around the mean. Skewness refers to a deviation from the normal bell curve and a lean of the curve towards either end.

9.3.4 MONTE CARLO SIMULATION

Quantitative security risk analysis can be performed rather simply when the variables to the security risk equation are single points or values. For example, if there is a 12% probability of a successful ransomware attack on an organization and the expected loss is $400,000, then we can simply multiple $400,000 by 12% to obtain a $48,000 risk (expected annual loss), see Figure 9.23.

However, it is not always possible or even useful to provide single point estimates for security risk variables. Estimate ranges allow the security risk assessor to provide a more insightful and useful estimate to be used in the qualitative security risk analysis. These estimate ranges are expressed in probability distributions or pdfs (e.g., normal distribution and lognormal distribution). These estimate ranges (expressed in probability distributions) allow the assessor to express uncertainty while still expressing a measurement. Furthermore, these probability distributions account for the range of all possible values instead of just the ML (mode) or average (mean) value.

The issue is that once probability distributions are adopted as the preferred method of the security risk assessment team (or the adopted security risk methodology), the assessment team cannot rely on straightforward mathematics to calculate the security risk. There is no straightforward mathematical function for multiplying a loss probability distribution with an expected loss probability distribution to determine the security risk (probability distribution). In fact, determining a result from probability

FIGURE 9.23 Simple quantitative security risk analysis. When the values of the security risk equation variables (loss probability and expected loss) are single points, computing the ALE to a security risk such as ransomware is straightforward using multiplication.

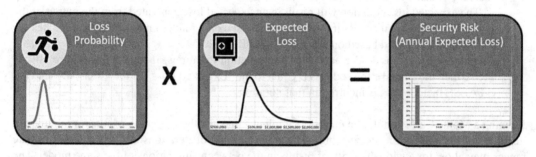

FIGURE 9.24 Quantitative security risk analysis through Monte Carlo Simulation. When the values of the security risk equation variables (loss probability and expected loss) are represented by pdfs (or probability mass functions), computing the ALE to a security risk such as ransomware can be performed through Monte Carlo simulations.

distributions has been a problem that plagued mathematicians until the invention of a mathematical technique referred to as Monte Carlo Simulation. This technique was invented by Stanislaw Ulam in the 1940s as a way to deal solving problems in neutron diffusion. The technique involves the generation of a solution probability distribution from two (or more) other probability distributions. Applying this technique requires running a simulation in which a random number is selected based on each of the probability distributions representing the security risk equation variables. The simple multiplication can be performed on the random numbers selected in each simulation or iteration. When this process is repeated, say 5,000 times, we have a large enough set of security risk solutions to allow us to create a graph of the probability distribution of those solutions, see Figure 9.24.

9.3.4.1 Ransomware Example—Monte Carlo Simulation

In our ransomware example, a random number would be selected based on the pdf representing the loss probability governed by values of 8% (minimum), 20% (maximum) and a pdf representing the expected loss governed by the values of $200,000 (minimum) and $1,200,000 (maximum).

- Loss Probability—Based on the example organization and research the loss pdf is assumed to follow the normal distribution curve (for the purpose of this example) and a minimum and maximum range of 8% and 20%, respectively. We can simulate this risk equation variable using Excel with the following formula:

```
=IF(RAND()<=NORMINV(RAND(),mean,standard_dev)
```

Where, mean = max + min/2 (0.20 + 0.08)/2 = 0.14, and
standard = max − min/3.29 = (0.20 − 0.08)/3.29 = 3.65

The loss probability equation will result in a TRUE (1) if the random number generated is less than the random number generated from the output of the loss probability distribution function based on a random number and a FALSE if not. This simulates the ransomware event with an 8%–20% chance of occurring.

- Expected Loss—Based on the example organization and research the expected loss pdf is assumed to follow the normal distribution curve (for the purpose of this example) and a minimum and maximum range of $200K–$1.2M. We can simulate this risk equation variable using Excel with the following formula:

$$=\texttt{NORMINV(RAND(),mean,standard\_dev)}$$

Where, mean = max + min/2 (200K + 1200K)/2 = 700K, and
standard = max − min/3.29 = (200K − 1200K)/3.29 = $303,951.37

The expected loss equation will result in an expected loss generated from the output of the expected loss probability distribution function based on a random number. This simulates the expected loss incurred based on a range of $200K to $1.2M.

- Annual Expected Loss—For each of the simulation iterations, if the "Ransomware Hit" is TRUE then the annual expected loss is equal to the "Expected Loss." If the "Ransomware Hit" is FALSE then no loss is incurred in that iteration.

Running a Monte Carlo simulation on this example we may get the following results for the first ten iterations of the simulation. Performing just a small number of iterations on across these estimate ranges may allow for a wide disparity of results in the between simulations of the same model. The sample small run of the simulation above gives us an 80% chance of $0 expected loss and a 10% chance of a $1.2M loss or $418K loss. It is easy to image how successive runs of this same model would give varying results, see Table 9.5.

TABLE 9.5
Sample (First ten) Monte Carlo Simulation Iterations

Simulation Iteration #	Ransomware Hit	Expected Loss	Annual Expected Loss
Simulation should run 1,000–10,000 iterations	Normal Probability Distribution [Min: 8%; Max: 20%]	Normal Probability Distribution [Min: $200K; Max: $1.2M]	Expected Loss = Expected Impact if ransomware hit = Yes
1	FALSE	$ 1,067,442	$ 0
2	FALSE	$ 1,168,788	$ 0
3	TRUE	$ 1,199,866	$ 1,199,866
4	FALSE	$ 776,814	$ 0
5	FALSE	$ 575,262	$ 0
6	FALSE	$ 911,942	$ 0
7	FALSE	$ 919,943	$ 0
8	FALSE	$ 783,564	$ 0
9	FALSE	$ 1,173,644	$ 0
10	TRUE	$ 418,160	$ 418,160

Note: The annual expected loss of a specific security risk (e.g., ransomware) can be derived from a simulation of the security risk equation through Monte Carlo simulations when the risk variables are described with probability distribution functions or probability mass functions.

To overcome this variation the Monte Carlo simulations, apply the law of large numbers theorem which states that as the number of simulations performed increases the average of the results gets closer to the expected value. Therefore, Monte Carlo simulations are typically run for 5,000 to 10,000 iterations. Running the same simulation above for a sufficient number of iterations produces a more accurate ransomware security risk result, see Figure 9.25.

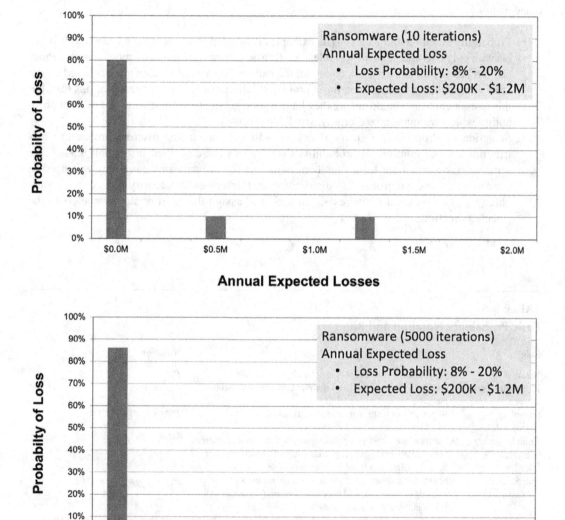

FIGURE 9.25 Monte Carlo Simulation—number of iterations. Performing a large number of iterations of the Monte Carlo simulations create an annual expected loss probability distribution closer to the expected outcome. Above we see the refinement of the probability distribution from a run of ten iterations to a run of 5,000 iterations of the simulation based on the ransomware example.

9.3.4.2 Building Monte Carlo Simulation Models

Monte Carlo simulations can handle a variety of security risk equations depending on the needs of the assessment team. When using Monte Carlo simulations to calculate the security risk, the security risk assessment team may employ a variety of equations, variables, and mathematical rules to create complex equations for specific scenarios. Those members of the assessment team building complex models of security risk will need to be well-versed in basic probability rules, the appropriate selection of probability density (or mass) functions and their parameters, and building security risk equations.

- Probability Notation and Rules—The examples illustrated in this text have been simple models with only two independent variables. As the assessment team employs more complex models to represent the security risk equation, the team must carefully create models based on the laws of probability. A primer on basic probability theory is beyond the reach of this text, but the assessment team should ensure they have a good grasp of the basic facts and rules of probability which are summarized briefly, see Table 9.6.
- Selection of Probability Density Functions—In addition to the discrete probability distributions, seven continuous probability distributions are described in Section 9.3.3.[6] The security risk assessment team members modeling the security risk equations will need to appropriately select a probability distribution that describes the security risk equation variable (e.g., loss probability and expected loss) and assign the appropriate parameters to the selected function.

TABLE 9.6
Basic Probability Notation and Rules

Rule	Description	Notation
Notation	The probability of an event A is notated:	$P(A)$
Probability values	A probability is expressed as a number between zero and one, inclusive.	$0 \leq P(A) \leq 1$
Sum of all probabilities	If all possible outcomes are events A, B, and C then.	$P(A) + P(B) + P(C) = 1$
Complementary events	When there are only two possible outcomes and those outcomes are mutually exclusive (e.g., a coin flip will result in either heads or tails) then those events are complementary.	$P(A') = 1 - P(A)$
Independent events	When the result of one event has no effect on the result of another event those events are said to be independent. (e.g., result of the first coin flip and the result of the second coin flip).	$P(A \text{ and } B) = P(A) \times P(B)$
Dependent events	When the result of one event has an effect on the result of another event those events are said to be dependent. (e.g., result of the first die roll and the total of the first and second die roll).	
Independent multiplication	The chance of both independent events occurring is equal to each probability multiplied by the other.	$P(A \cap B) = P(A)P(B)$
Dependent multiplication (conditional probability)	The chance of both dependent events occurring is equal to each probability that the first event occurs multiplied by the probability that the second event occurs given that the first event occurred.	$P(A \cap B) = P(A)P(B|A)$
Addition rule	The chance either of two events occurring is equal to the chance of the first event occurring plus the chance of the second event occurring minus the chance of both events occurring.	$P(A \cup B) = P(A) + P(B) - P(A \cap B)$

Note: Security risk assessment teams using quantitative methodologies, especially Monte Carlo simulations will need a basic understanding of probabilities and the basic notation and rules in order to build more complex security risk equations.

There are no specific rules for which functions to select for security risk equation variables but there are some observations that may guide the assessment team in the appropriate selection the appropriate functions.

- Discrete or Continuous—Determine if the security risk variable is best represented by discrete data or continuous data. Discrete distributions are best applied to events whose outcomes result in a discrete value such as *true* or *false* or an integer value. Continuous distributions are best applied to events whose outcomes cover a continuous data set such as the MTTF or the expected loss in dollars.

  - Discrete Data—When the security risk variable can take on only discrete values, a discrete distribution function should be used. Examples of such variables include events that happen or do not (e.g., True or False) and events that have a discrete number of hits (e.g., number of laptops stolen). When working with a discrete security risk equation variable the best approach to determining an appropriate probability distribution function is to first identify all of the possible outcomes, estimate the probabilities for each outcome using historical data, experience, or specific knowledge, and then choose the function that best fits the behavior of the variable, see Table 9.7.
  - Continuous Data—When the security risk equation variable can take on any value, a continuous distribution function should be used. For many variables we cannot list all possible outcomes and their functions can best be represented by continuous distribution functions., Examples include the length of a power outage or expected loss variables that are not based on a pre-set amount such as a fine. When working with a continuous security risk equation variable the best approach is to examine the identifying characteristics of the possible data values:
  - Symmetry—Does the data set exhibit a symmetric relationship (e.g., mirror image of data values on either side of the mode?)
  - Skewness—If the data values are not symmetric, are they skewed toward lower (positively skewed) or higher (negatively skewed) values? For example, you may expect between 15 minutes to 4 hours of downtime next year, but you are more likely to see values under 1 hour than above 2 hours.
  - Tails—Does the data show exhibit a very low probability of deviating more than a few standard deviations from the mean or is there a need to represent infrequent but possible very large values. Distributions that describe data values that can deviate substantially from the mean are said to have "fat tails." For example, an expected loss may typically range around $5K–$10K but a small percentage of the time cost over $1M.
  - Limits—Are there upper or lower limits on the possible outcomes? For example, you will not have a negative amount of downtime or fines will not exceed $1M.
  - Negative Values—Do you need to ensure that the data values cannot take on negative values? For example, expected losses should be positive.

    Based on the assessor's understanding of the possible data values, the appropriate continuous probability distribution function should be selected and tuned appropriately using the associated parameters, see Table 9.8.

- Building Security Risk Equations—In its simplest form, the security risk equation is *loss probability* times *expected loss*, see Figure 9.17. When the security risk assessment is able to obtain estimate data sufficient to create a probability distribution for each of these variables then building the security risk equation remains rather simple. However, if the assessment team cannot obtain adequate data for estimation, more complex security risk scenarios and associated security risk equations may be required. The creation of these equations cannot be bounded as they vary so greatly but there are a few guidelines that may assist the team:

  - Keep it Simple—Even when the assessment team feels that data is sparse and estimation could prove difficult, it is advisable to stick with the simple two variable security risk equation while increasing the range of estimation values to obtain the desired confident

TABLE 9.7

Selection of Discrete Probability Density Functions

Function/Parameters	Description/Parameters	Applications
Uniform	A flat distribution; all outcomes have an equal opportunity of occurring. $P(outcome\ 1, outcome\ 2, ...)$	Events with multiple possible outcomes but no data that one is more probable than the other such as day of the week laptop is stolen.
Binary	Only two possible outcomes: the event happens or not. • $P(outcome)$	Events with large impacts that happen infrequently such as a natural disaster or major data breach.
Frequency	The probability of each outcome is known. • $P(outcome\ 1)$ • $P(outcome\ 2)...$	Events in which the assessor has historical data such as lost laptops over the last 5 years.
Binomial	Probabilities of the number of "successes" or "hits" over a given number of trials. • #of trials • $P(success)$	Events that happen multiple times in a given time period for which you are able to determine the probability of each number of hits such as lost laptops.
Poisson	Measures the probabilities of a number of events occurring over a given time period. • Lambda (λ)—average number of events	Events that happen multiple times in a given time period such as malware incidents and exhibit asymmetry.

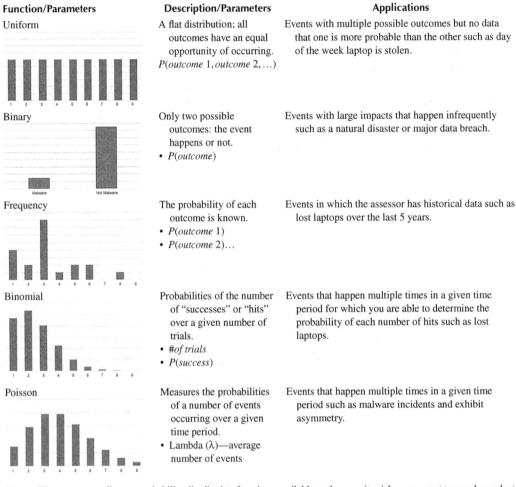

Note: There are many discrete probability distribution functions available to the security risk assessment team when selecting an appropriate model to represent the security risk equation variables. These are a few of the more popular ones.

level (e.g., 90%). There are many data sources and estimation techniques that the team can utilize to obtain adequate estimation data for both the *loss probability* and the *expected loss* functions for almost all security risk scenarios. Breaking the equation down further may be required in some instances but start with the principle of keeping it simple.

• Focus on Meaningful Difference—When creating more complex security risk equations the assessment team should only add variables to the equation when there is a meaningful difference in the associated values. For example, a security risk equation covering lost or stolen laptops could be expanded to include a variable indicating the probability that the laptop is protected though full disk encryption (FDE).

$$Security\ Risk = P\big(lost\ laptop\big) * \big(P\big(laptop\ FDE\big) * P\big(loss\ with\ FDE\big) + \begin{pmatrix} 1 - P\big(laptop\ FDE\big) \\ * P\big(loss\ without\ FDE\big)\big) \end{pmatrix}$$

    For variables with smaller differences in resultant values (e.g., loss of MacBook laptop vs. loss of PC laptop) the resultant expected loss distribution is rarely sufficiently different and worth the burden of complexity.

- Understand the Application Probability Theory—Creating more complex security risk equations will require the correct application of probability theory to ensure the correctness of the equations and solutions. Basic probability rules were introduced in Table 9.6. In addition to understanding dependent and independent events, conditional probabilities, addition, and multiplication rules, the assessment team should acquire a solid understanding of more advanced probability theory concepts such as Log Odds Ratio (LOR).

- Double-Check Dependence—The assessment team should double-check the security risk equation variables and the assumptions made on their dependence (or independence). The appropriate security risk equation elements differ greatly when combining probabilities of dependent vs. independent variables. The assessment team should review their initial security risk equation constructs to ensure that initial assumptions on these variables are correct. For example, consider the security risk equation above that differentiates between a laptop with and without FDE implemented. This example assumes that the variables for the probability of the lost laptop and the laptop FDE are independent. The assessment team should consider whether the laptops that are more likely to be lost or stolen are also more likely to have implemented FDE. If so, the appropriate security risk equation would use the dependent multiplication rule instead of the independent multiplication rule as in the equation above.

9.3.4.3 Quantitative Analysis Advantages

Quantitative methods, based on the objective measurements and mathematical calculations, have many benefits:

- Objective—A security risk decision variable determined through quantitative analysis can be considered objective. Because the calculations that determine the value of the security risk decision variables are based on pre-determined formulas, the resultant value can be considered objective and not as likely to be influenced by subjective measures or judgment.

- Expressed in "Real" Numbers—Asset valuation and safeguard valuation can all be expressed in terms of specific costs (e.g., U.S. dollars). When considering the value of a single asset, consider all direct and indirect values of the asset. It also helps to consider the value of the asset in light of a specific threat.

Consider a warehouse that stores inventory and that is threatened by a fire. First, consider the direct costs of the building itself, and the inventory and equipment inside the building. These values are relatively easy to obtain because market value and replacement costs can usually be easily computed. Then consider the indirect costs. These costs may include, but are certainly not limited to, lost business due to the fire, lost business due to loss of reputation of the organization, and potential loss of life. The calculation of the indirect costs is typically more complicated than that of direct costs. This calculation becomes difficult as unknown elements and values that are difficult to obtain enter the equation.

    In Table 9.9, three indirect costs are computed. The first indirect cost is that of lost business due to the fire in the warehouse. In the example, it was determined that lost business would be equal to the profit that would have normally been made from orders during the time it takes to get the warehouse functions back to normal. The second indirect cost is the damage to the organization through the loss of reputation due to a fire in the warehouse. In this example, loss of reputation is considered to be a 10% drop in business for 1 year. When considering the loss of future monies, you must also consider the present value of the future revenues. A present-value-of-money formula was used in the calculation in the example to account for the time value of money. The third indirect cost considered here is potential loss of life.

TABLE 9.8

Selection of Continuous Probability Density Functions

Function/Parameters	Description/Parameters	Applications
Uniform	A flat distribution: all outcomes have an equal opportunity of occurring.	All values in the range have an equal probability such as the day of the week for the first 100 days.
Normal	Common distribution exhibiting symmetry, data clustered around a central value, and few outliers. • Mean-central value (or LB and UB) • Standard Deviation (or a 90% CI with LB and UB)	Values clustered around a central value with few outliers. Examples include test scores and stock market returns.
Log Normal	Asymmetric distribution where values skew mostly positively. • Mean-central value (or LB and UB) • Standard Deviation (or a 90% CI with LB and UB)	Values positively skewed such as mean time to failure and failure rates.
Triangle	Symmetric or asymmetric distribution shaped by three values and no outliers. • Lower Bound (LB) • Upper Bound (UB) • Most Likely (ML)	Values clustered toward a center value but with strict limits on LB and UB such as expected losses with a cap.
Beta	Flexible distribution that can exhibit positive or negative skewness. • alpha (α)—shift • beta (β)—spread	Used in a variety of applications when the assessor wants flexibility with creating a curve.
PERT-Beta	Beta distribution where parameters are derived from LB, UB, and ML: • alpha (α) $(4*(ML-LB))/((UB-LB)+1$ • beta (β) $\dfrac{4*(UB-ML)}{UB-LB}+1$	Used when the assessor can estimate LB, UB, and ML.
Weibull	Asymmetric distribution with positive skew. • alpha (α)—time to failure • beta (β)—failure rate. • $\beta < 0$: descending failure rates • $\beta = 1$: steady failure rates • $\beta > 1$: climbing failure rates	Used in reliability analysis to model failure rates.

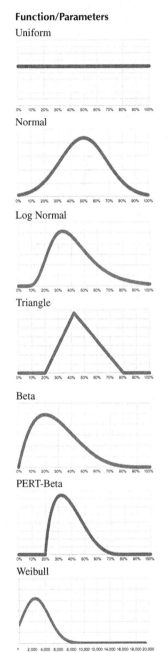

(*Continued*)

TABLE 9.8   *(Continued)*

Function/Parameters	Description/Parameters	Applications
Exponential 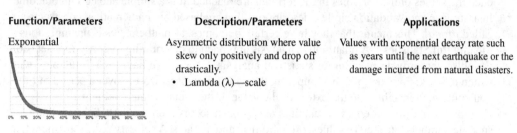	Asymmetric distribution where value skew only positively and drop off drastically. • Lambda (λ)—scale	Values with exponential decay rate such as years until the next earthquake or the damage incurred from natural disasters.

Note: There are many continuous probability distribution functions available to the security risk assessment team when selecting an appropriate model to represent the security risk equation variables. These are a few of the more popular ones.

TABLE 9.9
Quantitative Measurements

Asset Valuation Components	Value	Justification
Direct costs		
Building	$100,000	Cost to rebuild
Inventory	$50,000	Cost to organization
Equipment	$48,000	Replacement cost
Indirect costs		
Lost business	$24,000	4 weeks to return to normal operations; loss of $6,000 profit from orders per week
Lost reputation	$31,200[7]	Expected loss of business—10% of 1 year's business
Employee endangerment	$7,583	Risk of life is 0.076%[8]; value of life = $10 million

Note: Quantitative analysis of asset valuation and safeguard valuation results in a specific cost.

In the example of the warehouse in Table 9.9, a single security guard was considered. The warehouse has no full- or part-time employees assigned to the building except for a single security guard. Because the guard is posted outside the building and charged with detecting and reporting a fire but not with building evacuation, the chances that the fire would injure or kill the security guard are considered low. Valuation of a human life is perhaps the toughest of all the quantitative security risk decision variables. It is an absolutely political and moral nightmare to put a dollar value on a human life; however, such a value is required if you plan on performing a cost–benefit analysis that involves human life. The statistic is called "Value of a Statistical Life" (VSL). VSL refers to the value gained in the reduction of the average number of deaths by one instead of a specific human life.

If you plan to use quantitative analysis, you will need a dollar figure. Using a VSL from another source provides some level of credibility to your analysis. In 2016, the United States Environmental Protection Agency set the value of a human life at $10 million. The EPA seems to be the most generous agency, as the Department of Transportation uses a VSL of $9.6 million; the Food and Drug Administration and Health and Human Services uses a VSL of $9.5 million; and the U.S. Department of Agriculture uses a VSL of $8.9 million. In the warehouse example, a human life is considered to be worth $10 million, consistent with the highest of these VSLs. Further benefits of quantitative analysis include

- More Easily Understood—The expected loss is better understood. Formulas are mathematical equations. The simplest of formulas, like those listed previously, are very easy to understand. It is important to separate the concepts of understanding from those of agreement. I am not saying that you will not have heated debates about the value of a human life, for instance, but once the values of the variables in the formula are reached, it is a simple and certain outcome. In assurance and validation circles, descriptions that are based on mathematical constructs are called *formal*. This means that they have certain outcomes, as mathematics is unambiguous.

- Meaningful Statistics—A quantitative analysis approach to determining security risk decision variables can provide meaningful statistical analysis, because we have "real" numbers with which to work. For example, by comparing the ALE for an organization over a period of time, you could gain insight as to the extent of the value of the security improvements.
- Credible—Analysis based on a quantitative approach seems more credible because there are specific numbers attached to values, probabilities, and impacts. A security risk assessment that results in the statement, "The current annualized expected loss for this organization is $3.16 million due to breaches in cyber-security," seems more credible than the statement, "The current security posture of this organization is medium-high." Although both statements may be based on the same analysis and the same level of rigor in the assessment, the quantitative approach resulting in a dollar figure seems more credible.
- Provides a Basis for Cost–Benefit Analysis—Many corporate decisions requiring the expenditure of limited resources are made only after a careful cost–benefit analysis. This means that the perceived benefit of the project (e.g., develop a patch-management system) must outweigh the cost involved in such a project. Quantitative analysis, namely calculation of safeguard value, can provide the information necessary to analyze the costs and benefits of proposed security controls.
- Supports Budget Decisions—Similarly, the dollar figures provided by the quantitative analysis can be used to support budget estimates for upcoming projects and budget cycles.

9.3.4.4 Quantitative Analysis Disadvantages

Although quantitative analysis has many benefits, the complexity of this approach results in some perceived disadvantages as well:

- Complex—The formulas used in quantitative analysis and the resulting volume of tables upon tables of numbers can be quite complex. This leads to several problems for the project, including the need for more experienced project members and overall increased costs.
- Calculations Often Not Well Understood—The calculations and complexities of probability distributions and Monte Carlo simulations involved in the various formulas can appear daunting and confusing to the reader. This hinders the understanding of the analysis performed.
- Results Not Trusted—The complex formulas and lack of understanding of the calculations may lead to a general frustration and even mistrust of the results. It is difficult to accept the conclusion of a report if you do not understand the analysis. Understanding the analysis of some quantitative methods is a task on a par with understanding geometric proofs.
- A Lot of Work—A quantitative security risk analysis can be labor-intensive because of the number of data elements required and calculations that need to be performed. Substantial information gathering is required to obtain the values needed for the quantitative formulas. The derivation of the value for each of the asset, threat, vulnerability, and safeguard variables for a single team member is difficult enough. Add to that the difficulty of arriving at a team consensus for each and everyone of those values.
- Potential False Sense of Accuracy—Perhaps the biggest perceived disadvantage of a quantitative security risk assessment method is the false sense of accuracy it portrays to most consumers of the information. When consumers of a security risk assessment report are presented with specific figures for expected loss or safeguard value, they tend to believe that the numbers are derived with a large degree of accuracy. The fact is that an accurate value for many variables that go into computing these figures is difficult to obtain and typically is based on subjective elements such as opinion.

The use of quantitative methods in risk analysis has a long history of successful implementation and the application of these methods in security risk analysis have come a long way. Several well-known security risk assessment methods (see Chapter 14) and software tools have evolved and are commonly incorporated into security risk assessments and security risk management. The above disadvantages are listed and discussed as perceived disadvantages. Most of these disadvantages can be overcome through the adoption of solid quantitative methods, the use of estimation techniques, and the appropriate training of the security risk assessment team members.

9.4   SUMMARIZING SECURITY RISK ANALYSIS

Between asset valuation, threat frequency, vulnerability probability, and impact affect, there are many values or numbers of which to keep track. If the security risk assessment team is using a tool, the tool can be used to keep track of and report the values and numbers. If the team is using a process without an automated tool, then an approach is required to track these values.

One such approach is the creation of a table to track analysis and findings. The elements of such a table are dependent on the needs of the security risk assessment team and the assessed organization, but the assessment team should certainly include the following:

- Threat Agent/Action Pair—The root of all security risks is the threat agent and action pair. Any tabulation of security risk analysis results should begin with the threat agent/action pair.
- Threat Frequency Summation—Also called the likelihood of threat occurrence, a summation of any calculations used to arrive at the threat frequency should accompany the threat agent/action pair.
- Expected Impact—The expected impact is a total of the harm to the organization's assets should the threat action occur. This element should accompany the threat agent/action pair as well.
- Calculated Security Risk—This is the calculation result of the threat frequency and the expected impact and should be thought of as the expected annual loss associated with the threat action/agent pair.

This next set of security risk assessment elements may be useful to track and present to the assessed organization in the security risk table. As such, the assessment team should consider their inclusion:

- Threat Frequency Calculation Elements— If the team used any sub elements to estimate and/or calculate the threat frequency such as motive, opportunity, and means, it may be useful to include them in the tracking table as well.
- Expected Impact Calculation Elements—If the team used any subelements to estimate and/or calculate the expected impact such as the harm elements (operations, assets, fines, others) it may to be useful to include these also.
- Vulnerability Conclusions—Summations of the effectiveness of preventative, detective, and corrective controls and their impact on the threat frequency and expected impact values are useful to track.

The security risk tracking table should primarily serve the purpose of tracking the security risk assessment team's data gathering and analysis within the security risk analysis phase of the security risk assessment. There is no new information required to create this tracking table as it is a summary of the findings and analysis already performed. The example table below is a simplified example based on the worked examples in this chapter. The security risk assessment team may expand the tracking table to include additional elements, colors, and even calculations, see Table 9.10.

TABLE 9.10

Security Risk Summary Table: Worked Examples

		Threat		
Agent	**Action**	**Frequency**	**Expected Impact**	**Annualized Security Risk**
Human-Outsider	Ransomware	0.51 • 51% SMBs infected	$1,080,000.00 • 16 days downtime	$550,800.00
Human-Outsider	Laptop Theft	3.75 • 5% loss/year • 75% laptops w/FDE	$9,712.50	$36,421.88
Infrastructure	Power Outage	1.00 • 1.0 outages/year	$31,875.00 • 85-minute downtime	$31,875.00

Note: The security risk assessment team should track the security risk analysis in a security risk summary table. This table provides a common set of outcomes from the analysis and is an effective way to communicate amongst the assessment team.

9.4.1 Team Review of Security Risk Summary

Because of the large amount of data generally compiled during the data gathering stage, not all members of the security risk assessment team may have been in every discussion involving the research, data analysis, and security risk calculations for every threat action. It is a good idea for the security risk assessment team to ensure that all members review and concur with the security risk summary.

Arriving at a consensus for the elements within the security risk statements is an important step in the security risk analysis process. This step ensures that all members of the team have a chance to explain their findings and discuss the findings of others. Furthermore, obtaining a team consensus on the security risk statements allows all team members to gain a perspective of the overall security risk of the organization through a better understanding of all of the elements.

While obtaining consensus on these statements, the team should be wary of too much overlap. The following advice on obtaining security risk statement consensus may prove useful during this exercise:

- Avoid Overlap—While reviewing security risk summary, the team may find that some rows in the security risk summary table (e.g., threat actions and associated elements including security risk) may completely overlap or duplicate others. In this case, the statements should be reduced to a single statement or refocused to eliminate overlap. A best practice is for the team to institute some type of ordering of the statements (e.g., according threat agents) so that all duplicates may be more easily found.
- Group Like Findings—There are likely to be some threat agent/action pairs that have similar findings and likely will have similar recommendations in the next phase. For example, the rows of the security risk table associated with natural disasters (e.g., floods, high winds, and hurricanes) will likely have many analysis elements nearly identical (e.g., lack of response plans). Although the threat frequency may differ somewhat between these threat actions it may be useful to the customer to group these findings into relatively fewer findings with common recommendations, such as create disaster response procedures.

9.4.2 DERIVING OVERALL SECURITY RISK

Next, the security risk assessment team should derive an overall security risk. The overall security risk measurement should be consistent with the statement of work and the ranges used to describe individual security risks. For organizations regulated by information security laws such as the Health Insurance Portability and Accountability Act (HIPAA), the overall security risk should also indicate a level of compliance. For all other organizations, the overall security risk level should indicate a relative security risk, for example, Moderate Security Risk, and a comparison to others in the same industry. The details provided in such a measurement should be supported by the security risk summary table.

9.4.3 PRIORITIZATION OF SECURITY RISK

Lastly, the security risk assessment team should prioritize the security risk findings based on the overall security risk (e.g., ALE) calculated for each security risk scenario or threat action. The prioritized list of security risk findings will be used in the next phase of the security risk assessment: Security Risk Mitigation

www.infosecurityrisk.com	For a downloadable spreadsheet with the discrete and continuous probability distribution functions, Monte Carlo simulation, and a basic security risk equation built with these functions go to the website: www.infosecurityrisk.com and head to the downloads section for the Security Risk Assessment Handbook and go to Chapter 9 downloads.

EXERCISES

1. Quantitative vs. qualitative. For each of the following measurements, indicate if it is qualitative or quantitative in nature.
   a. Your grade in this class
   b. An evaluation based on the Likert scale
   c. Your last employee review (explain)
   d. A movie review consisting of one to five stars
2. What role does the creation of a security risk summary table play in security risk analysis?
3. What data is currently available to assist in determining the likely frequency of the following threat actions?
   a. A structure fire in the nearest warehouse area to your location.
   b. A programmer placing a backdoor in production code.
   c. A misplaced thumb drive with unencrypted customer records
   d. Misdelivery of medical results via e-mail or fax.
4. Requiring encryption on removable media reduces which element of the security risk equation?
   a. To what extent? (consider that this is a policy requirement that all removable media with sensitive information be encrypted).
   b. How would this change if the encryption was enforced through endpoint protection?
5. Using available public data, research, and your own estimations provide a quantitative security risk calculation for the threat action of lost removable media from your organization or university with 10,000 sensitive records. Include threat frequency and expected impact estimations. Include references of any statistics or other estimation aides. Document any assumptions you make.

6. Calculate a qualitative security risk measurement for the following risk scenarios. Use NIST SP 800-30 security risk assessment approach to calculate a qualitative security risk measurement for the following risk scenarios Document any assumptions you must make.
    a. Exfiltration of student information from a university server set up outside of the supervision of a central information technology department.
    b. Account takeover via social engineering of remote customer service agent.
    c. Unauthorized physical access into the nearest data center.
    d. Unauthorized access into corporate systems via unauthorized backdoor installed by trusted programmer.
7. Calculate a quantitative security risk measurement for the risk scenarios in question 6.

NOTES

1 Cohn, Mike, Agile Estimating and Planning, Pearson, November 2005.
2 Hubbard, Douglas W. How to Measure Anything: Finding the Value of Intangibles in Business, 2007.
3 What are the chances a hurricane will hit my home?, National Oceanic and Atmospheric Administration, August 20, 2018, https://www.noaa.gov/stories/what-are-chances-hurricane-will-hit-my-home
4 The assessor should be careful to note that the Poisson distribution assumes that events occur independently. This may not be valid in the case of lost or stolen laptops as several laptops could be stolen at once in a robbery at the office.
5 Log normal probability distribution curves (and other advanced probability distribution curves) will push your knowledge or recall from basic mathematics and statistical methods. We will limit our coverage of different probability distributions to their application in security risk assessment. For a primer or refresh on logarithms, exponents, the derivation of standard deviation, and adjusting the shape, placement, and height of probability distribution curves please consult any standard statistics textbook or your favorite statistics website.
6 There are many more probability distribution functions that could be used that are not covered in this book.
7 The reputation calculation is computed using a present-value-of-money formula with an interest rate of 6% and a loss of 10% of the business profit, or $600/week for a year.
8 2010 FEMA report "Nonresidential Building Fires" states 75 deaths in 98,900 fires in 2006. This equates to a risk of life in nonresidential building fires of 0.076% risk of life.

BIBLIOGRAPHY

Centolella, Paul, Farber-DeAnda, Mindi, et al., Estimates of the Value of Uninterrupted Service for The Mid-West Independent System Operator, https://hepg.hks.harvard.edu/files/hepg/files/voll_final_report_to_miso_042806.pdf
Glen, Stephanie, "Power Law and Power Law Distribution" From StatisticsHowTo.com: Elementary Statistics for the rest of us! https://www.statisticshowto.com/power-law/
Hubbard, Douglas W., How to Measure Anything: Finding the Value of Intangibles in Business, 2007.
Hubbard, Douglas W., Seiersen, Richard, How to Measure Anything in Cybersecurity Risk, 2016.
International Standards Organization, International Standard, ISO/IEC 27001, Information Technology – Security Techniques – Information Security Management Systems, – Requirements, Second Edition 2013-10-1.
Shalizi, Cosma, "So, You Think You Have a Power Law, Do You? Well Isn't That Special?" Statistics Department, Carnegie Mellon University, October 18, 2010. http://www.stat.cmu.edu/~cshalizi/2010-10-18-Meetup.pdf
U.S Department of Homeland Security, Information Technology Sector Baseline Risk Assessment, August 2009, https://www.dhs.gov/xlibrary/assets/nipp_it_baseline_risk_assessment.pdf

10 Security Risk Analysis Worked Examples

In order to demonstrate the concepts of threat assessment, vulnerability assessment, impact assessment, and security risk calculation, this chapter includes worked examples demonstrating the concepts in security risk analysis to illustrate the techniques presented in this chapter. These worked examples provide guidance on *how* to perform this step of the security risk assessment process no matter which method the team chooses to adopt. As such these worked examples will be used throughout this chapter of security risk analysis.

The worked examples will be demonstrated through an example security risk assessment method using both the qualitative approach and a quantitative approach. The assessment team may utilize the guidance and methods that most closely match their own approach or choose to step up their game to a more involved method.

- Qualitative—Qualitative security risk assessment uses methods based on ordinal (order but not scale) categories for security risk measurements. These approaches typically use categories such as low, moderate, high, and critical to order security risk components and overall security risk measurements. An extension of the qualitative approach is the semi-qualitative approach in which ranges of numbers are included in the measurement categories. These number ranges are ordinal (order) but not cardinal (order and scale) and therefore should not be considered quantitative in nature (e.g., very low: 0–15; low: 16–35; moderate: 36–70; high: 71–85; and critical: 86–100).
- Quantitative—Quantitative security risk assessments use methods for assessing security risk based on cardinal numbers that maintain context outside of the security risk calculations (e.g., 10%–20% chance of losing $1M–$2M due to a ransomware attack.)

The worked examples used to illustrate concepts in this chapter are listed and described in Table 10.1. These examples include a lost or stolen laptop, a non-targeted ransomware attack, and a power outage. For the purpose of illustrating the qualitative and quantitative techniques for measuring asset impact, the following threat action examples will be used as an example consulting organization of 75 employees in Austin, Texas.

- Lost or Stolen Laptop—The organization issues laptops for most all of its employees. These laptops are exposed to theft situations and carelessness by the employee, so the laptops could go missing. Employees travel extensively, take their laptops home, take their laptops to customers sites, and remote work locations such as coffee shops. There are ample opportunities for theft or loss. The laptops contain sensitive data for current customers and may not be full disk encrypted (FDE) as the organization has a policy for full disk encryption but has not yet implemented mobile device management. Employees are instructed to report laptops missing. Laptops are replaced, even while on travel, within two business days.
- Power Outage—Power outages are a frequent occurrence through the business world. This organization has a headquarters building that houses a computer operations center, customer services, accounting, the executive's suite, and some of the sales team. A power outage would affect all systems within the building.

TABLE 10.1
Qualitative Threat Action Assessment: Selected Example Threat Actions

Category	Threat Action	Threat Agent	Threat Action Elements	Rating
Invoked malware	**Ransomware** C&C malware Trojan horse Password Dumper Downloader Backdoor	Human–Insider	• Motive: Moderate • Opportunity: High • Methods: High	Very high
Theft & sabotage	Stolen sensitive paper **Stolen laptop—home/travel** Stolen phone—home/travel	Human–Outsider	• Motive: Moderate • Opportunity: Moderate • Methods: High	High
	Stolen laptop—office Stolen phone—office	Human–Insider	• Motive: Moderate • Opportunity: High • Methods: High	Very high
Socially engineered	Physical breach Phishing Spear phishing Pre-texting	Human–Outsider	• Motive: Moderate • Opportunity: High • Methods: High	Very high
Hacked	Brute force Intercept wireless access Vulnerability exploitation Use of stolen credentials	Human–Outsider	• Motive: Moderate • Opportunity: Moderate • Methods: Moderate	Moderate

Category	Threat actions	Threat source	Attributes	Rating
Abused trust	Privilege abuse Illicit content Theft Unapproved software	Human-Insider	• Motive: High • Opportunity: High • Methods: Low	Moderate
Environmental damage	Hurricane, flood high winds, tornadoes Earthquakes	Natural	• Frequency: Very Low–Moderate	Moderate Low Very low
	Power outage Water service interruption	Infrastructure		Moderate Low
Erred	Loss—laptop Loss—phone Misdelivery—e-mail Misdelivery—fax Misdelivery—e-mail Misconfiguration system Misconfigure privileges	Human-Insider	• Motive: Low • Opportunity: Moderate • Methods: Low	Moderate

Note: The security risk assessment team should enumerate specific threat actions like these, ensuring they only list those threat actions that are relevant to the assessed organization.

- Ransomware Attack—Ransomware attacks are popular methods among cybercriminals to infiltrate organizations and to extract payments. This malware may enter the organization's system through social engineering, insecure websites, trojan horse downloads, or weak account credentials. When a ransomware attack has successfully deployed it typically encrypts critical systems files disabling all systems.

10.1   RIIOT FRAME

This section introduces the RIIOT Framework Risk Assessment Method—Example (RIIOT FRAME). The RIIOT FRAME streamlines the security risk assessment process by aligning the assessment method to the data gathering process that has already been performed by the security risk assessment team. This is an example of security risk assessment method for the purposes of demonstration. However, the RIIOT FRAME is a complete process with a few unique benefits not seen in other security risk assessment methods:

- Utilizes RIIOT data gathering—RIIOT FRAME uses much of the work already accomplished by a team that has performed the RIIOT data gathering approach.
- Supports both Qualitative and Quantitative Methods—RIIOT FRAME may be used in a qualitative or quantitative method for the security risk measurement.
- Maintains Clear Link to Evidence—RIIOT FRAME requires that the security risk assessment team utilizes, document, and maintain the RIIOT data gathered evidence to arrive at a security risk measurement. The link to evidence is useful in assessment revisions, presentation, and defense of results.

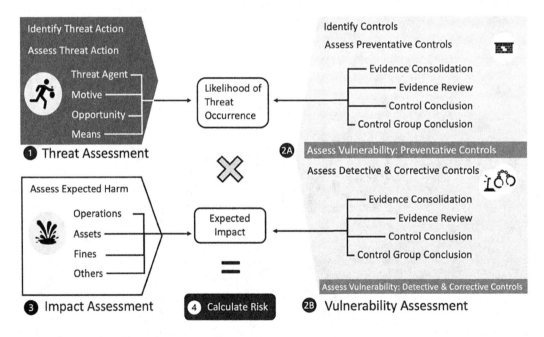

FIGURE 10.1   RIIOT framework risk assessment method—Example (RIIOT FRAME). Security risk is calculated based an understanding of the threats, vulnerabilities, and impact on organizational assets. This approach is based on the RIIOT data gathering and analysis methods.

The calculation of the security risk, at its highest level, is the likelihood that a threat action will occur and the expected impact of that action, see Figure 10.1 There are several steps involved within each of these security risk calculation variables, but one of the values of the RIIOT FRAME is that it keeps this basic security risk calculation simple. The RIIOT FRAME is presented below for both qualitative and quantitative security risk assessments.

10.1.1 RIIOT FRAME—Qualitative

The objective of the first two steps (step 1 and 2A) from Figure 10.1 is to identify the security risk equation variable: *Likelihood of Threat Occurrence*. This may be determined through a threat assessment and a vulnerability assessment of any relevant security controls that may prevent the threat action from taking place, see Figure 10.2.

10.1.1.1 Qualitative Threat Assessment: (Phase 1)

The goal of the threat assessment is to identify and assess threat actions relevant to the organization. Recall that threats comprise both a threat agent and a threat action. Threat agents are the entity that may cause a threat to happen and can be categorized by human–accidental, human–intentional, and natural. A threat action is what is caused by a threat agent, namely, invoked malware, theft & sabotage, socially engineered, hacked, abused trust, environmental damage, and erred. This basic grouping of threat agents and threat actions was introduced in Chapter 4 and used throughout Chapters 5, 6, and 7 to illustrate the threat agents and threat actions affecting or affected by the administrative, technical, and physical controls. Here we dive deeper into threat agents and threat actions to estimate their contribution to the security risk equation.

Threat actions (paired with the relevant threat agents that cause those actions) are analyzed to determine their relevance and potential for occurrence.

- Identify Relevant Threat Actions—Using the threat action categorization introduced in Chapter 6, the security risk assessment team should list all relevant and in scope threat actions to be considered for the security risk assessment. The assessment team may work from a list of threat actions specified in the statement of work, used within the assessing organization's standard practice, reference to an industry standard list, or create their own. The assessment team should only consider relevant threat actions for the assessed organization. For example, a volcano would be not applicable to Austin, Texas as there are no active volcanoes in the area. This list becomes a boundary for the assessment as the team will calculate the security risks for each of the relevant and documented threat action/agent pairs.

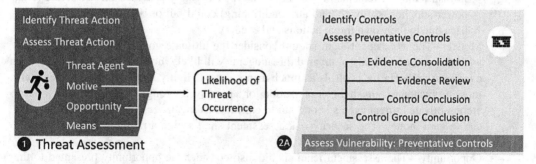

FIGURE 10.2 Determining RIIOT FRAME likelihood of threat occurrence. Threat actions and their associated elements along with preventative control vulnerabilities are analyzed to determine the likelihood of the threat occurrence for each threat agent.

FIGURE 10.3 RIIOT FRAME threat action categories. This categorization of threat actions can be used to enumerate threat actions for the security risk assessment.

The security risk assessment team may create a list of relevant threats using the seven threat action categories, see Figure 10.3. Each of the threat action categories can then be expanded to include threat actions relevant to the assessed organization. An example list of threat actions based on an expansion of the seven categories of threat actions used throughout this book, can be seen in Table 10.1. The worked examples have been bolded within the table.

Once the security risk assessment team has identified and compiled a list of relevant threat actions, they should assess each of these threat actions through a review of their important elements. Elements of the threat action that are important to be analyzed include the threat agent's identification, motive, opportunity, and means. The study of threat agent basic characteristics assists the security risk assessment team in their analysis of the threat actions. The following threat action characteristics should be considered: identification, motive, opportunity, and means.

- Threat Agent Identification—A threat agent can best be analyzed by first identifying it. A threat agent may be classified within any of the following categories and further described within these categories if necessary.
  - Human-Intentional—An insider or outsider may intentionally exploit a vulnerability in the organization's systems or physical controls to gain unauthorized access, modification, or interruption of services.
  - Human-Accidental—A trusted user or administrator may commit an error that leads to unauthorized access, modification, or interruption of services.
  - Nature—Any number of natural events can cause a damage to the organization's facilities and systems. These include fires, tornadoes, floods, and earthquakes.
  - Infrastructure—Elements of the organization's externally provided infrastructure (e.g., power supplies, software, and air conditioning) could fail or become unavailable (perhaps due to their own threat actions and events).
- Motive—The assessment team should consider the ultimate goal of the threat agent and what drives them. Highly motivated threat agents will likely increase the effort required to overcome preventative controls as much as necessary. Highly motivated threat agents are those motivated to punish the organization for a perceived wrong. An example of a moderately motivated threat agents is one out to exfiltrate as much sensitive information as they can to gain money. The security risk assessment shall assign a rating of Low, Moderate, High, and Very High for *Motive*.
- Opportunity—The assessment team should also consider the opportunity presented to the threat agent in which to conduct the threat action. For example, Internet-facing web applications present a high level of opportunity to threat agents. Low levels of opportunity are presented to outsiders attempting physical access as they generally lack the credentials for entry.

For many threat actions opportunity to initiate the threat action may have been witnessed and data available. For example, there are available statistics for the frequency of power outages, windstorms, and other natural events for any given region of the country. Likewise, the organization may be aware of identical or similar threat actions from the past within the organization or the industry. For example, industry wide estimates for the chance of a laptop being lost or stolen is 7%–10%, but an even better statistic is how many laptops were lost or stolen within the assessed organization in the last few years. The security risk assessment shall assign a rating of Low, Moderate, High, and Very High for *Opportunity*.

- Means—When considering threat agents, the team may gain a better understanding of the threat by considering the tools and techniques typically employed or even required to pull off the threat action. For example, a human-intentional threat agent executing a phishing attack typically has access to rather sophisticated tools and employs effective techniques. The security risk assessment shall assign a rating of Low, Moderate, High, and Very High for *Means*.

- Environmental Damage Exception—The threat agent for environmental damage is nature. Nature does not hold a grudge, or many other characteristics typically assigned to human-based threat agents. Therefore, it does not make much sense to assign motive, opportunity, or means to nature. Instead, these natural (and infrastructure) events typically have rather good data regarding the frequency of occurrence in any particular area of the world. For this reason, the motive, opportunity, and means approach is substituted here for environmental damage with a frequency measurement. The security risk assessment shall assign a rating of Low, Moderate, High, and Very High for *Frequency*.

Once the threat action elements for each threat action have been reviewed, the team then concludes on likelihood of occurrence for each threat agent. The RIIOT FRAME for Threat Action Review Approach starts with a qualitative synopsis of the threat agent elements, see Table 10.1. This table includes a qualitative value (e.g., Very High, High, Moderate, Low, and Very Low), the description of the qualitative rating can be found in Table 10.2.

The security assessment risk team now uses the RIIOT FRAME Assessment Scale (Table 10.2) to assign a qualitative value to the end of each row in the Threat Actions Table (10.1) indicating threat occurrence level based on the motive, opportunity, and means for human-based threat actions or based on known frequency of occurrence for natural threat actions. For the worked example, this assignment has been done for all of the selected sample threat actions in Table 10.2, see final column of Table 10.2.

TABLE 10.2
RIIOT FRAME Qualitative Assessment Scale

	Threat Action				
	Motive	Opportunity	Means	Frequency	Asset Harm
Rating		**Used in Phase 1**			**Used in Phase 3**
Very high	• All three *Highs*			More than 100 times a year	Catastrophic harm
High	• Two *Highs* and one *Moderate*			Between 10 and 100 times a year	Severe harm
Moderate	• Three *Moderates,* Two *Highs,* and one *Low*			Between one and ten times a year	Serious harm
Low	• One *Moderate* and two *Lows*			Less than one a year	Limited harm
Very low	• Three *Lows*			Less than once every 10 years	Negligible harm

Note: Within the RIIOT FRAME approach this assessment scale can be used for the determination of qualitative ratings.

10.1.1.2   Qualitative Vulnerability Assessment: (Phases 2A and 2B)

Once threat actions have been identified and assessed the security risk assessment shall consider the affect that organizational controls have on the likelihood of the threat occurrence. This step involves identifying the relevant controls to each of the identified threat actions. Once these controls have been identified the evidence gathered during the data gathering phase of the security risk assessment is then analyzed to determine the strength of the control and its ability to affect the security risk equation.

- Identify Controls—The assessment team should determine all controls relevant to the threat actions in scope of the security risk assessment. For our worked examples, the relevant set of controls contributing to the security risk equation either by affecting the threat likelihood (phase 2A—preventative controls assessment) or by affecting the expected impact (phase 2B—detective and corrective controls assessment) include the following:
    - Relevant Administrative Controls—The administrative controls of policy (reporting security incidents and lost laptops), requiring full disk encryption on laptops, security awareness training (briefings on the threats of laptop theft and ransomware), and recovery procedures (lost device and ransomware procedures) are relevant to at least one of the three worked examples of lost laptop, power outage, and ransomware.
    - Relevant Physical Controls—The physical controls of locks are relevant to lost laptop vulnerabilities and Uninterrupted Power Supply (UPS), and on-site generators are relevant to a power outage.
    - Relevant Technical Controls—The technical controls of anti-malware, e-mail scanning, web filtering, patch management, full disk encryption technologies, backup technologies, and laptop capabilities (battery operation) are relevant to at least one of the worked example scenarios.[1]
- Assess Controls—The security risk assessment will have already gathered data on each of the controls listed above and recorded this data for review. It is at this point in the process that the assessment team should review that data gathered to determine the associated control effectiveness. The RIIOT FRAME method of assessing a control is introduced here and demonstrated through the continued use of the worked examples of lost laptop, power outage, and ransomware.

10.1.1.2.1   The RIIOT FRAME for Qualitative Vulnerability Review Approach

The RIIOT FRAME approach for assessing security control vulnerabilities utilizes the various methods of data gathering (namely, Review, Interview, Inspect, Observe, and Test) to structure the assessment of each security control's effectiveness. The RIIOT FRAME for Vulnerability Review Approach (VRA) is a four-step process that includes the following elements:

- **Step 1: Control Evidence Consolidation**—The assessment team consolidates all of the evidence collected during the data gathering portion of the assessment. In this phase the team may review, follow up, or request additional information if needed but for the most part the team should already have the data collected. Evidence is consolidated and tabulated in a shared table that supports collaboration and review. For each of these controls relevant to the worked examples, a short synopsis of the evidence collected in noted in the table, See Table 10.3.
- **Step 2: Summarize Evidence Elements**—Once the control evidence is consolidated in a synopsis table, the team then determines the meaning of the data in terms of positive or negative indication as to the control effectiveness. For each data element the team substitutes the evidence synopsis description with a "✓" or an "×" indicating positive and negative evidence toward the control's effectiveness, see Table 10.4.

TABLE 10.3
RIIOT FRAME Approach for Vulnerability Identification

	Review Documents	Interview Staff	Inspect Controls	Observe Behavior	Test Controls
Administrative Controls					
Reporting requirements	• Lost devices and suspicious behavior reported	1/3 users unaware of reporting requirement			
Mobile device protection	• Passwords required • FDE required	2/3 users unaware FDE capabilities			
Security awareness training	Staff briefed on threats to device loss, social engineering, and ransomware	Three of three users aware of threats		• Laptops unlocked in public areas • Badges not worn consistently • Frequent tailgating	Phishing exercises 37% positive rate
Recovery procedures	• Lost devices procedures • No ransomware procedures • Power outage procedures	• Lost devices procedures • No ransomware procedures • Power outage procedures			
Physical Controls					
Laptop locks	No laptop lock usage policy	Laptop locks issued to staff		Laptops unlocked in public areas	
UPS		Inline UPS 15 min	Inline UPS 15 min		
Generator		No generator	No generator		
Technical Controls					
Anti-Malware		Anti-malware is installed on all laptops			
E-mail scanning	E-mail is scanned for malware	E-mail scanning is in place			Test malware filtered
Web filtering		No web filtering in place			
Patch management		• Users subscribe to updates • No patch management			
Full disk encryption	Built in FDE implements AES 256	2/3 users unaware of FDE setup			

(Continued)

TABLE 10.3   *(Continued)*

	Review Documents	Interview Staff	Inspect Controls	Observe Behavior	Test Controls
Backup	No backup policy or procedure	• Daily server backup • Cloud storage			
Laptop capability			Laptop battery power		

Note: Various pieces of evidence are available for each of the listed administrative, physical, or technical controls. The assessment team must review available evidence to determine the effectiveness of the controls.

TABLE 10.4
RIIOT FRAME Control Vulnerability Summary Table

RIIOT Data Gathered

Relevant Controls	Review	Interview	Inspect	Observe	Test	Control Vulnerability Conclusion
Reporting requirements	✓✓	×				Moderate
Mobile device protection	✓✓	×				Moderate
Security awareness training	✓	✓		×××	×	High
Recovery procedures lost devices	✓	✓				Low
Recovery procedures ransomware	×	×				Very high
Recovery procedures power outage	✓	✓				Low
Laptop locks	×	✓		×		High
UPS		✓	✓			Low
Generator		×	×			Very high
Anti-Malware		✓				Low
E-mail scanning	✓	✓			✓	Low
Web filtering		×				Very high
Patch management		✓×				Moderate
Full disk encryption	✓	×				Moderate
Backup	×	✓✓				Moderate
Laptop's battery			✓			Low

Note: Various pieces of evidence are available for each of the listed administrative, physical, or technical controls. The assessment team must review available evidence to determine the effectiveness of the controls.

- **Step 3: Control Vulnerability Conclusion**—The security risk assessment team reviews the evidence review table row by row to determine the overall control conclusion. The control effectiveness conclusion is based on the evidence in the control row. There are several approaches that may be applied to assist in the review of the data gathered.

- Corroborating Evidence—The simplest principle of reviewing evident to apply is when all evidence sources point to the same conclusion. If all evidence points to an either strong or weak control, then the conclusion as to the effectiveness of the control is rather straightforward. For example, in Table 10.4, both the interview and the inspection of the data center revealed that no generator is in place to back up the UPS during a power failure. The control of generator is non-existent. Another example, in Table 10.4 of corroborating evidence can be found in the row for the e-mail scanning. In this row we find that the evidence from policy review, the interview, and a test of e-mail scanning of malware all point to an effective control. Controls with corroborating evidence are the easiest controls in which to summarize the evidence collected.
- Rebutting Evidence—A more difficult evidence review concept is applied when pieces of evidence do not align or agree. This is referred to as "rebutting evidence." For example, in Table 10.4, security awareness training covers laptop theft threats, interviews revealed that users were aware of these threats, yet laptops were observed unattended and unlocked in public areas on-site (cafeteria, lobby, break room). In cases were evidence sources reveal non-aligning results the security risk assessment team must apply judgment to arrive at a measurement of the controls' effectiveness. Although there is no calculus for this judgment, there are a few pointers the assessment team should consider.
  - Negative Observations and Tests—If the team observes control weaknesses or is able to demonstrate a control weakness through a test, then the control should be considered weak despite evidence from other methods such as documents and interviews.
  - Negative Interviews—If the team receives an admission that a control is not in place or is weak from an assessed organization's staff member that should know, then the control should be considered weak despite evidence from other methods such as documents, observations, and some tests.
- Scant Evidence—There may be several controls in which the team was not able to gain evidence from multiple sources using the RIIOT method. For example, in Table 10.3, the only piece of evidence regarding the installation of anti-malware controls placed on laptops is from an interview with the laptop administrator. In this case the team should consider gaining additional evidence to confirm, such as an inspection of a sample of laptops. However, if this is the only piece of evidence then the control should be considered to be in place but the confidence level in that result is low. When it comes to providing estimates on the effectiveness of this control, the estimates would likely have a wider range to accommodate the low confidence level based on the scant evidence.

  Once the evidence for each control has been reviewed, using the evidence review rules presented above, the team then concludes on each control. The RIIOT FRAME for Vulnerability Assessment can use a qualitative synopsis of the control vulnerability. The security assessment risk team now uses the Control Vulnerability Conclusion Key (Table 10.5) to assign a qualitative value to each of the controls. For the worked example, this assignment has been done on the controls associated with the worked examples of lost laptop, power outage, and ransomware, see the last column of Table 10.3.

- **Step 4: Control Group Vulnerability Conclusion**—Once the security risk assessment team has concluded on the vulnerabilities in each of the associated controls, the team will next conclude on the group of controls associated with a specific threat action. This requires the grouping of the preventative controls with the associated threat actions, which is a subset of Table 10.4. That grouping is then used to create the control group vulnerability table and ultimately the control group vulnerability conclusion, see the last row of Table 10.6. The qualitative assessment of the control group vulnerabilities uses the same key, Table 10.5, as the individual control vulnerability conclusions.

Determining the conclusion for the control group can be a bit difficult as it is unclear as to the contributing factor of each control in the group with respect to the threat action. For example, a

TABLE 10.5
RIIOT FRAME Control Vulnerability Conclusion Key

Qualitative Value	Control Description	Control Group Description
Very high	• Strong negative evidence. • No rebutting evidences.	• No associated controls in place or effective.
High	• More negative than positive evidence.	• Most associated controls are not in place or ineffective.
Moderate	• Equal or more positive than negative evidence.	• A least one key control is only somewhat effective.
Low	• Positive evidence. • No rebutting evidence.	• Several controls are in place and functioning well. • Minor vulnerabilities noted with some room for improvement.
Very low	• Strong positive evidence • No rebutting evidence	• Several effective controls are in place and effective. • No obvious vulnerabilities.

Note: The team should assign a qualitative value to the end of each row in the Vulnerability Control Summary Table indicating vulnerability level of the control based on the evidence gained during the security controls assessment.

TABLE 10.6
RIIOT FRAME Preventative Control Group Vulnerability Conclusion: Qualitative Worked Example

Associated Controls	Worked Example – Threat Scenarios		
	Lost Laptop	Power Outage	Ransomware
Administrative Controls			
Reporting requirements	Moderate		Moderate
Security awareness training	High		High
Physical Controls			
Locks	High		
UPS		Low	
Generator		Very high	
Technical Controls			
Anti-Malware			Low
E-mail scanning			Low
Web filtering			Very high
Patch management			Moderate
Laptops		Low	
Control Group Conclusion	**High**	**High**	**Moderate**

Note: The team assigns a qualitative value to the bottom of each column in the Control Group Vulnerability Conclusion Table indicating vulnerability level of all preventative controls affecting the likelihood of occurrence for each threat action.

generator is likely to have a much higher effect on the prevention of a power outage to the data center than a policy regarding a requirement for a generator. The Control Vulnerability Conclusion Key (Table 10.5) is provided as a reference, but the team may choose to deviate from the table's conclusion because it is not possible to cover all the weighting options required to come up with a calculation here. This is an estimate. There are several approaches that may be applied to assist in the team in the conclusion of the control group vulnerability.

- Averaging—One approach is simply to take an average of the individual vulnerability control assignments. As these assignments are qualitative in nature, the assessor should be aware that it is not appropriate to apply mathematical concepts such as addition, multiplication, and averaging on ordinal concepts of numbers. However, the assessor may get a general sense of the control group vulnerability level based on a consideration of the individual vulnerability ratings and their "centering" on a vulnerability level. For example, the individual controls for the lost laptop scenario include policy, security awareness training, and laptop locks. These individual controls have vulnerability assignments of moderate, high, and high, respectively. It seems reasonable to consider a high rating in this case.
- Check Your Work—Once a vulnerability has been assigned to a group of controls, as in applying the averaging approach, the team should review the set of associated vulnerabilities holistically and determine if the initial assignment is appropriate. For example, the team may have initially assigned a moderate vulnerability rating to the power outage control group based on a very high, low, and low individual control rating. However, since most power outages last well over the 15-minute limit of the UPS and many critical systems are not implemented on laptops the team may decide to bump the vulnerability rating of the control group to high.

A worked example of the control group vulnerability conclusion is provided in Table 10.6. This table is a subset of Table 10.4 in that we can remove the RIIOT evidence column as the control conclusion has been determined and we can assign the preventative controls to each of the worked example threat actions of lost laptop, power outage, and ransomware.

10.1.1.3 Qualitative Threat Occurrence Likelihood

Once the security risk assessment team has performed the threat action assessment (see Table 10.1) and the preventative controls group assessment (see Table 10.6), the likelihood of threat occurrence can be determined. At this point the team uses the first of the lookup tables for the RIIOT FRAME—Qualitative, see Table 10.7.

TABLE 10.7
RIITO FRAME Likelihood Likelihood of Threat Occurrence Qualitative Lookup Table

Threat Action (Table 10.1)	Preventative Controls Group Vulnerabilities (Table 10.6)				
	Very High	**High**	**Moderate**	**Low**	**Very Low**
Very high	Very high	Very high	High	Moderate	Low
High	Very high	High	Moderate	Moderate	Low
Moderate	High	Moderate	Moderate	Low	Low
Low	Moderate	Moderate	Low	Low	Very low
Very low	Low	Low	Low	Very low	Very low

Note: The team determines the threat action likelihood of occurrence based on the threat action likelihood rating (Table 10.1) and the associated preventative controls group vulnerabilities affecting the likelihood of occurrence according to this lookup table.

TABLE 10.8

RIITO FRAME Likelihood of Threat Occurrence: Qualitative Worked Example

Worked Example Threat Action	Threat Action Likelihood (Table 10.1)	Preventative Controls Group Vulnerability Rating (Table 10.6)	Likelihood of Threat Occurrence (Table 10.7 Lookup)
Lost laptop	High	High	**High**
Power outage	Moderate	High	**Moderate**
Ransomware	Very high	Moderate	**High**

Note: The likelihood of occurrence for the worked example threat actions is determined based on the threat action likelihood rating (Table 10.1) and the associated preventative controls group ratings (Table 10.6) according to Table 10.7.

For the worked examples of lost laptop, power outage, and ransomware we can determine the likelihood of threat occurrence, see last column of Table 10.8.

10.1.1.4   Qualitative Expected Impact

The second key element of the RIIOT FRAME is to determine the expected impact of the threat action if it does occur. This may be determined through an impact assessment of the threat actions and a vulnerability assessment of any controls that may detect and correct damage once the threat action has taken place, see Figure 10.4.

10.1.1.4.1   Qualitative Impact Assessment (Phase 3)

The goal of the impact assessment is to determine the expected impact of the given threat action based on the impact elements: harm to operations, harm to assets, other fines, and harm to others. The harm that results from a successful threat action against exploitable organizational assets is based on available evidence. The team should consider the following elements when determining the harm associated with the threat action.

- Harm to Operations—A successful threat action may result in measurable harm to the operations of the organization. The harm to operations can include interruptions to providing goods and services. Here it is very useful for the security risk assessment team to understand the mission and operations of the organization being assessed.

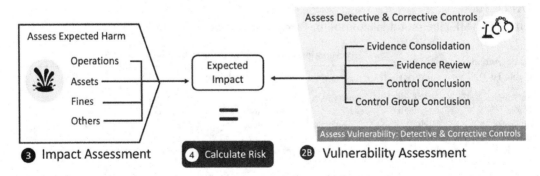

FIGURE 10.4   Determining RIIOT FRAME expected impact. The elements of expected harm and the detective and preventative controls that may affect the impact of the threat action are analyzed to determine an overall expected impact for each threat action.

TABLE 10.9

RIIOT FRAME Expected Harm: Qualitative Worked Examples

	Worked Example—Threat Scenarios		
Harm Elements	**Lost Laptop**	**Power Outage**	**Ransomware**
Harm to operations	• Operational delay	• System shutdown	• System shutdown
Harm to assets	• Lost laptop	• None	• Lost data
	• Some lost data		
Harm to other organizations	• Delay in services	• Delay in services	• Delay in services
	• Loss of sensitive data		• Loss of sensitive data
Fines and fees	• None	• None	• Potential fines
Harm to Assets (Impact Ratings)			
Rating	Moderate	Low	High

Note: The harm to assets for the worked example threat actions is determined based on the harm elements for each of the threat actions.

- Harm to Assets—A successful threat action may result in damage or loss to the organization's buildings, information systems or information system components, loss of intellectual property, loss of critical data, or other assets.
- Fines and Fees—A successful threat action may also result in fines or fees associated with non-compliance to industry standards and/or laws and regulations.
- Harm to Other Organizations—A successful threat action may result in harm to other organizations such as customers or prospective customers. Elements of this area of harm includes costs of contract penalties or breaches and lost future revenues and sales.

The harm elements of the threat action for each of the worked examples are summarized in Table 10.9. Using the RIIOT FRAME assessment scale, see Table 10.2, the last two rows of Table 10.9 are completed with the asset harm determined for each of the worked examples.

10.1.1.4.2   *Qualitative Vulnerability Assessment: Detective and Corrective Controls (Phase 2B)*

Once harm to assets has been identified and assessed the security risk assessment shall consider the effect that organizational detective and corrective controls have on the harm to assets for each of the threat actions. This step involves identifying the relevant controls, in this case detective and preventative controls, to each of the identified threat actions. Once these controls have been identified the evidence gathered during the data gathering phase of the security risk assessment is then analyzed to determine the strength of the detective and corrective controls and their ability to affect the harm to assets. This phase will mirror phase 2A (preventative controls vulnerability assessment) in terms of the process description as it is the same process except for the identification of controls. Here we see the similar process demonstrated with the worked examples of lost laptop, power outage, and ransomware, using detective and corrective controls as the relevant controls for the vulnerability assessment.

- Identify Controls—The assessment team should determine the detective and corrective controls relevant to the threat actions in scope of the security risk assessment. For our worked examples, the relevant set of controls affecting the expected impact (phase 2B—detective and corrective controls assessment) include the following:

- Relevant Administrative Controls—The administrative controls of policy (reporting security incidents and lost laptops), requiring full disk encryption on laptops, security awareness training (briefings on ransomware), and recovery procedures (lost device and ransomware procedures) are relevant to at least one of the three worked examples of lost laptop, power outage, and ransomware.
- Relevant Physical Controls—The physical controls of UPS and on-site generators are relevant to a power outage.
- Relevant Technical Controls—The technical controls of anti-malware, full disk encryption technologies, backup technologies, and laptop capabilities (battery operation) are relevant to at least one of the worked example scenarios.
- Assess Controls—The security risk assessment will have already gathered data on each of the controls listed above, recorded this data for review, and determined the associated control effectiveness, see Table 10.4.
- Control Group Vulnerability Conclusion—Since the security risk assessment team has already concluded on the vulnerabilities in each of the associated controls, the team will next conclude on the group of controls associated with the harm from a specific threat action. This requires the grouping of the detective and corrective controls with the associated harm, which is a subset of Table 10.4. That grouping is then used to create the control group vulnerability table and ultimately the control group vulnerability conclusion, see the last row of Table 10.11. The qualitative assessment of the control group vulnerabilities uses the same key, Table 10.5, as the individual control vulnerability conclusions.

The worked example of the control group vulnerability conclusion for detective and corrective controls is provided in Table 10.10. This table is a subset of Table 10.4 in that we can remove the RIIOT evidence column as the control conclusion has been determined and we can assign the detective and corrective controls to each of the worked example threat actions of lost laptop, power outage, and ransomware. The last row of the table is the conclusion of the effectiveness of the control group to affect the threat action impact.

TABLE 10.10

RIIOT FRAME Detective and Corrective Control Group Vulnerability Conclusion: Qualitative Worked Example

	Worked Example—Threat Scenarios		
Associated Controls	**Lost Laptop**	**Power Outage**	**Ransomware**
Administrative Controls			
Reporting requirements			Moderate
Mobile device protection	Moderate		Moderate
Security awareness training	High		High
Recovery procedures	Low	Low	Very high
Physical Controls			
UPS		Low	
Generator		Very high	
Technical Controls			
Anti-Malware			Low
E-mail scanning			Low

(Continued)

TABLE 10.10 *(Continued)*

	Worked Example—Threat Scenarios		
Associated Controls	**Lost Laptop**	**Power Outage**	**Ransomware**
Web filtering			Very high
Patch management			Moderate
Full disk encryption	Moderate		Moderate
Backup	Moderate		
Laptop capability		Low	
Control Group Conclusion	**High**	**High**	**Moderate**

Note: The team assigns a qualitative value to the bottom of each column in the Control Group Vulnerability Conclusion Table indicating vulnerability level of all preventative controls affecting the likelihood of occurrence for each threat action.

10.1.1.5 Qualitative Expected Impact

Once the security risk assessment team has performed the impact assessment (see Table 10.9) and the detective and corrective controls group assessment (see Table 10.10), the expected impact can be determined. At this point the team uses the second of the lookup table for the RIIOT FRAME, see Table 10.11.

For the worked examples of lost laptop, power outage, and ransomware we can determine the expected impact, see last column of Table 10.12.

TABLE 10.11

RIIOT FRAME Qualitative Expected Impact Lookup Table

Impact Rating (Table 10.9)	**Detective and Corrective Controls Group Vulnerabilities (Table 10.10)**				
	Very High	**High**	**Moderate**	**Low**	**Very Low**
Very high	Very high	Very High	High	Moderate	Moderate
High	Very high	High	High	Moderate	Low
Moderate	High	Moderate	Moderate	Low	Low
Low	Moderate	Moderate	Low	Low	Very low
Very low	Low	Low	Low	Very low	Very low

Note: The team determines the expected impact based on the Impact Rating (Table 10.9) and the associated detective and corrective controls group vulnerabilities (Table 10.10).

TABLE 10.12

RIIOT FRAME Qualitative Expected Impact: Worked Examples

Worked Example Threat Action	**Impact Rating**	**Controls Group Vulnerabilities**	**Expected Impact**
Lost laptop	Moderate	High	Moderate
Power outage	Low	High	Moderate
Ransomware	High	Moderate	High

Note: The expected impact for the worked example threat actions is determined based on the impact rating and controls group vulnerability rating for the associated threat actions.

TABLE 10.13
RIIOT FRAME Qualitative Security Risk Lookup Table

Expected Impact (Table 10.11)	Likelihood of Threat Occurrence (Table 10.8)				
	Very High	**High**	**Moderate**	**Low**	**Very Low**
Very high	Very high	Very high	High	Moderate	Moderate
High	Very high	High	High	Moderate	Low
Moderate	High	Moderate	Moderate	Low	Low
Low	Moderate	Moderate	Low	Low	Very low
Very low	Low	Low	Low	Very low	Very low

Note: The team determines the security risk for each threat action based on the expected impact (Table 10.11) and the likelihood of threat occurrence (Table 10.8).

TABLE 10.14
RIIOT FRAME Qualitative Security Risk: Worked Examples

Worked Example Threat Action	Expected Impact (Table 10.13)	Likelihood of Threat Occurrence (Table 10.8)	Security Risk
Lost laptop	Moderate	High	**Moderate**
Power outage	Moderate	Moderate	**Moderate**
Ransomware	High	High	**High**

Note: The expected impact for the worked example threat actions is determined based on the impact rating and controls group vulnerability rating for the associated threat actions.

10.1.1.6   Qualitative Security Risk Calculation

The final key element of the RIIOT FRAME is to calculate the security risk for the selected threat actions. Since the first two key elements (likelihood of occurrence and expected impact) have already been calculated this is simply a lookup table.

For the worked examples of lost laptop, power outage, and ransomware we can determine the Security Risk, see last column of Table 10.14.

10.1.2   RIIOT FRAME—QUANTITATIVE

This section implements the RIIOT FRAME with the same worked examples but using quantitative methods. This demonstration will step through the RIIOT FRAME process using quantitative values in each of the security risk analysis steps. The elements of these phases will follow the same order as the qualitative example with fewer descriptions of the process as the process elements have already been introduced.

10.1.2.1   Obtaining Quantitative Data

Throughout the quantitative security risk assessment method, the security risk assessment team will be required to determine quantitative estimates of threat action frequency and expected impact.

Rather than simply estimating the security risk equation variables of threat frequency and expected impact, the assessment team should seek relevant data to support a calibrated estimate.

The assessment team may use several methods to obtain adequate data in order to appropriately estimate quantitative measurements. These methods may involve obtaining the threat frequency or impact data directly or indirectly. Direct threat frequency and expected impact measurements may be available through historical data from the assessed organization on similar threat scenarios, or through crime statistics, analysis from previous security risk assessments, industry studies, or organizational knowledge regarding related industries. Indirectly threat frequency and expected impact data will need to be developed or calculated by the assessment team using several approaches outlined below.

10.1.2.1.1 Direct Threat Frequency or Impact Data

When the assessment team needs data to support a security risk equation variable estimate such as the threat frequency or the expected impact, the best data is data that may directly support these estimates. Direct threat frequency or impact data may come from a variety of sources, such as those listed below:

- Organizational Historical Threat Frequency Data—The assessed organization may have available data on the frequency of threat actions that have occurred in the past. This data on past events provides some indication as to the likelihood of similar events. For example, if the organization lost four laptops last year and three the year before without any significant safeguard improvements, it may be reasonable to assume that there will be between three and four laptops lost in the next 12 months.
- Organizational Expected Impact Data—The assessed organization may have available data on the expected impact of foreseeable events as part of their business continuity planning process. For example, the organization may have a mature business continuity planning process and may have determined several expected loss impact estimates including hourly and daily downtime costs. When available, this data is a great source for the security risk assessment team as the data is directly applicable to the assessed organization and the data fits the security risk equation variables without the need to scale or project.
- Industry-Specific Frequency or Impact Data—The team can perform some basic Internet research for data specific to the assessed organization's industry. Available data involving threat actions and expected impacts may be found in annual studies, surveys, reports, and other available data sources produced by survey organizations, information security analysts, information security technology vendors, information security service vendors, universities, industry trade groups, and government organizations. In many cases these reports provide a breakdown of the data into industry groups such as health care, retail, higher education, service providers, and manufacturing, for example. The industry breakdown of the data should be used when available as it is more applicable to the assessed organization.
- Country-Specific Frequency or Impact Data—The same reports and data sources listed above may also breakdown the data according to country or region. The country or region breakdown of the data should be used when available as it is more applicable to the assessed organization.
- Assessing Organization's Frequency or Impact Data—Organizations performing security risk assessments as a service should be compiling frequency and impact data from the sources above and from their own customers. This data should be made available to all security risk assessment team members upon which to standardize the security risk assessment approach and as a way to support continual improvement. This data is best organized by the major security risk equation elements (i.e., threat action and expected impact) with meta-data such as industry, region, data, organization size, and other elements that may assist the security risk assessment team in tailoring the compiled data for the current assessed organization.

10.1.2.1.2   Indirect Threat Frequency or Impact Data

There will likely not be threat frequency and expected impact data available for all security risk equations that the assessment team must compute. In the case that such data is not available directly the team will need to derive these values from indirect data. Three approaches to deriving relevant estimates from indirect data are presented below:

- Approach 1: Create an Equation: Consider that a 2009 (dated) study states that the average cost of a lost laptop is $49,246.[2] This statistic may give the assessment team a starting point for determining the expected impact of a lost or stolen laptop at the assessed organization, but the study includes many organizations that may have tens of thousands of records on a laptop and the assessed organization has only ten to 20 customer reports on the laptops. The assessment team will need to provide an estimate of the expected impact of a lost laptop based on more relevant data.

  The following three-step process may be used to create equations that will assist the assessment team in determining appropriate quantitative estimates, see Figure 10.5.

  - Step 1: Assessment team equation—The assessment team develops an equation that seeks to determine the quantitative value for a security risk equation component. In this example, the equation computes the expected impact of a lost laptop based on the cost of the laptop itself, operational days impacted and their cost, and when the laptop has not been FDE, the team also includes the cost of lost records and lost customers.
  - Step 2: Assessed Organization's Data—The assessment team reviews documents or interviews key staff members to complete as many equation variables as possible. In this example, the assessment team is able to obtain data for number of records per laptop, cost of a lost record, value of customers, operational days impacted, cost of a lost operational day, and the cost of the laptop itself.

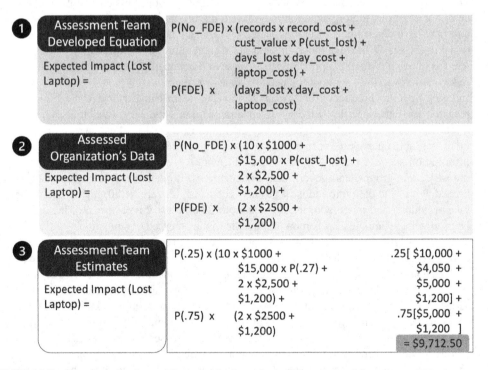

FIGURE 10.5 Equations for determining quantitative values. The security risk assessment team may need to develop their own equations for determining quantitative values. In this example the team uses a three-step process to determine the expected impact of a lost laptop.

- Step 3: Assessment Team Estimates—The assessment team now estimates the remaining equation variables based on team experience and available industry or research data. In this example, the assessment team estimates that only 75% of laptops are FDE based on the "High" level of vulnerabilities for the laptop detective and corrective controls, see Table 10.11. The team is also able to estimate the probability of losing a customer due to a data breach based on a recent survey. 21% of U.S. customers and 41% of Australian customers say they will never return after a data breach.[3] The team decides to use a 27% figure here.

Now all of the variables have values based on the assessed organization's own data and the research and estimations by the assessment team. The team computes the expected impact of a lost laptop at $9,712.50.

- Approach 2: Bound the Problem: When attempting to determine security risk component factors through the use of judgment, it is useful to first bound the problem with best- and worst-case scenarios. The team developing the values should use reasonableness when considering the best and worst cases. For example, a lost laptop could represent a significant impact or a rather negligible impact depending on the circumstances. The assessment team can provide better estimates by estimating the lower and upper end of the expected impact. For this approach is may be useful to think of the lower end as "95% of the time the impact will be higher than…" and the higher end as "95% of the time the impact will be less than…."

    On the lower end of the impact range the team may determine that the laptop stands a good chance of properly implementing full disk encryption and being lost while not on the customer site. In such a case the expected impact would be a single day of operational interruption and no data breach impact. On the higher end of the impact range the team may determine that the laptop would not have properly implemented full disk encryption, contain 15 customer reports, and be lost or stolen while on-site. The lower end here could be $3,600 and the higher end would be $76,000, see Table 10.15.

- Approach 3: Choose or Develop a Probability Distribution: Once the problem has been bound, the team should consider if there is value in developing a range of values with probabilities for each value. This is called a probability distribution. There are a number of probability distributions that occur frequently such as the normal distribution that the team may elect to use in probability calculations, but the team may elect to create its own distribution to more appropriately represent the data.

    Table 10.16 provides an example of reducing uncertainty through bounding the problem and developing a probability distribution. For example, it is reasonable to consider that a

TABLE 10.15

RIIOT FRAME Quantitative Security Risk: Low- and High-End Estimations

	Expected Impact Estimation: Lost Laptop	
	Low End	High End
Cost of laptop	$1,200	$1,200
Operational days	1 day @ $2,400/day	2 days @ $2,400/day
Data breach fees	$0	Ten records @ $1,000/record
Customer loss	$0	Four customers @ $15,000/customer
Total	**$3,600**	**$76,000**

Note: When direct data is not available the assessment team may arrive at estimation data through bounding the problem on the low and high end. Here we estimate the expected impact of a lost laptop based on a laptop lost when not on-site with a customer and with proper FDE implementation vs. a laptop lost while on-site without proper FDE

TABLE 10.16

Probability Distribution for Duration of Power Outage

Upper and Lower Bound	Range of Values	Probability Distribution
5 minutes	5–10 minutes	7%
	10–15 minutes	8%
	15–30 minutes	34%
	30–60 minutes	18%
	1–2 hours	14%
	2–4 hours	8%
	8–16 hours	6%
	16–24 hours	3%
2 days	1–2 days	2%

Note: The use of judgment can be improved through the use of a range of values and probability distributions.

power outage would last a minimum of 5 minutes and a maximum of 2 days. Most power outages are estimated to last less than 1 hour. In this example, experts are polled to determine probable occurrences of various power outage times.

The use of probability distributions adds another level of accuracy in the estimation or measurement of security risk to an organization's assets. This additional information allows the use of statistics, probability functions, and mathematical modeling.

- Approach 4: Use of Conditional Probabilities: Some threat actions should be considered with respect to the chain of events that must occur for the threat action to ultimately impact the organization's assets. In such a chain of events, each event must occur for the next event to be considered. These are referred to as "conditional probabilities." It is the probability of the summation of the events taking place (considering all the other events in the chain), not a single event, that is used as the frequency of the threat action.

When determining the threat action frequency probabilities, consider the chain of events that must take place for the threat to ultimately exploit the organization's vulnerabilities. For example, consider the threat action of an ex-employee gaining access to your routers and switches by logging in remotely and using the administrator password. The probability of such an event may seem difficult to determine because there are so many factors involved, but by considering the chain of events, determining the probabilities becomes more tractable.

- First, determine all of the events that are part of the threat action. In this case, the following events are part of the example threat action:
  1. An employee with access to the network infrastructure is terminated.
  2. Employee has desire to gain access.
  3. Passwords are not changed before employee attempts access.
- Second, determine the probabilities of each event (see Table 10.17):
  1. Terminated Administrators—Continuing with this example, start with how many employees are likely to be terminated this year. In the absence of any other knowledge, such as a planned layoff or merger, historical records will provide a fairly accurate measurement. In our example, an organization has 50 administrators with access to the network infrastructure. The organization has an industry average turnover rate of 30%. Most terminations were friendly, such as the employee changing careers or moving away, but 33% of the terminations were for cause. This gives us 15 terminated

TABLE 10.17
Conditional Probabilities

Event Number	Event	Probabilities	Discussion
1	Admins with access terminated	• 15 admins terminated/year	• 50 admins have passwords to network. • 30% turnover rate among admins.
2	Terminated admin has desire to gain access	• 10 admins terminated (not for cause) • 5 admins terminated for cause • 2 (20% of 10) admins terminated (not for cause) seek to gain access • 2.5 (50% of 2.5) admins terminated for cause seek to gain access	• 67% of terminations are for cause. • 20% of terminated admins (not for cause) seek to gain access. • 50% of admins terminated for cause seek to gain access.
3	Passwords are not changed in time	• 4.5 terminated admins seek to gain access • 33% passwords not changed • 1.5 terminated admins gain unauthorized access	• Passwords are typically changed prior to the terminated employee leaving the building, but occasionally (33% of the time) personnel performing this duty are busy on other tasks and cannot get to it until the end of the day.
Annual Threat Frequency		1.5 terminated admins gain unauthorized access	

Note: Determining the probability of an ex-employee gaining access to the organization's routers and switches by logging in remotely and using the administrative password can be a rather difficult figure to develop. The use of conditional probabilities together with some known data reduces the complexity and uncertainty of such an estimate.

administrators with network access terminated a year, ten terminated not for cause and five terminated for cause.

2. Terminated System Administrators with Desire to Gain Access—Not all terminated system administrators would even want to gain access to the routers and switches of their ex-employer. After all, if they get caught, their career (and freedom) could be jeopardized. Here we must use some judgment. Based on experience and intuition, let us say the team comes up with the judgment that 20% of the system admins would have the desire to attempt access. This may seem like a high number, but consider that (a) they might just be "checking" the system to see if the passwords were changed, (b) anyone who would catch them would likely be their friend and may not turn them in, and (c) the system administrators' knowledge of the system allows them to believe that they can get around without anyone detecting their presence. The percentage for system administrators terminated for cause increases to 50% because the same reasons (a)–(c) apply, but now we have reason (d): they are out to hurt the organization for hurting them. At this point in the chain of events, we have two terminated system admins with desire to access the routers and switches (20% of the ten terminated) and 2.5 system administrators terminated for cause with the same desire (50% of the five terminated for cause) for a total of 4.5 terminated administrators attempting access.

3. Terminated System Administrators with Desire and Means to Gain Access—Fully realizing the dangerous situation of terminated employees with sensitive passwords,

this organization has procedures in place to change all passwords on systems if the passwords are known by an employee being terminated. The procedure calls for the system administrators to change the passwords as a part of the termination procedures. However, because system administrators are understaffed and overworked, the procedure is not always completed prior to the employee's leaving the building. About 1/3 of the time, the personnel performing this task cannot get to it until the end of the day. It is only in these circumstances that the terminated system administrator can access the system. At this final stage, we are now considering 4.5 terminated admins with the desire and means to access the routers and switches, and 1/3 of them will be successful. This gives us an annual frequency of this threat action of 1.5.

10.1.2.2 Quantitative Threat Occurrence Likelihood (Phase 1 and 2A)

For a quantitative assessment the goal is to estimate the likelihood of the threat occurrence at the assessed organization for each of the selected threat actions. We can reuse the data analysis findings from the qualitative example as this data is available to the security risk assessment team to provide some context for the estimations. Assessed Organizational Data—Having selected the relevant threat actions, the security risk assessment team can make a plan prior to the RIIOT data gathering stage to gather data that will be useful in estimating the frequency of occurrence for each of the threat actions. For the worked example threat actions, the team could request any records of security incidents involving lost laptops, power outages, or ransomware over the last 24 months and ask the same question of the appropriate personnel during the data gathering portion of the assessment

The security risk assessment team will need to do some research to get the quantitative data for threat action occurrence. Some Internet research provided some basic frequency estimates on all three of the worked example threat actions. References for all of this data is provided in the footnotes and the security risk assessment team is encouraged to perform their own research, compile basic statistics used for all of their security risk assessments, and adjust the estimate ranges based on the preventative control vulnerabilities. For the worked examples the following analysis is provided as an example of an assessment team's analysis for determining expected frequency.

- Lost Laptop Expected Frequency—In general lost laptops would be estimated be to lost or stolen 10% of the time over a 3-year period, or 3% of the time annually.[4] Due to the "High" vulnerabilities for this organization in preventative controls for lost laptops (e.g., use of locks) the assessment team estimates the chance of a lost laptop at 5% annually, see Table 10.6. An organization with 75 laptops issued to traveling consultants may expect (75 × 5% = 3.75 laptops) 3.5 laptops to be lost or stolen a year. The security risk assessment team may also decide to gather additional data such as the number of laptops lost or stolen in the last several years. This additional data will improve the team's ability to provide a better estimate.
- Power Outage Expected Frequency—The reliability of electrical systems is measured by the U.S. Energy Information (USEIA) Administration. One of the metrics available online from the USEIA's Annual Electric Power Industry Report is the average number of interruptions from of power outages. System Average Interruption Frequency Index (SAIFI) measures the average frequency of power outages and is available from most all utilities in the United States. Austin Energy SAIFI) is one. The power outage preventative control vulnerabilities are rated at a "High" for the assessed organization, see Table 10.6. The assessment team determines that there is no reason to lower the expected frequency (e.g., if the assessed organization had longer UPS protection or an on-site generator then many power outages could be avoided) so the expected frequency for a power outage is one.
- Ransomware Expected Frequency—A recent survey finds that 51% of surveyed businesses were hit by ransomware in the last year. The assessed organization does not have very strong controls to prevent ransomware (e.g., no web filtering, weak security awareness, and moderate

reporting requirements), see Table 10.6. The assessment team determines that the chance for this organization to be hit by ransomware is as good as any surveyed organization and sets the expected frequency of ransomware at 50%.

The quantitative option to RIIOT FRAME is based on the assumption that the assessors providing estimates are calibrated estimators. The idea of calibrating a person for estimation work is introduced and presented well in the work of Douglas Hubbard's "How to Measure Anything: Finding the Value of Intangibles in Business" and his follow-on work "How to Measure Anything in Cybersecurity Risk." In these books Mr. Hubbard lays out a strong approach for calibrating estimates and computing the probability of results based on a range of values.[5]

The worked examples, along with example relevant data for the team to consider are presented in Table 10.18. The last column of this table includes the likelihood of threat action. This number represents the assessment teams estimate for the likelihood that a laptop will be lost or stolen, the organization will experience a power failure, and the organization will get infected with ransomware. The data used in these security risk equation values are computed based on various techniques presented in Chapter 9.

TABLE 10.18
Expected Frequency: Quantitative Worked Examples

Threat Action	Preventative Control Group Vulnerabilities	Quantitative Data to Consider	Expected Frequency
Lost laptop	High	• Consulting organization of 75 employees. • 86% of companies have had a laptop stolen.[6] • 52% of laptop thefts would be prevented by a lock.[7] • 10% of laptops will be lost/stolen in their 3 years lifetime.[8] • Laptop Preventative Control Vulnerabilities: High	3.75
Power outage	High	• Austin Energy System Average Interruption Frequency Index (SAIFI) is one. • Power Outage preventative control vulnerabilities: High.	1.0
Ransomware	Moderate	• 42% of businesses had ransomware attacks by 2019.[9] • Businesses had a 47% chance of getting infected with ransomware in 2017.[10] • 51% of surveyed businesses were hit by ransomware in 2020.[11] • Ransomware Preventative Control Vulnerabilities: Moderate.	0.51

Note: The assessment team estimates the likelihood of occurrence based on relevant data and the effectiveness of detective controls.

10.1.2.3 Quantitative Expected Impact: Phase 3 and 2B

The second element of the security risk equation needed is the expected impact that would result from the threat action. In the quantitative assessment the goal is to estimate the range of damage. We can reuse the data analysis findings from the qualitative example as this data is available to the security risk assessment team to provide some context for the estimations. Additional information used to form an estimation can come from the same sources as mentioned in the previous phase.

The security risk assessment team will need to do some research to get the quantitative data for threat action impact. Some Internet research provided some basic harm estimates on all three of the worked example threat actions. References for all of this data is provided in the footnotes and the security risk assessment team is encouraged to perform their own research, compile basic statistics used for all of their security risk assessments, and adjust the estimate ranges based on the detective and corrective control vulnerabilities. For the worked examples the following analysis is provided as an example of an assessment team's analysis for determining expected impact:

- Lost Laptop Expected Impact—In general the average cost of a lost laptop is $49,246.[12] However, the assessed organization was found to (1) have a higher than average vulnerability for controls designed to detect and correct the threat action of laptops (e.g., recovery procedures and full disk encryption) and (2) have a much lower than average number of records per laptop.. The estimate recorded for this worked example is worked out as a demonstration of the three-step process for deriving quantitative data when there is no direct frequency or impact data available, see Figure 10.6. In this example the expected impact of a lost laptop was computed as $9,712.50.
- Power Outage Expected Impact—The reliability of electrical systems is measured by the USEIA Administration. One of the metrics available online from the USEIA's Annual Electric Power Industry Report are the average duration of power outages. System Average Interruption Duration Index (SAIDI) measures the average length of power outages and is available from most utilities in the United States. Austin Energy SAIDI is of 85 minutes. The assessed organization's senior executive states that power outage will cost the organization $2400/day/employee or $37,500/hour.
- Ransomware Expected Impact—The expected impact of ransomware on the example assessed organization is based on downtime. On average small to medium businesses (SMBs) report 5 to 20 days of downtime when hit by ransomware.[13] The example assessed organization has "Moderate" vulnerabilities in their detective and corrective controls and notably no recovery procedures. Based on this data the assessment team assigns the ransomware downtime duration at 16 days. Next the assessment team asks the assessed organization for an estimate of the downtime cost for the organization. The senior executive states that a consultant's daily charge rate to the customer is $2400/day and only 33% of them would be affected by the power outage. Therefore a 16-day power outage would affect 25 consultants at $2400/day or $960,000. The team also decides to add operational costs of cleaning up the ransomware incident of $3000/day for 16 days. This adds an additional $48,000 for a total of $1,080,000.

The worked examples, along with example relevant data for the team to consider are presented in Table 10.19. The last column of this table is the expected impact. This number represents the assessment teams estimate for the expected cost if a laptop is lost or stolen, the organization experiences a power failure, or the organization gets infected with ransomware.

10.1.2.4 Quantitative Security Risk Calculation

The final key element of the RIIOT FRAME—Quantitative approach is to calculate the security risk for the selected threat actions. We have values for both the likelihood of threat action and expected

TABLE 10.19

Expected Impact: Quantitative Worked Examples

Threat Action	Detective and Corrective Control Group Vulnerabilities	Quantitative Data to Consider	Expected Impact
Lost laptop	High	• Only 10 customer data records on a laptop. • Chance lost laptop having FDE is 75%. • The cost of lost records is $1,000 record.[14] • Each customer is valued at $15,000. • Chance of losing a customer is 27%.	$9,712.50
Power outage	High	• Austin Energy System Average Interruption Duration Index (SAIDI) is 85 minutes. • Downtime cost is $2,400/employee/day.	$31,875
Ransomware	Moderate	• Downtime cost is $2,400/employee/day. • 75 employees • Ransomware affects 33% of the employees' productivity. • Ransomware downtime for assessed organization is 16 days.[15] • Cleanup costs include 16 days @ $3K/day.	$1,080,000

Note: The assessment team estimates the expected impact based on relevant data and the effectiveness of detective and corrective controls.

impact. By multiplying these values, we have the overall expected loss due to the three worked example threat actions.

For our equation we have values for the likelihood that a threat action will occur. (e.g., 3.75 laptops will be lost or stolen in the next 12 months) and we have a range of values that represent the expected impact of that event (e.g., a lost or stolen laptop has an expected impact of $9,712,50). For each threat action scenario, we multiple these two variables to obtain the expected loss.

10.1.3 QUALITATIVE AND QUANTITATIVE COMPARISON

In the sections above, three worked examples of security risks were calculated through an example security risk assessment method (RIIOT FRAME) using both qualitative and quantitative methods. The results of these worked examples (lost laptop, power outage, and ransomware) are summarized in Tables 10.20 and 10.21 for comparative purposes.

Once the security risk equation variables are estimated in ranges, the next issue is how to compute the security risk for the threat action scenario. For this calculation we must calculate an equation with two ranges. These ranges are probability distributions, meaning that there is a distribution of probabilities that the true value is represented by the range. However, not all of the values between the low and high values of the range have an equal probability of occurrence. For example, the true value of the ransomware impact (if the organization is infected) is more likely to be near $750,000 (toward the middle of the range) than $315,000 (at the beginning of the range). This distribution of probabilities is called a probability distribution. Different data sets can exhibit different shapes of the probability distributions such as the common "bell shape." For the purposes of this discussion, we will stick with the normal distribution to describe the probability distribution for our estimates

TABLE 10.20

Security Risk: Quantitative Worked Examples

Threat Action Scenario	Expected Frequency (Table 10.15)	Expected Impact (Table 10.16)	Expected Loss
Lost laptop	3.75	$9,712.50	$36,421.88
Power outage	1.00	$31,875.00	$31,875.00
Ransomware	0.51	$1,080,000.00	$550,800.00

Note: The assessment team provides quantitative estimates of the expected impact based on relevant data and the effectiveness of detective and corrective controls.

TABLE 10.21

Security Risk: Quantitative Worked Examples

Threat Action Scenario	Qualitative Expected Loss	Quantitative Expected Loss
Lost laptop	Moderate	$36,421.88
Power outage	Moderate	$31,875.00
Ransomware	High	$550,800.00

Note: The assessment team provides qualitative estimates of the expected impact based on relevant data and the effectiveness of detective and corrective controls.

SIDEBAR 10.1   USE OF BINOMIALS AND RANGES IN MEASUREMENTS

In the quantitative worked examples above, we used a single value for threat frequency (e.g., likelihood of threat occurrence) and a single value for expected impact to calculate the expected loss (e.g., security risk) for each of the threat actions. In these cases, the assessment team had sufficient evidence to arrive at a single value estimation. When the assessment team feels that they cannot provide a single value measurement, they many opt for a measurement range.

A measurement range is a range of values in which the assessment team is confident. This range is bounded by a low value and a high value. The assessment team shall be confident that the true value resides somewhere in between. We call the range of values a confidence interval and the confidence that the true value resides within the confidence interval is a confidence level.

The use of measurement ranges is a useful tool for the security risk assessment team when performing security risk analysis on security risk equation elements that are difficult to measure. For example, in the worked example of ransomware we had the following quantitative (single value) measurements:

- Expected Frequency (Ransomware): 0.51
- Expected Impact (Ransomware): $1,080,000

If the security risk assessment team was unsure of their measurements here (i.e., they had a low confidence level in their estimations), they could increase their confidence level by using measurement ranges. Reviewing the available and researched data for the ransomware attack scenario the assessment team may have chosen to provide a set of measurement ranges instead, see Table 10.22. In this worked example, the quantitative measurement variables for the security risk equation are given in ranges instead of single values. The assessment team may now have a greater confidence level in their measurements.

TABLE 10.22

RIIOT FRAME Security Risk: Quantitative Ranges Ransomware Worked Example

Threat Action:

Ransomware	Threat Frequency		Expected Impact	
Analysis	• 42% of businesses had ransomware attacks in 2019 • 47% of businesses infected with ransomware in 2017. • 51% of surveyed businesses were hit by ransomware in 2020. • Ransomware Preventative Control Vulnerabilities: Moderate		• Downtime cost is $2,400/employee/day. • 75 employees • Ransomware affects between 33%. • Ransomware downtime for assessed organization is 5–20 days. • Cleanup costs include 16 days @ $3K/day.	
	Low	High	Low	High
Measurement	42%	51%	$312,000	$1,248,000

Note: The assessment team estimates the threat frequency and the expected impact based on relevant data and the effectiveness of detective and corrective controls. However, in this example, the assessment team provides a range of measurements for these security risk equation variables.

For the ransomware event, it either happens or it does not. In statistics this is referred to as a binomial as the result is either a one or a zero (e.g., the event happens or it does not). There is no 46% of a ransomware attack. Instead, the chance of a ransomware infection is between 42% and a 51%. So nearly half of the time our assessed organization would not be infected. For this element of the calculation, we set up a binomial probability distribution across the 42% to 51% chance of occurrence and then select a random number between zero and one. If the random number is equal or greater than an individual trial run of the ransomware infection distribution then we assume a ransomware infection and include the individual trial run result of the ransomware impact distribution.

Using this approach, we get a more nuanced result to the security risk of the ransomware threat action. Both results are accurate in that the provide a measurement based on the assessment team's analysis. However, the quantitative result based on binomials and ranges in the measurements provides a more insightful measurement and report, see Figure 10.6.

SIDEBAR 10.2 INTERPRETING REQUIREMENTS

Many security risk assessment projects include a requirement to compare the current security posture against a set of requirements, a regulation, or a standard. These will collectively be referred to as *requirements*.[16] Despite the intentions of those who develop the requirements, security compliance requirements rarely have a straightforward interpretation. Because of the ambiguity of the language, an interpretation process or professional judgment is required to resolve areas of confusion.

Some requirements, such as the "Common Criteria for Information Technology Security Evaluations," have a formal interpretation process. Such a formal process requires procedures for requests for interpretation, draft and formal rulings, and a catalog of previous rulings.

Other requirements simply depend upon the professional judgment of the security risk assessment team and the team leader. The judgment of adequate interpretations is based on the situation and an understanding of the intention of the requirement. Table 10.23 provides an example of the interpretation process.

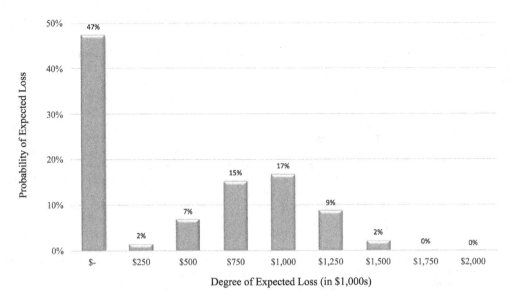

FIGURE 10.6 Quantitative Security Risk with Measurement Ranges. The security risk of ransomware threat action worked example can be calculated using a probability distribution range for both the threat frequency and the expected impact. Using the measurement ranges in Table 10.18 we arrive at a probability distribution that shows a 47% chance of no loss and a probability distribution of expected losses for the other 53% of the time of between $250,000 to $1.5 million.

TABLE 10.23
Interpretation Process Example

Step	Discussion/Example
Requirement	Automatic log-off: Implement electronic procedures that terminate an electronic session after a pre-determined period of inactivity. HIPAA 164.312(a) (2)(iii).
Interpretation	The organization must ensure that any session with protected health information (PHI) is terminated after a reasonable period of inactivity (5 and 15 minutes). The termination of the session can take place on any of the following elements of the session: • *The user terminal.* This can be a workstation or a remote computer. • *The media.* This could be a VPN connection or an application login. • *The sensitive system.* This could be an organizational system with PHI or an application that grants access to the end system.
Discussion	After interviewing the organization's systems administrators, it is found that workstations' default configuration currently locks after 15 minutes of inactivity, but this is not documented in policy and is not enforced. Session controllers have the capability to automatically disconnect the session after a period of inactivity, but this is not configured. Session disconnect is a problem for some suers because the session looks inactive, but a process could still be running.
Findings	The organization *does not* currently meet this requirement because it does not automatically terminate idle and inactive remote sessions.
Recommendation	Use of the system automatic disconnect feature would likely interfere with operations if it is set to a reasonable limit such as 5–15 minutes. However, the organization should set this control to terminate access after 4 hours of recorded inactivity. Because this control does not adequately protect unattended workstations, the organization should document and implement a policy to lock workstations after 5–15 minutes of inactivity.

Note: The interpretation process involves an interpretation of the requirement, a discussion of the environment, and application, a finding, and a recommendation to the organization based on the interpretation.

and

www.infosecurityrisk.com 	For a downloadable tool/spreadsheet with the RIIOT FRAME method and worked examples go to the website: www.infosecurityrisk.com and head to the downloads section for the Security Risk Assessment Handbook and go to Chapter 10 downloads.

EXERCISES

1. Build an Excel spreadsheet implementation of RIIOT FRAME – Quantitative for the 3 worked examples. Answer the following questions:
   a. Of which of the values used for the security risk equation variables are you most skeptical?
   b. How would you address this skepticism if this was your assessment, and the skepticism came from the project sponsor?
   c. Create alternative values for the variables in question and re-calculate the security risk.
   d. How could you incorporate the re-calculation of security risk into security risk management?
2. Perform a security risk assessment using RIIOT FRAME Qualitative for the following threat scenarios. Document any assumptions you make to complete the exercise:
   a. Spear-phishing
   b. Earthquakes
   c. Mis-delivered Fax
   d. Mis-configure Privileges
3. Perform a security risk assessment using RIIOT FRAME Quantitative for the following threat scenarios. Document any assumptions you make to complete the exercise:
   a. Spear-phishing
   b. Earthquakes
   c. Mis-delivered Fax
   d. Mis-configure Privileges

NOTES

1 The reader may observe that some controls appear in both the identification of preventative controls table (Table 10.3) and the identification of detective and corrective controls table (Table 10.11). This is because some controls impact both the prevention and either detection or corrective capabilities. For example, The reporting of suspicious behavior could prevent a ransomware attack from successfully installing and could decrease the response time thus lowering the impact of the attack.
2 https://www.absolute.com/blog/cost-of-a-lost-laptop-is-nearly-50000
3 https://businessinsights.bitdefender.com/
businesses-can-lose-up-to-58-of-customers-after-a-data-breach-research-shows
4 https://www.infoworld.com/article/2624968/corporate-america-s-lost-laptop-epidemic.html
5 For more information regarding the calibration of you and your team as an estimator and the use of the Mr. Hubbard's techniques please refer to his excellent texts. The assessment team is highly encouraged to obtain training on becoming a calibrated estimator prior to providing estimates for the security risk assessment using quantitative techniques.
6 https://securityboulevard.
com/2018/09/7-shocking-statistics-that-prove-just-how-important-laptop-security-is
7 https://cdn.cnetcontent.com/7d/e5/7de53b29-1e11-4592-b130-2527928779ad.pdf
8 https://www.infoworld.com/article/2624968/corporate-america-s-lost-laptop-epidemic.html
9 https://www.sentinelone.com/blog/what-is-the-true-cost-of-a-ransomware-attack-6-factors-to-consider
10 https://www.apextechservices.com/topics/articles/435355-what-the-odds-a-ransomware-attack.htm#
11 https://www.sophos.com/en-us/medialibrary/Gated-Assets/white-papers/sophos-the-state-of-ransomware-2020-wp.pdf

12 https://www.absolute.com/blog/cost-of-a-lost-laptop-is-nearly-50000

13 https://www.coveware.com/blog/2020/1/22/
    ransomware-costs-double-in-q4-as-ryuk-sodinokibi-proliferate

14 IBM Security, Cost of a Data Breach Report, 2019 [$150 / record, the assessment team increased the range
    as the reports have significantly more value than a single data record.]

15 https://www.coveware.com/blog/2020/1/22/
    ransomware-costs-double-in-q4-as-ryuk-sodinokibi-proliferate

16 The term *requirements* is used loosely here to mean any statement within the standard, regulation, or guid-
    ance that speaks to the security controls that should be in the information system being assessed.

11 Security Risk Mitigation

Once the security risks to an organization's assets are known and prioritized, the security risk assessment team should create a set of recommendations for the assessed organization to implement in addressing security risks. For each threat action (or security risk scenario), the security risk assessment team can create a set of recommendations that, when followed, will result in the lowering of the security risk for that threat action. Recommendations may include the implementation of additional preventative, detective, or corrective security controls or improvements of existing security controls. This process is referred to as security risk mitigation.

There will be some security risks that are present a low overall security risk (e.g., annual expected loss) and will be accepted by the organization without the implementation of additional security controls. While other security risks will present an annual expected loss of such a magnitude that the assessed organization will choose to implement the additional security controls to eliminate or reduce the security risk presented by the specific threat action.

The determination of which threat actions must be addressed to reduce the security risks and which threat actions present an acceptable level of security risk is addressed in the security risk appetite of the assessed organization. For any security risks beyond the security risk appetite, the security risk assessment team should provide recommendations for the assessed organization to address the security risks and eliminate or reduce them to a level below the security risk appetite.

11.1 DEFINING SECURITY RISK APPETITE

The formal definition and management of the security risk appetite is an element of the assessed organization's security program that should be in place. If so, then the security risk assessment team's statement of work will have already specified the metrics to be used for security risks and the limitation of security risk acceptance. For example, the if the assessed organization has qualitative security risk assessments performed, it may have specified a security risk appetite that limits security risk acceptance of low and medium risks or any security risks above 30 on a 0-100 scale such as the scale used in NIST SP 800-30. If the assessed organization has quantitative security risk assessments performed, then the security risk appetite will be specified in terms of annual expected loss (e.g., all security risks estimated at $100,000 per year or more shall be eliminated or reduced below $50,000 per year). There will also be assessed organizations that have yet to establish and document a formal security risk appetite. In these cases, the security risk assessment team should use their judgment to suggest a security risk appetite for the assessed organization based on their knowledge of the organization, its current security program maturity, and the current security risk environment.

At this point in the process, the security risk assessment team will have compiled a security risk summary and prioritized its findings. The security risk appetite definition provides the assessment team with a method to identify those security risks that should be mitigated versus those security risks that will be accepted by the organization. Once a security risk appetite is defined, the security risk assessment team shall apply the security risk appetite statement to their security risk findings, see Figure 11.1.

For any security risk scenarios or security risks presented by threat actions that lie above the assessed organization's security risk appetite, the security risk assessment team must develop recommendations to mitigate or reduce the security risk. These recommendations are referred to as *safeguards* or *countermeasures*. This chapter discusses the selection of safeguards, the compiling of safeguard solution sets, justifying the safeguard implementation, and an understanding of the security risk parameters regulating the acceptance of safeguard recommendations.

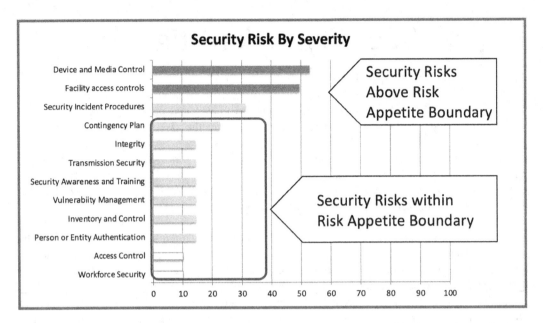

FIGURE 11.1   Security risk appetite application to security risk summary. The assessed organization's security risk appetite may be applied to the prioritized security risk summary table to identify those security risks that require security risk mitigation.

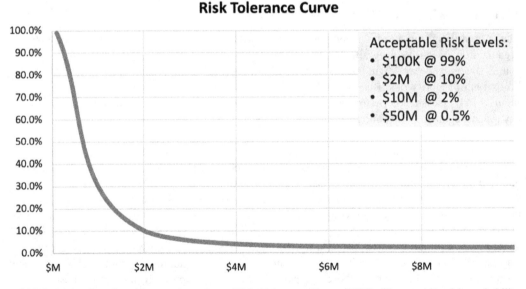

FIGURE 11.2   Security risk appetite using a Risk Tolerance Curve (RTC). The security risk probability distributions may be plotted against the assessed organization's security risk appetite (RTC) to identify those security risks that require security risk mitigation.

For those security risk assessment teams implementing quantitative security risk analysis through the use of probability distributions, see Chapter 9, Section 9.3.3, a risk tolerance curve (RTC) can be created based on the assessed organization's security risk appetite. Similar to the discussion above, any expected losses (e.g., risks) that lie above the RTC would be identified as security risks to mitigate. The RTC is plotted along with a curve representing the total security risk (total expected loss), see Figure 11.2.

FIGURE 11.3 Security risk appetite application to security risk summary. The assessed organization's security risk appetite may be applied to the security risk summary (combination of all expected losses) to identify any exceedance of the risk tolerance curve.

Where the total security risk curve exceeds the RTC, the assessed organization should seek to mitigate selected security risks to lower the total expected loss. The security risk assessment team may create additional plots of selected security risks (especially any that exceed the RTC by them-selves) to demonstrate those security risks most in need of remediation. Care should be taken when plotting multiple probability distributions on a single chart as they can get busy rather easily. The team may determine that only one or two security risks should be plotted at a time against the RTC, see Figure 11.3.

11.2   SELECTING SAFEGUARDS

Safeguards are selected based on their effectiveness in addressing the indicated security risks. In other words, safeguards are put in place to reduce the security risk. The pool of available secu-rity safeguards (e.g., policies, procedures, training, two factor authentication, full disk encryption, integrated badge access, automated backups, intrusion detection systems) to employ is large and is expanding all the time. The security risk assessment team can only suggest those safeguards with which it is familiar. The more experienced the team, the larger the pool of safeguards it has to draw from during this stage of the security risk assessment. The safeguards listed in Chapters 6, 7, and 8 are a good start, but the team should not limit itself to those listed in this book.

When selecting improvements in existing security controls or new security controls to address a given security risk scenario, it is not always a simply process. At times, recommendations for improvements simply involve pointing out obvious (to the assessors) implementation gaps or mis-configurations of security controls. While more often than not, the selection of security controls and security control sets can be rather involved and take a considerable amount of analysis, planning, and write-up.

Another way to view the process of security risk mitigation is to review the security risk equation:

$$Security\ Risk = Likelihood\ of\ Threat\ Action \times Expected\ Impact$$

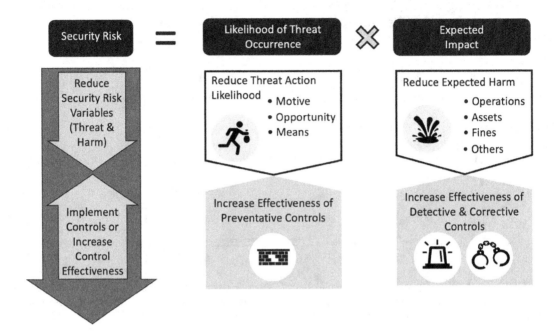

FIGURE 11.4 Security risk reduction. Security risk can be reduced by lowering the security risk equation variables of threat action likelihood or expected impact or through the implementation of preventative, detective, and corrective controls.

The reduction of security risk can be accomplished by lowering the value of either of the security risk variables or increasing the effectiveness of security controls. The value of the security risk variables (i.e., likelihood of threat action, expected impact) can be reduced by addressing the elements of the threat action (e.g., motive, opportunity, and means) or elements of the expected harm (e.g., harm to operations, assets, fines, and others). The effectiveness of security controls can be addressed through the improvement or implementation of preventative, detective, or corrective security controls, see Figure 11.4.

Security risk mitigation can best be described as appropriately selecting security safeguards through a purposeful process. There are many approaches to the process of selecting appropriate safeguards. The security risk assessment team or the employed security risk assessment method may have its own approach that the team is comfortable and experienced using. On the other hand, this may be an area in which the security risk assessment is looking for a bit of guidance. To assist in this difficult process, four different methods are listed and described here. The methods listed below are offered as examples of methods used in the industry.

11.2.1 METHOD 1: MISSING CONTROL LEADS TO SAFEGUARD SELECTION

Many times, the description of a security risk scenario can lead to a logical or even an obvious choice for a safeguard to address it. For example, if an organization is missing key controls in their cybersecurity program such as a documented incident response plan—the lack of which would increase the impact of most security breaches—the obvious safeguard is to create an incident response plan. On the surface, this method may seem rather simplistic, but many times, the best way to treat a security risk scenario is to simply implement missing controls closely associated with the threat action. This method works well for "essential elements" of security programs and is probably best employed for less mature security organizations.

11.2.2 METHOD 2: PEOPLE, PROCESS, TECHNOLOGY

This approach provides a systematic way of considering possible safeguards within the people, process, and technology categories. These three categories are used rather extensively within the information technology arena, and for good reason, because they effectively describe three separate areas from which information technology is affected.

These categories are a good fit for framing the discussion of safeguard selection.[1]

- People Safeguards—The team should consider people-based safeguards such as qualified and trusted individuals.
- Process Safeguards—The team should consider process-based safeguards such as security awareness training, account review, or change management.
- Technology Safeguards—The team should consider technology-based safeguards such as two-factor authentication, intrusion detection systems, or spam filtering.

11.2.3 METHOD 3: THE "NINE-CELL"

An expanded approach similar to the "people, process, technology" method is the "nine-cell," which gets its name from the 3 × 3 matrix representing different categories and types of security controls. In this approach, a matrix is created with the different types of security controls: preventative, detective, and corrective as columns and the different categories of security controls: administrative, technical, and physical as rows in a 3 × 3 matrix, see Figure 11.5.

This approach provides a systematic way of considering possible safeguards by considering standard safeguard types and categories. They types are aligned with the primary objective of the

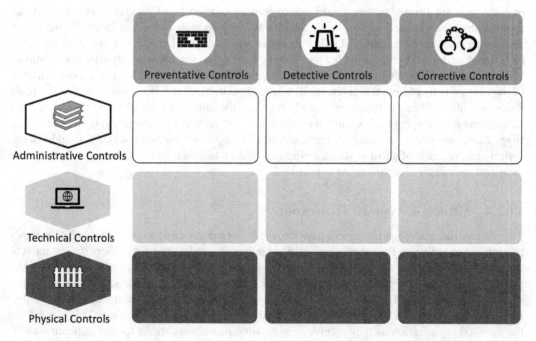

FIGURE 11.5 The "Nine-Cell." This approach to guide the selection of appropriate safeguards to address security risks asks the assessment team members to brainstorm appropriate controls for each of the cells of a matrix created by safeguard types (preventative, detective, and corrective) and safeguard categories (administrative, technical, and physical).

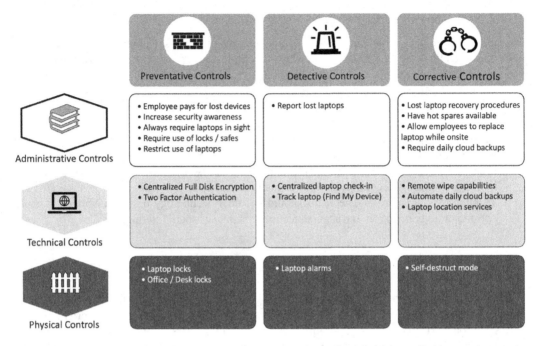

FIGURE 11.6   Nine-Cell worked example: lost laptop. The nine-cell approach is applied here to the security risk scenario of a lost or stolen laptop. The worked example brainstorming session yielded many results for potential safeguards to address the threat action.

control: preventative, detective, or corrective. The categories here are "administrative, technical, and physical" and are a common way breakdown of security controls (see Chapters 6, 7, and 8).[2] As an application of the nine-cell approach, consider the worked example of the lost laptop. Typically, an assessment team would recommend rather obvious controls such as laptop locks or centrally administered mobile device management, but they may be leaving out some potentially effective solutions. The nine-cell approach challenges the assessment team to come up with at least one control in each of the nine cells to address the given security risk (e.g., lost laptop). It is important that the team follow the rules of brainstorming and simply populate the nine-cell without being critical of each suggestion or even trying to determine the effectiveness of each suggestion just yet. This way other suggestions may come up based on previous ones. A populated nine-cell seeking to address the security risk scenario of a lost or stolen laptop may yield a large number of potential safeguards for the assessment team to consider, see Figure 11.6.

11.2.4   METHOD 4: AVAILABLE TECHNOLOGY

The security risk assessment team will have knowledge of the available technologies and safeguards to apply when analyzing the security risk assessment results. In fact, team members should actively continue their education through reading, seminars, and implementation in order to be up on the latest methods. The team members should utilize their knowledge of available safeguards and apply them to each security risk assessment. The benefit of this method is the vast amount of knowledge the assessment team will have on available technology in which they are familiar. This is good for the assessed organization as they receive very detailed recommendations for the implementation. The drawback, however, is that when an assessing organization "pushes" certain technology, especially technology that they sell, the impartiality of the security risk assessment comes into question. This potential impartiality can be addressed by the assessment team offering several alternative solutions outside of those products and services they offer as a follow-on sale.

Similarly, the members of the assessed organization will sometimes push for the implementation of a specific technology. The security risk assessment team should actively seek out and review the security technology implementation plan (e.g., what do you plan to buy or implement this year?) and consider each of those technologies and their capability to reduce security risk. This will provide valuable guidance to the security risk assessment customer and possibly lead to an adjustment in the implementation order.

11.3   SAFEGUARD SOLUTION SETS

The previous discussion regarding safeguard selections assumes a one-to-one relationship between threat actions or missing controls and safeguards. For example, for misconfigured or unpatched systems that are suspectable to known security vulnerabilities, the obvious safeguard is to securely configure the system or apply latest security patches. The relationship between many safeguards and threat actions, however, is many-to-many. This means that some safeguards address more than a single vulnerability, and some vulnerabilities are addressed by several safeguards, see Table 11.1.

In fact, the application of several safeguards to address a single vulnerability, or a closely related set of vulnerabilities, is the implementation of the design principle of defense in depth. The team should keep this principle in mind when coming up with safeguard recommendations and provide recommendations for control sets along with a plan or roadmap for implementing those controls.

Determining a recommended mix of safeguards to effectively address the identified security risk scenarios and recompute the residual security risk can be something of a trial-and-error exercise. Team members with a working knowledge of the application and effectiveness of current industry solutions will be of particularly good use at this stage.

A solution set is a composition of complementary and compensating safeguards that work well together to address the identified security risks and provide cost-effective solutions to reduce the security risk to an acceptable level. For example, a solution set that addresses the security risk of the unauthorized access to the assessed organization systems due to weak passwords could include the following elements:

- Modification of the Acceptable Use Policy to require users to pick strong passwords.
- Improvements to the Security Awareness Training to include discussion of password strength determination, tips on picking strong passwords that can still be remembered, and the results of the latest results from password-cracking exercises.

TABLE 11.1
The Many-to-Many Relationship between Safeguards and Threats

Applicable Safeguards	Threat Action				
	Structure Fire	Internal Theft	External Theft	Hurricane	Sabotage
Fire detection system	✓				✓
Loss control team	✓	✓	✓	✓	✓
Roving guards	✓	✓	✓		✓
Intrusion detection		✓	✓		✓
Power generator				✓	✓
Backup plan	✓			✓	✓

Note: Any given safeguard measure can address more than one threat action. Conversely, any threat action can be addressed by multiple safeguards.

- Regular use of password-cracking software by security personnel to expose weak passwords.
- Implementation of two factor authentication for all systems and applications
- Improvements in the password reset procedures
- Improvements in the initial account authorization procedures.

The security risk assessment team should work together to produce a variety of safeguard solution sets prior to settling on a recommended set. The three factors that will determine the recommended set are cost, effectiveness, and accepted residual security risk.

11.3.1 Safeguard Cost Calculations

Many security risk assessments include (as specified in their statement of work) a rough calculation of the safeguard cost as well as the indication of the effectiveness of the safeguard. The cost of a safeguard includes several components, namely, purchase price, installation charges, training costs, operational costs, and maintenance costs. Each of these safeguard costs is described below:

- Purchase Price—Many technology-based safeguards are additional system components that must be purchased. The purchase price is simply the cost to purchase the safeguard component from the vendor.
- Installation/Integration Charges—Many safeguards have an associated cost for installing or implementing the safeguard. The installation cost is the cost of integrating the safeguard into the organization's information system including changes to formal processes and procedures.
- Training Costs—The implementation and operation of many safeguards will require that the organization's staff receive training on the safeguard. The training costs are the costs associated with properly training the affected staff on the security safeguard.
- Operational Costs—All safeguards have some operational cost associated with them. The operational cost is the day-to-day cost of ensuring that the safeguard is working as intended.
- Maintenance Costs—Many safeguards have an associated cost for maintaining the safeguard. This could be in the form of a software update/maintenance contract or the cost of yearly maintenance. The maintenance cost is the annual cost of maintaining the safeguard in good working order.

11.3.2 Safeguard Effectiveness

Safeguard effectiveness is measured by its ability to reduce the frequency of occurrence or to reduce the impact of the event. Effectiveness measurement is typically difficult to quantify but approaches such as cost estimation and reliance on available data are used. Once the cost and effectiveness of safeguards and safeguard solutions sets are known, the next task is to justify the recommended safeguards to the senior management of the organization.

11.3.2.1 Justification through Judgment

Safeguard justification typically comes down to a cost–benefit analysis, but there are many safeguards that should be implemented without the cost of justifying them through a cost–benefit analysis. These safeguards include those required by law as well as low- and moderate-cost safeguards.

- Required by Law—For those organizations within regulated industries, many of the recommended safeguards are simply those required by the regulations. For example, all financial institutions with individual financial records must comply with the Gramm–Leach–Bliley Act, which requires, among other things, annual security awareness training. It would be a waste of effort to perform a cost–benefit analysis on security awareness training. Rather the organization should accept the safeguard because it is required by law.

- Low Cost with Material Benefit—Many safeguards have a very low cost and a clear benefit to the organization's security posture. Such safeguards should not undergo rigorous cost–benefit analysis calculations in order to justify their implementation. These safeguards should simply be accepted at face value and implemented to improve the protection of the organization's assets. For example, applying security patches to servers has a relatively low cost and certainly provides a clear benefit to the organization's security posture.
- Moderate Cost with Critical Reductions in Security Risk—Other safeguards have a moderate or reasonable cost, with the potential to avoid a fatal loss. Again, these safeguards should not be subject to cost–benefit analysis and instead should be accepted as an improvement to the organization's security program. For example, implementing an effective security awareness program has a moderate cost but provides a great potential for avoiding fatal losses through social engineering, user error, and system misuse.

The use of safeguard justification through judgment should not be overlooked. Even though there exist formulas for determining safeguard cost and approaches for estimating safeguard effectiveness, it is not always in the best interest of the organization to spend valuable engineering time on the exercise of formally justifying all recommendations. Many business decisions are based on the judgment of experienced and trusted consultants. In many instances, it makes sense to take the recommendations as presented without asking for extensive and costly additional analysis. For example, organizations in the early stage of developing a security program to protect their assets are likely to have predictable gaps in their security program, such as security policies, awareness training, adequate staff, and review of logs.

If the conclusions of the security risk assessment recommend the selected safeguards, most organizations would be well advised to get busy implementing, instead of calling for more data. On the other hand, there are times when a more complete cost–benefit analysis is required.

11.3.2.2 Cost–Benefit Analysis

Cost–benefit analysis is a precise method for determining and comparing the value and cost of a proposed safeguard. Cost–benefit analysis, therefore, provides a quantitative method for justifying proposed safeguards. However, this precision comes at a cost and has several required components:

- Common Unit of Measurement—A cost–benefit analysis is a mathematical comparison of costs and benefits and requires that all costs and benefits be expressed or converted into a common unit of measurement. The unit of measurement used could be security risk or even societal benefit, but it is typically dollars. In the case of dollars as a common unit of measurement, all dollars must be expressed in terms of "today's dollars." Although this expression may sound like a complicated economic concept, it is actually quite simple and is based on the concept that being paid a dollar today is worth more than being paid a dollar next year. This concept is referred to as *present value* of money.
- Estimating the Costs—When performing the cost–benefit analysis for any recommended safeguard, the complete costs of the safeguard must be accounted for. These costs include all costs over the life cycle or useful life of the safeguard and include acquisition, implementation, training, operational, and residual security risk costs.
- Discount Costs and Benefits—The costs and benefits of the recommended safeguard may not be required or realized right away. Some costs or benefits are attributed to the start of the safeguard implementation project, while others are applied later in its life cycle. As discussed previously, a dollar two years from now is worth less than a dollar today, and its exact value depends upon the rate of inflation or return you could otherwise get for investing the dollar somewhere else. The technique of converting future dollar costs and revenues to today's dollars is called *discounting*. The next step requires that the costs and benefits be discounted.

SIDEBAR 11.1   ECONOMIC TERMS

Many of the examples throughout this book use simplified cost and loss figures. In these figures the time value of money is not incorporated into the dollar figures for expected loss, cost, or other calculations. However, in business the time value of money is always a factor. Some of the terms most frequently used when considering the time value of money are listed and described below:

- Present Value of Money (PV)—PV relates the value of a future dollar to a present-day dollar. An investment that would pay $1,000 five years from today and earns 10% per year interest has a present value of $620. In Excel, the present value function is:

$$PV(rate, nper, pmt, [fv])$$

  - rate: the interest rate per period (e.g., annual)
  - nper: the total number of payment periods (e.g., 5)
  - pmt: the payment made each period
  - [fv]: [optional parameter] the future value
- Net Present Value of Money (NPV)—NPV relates the combined negative and positive cash flows from the project in today's dollars. A positive net present value indicates a worthwhile project, while a negative NPV indicates that the organization should forgo the project. In Excel, the net present value function is:

$$NPV(rate, value1, value2, ...)$$

  - rate: the interest rate per period (e.g., annual)
  - value1, value2, ...: equally spaced values of expected cash flows
- Internal Rate of Return (IRR)—IRR is the return an organization requires to invest in internal projects. In Excel, the internal rate of return function is:

$$IRR(value\_array)$$

  - value_array ...: an array of referenced cells containing cash flows and expenses. The array must contain at least one positive and at least one negative cash flow to calculate the internal rate or return.

- Compute Cost Benefit—Projects have both negative cash flows (expenses) and positive cash flows (revenues). These cash flows can be realized at different times. In order to compare these values fairly, all cash flows are normalized to "today's dollars" (net present value, NPV). Even projects with positive NPV may not be selected by management. Management has a limited budget, and only those projects with the best returns get funding. The hurdle rate for funding within the organization is called the internal rate of return (IRR).

In the following example, the safeguard of implementing a secure coding effort is reviewed. The costs of a secure coding effort include the development of standards, training, additional coding steps, and additional review steps, see Tables 11.2 and 11.3.

PV(rate,nper,pmt,[fv])

The benefits of this effort include reduction in rework and reduction of threat impact. The net present value of the effort is computed based on the expected incomes or costs over a number of years:

$$NPV = \sum_{i=1}^{n} \frac{incomes_i}{(1+rate)^i}$$

TABLE 11.2

Estimating Costs: Cost Benefit Analysis Worked Example Secure Coding Effort

Estimate Costs	1st Year	2nd Year	3rd Year	4th Year	5th Year	Assumptions
Secure coding standards	$8,000	$1,000	$1,000	$1,000	$1,000	1st year: 80 hours to develop (in-house); 10 hours to maintain in later years
Secure coding training	$14,000	$7,000	$3,500	$3,500	$3,500	1st year: 20 developers, 2 sessions; same course 1 session next year; self-taught from recordings in later years
Impact on coding	$200,000	$100,000	$50,000	$50,000	$50,000	1st year: 10% additional effort: 2 extra developers; savings over later years due to organizational maturity
Impact on review cycle	$200,000	$200,000	$200,000	$200,000	$200,000	$20,000 per app.; 10 apps. per year
Total costs	**$422,000**	**$308,000**	**$254,500**	**$254,500**	**$254,500**	

Note: The costs of a secure coding project include the development of standards, training, additional coding steps, and additional review steps.

TABLE 11.3

Estimating Benefits: Cost Benefit Analysis Worked Example Secure Coding Effort

Estimate Benefits	1st Year	2nd Year	3rd Year	4th Year	5th Year	Assumptions
Reduction in rework	—	$120,000	$240,000	$360,000	$360,000	1st year, no reduction 2nd year, 10% reduction 3rd year, 20% reduction 4th and 5th year, 30% reduction; rework is 30% of coders' time
Reduction of threat impact:						
Disclosure	$180,000	$180,000	$180,000	$180,000	$180,000	$10,000/disclosure; ALE = 1.5 disclosures per app. Reduction = 60%
Integrity	$75,000	$75,000	$75,000	$75,000	$75,000	$5,000/mistake; ALE = 1 mistake/app. Reduction = 75%
Availability	$125,000	$125,000	$125,000	$125,000	$125,000	$25,000/hour; ALE = 1 hour/app. 50% reduction in DOS
Total benefits	$380,000	$500,000	$620,000	$740,000	$740,000	
Total costs	$422,000	$308,000	$254,500	$254,500	$254,500	
Net benefit	**$(42,000)**	**$192,000**	**$365,500**	**$485,500**	**$485,500**	

Note: The benefits of a secure coding project include reduction in rework and reduction of threat impact.

11.4 ESTABLISHING SECURITY RISK PARAMETERS

It is the duty of senior management to accept the security risk to the organization's assets. With this in mind, the security risk assessment team must have a good indication as to the security risk adversity of the organization's senior management. Recall the earlier discussion regarding the assessed

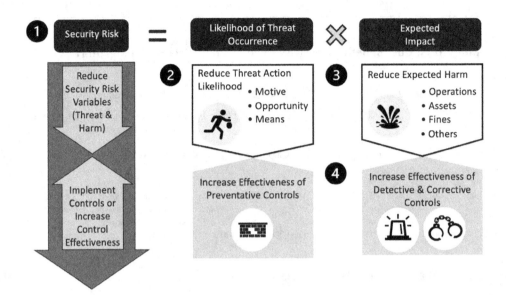

FIGURE 11.7 Security risk treatment. The assessed organization has four ways to address each security risk: 1—accept, 2—avoid, 3—assign, and 4—reduce. It is the objective of this phase of the security risk assessment process to reduce security risk through the selection of safeguards.

organization's security risk appetite. The organization's level of security risk appetite should be considered when selecting recommended safeguards.

The security risk for each vulnerability found during the data gathering phase can be addressed through one of four ways:

1. Accept Security Risk—Based on business mission and other factors, accept the identified security risk. When the expected loss is within the RTC, the organization may choose to accept the risk.
2. Avoid Security Risk—Avoid the security risk by eliminating the security risk cause, for shutting down a system at high or critical risk, thus eliminating the threat to the system..
3. Assign Security Risk—Purchase insurance to assign or transfer the security risk to another party.
4. Reduce Security Risk—Implement recommended safeguard to reduce specific security risk.

The objective of the safeguard selection process is to address the fourth way: reduction of security risk, see Figure 11.7.

EXERCISES

1. Section 11.2.3 introduces the safeguard selection approach of the "nine-cell." Create and complete a nine-cell diagram for the following security risk scenarios:
   a. Front entrance is susceptible to piggybacking.
   b. In-house-developed Web applications are susceptible to SQL injection attacks.
   c. Critical patches are not applied within 7 days.
   d. USB thumb drives containing sensitive data are lost outside of the building.
2. Estimate (quantitatively) the cost of implementing the following controls:
   a. Secure code development training for 20 developers.
   b. Fire suppression system for 2,000 sq. ft. (24,000 cu. ft.) data center.
   c. Whole-disk encryption for 100 laptops.
   d. the development of a vendor security risk management program within a major retailer.

3. Estimate the costs for the same controls above using the following qualitative scale:

Very high:	> $1 million
High:	< $1 million
Medium:	< $200,000
Low:	< $10,000

4. Consider the safeguards described in 2a–d.
   a. Suggest a quantitative measurement approach for effectiveness of 2a–d.
   b. What would it cost to obtain that measurement?
   c. Is it worthwhile to do so?
5. Estimate the effectiveness of 2a–d using the qualitative scale of Very High, High, Medium, and Low.
   a. Using only the qualitative measurements for cost and effectiveness, what controls would you suggest be implemented?
   b. Is it likely that quantitative methods would produce different results?

NOTES

1 The categories are sometimes extended to include "environment" as well.
2 I have been asked why I do not include the "familiar" control sets of "deterrence, recovery, and compensating." Quite simply I do not find them to be familiar. In fact, I find them to be either superfluous or even confusing. "Deterrence" is often described as a "weak preventive," e.g., a no trespassing sign vs. a fence. I find that most security professionals equate both the sign and the fence as having the intention to "prevent." "Recovery" has a similarity to "corrective," but you can differentiate between the two. For example, putting a spare tire on a car is corrective, but it is not until you get the original repaired that you have actually corrected. However, this distinction between "recovery" and "corrective" adds little value to the categorization approach. Lastly, the concept of "compensating" controls does not belong in this categorization at all, because any of the controls can be a compensating control. "Compensating" simply means that a control is used where another control does not make sense. Nevertheless, if the security professional is more "familiar" with the complete list of categories—deterrent, preventive, detective, corrective, recovery, compensating—feel free to use them.

12 Security Risk Assessment Reporting

To the customer of the security risk assessment, the project is not complete until it is documented. One of the most important elements of the security risk assessment effort is the reporting of the results. The security risk assessment team may have a clear understanding of the risks to the organization and the safeguards that should be employed, but that information must be conveyed to the organization in a clear and effective manner.

Recall that a security risk assessment is an objective analysis of the current security controls effectiveness to protect an organization's assets and a determination of the probability of losses to those assets. The goal of the security risk assessment is to provide information regarding security risks to the organization's assets and recommendations for reducing those security risks to senior management in support of their safeguard selection decisions or security risk acceptance. Clear and effective security risk assessment reporting requires that the contents of the report be perceived as accurate, non-threatening, relevant, and unambiguous. Each of these aspects of a quality report is discussed in this chapter.

12.1 CAUTIONS IN REPORTING

A security risk assessment team can deliver a technically accurate report but still miss the objective of the security risk assessment effort by alienating those who receive the information or those who provide support to those senior managers. The security risk assessment team must be careful about not only what they say, but also how they say it. The following discussion is meant to provide some advice on framing the assessment results in a manner that will be well received:

- Include Positive Findings—The security risk assessment report is an extremely important tool for the senior management of the organization. However, much like an audit report, it is filled with a list of many areas for improvement. The security risk assessment team must understand that a list of all these findings in a single report, delivered to the senior management of an organization, is understandably met with a mixed reaction from those who will eventually be asked to implement many of the recommendations.
- Avoid Delay in Reporting—Although security risk assessment reports include tactical and strategic analysis, many of the observations, findings, and recommendations are operational. This means that time is of the essence in delivering the security risk assessment report. On the other hand, the security risk assessment team needs to ensure that the report is accurate. Therefore, it is essential to create a draft report that can be delivered for initial customer review with the expectation that some components of the draft report may need to be revised to ensure accuracy and completion of the deliverable objectives. This first draft should be delivered without delay. The elapse of too much time between the last interaction with the organization and the first draft of the report leads to an impression of irrelevance of the report. The following quote, taken from Rochester Institute of Technology's first experience with security risk assessment vendors, demonstrates the importance of timely delivery of the security risk assessment report:

TABLE 12.1

Non-confrontational, Non-judgmental Risk Statements

Avoid These Phrases	Instead Use These Phrases
Finding. Administrators in group A failed to properly harden all servers in their area.	*Finding.* Procedures for hardening servers in group A were not completely effective.
	Evidence. Some servers in group A were not hardened in accordance with the stated policy.
Finding. Bad user habits leave passwords written in the clear around their workstations.	*Finding.* Security awareness training is not completely effective for all users.
	Evidence. Many user workstation areas had recorded passwords in plain sight (e.g., sticky notes on monitors, taped to pull-out drawer).

Note: The security risk assessment team must avoid confrontational or judgmental findings. Remember, the objective of the assessment is to prioritize risks and not to assign blame.

> Some analysis was no longer relevant by the time the final report was delivered.... Our vendor estimated the delivery of the final report to take about three times the amount of time spent during the onsite interview and scanning phase.
>
> ("Lessons Learned", 22004)

- Avoid Pointing Fingers—Again, the objective of the security risk assessment is to determine risk and recommend safeguards, not to assign blame. The security risk assessment team should avoid statements that may be interpreted as assigning blame (see Table 12.1).

12.2 POINTERS IN REPORTING

Too many engineers believe that the important work is in the data gathering and analysis, and they can forget that nothing matters unless it is communicated effectively. Security risk assessment reports are especially difficult to create because they are based on technical information that needs to reach both managerial and technical audiences. A few tips are provided below to assist the team in preparing a quality document:

- Use Tables and Figures—Many ideas are best presented in a table or a figure. Also understand that about half your audience will gain most of their information through visuals. Use them generously. Be sure to refer to every table or figure in the body of the report. Label tables and figures correctly and consistently. Include a list of tables after the table of contents.
- Use Consistent Terminology—In any field, there are many ways to say the same thing. Within security risk assessments, the terms *safeguards, countermeasures,* and *compensating controls* are used interchangeably. This is fine among other professionals, but in a report to a diverse audience, the switching from one term to another can completely lose your audience. It is a good idea for the team leader to produce a term sheet to be used throughout the report. The term sheet should cover technical terms to be used, as well as the long and short name to be used for the customer, the name of computer systems, and the name of locations.

12.3 REPORT STRUCTURE

The structure of the report can greatly enhance its readability and usability. Because the report is designed for different audiences, it should have different sections for each type of audience. These include executives and technical resources.

12.3.1 EXECUTIVE-LEVEL REPORT

The executive report is clearly designed for the senior management of the organization. As such, the executive section should cover the information the senior management requires to make an informed decision. The following recommendations should be followed when compiling the executive summary:

- Length—The executive management section is typically a 2- to 4-page summary of the entire report.
- Key Elements—Describe the purpose of the assessment, the assessment approach, major findings, recommendations, and next steps.
- Clear Recommendations—The executives are quite comfortable making decisions based on recommendations and available information. They are typically not comfortable with analysis that provides no clear recommendation. You are the expert—state your opinion.
- Technical Detail—The executive summary should never contain detailed technical information. However, the report should be structured so that finding detail on high-level findings and recommendations is easy.

12.3.2 BASE REPORT

The main body of the report should provide almost all of the information gathered during the assessment process. The structure of the report could be dictated by the statement of work (SOW). If so, follow the dictated structure. If not, the following recommended structure could be followed:

- Introduction—This section provides an introduction to the security risk assessment. It should contain all the information required for someone to come up to speed on the reason for the project and what the project entailed. Those familiar with the project should be able to skip this section without missing any required information to make security risk decisions. This section should include the following subsections:
  - Background—Provide a background on why and how the security risk assessment was performed. This may include regulatory requirements or other driving factors.
  - Security Risk Management Overview—Provide a primer on risk management to properly frame the role of the security risk assessment. Section 1.4.1 provides a nice example of the security risk management overview.
  - Scope—Provide a description of the scope of the assessment. This scope should be taken directly from the SOW and logical and physical boundaries as well as coverage (e.g., administrative, physical, and technical) and rigor descriptions.
  - Approach—Provide a description of the security risk assessment approach. If you are using a common approach or tool, use the standard description of the security risk assessment approach provided by the product literature. If you are using a proprietary method, you may use the marketing literature or proposal response language.
- Site Characteristics—Describe the existing physical safeguards, environmental factors, and geographic location of the information systems to be assessed. This should include facility access controls, visitor procedures, restricted areas, power sources, safety features, and environmental systems.
- Information System Characteristics—Describe the existing technical safeguards. This should include data classification, virus protection, backup software, identification and authentication systems, and all other technical controls.
- Organizational Characteristics—Describe the existing administrative safe-guards. This should include policies, procedures, and security activities currently performed by the organization's personnel or outsourced to trusted partners. An organizational chart highlighting the security organization should also be included and discussed.

- Asset and Threat Analysis—Include a report on the asset and threat analysis of the organization.
- Vulnerability Analysis—Include a report on the identified vulnerabilities.
- Security Risk Analysis Summary—Include a discussion of the security risk analysis results and a clear and prioritized table of the security risk analysis summary. This could be recorded in tabular or other formats.
- Countermeasure Recommendations—Include a list of countermeasures recommended.

12.3.3 Appendices and Exhibits

A report can be made more clear by including details for those who want additional information to support the findings. Appendices can include anything that would assist in making the case for any recommendations in the body of the main report. The typical appendices of a security risk assessment report are as follows:

- Resources and Evidence Information—Provide a list of the evidence used to determine asset values, threat statements, and identified vulnerabilities. Many of the findings within the report will be accepted at face value because of the credentials of the security risk assessment team and the recognition of the problem areas by the organization. However, some findings may be questioned. The evidence appendix can provide the required information to back up the findings of the team. Production of this appendix throughout the security risk assessment process is imperative to ensure its accuracy.
- Detailed Findings—Many findings are too detailed for the body of the report but provide information that will be needed by the organization. For example, the output of a vulnerability scanner provides in-depth information that will be needed by the organization's administrator tasked with fixing the problems.
- Cost Estimate Worksheets—If considerable effort was put into calculations such as cost–benefit analysis or recommended countermeasure estimates, these calculations can be recorded in an appendix.
- References—It is common practice to provide a list of references used and cited throughout the report.

12.4 DOCUMENT REVIEW METHODOLOGY: CREATE THE REPORT USING A TOP-DOWN APPROACH

The first description of what the customer expects in the final security risk assessment report is in the SOW. Although the SOW does not provide great detail as to the contents of the report, the project manager should ensure that the final report meets the minimum description contained in the SOW.

A good start for the report development is a description of what the report will look like: format, approximate length, key concerns of the customer, details contained within, and so on. This information is captured in a document specification. The document specification should be reviewed and approved by the customer. The customer may comment on certain elements of the document specification, such as the key concerns or the extent to which recommendations will provide details. Comments such as these should be encouraged and even solicited from the customer. A careful review and wording of the document specification assists in a greater understanding of the intended contents of the final deliverable.

The security assessment team leader should negotiate requested changes to the document specification to address the comments of the customer and seek approval of the revised document specification. Once approval has been obtained, the document specification becomes the new deliverable description. This is advantageous to both the customer and the assessment team, because it is a refinement of the SOW. Any differences between what is expected and what is planned to be delivered should be dealt with as early as possible.

The next level of document development is an annotated outline. These refinements of the deliverable will lay out the topics to be covered in the document and the order in which they are to be presented. Moreover, an annotated outline contains a one- or two-sentence description of the document sections to more clearly identify the topics to be covered. The document authors should not assume that a section title alone explains its contents. For example, a section of a risk assessment report called "security controls" could have a subsection entitled "security policies." It is not immediately clear if this section is intended to discuss rules and regulations that govern the behavior of authorized individuals or if this section is referring to the rulesets for the firewalls. As *security policies* is an overloaded term, different individuals could infer quite different meanings. This inference regarding the contents of the final deliverable could lead to a miscommunication and, perhaps, ultimately to a dissatisfaction or rejection of the final report.

12.4.1 DOCUMENT SPECIFICATION

A document specification is a formal document describing the deliverables of the engagement. Even though the deliverables may have been listed in the SOW, the document specification is a useful document that can lead to project efficiencies through increased communication and feedback. The document specification identifies the following aspects and details of the security risk assessment report to be created and delivered:

- Project—The official name of the project. This should be consistent with the SOW and be used on-site as well. Use of a consistent name can eliminate confusion, especially if there are multiple assessment projects within the organization at any one time.
- Audience—Clearly state the primary and secondary audience of the document. In the case of a security risk assessment, the primary audience is the senior management of the organization being assessed, and the secondary audience is the staff who will be asked to implement some of the controls described in the report. An understanding of the audience helps to ensure that the report is compiled and written in a manner that assists its audience in reading, understanding, and using the document. For example, inclusion of an executive summary and a technical appendix would satisfy the needs of two disparate audiences.
- Key Topics—List any specific considerations for this particular assessment of which the team or the customer should be aware, for example, "This assessment is being performed as a pre-audit for a Sarbanes-Oxley assessment." Such instructions give the project leader and the team members a heads-up for unique considerations within the environment.
- Production Issues—Identify any specific production or delivery issues regarding the final or intermediate deliverables. For example, identify the format, number of copies, and delivery method for the final report. Mention here if a formal presentation is expected and if other formats of the report, for example, slides or a summary, are expected.
- References and Prototypes—List any references such as regulations or security risk assessment methods to be followed. Also list any previous work, such as last year's security risk assessment, that could be used to garner information.

The sample document specification in Table 12.2 illustrates the format and use of a document specification in structuring the document development methodology.

TABLE 12.2
Document Specification Example

Project: 081503001—ABC Corporation Security Risk Assessment

Title: ABC Corporation Security Risk Assessment

Type: Security Risk Assessment Report

Audience:

- **Primary:** ABC Corporation management will use the findings of this report to determine required changes in their security program. Specifically, they will look for existing vulnerabilities and how to patch them, missing elements of the security program and how to implement them, and residual risk and how to mitigate it.
- **Secondary:** This document will be used in subsequent efforts to assess and improve the security posture of the ABC Corporation. Secondary audience may include security engineers/auditors and managed security vendors.

Purpose/Problem Statement:

- Assess ABC Corporation's current security architecture. ABC Corporation wants to be certain that it has done due diligence in analyzing its current security architecture.
- Provide recommendations for solutions to security deficiencies. Provide options, recommendations, and proposed solutions necessary to provide a secure environment.
- ABC Corporation also wants to prepare itself for a mandatory SSAE 16 audit that will be performed early next year.

Key Topics:

- An executive summary highlights the most pertinent issues, high-level findings, and an assessment of the overall security posture of the network.
- The body of the report provides a description of the approach, findings sorted by area, recommendations for improvements, and appendices containing detailed findings.
- This report will give ABC Corporation a straightforward description of the actions needed to address areas of concern.
- Specifically, the report will summarize the customer's security needs; identify relevant threats and vulnerabilities given the customer's current architecture, operational procedures, and risk level; specify architectural improvements and considerations; and summarize findings and recommendations, providing a framework for moving forward. The report is organized as follows:
- Introduction (background, security risk management overview, scope, approach)
- Site characteristics
- Information system characteristics
- Organizational characteristics
- Asset and threat analysis
- Vulnerability analysis
- Security risk analysis
- Countermeasure recommendations

Specific Considerations:

Project management, project contributors, and document reviewers need to be aware of cost and time constraints and the impact of overages on other tasks.

Document Specification History:

Date: V1.0 Initial draft document specification

Date: V1.1 Changed _ in response to _

(Continued)

TABLE 12.2 *(Continued)*

Production Issues:

- **Review:** Delivery relies upon timely review of document specification and rough draft of the assessment report by ABC Corporation.
- **Up-to-date:** Assessment findings and solution recommendations are based on available information of existing products and services, and known vulnerabilities at the time of the review.
- **Coordination:** Various sections of the report will rely on input from several different security engineers. However, recommendations for overall solutions will overlap these areas. Coordination in findings and recommendations is necessary for overall recommended security plan.
- **Changing Environment:** Assessment requires a freeze on the scope of the assessment. This includes the infrastructure, policies, organization, and configurations. The assessment team lead must be notified of any changes that will take effect during the assessment. We would expect such changes to follow a change-control process.

References/Prototypes:

1. *ABC Corporation/Lantego. Statement of Work for Security Assessment*, September 26, 2020.
2. Landoll, Douglas J. *The Security Risk Assessment Handbook, 3rd Edition,* CRC Press, 2020

Resources:

Project lead: Dara Lee

Document lead: Thomas Benton

Principal writers: Kasey Nicole

Secondary writers: Rachel Rose

Technical support: Dacy V.

Reviewer(s): Internal: Denver W., Dex R.

Customer: ABC (Dala L.)

Note: A document specification describes the content, layout, key issues and production issues of the deliverable in order to increase communication with the customer and the ultimate acceptance of the deliverable.

12.4.2 DRAFT

The development of a draft security risk assessment report is essential to the success of the project. A draft report provides two important functions:

- Immediate Feedback—The draft security risk assessment report provides an immediate feedback to the customer for security gaps of high risk. If the assessment team has uncovered and documented high-risk security gaps that should be addressed immediately, the draft report is a useful vehicle for delivering a documented record and recommendations for addressing these areas. For example, a draft report could contain the results of vulnerability scans and recommendations for patches.
- Opportunity for Correction—In the course of reviewing documents, performing interviews, inspecting controls, observing behavior, and testing controls, mistakes will be made by the security risk assessment team. Those mistakes may be as simple as misspelling the name of an interviewee to as complex as incorrectly documenting the current system architecture. In either case, it is important to get the facts right so that the findings may be considered without undue prejudice.

12.4.3 FINAL

The final security risk assessment report is the corrected version of the draft report. The team leader should be careful to ensure that the final report contains only those corrections from the draft that have been discussed with the customer. This point is important and deserves clarification. It is not necessary that the final report findings be accepted or approved by the customer, but it *is* necessary that they be discussed with the customer and that the customer is given an opportunity to clarify any misunderstandings.

The objectivity of the security risk assessment is essential to its value. The team must ensure that the final security risk assessment documents the beliefs and findings of the security risk assessment team.

12.5 ASSESSMENT BRIEF

It is recommended that the final security risk assessment report be presented to the organization's senior management. The assessment briefing is outlined here:

- Attendees—The attendees for the security risk assessment briefing should include representatives from the organization's senior management and the security risk assessment team. At a minimum, the attendance should include the project sponsor and the security risk assessment team leader.
- Meeting Agenda—The presentation of the final report should be rather straightforward and follow the outline of the report itself. The meeting should start with introductions and a brief explanation of the effort. The security risk assessment team leader should briefly describe the process of the security risk assessment and then provide a review of the high-level findings, starting with positive findings. Next, the team leader should list the recommended safeguards and a suggested timetable for implementation.
- Briefing Tips—As mentioned in many other places throughout this book, the security risk assessment can be a controversial effort within the organization. The team leader should be aware that the final presentation could be a place where such controversy comes to the surface. The following tips are provided to help ensure that the final briefing is successful and runs smoothly:
  - Iron out wording problems in the draft.
  - Ensure that all draft reviews included appropriate parties.
  - Bring enough of copies for everyone.
  - Be sure to highlight positive findings, including the security risk assessment project itself.
  - Invite all interested parties.
- Keep findings non-judgmental (provide solutions, not blame).

12.6 ACTION PLAN

The final phase of the security risk assessment is to ensure that the organization creates an action plan that addresses all security risks identified in the final report. Each item should be assigned to a named individual; a date for action should be identified; and the results should be tracked. Each of these identified risks should be either reduced, accepted, rejected, or assigned. A good practice is to record the disposition of the risk on a master copy of the final security risk assessment report, with a date and a signature of the senior officials who choose to accept an identified residual risk instead of implementing the proposed remediation approach.

If the customer has already established and maintains a risk register, the action plan can be formatted to ease the transfer of identified risks from this report to the assessed organization's risk register. If the customer does not already have a risk register the following items are recommended (as a minimum) to be included in a risk register and should be attributes of the action plan to give the assessed organization a good start at establishing a risk register.

- Last Modified (date at which the risk register was last modified)
- For each risk
  - Risk rank
  - Risk identification number
  - Name of risk
  - Description of risk
  - Date risk identified and by whom/by which activity
  - Description of threat and threat aspects
  - Identification of associated vulnerabilities
  - Value and parameters of loss probability
  - Value and parameters of expected loss
  - Assigned owner of risk
  - Recommended risk reduction measures
  - Selected risk reduction measures
  - For each risk reduction measure:
    - Person assigned responsibility for completion
    - Date of expected completion
    - (When risk reduction measures are completed) risk reductions (e.g., loss probability, expected loss, and risk)
    - Date risk reduction measure was completed

EXERCISES

1. Find an organization that has had a recent security risk assessment. Through an interview with at least one of the consumers of the assessment report, determine what they liked most about the report and their biggest complaint regarding the report.
2. Why is it important to have each of the following deliverables in a security risk assessment engagement?
   a. Statement of work
   b. Document specification
   c. Draft deliverable
   d. Final deliverable
3. When preparing for a security risk assessment brief, what documents and information should be provided to the customer? When and why?
4. Create an example of an action plan. Include a sample of a few security risks, their associated recommended safeguards, assignment of an action to an individual, and other items you feel are warranted.
5. What percentage of total hours for the security risk assessment effort should be devoted to the creation of a security risk assessment report? What factors would influence your answer?

BIBLIOGRAPHY

United States General Accounting Office, Accounting and Information Management Division, *Information Security Risk Assessment: Practices of Leading Organizations*. A Supplement to GAO's August 1999 Executive Guide on Information Security Management, November 1999. GAO/AMID-99-139. https://www.gao.gov/assets/80/76441.pdf (Accessed October 21, 2020).

U.S. General Accounting Office, How to Get Action on Audit Recommendations. July 1991. https://www.gao.gov/special.pubs/p0921.pdf (Accessed October 21, 2020).

Rochester Institute of Technology, Lessons Learned from RITs First Security Posture Assessment. January 1, 2004.

Rugh, David E., and Robert E. Manning, *Proposal Management Using the Modular Technique*, Los Altos Hills, CA, Peninsula Publishing, 1973.

13 Security Risk Assessment Project Management

A security risk assessment is a project—a rather unique project that requires a specific skill set and activities, but a project, nonetheless. For the security risk assessment to result in a successful effort, the project must be well managed. In this chapter, the fundamental elements of project management are discussed. These elements are planning, tracking, correction, and reporting.

13.1 PROJECT PLANNING

A project manager has the ultimate responsibility for the successful completion of a project. Success is defined in terms of customer satisfaction, technical quality of the work, and completion within budget and time constraints. In order to ensure a successful project, the project manager must properly plan the project.

13.1.1 PROJECT DEFINITION

Project planning begins with the project definition. A project is defined within the statement of work (SOW). This is the portion of the contract that is the basis for defining the work and the time and resource constraints on the project. Ideally, a project manager will have been involved in the negotiation process and the creation of the SOW, but this is not always the case.

The first thing a project manager needs to do is to read the SOW and ensure that the project expectations are understood. The project manager must then confirm that the deadlines and resource constraints are able to be met. If the project manager sees any problem with the SOW, including the deliverables, resources, or deadlines, these problems must be dealt with as early as possible in the process. The project manager must articulate what changes need to take place before accepting the project from the senior manager or whoever signed the SOW. The project manager and senior management need to come to an agreement as to the parameters of the SOW. Any required changes could be to the SOW or as an internal charge or expected overrun.

At this point, the project manager accepts the project and its parameters. It is now up to the project manager to ensure that the project completes successfully.

13.1.2 PROJECT PLANNING DETAILS

In order to effectively allocate hours and still ensure that the project will finish on time, the project manager will typically divide the project up into phases and activities within each phase. Tools such as Microsoft Project® provide a useful way to quickly create project plans.

13.1.2.1 Project Phases and Activities

The first step is to divide the project into phases. There is no hard-and-fast rule about phases. Project managers want to strike a balance between the ability to adequately track progress (thus siding for small phases) and the overhead of managing many phases (thus siding for larger phases). But a good rule of thumb is that each phase should be at least a few days and not more than a month. For example, an average security risk assessment project may be divided into the phases shown in Table 13.1.

Each phase can be further broken down into activities. Again, there are no hard-and-fast rules here either, but a good rule of thumb is that each activity should be at least a day and not longer than

TABLE 13.1

Project Phases—Divide the Project into "Manageable" Phases

Phase	Name	Description
1	Pre-on-site	Complete project initiation tasks and prepare for on-site activities
2	On-site assessment	Perform on-site data gathering and testing
3	Results analysis	Review data gathered and compile results
4	Reporting	Document and present findings to the customer

Note: The average security risk assessment can be well-managed by breaking it up into four phases of preparation, onsite, analysis, and reporting.

TABLE 13.2

Project Tasks—Divide Each Phase into an "Assignable" Task

Phase	Tasks
Phase 1: Pre-on-site	1.1 Project initiation (letter of introduction, kickoff meeting, obtaining proper signatures, permissions and accesses, requests for documents) 1.2 Document review (review of policies, procedures, training material, previous risk assessments, organizational charts, etc.) 1.3 Interview preparation (preparing interviews with key personnel)
Phase 2: On-site assessment	2.1 Document follow-up 2.2 Observation of security practices (walk-throughs, "trash intelligence," TRASHINT) Interviews 2.3 Technical assessment (internal security scanning, war dialing, firewall ruleset review, architecture review)
Phase 3: Results analysis	3.1 Data analysis 3.2 Create risk statements (including recommendations) 3.3 Team review and consensus of risk statements 3.4 Additional research for recommendations
Phase 4: Reporting	4.1 Document specification 4.2 Annotated outline (with section assignments to team members) 4.3 Draft 4.4 Final 4.5 Briefing (if required)

Note: The average security risk assessment can be well-managed by breaking it up into four phases of preparation, onsite, analysis, and reporting.

a week or two. You will find that exceptions are more the rule, though. For example, reviewers are typically given 4–8 hours to review a document. Continuing the security risk assessment example, each phase can be broken into assignable tasks, as shown in Table 13.2.

13.1.2.2 Phases and Activities Scheduling

Now that the project has been divided up into phases and activities, the project manager needs to schedule the phases and activities such that the project will complete on time. Experience is the best teacher for doing this correctly, but a few tips are offered here:

- Determine Start Times—Work backward from the due date.
- Review Time—Be sure to leave adequate time for internal and customer review. Customer review time is typically 2–3 times as long as the security risk assessment team's review time because we do not have control over how the customer spends the time.

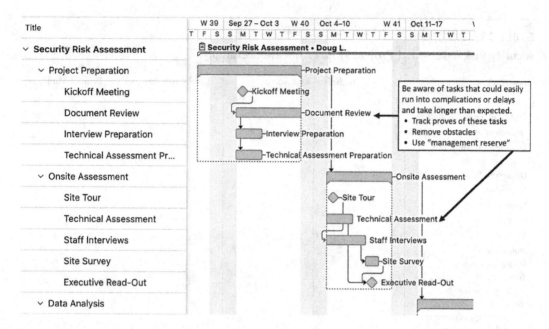

FIGURE 13.1 Using a Gantt chart to schedule tasks. The Gantt chart view in project management software is a useful way to plan and visualize how the project tasks interrelate.

- Critical Paths—Be aware of dependencies and critical paths. Some activities can be performed at any time, while others require the results of a previous activity being performed.
- Efficiencies—When defining activities, consider time and travel efficiencies by grouping activities using identical resources or requiring travel to the same location together. For example, both internal scanning and key personnel interviews will require the security risk assessment team to be on site. Consider scheduling these activities in the same timeframe (e.g., in the same week). On the other hand, consider the resources required to support these activities and ensure that enough slack time is allowed for slips in the schedule due to testing delays, organizational meetings, or key personnel who may be needed for both activities.

If you are using a tool to create a project plan such as a Gantt chart, the tool can take these inputs and assist with efficient planning. Throughout the project engagement, the security risk assessment project lead can track progress of each of the tasks and the expenditure of hours to manage a successful project, see Figure 13.1.

13.1.2.3 Allocating Hours to Activities

With resources allocated to activities, the project manager now assigns hours to activities. This is a careful balance. The project manager needs to assign enough hours to the activity so that the resource can complete the task. At the same time, the project manager needs to ensure that the project can be completed within budget. Again, experience is the best teacher here, but below are a few tips:

- Management Reserve—Set aside a 10% "management reserve." As stated previously, something always comes up, or you will find that you underestimated at least one of the tasks. This reserve can be dipped into if you are going over budget.
- Project Management Hours—Be sure to assign hours to project management. This typically translates to 5%–10% of the total hours on many projects.
- Engineering Estimates—Don't be afraid to ask the resource directly, "How many hours would you need to review a company's security policies?" or "Can you review their policies in 16 hours?"

TABLE 13.3

Security Risk Assessment Project Hours Allocation Example

Phase/Task	Technical Assessor	Lead Assessor	Project Manager
Pre-on-site:			
Project planning			2
Document review		20	
Interview preparation		3	
On-site assessment:			
Document follow-up		3	
Interviews		10	
Inspection		5	
Observations		3	
Testing	16		
Results analysis:			
Data analysis	8	8	2
Team review	6	6	6
Additional research	8	8	
Reporting:			
Document specification		2	
Annotated outline		4	
Draft	8	20	
Final	2	6	2
Briefing	2	2	
Task total: 162 hours	50	100	12
Management: 18 hours			
Net: 180 hours			

Note: The project manager should sketch out the allocation of the hours to the project's tasks in order to determine how the project can be completed within budget. Notice the "management reserve" under the heading "Management."

- Organizational Standards—For organization's that perform many information security risk assessments, common tasks should be measured and monitored. Over time, the organization will develop standard assignment of hours to tasks. If your organization has yet to implement this standard measurement and monitoring, begin now.

Let us say that a security risk assessment project was bid at $45,000 and four weeks to complete the project. At the current rate of $250/hour, that gives you 180 hours of labor to complete the project in four weeks. Sketch out the hours and calendar time it may take to get the job done. Ideally, this was already done during the proposal stage. An example is provided in Table 13.3.

The team leader should share with the project members the Gantt chart and the hours-allocation table. Now your project members know what you expect from them, when you need it, and with whom they will be working. Be sure to give them enough information, worked examples, and guidance so that they understand how to complete the task. One of the keys to successful project management is effective delegation.

13.1.3 PROJECT RESOURCES

The project manager needs to ensure that the project can be performed successfully with the resources assigned. The project manager should first consider any contractual requirements on resources. The contract may have specified a named individual or specific experience or credentials for some of the team. Given these constraints, the project manager must first address contractual issues.

Once contractual issues are handled, the project manager must then ensure that the project team has the necessary skill sets and availability to get the job done. A successful risk assessment project will depend largely on the skill of the project manager and the quality of the project team. The ability of the project team members is dependent on their objectivity, knowledge of the system, and security risk assessment skills.

13.1.3.1 Objectivity vs. Independence

An objective team member is one whose view is not distorted or influenced by emotion or personal bias. Those who assess the relative strengths and weakness of the security controls must be able to do so without pride of ownership, undue influence from bosses, internal political pressures, or any other factor that may pollute neutral analysis. Even if a team member is able to professionally perform the tasks within a security risk assessment, there may remain the appearance of a conflict of interest. Furthermore, team members with the best intentions of remaining objective are typically

---

SIDEBAR 13.1   SHOULD YOU HIRE A CYBERCRIMINAL?

Short answer: No, but first a quick disclaimer on the use of the term *cybercriminal* and the term *hacker*. Throughout this book, the term *cybercriminal* is used to describe an unethical lawbreaker who targets an organization's assets through information security vulnerabilities. The term *hacker* has been used in the past to describe this criminal element but the use of this term to mean criminal has fallen out of favor.[1] Today the term "hacker" refers to someone who enjoys exploring complex systems to find unique ways to make the system do what it was not intended to do. There is not necessarily a criminal element or intent associated with the term *hacker*. The term *cybercriminal* here is used to describe the criminals who may use hacking techniques to gain unauthorized access or otherwise circumvent security controls.

When shopping for a quality organization or individual to test an information system or to assist in securing an organization's information system, some people are confused as to whether they should hire an "ex" cybercriminal. Some would argue that cybercriminals are likely the best people suited to help organizations protect their assets. They often ask, "Who else would know better how to defend against cybercriminal attacks than a cybercriminal himself?" This misguided concept based on little more than guesswork. The fact is that cybercriminals may be skilled at breaking into systems, but that skill does not always translate into the same skills required when performing a security risk assessment. In fact, there are five principle reasons not to hire a cybercriminal to defend your system or to defend information systems of your customers: trust, skill, threats, negligent hiring, and better alternatives.

- *Trust.* An information system security consultant must be a trusted individual with the highest integrity. These consultants, by the nature of their work, will have knowledge of your system vulnerabilities and often physical and logical access beyond that of an outsider. Trust in such an individual is paramount. Cybercriminals have already demonstrated that they are willing to commit cybercrimes. Known or admitted cybercriminals have violated laws and the ethics held by information security professionals.

Furthermore, many cybercriminals are skilled in the art of social engineering, meaning that they are good at making people believe they are one of the good guys and are here to help yet they are simply lying and preparing to violate your trust. In the words of Maya Angelou, "When someone shows you who they are; believe them the first time."

- *Skill.* An information security professional must also have a broad set of skills to determine all the possible vulnerabilities of your system and to provide recommendations for how to mitigate your overall security risk. These consultants must be knowledgeable in all domains of information security. Security will often break at the weakest link, but there are a lot of links in the chain.

  Cybercriminals are much like cat burglars, or any career criminal; they typically rely on a small set of techniques to breaking into systems that they use again and again. This approach is often referred to as their modus operandi or MO. A cat burglar who breaks into homes knows one or two tricks for breaking in. For example, he knows how to jump a sliding glass door off the tracks or how to pop a garage door off its tracks. If you hired this "reformed" thief to protect your home, he would be great at showing you how to put a safety bar on your glass door and how to lock your garage door instead of just closing it. However, this thief would likely know nothing about quality alarm systems, lighting, camera placement, strength of door jambs, and teaching your kids not to answer the door or the phone when you are out for the evening. The "credential" of being a "reformed" cybercriminal is not an indication of a skilled cyber-defender.

- Threats. The idea that cybercriminals are the best suited to help protect an organization's assets is misguided because it also assumes the organization is exposed to the limited set of threats formerly represented by the cybercriminal. It should be clear to any reader of this book that threat sources come from many types of external actors but also from internal employees or from acts of nature. It would be a severe error in security risk management to disregard the other threats such as errors and omissions, loss of physical or infrastructure support, malicious code, and fraud.

- Negligent Hiring. Under the doctrine of negligent hiring, an employer is liable for harm its employees inflict on their customers when they knew or should have known the risks posed by their employee. Negligent hiring lawsuits cost an average of $1.5 million. When these cases are brought to court, employers lose about 70%–80% of the time. Would you want to defend your company for the criminal actions of an employee when they had a documented past of similar criminal activities?

- Better Alternatives. The cybersecurity industry has grown and matured over the last several decades and offers an incredible array of services from qualified and professional individuals. There really is just no reason to take your chances with a cybercriminal. Your best bet when selecting outside assistance for the testing or securing of your organization's assets is an information security professional and not a hobbyist or criminal.

---

unable to remain objective because they are too close to the "problem." A security architect who designed and assembled the current system architecture is unlikely to look at the problem with a fresh set of eyes. The architect will naturally be hesitant and perhaps unable to view the current architecture with the same detached emotion as an outsider.

Human nature practically dictates that independence is required to ensure objectivity. There are many reasons why a member of a security risk assessment team may not be able to provide an objective review. The customer and project leader should take reasonable precautions to ensure that team members are objective. The customer and the team leader should carefully consider removing any team member who fits one of the following categories as a voting member of the security risk assessment team:

- Builder—A team member who was or is currently involved in the design, development, or operation of any of the security controls under scrutiny (e.g., members of the current security team).
- Interested Party—A team member who is in a position within the organization that will be affected by the results of the security risk assessment (e.g., candidates for a security team, project managers for projects that may require additional security measures).
- Stakeholder—A team member who is in a position to benefit or be harmed from the results of a security risk assessment (e.g., project managers, "competing organizations").

13.1.3.2 Internal vs. External Team Members

Many arguments have been made for the inclusion of internal resources on the security risk assessment team. These arguments point out that complex systems and security controls can best be understood by those who are most familiar with these systems. There is no doubt that internal resources will have a better understanding of the systems and even the business objectives if these internal resources include members sufficiently high up in the organization. However, the inclusion of internal resources on a security risk assessment team can have many setbacks as well.

Internal resources added as members of the security risk assessment team tend to be biased and inexperienced in security risk assessment methods. Anyone who cannot provide an objective assessment of the security controls should not be a voting member of the security risk assessment team. Moreover, internal resources tend to have expertise in the organization's systems and not in the security risk assessment method being employed on the project. Unfamiliarity with general security risk assessment concepts can slow the team down or lead to inaccurate results. For these reasons, internal resources should not be part of a security risk assessment team.

That being said, internal resources are incredibly valuable to the security risk assessment process. The team will rely on these resources to explain the operation of systems and security controls employed. It is not unusual to have internal resources "drive" when reviewing configurations or performing some internal testing of the systems and their controls.

13.1.3.3 Skills Required

The project manager or customer will also want to ensure that an appropriate team is assembled for the security risk assessment. It is not always possible for the project manager to choose the team. However, if the project manager has a choice, a team composed of objective and experienced members would be best. When assembling the team, the project manager should consider both team expertise and team member expertise.

- Team Skills—The team as a whole will require the skills necessary to test all security controls within the defined scope of the project. The team will require skills of leadership, writing, presentation and, depending on the scope of the project, various technical skills.
- Team Member Skills—Each member of the team needs to have specific security risk assessment skills, general consulting skills, general team member skills, and general writing skills. Specific security risk assessment skills are largely discussed in this book. The other required team member skills mentioned here are discussed briefly below. Security professionals should refer to other texts or courses to develop the proper skills listed here.

13.1.3.3.1 Specific Security Risk Assessment Skills

This book is intended to assist in the teaching of specific security risk assessment skills. By reading this book and referring to its contents throughout the security risk assessment process, team members can increase their specific security risk assessment skills and become more productive team members. However, it is expected that the members of the security risk assessment team have a general knowledge of security, experience with the review and implementation of security controls and specific security risk assessment skills.

A general knowledge of security can be gained from working within the information security profession on a variety of assignments and roles. Information security assignments can vary from the development of policies and procedures, to an understanding of the laws and regulations, to technical knowledge of the security controls. A general knowledge of the security controls, organizational structures and processes, incident response, and regulations can all be gained from these assignments.

More specific and applicable experience in the information security field can also be gained from more relevant assignments. In addition to a general exposure to the information security profession, experience with the implementation and review of information security controls can be a great benefit to an information security risk assessment team member. Relevant assignment areas generating such experience include governance and compliance, policy and procedure, logging and monitoring, audit, and testing and assessment.

There is another set of specific security risk assessment skills that are more difficult to define and find when selecting security risk assessment team members. These skills are more character traits than learned skills and difficult to cultivate, but the best risk assessors tend to have many of the following qualities:

- Analytical and Critical Thinker—Security risk assessment relies on the ability to investigate and to think analytically. A major component of many security risk assessment activities is problem-solving. Whether determining the best approach to gather data or creating risk equations the security risk assessor must be comfortable with a process that requires innovation, adaptability, and analysis. Security risk assessment is not a plug-and-play process. Each situation will require creative thinking and analytical skills.
- Confident—Security risk assessors must be able to present their findings and recommendations with confidence. The audience for the findings and recommendations may be hostile and the ramifications for the suggestions can be high stakes. Nobody wants to take hesitant strategic direction from a timid messenger.
- Mentally Tough—The role of a risk assessor is the role of a critic. As you comment on how others could do their work better you will receive push back, criticism, and opposition to your findings and suggestions. It is important to be able to remain unaffected by such attacks and focus on delivering an objective assessment-based evidence. Fragile assessors can be bullied, frustrated, or distracted.
- Humble—Although the assessor is playing the role of critic, they must also remain humble. There may a misunderstanding or the presentation of additional evidence that leads an assessor to reevaluate findings and conclusions. A skillful assessor remains humble and looks for opportunities to learn and always ensure that the analysis is correct.
- Critical Listener—Much of the data gathering tasks with the performance of a security risk assessment requires critical listening skills. It is not always easy to obtain clear answers when seeking information about the implementation and effectiveness of security controls. Assessors performing interviews require critical listening skills, see Chapter 5, Section 5.3.2.2.
- Pragmatic—When developing recommendations for safeguards to address security risks, the assessor must remain cognizant of business objectives, obstacles, and budget limitations. The best recommendations are not only effective but overcome the business constraints that may otherwise block implementation.
- Curious and Cynical—A skillful security risk assessor is respectfully suspicious. This skill will lead the assessor to asking the next question or testing the next assertion when gathering data. This skill needs to be applied to the security risk assessment team's own work as well. A skeptical and inquisitive review of findings, approaches, and recommendations is essential in ensuring a quality security risk assessment.
- Methodical—Some elements of security risk assessment work are tedious. There are many tasks within these projects that require diligent adherence to a process or pouring over large amounts of data. The skillful security risk assessor understands the value of pushing through a monotonous task.

13.1.3.3.2 Certifications

The best indication of a professional's experience is gained from observing the person's work. However, customers do not always have previous experience with the information security professionals, and therefore an observation of their work is not possible until they are under contract and working for the customer. More and more organizations are relying on a review of the certifications held by information security professionals as a measurement and indication of their experience, trustworthiness, and knowledge.

Within the information security field, the number of certifications can be overwhelming. Sorting of these certifications can be a monumental task. Although there are well over a dozen information security certifications available, they can be categorized as major certifications, advanced certifications, vendor certifications, specialty certifications, and other certifications. The purpose of this section is to highlight the most recognized and therefore sought-after certifications in the information security field.

There are a number of recognizable certifications within the information security industry that demonstrate skills useful to information security risk assessment team members. These certifications include major, advanced, vendor, specialty, and other information security certifications:

- Major Information Security Certifications—The certifications discussed in this section are considered the major information security certifications. These certifications are among the most popular within the industry, recognized by other professionals, and most frequently found in job descriptions or listings.
  - CISSP®—The International Information Systems Security Certification Consortium, (ISC2), calls the Certified Information System Security Professional (CISSP) the "Gold Standard in information system security certifications." It is hard to argue with this bold statement. The stringency of the requirements, the breadth of the tested knowledge, and the recognition of the CISSP have made this the most sought-after information security certification in the industry. Candidates wishing to obtain a CISSP certification must pass a 100 to 150-question, 3-hour exam covering eight areas of information security, called the Common Body of Knowledge (CBK). This certification also requires that candidates have a minimum of four years of experience, comply with a strict code of ethics, be endorsed by an information security professional, and attest to a clean criminal history.
  - CISA—The Information Systems Audit and Control Association (ISACA) has created the longest standing of any of these certifications. The Certified Information Security Auditor (CISA) certification is the information security auditor credential. The exam is 150 questions, 4 hours long. CISA candidates must also adhere to a strict code of ethics and have five years of experience to obtain this certification.
  - CISM—The ISACA has also created a security management certification: the Certified Information Security Manager (CISM) certification. The exam is 150 questions, 4 hours long. CISM candidates must also adhere to a strict code of ethics and have five years of experience to obtain this certification.
  - GSEC—The SANS (SysAdmin, Audit, Network, Security) Institute developed the Global Information Assurance Certification (GIAC) Security Essentials Certification (GSEC) to validate a security professional's skills. The GSEC has established itself as the "technical" security certification, largely because it tests the candidate's knowledge on a more granular level of detail. GSEC candidates must complete a 180 questions exam covering 31 cybersecurity topics within 5 hours.
- Advanced Information Security Certifications—The certifications discussed previously are only part of a more complex structure of certifications in which more advanced credentials can be obtained by specializing in other areas. Professionals wishing to expand their knowledge on specific aspects of information security can obtain these advanced credentials.

- (ISC2), the organization that administers the CISSP certification, also offers additional advanced certifications for professionals who have already obtained the CISSP and want to specialize in architecture (Information Systems Security Architectural Professional—ISSAP®), management (Information Systems Security Management Professional—ISSMP®), or government criteria and processes (Information Systems Security Engineering Professional—ISSEP®).
- ISACA, the organization that administers the CISA certification, also offers a companion certification for professionals who want to specialize in management (CISM).
- SANS, the organization that administers the GIAC GSEC certification, has the most complex—or robust (depending on your point of view)—certification scheme for information security professionals. The scheme is based on a fundamental certification (GSEC) and can be built on from there. Specific areas of concentration include technology such as firewalls, intrusion detection, and forensics. The SANS tops off the information security certification mountain with the GIAC Security Expert (GSE). GSEs must complete all GIAC certifications.

- Vendor Information Security Certifications—Nearly every security product has an accompanying certification associated with the product or product lines. These certifications are valuable for those who will be working extensively with the products, especially those who work with these products on a daily basis.
- Specialty Security Certifications—The major information security certifications recognize the need for information security professionals to have a working knowledge of associated fields such as computer forensics, physical security, and business continuity planning. But each of these areas has its own credentials as well. For those who will specialize in these fields such certifications should be investigated.
- Other Information Security Certifications—There are still more information security certifications available for those who do not meet the experience requirements of the major certifications or who just want another approach. The most popular of these is the Computing Technology Industry Association (CompTIA) Security+ certification. CompTIA is best known for its A+ certification for entry-level computer technicians. Although the Security+ certification does not carry the weight of any of the major security certifications, it is well known. Security+ candidates are required to have two years of experience in networking, with an emphasis on security. The exam covers general security issues, cryptography, communications, infrastructure, and organizational security.

13.1.3.3.3 General Consulting Skills

Consulting is the process of assessing a business problem or challenge from an outside perspective and providing recommendations to resolve the problem or overcome the challenge. Consultants need to understand the many obstacles they may face in their endeavor to assist an organization.

13.1.3.3.3.1 Criticisms of Consultants

Consultants belong to a much-maligned profession. Criticisms of the profession are a mixture of reality and perception. At worst, consultants are sometimes considered insensitive, inexperienced, and unable to produce real results:

- Insensitive—Whenever a consultant is on the job, that person is also a visitor in someone else's workplace. Every workplace has a unique culture and set of normative values that have evolved within the group of people who work together daily. Any visitor to the workplace may be considered insensitive if that person violates these normative behaviors. Furthermore, consultants are sometimes called in to assess a current situation or assist in a project that has been stalling. In either case, the consultant's advice or mere presence can be taken as criticism of the existing work.

- Inexperienced—Every project a consultant works on is unique. Even if the consultant is an expert in a specific service and has led numerous efforts within the area, each project presents unique characteristics. These unique characteristics include the customer mission, custom systems and application, and specific technology. No consultant is going to know as much as the customer regarding these characteristics. Employees within the customer organization may sometimes criticize the consultants for not understanding their systems. Often, this is a reaction to the real or perceived criticism mentioned previously—insensitivity.
- No Real Results—As mentioned previously, consulting is the process of assessing a business problem or challenge from an outside perspective and providing recommendations to resolve the problem or overcome the challenge. This type of engagement is complete once the recommendations are submitted and the report is accepted. The process of implementing the results would be a different contract and is often not part of the engagement. When the customer organization has determined that they will implement the recommendations without the assistance of the consultants (for cost or even independence reasons), the consultants are often viewed by others within the organization as a group that cannot produce real results.

13.1.3.3.3.2 *Overcoming Critics*

Not everyone is cut out to be a consultant. The business of consulting can be demanding and tricky. Just because you have technical skills does not mean you will be a good consultant. Consulting is not simply the application of technical know-how. The underlying technical skills required are a necessary but by no means a sufficient skill. Consulting is, instead, a mix of listening, observing, analyzing, researching, presenting, and teaching, with an emphasis on diplomacy. To be a productive consultant and overcome the criticisms mentioned previously, the consultant should first understand the criticisms and then consider the following advice:

- Sensitivity—Consider that you are a guest in someone else's workplace. Do your best to understand and comply with the normative values of the organization. Also understand that you may have been called into a situation that has already accumulated baggage. Various members of the organization may have already drawn up sides on issues that you have yet to discover. Be aware that when you point out areas for improvement, you may also be pointing out gaps in someone else's work. Carefully phrase your speech when conducting interviews, briefing findings, and creating the report.
- Experience—Seek to understand the unique elements of the specific job as early as possible. Research the organization's mission from its website, annual reports, press releases, and other sources. Ask for a brief description of the company mission and the systems and applications that are within the project scope. Attempt to talk less and listen more during interviews. This will not make you an expert on the organization and its systems, but it will lead you to a reasonable understanding of the project's unique characteristics and toward more targeted analysis. The result will be recognition by the customer that you understand that they are unique and will treat them with respect and not apply "cookie cutter" solutions.
- Results—Much of the problem with the criticism of "no real results" comes from a lack of understanding within the organization regarding the scope of the contract. Most contracts are limited to providing recommendations and stop short of having an assessment team implement recommendations within the same contract. When you are part of a team that will not be providing the implementation of the recommendations, be clear in interviews, presentations, and the final report regarding the scope of the work. Recommendations should provide as much detail as possible to the implementation team. Specific information regarding the implementation will be appreciated by those who inherit these recommendations.

13.1.3.3.3.3 Conflict of Interest

To avoid a conflict of interest, many contracted assessment efforts cover strictly the assessment and not any follow-on work. The concern is that the assessment team may have a conflict of interest between providing well-researched, targeted recommendations and "cookie cutter" solutions that lead the organization into purchasing more services or products from the assessment team. This concern is reasonable and should be carefully considered by both the customer and the security service consultant vendor.

13.1.3.3.4 General Writing Skills

All team members should have the ability to write effectively. They should be able to present their ideas in a clear and concise manner. In this section, we offer some high-level advice for general technical writing skills that should be well understood and practiced by each member of the security risk assessment team.

- Understand and Write to Your Audience—The audience of the security risk assessment report can be rather mixed. You should expect senior-level managers, mid-level managers, and technical personnel within the organization to read the security risk assessment. Writing to such a diverse audience can be problematic. Therefore, you should create, for example, (a) an executive summary designed specifically for the senior-level executive who wants the "bottom line" and (b) technical appendices for the technical readers who want to know the results of the vulnerability scan. However, the body of the report should be written to address the security risk assessment sponsor or mid-level managers. The report should be thorough in terms of explaining the findings, their impacts, and the recommendations.
- Don't Lecture—The authors of the document should state facts and opinions but never emotions. Understand that you must carefully word your descriptions and findings within the report to ensure not only accuracy, but also sensitivity. Leave emotion out of it. Simply state the facts as they present themselves and render a neutral opinion as to the findings.
- Write Clearly—The contributing authors to the security risk assessment report must be able to clearly express their technical ideas and findings to a wide audience that does not necessarily include security experts. Indeed, the audience reading the report is likely to have very different expectations, expertise, and motivations. It is for this reason that the report should be divided into distinct areas designed for the different groups who will read the report. An executive summary is designed for the executives and those who need a high-level understanding of the report's results and conclusions. The body of the report is designed for the majority of the audience who are interested in the approach, techniques, and findings of the report to a greater level of detail. Lastly, appendices may be developed to provide more technical and detailed information (scanning reports, lists of tools used, or other technical information) for those who would appreciate this information.

The authors of the report must be able to determine their intended audience and use the appropriate terms and concepts to convey the information most appropriately. For example, someone reading the executive summary is not interested in the tools used to scan a workstation or in a listing of the ports that remain open. In fact, such information is likely to be confusing or, at the very least, distracting within the executive summary. Instead, the author of the executive summary should state that some workstations remain vulnerable to Internet-based attacks. The body of the report could contain a description of the techniques used to determine susceptibility, and the appendix should contain the results of a vulnerability scan on that system.

SIDEBAR 13.2 HOW TO DESTROY CREDIBILITY IN FIVE LETTERS OR LESS

Every interaction between a consultant and the customer results in the establishment or the modification of the credibility of the consultant. This is why it is just as important to dress and communicate appropriately as it is to perform quality work. I once gave a seminar on the Health Insurance Portability and Accountability Act (HIPAA) to a group of state auditors, hospital administrators, and healthcare organizations. During this two-day seminar, we discussed the history of the legislation, covered entities, dates, and penalties as well as the privacy and security regulations and their implications on their organizations' administrative, physical, and technical controls.

The seminar was cosponsored by a company that intended to resell HIPAA integration services. As a sponsor of the seminar, they added several slides to the end of the presentation that described the services they offered. There was a small but noticeable mistake in these final slides. The final slide describing their credentials claimed that the company employed "HIPPA experts." It is rather difficult to establish credibility if you cannot even spell the topic in which you claim to be an expert.

13.2 PROJECT TRACKING

An essential element of project management is tracking the progress of the project. Project tracking is required to correctly report on the project status and to detect and correct any deviations from the plan. A project manager may choose to track the progress of the project on several different levels, including tracking hours only, tracking time elapsed only, or tracking both hours and calendar time against the completion of tasks within the project. The level of tracking performed by the project manager should be determined based on the complexity and length of the project.

13.2.1 HOURS TRACKING

Security risk assessments that are less rigorous and involve a relatively small scope could be adequately managed simply by tracking the hours expended on the effort against the completion of the tasks within the project. For example, if the task of reviewing the existing security policies and procedures is expected to take 8 hours and the task of performing interviews with key personnel is expected to take 12 hours, then it may be adequate to simply record the number of hours actually expended for each of these tasks.

In this case, project tracking could be accomplished in a simple table (see Table 13.4) that indicates the planned and actual hours for each task, along with an indication of their completion. For simple security risk assessments, the information available from this type of tracking is adequate to record hours expended and to determine when it may be time to take corrective action.

13.2.1.1 Calendar Time Tracking

Another way to track the progress of security risk assessments that are less rigorous and involve a relatively small scope is to track planned and actual completion times for each task. For example, if the task of reviewing the existing security policies and procedures is expected to start on September 1 and take one day, while the task of performing interviews with key personnel is expected to start on September 3 and take two days, then it may be adequate to track planned and actual calendar time.

TABLE 13.4

Security Risk Assessment Project Hours Tracking Example

Phase/Task	Resource 1		Resource 2		Resource 3		Hours Tracking
	Planned	Actual	Planned	Actual	Planned	Actual	
Preparation							
Project planning	6	4			2	3	−1
Document review			8	10			+1
Interview preparation			3	4			+2
Onsite							
Document follow-up			3	6			+5
Interviews			3	4			+6
Inspection			5	4			+5
Observations			2	4			+7
Testing	16	12					+3
Analysis							
Data analysis	8	8	8		2		
Create risk statements	6	6	6				
Team review	6	6	6		6		
Additional research	8	8	8				
Reporting							
Document specification			2				
Annotated outline			4				
Draft	8		20				
Final	2		6		2		
Briefing	4		2				
Task total: 162 hours	64		86		12		
Management: 18 hours							
Net: 180 hours							

Note: Project managers can effectively track the progress of small and simple projects through tracking the hours planned and expended on each task. Here we see that the project is trending over budget going into the results analysis task.

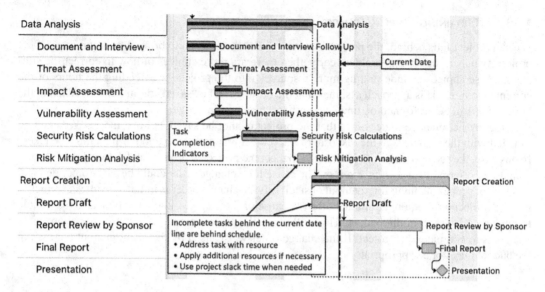

FIGURE 13.2 Using Gantt charts to track your project. The tracking Gantt chart view in project management software is a useful way to track progress on your project tasks to present to the customer or to provide you with an indication of when to take corrective action.

Project tracking using only calendar time could be accomplished in a simple table that indicated the planned and actual start and completion dates for each task. For simple security risk assessments bid at a firm fixed price (FFP), the information available from this type of tracking is adequate to track completions and to indicate when it may be time to take corrective action.

13.2.2 PROJECT PROGRESS TRACKING

While hours and calendar tracking may be adequate for relatively small security risk assessment projects, larger and more complex projects require more insight into indications of project progress. It is not enough to know how many hours over- or under-budget the project is or how many days behind it may be. Instead, the project manager needs to be able to view both of these indicators—and more—to properly manage the project.

The project manager should continually track progress on the project to ensure that the technical, calendar, and budget constraints are met. The technical constraints (quality of the work) can be tracked through your technical lead or through involvement in the technical reviews of the work products. The calendar and budget constraints may be tracked through updating the project plan and comparing the planned calendar time and budget to the expended calendar time and budget. Again, Microsoft Project or other project-management software can provide useful tools for tracking project progress (see Figure 13.2).[2]

13.3 TAKING CORRECTIVE MEASURES

If the project manager notices that the project is no longer on track, the project manager must take corrective measures to get it back on track. These measures can range from getting more resources, working longer hours, or asking the customer for a larger budget.

13.3.1 Obtaining More Resources

When a project falls behind, the project manager must create a plan to bring it back "in line." If the project manager notices this problem early, then there are more choices of how to correct the situation. These choices include putting more resources into the project or extending the hours of the current resources. This approach assumes that the project can be "saved" or, in other words, that the project can still be performed on time and perhaps even within budget.

If the project manager determines that the project cannot be saved and that the SOW cannot be satisfied with the resources at the disposal of the project manager, then another path must be taken. In this case, the scope of the work is changed to meet the projected product and delivery date. This is commonly referred to as a *change order*. The cause for a change order could be a customer demand or a lack of proper planning for potential obstacles. If the change order is initiated by the customer—and the project will require additional effort because of the change—then it is typically reasonable to pursue an increase in the budget. This will allow the project manager to obtain the appropriate resources to complete the project. If the change order was caused by the team, then an increase in the budget may not be appropriate.

13.3.2 Using Management Reserve

A management reserve of hours and calendar time can come in handy in the situation when you find your project is running behind schedule. Management reserve should not be thought of as a "fudge factor," as if the project manager is not skilled at estimating the project. Instead, the reservation of a small number of hours and time as a buffer is a technique used by project managers to give them the capability to actively manage the project and meet customer satisfaction goals.

Any good project manager will tell you that every project, no matter how well planned, will have obstacles and unforeseen delays. You know there will be some challenges during the project, but you just don't know what they are going to be. Based on the complexity of the project and an experienced estimate of the magnitude and frequency of delays, a good project manager can provide reasonable estimates for management reserve. This ability to estimate adequate management reserve will come with experience. If you have such experience—use it. If not, for now, just use 10% for both hours and calendar time. If the deviations from the project are caught soon enough or are small enough, you can basically make an adjustment without affecting the final deliverable or the bottom line.

SIDEBAR 13.3   KEYS TO ENSURING PROJECT SUCCESS

This book is filled with practical approaches for performing a security risk assessment. This viewpoint, however, is mostly from the perspective of the information security engineer performing the security risk assessment. It is the organization management, and not the information security engineer, who commissions or coordinates the security risk assessment project and, in many ways, is responsible for its success through the organizational treatment of this task.

In 1999, the General Accounting Office (GAO, renamed in 2004 as the Government Accountability Office) performed a study of best practices in industry for performing security risk assessments. The GAO report (1999) concluded that the following success factors were crucial to the organization's success in performing security risk assessments.

- Obtain Senior Management Support and Involvement—This has been stated several times, but it deserves reiteration here. The GAO study found that senior management support was important to ensure that lower-level organizations took the security risk assessment seriously, that adequate resources were made available for the project, and that the results of the assessment were implemented. Senior management involvement is not simply the provision of adequate budget. The study found that successful organizations involve senior management in the determination of the security risk assessment scope, selecting participants in the process, and approving the final action plan resulting from the assessment.
- Designate Focal Points—Security risk assessment projects that had oversight by champions at a senior level within the organization were more successful and coordinated than those security risk assessment projects that did not have designated focal points. Security risk assessment focal points assisted with the organizational planning, performance, and reporting associated with multiple security risk assessments within the organization.
- Define Procedures—All organizations within the GAO study had developed and documented security risk assessment procedures and even tools to facilitate and standardize the process. These procedures helped to ensure consistency between security risk assessment projects within the organization, but they also had an added benefit. Security risk assessment procedures limited the time and cost of security risk assessments because the security risk assessment teams did not have to perform the effort from scratch and could leverage techniques, processes, and templates developed previously in other security risk assessments.[3]
- Involve Business and Technical Experts—The GAO study found that the use of business managers and technical specialists was helpful to the security risk assessment process. Business managers were considered valuable for their deep understanding of business operations, criticality of systems, and sensitivity of data. Technical personnel were found to be experts in system architecture, system vulnerabilities, and the effect of changes on operational procedures. The involvement of other experts, such as internal auditors, contractors, and even federal agencies, proved to be useful to some organizations studied.
- Hold Business Units Responsible—When it comes to assigning responsibility for implementing the recommendations of a security risk assessment, the organizations studied concluded that individual business units were best positioned for ensuring follow-through. Business units were also determined to be well suited for determining when the next security risk assessment should be performed.
- Limit the Scope of Individual Assessments—The organizations that were the subject of this study found that conducting individual assessments with a narrow and specific scope helped to keep each security risk assessment more manageable. These organizations conducted a series of individual security risk assessments and used the results to compare and rank business units.
- Document and Maintain Results—Documentation of a security risk assessment is essential. The final security risk assessment report must be maintained and made available to the appropriate individuals. Uses of the security risk assessment report include providing a record of the security posture of the system, providing valuable information to internal auditors and future security risk assessment teams, and being a method for holding management accountable.

13.4   PROJECT STATUS REPORTING

One of the most important aspects of project management is project reporting and control. This is because project reporting serves two major functions:

1. *It provides the customer with the confidence that the project is going well, and they are getting value.* Even though the technical team may be making great progress, the lack of clear project reporting to the customer may leave the customer thinking that nothing much is going on. Similarly, the lack of efficient and complete information exchange with the customer concerning the project reflects on the professionalism of the company.
2. *It provides team members and senior management with a view of the project's progress.* Team members and senior management tend to become frustrated when they are left in the dark as to the progress of the project.

13.4.1   REPORT DETAIL

The detail provided in the status report depends upon the customer's need for insight and oversight of the project. The report should provide enough detail to let all those concerned understand the project's progress and current action items. However, the team leader should be careful not to include so much detail in the report as to spend a disproportionate amount of effort on tracking and reporting progress and less on performing the other tasks within the effort, see Figure 13.3

13.4.2   REPORT FREQUENCY

The optimal frequency of project reports is determined by the complexity of the project, the length of the engagement, the number of people involved, and the preference of the project sponsor. Although almost any frequency could be demanded, weekly, biweekly, or monthly are the most popular.

13.4.3   STATUS REPORT CONTENT

The content of the project status report may be specific to a project, i.e., it is specified in the SOW. If the SOW requires a specific format or specific content in the status report, then clearly a compliant status report should be developed. However, if no format or content is stated, the security risk assessment team should use their standard template. This standard template should include the following information:

- Project Name and Date of Report—The status report should be clearly labeled and named so that the reader can quickly ascertain the project and the time frame for which this report was created.
- Progress Indication—To the customer, this should be in terms of milestones reached and progress made on others. MS Project creates a nice chart for this. To the team members and senior management, progress indication also includes hours expended and hours left.
- Plans for Next Period—This is what the team is doing next. The Gantt chart mentioned previously would also cover this as well.
- Action-Item Tracking—All projects have a series of action items for the team or for the customer. These are specific tasks that need to be completed to accomplish the project, for example, schedule interviews with key personnel, get access badges, and so on. It is best to record, assign, and track these for the project. It is not an action item until it is specified, assigned, and given a due date. Issues—Include any issues that cannot be resolved by the team.

ACME Bank Security Risk Assessment Status Report		Period: 5//25/2020 – 6/3/2020
Overall Status	**Schedule Status**	**Scope Status**
Green	Green	Green

Client Contact:	ACME Bank	Assessment Lead:	Doug Landoll
Scope:	Lantego will perform an information security risk assessment and develop an accompanying process for the cusotmer based on FFIEC's Cybersecurity Assessment Tool (CAT) and the SANS Center for Information Security (CIS) Top 20 Critical Security Controls (CSC)		
Summary:	• Project Kickoff (5/15/2020) • Document collection sheet to customer (5/18/2020) • Interview topic / request sheet (5/24/2020) • Onsite interviews for IT and Security set for 6/8/2020 – 6/13/2020 • Onsite Interviews for departments set for week of 6/19/2020 (6/20-6/23) • Risk Assessment Completion (7/15/2020) • Risk Assessment Process Complettion (8/10/2020)		

Milestones / Deliverables

Completed

Name	Planned	Actual	Variance	Comment
• Project Kickoff	5/15/2020	5/15/2020	0	
• Document and Interview Collections Sheets	5/24/2020	5/24/2020	0	

Active

Name	Planned	Actual	% Complete	Comment	Status
• Draft Risk Assessment Report	7/12/2020		0%	•	
• Draft Risk Assessment Presentation	7/13/2020		0%	•	
• Risk Assessment Process	8/4/2020		0%	•	

Priority Issues & Risks

Issues

Title	Owner	Due Date	Comments	Status
List of Systems In Scope	J.F. Duit	6/1/2020	A list of cloud and on-prem systems together with a basic network diagram.	Complete
Basic Document Set	J.F. Duit	6/1/2020	Customer is uploaded documents. These will be reviewed prior to first onsite.	In Progress
Interview Scheduling	J.F. Duit	6/1/12020	Lantego will be onsite 6/8 – 6/12. List of staff members to be interviewed is complete.	Complete
Inherent Risk Profile Walkthrough	Doug/J.F. Duit	6/5/2020	Walk through the FFIEC CAT's Inherent Risk	To be completed onsite (6/8/2020)
Review Available Documents	Doug	On-Going	Doug reviewing as available	On going
Worksheet to IT controls interviews	Doug	6/6/2020	Doug to complete by end of day.	In Progress

FIGURE 13.3 Project status reporting. The creation and delivery of project status reports provides the customer confidence in the project's progress and provides the team members and senior management a view of the project's status to assist in the effective management of the project

13.5 PROJECT CONCLUSION AND WRAP-UP

Don't let down your guard just because the project is coming to a close. This is one of the most critical stages of the project. Dangers here include "scope creep," project run-on, and the inability to effectively go after follow-on work.

13.5.1 ELIMINATING "SCOPE CREEP"

This refers to the phenomenon suffered by many projects where the customer keeps expecting more. As the customer asks for more, the inexperienced project manager gives more, and it becomes increasingly difficult to ever end the engagement for which you were tasked.

For FFP contracts, this results in cost overruns for which the contractor cannot charge, because the deliverable is the final report, and individual hours are not charged. For time-and-materials (T&M) contracts, this is not good either, because the customer will end up being charged more than was originally expected. Even though this will lead to more contracted hours and therefore more money for the contractor, this is not a good way to operate a consultancy, because there is a big danger that the customer will be unhappy.

The best way to control these situations is to clearly define the scope of work and to manage the expectations of the customer throughout the project. If a customer wishes us to extend the scope of work, the project manager should write up a new task order, complete with an estimate of the hours it would take or the extra cost to complete the new task.

13.5.2 ELIMINATING PROJECT RUN-ON

Whereas "scope creep" is the customer pushing for more work, "project run-on" is the project members not knowing when to quit. In almost all security risk assessment engagements, the team is limited by time or the customer's budget for the project. Many times, this means that the completed work could be better. The team can *always* find ways to spend more time writing up recommendations for a security risk assessment. The team can always provide more references for why a security policy statement should be included in an acceptable-use policy. The team can always continue to try to penetrate a system. However, if the consultancy is to remain viable over the long term, it is essential that it (a) clearly communicates to the customer the extent of the services, (b) ensures that the team delivers and delights the customer, and (c) completes the project within the budget.

The best way to eliminate project run-on is to be diligent about allocating hours to team members, tracking the project, and taking appropriate corrective action when the project gets behind.

EXERCISES

1. Section 13.1.1 refers to a statement of work. In the event the security risk assessment is performed internally, and a statement of work is not issued, how does a project manager determine the project parameters and requirements?
2. When discussing project plans and tasks, what is a critical path? Referring to Figures 13.1 and 13.2, what tasks are on the critical path?
3. Using the discussion in Sections 13.1.3.1 and 13.1.3.2, what do you feel is the strongest reason not to include internal resources on the security risk assessment team?
4. Review the code of ethics statements for several major security certifications (e.g., CISSP, CISA, and Security+).
   a. How does each of these codes of ethics address conflict of interest?
   b. How would you apply these ethics to the selection of security risk assessment team members?
   c. What do these codes of ethics say regarding the hiring of cybercriminals?
   d. How would you apply these ethics to team members with a "cybercriminal past"?
   e. How would the legal concept of due diligence apply to the assessing organization if a team member with a known cybercriminal past breach the trust by exposing vulnerabilities to the public?
5. Describe the difference between "scope creep" and "project run-on." How would you handle each of these project risks?

NOTES

1 In fact, previous editions of this book used the term *hacker* to describe the criminal element. That term has been replaced throughout the book in this edition with the term *cybercriminal*.
2 Be careful of using the resource-usage features of these software packages. They are typically far too complex to be useful for projects of this size and do not translate well to projects in which your resource may be working on other projects at the same time. Stick with the pretty Gantt chart they make.
3 This is precisely why security risk assessments performed by information security professionals are so efficient. Information security professionals perform security risk assessments for multiple organizations and have well-developed processes and tools.

BIBLIOGRAPHY

Landoll, Douglas J. Benefits of IT Certifications. *Certification Magazine*, March 2004.
Western Reporting, Negligent Hiring Claims Top $50 million, https://westernreporting.com/blog/negligent-hiring-claims-top-50-million/

14 Security Risk Assessment Approaches

There are nearly as many security risk assessment approaches as there are organizations that perform them. It is not the intent of this book to define the best or only approach for performing security risk assessments. In fact, it seems clear that different approaches to performing a security risk assessment are required for different situations. Various security risk assessment approaches are discussed here for two reasons.

First, it is important to understand the different approaches that have been developed and are currently in use to perform a security risk assessment. Those performing these assessments should always be looking for ways to improve the process through the adoption of new techniques or the modification of current ones. To allow for the process of continuous improvement, those defining and performing security risk assessments must have an understanding of the other approaches currently being used.

Second, various security risk assessment approaches are discussed here to demonstrate the applicability of the advice in this book, regardless of the security risk assessment taken. Most activities described in this book (e.g., understanding business objectives, gathering data, conducting interviews) are required in all security risk assessment approaches. However, most other security risk assessment approaches lack a detailed description of the activity and offer little advice on actually performing the task. The reader can use the descriptions and advice in this book to gain a better understanding and more efficient approach to completing his own security risk assessment using nearly any security risk assessment approach.

The reader will also find specific activities described in detail in this book that are not discussed elsewhere and may not be a part of the current security risk assessment approach taken. For example, the document review methodology, physical security walk-throughs, or specific checklists are not typically described or used in other security risk assessment approaches. Readers should carefully consider these activities as possible improvements to their current processes.

The first step in performing a security risk assessment is to clearly define and understand the specific security risk assessment approach to be taken. Each of the security risk assessment approaches will vary in terms of the type and rigor of analysis, data collection or measurement, use of tools, and the definition of the project phases. There are strengths and weaknesses within each approach, but the applicability of the approach to your specific environment, objective, and available resources will be the biggest driving factor in selection of the appropriate approach. The following sections briefly describe some of the differences between currently available approaches to assist in your understanding and to aid in the selection process.

14.1 SECURITY RISK ASSESSMENT METHODS

All security risk assessment methods are a prescribed process that includes threat analysis, vulnerability analysis, impact analysis, and ultimately a measurement of security risk. Any process that results in an assessment of the current security controls, their ability to protect the organization's assets from foreseeable losses due to relevant threats and provides a measure of security risk is a security risk assessment method. To be useful to security assessment teams, these methods require a set of procedures and activities that structures the security risk assessment process. Security risk

Impact Assessment	Threat Assessment	Vulnerability Assessment
Identify Assets in scope	**Identify Relevant Threats**	**Identify Relevant Controls**
• Estimate Impact / Harm • Determine vuln. Influence (opt.)	• Estimate Likelihood of Occurrence • Determine vuln. Influence (opt.)	• Estimate control vulnerability (optional)

Risk Calculation

Calculate Risk
• Perform risk calculations

FIGURE 14.1 Generic security risk assessment method. All security risk assessment methods include the phases of threat assessment, impact assessment, (optionally vulnerability assessment), and risk calculation.

assessment methods generally have the same basic elements, namely: threat assessment, impact assessment, vulnerability assessment, and risk calculation (Figure 14.1).

- Threat Assessment—A process, method, or series of steps for determining the likelihood of a threat (or loss) event occurrence. This assessment phase typically involves the following elements:
  - Threat agents and actions—Threat may be broken up into threat agents and threat actions (or threat events). A security risk assessment method may include a set of threats agents and actions or a taxonomy for describing the elements of the threat.
  - Frequency/Likelihood—Most importantly the security risk assessment method includes a technique for measuring the likelihood of the threat action occurrence or the frequency in which the threat may occur within a timeframe (e.g., annual).
  - Threat Subelements—Some security risk assessment methods may subdivide the process of threat measurement into elements of the threat agent or action such as capability, intent, targeting, motivation, and relevance. These subdivided elements roll up to assist in the measurement of the threat event frequency.
  - Estimation Technique—A security risk assessment will use either a qualitative or quantitative measurement technique to summarize the threat assessment.
    - Qualitative estimations are typically implemented through a qualitative lookup table with selectable measurements, for example, high, moderate, low.
    - Quantitative estimations are typically implemented through the assessor's assignment of a frequency or probability of occurrence. These quantitative estimates can be as simple as a single point estimation (e.g., 50% probability or twice a year) or the assessor may provide an estimate range (e.g., between 40% and 65% probability or 1–3 times a year). Probabilities are always expressed as a number between 0 and 1 (e.g., 0–100%).
- Impact Assessment—A process, method, or series of steps for determining the expected loss or impact to the organization. This typically involves the following elements:
  - Direct Loss (Primary Loss)—Losses incurred as a direct result or liability attached immediately upon the happening of the occurrence are considered a direct or primary loss. These typically include harm to assets directly affected by the occurrence (e.g., lost laptop),

operational losses directly affected by the occurrence (e.g., system downtime), and fines and judgments incurring directly from the

- Indirect Loss (Secondary Loss) —Losses incurred as an indirect result or liability attached after the primary losses have been addressed or fulfilled. These typically include harm and loss conditions that may come to fruition such as lost future sales, reputation, and secondary fines and judgments.
- Estimation Technique—A security risk assessment method includes a technique for measuring the magnitude of the expected loss with respect to the associated threat action, including rolling up the expected impact elements. The measurement technique here is again either a qualitative or quantitative:
  - Qualitative techniques are typically implemented through a qualitative lookup table with selectable measurements, for example, high, moderate, low.
  - Quantitative techniques are typically implemented through the assessor's assignment of a dollar figure for the expected loss. These quantitative estimates can be as simple as a single point estimation (e.g., $47,500 for a lost laptop) or the assessor may provide an estimate range (e.g., between $10,000 and $60,000 for a lost laptop).
- Vulnerabilities Assessment—Depending on the security risk assessment method, vulnerabilities of existing security controls may play a role in security risk assessment methods by affecting one or both of the security risk calculation variables of threat frequency and expected impact. Security control vulnerabilities generally increase the threat frequency as a threat agent and action are more likely to cause harm to the organization and its assets if the security control is more vulnerable. Some security risk assessment methods also account for the effect of a security control's vulnerability in increasing the magnitude of the expected loss. For example, vulnerabilities in corrective security controls such as incident response increase the magnitude of harm to an organization in dealing with a security incident. The measurement of the severity of control vulnerabilities are generally incorporated into the security risk assessment method's qualitative or quantitative calculations. Other security risk assessment methods either do not account for vulnerabilities in the calculation of security risk (e.g., OCTAVE Allegro) or account for the vulnerabilities of security controls in the creation of security risk mitigation controls (e.g., OCTAVE).
- Risk Determination/Calculation —A process, method, or series of steps for determining the security risk to the organization's assets. All security risk assessment methods include an overall security risk is a calculation based on the threat frequency and expected impact. The measurement technique is either a qualitative or quantitative:
  - Qualitative techniques are typically implemented through a qualitative lookup table with selectable measurements, for example, high, moderate, low.
  - Quantitative techniques are typically implemented through a quantitative calculation. When the assessor has worked with single point assignments this can be a simple multiplication (e.g., twice a year at $47,500 = $95,000 loss per year) or a more complex mathematical techniques for combining probability and loss ranges (e.g., Monte Carlo estimation).

Any given method for performing a security risk assessment may be ideal for one situation, budget, organization, assessment team, or industry but not for others. Security risk assessment methodologies are not a one-size-fits-all situation. Because of the various needs and various situations, a variety of security risk assessment methods have been developed. The following popular security risk assessments methods are covered below:

- NIST SP 800-30
- OCTAVE, OCTAVE-S, OCTAVE-Allegro
- IRAM2
- FAIR-BRAG, FAIR
- RIIOT FRAME (Qualitative), RIIOT FRAME (Quantitative)

14.1.1   NIST Guide for Conducting Risk Assessments (NIST SP 800-30)

The National Institute of Standards and Technology (NIST) has provided guidance for conducting information security risk assessments for federal information systems and organizations. This guidance is published in the NIST Special Publication 800-30: Guide for Conducting Risk Assessments. Although intended for federal information systems the NIST SP 800-30 Risk Assessment method has been adopted by many organizations to perform information security risk assessments within their own environments. The NIST SP 800-30 method is intended to be performed by information security professionals with experience in information system assessment and information security risk assessment. The method is integrated into an overall Risk Management Framework (RMF) that provides guidance on managing, applying, and monitoring information security risk with a set of related publications that provide additional guidance on each of these topics. The NIST SP 800-30 method provides a process complete with guidelines, checklists, process descriptions, and supporting appendices for this thirteen-step security risk assessment process. The NIST SP 800-30 method is can be tailored within many of the process steps for different organizational information security needs based on environment, threats, data sensitivity, and security requirements.

The NIST SP 800-30 method takes a threat-based approach to information security risk assessments by first identifying all potential threat events and associated threat sources. Each of the identified threats are rated for relevance (e.g., confirmed, expected, anticipated, predicted, possible, or not applicable). The assessment team sets a threshold for "relevant" threats and the set of threats to be considered is narrowed. For each relevant threat, the risk assessment team determines the Level of Impact, Overall Likelihood, and Level of Risk, see Figure 14.2.

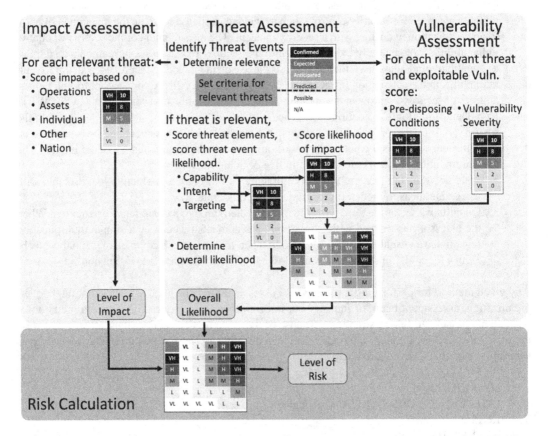

FIGURE 14.2   NIST SP 800-30. The NIST SP 800-30 method is a qualitative threat-driven approach that determines the level of risk based on a lookup table using a level of impact and overall likelihood.

- Level of Impact—The impact of each relevant threat is scored based on its potential harm to operations, assets, individuals, other organizations, and the nation. This gives us the "Level of Impact."
- Overall Likelihood—The likelihood that the threat event will occur is determined based on scoring each threat source's capability, intent, and targeting. The likelihood that the threat will occur and result in an adverse impact is determined based on scoring the threat source's capability, predisposing conditions, and the severity of related vulnerabilities. Both the likelihood of the threat occurring and the likelihood of the threat resulting in an adverse impact are used in a lookup table to determine the overall likelihood.
- Level of Risk—The final calculation is performed in a lookup table using both the level of impact and the overall likelihood to determine the level of risk.

14.1.2   OCTAVE

Operationally Critical Threat, Asset, and Vulnerability Evaluation (OCTAVE) is an information security risk evaluation approach created by the Computer Emergency Response Team (CERT) Coordination Center (CERT/CC). OCTAVE is a self-directed evaluation approach that utilizes business and technical personnel to perform information security risk evaluations and a set of recognized information security practices to drive information security risk mitigation. The OCTAVE method provides a process complete with guidelines, checklists, time estimates, and process descriptions for this three-phased security risk assessment process.

The OCTAVE method is highly flexible and can be tailored within many of the processes of the method for different organization types and sizes. In fact, OCTAVE has several formalized information security risk assessment methods to address different organizational types and sizes:

14.1.2.1   OCTAVE (Original)

The original OCTAVE information security risk assessment method was designed for larger organizations (e.g., 300+ employees). The OCTAVE method is performed by an internal interdisciplinary team through a series of workshops. OCTAVE takes an asset-driven approach to information security risk assessments by first identifying all assets and then narrowing the evaluation to "critical assets." For each critical assets the key security requirement (confidentiality, integrity, availability) is identified, and a qualitative impact value (high, medium, low) is assigned. Threat assessment is limited to only relevant threats to critical assets, selected by reviewing "areas of concern" and generic threat trees to create asset-based threat profiles. For each threat profile, a qualitative probability (high, medium, low) also called the "frequency of occurrence" is assigned based on the asset, actor, motive, access, and outcome of the threat. The "expected [impact] value" is determined through a lookup table using the values of impact value and probability.

It should be noted that the OCTAVE method does not utilize the review of security control effectiveness in determining the security risk (expected value). Instead, these elements are used in the creation of actions and recommendations for information security risk mitigation. OCTAVE includes a "catalog of practices." The internal assessment team surveys the assessed organization on their opinion if each security practice in the catalog is in place or not. The team also ensures that vulnerability scanners are run on system components relevant to critical assets. The survey results and the vulnerability scans are assigned severity levels. These results are used to form actions and recommendations for security risks the organization wishes to deter or mitigate, see Figure 14.3.

14.1.2.2   OCTAVE-S

OCTAVE-S is a variation of the original OCTAVE designed for small (e.g., less than 100 employees) manufacturing organization. This information security risk method drops many of the formal data gathering workshops in favor or a small team with broad knowledge of the small organization.

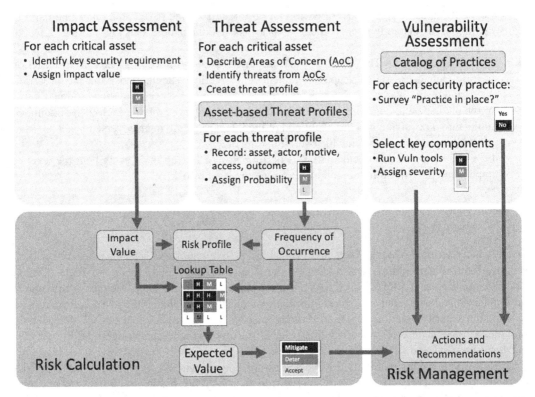

FIGURE 14.3 OCTAVE. The OCTAVE method is an asset-driven approach that determines security risk through a qualitative lookup table based on critical asset impact and threat probabilities.

OCTAVE-S also drops the vulnerability scanning as most small manufacturing businesses are believed to frequently outsource IT services and functions.

OCTAVE-S also takes an asset-driven approach to information security risk assessments by first identifying all assets and then narrowing the evaluation to "critical assets." For each critical asset, the most important security requirement (confidentiality, integrity, availability) is selected, and threats are enumerated using recorded areas of concern and expanded through the use of threat trees. For each critical asset/threat scenario pair, a qualitative impact value (high, medium, low) and threat probability (high, medium, low) is assigned. The internal assessment team determines the effectiveness of the assessed organization's security practice by assigning a qualitative value (red, yellow, green). All of this information is recorded into a risk profile worksheet for tracking purposes. There is no lookup table used in OCTAVE-S, instead the assessment team decides which risk profiles to mitigate based on threat impact and probability values, most important security requirements, security practices effectiveness, and areas of concern, see Figure 14.4.

14.1.2.3 OCTAVE-Allegro

OCTAVE-Allegro is a variation of the original OCTAVE designed to streamline the OCTAVE approach. OCTAVE-Allegro assessments are designed by be implemented by a single individual without extensive organizational involvement, although it still supports larger teams. OCTAVE-Allegro also takes an asset-driven approach to information security risk assessments but focuses the assessment on the context of critical asset use, location, threats, and vulnerabilities.

The OCTAVE-Allegro method begins with the definition of qualitative impact criteria for the five impacts areas of reputation, financial, productivity, safety, and fines with an optional 6th impact area

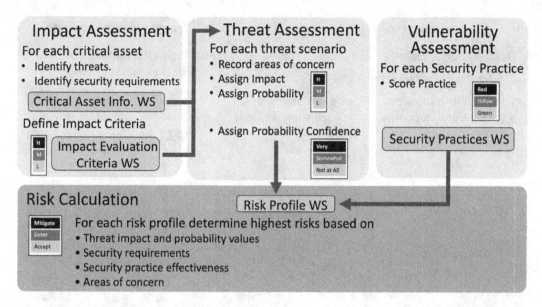

FIGURE 14.4 OCTAVE-S. The OCTAVE-S method is an asset-driven approach that determines security risk through a team decision based on qualitative values (impact, probability, control effectiveness) contained in the developed risk profile worksheet.

that is user-defined. The assessment team ranks these impact areas (1–5 or 6) in terms of priority. These impact areas are then scored for each critical asset and a sum product of the priorities and scores is calculated for each asset to arrive at a relative risk score. Threats are assessed by brainstorming areas of concern and expanding these concerns into threat scenarios. The actor, means, motive, and outcome of each threat scenario along with an assigned threat scenario probability are recorded for each threat scenario. The risks are sorted into "risk pools" determined through a lookup table using the values of relative risk score and threat scenario probability. The highest risks are assigned to the "mitigate" risk pool; the second highest are assigned to the "deter" risk pool; and the balance are assigned to the "accept" risk pool, see Figure 14.5.

It should be noted that the OCTAVE-Allegro method eliminated the survey of security practices and vulnerability testing. There is no analysis of the effectiveness of controls within the OCTAVE-Allegro method unless the team incorporates such analysis in threat probabilities.

14.1.3 INFORMATION SECURITY ASSESSMENT METHODOLOGY 2 (IRAM2)

Detailed and specific qualitative method for performing an information security risk assessment. Asset impacts, threats, and control vulnerabilities are scored on a qualitative scale (0–3 or 0–4). Threat likelihood and security risk are determined based on lookup tables (negligible, low, moderate, high). Information Security Forum (ISF) provides some guidance in terms of a common threat list and a threat event catalog. This is a well-supported method with a membership organization, annual meetings and several commercial tools have implemented the process.

The ISF developed the IRAM2 method to support information security risk management. The ISF has created the methodology, associated tools, guidelines, and a support organization for the IRAM2 method of performing information security risk assessments.

The IRAM2 method takes a threat-based approach to information security risk assessments and implements a process that includes an impact assessment, threat assessment, vulnerability assessment and final risk calculation, see Figure 14.6.

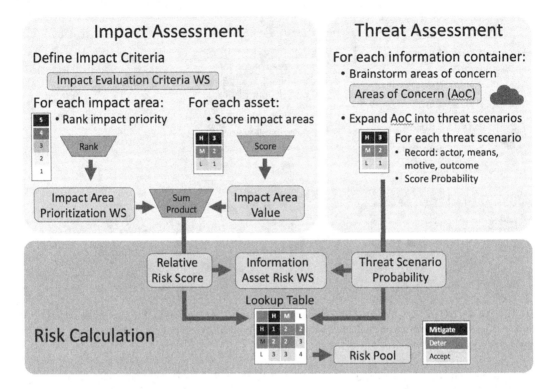

FIGURE 14.5 OCTAVE-Allegro. The OCTAVE-Allegro method is a qualitative asset-driven approach that sorts security risks into risk pools based on a lookup table using a relative risk score and threat probability. This method is a streamlined approach designed to reduce the need for large teams and extensive risk assessment knowledge.

- Scope Assessment—The IRAM2 assessment begins with a scoping of the assessment environment to set boundaries of the assessment and list the associated information assets.
- Impact Assessment—The *residual impact* of each asset is scored based on the maximum potential impact to confidentiality, integrity, and availability using a 0-3 scoring method.
- Vulnerability Assessment—The *control strength* of each security control is assessed using a 0-4 scoring method based on the control's relevance and implementation.
- Threat Assessment—Each relevant threat is assessed to determine the likelihood of initiation and the threat strength.
  - Likelihood of Initiation: Threats are scored using a 0–3 scoring method based on the threat history and threat motivation.
  - Threat Strength: Threats are also scored using a 0–3 scoring method based on the threat capability and commitment.
  - Likelihood of Success: The likelihood that a threat would successfully impact the organization is computed in a lookup tables using the results from *threat strength* and *control strength*.
  - Residual Likelihood: The residual likelihood of the threat is computed in a lookup table using the results from *likelihood of initiation* and *likelihood of success*.
- Residual Risk—The final calculation is performed in a lookup table using both the *residual impact* and the *residual likelihood* to determine *residual risk*.

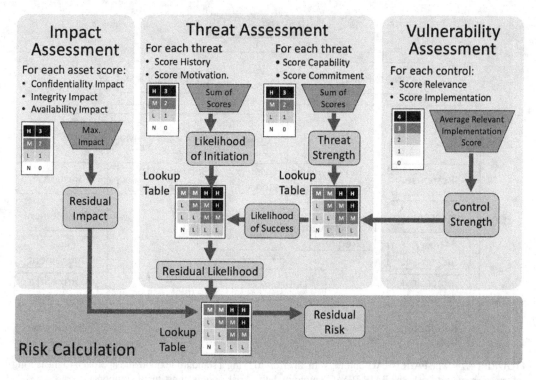

FIGURE 14.6 IRAM2. The IRAM2 method is a qualitative threat-driven approach that scores asset impact, threat likelihood, threat strength, and control strength to determine residual risk using lookup tables.

14.1.4 Factor Analysis of Information Risk (FAIR): Basic Risk Assessment Guide (BRAG)

The Factor Analysis of Information Risk (FAIR) original ontology provides a set of risk element definitions and relationships that provides the basis for the FAIR Basic Risk Assessment Guide (BRAG). The FAIR BRAG is a "quasi-quantitative" threat-based security risk assessment approach. Guidance on implementing this approach is available with the "FAIR Book" and the original 2005 paper by Jack Jones. The FAIR approach is intended to bring a standard lexicon and approach to measuring information security risk. The ontology that provides the basis of the BRAG approach defines information security risk as a summation of primary risk and secondary risk, each of which is a calculation of loss event frequency and magnitude, see Figure 14.7.

The FAIR BRAG method takes a threat-based approach to information security risk assessments by first identifying all assets at risk and the threat communities associated with those assets. For each of the threat communities identified the threat event frequency, threat capability, and threat difficultly are estimated. A vulnerability measure is determined through a lookup table using both the threat capability and threat difficulty. The primary loss event frequency is determined using both the threat event frequency and vulnerability. Also estimated is the secondary loss frequency, which is used to convert to a secondary loss percentage. Both the secondary loss percentage and the primary loss event frequency are used to determine the secondary loss event frequency through a lookup table. Both the primary and secondary loss are estimated for each of the five areas of loss (response, replacement, fines & judgment, competitive advantage, and reputation). These five areas of loss are

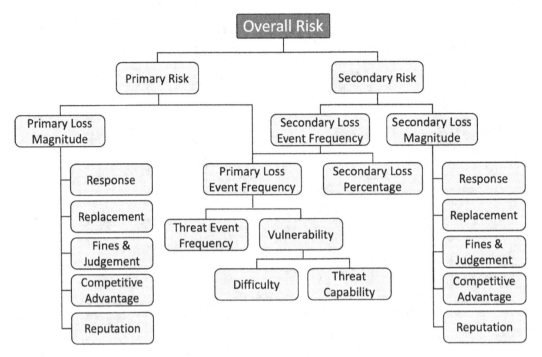

FIGURE 14.7   The FAIR BRAG ontology. In an effort to bring a standard lexicon and approach to measuring information security risk, the FAIR BRAG ontology defines risk and its constituent component.

"summed" to compute the primary and secondary loss magnitude. Next, primary and secondary loss magnitude and loss event frequency are used to determine primary and secondary risk through a lookup table. Finally, primary and secondary risks are used to determine overall risk through the use of a lookup table, see Figure 14.8.

14.1.5   FACTOR ANALYSIS OF INFORMATION RISK (FAIR): QUANTITATIVE

The FAIR model for information security risk is based on an updated ontology, The FAIR model is quantitative threat-based security risk assessment approach. Guidance on implementing this approach is available with the "FAIR Book" and the through the FAIR Institute (website, blog, conferences, and training) as well as implemented in several tools. The ontology that provides the basis of the FAIR approach defines information security risk as a summation of loss event frequency (a product of threat event frequency and vulnerability) and loss magnitude (a product of primary and secondary loss), see Figure 14.9.

The FAIR method takes a threat-based approach to information security risk assessments by first identifying all assets at risk and enumerating risk scenarios for each asset. Risk scenarios include the associated asset, the threat community (e.g., cyber criminals, internal, privileged internal, customers) and type (e.g., malicious, error, fraud), and effect (e.g., confidentiality, integrity, availability). For each risk scenario, both the *loss magnitude* and the *loss event frequency* are estimated or derived through a Monte Carlo simulation of the next level variables. Assessors of the FAIR method are required to estimate the lower bound, upper bound and most likely values for security risk variables in support of Monte Carlo simulations of both *loss magnitude* and *loss event frequency*, see Figure 14.10.

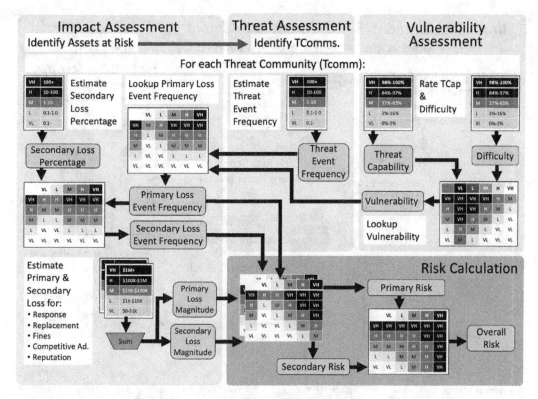

FIGURE 14.8 Open FAIR basic risk assessment guide. The Open FAIR BRAG method is a qualitative threat-driven approach based on the FAIR ontology, estimates, and lookup tables.

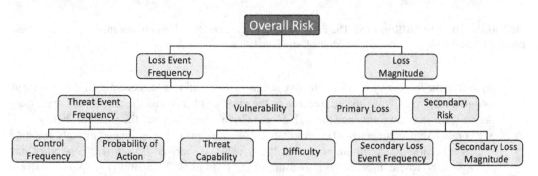

FIGURE 14.9 The FAIR method ontology. The original FAIR ontology has been updated for the FAIR quantitative method.

- Loss Magnitude—The *loss magnitude* comprises both the *primary loss* and the *secondary loss*. Estimates include a minimum, maximum, and most likely value. *Primary loss* a sum of the estimated loss from productivity, response, replacement, competitive advantage, fines and judgments, and reputation. *Secondary loss* is the probability of *secondary loss* multiplied by the sum of loss factors: response, fines and judgment, and reputation.
- Loss Event Frequency—The *loss event frequency* is either estimated directly or derived from *threat event frequency* and *vulnerability*. As above, estimates include a minimum, maximum, and most likely value. When there is sufficient historical data available to the assessment team

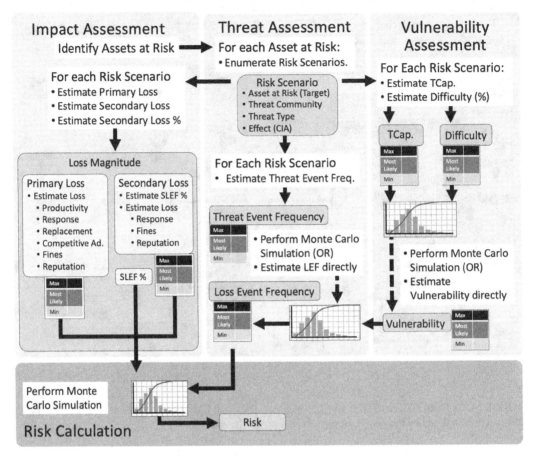

FIGURE 14.10   The FAIR method. The FAIR method is a quantitative threat-driven approach based on the updated FAIR ontology, estimates, and Monte Carlo simulation.

regarding the frequency in which the risk scenario may lead to a loss event then the *loss event frequency* is typically estimated directly. In the absence of this data the assessment team may derive the loss event frequency through Monte Carlo simulation and the variables below:

- Threat Event Frequency—The *threat event frequency* is either estimated directly (including a minimum, maximum, and most likely value) or derived from *threat capability* and *difficultly*, where *difficultly* is a measure of the level of skill (capability) required to overcome existing controls.
- Vulnerability—The *vulnerability* is the probability (percentage) that the threat source will result in a loss. The *vulnerability* estimate includes a minimum, maximum, and most likely probability. This can either be estimated directly or derived from the *threat capability* and *difficultly*. Direct estimations are the typical approach to estimating *vulnerability* but when insufficient data exists the team may decide to derive the vulnerability estimate value through a Monte Carlo simulation and the variables below:
  - Threat Capability—The *threat capability* is the ability or skill level of the threat source. *Threat capability* is a probability and is expressed in terms of minimum, maximum, and most likely value.
  - Difficultly—The *difficulty* is the level of resistance that the threat source must overcome. *Difficulty* is a probability and is expressed in terms of minimum, maximum, and most likely value.

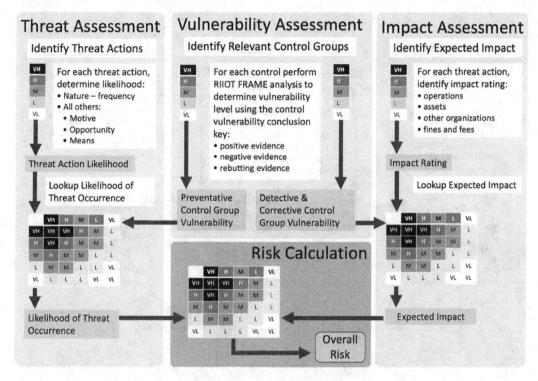

FIGURE 14.11 RIIOT FRAME—Qualitative. The RIIOT FRAME (Qualitative) method is a qualitative threat-driven approach utilizing the RIIOT data gathering approach, and lookup tables.

14.1.6 REVIEW, INTERVIEW, INSPECT, OBSERVE, TEST (RIIOT) FRAMEWORK RISK ASSESSMENT METHOD: EXAMPLE (FRAME)—QUALITATIVE

The RIIOT FRAME was introduced in Chapter 10 (Section 10.1) as a demonstration method for this text. This method, however, is a fully functional method that may be used in the execution of information security risk assessments. As the name suggests, the RIIOT FRAME—Qualitative is a qualitative risk assessment method that incorporates the RIIOT data gathering methods and simplifies the security risk assessment approach.

The RIIOT FRAME method takes a threat-based approach to information security risk assessments by first identifying relevant threat actions and performing a controls vulnerability assessment. For each threat action the likelihood and impact rating are determined using a qualitative scale (very high to very low). For each control, a vulnerability level is determined. The threat action likelihood and impact ratings are adjusted based on preventative and detective/corrective control vulnerability levels resulting in the likelihood of threat occurrence and the expected impact ratings using lookup tables. The final overall risk is determined by using a lookup table and the likelihood of threat occurrence and expected impact ratings, see Figure 14.11.

14.1.7 REVIEW, INTERVIEW, INSPECT, OBSERVE, TEST (RIIOT) FRAMEWORK RISK ASSESSMENT METHOD: EXAMPLE (FRAME)—QUANTITATIVE

The RIIOT FRAME was introduced in Chapter 10 (Section 10.1) as a demonstration method for this text and included both a qualitative and quantitative option. This method is a fully functional method that may be used in the execution of information security risk assessments. The RIIOT FRAME—Quantitative is a quantitative risk assessment method that incorporates the RIIOT data

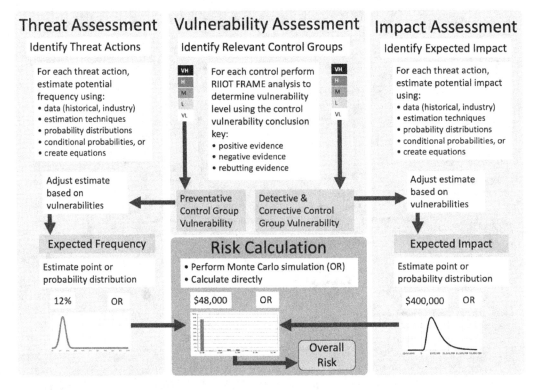

FIGURE 14.12 RIIOT FRAME—Quantitative. The RIIOT FRAME (Quantitative) method is a quantitative threat-driven approach utilizing the RIIOT data gathering approach, estimates, and Monte Carlo simulation.

gathering methods, estimation, and Monte Carlo simulation, and simplifies the quantitative security risk assessment approach.

The RIIOT FRAME quantitative method is a threat-based approach to security risk assessment that starts by identifying relevant threat actions and performing a controls vulnerability assessment. For each threat action, the potential frequency and the potential impact are estimated. For each control, a vulnerability level is determined in the same manner as in the qualitative version of the RIIOT FRAME. The threat action potential frequency and potential impact estimates are adjusted based on preventative and detective/corrective control vulnerability levels resulting in the expected frequency and the expected impact estimates. These estimates may be made as a point estimate or using a probability distribution. The final overall risk is determined by calculating directly or by performing a Monte Carlo simulation on the probability distributions, see Figure 14.12.

14.2 SECURITY RISK ASSESSMENT FRAMEWORKS

There is a bit of confusion within the cybersecurity community as to what makes a security risk assessment method vs. a security risk assessment framework. A security risk assessment framework does not include a prescribed process or set of steps to be followed to produce a security risk assessment. A security risk assessment framework typically specifies expected elements of a risk assessment, for example, security risk assessment shall include a review of threats, vulnerabilities, and impacts. Moreover, a security risk assessment framework, or more aptly a security RMF, specifies the need for security risk assessments, the organizational statement of a security risk appetite, the security risk mitigation process, and overall security risk management. The following is a list of security risk assessment/management frameworks—not to be confused with a security risk assessment method.

- COBIT 5 for Risk—COBIT 5 for Risk does not define a detailed security risk analysis method. COBIT 5 for Risk describes what is needed to establish a risk function within an organization. This includes establishing organizational processes for identifying, analyzing, and responding to risk appropriately.
- ISO's 27005—This International Standards Organization (ISO) standard for information security risk management discusses how the security risk assessment integrates into the security risk management process. This standard includes some basic criteria for security risk management and security risk assessment, definitions for threats, vulnerabilities, impacts, and risks. The ISO 27005 describes how a risk assessment process consists of risk identification (assets, threat, controls, vulnerabilities, and consequences) risk analysis (qualitative or quantitative, consequence assessment, incident likelihood assessment, risk level determination) and risk evaluation. In annexes and appendices, the standard provides quite a few detailed examples including 43 specific threats across 5 human and 7 general threat types; 85 example vulnerabilities across 6 vulnerability types; 4 types of direct and 5 types of indirect impacts; and 3 table-based qualitative examples of how to compute security risk scores. Yet these are examples that fit the basic criteria for information security risk assessment and not methods themselves. ISO 27005 remains a solid framework for analyzing the completeness of an information security risk assessment method but is not a method itself.

www.infosecurityrisk.com	For a downloadable full version of the security risk assessment method figures, go to the website: www.infosecurityrisk.com, head to the downloads section for the Security Risk Assessment Handbook, and go to Chapter 14 downloads.

EXERCISES

1. Explain how the simple risk equation (Security Risk = Assets × Threats × Vulnerabilities) is implemented within the following information security risk assessment approaches:
   a. NIST SP 800-30
   b. FAIR
   c. IRAM2
   d. OCTAVE
   e. RIIOT FRAME
2. Compare and contrast any two security risk assessment methods or models.
   a. How are the models alike and how are they different?
   b. Which of the two models do you prefer and why?
   c. What is the biggest drawback to the model you prefer?
   d. How would you improve that drawback?
3. Checklists and tools provide many benefits such as adding structure and ensuring constancy, but there are some dangers to using these during an engagement.
   a. What are the dangers of using checklists or tools in the execution of a security risk assessment project?
   b. Are the dangers increased or decreased when applied to a self-assessment? Explain.
   c. What controls could you implement to reduce the disadvantages of using checklists and tools?

4. There are many security risk assessment methods described in this chapter.
   a. Identify a security risk assessment method not covered in this chapter.
   b. Create a diagram in the style of Figures 14.2 through 14.6, 14.8, and 14.10.
   c. What benefits might this other approach have?
5. What elements of this text will be helpful to you in your next security risk assessment? Describe how you would put that information to use.

BIBLIOGRAPHY

Alberts, Christopher J., and Dorofee, Audrey J., *OCTAVE(SM) Catalog of Practices, Version 2.0*, October 2001a.

Alberts, Christopher J., and Dorofee, Audrey J., *OCTAVE(SM) Method Implementation Guide, Version 2.0*, Volumes 1–2, June 2001b.

Alberts, Christopher J., and Dorofee, Audrey J., *OCTAVE®-S Implementation Guide, Volumes 1-10, Version 1.0*, January 2005.

Caralli, Richard A., Stevens, James F., Introducing OCTAVE Allegro: Improving the Information Security Risk Assessment Process, May 2007. https://resources.sei.cmu.edu/asset_files/TechnicalReport/2007_005_001_14885.pdf

Freund, Jack. Jones, Jack. Measuring and Managing Information Risk: A FAIR Approach, 2015.

International Standards Organization, International Standard, ISO/IEC 27005, Information Technology – Security Techniques – Information Security Risk Management, Third Edition 2018-07.

ISACA, COBIT 5: An ISACE Framework: COBIT 5 for Risk-An Overview, December 2014. http://www.alrim.lu/sites/alrim/files/download_center/cobit_5_for_risk_-_overview_-_isaca_luxembourg_chapter_december_2014.pdf

ISO/IEC 27005:2018 Information Technology – Security Techniques – Information Security Risk Management, https://www.iso.org/obp/ui/#iso:std:iso-iec:27005:ed-3:v1:en

Oredsson, Mattias, Bridging the Gap Between Information Security Risk Assessments and Enterprise Risk Management – How to Ensure a Balanced Reporting of Information Security Risks to the Top Management and the Board, Master's Thesis, University in Stavanger, Spring / Autumn 2018. https://uis.brage.unit.no/uis-xmlui/bitstream/handle/11250/2565842/Oredsson_Mattias.pdf?sequence=1

U.S. Department of Commerce, National Institute of Standards and Technology, Guide for Conducting Risk Assessments, Special Publication 800-30 Revision 1, September 2012. https://csrc.nist.gov/publications/detail/sp/800-30/rev-1/final

U.S. Department of Transportation, Office of the Secretary of Transportation, Memorandum to Secretarial Officers, Modal Administrators, "guidance of Treatment of Economic Value of a Statistical Life (VSL) in U.S. Department of Transportation Analysis 2016 Adjustment. https://www.transportation.gov/office-policy/transportation-policy/revised-departmental-guidance-on-valuation-of-a-statistical-life-in-economic-analysis

Index

Page numbers in **bold** indicate tables, page numbers in *italic* indicate figures.

Printed in the United States
by Baker & Taylor Publisher Services